T0305208

JEWISH ENTREPRENEURSHIP IN SALONICA, 1912–1940

JEWISH ENTREPRENEURSHIP IN SALONICA, 1912–1940

An Ethnic Economy in Transition

ORLY C. MERON

sussex
ACADEMIC
PRESS
Brighton • Portland • Toronto

2 4 6 8 10 9 7 5 3 1

First published in 2011 in Great Britain by
SUSSEX ACADEMIC PRESS
PO Box 139
Eastbourne BN24 9BP

in the United States of America by
SUSSEX ACADEMIC PRESS
920 NE 58th Ave   Suite 300
Portland, Oregon 97213-3786

and in Canada by
SUSSEX ACADEMIC PRESS (CANADA)
8000 Bathurst Street, Unit 1, PO Box 30010, Vaughan, Ontario L4J 0C6

British Library Cataloguing in Publication Data
A CIP catalogue record for this book is available from the British Library.

Library of Congress Cataloging-in-Publication Data
Meron, Orly C.
Jewish entrepreneurship in Salonica, 1912–1940 : an ethnic economy in transition /
  Orly C. Meron
p. cm.
Includes bibliographical references and index.
ISBN 978-1-84519-261-7 (h/b : alk. paper)
  1. Jews—Greece—Thessalonike—Economic conditions—20th century.
2. Entrepreneurship—Greece—Thessalonike—History—20th century. 3. Jews—Greece—
Thessalonike—History—20th century. 4. Thessalonike (Greece)—Economic
conditions—20th century. 5. Thessalonike (Greece)—Ethnic relations. I. Title.
DS135.G72T498 2011
338.09495'4—dc22

2010041529

MIX
Paper from
responsible sources
FSC® C013056
www.fsc.org

Typeset & designed by Sussex Academic Press, Brighton & Eastbourne.
Printed on acid-free paper by TJ International, Padstow, Cornwall.

Contents

List of Tables, Figures and Maps

Tables

Figures

Maps

List of Illustrations

Acknowledgements

Above all, I acknowledge and marvel at the magnificent, driving entrepreneurial force that once was at the heart of the Jewish community of the port city of Salonica – the glorious "Jerusalem of the Balkans". As I put the finishing touches on the text, I cannot help but think of the current financial crisis that finds Greece under the burden of a huge foreign debt, high unemployment, and the real possibility of economic collapse were it not for the EU bailout. I wonder if the Jewish entrepreneurs of Salonica who weathered heavy losses with admirable aplomb due to Greece's forgotten suspension of its foreign debt in 1932 had been allowed to survive and thrive, then maybe Greece might have been spared repeating its economic history in the early twenty-first century. With their unique geographical position on Greece's northern seacoast, their ability to network, and their keen business acumen, Salonica's Jewish minority's entrepreneurs established a highly productive local and worldwide business environment. Their success at finding viable niches contributed disproportionately to the New Greece's overall economy throughout the 1930s right up to the eve of the destruction of this, the greatest Sephardic Jewish community in Europe. Today, modern Greece's Jewish population numbers around a mere thousand in Salonica and another several thousand in Athens.

This multidisciplinary and interdisciplinary research project reflects many years of study in various departments at Bar-Ilan University, beginning with the study of mathematics via Jewish history and ending with sociology. I express my gratitude especially to my devoted mentors from the beginning of my academic career: Professors Emeriti Yehuda Don of the Economics Department, an expert on Jewish economy; Ernest Krausz of the Sociology and Anthropology Department, a renowned scholar in the sociology of Jewish communities; and Ariel Toaff of the Jewish History Department, a specialist historian of Italian Jewry. They are my advisers and the source of my inspiration to this very day.

Special thanks are owed to Professor Moises Orfali, the former Dean of the Jewish Studies Faculty, Bar-Ilan University, who gave me the confidence to write this book.

I acknowledge with thanks the senior and prominent professors of the Israeli academic world who encouraged me to develop this unique multidisciplinary and interdisciplinary research method: Israel Prize laureate, Professor Emeritus Jacob Landau, who read selected chapters; Professor Gad Gilbar, the former Rector of Haifa

University, a source of consistent support; and Professor Emeritus Sergio Della Pergolla of the Hebrew University of Jerusalem, whose profound, cumulative knowledge of Jewish populations all over the world inspired this research. I am also most obliged to two prominent figures from the Greek and Turkish academic worlds for their kind help: Professor Gelina Harlaftis, Ionian University, Corfu, and Professor Edhem Eldem, Boğaziçi University, Istanbul.

Warm thanks go to my colleagues in Salonica, especially Professor Alexandros Dagkas of the Aristotle University, an expert in the indigenous conditions and terminology of the past; Dr. Ariadni Mutafidou of the Hellenic Open University was tireless in her readiness to assist my research at the local libraries.

I would like to express my appreciation to all the archives and libraries around the world that put their treasures at my disposal. I am most obliged to Fruma Mohrer, Chief Archivist of the YIVO Institute, New York; Devin Naar, the director of the YIVO Salonika Project, and Trudy Balch, project archivist, who assisted me in finding the materials on the Bank Union SA; Elias Messinas, who kindly steered me through the obscurity of the Jewish Community of Salonica at the Central Archives for the History of the Jewish People (CAHJP), Jerusalem. I owe a debt of gratitude to the Bar-Ilan University interlibrary loan service headed by Hadassah Vargon, which managed to produce every item required for my research.

Many thanks to Yannis Megas, Salonica, who gave me permission to publish selected items from his extensive private archive. Erika Perahia Zemour, executive secretary of the Jewish Museum of Thessaloniki, skilfully selected illustrations for the book from Megas' private archive. Also thanks to her staff, especially Mrs. Eleni Tsuka who as a local resident made the past come alive for me.

I am indebted to prominent members of the leadership of Salonica's Jewish community, who have given so much of their time and effort in order to preserve Jewish memory. Special mention goes to my personal friends, Stella Salem, Adv., Kelly and Jacky Benmayor, and Professor Rena Molho.

I note with gratefulness the Israeli businessmen of Salonican origin who opened their doors to me: David Recanati for putting at my disposal his valuable documents; Marcel Yoel, who encouraged me along the way and gave me the idea for the cover illustrations; and Jacky Allalouf, a wonderful raconteur, whose stories instilled in me a sense of understanding of the late 1930s Jewish business world.

In the multi-linguistic research demanded by the subject matter, I was warmly assisted by my expert friends. Moshe Ha-Elion, Chairman of the Association of Survivors of Concentration Camps of Greek Origin Living in Israel, was a youth in 1930s Salonica; his language skills aided me in reading the Greek resources. Daniel Frisch, a relative and an expert in the French and German languages and in banking, shed much light on the translation difficulties pertaining to the financial aspects covered in the book.

The publication of this book was supported by research grants from the Interdisciplinary Department for Social Sciences, Bar-Ilan University; The Israel and Golda Koschitzky Fund attached to the Jewish History Department of Bar-Ilan University; The Aharon and Rachel Dahan Centre for Culture, Society, and Education in the Sephardic Heritage, also at Bar-Ilan University.

In matters of the writing and book production: I owe a great deal to Nina Reshef for the English language editing from the very first draft of this research and throughout its development until the end; to David Brauner for his concerned, constructive, and detailed final editing; Joan Hooper for her incisive proofreading; to the staff of Sussex Academic Press in seeing this complicated book through its publication; and to the Anonymous Reader, whose wise counsel I made a guiding principle for the final editing. Despite every effort to be accurate, any errors that may be found are entirely my responsibility.

I am most grateful to my youngest brother, Dr. Nissim Leon, anthropologist and expert in contemporary Sephardic Jewry in Israel, for his professional advice as well as his emotional support.

Throughout this long journey, my loving family – my parents Shalom and Hana Leon; my children Shira-Rivka and her family; Meir, Shelly, and Nethanel – have been a constant source of forbearing, encouragement, and inspiration.

Last but never least, to my husband of my youth, Michael, who functions as the steady anchor of our family, this book is dedicated to him with love.

ORLY C. MERON
Bar-Ilan University
April 2011

Explanatory Notes

1. After November 1912 all Jewish subjects automatically became Greek citizens, unless they renounced Greek nationality in favour of another citizenship. The term "Jew" includes Jews of all nationalities. "Greek" includes generally Orthodox Christians. In this book, Greek and Jewish are denotations that distinguish religious affiliation.

2. The book contains a vast number of names. Alternative spellings of the same name are quite common, often resulting from the transliteration of names from non-Latin languages, viz., Hebrew, Ladino, and Greek, into French, Spanish, and English. In order to deal with the spelling problem, we have consistently used only one version of the name. The first time a name that has several spellings is mentioned in the text, we add in brackets all various spellings that were found in the documentation. However, any apparent inconsistencies the reader may note are due to strict adherence to the original sources.

3. Regarding the handling of the multilingual sources in the bibliography, the non-English language quotations are italicised. The bibliographical entries from Hebrew and Greek are written in English transliteration followed by an English translation in brackets.

4. The French in the original documents is often written in an ancient or local dialect. Frequent mistakes in French grammar and syntax were left unchanged, i.e., the quotations remain faithful to the French as it was written in the original. Many of the anomalies are noted, but not always. Thus, the English translations may not always be entirely complete, as we sought rather to give the flavour of the quotations rather than a verbatim rendering.

5. When the text refers the reader to the number of a firm in parenthesis, and the number of the Appendix does not appear (only the number of the firm), then such numbers in Chapter 4 refer to Appendix 4.1; Chapter 5 to Appendix 5; and Chapters 8 and 9 to Appendix 8.

Map 1 Sketch map of Greece, 1923, integrating "Old Greece" with "New Greece"

"Old Greece" included the five regions: Central Greece and Eubée, Thessaly, Ionian Islands, Cyclades Islands, and Peloponnese. "New Greece" includes the provinces acquired by Greece after the Balkan Wars (since 1913): Macedonia, Epirus; Crete, Western Thrace, and several Aegean Islands including Lesbos, Samos and Chio, but excluding Rhodes and the Dodecanese, which became Greek only in 1947.

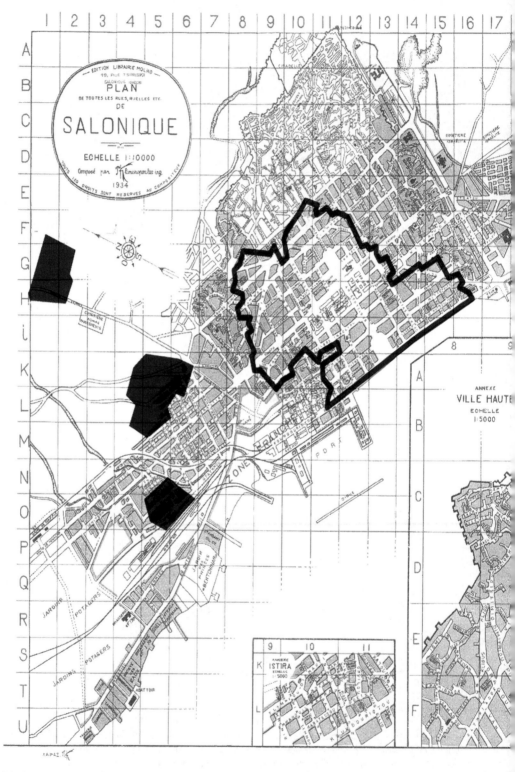

Map 2 Sketch map of the Jewish neighbourhoods in Salonica during the 1930s

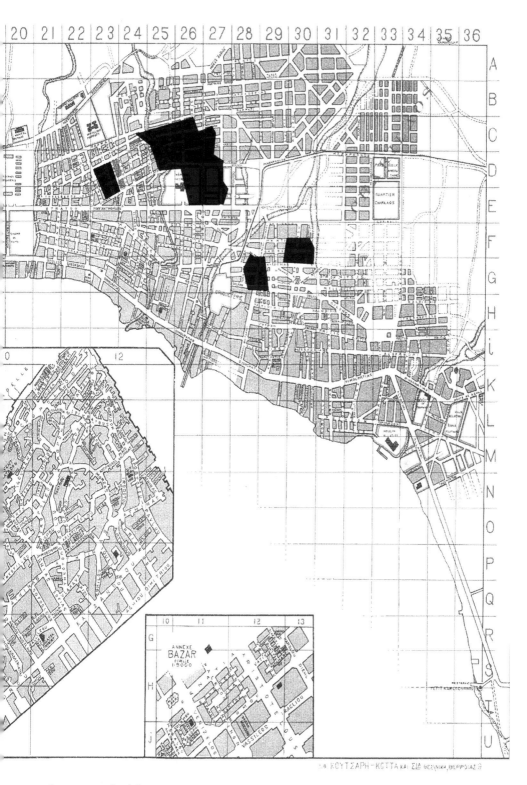

See page xvi for full caption.

Map 2   Sketch map of the Jewish neighbourhoods in Salonica during the 1930s

Based on a scanned city map of 1934 (Courtesy of the Yannis Megas Archive, Salonica)
The city centre's burned-out area indicated by a heavy back line was sketched according to the map published (1967) in Salonique, Ville-Mère en Israël. *Jérusalem and Tel Aviv: Centre de recherches sur le Judaïsme de Salonique (Hebrew).*
The Jewish neighbourhoods (blackened areas) were sketched according to Vilma Hastaoglou-Martinidis (1997). "On the Jewish community of Salonica after the Fire of 1917: An Unpublished Memoir and Other Documents from the Papers of Henry Morgenthau, Sr." In I. K. Hassiotis (ed.), The Jewish Communities of Southeastern Europe from the Fifteenth Century to the End of World War II. *Thessaloniki: Institute for Balkan Studies, p. 174.*
I thank Prof. Vilma Hastaoglou-Martinidis, who kindly allowed me to use this map as a basis for delineating the Jewish neighbourhoods.

For Michael

Introduction

This book traces the transformations in the Jewish-owned economy in Salonica from the incorporation of Salonica and its Macedonian periphery into the Greek nation-state in 1912 until the Italian offensive in Albania began on 28 October 1940, an event that marked Greece's entry into World War II. The book's main hypothesis is that the scope and character of the Jewish economy were determined by the interplay between the opportunity structure provided by the host environment, endogenous factors, and the group's internal sociocultural resources. Through a detailed examination of the evidence, this book also discusses the networks established by Salonican Jews transplanted to France, Italy, Great Britain, and America as well as British Mandatory Palestine.

Macedonia was already in the midst of an entrepreneurial boom during the decline of Ottoman rule. Several scholars, including Paul Dumont[1] and Donald Quataert,[2] in their comments on the spectacular industrial and commercial development and its impact on the local population, have emphasised the significant role of individual Jewish entrepreneurs – Allatini, Modiano and Mizrahi, to name just three – active in Salonica at the turn of the twentieth century. Quataert, who documented and analysed industrial development throughout the Empire,[3] stated that Salonica was unique in that its major industrialists were Jews.[4] In this book we depart from the Ottoman era and focus not only on "the exceptional individual case" but also on the "mass of small and medium business that determine the group function".[5] We view this class of businessmen as job creators for their fellow Jews because their enterprises provided a protected labour market once increasing competition and institutional discrimination began to plague the Greek national labour market.

The study of Jewish entrepreneurship has found a secure place within the broader research conducted during the last decade in Salonica. That research is aimed at divulging the neglected contributions of Greek Macedonia to the development of the New Greek nation-state and its economy. Comprehensive research has since identified Jewish entrepreneurship as an integral and important segment of the larger Greek economy. The series on this subject, published by Evangelos Hekimoglou (2004) and supported by Greek firms and the National Bank of Greece, includes two magnificent volumes, written in Greek, which focus on the period 1900–1940. Volume C is dedicated to monographs on Greek entrepreneurial families (of which only two out of thirty-two were Jewish), while Volume D provides a directory of the firms operating in Salonica during the same period. This volume is based on reports prepared by the Salonica Chamber of Commerce and Industry in 1919, 1924, 1932, 1933, 1934, 1939, and 1940, and additional data derived from contemporary Greek commercial guides published in 1920, 1925, 1927, and 1940.[6] About one-third of the firms involved were of Jewish ownership.

The present book is not intended to provide a history of individual firms, as the relevant details can be found in Hekimoglou's directory. Instead, we focus here on the inter-ethnic aspects of Jewish entrepreneurship from the perspective of changing minority–majority relations. After its incorporation into Greece in 1912, Salonica's population consisted of multiple ethnic elements; this was to change following the entry of Greek refugees, beginning in September 1922; Salonica would henceforth become a dual, ethnically stratified society (Chapter 3). In consequence, research of Jewish entrepreneurship in Salonica during the 1920s must consider the ethnic dimension and its implications. Local Greek research has previously treated the Jewish entrepreneurial segment active during this period as an integral part of the local indigenous Greek bourgeoisie, not as members of an ethnic minority living in such a society. By doing so, scholars have, in effect, denied the discrimination experienced by this group, which was finally deported from Nazi-occupied Greece and perished in the Holocaust.

The book employs an innovative inter-disciplinary methodology integrating economic sociology with historical archival analysis. These methods, previously acknowledged as fruitful for the investigation of entrepreneurial behaviour of indigenous and migrant minorities active in Western countries operating in advanced economies,[7] is now applied to a different context, that of an indigenous Jewish minority and repatriated refugees active during consolidation of the Greek nation-state. The research examines Jewish entrepreneurship in changing environments, from the European economic semi-colonialism that thrived in Ottoman Macedonia to the emergence of a new national entity; from a city in which the Jews were a dominant demographic minority to one in which they were an ethnic–religious minority but perceived as a national minority by the majority; from a market integrated into the developing global economy to a national autarky.

The book also expands the theoretical discussion on Jewish entrepreneurial patterns among Ashkenazi minorities (Kuznets 1960; Kahan 1978; Garncarska-Kadary 1985 (in Hebrew); Mosse 1987; Don 1991; Green 1997; Godley 2001) to the Sephardic cultural region that thrived in the Balkans prior to the outbreak of World War II. The empirical findings therefore contribute the material for new theoretical insights regarding the vital connection between institutional contexts and the strategies adopted by minority entrepreneurs in order to survive political and economic discrimination in ethnically stratified societies.

This book stresses Jewish business initiatives in the private sector, which was less vulnerable to ethnic discrimination when compared with public and semi-public sectors (e.g., the port). It examines Jewish-owned firm behaviour during three crucial periods when new conditions for entrepreneurship arose. Jewish private-sector entrepreneurs took an active part in community life and contributed to its well-being at the same time that they provided places of work for individual co-ethnics.

The research examined macro-level, historical features of the Jewish economy in addition to the micro-level details relating to the Jewish-owned economy. It provides an empirical analysis of Jewish entrepreneurship in Salonica based on a combination of qualitative and quantitative methods, an approach appropriate to the sphere of historical economic sociology. Both micro data and macro data were derived from various primary sources: official and unofficial documents; published and unpublished documents from Jewish and non-Jewish sources, such as documents written in Ladino, which includes the Jewish community's budgets and almanacs; also used were the Salonica Jewish community's correspondence with Zionist institutions and representatives. In addition, unpublished Jewish multi-lingual archival material, much of it translated and analysed for the first time, was made available. All these sources are detailed in the Bibliography.

Several sources were especially relevant to the empirical research. I am referring to consular reports, the yearbook of Salonica's local Chamber of Commerce and Industry for 1922 and *Guide Sam* for 1930. The micro data derived from these sources, complemented and compared with other documents, enabled us to sketch an overview of the structure of Jewish entrepreneurial activity at two turning points in time: 1922 and 1929. The mapping of Jewish entrepreneurship on the eve of the Great Depression, facilitated by information gleaned from the 1930 edition of *Guide Sam*, covering firms active in 1929, provided the infrastructure for the detailed empirical analysis of Jewish entrepreneurial strategies adopted during the 1930s. *Guide Sam*, published for ten consecutive years (1920–1930), was meant to be "le miroir fidèle de l'Orient" according to its editor, the former Salonican journalist and publisher Sam Lévy.[8] Lévy attempted to keep the Sephardic Jewish commercial networks in the Near East well informed after their centre shifted to Paris, where Jews of Salonican as well as Levantine origin had begun to concentrate. The conspicuous placement of advertisements for Jewish firms, in addition to the "Our Announcers" column, clearly demonstrate that the *Guide*'s target audience was the Sephardic Jewish entrepreneurial community residing in the Levant,[9] which represented one segment of the Jewish transnational Diaspora. The section devoted to Greece in the *Guide* focused on Salonica also referred to Athens, which had recently become the centre of the Greek national economy. Data were likewise provided on Kavalla, the second largest urban centre in Macedonia after Salonica thanks to its tobacco industry and large population of Jewish tobacco workers.

The depiction of the Jewish economy on the eve of the Great Depression (1929) provided the foundations for our portrayal of the events that took place in the 1930s. Using previously unstudied archival documents obtained from two Jewish banks located in Salonica, Banque Union and Banque Amar,[10] we investigated Jewish entrepreneurship for two sub-periods, each with its own focus: 1930–1933, when Jewish entrepreneurs were forced to cope with the Depression; and 1934–1937, when Jewish entrepreneurial activity responded to the wave of Jewish emigration to the Land of Israel, then under the British Mandate.

Banque Union (*Enossis*) SA (*Société Anonyme*), previously Banque Mosseri (see Appendix 4.1, no. 673), was founded in 1926 by Joseph Nehama with capital of £50,000 and reserves amounting to £10,000 and GRD 1,374,000; it was managed by his brother Albert Nehama together with a governing board including Jews, Joseph Nehama (president), Albert Matarasso, and Jeshua Perahia but also a Greek business leader, Ioannis Athananasiadis.[11] The bank had wide-ranging connections with European financial institutions, such as the Union de Banques Suisses. Evidence for these ties is demonstrated by the numerous proposals received requesting that the Salonica bank advertise itself within Union yearbooks and almanacs[12] as well as take advantage of Union banking services in their branches spread throughout Europe. Other European firms, such as London's Hotel Plaza,[13] offered their services to travelling Banque Union officials. This Jewish bank also cooperated with foreign banks with regard to financial information. Correspondence between Banque Union and European banks during the summer of 1932 shows the reciprocal flow of solvency-related information, so crucial during the 1930s credit crunch. About 300 of these documents are preserved at the YIVO Institute for Jewish Research in New York. Some of these documents contain correspondence between Banque Union and European firms and banks during the short but significant period extending from July to November 1932, some three months after Greek Premier Venizelos suspended payments on all foreign debts (27 April 1932). Generally written in French, the *lingua franca* of Mediterranean commerce (see Appendix 7.2), these documents shed light on how Jewish entrepreneurs faced the international financial crisis (see Chapter 7).

Banque Amar was a successor of the banking firm established by Abram Ascer. This SA (*Société Anonyme*) firm was founded in 1920 with an initial capital input of GRD 1,200,000 and reserves of GRD 22,600,000. The bank was tied to Bank Saul Amar, Paris. Its board of directors was comprised of Abram Amar (president), Saul Amar, Moïse Assael, Eli Amar, Eli Allalouf, and another Amar family member.[14] The Banque Amar archive was also seized by Nazi troops in August of 1941.[15] According to Michael Molho and Joseph Nehama, the so-called Rosenberg *Sonderkommandos* ransacked the Banque Union archives in search of evidence to substantiate their theories about an international Jewish financial plot to control the world.[16] Strangely, Molho and Nehama, who witnessed the events, made no mention of Banque Amar. This bank, like Banque Union, had Jewish staff and held Jewish capital; it was one of the most important Jewish financial institutions operating in the Greek state. The archive's documents[17] miraculously survived and are now preserved in the Central Archives of the History of the Jewish People (CAHJP) in Jerusalem.[18] They shed new light on the entrepreneurial activity of Salonica's Jews in addition to that of the Greek majority on the eve of the Nazi occupation.

Reliable financial information, exchanged between Banque Amar and its clients (see Chapters 8–9), is recorded in about 800 statements. Filed under the heading "Renseignement" (Information) and ordered by reference number and date, these documents reveal banking information about those Greek as well as Jewish firms that had applied for loans.[19] These "due diligence" type of documents, spanning from 1935 to 1937, shed further light on the business practices and dynamics current during the 1930s, and often introduce the history of the entrepreneurs between the wars. Most were written in antiquated, informal French; the fifty-two documents written in Greek generally contain information pertaining to Greek clients. These original bank documents contain the name of the firm; year of its establishment; address; partners' names and demographic details (origin, nationality, age, marital status, family members); the firm's economic activity and net worth (cash and immovable assets); number of employees and/or workers; and moral standing, especially solvency. They frequently contain a brief history of the firm and details meant to influence bank officials responsible for approving loans. They provide data facilitating exploration of the microeconomics of self-employment in the Greek historical markets of the mid-1930s, together with indications of the level of competition waged between the city's veteran Jewish population and the Greek entrepreneurs. These data are used to distinguish between the Jewish entrepreneurial elites and their Greek peers throughout this book (see especially Chapters 8 and 9). Appendices 8 and 9, constructed on the basis of the original documents, support achievement of previously impossible in-depth analysis.

The book consists of three parts. **Part One** contains the theoretical framework and historical background. Chapter 1 introduces the interdisciplinary approach to the research of ethnic economies established by immigrants or by permanent ethnic minorities. Chapter 2 provides an historical background of Jewish entrepreneurial activity in Salonica.

Parts Two and **Three** follow a chronological division: **Part Two** (Chapters 3–5) covers the period 1912–1929, divided into two phases (de-colonisation and post-colonisation, before and after the compulsory population exchange between Turkey and Greece), beginning with the incorporation of Macedonia and its capital, Salonica, into the Greek nation-state and closing with the Great Depression. **Part Three** (Chapters 6–10) covers the period from 1930 to the eve of Greece's entry into World War II.

Chapter 3 describes the post-1912 transformations experienced by the Jewish community. It focuses on the area's political transformation subsequent to the incorporation (1912–1921), which was followed by the radical demographic changes initiated with the entry of more than 100,000 Greek refugees into Salonica after the Turks defeated Greece in the Greco-Turkish War. This "Transfer", as it is called, stimulated labour market competition and also intensified nationalism. While this chapter concurrently traces the meaning of the new exogenous conditions for Jewish entrepreneurs, it also examines their impact on Jewish entrepreneurial power and on the ethnic resources available for entrepreneurship. Chapters 4 and 5 provide an overview of the scope and structure of the Jewish economy before (1912–1921) and after (1922–1929) these radical demographic transformations.

Part Three is based on innovative empirical research. It provides a detailed analysis of the business strategies adopted by Jewish entrepreneurs during the international economic crisis of the 1930s. Chapter 6, like Chapter 3, describes the opportunities opening up to Jewish entrepreneurs together with the ensuing changes in group resources; it focuses on the decline in the number of entrepreneurs and the supply of labour following the new wave of Jewish emigration (1932–1936). Through an analysis of their correspondence, primarily with European firms, Chapter 7 examines the short-term solutions adopted by Jewish companies as they confronted the financial crisis. Chapters 8 and 9 examine long-term Jewish entrepreneurial responses while focusing on the quantitative and qualitative features of Jewish firms on the brink of World War II. Chapter 10 describes the final phase of Salonican Jewish entrepreneurship (1938–1940), while proposing some explanations for its tragic end. The chapter also offers several insights based on a comparison between the Jewish entrepreneurial experience in Salonica and that of their fellow Jews in Central Europe on the one hand, and of non-Jewish minorities responding to similar opportunity structures on the other.

Research on the patterns of Jewish entrepreneurship during the 1930s also sheds light on the conduct of Jewish life in the city prior to the Holocaust. Visual data from historical photographs and postcards[20] supports the socio-economic research.[21] Testimonies and memories add a human voice to the empirical analysis. These documents, which were in effect rescued from the ashes, commemorate the silenced Jewish voices and make this book a memorial to Jewish life in Salonica before the Holocaust.

PART ONE

The Rise of a Jewish Economy in Ottoman Salonica, 1881–1912

1 | Theoretical Framework

Le samedi, d'abord, c'était la fête générale à Salonique, les musulmans, les ortho-
doxes, les Bulgares, tout le monde fermait les magasins, samedi, c'était sacré . . .
la douane, la poste, tout était fermé.[1]

Due to the demographic and economic superiority of the Jewish population during the last decades of Ottoman rule in multi-ethnic Salonica, port activity ceased on Saturday, the Jewish day of rest, rather than on Friday, the Muslim day of rest (see Chapter 2). Following Salonica's incorporation into the new Greek nation-state (1912), the city's Jewish economy gradually shrank until its tragic end after the German invasion (9 April 1941).

Salonica's Jews were, first and foremost, members of a distinct ethnic minority,[2] at times a minority among the city's international heterogeneous populace, and at other times a minority within the relatively homogenous national population. Against this historical background, this chapter proposes a theoretical framework that will enable us to understand the longitudinal dynamics of Jewish economic activity, its static latitudinal patterns as well as the factors that anchor this analysis within inter-ethnic comparative perspectives.

Writing within the developing interdisciplinary approach of economic sociology,[3] Light and Gold (2000) defined the comprehensive concept "ethnic economy" in practical, operational terms so as to make its subject amenable to comparative inter-ethnic empirical research. An ethnic economy consists of two complementary components: an *ethnic-owned economy* and an *ethnic-controlled economy*. While the ethnic-owned economy is comprised of self-employed entrepreneurs or businessmen,[4] their unpaid family members and their co-ethnic employees, the ethnic-controlled economy includes firms not under ethnic ownership in addition to government-owned or controlled firms. In the latter, ethnic groups exercise control over hiring, wages, and working conditions, usually due to their size, clustering, and organisation but also their political or economic power.[5] This book focuses on the Jewish ethnic-owned economy; it therefore stresses the central role of ethnic entrepreneurs in creating employment for themselves and for their co-ethnic workers.

1.1 Determinants of Ethnic Entrepreneurship

Here we delve into the world of entrepreneurship[6] in the commercial and industrial sectors, to the exclusion of the free professions (law, medicine, engineering, and so forth). When examining an ethnic economy, we refer mainly to owners and managers of their own businesses,[7] who identify themselves with their respective ethnic group. For purposes of the quantitative study, we define an *entrepreneur* as a firm founder or owner who has chosen self-employment over salaried employment.[8]

Ethnic entrepreneurs tend to suffer from discrimination and exclusion at the hands of the dominant population, mainly due to their subordinate political status (see below). At the same time, as members of an ethnic community,[9] ethnic entrepreneurs enjoy the benefits of "ethnic resources",[10] material and non-material capital often unavailable to majority entrepreneurs. These resources include the group's prominent social traits, what can serve as the basis for collective action and social solidarity. We therefore find that ethnic resources can include the kinship relations that create social networks; the cultural heritage that transmits traditional skills; clustered residence that is conducive to increased solidarity and institutions established for the provision of mutual aid,[11] including cheap credit.[12] Because social "closure" (in-group marriage, spatial concentration, etc.) facilitates the creation of mutual obligations,[13] expectations and trustworthiness among group members, it increases the social capital available to ethnic entrepreneurs. These entrepreneurs, who find it more difficult to borrow from banks than do members of the majority population, go on to use ethnically grounded social capital to facilitate the conclusion of their market transactions.[14]

Ethnic networks are one source of social capital because they channel co-ethnics into jobs and training opportunities. Belonging to such a network enables both employers and employees to acquire the qualitative information that reduces risk.[15] An ethnic community's scale (size, concentration, and efficient communal institutions) thus affects the quantity and quality of the social capital available to its entrepreneurs. Ethnic entrepreneurs thus enjoy the advantage of being able to mobilise the collective ethnic resources (cheap ethnic credit, loyal ethnic labour, etc.) that enhance those individual "class resources" (real capital, human capital such as education, job skills, citizenship, and so forth)[16] that support the organisation and conduct of business.[17] These advantages promote the optimal use of the minority entrepreneur's personal capabilities (e.g., innovation, risk-tolerance, linguistic skills) in his endeavours.[18]

Research conducted among various minorities in different host societies has nevertheless shown that the interplay between opportunity structures and group characteristics is what determines the specific entrepreneurial patterns adopted by ethnic entrepreneurs. The former consist of (1) market conditions (ethnic structure of consumer markets and "business vacancies" in the non-ethnic market) that favour growth and (2) access to entrepreneurial opportunities. The latter depend, of course, on individual "class resources" (e.g., linguistic skills, real capital) but are highly influenced by government policies toward minorities (institutional discrimination) as well as by inter-ethnic competition.[19] Ethnic group access to opportunities is also influenced by the entrepreneurial culture of the dominant population, which impacts on the quantity of business vacancies available to minority entrepreneurs.[20]

Because exclusion of and discrimination against minorities in the mainstream labour market contribute to the construction of structural barriers preventing immigrants from equitably competing with native-born workers in the labour market, migrants often pursue self-employment to offset the risk of unemployment.[21] Once they adopt this option, a ready supply of cheap co-ethnic labour enables ethnic entrepreneurs to work at levels of monetary gain below those demanded by majority entrepreneurs in the same industry or branch. The disadvantages of exclusion and discrimination thus provide ethnic minority businessmen with the economic advantage of potentially being able to undersell majority competitors. Furthermore, because recently arrived immigrants prefer to work in co-ethnic labour markets in order to side-step barriers (lack of linguistic skills, discrimination) to entry in the new host society,[22] ethnic entrepreneurs are able to hire co-ethnics at below-standard wages. For these reasons, ethnic entrepreneurs are often accused of *exploiting* their co-ethnic employees.[23]

To summarise, the phenomenon of ethnic entrepreneurship is cumulatively affected by the interaction between group resources, individual resources, market growth potential as well as the prevailing attitudes towards ethnic group participation in the mainstream labour market. These same factors impact on the scope as well as structure of the ethnic-owned economy. In recognition of this framework's effectiveness, we apply it here to deepen our understanding of the ethnic-owned economy maintained by Salonica's Jewish community before the Nazis rang their death knell.

1.2 Ethnic Entrepreneurial Strategies and the Ethnic-Owned Economy

The reciprocities between ethnic group characteristics and the opportunity structure within which an ethnic entrepreneur operates determine the scope of the ethnic-owned economy (see section 1.1) but also the entrepreneurial strategies devised to respond to each phase of economic change.

The late economist Simon Kuznets, winner of the 1978 Nobel Prize, offered a concise formulation of the three main factors that impact on the economic structure of small, permanent migration-generated ethnic groups: unique pre-migratory skills (or "economic heritage"), attempts to maintain internal cohesion (in-group endogamy, clustered residence, mutual assistance institutions), and environmental conditions (state policy and public attitudes towards minorities, the structure of opportunities).[24]

The validity of the Kuznets model appears to be confirmed by the similarities in the strategies adopted by an array of similar ethnic groups active in capitalist societies around the world.[25] Ethnic entrepreneurship (in contrast to non-ethnic small-scale entrepreneurship) is driven by labour market disadvantages and discrimination; participants are consequently forced to cut the costs of labour and operations to ensure survival. In the face of these challenges, ethnic resources provide the cushions allowing the group's entrepreneurs to adapt their activities to changing circumstances and, ultimately, to enhance class resources. The following three strategies are those found to be typical of ethnic entrepreneurship in commerce and manufacturing, the two main areas of Salonica's Jewish-owned economy covered in this book:

1. Attraction to portable businesses due to their status as immigrants or, alternatively, as a response to their politically unstable status. These endeavours are attractive due to the inferior political status allotted to immigrants or, alternatively, as a response to political instability. Ethnic entrepreneurs tend to acquire skills that are

easily transferable from one region to another; they favour businesses requiring relatively liquid assets and few fixed assets; they prefer goods that have high turnover and low profit margins.[26] In line with these preferences, products are often sold directly to customers in the open market.[27]

2. Concentration: Intense competition compels ethnic entrepreneurs to increase efficiency without, however, changing the structural basis of their costs. They prefer to take advantage of ethnic cohesion, community solidarity and informal networks, assets which contribute to horizontal cooperation between co-ethnic businesses operating in the mainstream market. Ethnic entrepreneurs also lean toward niching, a strategy supporting group embeddedness within the mainstream economy. Among the principal stimuli motivating niche creation are an industry's reduced profitability and loss of attractiveness for the indigenous population; rising demand for ethnic consumer products engendered by a taste for things exotic; demand for new, specialised skills during industry formation; and identification of under-served non-ethnic markets. Ethnic information and recruitment networks support the channelling of recently arrived immigrants to the new niches. The concentration of co-ethnics in these niches also occurs through vertical as well as horizontal integration, which strengthens the niche's ethnic identification.[28]

3. Organisation as a family business, a structure often decisive for success: Initial investments in such enterprises are often small in scale and based on labour-intensive technologies. Members of the nuclear and extended family provide cheap (even unpaid) and devoted labour, prepared to work long hours. With relatives normatively indebted to their employers, reduced production costs and extensive guaranteed credit, the family business often promotes family cohesion by encouraging marriages between far-flung family members.[29] Ethnic entrepreneurs are also able to hire high-quality co-ethnic workers at the low wages that their disadvantaged status compels them to accept.[30] Family businesses likewise provide informal vocational training to young co-ethnic workers and future entrepreneurs.[31]

The ethnic entrepreneurial strategies determined the structure of the ethnic-owned economy. As competition and institutional (overt or latent) discrimination intensify, the ethnic economy tends to become narrower and more concentrated. We can therefore understand why Kuznets considered the structure of a minority economy to be "abnormal" in comparison with the mainstream economy.

> If the economic structure of a country's total population is "normal", then, almost by definition, the economic structure of a small and permanent minority must be abnormal. Otherwise the minority will not long survive as a distinctive group.[32]

Kuznets's attribution of "abnormality" to ethnic economy structure should be applied particularly to that of the Jewish-owned economy, the subject of this book. Any analysis of the minority entrepreneurs' adjustment to the larger, majority economy should likewise refer to the way that the minority entrepreneurs retained the distinct structure of the resulting Jewish-owned economy.[33]

1.3 Ethnic Economies and Levels of Analysis

Based on their analysis of ethnic entrepreneurial behaviour in the Netherlands, Kloosterman and Rath (2001) caution us about automatically treating group traits as explanatory variables when referring to ethnic entrepreneurship. Instead, they stress the importance of analysing this phenomenon within its "specific context".[34] Casson and Godley (2005) also determined that variations in institutional regimes and the backgrounds of the actors involved appear to significantly influence the process by which ethnic entrepreneurs are able to overcome economic discrimination, build prosperous businesses, and acquire social acceptability.[35]

This book addresses a slightly different but related phenomenon, that of the "classic" middleman minority.[36] Such a minority's entrepreneurial activity is conducted in the historical context of a political entity's transition from European colonialism/semi-colonialism[37] to nation-statehood.[38]

The initial phase of this historical situation can be outlined as follows: European colonialism/semi-colonialism creates new economically profitable opportunities for small demotic ethnic communities (see note 9, above) whose elites had enjoyed a privileged, economically favoured status, conferred in return for their political loyalty to the colonial elites present in the heterogeneous, rigidly stratified host society. This situation regenerated the group's ethnic resources (promoting demographic growth mainly in consequence of chain migration, reinforced social solidarity) as well as those "class resources" available to its members, especially marketable skills such as linguistic capacities and the ability to mobilise "ethnic resources" for business ventures.[39] All these regenerated resources allowed the group to adapt its economic activities in general, and entrepreneurial activity in particular, to the new circumstances. Under these conditions, by virtue of these competitive advantages over the majority as well as other minorities, the respective ethnic group is able to fulfil functions that the indigenous majority is unable or unwilling to undertake.[40] This functional version of the "classic middleman minority" model does not treat the minority as a monolithic population segment.[41] Rather, it stresses the minority's mercantile legacy and business activities,[42] and consequently enables us to analyse the entire ethnic-owned economy, the middleman minority's entrepreneurs as well as their recruited co-ethnic workers.

The "ethnic economy" of middleman minorities thus encompasses all ethnically owned or controlled enterprises active in the broader economy.[43] From an operational perspective, the term can serve as "an inclusive umbrella" for the systematic examination of longitudinal changes in the respective group's economy at each phase in which a new opportunity structure emerges. Because industrial and occupational clustering is measurable, the concept can be used to conduct comparative research on the mobility and economic integration of ethnic minorities in different contexts.[44]

The weight of research on the entrepreneurial patterns of immigrants and migrant-generated minorities has so far focused mainly on contemporary advanced Western economies. This book extends that research to the ethnic economies of "former" middleman minority entrepreneurs in an emerging nation-state undergoing globalisation/de-globalisation, a process that apparently reached its conclusion in Greece as the worldwide recession of the late 1920s was about to begin. That traumatic event provoked the rise of national autarkies and disrupted "the first era of globalisation".[45] Two salient phases link the rise of the nation-state to the final stage of the "first era of globalisation".[46] The first phase, what I refer to as the *de-colonisation* phase, saw the end of colonial rule. It somewhat overlapped the birth of the independent nation-state and the nation-building process that helped initiate the modern world-system.[47] The second historical context, the *post-colonial* phase, was marked by the emerging nation-state consolidation.[48] This phase promoted the introduction of economic and political barriers to prevent the free transfer of people and goods within the world-economy.[49] Each phase was accompanied by multi-dimensional transformations in opportunity structures; new market conditions; new ethnic relations, as well as revised national preferences.[50] As the region's incorporation within the modern world-system progressed, new competitive components were formed.[51]

Two major historically interrelated factors affected the nation-state's economic opportunity structure and thus the ethnic economy: The first, major demographic shifts, involved repatriation of persons (including political refugees) belonging to the national "majority" from their former location in the diaspora. The repatriated population came well-equipped with political and some specific economic resources.[52] Population movements strengthened the emerging state's hold on territory, homogenised population makeup and increased economic competition between veteran ethnic group residents and the repatriated majority, especially in the main-stream labour market.[53] The second, economic nationalism, often evolved into economic chauvinism, expressed in behaviour patterns and policies that helped consol-idate the mainstream economy: a preference for persons belonging to the national majority in the spheres of commerce, labour, and marriage; and protection of majority labour from the risks of economic competition.[54] Government policies thus exacer-bated inter-ethnic market competition by applying legal and political measures meant to favour the national majority and concurrently discriminate against minorities.[55] Government intervention assured control not only in the public sector, where the state acted as the employer, but also in the private sector.[56] In return, the new nation-state expected its majority entrepreneurs to express the same nationalistic "taste for discrim-ination", meaning a readiness to pay the material price of lost "efficiency" incurred with the replacement of experienced minority labour by often inexperienced labour belonging to the national majority.[57]

Yet, such socio-political environments often regenerate the "sojourning"[58] features typical of migrant ethnic groups, but this time among indigenous permanent (non-assimilating) small minorities.[59] During the de-colonisation as well as post-colonisation phases, such features may appear most intensively among long-resident ethnic migrants. Salonica's Jews represented one such minority in the period in question, 1912–1940[60] (see Chapters 3, 6).

Research on middleman minorities active in plural societies[61] undergoing transition from a patrimonial/colonial regime to that of independent nation-statehood stresses modifications in the respective society's ethnic preferences and subsequent intensified inter-ethnic competition.[62] During these periods of change, minority group members, as former "privileged insiders", become "ethnic outsiders", objects of discrimination at the hands of the new ruling elites.[63] As agents for the rising politically dominant group, the new state's government prefer cooperation with co-national partners. Among the methods these governments choose to realise this preference is reduction of local market competition through implementation of policies geared at protecting those sectors in which the dominant group is most heavily involved.[64] Such acts impact on minorities' access to new entrepreneurial opportunities as well as on their ability to preserve their established economic and social positions. Lacking sufficient political power to counteract these measures, minority entrepreneurs strive to protect their interests by increasingly transferring assets abroad or even emigrating. Yet, the remaining minority entrepreneurs – the subject of this book – continue to experience shifts in their entrepreneurial activity.[65]

Regarding the ethnic-owned economies themselves, past research has focused primarily on voluntary migrants, individuals who made a decision to immigrate with various degrees of free will. These studies, which dwelt on the private sector, generally included small-scale ethnic entrepreneurs who created limited job opportunities for their co-ethnics and thereby saved them from suffering discrimination in the mainstream economy. The theoretical foundations of those studies were, for the most part, embedded within the experiences of North American or other advanced capitalist economies,[66] and based on the assumption that the immigrants involved came from less-developed backgrounds than that of the majority population. Reflecting the experiences of advanced capitalist economies, their authors concluded that ethnic resources – which include access to cheap but loyal co-ethnic labour – could compensate for large-scale exclusionary and discriminatory treatment.[67] Given the specific context of that research, which was conducted in relatively liberal competitive markets, the universality of their conclusions should not automatically be assumed.

This book expands the research on ethnic economies to the dynamic context of an emerging nation-state. It examines the extent to which Jewish entrepreneurs were able to economically adapt to the consolidating national autarky. In examining the entrepreneurial strategies adopted by these ethnic entrepreneurs, we focus on the strength of their ethnic resources and the extent to which formation of inter-ethnic ties (e.g., ethnically mixed joint ventures) assisted Jewish entrepreneurs in sustaining the socioeconomic status achieved during the semi-colonialism phase. We also delve into how the phenomenon described as "reactive ethnicity" supported their adjustment.[68] More crucially, the book traces the Jewish entrepreneurial responses to the multi-dimensional transformations in the structure of opportunities as well as ethnic collective resources throughout every phase of Greece's passage to an autarkic economy during the 1930s.

This book thus presents the product of research conducted on three geopolitical units: the city of Salonica including the Macedonia region, the Greek nation-state, and the modern world-system. Different sets of factors shaped the opportunity structures at each level.[69] After arguing that the Jewish community of Salonica acted as a middleman minority during European semi-colonialism in Ottoman Macedonia, the book goes on to conduct a dynamic analysis of the type of entrepreneurship practiced by this stateless minority within the inchoate Greek nation-state from the broad perspective of the *longue durée* of de-globalisation.

2 | The Jewish Economy on the Eve of the Greek Annexation, 1881–1912

In this chapter we survey the history of the Jewish minority in Salonica together with the Jewish-owned economy as it emerged at the turn of the twentieth century. Who belonged to the entrepreneurial elites? How were they distributed among the various sectors? Was capital available and where were the boundaries of the Jewish economy prior to Salonica's annexation by the Greek nation-state?

2.1 Historical Roots of the Jewish Population in Ottoman Salonica, 1492–mid-1800s

Since the beginning of the first century BC, when the city served as the administrative centre for the Roman government of Macedonia, Salonica has been home to a small Jewish community. This presence continued well into the fifteenth century, through the Ottoman occupation of the city in 1430, and is recorded in the Imperial Census of 1478. Following that census, all signs of a Jewish presence in the city suddenly vanished. The census data appear to confirm the commonly held view that Salonica's Jews, like the city's other ethnic residents, were forcibly transferred (*surgun*) to Istanbul by the Ottomans after they seized the region from the collapsing Byzantine Empire.[1]

Signs of a renewed, prosperous Jewish presence in Ottoman Salonica began to appear toward the end of the fifteenth century. Drawn by the incentive of asylum as well as the new opportunities in the nascent area of international commerce and crafts (e.g., preparation of "court attire"), Jews began settling in Macedonia and its capital after fanatical Catholic rulers expelled them from the Iberian Peninsula (1492, 1497), Sicily (1493), and Napoli (1510, 1541). Their arrival caused a demographic upheaval in Salonica; Jews became the dominant component in the city's ethnic fabric almost consistently until the eighteenth century.[2] The Judeo-Spanish-speaking migrants, who formed the majority among the Jewish population that also included relatively small numbers of Greek Jews[3] and Jewish refugees from central Europe, created the largest of the Sephardic Jewish communities in the Ottoman territories by the sixteenth century. The Iberian Jewish immigrants transferred the advanced technologies and skills of the Western textile industry to the Ottoman Empire, to make Salonica the most important centre of woollen cloth production in the empire.[4]

Salonica's Jewish population growth stalled and then began to decline in the late 1600s, together with the Ottoman Empire's waning economic and political strength,[5] especially after the economic crisis that struck the Empire's textile centres. Salonica's Jews, like other Ottoman textile manufacturers, were unable to effectively compete with their European rivals. The latter, equipped with the latest technologies and more favourable trade conditions, had gained control over the production of raw materials, which forced up input prices. Europe then flooded the Empire with high-quality textiles that could be purchased at relatively low prices. The Jewish manufacturers who had committed themselves to supplying uniforms for the Ottoman Janissaries were forced to absorb heavy losses, and many Jewish textile manufacturers were compelled to emigrate in search of new economic horizons. Furthermore, the continued decline of Salonica's port, caused in part by the diversion of international trade routes in the previous century as well as the blossoming of new centres of international trade in Izmir, motivated Salonican Jewish businessmen bent on taking advantage of the new opportunities offered in Western Anatolia and Western Europe to depart from the city.[6]

Jewish demographic decline was also driven by mass conversions to Islam (1683, 1686) following the death of the false prophet Sabbatai Tsevi in 1676. These new converts (the *Dönme*), who imitated their prophet's conversion to Islam while in Istanbul (1666), transformed Salonica to the region's largest *Dönme* centre, followed by Edirne, Izmir and Bursa.[7] Emigration was also stimulated by various natural disasters. Regional insecurity, fires, epidemics and poor sanitation caused a drop in total population as morbidity increased among adults; infant mortality rose precipitously. Following the 1709–1719 epidemic, the Jewish population of Salonica declined from 30,000 (1715) to about 12,000 (1800) (see Appendix 2, Table A).

The Jewish population in Salonica was documented by an official census in 1831. Although the figures recorded in that census suffer from under-registration (i.e., they exclude women and children) and inconsistencies by administrative region, they do provide official preliminary estimates of the number of Jews that lived within the district of Salonica (the minimal administrative unit that included the city). If we adjust the 1831 figures by multiplying the 5,667 Jewish males listed by 5 (average Jewish family size), we arrive at an estimated Jewish population of about 28,000 living in the city,[8] just when Salonica was on the verge of entering a new phase, that of European semi-colonialism.

2.2 The New Structure of Opportunities in Ottoman Macedonia

The specific historical geopolitical framework relevant to our discussion was demarcated by the geographical boundaries of the Ottoman Province (*vilâyet*) of Salonica, roughly the area of Greek Macedonia (as of November 1912).[9] It is within this space that Macedonia's transition from part of the Ottoman Empire to a modern economic unit joined to the Greek nation-state occurred. Economic growth was driven by regional and world market trends, with new opportunities for entrepreneurs created in a region where the majority (87 percent or 37,206 out of 42,714) of Macedonia's Jewish population had concentrated by 1893.[10]

2.2.1 European Semi-Colonialism in Ottoman Macedonia

With the abolition of Ottoman trade monopolies and the establishment of free trade zones (1838), the control of imports was effectively transferred from the Empire's authorities and guilds to European hands.[11] European semi-colonialism was based on a division of power between the economic (European) and the political–legal (Ottoman) spheres.[12] The Ottoman Public Debt Administration (est. 20 December 1881), assigned the task of restoring the Empire's financial stability, imposed substantial foreign control over most of the economy's crucial sectors, and spurred Ottoman Macedonia's incorporation into the expanding capitalist world-economy.[13] According to an agreement reached between the Empire and the Administration, which represented the Empire's foreign and local creditors, about one-fifth of the state's revenues would be relinquished to the Administration until the outstanding debt had been settled. Ottoman financial integration with Europe was, in effect, akin to European imperialism. Yet, this arrangement did open the way to development as Western capital began to enter the Ottoman market at an increasing rate.[14]

2.2.2 Official Attitude towards Minorities

The Sultan's declaration (1839, 1856) of equality before the law of all the Empire's subjects, regardless of religion, expressed his commitment to Western values, a prerequisite for the conclusion of the Treaty of Paris (30 March 1856), which settled the Crimean War. The Great Powers' guarantee to preserve the Empire's territorial integrity was, however, to be realised on terms decidedly partial to the West; it included the right to interfere in the Empire's internal matters, including enforcement of reforms, especially the protection of non-Muslims.[15] The subsequent series of new, enlightened Ottoman laws, the *Tanzimat* (1839, 1856, 1869, 1876), provided equal legal status for non-Muslims while they encouraged foreign investment in Ottoman territories. They thus paved the way for foreigners and non-Muslim minorities to gain access to new entrepreneurial opportunities.[16]

   These liberal legal reforms removed several major obstacles to capital accumulation among Ottoman subjects (the majority of the Jewish population), as described by the historian Isac Emmanuel (1972:135): "In this way, a father could bequeath his property to his son, without the authorities confiscating it; the merchant would know that he would not arrive empty-handed." Other reforms included protection of the private assets of Ottoman subjects from arbitrary confiscation, cancellation of the prohibition against the sale of real estate to foreigners (1856), and consent to foreign ownership of real property (1867). The last reform enabled foreigners to enjoy property rights, tax protection, and other benefits (originally stipulated in the capitulation agreements) designed to encourage foreign investment in infrastructure.[17]

2.2.3 Consolidating New Markets: Salonica and its Macedonian Hinterland

Ottoman legal reforms played a decisive role in the Macedonian market's formation. Salonica, with its safe natural harbour, had been a major administrative capital and the site of a fortified strategic casern for Ottoman troops. Foreign entities now began to invest in the Macedonian infrastructure, especially in the railway line connecting Salonica's port to the hinterland,[18] as well as in urban transportation (e.g., trams). The new transport system promoted consolidation of the city with its hinterland[19] and solidified the economic unification of the area. New opportunities opened to entrepreneurs, particularly in connection with primary exports from Salonica's hinterland to Western industrialists, imported industrial products as well as semi-raw materials for growing local industry, and imported luxury goods geared to growing domestic demand. At the same time, improved accessibility between the city and the agricultural environs cut the costs of manufacturing as well as distribution. Together these promoted local crafts, goods manufacture (including furniture and clothing), and the shipment of construction materials.[20]

Salonica's rapid urbanisation in this period was largely due to an influx of refugees from various parts of the Ottoman Empire, a pattern to be repeated in the next century. The national conflict over Macedonia, which intensified during the second half of the 1800s, pushed Orthodox Christian merchants from the nationalist and terror-fraught interior to Salonica. These immigrants were joined by labourers from western and central Macedonia, attracted by the burgeoning industrial and construction sectors as damage from recurring fires during the 1890s spurred substantial new building. Wealthy Muslims from the lost Ottoman provinces of Bosnia, Thessaly and Eastern Rumelia also came to the city.[21] This rapid population growth changed Salonica's status in the 1880s to that of a city (i.e., its population now numbered more than 100,000).[22]

At the beginning of the twentieth century, growing demand for goods by the Ottoman military; rising world demand for Macedonian products; increasing remittances from Macedonian migrant labourer working in the west; an emerging new class of returning emigrants with sufficient means to buy land at any price and start businesses in the towns (which meant filling the gap left by the declining number of Muslim landlords) stimulated consumption both in the hinterland and in metropolitan Salonica. These trends fed activity in Salonica's port, which served as a major *entrepôt* for goods imported to Macedonia as well as for agricultural exports. Although cash crop exports were not large due to the use of outdated agricultural methods as well as multiple droughts, the consumption of imports such as sugar, coffee, beer, petroleum, domestic wares, furniture, glassware, and other "luxuries" was democratised, attracting peasants and urbanites alike.[23]

In parallel, the Ottoman Public Debt Administration encouraged foreign investment in transportation, increased agricultural efficiency through the introduction of new technologies, and assisted in maintaining security throughout the hinterland.[24] Institutionalisation of the foreign financial sector led to substantial changes in production, trade, and consumerism. New socio-economic conditions and lifestyles were created in turn.[25]

2.2.4 Inter-Ethnic Competition: Turks, Jews and Greeks

During the last decades of the Ottoman regime, improved Jewish–Ottoman relations eased Jewish access to new entrepreneurial opportunities but simultaneously impacted on Jewish–Greek competition. Inter-group relations between Macedonia's Ottoman Turks, Jews, and Greeks during the last decades of Ottoman rule in Macedonia were determined mainly by the population's ethnic make-up and the rising nationalism. Inter-communal relations in Salonica after the Berlin Congress (1878) were influenced primarily by the "Macedonian Question",[26] that is, the debate over which national entity would replace Ottoman rule in Macedonia.

These multifaceted relations had also been traditionally influenced by Jewish collective memories of this community's history in Salonica. Jews had been the only non-Muslim group to choose to be Ottoman subjects; the Jewish community was therefore considered faithful to the Sultan, a loyal and valuable element within the city's social fabric.[27] This community later expressed pro-Turkish sentiments, even during the brief period of the chauvinistic Young Turks regime.[28] Importantly, Ottoman Jews, in contrast to other Balkan national minorities, lacked political and territorial ambitions; they thus became favourites of the Ottoman elites. These sentiments were illustrated by the absence of any official connection between Salonica's Jewish community and the Central Zionist Organization prior to the Greek Occupation (1912).[29] In contrast, Jewish expulsion from Christian lands had negatively coloured the Jewish collective memory pertaining to Christian rule in Macedonia.

Jewish–Greek economic rivalry in the Balkans likewise burdened inter-communal interactions.[30] The similarities between these two middleman minorities, both active in Ottoman territories, resulted in long-standing competitive conflict, especially following establishment of the Greek ethnic state (1830) (see below).[31] This religious and economic rivalry provided a firm basis for the ethnic conflicts that appeared on the eve of Greek nation-state formation.[32] They intensified during the increasingly international struggle over Macedonia and its capital, especially after the military conflict reached a watershed in the Turkish–Greek War (1897), and encouraged anti-Jewish feelings among Greek nationalists.[33]

Following the Young Turks revolution (1908), during which Salonica's Jews retained their pro-Turkish sentiments,[34] "the Greeks lashed out against the Jews, claiming to find in their attitude an insult directed against the Greeks and a manifestation of the hatred which the Jews . . . bore against the Greeks".[35] Greek antagonism towards the Jews was nourished by cooperation between the Jewish public and the Muslim elites during Salonica's November 1908 elections, the results of which effectively stymied the city's early Hellenisation.[36]

External political events often exacerbated these relations. The Italian invasion of Ottoman Tripoli (1911) transformed Italian residents of Salonica, Jews as well as non-Jews, into enemies of Ottoman rule, a change in attitude that motivated the exit of Italian Jews from the city.[37] At the same time, increasing "Turkification" helped Salonican Jews prosper in the face of Greek economic rivalry. As a display of gratitude, Salonica's Jews joined the "Unionist" Turks, who were actively engaged in a general boycott of Greek commerce as punishment for Athens' support of Crete's declaration of union (*enosis*) with Greece in October 1908.[38] In retribution, the Greeks declared economic war against the Jews, with calls for boycotts of Jewish businesses regularly published in the local Greek newspaper (*Pharos tis Thessaloniquis*) on the eve of the Greek annexation of Salonica (1912).[39]

2.3 The Jewish Minority in Ottoman Salonica, 1880s–1912

On the eve of European semi-colonialism in Ottoman Macedonia, the Jewish population was impoverished and lacked modern education or skills.[40] According to a published report (1884) prepared by an Alliance Israélite Universelle informant in Salonica, the province's Jewish labour force consisted of 4,000 tradesmen, 4,000 shopkeepers, 2,000 porters, 600 boatmen, 250 brokers, 250 butchers, 250 tinkers, 150 fishermen, 150 donkey drivers, 100 domestic servants, 60 coal dealers, 60 turners, 50 chair manufacturers, and 500 people plying various other trades.[41] This situation resulted from the continued weakening of the local Jewish craft guilds that began in the eighteenth century and reached its peak in 1826, following disbandment of the Janissaries (an elite unit of Turkish guards)[42] and the sultan's cancellation of orders for their woollen uniforms. A long-standing failure to compete with British and continental manufacturers in quality and costs also led to reduced local demand as well as shrinking international markets (especially Italian and French) for Salonica's woollens. Stagnation of local craft and commerce in wool ensued, together with broadening poverty among Jews active in all parts of the sector.[43]

European semi-colonialism, with its economic stimuli and demographic pressures, enabled the Jewish minority to renew the group's ethnic as well as private resources, both prerequisites for profit maximisation in the new environment. Anti-Semitic incidents in Europe and the Ottoman Empire functioned as a reactive ethnic resource,[44] reviving solidarity between the local Jewish elites and the larger Jewish population as well as with their co-religionists in other European states. Secularisation of the Jewish community through the *millet* system (1865) enabled Salonica's Jewish elites, aided by Jewish philanthropic associations (the most prominent being the Alliance Israélite Universelle (AIU)), to bolster weakened communal institutions and to invest in education and welfare. The educational revolution spawned, led mainly by the AIU, aimed at Westernising the city's Jewish youth and preparing them to seize the new opportunities emerging in the world-economy.[45] The Jewish elite's entrepreneurial wealth thus allowed them to utilise their accumulated financial and human capital to stimulate the entire Jewish community's adaptation to modern Western culture as well as to greater Ottoman society.[46]

2.3.1 Demographic Developments

During the second half of the nineteenth century, the demographic profile of the Jewish population in Salonica changed, [47]subsequent to the arrival of Jews found among the new immigrants from former Ottoman territories. Many of these immigrants preferred the Sultan's sovereignty to the new nation-states;[48] others were Italian Jews attracted by the favourable economic conditions offered by the Ottoman capitulation regime.[49] As Salonica entered the twentieth century, the city's Jewish population experienced another upward turn: rapid population growth resulted from lower infant mortality rates in addition to immigration.[50] Two official Ottoman census reports (1893, 1906) reveal a 40 percent increase in the Jewish population living in the Province of Salonica in this period.[51] The mass of Jews, who were concentrated in the central district (*kaza*; in the sub-province of Salonica), became the dominant ethnic component.[52] According to other official data for 1905/6, the Jewish population constituted the city's majority (55 percent), and was greater in number than either the ruling Muslim segment (*c.* 31 percent) or the indigenous Greeks (*c.*13 percent).[53] Salonica's Jewish population eventually reached an estimated 65,000 to 70,000[54] (Appendix 2, Table B). Given these figures, we can understand why the plural society[55] of semi-colonial Ottoman Salonica was described by a contemporary as "*une moderne Babel de races, de langues, de croyances, de coutumes, d'idées, d'aspirations*".[56]

This diversified social structure was mirrored in the Jewish community itself, with Jews maintaining an internal system of sub-ethnic affiliations. "Recently arrived"

Italian Jewish immigrants, like the old-time Italian Jews already living in Salonica, differed from the majority of Ottoman Jews not only by their civil status but also by their culture. The Italians belonged to the "Western Sephardic culture area"[57] whereas the majority of Ottoman Jews (including the *beratli*),[58] the group demographically and culturally dominant in the city and the province, belonged to the "Eastern Sephardic culture area". The former spoke Italian, whereas the latter spoke Ladino, the Judeo-Spanish language. The demographic supremacy of Eastern Sephardic Jews over all the other Jewish sub-ethnic groups in Salonica, together with the superior reputation enjoyed by that culture area, motivated Ashkenazi and Romanioti Jews to assimilate into that culture by adopting Ladino at the very least.[59] The Italians also adopted Ladino but continued to speak Italian at home.[60]

2.4 Formation of a Jewish Entrepreneurial Elite

In this book, the term "entrepreneur" excludes peddlers or micro-vendors but does refer to participants in small- to large-scale business activities; in general, these firm-owners were registered with the Salonica Chamber of Commerce. While Jewish professionals are considered to be entrepreneurs, they are generally excluded from this book.

Jewish entrepreneurial elites, by virtue of their extensive business experience, linguistic skills, commercial skills as well as renewed collective ethnic resources, were well equipped to take advantage of Macedonia's incorporation into the world-economy prior to its incorporation into the Greek state (1912). These Jewish businessmen also enjoyed a favourable position within the inter-ethnic fabric of Ottoman Macedonia (section 2.2.4). In contrast with Greeks (Armenians and other national minorities living in the region), who were suspected of disloyalty to the Ottoman regime either because of nationalist aspirations, collective Russian protection, or the Greek citizenship some of them held,[61] these Jews had close ties with the Ottoman elites as well as with European elites. Ottoman Jews, well known for their loyalty to the Ottoman elites, together with their "foreign" co-religionists who served as representatives of European economic semi-colonialism,[62] were ready to take advantage of transformations in commerce and manufacturing.

2.4.1 Size and Sub-Ethnic Make-up

Inauguration of the Ottoman regime's liberal immigration policy in 1857, which encouraged foreigners to immigrate and invest in the empire, [63]stimulated the arrival of foreign Jewish investors from the Austro-Hungarian Empire, Germany, and France, especially to Salonica.[64] The most prominent group of immigrants came from Livorno (Leghorn) in Tuscany. As early as the opening decades of the eighteenth century, Jews from this port city had immigrated to Salonica to join veteran Jewish "foreigners", known as Francos,[65] living under the protection of the European consulate of the nation that controlled Tuscany at the time (Austria as of 1737, England as of 1796, and France between 1800 and 1815). Beginning in 1859, when Livorno was annexed to the Kingdom of Italy and lost its status as an international free port, Italian Jewish merchants were deprived of their former privileged status in this port. As commercial opportunities in Livorno diminished ("push" factors) these traders were attracted by the favourable trade conditions (a "pull" factor) offered by the Ottoman capitulation regime to foreigners settling in their port cities. By the end of the nineteenth century, it was estimated that Salonica's "recently arrived" Italian Jews, the majority of whom enjoyed the advantages gained from being naturalised Italian citizens in the wake of Italy's unification (1861), numbered about 1,000.[66] Together with their precursors who had arrived since the mid-eighteenth century, the Italian community numbered almost 4,000 or about 5 percent of the city's 70,000 Jews in 1914.[67] These Italian Jews belonged to the upper socio-economic stratum – the so-called *gente alta* of Salonica's Jewish society – and comprised its dominant elite. The sociologist Edgar Morin, a descendant of the Livornean Nahum family, described the Western features of Italian Jewish identity in these words:

> Ces Livournais sont en quelque sorte des néo-marranes, non pas christianisés, mais laïcisés: ils portent le costume européen, se rasent le menton, parlent l'italien en famille. . . . Pendant tout le XIXe siècle . . . rassemblés dans le quartier franc, vivent en endogamie, se mariant dans leur micro-communauté.[68]

Recently arrived Italian Jews joined the tiny established Jewish elite comprised of foreign *protégés* as well as Ottoman Jews holding *berats*, that is, a group enjoying the favoured commercial conditions guaranteed by capitulations. Speaking French and Francophile in attitude, common cultural and social bonds distinguished this group from the Jewish masses who generally spoke Ladino.[69]

It should be noted that when individual German Jewish merchants, members of a cultural area foreign to that of the local Sephardic community, came to Salonica around the turn of the twentieth century, they preferred integration within Salonica's local civil society.[70] Their relatively small numbers, their concentration within the *franc* quarter, and their linguistic barriers (they spoke German) significantly raised the costs of their social integration within the larger Jewish community of primarily Sephardic Jews.[71]

2.4.2 Initial Capital for Entrepreneurial Activity

In contrast to Ottoman Jews, who were exposed to arbitrary confiscation of their property before enactment of the Ottoman reforms, Italian Jews were shielded by their *protégé* status. They were thus able to accumulate sufficient capital for new investment. At the same time, Jewish entrepreneurs who were Ottoman subjects dominated intermediary economic activity in regional and metropolitan markets through their development of regional networks, aided by the rejuvenating Ladino.[72]

In 1909, M. Benghiat, a teacher employed by the Alliance Israélite Universelle, wrote a succinct description of Jewish domination of capital in Macedonia.

> No significant business can be carried out without one of these brokers [in Salonica] as an intermediary agent. It happens that almost all of these brokers are Jews. They are rather well-off; often they advance funds to the merchants and they almost always act as guarantors for their clients in their dealings with the large commercial enterprises. Even the banks sometimes grant credit to the merchants only because of the recommendation and the guarantee of the brokers.[73]

This description explains how the merchant houses owned by the Allatini, Fernandez, Mizrahi, and Tiano families were able to develop into small empires during the second half of the nineteenth century, with branches and business extending beyond Macedonia to most European commercial centres. These same families became lenders to the Ottoman regime, providing loans to Ottoman officials and landowners.[74] In 1888 the Jewish firm Allatini Fratelli mobilised the Viennese Länderbank and the Parisian Comptoir d'Escompte; together they founded the Banque de Salonique, which provided credit for the majority of Jewish industrial initiatives.[75] Jewish banks remained firmly attached to the interests of their co-religionists because

> The Greeks wanted to supplant the Jewish brokers and replace them with Greek brokers. And as the Greek brokers did not have the necessary funds to replace the Jewish brokers, the Greeks began by founding Greek financial institutions in Salonica. . . . The Jewish brokers began to sound the alarm, and in a spirit of solidarity, the Jewish merchants refused to grant these [i.e., Greek] brokers the payment and credit terms they granted the Jewish brokers, so that, in spite of the intervention of the Greeks, businesses were still obliged to work through the Jewish brokers.[76]

These bankers, highly experienced in money market transactions, bought and sold bills of exchange while relying on their information sources for reports on their Jewish clients' creditability and financial health.[77] Jewish bankers thus preferred Jewish borrowers. As suspension of payments in the wake of commercial crises was frequent in Salonica, bankers were able to accumulate great fortunes in land and other properties after their owners had defaulted on their mortgages and loans.[78]

Although Greek banks supplied credit to Greek entrepreneurs, Jewish entrepreneurs became the chief debtors of the Banque de l'Orient because they held the largest accounts in Salonica.[79] Jewish clients thus constituted about two-thirds of the clients of the Banque de l'Orient.[80] The estimated value of their assets indicates their position within Salonica's entrepreneurial elite. Figure 2.4.2 shows the distribution of Salonican firms, Jewish as well as non-Jewish, according to their total assets.

Analysis of the firms' names indicates that two Italian Jewish families, Allatini and Modiano, which owned three major firms (Fils Allatini, Saul Modiano and Levi Modiano), were considered to be among Salonica's wealthiest families.[81] Each of these firms was estimated to have assets of more than 300,000 Gold Turkish Liras (GTL).[82] The second level contains firms with capital valued at about 25 percent of the capital held by the two aforementioned families. Other than the two Italian firms Fils Konfino and E[riko] Mizrahi (Mizrahi was related by marriage to the Modiano family), only one non-Jewish entrepreneur, Alfred Abbot, belonged to this economic level. Only on the third economic level two Greek-owned and well-known spinning mills were to be found: C. Kyrtsis & Sons and Longos, Kyrtsis & Tourpalis. These findings corroborate the testimony of a contemporary, George Frederick Abbot (1903: 20), who stated that the Greeks "in multitude and in wealth . . . are immeasurably inferior to the Jews".

This figure also sheds light on the internal layers within the Jewish elite according to sub-ethnic origin, Italian and Sephardic.[83] All of the firms with nominal assets of GTL 40,000 or more were owned by Italian Jews. Only on the fifth level, that of GTL 30,000, do Sephardic Jewish names (e.g., Aelion [no first name discovered] and Gabriel Almosnino) appear. The prominence of Italian Jews in this group may be attributed

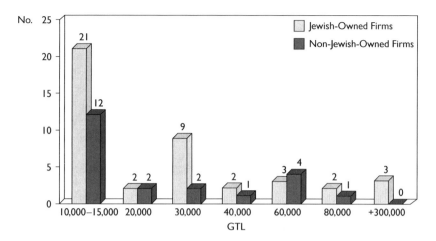

Figure 2.4.2   Nominal Assets of Jewish-owned Firms and non-Jewish-owned Firms, Salonica, 1906–1911 (in Gold Turkish Liras, GTL)

Source: Adapted from Hekimoglou 1997: 178, Table 1.
Notes: Hekimoglou derived his data from the Banque de l'Orient archive, and classified clients' names according to their nominal assets. I used his data but classified these names according to their ethnic origin. Non-Jewish firms were owned by Muslims (Turks) and Greeks.
One Gold Turkish Lira was worth nine-tenths of an English sovereign in this era: see Hekimoglou 1997: 177, note 9.

to the capital that they had succeeded in accumulating over the generations,[84] during a period when Ottoman Jews were still exposed to arbitrary confiscation of assets by the sultan's officials.[85]

2.4.3 Entrepreneurial Strategies

Figure 2.4.3 delineates the complex business network consisting of the prominent Jewish families of Italian origin as the nineteenth century welcomed the twentieth. The network of family ties, reinforced by marriage, was maintained throughout this period. The Allatini family used its marital ties to the Modiano, Fernandez, Mizrahi, and Torres families to expand its already extensive commercial network, to enlarge its capital base, and to encourage intra-familial transfer of wealth. The Allatini concern was considered the most important industrial cartel in the European segment of the Ottoman Empire.[86] Using vertical integration strategies and relying on family ties, the Allatinis created inter-dependence between different parts of its diversified enterprise. The family's bank financed its industrial and commercial enterprises as follows: their quarries provided raw materials for a brick and shingle manufacturing plant (est. 1880); their tobacco trading firm provided the cigarette manufacturers with raw leaf; trade in cotton ensured supply for the cotton spinning mill (Torres, Mizrahi et Cie., est. 1885);[87] trade in grain provided inputs for their flour mill (est. 1854)[88] and bakery (est. 1912)[89] on one hand, and for their brewery (Mizrahi, Fernandez et Cie., est. 1893) on the other. In addition, its jute-weaving mill and sack manufacturing facility (Elie [Abram] Torres et Cie., est. 1906) provided commercial inputs for its tobacco and flour

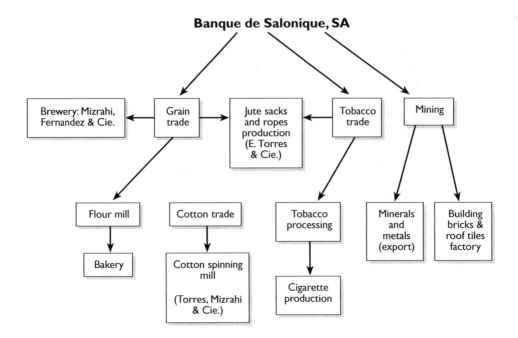

Figure 2.4.3   Allatini Group (1881–1912)

production.[90] We should note here that this list represents only some parts of the concern's operations; many items could be added to the list if we were to include firms whose owners were only associated with the Allatinis, for example, Moises Is. Tiano Cie. (Tiano was related by marriage to the Fernandez family), which traded in grain and wheat.[91]

The Allatinis' pioneering commercial activities, reflected in the network's inclusion of anonymous firms (*Société Anonyme* or SA), indicates how well they had internalised the organisational patterns characterising modern capitalistic commerce. Banque de Salonique was founded as an Ottoman *Société Anonyme*.[92] Other companies belonging to the Allatini Group had been transformed into SA companies since 1895. Transformation of a privately owned tobacco firm into The Commercial Company of Salonica, Ltd. in 1895 (see illustration on the book's back cover) enabled expansion of the family's financial base and tobacco operations. Thanks to their commercial and organisational acumen, the Allatinis were able to face European competition and achieve second place in the Salonican Tobacco industry behind the Austrian–Hungarian firm Herzog et Cie.[93] In 1910, the Commercial Company of Salonica Ltd. was among the five principal commercial enterprises dealing with tobacco leaf in the city.[94] Similarly, the Société Anonyme Ottomane Industrielle & Commercial de Salonique was established in 1897 to support the operation of the Allatini flour mill as well as its brick factory. This company also operated the new steam-driven mill as of 1900 (see illustration on the front cover of this book). Mizrahi, Fernandez et Cie. (est. 1893), owned by the Allatinis, became SA Olympos Brewery in 1911;[95] the mechanised cotton-spinning mill Torres, Mizrahi et Cie. (est. 1885) was transformed into La Nouvelle Filature Société Ottomane Anonyme de Salonique in 1905.[96] Yet, these anonymous companies continued to be dominated by their Jewish founders, e.g., the main shareholder (70–75 percent) in the Olympos Brewery was the Banque de Salonique.[97]

The Jewish Italian entrepreneurial elite spread its far-reaching business networks, based on ramified family ties, throughout the Ottoman Empire's capitals. Doing so provided Italian Jews with diversified, essential information while it eased their access to mediator positions bridging core European corporations with Ottoman clients in the international commercial services, e.g., insurance and maritime services. The Allatini, Fernandez, and Morpurgo families were bound through marriage to the Camondo family,[98] also of Italian Jewish origin, which was active in Constantinople until the late nineteenth century, when they left for Paris.[99] Consider the wealthy Jewish Morpurgo family. Originally from Trieste, the family controlled the city's Assicurazioni Generali (the Italian re-insurer) as well as the local Chamber of Commerce and the main navigation company. It is consequently not surprising that Moise Morpurgo was considered suitable to serve as the president of the Syndicate des Companies d'Assurance in Salonica from 1905 on[100] (see 5.3.3).

Edgar Morin described the complex commercial network built by the Nahum family of Livorno as consisting of brothers, uncles, and cousins living in Livorno, Alexandria, Usküp, and great Western European cities such as Paris and Vienna.[101] These wide-ranging arrangements, based on trust, supported the entrepreneurial pattern prevailing in the Balkans. This pattern had developed in response to two major factors: first, delay in the passage of Turkish legislation regarding public companies, and second, distrust among the Balkans' different ethnic segments, especially in Macedonia, where the lengthy Ottoman occupation had reinforced traditional loyalties. And so, although Italian entrepreneurs were considered *avant garde* with respect to their corporate business organisation and participation in Jewish–Gentile joint ventures,[102] most Italian businesses in Salonica were conducted according to traditional methods of trade based on personal intergenerational trust, sustained by participation of the extended family. A contemporary account illustrates this approach: "Visitors lingered longer over their cups of coffee and transactions took on an even more personal character."[103] The Italian commercial elite thus remained inherently closed, rigid, and traditional. Consider this comment by Leon Sciaky describing relations in the Macedonian grain market (*Ishtira*): "The *Ishtira* was more than a business neighbourhood. It was an institution, the headquarters of a mercantile aristocracy having its traditions and strict code. One did not come to it. One was born and raised in it."[104]

While foreign protection could be inherited, a factor that perpetuated this group's preferred status,[105] in-group marriage patterns also assisted the Jewish elite to keep their circle closed. The endogamy patterns used by its members to fortify these trust networks also tightened the group's favourable status. However, although the sub-ethnic boundaries between Italian and Sephardic Jews were diligently maintained by the Italian community,[106] the close of the nineteenth century saw a shift away from sub-ethnic intra-class endogamy towards class endogamy, illustrated by marriages between well-to-do Italian and Sephardic families.[107] The latter also used intra-class marriage to concentrate their business affairs within the hands of a few families of the same socio-economic rank, thereby promoting intra-familial capital accumulation.[108]

2.4.4 Recruitment of Jewish Workers and the Scope of the Jewish-owned Economy

Jewish entrepreneurs found it difficult to hire Jewish workers to do manual labour in brick and tile manufacturing and brewing, for example, even if the concerns were owned by Jews; many more profitable job opportunities, e.g., the developing mercantile tobacco industry, were abundant in the mainstream economy. Chronic labour shortages instigated by the emigration of farmers from the nationalist terror-fraught Macedonian hinterland to the New World, resulted in growing remuneration in now-flourishing sectors, such as transport services in the port.[109] When faced with the choice between employing expensive Jewish workers or cheaper Slavic workers from the hinterland, whose employment also allowed the operation of plants throughout the week, including the Jewish Sabbath and holidays, Jewish employers tended to hire the latter. Yet, due to the importance of trust relations, jobs in the finishing phases of manufacturing as well as in the upper levels of marketing and management within Jewish firms remained subject to ethnic preferences. Contemporary descriptions of the ethnic make-up of labour within Jewish-owned industrial plants (e.g., the Allatini flour mill and the Olympos Brewery) indicate that Jewish unskilled or semi-skilled labourers preferred working in either Jewish or foreign-owned tobacco plants (e.g., the warehouses run by the Régie Co-intéressée des Tabacs de l'Empire Ottoman)[110] rather than as semi-skilled manual labour in Jewish-owned industrial enterprises that, being less profitable, thus paid lower wages.[111]

Importantly, Jewish tobacco workers, the group most profoundly involved in unionisation and the most active faction in the Socialist Federation, controlled hiring in Jewish-owned and non-Jewish-owned factories. Jews were the predominant group in the labour-intensive tobacco industry that, as a profitable growth industry, attracted unskilled and semi-skilled labour at the expense of even more arduous employment in the traditional textiles industry. When employment opportunities began to open up, Jewish workers of both genders flocked to tobacco.[112] According to a report by the Union des Associations Israélites (1912),[113] about 8,000 Jewish workers were employed in the tobacco industry. Even if the figure provided by the Jewish Union was exaggerated,[114] it was known that about 63 percent of those registered with the Tobacco Workers Syndicate (1908) in Salonica were Jewish, and that 90 percent of the workers in the cigarette manufacturing factories owned by the tobacco monopoly were Jewish women.[115] Furthermore, the Jews who launched the campaign to organise the industry's labour[116] were also active in the Tobacco Administration (1913).[117] This industry consequently became a major component of the Jewish-controlled economy in the Ottoman period.

Overland and maritime transportation in both the private and public sectors was also controlled by Jewish workers, whether self-employed or salaried: there were 500 Jewish workers operating carriages and carts, 600 working as porters, and 400 working as seamen and stevedores.[118] Jewish workers also provided loading/unloading services on the docks as well as in the nearby mercantile area. According to contemporary accounts, "the porter's trade in Salonica was almost entirely Jewish . . . ".[119] Guilds of Jewish porters, which had survived even after the other guilds operating during the Ottoman Empire were disbanded in 1860, continued to monitor labour competition within this sector through internal allocation of raw goods by storage area. Hence, the monopoly enjoyed by the porter guilds was especially active in the movement of raw goods such as wood coal (charcoal), hides, wheat and barley, silkworms, opium, and flour traded by Jewish merchants.[120]

The influence of Jewish entrepreneurs on the scope of the Jewish-owned economy was expressed in the number of places of employment they created for their fellow Jews, and in the satellite services created around their core activities. Yet, during the last decades of Ottoman rule in Macedonia, the Jewish-owned economy was able to benefit from the availability of a broad range of employment opportunities now open to Jews in the mainstream economy. Jewish entrepreneurs could therefore act in an economically rational way and hire non-Jews when interested in doing so.

2.5 The Jewish Economy from an Inter-Ethnic Perspective

Analysis of the structure of the Jewish entrepreneurial sector in Salonica requires an inter-ethnic perspective.[121] While Europeans dominated large-scale entrepreneurial activity, especially in infrastructure, a sector where Ottoman state involvement was glaringly absent, Jewish entrepreneurs owned the majority of firms situated in urban locations; they were thus also able to dominate the local Chamber of Commerce, founded in 1909.[122] The residential concentration of Jews in the Macedonian metropolis explains the density of Jews in urban professions: commerce (46 percent), industry and crafts (41 percent), transportation (6 percent), finance and brokerage (5 percent), and professional services (2 percent).[123] This trend, a continuation of the Jewish urban economic tradition, resulted from historical preferences but also from necessity.[124]

Jewish entrepreneurs filled, in effect, the entrepreneurial vacuum created by the paucity of Muslim Turks interested in business, a product of their elites' traditional inclination for employment in government and the military. Delayed development of a modern Ottoman public education system had led to a shortage in Western business and linguistic skills, essential for exploiting emerging opportunities.[125] The *Dönme* (see section 2.1, above), a minority group that was also familiar with the workings of modern administration, thus monopolised the municipal bureaucracy,[126] where they played a key role in promoting cosmopolitanism in Salonica.[127] Although several *Dönme* were large-scale traders in grain, tobacco, and textiles,[128] they represented a small portion (about 13 percent) of the Muslim population,[129] even smaller than the Jewish population, as described by a contemporary Jewish traveller to Salonica: "The Turks are officials, large landowners and small shopkeepers, but not of any commercial importance."[130] A similar description was given by a contemporary Greek businessman who expressed contempt towards the few Turkish merchants living in their midst while describing the Jews as "arbiters of the commerce of Salonica".[131] These comments strengthen Gounaris's determination (1997: 115) that "Beyond all doubt, the Jewish community was the dominant element in the city's economy . . . ".[132]

Although the small size of the modernising Muslim element in the growing city left space for the Jewish elites, Jewish participation in Salonica's provincial and municipal government administrations and in the senior Ottoman military command remained negligible even after the *Tanzimat* (1839) reforms that theoretically opened its doors to non-Muslims.[133] The relatively few Jewish professionals (physicians, lawyers, and engineers) found practicing in the city resulted from the absence of opportunities to acquire higher education within the Ottoman Empire.[134]

Within the rural economy, Jews, in contrast with the Turkish population dispersed throughout the Macedonian hinterland, were absent from agricultural production. According to a contemporary account (1900), "Except for the peasantry, you can find them [Salonican Jews] in all professions and works . . . ".[135] The Jewish owners of agricultural estates (*ciftliks*)[136] bought the estates largely as speculative investments, or to facilitate access to agricultural raw materials (e.g., wine and wood) for their industrial facilities.[137] Most unusual was the participation of Jews in maritime agriculture. A mere 100 Jewish families earned their livelihood from fishing in the Bay of Salonica or on the open seas.[138]

Absence from agricultural production did not, however, mean absence from commerce in agricultural produce, from the small-scale sale of fruit and vegetables to the large-scale export of tobacco, opium, and silk cocoons. Jewish entrepreneurs thus dominated urban industrial development (see above) but also small- and large-scale commercial activity in the Macedonian hinterland. Several factors explain this distribution of opportunities. Jewish entrepreneurs maintained contacts between the industrialists of in the urban centres and the cultivators in the periphery,[139] with both areas participating in the classic division of labour characterised by the export of raw material from the periphery to core states, and export of manufactured goods from core state industrialists to periphery consumers.[140]

Jewish traders took advantage of their demographic superiority in the metropolitan consumer goods market to control the city's wholesale as well as retail trade in fruit and vegetables.[141] The failed attempt of Greek rivals to boycott Jewish fruit merchants (spring 1908) inadvertently helped consolidate Jewish domination of the sector. The same M. Benghiat, cited above, described the market's structure: "The owners of the groves surrounding Salonica are almost all Greek; the fruit and vegetable merchants in Salonica are almost all Jewish. The intermediaries between the producers and the merchants are Jewish agents." However, when Greek growers attempted to sell their cherries only through Greek agents, "the Jewish fruit merchants came together and decided they would buy fruit only through the Jewish agents. For three days the producers held their ground, but when they began to see their cherries rotting in baskets, they gave in."[142]

The Greeks' struggle against their Jewish rivals included the establishment of new banks to finance industrial and commercial initiatives in Salonica (section 2.4.2). The opening of the Anglo-Hellenic Commercial Company in 1909 was a major step forward in the Greeks' competition with Jewish commercial houses such as Errera (see Appendix 4.1, no. 243), regardless of the fact that its Jewish owners employed numerous Greeks.[143]

In consideration of the strategic importance of Salonica's port, which was the last portal to the sea available to the Ottoman Empire in the Balkans, the Ottoman authorities viewed Jewish workers as appropriate alternatives to the inexperienced Muslim workers who began flooding Salonica after the turn of the century.[144] And, unlike the Jews, the Greeks were considered accomplices of the Empire's competitor for control over the port, the Greek nation-state.[145] The Ottoman regime thus supported Jewish dominance in port management and labour. The Jewish work force was sufficiently large to meet the demand for manual labourers, adequately trained and knowledgeable of European languages; these features made their integration into the port's lower management a simple task.[146] Salonica's port therefore became a site for Jewish entrepreneurship, and Jews held positions ranging from the owners of warehouses and boats, to semi-skilled jobs as sailors, stevedores, lighters, and porters, to menial jobs as custom porters and customs clerks.[147]

Reciprocities between the mainstream economy and the Jewish economy were particularly thick in the port. Hence, the Jewish economy and the port economy frequently overlapped and were mutually dependent on one another. While ignoring here the structural boundaries separating other aspects of the two economies, we can nonetheless state that Jews exercised dual control over the port: horizontal control over activities associated with international trade, and vertical control over entrepreneurial investment. This was accomplished through the supply of commercial services, from customs and insurance to unloading and delivery. Further evidence of the importance of the Jewish presence can be found in the 1 December 1911 judgment by Salonica's Chamber of Commerce declaring that Jewish porters need not work on the Sabbath.[148] Salonica's customs offices and other port activities therefore ceased on Saturdays but not on Sundays or Fridays, the Christian and Muslim days of rest.

2.6 Conclusion: A Jewish Middleman Minority in a Colonial Environment

During the European semi-colonial era in Ottoman Macedonia (1881–1912), Jewish entrepreneurs figured among Salonica's most prominent entrepreneurs. These businessmen functioned as surrogates for the Ottoman entrepreneurs who were conspicuously absent from all levels of the city's commercial and industrial sectors. The Jewish minority, because of its economic resources, internal cooperation, market skills, and favourable position as a community loyal to the Ottoman elites and free of independent political aspirations, filled the role of a "middleman minority" (see section 1.3) at this juncture in the city's history.

On 12 November 1912, after Greeks, Bulgarians, and Serbs had completed their occupation of Salonica, Joseph Nehama reported that

> the Jews are currently in a critical situation. The Greeks from our region envy our commercial success and would like to supplant us for good. . . . They ignore the Turks, few in numbers and nonexistent as commercial competitors, and move directly to attack the Jews.[149]

The Young Turks government that ruled Salonica from 1908 to 1912 aspired to establish a national economy and a national bourgeoisie comprised exclusively of Muslims. However, the chaos that marked their brief rule prevented the formation of any mechanism capable of realising their nationalistic aspirations. Greece's annexation of Salonica and its port (1912) consequently became a watershed in the development of the Jewish economy. In the following chapters, we will trace the transformations experienced by Jewish entrepreneurs and the Jewish-owned economy as their political status changed from a protected minority in a multi-national empire to marginalised citizens of a nation-state, whose businesses were now forced to contend with an institutionalised autarkic framework.

PART TWO

From European Semi-Colonialism in
Multi-National Ottoman Macedonia to
Greek Nation-Statehood, 1912–1929

3 | New Conditions for Jewish Entrepreneurship

The incorporation of Salonica into Greece in 1912 created a new environment for Jewish entrepreneurs. According to Article 3 of the Greek National Constitution from 1928, "The prevailing religion in Greece is that of the Eastern Orthodox Church." Nevertheless, Article 4 guaranteed the rights of non-Greek minorities including the Jews: "All Greeks are equal before the law. All Greeks living within Greek territory shall enjoy full protection of their life, honour and freedom, irrespective of nationality, race, or language and of religious or political belief."[1]

The incorporation of Salonica into the Greek nation-state transformed the Jewish population from a cosmopolitan community, fluent in diverse languages and living in a multi-national empire, into a national minority.[2] Officially, Jewish entrepreneurs as well as their workers and other co-religionists changed their legal status from members of a protected religious minority to citizens subject to national discrimination against them. Under the new circumstances these groups were in need of special international protection as early as 1924.[3]

The three main traits distinguished Jewish national identity during the consolidation of Greece; these were language (Ladino or Judeo-Spanish, French, and Greek), religious affiliation (Judaism), and political stance (Zionism, Communism and Greek patriotism). This multi-dimensional distinctiveness caused the Jewish population of Salonica to exclude itself from the New Greek majority, which responded in similar terms. These traits thus determined the Jewish population's minority status in Salonica, the second largest city in the Greek nation-state. The great fire of 1917, coupled with the effects of the Lausanne Treaty (30 January 1923),[4] accelerated the creation of changes that would affect the practice of Jewish economic life.

The latter part of the period discussed in this chapter (1912 until the late 1920s) saw Eleftherios Venizelos, who accelerated Hellenisation, return to the post of prime minister (1928), together with the beginnings of the global economic slump that revised the structure of opportunities available to Jewish entrepreneurs as well as the framework of Jewish business activity. This period could be divided into two sub-periods, with 1922 as the turning point: before 1922, the Jewish minority still represented the dominant group within Macedonia's plural society (see section 2.2); while after 1922, consecutive waves of refugees began to flood into Greek Macedonia, particularly

Salonica, an event that transformed the Jews into a minority within an otherwise homogenous population.[5]

New or modified environments often influence the business practices adopted by minorities; this certainly was the case here. Therefore, in the following sections we describe some of the major internal and external transformations that materialized, excluding those transpiring in the economic structure of opportunities, which are discussed in Chapters 4 and 5.

3.1 Demographic Transformations, 1912–1929: A Survey

Immediately following the Greek occupation of Salonica at the beginning of 1913, the Greek civilian governor-general of Macedonia, Constantine Raktivan, conducted a census, requiring specially designated local committees in each ethnic community to visit each household. The census results were considered accurate thanks to this method, which contrasted sharply with the former Ottoman practice of inviting house-holders to come and register at local government offices.[6] As to the results for the Jewish population in Salonica,[7] the indigenous Judeo-Spanish-speaking population was found to number 61,439 (or 39 percent of the city's 157,889 residents in 1913) immediately after this multi-ethnic metropolis had been incorporated into the Greek nation-state (1912). The two other major ethnic components were the Turks, with 29 percent (or 45,867 residents), and the Greeks, with about 25 percent (or 39,956 residents).[8]

Although the unpublished census results provide a figure below the 70,000 Jews estimated by David Florentin for the very same period (January 1913), they do corroborate Florentin's description of Salonica as a "Jewish metropolis", to be contrasted with the multi-ethnic Macedonian hinterland, divided into regions according to the ethnic concentration of Serbs, Bulgarians, and Greeks.[9] In 1913 occupied Salonica was described as "for centuries the centre of the Spanish-speaking Jewry and relatively the most Jewish city in the world."[10]

The Jews' demographic superiority, when added to their residential concentration in the city centre until 1917, intensified the community's cultural superiority, as described by the indigenous Jewish historian Joseph Nehama (writing under the pseudonym Risal):

> The Greeks, Dönmes, Turks, and foreigners are all minorities. The Jews comprise the bulk of the population. Everything here is Jewish: the city's language, appearance, and religion. They are the undisputed masters of commerce, banking, education, and the legal profession. Saturday is a public holiday. On the Day of Atonement, you see nobody in the streets, the cafes are deserted. . . . The language of all [Jews] is the Castilian language . . . and this was imposed throughout the city as a kind of Esperanto that the Greeks, Turks, Albanians, Bulgarians, and foreigners jabber. The Turkish tram driver, the Greek waiter, the Gypsy bootblack will converse with you in the language of Cervantes when they conceive a doubt about your nationality.[11]

The suppressed publication of the 1913 census, the submission of fabricated statistics by Greek Prime Minister Venizelos to the Paris Conference (18 January 1919 to 20 January 1920), and the absence of transparent data on the population's ethnic composition in the regions comprising "New Greece" – especially when compared to the accessibility of detailed data on "Old Greece" from the 1920 census[12] – indicate the Greek government's trepidation before the European powers, whose support was sought for its annexation of Macedonian territories lacking a Greek majority[13] (see Map 1). This was especially true with respect to Salonica, Macedonia's desirable capital,[14] given the presence of such a large Jewish community there during the first decade of Greek rule in the city.

However, after the fateful fire of 1917 that decimated Salonica's ancient city centre, where the majority of indigenous Jews had been concentrated, "foreign" Jewish entrepreneurs likewise soon deserted the area;[15] others left still later, with the departing Allied armies.[16] Nevertheless, as we shall see (see section 3.4), the absolute size of the city's Jewish population remained stable despite its decline as a percentage of total population, to about 36 percent (170,321) in 1920, because the exit of foreign Jews coincided with the entry of Jewish immigrants, including businessmen, from the new Balkan states.[17]

At the same time, a continuous flow of Greek migrants from the new Balkan states and other former Ottoman territories, as well as from Crete and the city's rural surroundings,[18] spurred the growth of Salonica's soon-to-be-dominant Greek population. As to the Turks and Bulgarians, their population declined both in absolute terms and as a percentage of the population.[19] The evolving demographic trends thus altered the ethnic composition of Salonica and its hinterland.

Exploitation of the August 1917 fire for the purpose of land expropriation transformed the old Jewish inhabitants into an uprooted population, which inflated the number of potential migrants. Only the wealthy Jews who remained in the city repurchased their old plots and re-built their old residences in the renewed city centre. The rest of the now homeless Jewish population resettled in eight ethnic enclaves in the city's periphery. Thanks to this redistribution, the visibility of the Jewish minority was diminished.[20]

With the entry of Greek refugees following the Greek military defeat at Smyrna in September 1922, the demographic Hellenisation of "New Greece" was completed,[21] with about half of the total refugees settling in Macedonia.[22] One result of the coerced transfer was the decline of Salonica's Jewish segment in both absolute numbers and relative terms. According to the published census of May 1928, there were 55,250 Jews in Salonica, or 23 percent of Salonica's total population (244,680). Nevertheless, assuming that the majority of these Jews were born in Salonica or had immigrated to the city during the 1910s,[23] thereby compensating for the native Jews who had previously emigrated,[24] it can be concluded that Jews represented about 63 percent of the city's 88,050 "indigenous" residents, or 37 percent of the city's "non-refugees", (numbering 147,655; see Appendix 3.1, Table B).

The entry of more than 100,000 Greek refugees into Salonica, together with the exit of 19,905 Muslim and Bulgarian residents to Turkey and Bulgaria,[25] stimulated ethnic unification of the city's metropolitan Greek population while it put pressure on the Jewish segment. A minority–majority environment thus replaced the multi-national environment. Whereas the transfer transformed the greater Greek population into a religiously homogeneous population, in metropolitan Salonica the ethnic make-up was revitalised. Between the two world wars, Salonica's metropolitan population had formed a dual, ethnically stratified society: the primary and deepest division was forged by the religious–linguistic boundary between the Greek Orthodox (representing 75.5

percent or 184,784 out of 244,680, including the repatriated refugees), and the non-Greek Orthodox population, mainly Judeo-Spanish-speaking Jews (22.6 percent or 55,250 out of 244,680),[26] who now formed the only significant religious–linguistic minority group in the city.[27] A second ethnic boundary within the Greek population divided the Greek Orthodox into veteran Greeks and refugees. This cleavage evolved in three Greek metropolitan populations (Athens, Piraeus, and Salonica),[28] because the new arrivals experienced exclusion and discrimination by indigenous urban Greeks; they responded with the inclusive behaviour typical of ethnic segregation in general.[29] Yet in Salonica, home of Greece's largest Jewish community,[30] Greek Orthodoxy functioned as the denominational factor facilitating integration of recently repatriated Greek refugees from Anatolia into the resident Greek population,[31] a process that naturally excluded veteran Jews. Language also differentiated Jews throughout New Greece from their co-religionists in Old Greece. The latter, including Jews from Athens and Piraeus, declared Greek as their native language;[32] they were consequently considered to be Greek Jews.[33]

3.2 Legal and Political Aspects of Hellenisation Policies

So-called Hellenisation – the official policy adopted by various Greek governments toward minorities – was aimed at enforcing cultural and national uniformity while actively discouraging continuation of separate ethnic identities.[34] The Greek government began to adopt this policy in 1917, and pursued it more vigorously following the previously mentioned demographic Hellenisation executed in 1923.

Yet during the first decade of the incorporation of Salonica into Greece, the official Greek attitude toward the city's Jewish population was relatively tolerant. This was motivated by Venizelos' interest in gaining the confidence of the local Jewish community; this confidence was viewed as a precondition for ensuring the rights of the Greek Diaspora, especially in Ottoman-held lands. At the same time, Venizelos hoped to use this tack to recruit the support of the Great Powers, imperative for the realisation of Greek irredentist aspirations in Asia Minor.[35]

The London Agreement (20 May 1913), which was reaffirmed at the Paris peace conference of 1919, granted formal and continuous protection to the Jewish minority's civil rights as well as to its unique religious culture following the Greek incorporation.[36] These documents secured the minority's right to act autonomously in the areas of public welfare, religion and education for the Jewish community. The agreement's conditions included exemption from military service in return for payment of a fee, effective three years after the arrival of the Greek army, without forfeiting the right to vote; preservation of the Sabbath, which meant permission to open shops on other days, including Sunday, the Christian day of rest; exemption from all taxes on the imported unleavened bread used during Passover; collaboration between civil veterinary officials and the official Jewish slaughterer to ensure observance of Jewish dietary laws; the right to continue to keep accounts in Ladino or French; freedom for the Jewish press; and government support for Jewish social welfare and educational institutions.[37] The Jewish community of Salonica was subsequently recognised as a "legal body under state law", a status eventually anchored in Law 2456 *Concerning Jewish Communities*, on 27 July 1920.[38]

The forced population exchanges between Greece and Turkey (1923) removed concerns regarding the Greek Diaspora from the national agenda. In its place, the transfer proposed a new solution for inter-ethnic tensions by creating what was an essentially mechanical ethnic homogeneity.[39] Greek government attitudes toward minorities found expression in an accelerated and multi-faceted Hellenisation policy.[40] This discriminatory policy abrogated the Salonican Jewish minority's unique religious, cultural and social rights, which had been agreed to by Greece within the comprehensive framework of the Lausanne Treaty.[41]

The first major opportunity for enforcing spatial Hellenisation presented itself in 1917, in the wake of the catastrophic fire that decimated the city's centre. Expropriation of properties in the devastated ancient area, about three-fourths of which were owned by Jews, effectively eliminated the Jewish presence there. The official architectural "new plan" set the groundwork for the area's conversion into a Hellenic city. Former property owners became holders of undervalued bonds, issued to cover the current value of their plots. Unification of the plots by the planners reduced the total number available from 4,101 to only about 1,300, which increased competition between potential buyers. By shifting the substantial cost of planning to the new owners, the government ensured that the lower middle-class former owners would be unable to repurchase their properties. Speculation in these bonds made repurchase of their properties even more difficult for the original owners[42] (see section 3.5.1 below).

Hellenisation of the day of rest (*dies non*) was a clear act of discrimination against the Jews, who observed the Sabbath on Saturday. Throughout the nineteenth century and up to 1922, every community had enjoyed the right not to work one day a week as prescribed by its religious traditions, even in central Greece. Following the incorporation of the new territories with their sizeable populations of Jews and Muslims, these non-Christian populations were permitted to observing a day of rest other than the Christian Sunday. However, on 21 July 1924, Law 3103, which was published in the official law journal, reversed Law 2456 and imposed Sunday as the universal day of rest. This law, because it required observant Jews to close their businesses for two consecutive days (i.e., Saturday and Sunday), was considered to be grossly discriminatory.[43] This anti-Jewish law, however, was also economically motivated: it provided one means for solving the economic difficulties encountered by refugees, specifically, the progressive removal – or at least circumscription – of the competitive strength of their Jewish rivals.[44]

In 1924, the Minister of the National Economy annulled Article 25 of Law 2456 (1920) and obliged all businesses to maintain accounts of their commercial dealings in the Greek language.[45] Hellenisation of accountancy compelled Jewish entrepreneurs to alter their business culture by making acquisition of the Greek language essential for the continued operation of all firms. While Judeo-Spanish was used for internal Jewish transactions and by Jewish micro- to small-scale traders, French, the *lingua franca* of Mediterranean commerce, had been traditionally used for official ledgers in Salonica. According to a contemporary,

> French thus became the second language of all educated people. It is used in all offices, in all administrations, for accounting, correspondence, and service relationships. It is used in notices and posters. . . . Meetings, speeches, reports of financial companies, associations, everything is in French. A foreigner who is not in contact with the common people and who is familiar only with hotels, restaurants, cafes,

merchants' offices, and people in good society would have the illusion of living in a provincial town in France.[46]

Consequently, it can be understood why Jewish businesses found it difficult to keep their books in Greek.

This type of legal nibbling away at their previous privileges and customs dampened initiative. It is also clear that the linguistic regulations, which included a prohibition on the use of Hebrew letters in store signs and in offices,[47] imposed additional linguistic barriers. This was especially true for the older generation of Jewish entrepreneurs, who had been educated during the Ottoman regime and was totally ignorant of Greek.[48]

Nevertheless, in order to prepare the younger generation to live as Greek citizens, the Greek authorities took an additional step toward Hellenising Jewish education through the Compulsory Education Law (1929),[49] which made Greek the language of instruction in all elementary schools under government supervision. The Jewish community's schools became cultural melting pots for Jewish youngsters and provided them with tools for conducting business with Greek companies. Yet Jewish parents, dissatisfied with the new Hellenised public education system, sent their children to foreign schools in order to equip them with knowledge of international languages, such as French, so that they would be able to sustain their international commercial ties.[50]

Government policies toward the Jews were influenced by various factors, including the community's historical relationship with its former Ottoman rulers (see section 2.2). The Jewish community continued to be viewed as an ally of the former Turkish "conquerors",[51] or at best as unwilling supporters of Greek sovereignty, and any Jewish adherence to a political ideology other than Greek nationalism was viewed as potentially threatening if not seditious. For their part, the Jews feared the city's separation from its traditional markets in the Macedonian hinterland as well as the installation of a prejudiced Christian regime. Many Jews hoped that Turkish forces would regain control of Salonica during the Balkan wars (1912–1913).[52]

Following the Greek occupation of Salonica on 26 October 1912,[53] the Ottoman Jews of Salonica became Greek citizens, a status similar to that held by the Jewish minority of Old Greece within the National Greek Space.[54] Nevertheless, while the Jews of Old Greece were considered a religious minority, the Jewish population of Salonica was subject to incomplete political absorption, which excluded them from being part of the new Greek majority. They thus continued to be perceived as a disloyal "national minority" and a threat to the territorial and political integration of Macedonia into the Greek nation-state.[55]

Although Jewish nationalism in the form of Zionism remained nascent during the 1910s, Greeks interpreted the financial support given by Salonican Jews for Zionism activity and propaganda as expressions of a lack of patriotism.[56] Similarly, Jewish Socialism was viewed with suspicion due to the Bulgarian origins of the movement's Jewish founder, Abraham Benaroya, and its link to the labour movement in Bulgaria, Greece's enemy. The Socialist Federation of Salonica (1909), which supported the Jewish workers' goal of creating an international movement of Balkan workers, continued to be the subject of mistrust by Greek officials due to its close relationship with the International Macedonian Revolutionary Organisation (IMRO), a group that hoped to establish an autonomous Macedonia.[57] In addition, Jewish propaganda supported the Austrian plan for internationalisation of Salonica, the purpose of which was to prevent the city's separation from the old markets in the Macedonian hinterland, an economy necessity.[58] The decision by individual Jewish businessmen to avoid Greek nationalisation by declaring foreign citizenship[59] also strengthened the Jews' image of disloyalty. Indeed, the Greek "government decided in the general interest of Salonica not to summon Jews as recruits for the army in the first three years, fearing it would lead to emigration on a large scale, to the detriment of commerce"[60] – yet the Venizelos revolutionary nationalistic government in Salonica, after joining the Allies in World War I, decided in 1916 "to apply to Jews in the new provinces compulsory military service similar to [that imposed on] their coreligionists in Old Greece, and also [forbade] departure of Jews (over 21 years of age)".[61] According to the testimony of the Jewish lawyer Asher Moissis, the Jews in New Greece were actually exempted from military service for the first decade of Greek rule, in contrast to the Jews from Old Greece, about 400 of whom served in the Greek army during World War I in order to show their Greek patriotism.[62] Since the mid-1920s, Jewish males of Salonica gradually integrated into the Greek army (Law 3298 of 8 March 1925).[63] Yet, the fact that Jews holding foreign citizenship were exempted from military service inflamed the Greek authorities, who therefore prohibited foreign Jews from participating in the management of Jewish communal institutions beginning in 1930.[64]

Jewish electoral behaviour also enforced their unpatriotic image. Disagreements between the Royalists (anti-Venizelists) and the Liberals (Venizelists) appeared to threaten Greek irredentist aspirations. Venizelos himself attributed his relatively weak support in Salonica during two election campaigns (1915, 1920) to the decisive Jewish vote, which had gone to the Royalists rather than to his party.[65] While anti-Venizelists were considered protectors of minorities in the face of Greek policies,[66] Venizelists were united around the "Great Idea" (*Megali Idea*) of redeeming the Greek Diaspora and its Ottoman lands.[67]

Due to their support for the Royalists in the 1920 election, which led to the removal of Venizelos and the fall of his government, Salonica's Jews were blamed for the Greek army's resounding defeat, under Royalist command, in Asia Minor. The Jews were likewise accused of complicity in the catastrophic territorial losses incurred by Venizelos in Eastern Thrace as well as in Asia Minor.[68] Consequently, in October 1923, following the Transfer, the recently elected Venizelist government reduced Jewish electoral power by setting up a separate minority electoral college (*curia*) for Salonica's Jews. This blatant political discrimination, manifested by the repeal of equal civil rights for the Jewish minority (as well as for the Muslim minority in Western Thrace) in New Greece, was part of the new manipulative regional election system installed in the wake of the Venizelos' political defeat in 1920.[69] This system clearly made it easier for the administration to exert political pressure on Greek refugees and other ethnic and religious minorities. The special legislation (*Katochyrotikon*)[70] enacted to "protect the republic" (23 April 1924) from political agitators reflected the anxiety felt by the Greek leadership when faced with any behaviour that could be interpreted as threatening the territorial integrity of the Greek nation-state.[71] Within this context, the government desired to limit access to political power for residents of the newly annexed regions.[72] Hence, the forced Hellenisation of Macedonia's Jews was part of a larger plan aimed to merge this group with all other population components in the new borders of territorially consolidating Greece and create a homogenous nation.[73]

National loyalty thus became a core issue for all Greek governments, especially after refugees began to enter New Greece (see Map 1), where territorial consolidation was crucial. Awareness of the considerable size of the Jewish community and its residence in New Greece's northern districts, areas only recently incorporated into the national territorial core and still contested by neighbouring states, intensified the government's anxieties.[74] In Venizelos' own words (1934): "The Salonican Jews are not Greek patriots but Jewish patriots. They are closer to the Turks than to us. . . . I will not allow the Jews to influence Greek politics."[75] This same attitude, also expressed towards other minorities residing in the new territories, influenced policy during all of the Venizelist administrations, into the mid-1930s (see section 6.2).

Hence, with the forced transformation of their political status, the stateless Jewish community in Salonica was compelled to undergo nationalisation. They were, in fact, required to redefine their former nationality of "Israélite du Levant" in the "petit patrie, la cité de Salonique",[76] a situation which contrasted sharply with that of their co-religionists in Old Greece (see Map 1), who had already gained Greek citizenship in the nineteenth century.

3.3 Unofficial Attitudes toward Salonica's Jews

The incorporation of Salonica into Greece exacerbated the historical economic competition between Jews and Greeks in the city[77] (see section 2.2). With the entry of Greek refugees in 1922, a new factor – refugee-Jewish relationships – aggravated the already fraught relations between Greeks and Jews. The enmity between these two groups found expression during the battles in Asia Minor in the summer of 1921, before the evacuation of Smyrna,[78] when Greek forces invaded the Jewish and the Muslim quarters in the city. According to a short report published in the *Bulletin de l'Alliance Israélite Universelle* on 2 September 1921, the Greek army committed atrocities against the two populations, which included burning their houses as well as killing 200 Jews and Muslims.[79]

Salonica thus became a symbol of the battle for the reconfiguration of Greek national identity after 1923. It was a juncture where several issues – forced emigration from Anatolia, insecurity about the territorial status of northern Greece, shifts in the ethnic composition of the city, inter-ethnic competition for physical, cultural, economic and political space, the wider political battle between Venizelism and its opponents, and intensified anti-Semitism across the continent – intersected and combined.[80]

The Greeks who had been forced to leave their homes in the consolidating Turkish Republic and Balkan States as of 1922 (see Appendix 3.1, Table B) were officially treated as repatriated co-nationals. As such, the government assigned them the task of internal colonisation, considered important for the consolidation of a homogeneous Greek society within the new territorial boundaries.[81] Thus, as refugees, the returning Greeks enjoyed some politically motivated benefits, such as access to international and local government assistance. Cooperation between the Greek regime and the League of Nations led to the creation of the autonomous Refugee Settlement Commission (RSC), funded by extensive international bank loans (1924, 1927). Furthermore, major international agencies, like ethnic philanthropic organisations, tried to supplement the impoverished state's absorption program.[82] Greek migrants in the West also increased remittances targeted at the implementation of this national goal.[83] All this activity did not, however, produce adequate outcomes: The construction of fifty segregated colonies, established especially for refugee families unable to find lodgings in houses abandoned by Muslims along Salonica's periphery, merely resulted in marginal inclusion of the refugees.[84]

Although officially absorbed into the indigenous majority as co-religionists and co-nationals, the refugees retained their unique identities as a result of the regional cultures they had internalised during their residence in Ottoman lands (see Appendix 3.1, Table B). Their cultural exclusion led to the founding of autonomous refugee-oriented associations, of which there were more than 100 by the late 1920s. These associations acted for the preservation of local cultures and ethnic cohesion; they also promoted the refugees' interests,[85] facilitated co-ethnic labour recruitment and provided financial support for refugee entrepreneurs (see section 6.2).

The 1926 commercial boycott against the Jews initiated by the National Macedonian Organisation provides an example of the intensifying economic competition between Greek refugees and indigenous Jews.[86] By 1927, the refugees represented the backbone of the National Union of Greece (*Ethniki Enosis Ellas* or EEE), the most extremist nationalist and anti-Semitic organisation active in Salonica.[87] Refugee–Jewish tensions in Salonica were not, however, limited to competition in the market or in housing, where continued shortages forced Jewish victims of the 1917 fire to vie with the newly arrived refugees. Much of the provocation for inter-group strain came from the political arena. Refugees felt that they owed unqualified allegiance to Eleftherios Venizelos and backed the "Liberal" party in the elections of 1923, 1926, and 1928.[88] They thus supported the Venizelist ethno-exclusive nationalistic policy, aimed at forcibly imposing cultural assimilation onto Salonica's Jewish minority.[89] In contrast, the majority of Salonica's Jews aligned themselves with the two anti-Venizelist options – the conservative Popular Party (the Royalists) and the nascent communist movement – while trying to avert aggressive Hellenisation.[90]

Public opinion pertaining to the Jews in Salonica was ignited by campaigns waged in the press. The anti-Semitic propaganda spread by the regional daily *Makédonia* made the situation worse. Its pages published references to the Jews as little more than Turkophilic foreigners, living off government resources, which rightly belonged to the Greek refugees who had returned to their homeland. Jews continued to be vilified in Greek popular literature, too, by means of demonising stereotypes. For instance, one rumour published was that the Jewish doctors and nurses working in a Greek hospital suffered from leprosy.[91] In February 1928, feelings of anti-Semitism were further roused by the publication of the forged *Protocols of the Elders of Zion*.[92]

3.4 Scattering and Shrinking of the Jewish Population in Salonica

Emigration became a response to the Jew's political and legal hardships. The exodus of Jews out of Salonica can be readily divided into two periods: before and after 1921. While the first period was linked with the incorporation of Salonica into Greece, the second resulted from the enforcement of Hellenisation and from the mass entrance of Greek refugees beginning in 1922, which intensified the process. The first émigrés were mainly foreign Jews who had the resources to move without great difficulty. Yet, these initial demographic losses were balanced by the continuing entry of Sephardic Jews from the neighbouring Balkan states that had previously comprised Salonica's hinterland. However, after 1921, when the fate of the expropriated Jewish plots in the decimated city centre clarified, Jews who were Greek citizens, usually indigenous residents with meagre resources, also began to emigrate.[93] The mass emigration of these Jews during 1921–1922 caused a deficit in this population.

Jewish emigration from Salonica had begun earlier, during the final years of the Ottoman regime. It's causes were varied; they included avoidance of the compulsory conscription of non-Muslims in 1909 and escape from "the insecurity of life and the disturbed business conditions" typifying the Young Turk regime, "together with the pervading poverty at home . . . [and] the lure of the pictured fortunes to be made in peaceful America".[94] Italian Jews left Salonica following Italy's invasion (1911) of Ottoman Tripoli since the Turkish government had reacted by threatening to expel them from Salonica and confiscate their property. However, after the relatively short battle, many of these Italian families returned to Salonica, now protected by Italy's membership in the Allies, and they remained active in the military market throughout World War I.[95] In terms of numbers, these émigrés had no significant effect on the overall size of Salonica's Jewish "Ottoman" (later "Greek") population.[96]

Following the incorporation of Salonica into the Greek nation-state, some upper-class Jews left for Turkey.[97] "Pushed" by increasing Greek hostility and fearing Christian rule as well as economic uncertainty, while "pulled" by official Turkish invitations promising exemptions from taxes for seven years, more than 200 Salonican Jews reached Constantinople and Smyrna.[98] At about the same time (1916), 602 Jews from Salonica arrived in the US; these represented about 42 percent (602 out of 1,445) of all Jewish émigrés from Salonica to the US prior to the imposition of literacy tests in 1917.[99] Whereas their lack of Greek literacy pushed Jews to emigrate, the US literacy test put Salonican émigrés who had not benefited from modern education at a great disadvantage. Hence, even before the Immigration Restriction Act of 1924, Salonican Jews belonging to the working class or the lower middle class were often denied entry to the US.[100] The second major group of 430 émigrés to the US arrived between 1920 and 1921. All told, the Jewish population of Salonica lost 1,930 members due to emigration to the US during the respective decade (1913–1924).[101]

The spatial distribution of Salonica's Jewish population had also begun to change before the arrival of the Greek refugees. The instigating factor was the fire (1917) that ravaged Salonica's centre, which led to the immediate legal expropriation of their plots in the area.[102] Although the expropriation process resulted in the emigration of hundreds of Jews, mainly to the West,[103] a delay in implementation of the respective law postponed this mass movement until the early 1920s. This delay was the product of Venizelos' wish to recruit Jewish votes in the 1920 national election. Jewish property owners, forced to wait until after the elections to learn about the fate of their properties, were able to recruit the international Jewish community in order to wage a political battle against the Venizelos government's decisions.[104] Only after the official approval of the city's plans for the area's reconstruction in 1921,[105] when Jewish property owners realised that their plots would truly be expropriated, did the mass emigration of Salonican Jews who were Greek citizens begin.[106]

Hellenisation, together with the hostile treatment received at the hands of Greek authorities and the local population, also pushed Jewish Greek nationals toward emigration. More than 6,000 Jewish Greek nationals emigrated, mainly to France[107] and, to a much lesser extent, to the US and to British Mandatory Palestine.[108] Only a few dozen moved to the national capital, Athens, as can be deduced from the linguistic composition of the Jewish population: about 17 percent declared Judeo-Spanish as their mother tongue in 1928,[109] the linguistic identity of Salonica's Jews, in contrast with Greek Jews in the capital, whose mother tongue was generally Greek (see above).

Paris, Marseilles, and Lyon were the preferred destinations for the Jewish émigrés. The fact that relatives and compatriots had immigrated to these cities made them preferred locations.[110] Yet, why was France the preferred destination for so long? The answer: Entry was considered easy. In contrast to the US, the most popular destination for European migrants, France had yet to establish an immigration authority to administer a systematic immigration policy.[111] Molho stressed that this stream was especially strong between 1922 and 1926,[112] precisely the period juridical instability and the stated lack of an immigration office made it impossible for France to control immigration.[113] The impact of World War I on the French population and the demographic stagnation of the 1920s had undermined the country's military strength, manufacturing base, and general prestige; hence, the country welcomed immigrants prior to 1926. France was also considered the most liberal and advanced of possible host countries,[114] especially for these French-speaking Salonican Jews, who were neither Greek nor Turkish, i.e., those identified as "Levantine Jews". It assigned them a special status, that of minority immigrants, which offered all the advantages of French national protection without the disadvantage of induction into the military. Until 1927, these immigrants, who arrived in great numbers especially after the great fire (5 August 1917), could obtain identity cards on presentation of residence permits alone, and without naturalisation.[115]

While these last two factors also applied to other migrants, only Jewish immigrants from Salonica had easy access to the developing trans-national Jewish Diaspora in France, a group that shared the "Mediterranean citizenship" unique to the former Ottoman Sephardic Jewish stateless Diaspora. Their knowledge of the French language and culture also resulted in relatively low migration costs for the Jewish Alliance alumni from Salonica (see below, section 3.4). One thinks of Nehama's description "*car tous les Israélites, ici, sont d'éducation purement française; tous pensent dans la langue de Racine; beaucoup ont fait leurs études en France*".[116] The formation of the *Association Amicale des Israélites Saloniciens* (AAIS) in France in January of 1921, meant to assist these immigrants in finding employment,[117] also bears witness to the size of the Salonican Jewish Diaspora in France.[118] At the same time, the Association's founding alludes to the socio-economic status of the Jewish immigrants arriving from Salonica. The composition of this group broadened in the 1920s, to include Greek Jews from the entrepreneurial and lower middle classes.

British restrictions on the entry of immigrants were focused on their financial status. According to the records of the Jewish Agency's Immigration Department, between 1919 and 1923, there were only 158 registered immigrants to British Mandatory Palestine from all of Greece. However, following the Transfer, the number of registered immigrants from Greece (including Salonica) grew to 815 (1924–1931).[119]

3.5 Jewish Communal Resources

The movement of Jews from their residential concentration in Salonica's old city centre to dispersion throughout the rebuilt centre and the peripheral neighbourhoods, together with emigration, depleted Jewish ethnic resources in the city. While the former resulted in weakening of internal solidarity, the latter reduced capital as well as entrepreneurial resources.

3.5.1 Internal Solidarity and Spatial Redistribution

The intensive efforts by the Jewish community to secure its members' well-being and relocation,[120] in addition to the aid arriving from Jews abroad, point to the high level of solidarity of the local Jewish community and its connections with international Jewry. Nevertheless, it should be noted that this social solidarity bore heavy traces of paternalism, a characteristic typical of larger Greek society.[121]

Hellenisation of the city centre and the resulting spatial redistribution of the Jews according to socio-economic criteria emphasised the social gaps that would eventually weaken Jewish solidarity. Up until 1917, the entire Jewish minority had been concentrated in the city's geographic core (including quarters evidencing ethnic integration), a factor that helped blur internal socio-economic differences and support communication between the classes. The geographic redistribution following the fire more accurately reflected socio-economic boundaries. Specifically, (a) Jewish labourers and small landowners who were unable to repurchase their properties in the city centre were subsequently concentrated in about eight neighbourhoods located on the periphery; and (b) medium and large property owners who could repurchase their land in the area damaged by the fire, including locations near the Monastirlis synagogue and in the Kampanias quarter, were scattered throughout the city.[122] That is, the middle and upper classes reintegrated, mostly on an individual basis, into the city's fashionable neighbourhoods while the poor lived in difficult conditions in neighbourhoods resembling ghettos[123] (see Map 2). Following this weakening of the residential fabric, political rifts began to appear in the 1920s, often according to individual socio-economic status. New ideological factions (Zionists, moderates, communists) arose. The moderates, including the bourgeoisie, were known for their tendencies toward cultural assimilation, and returned to settle in the reconstructed city centre. The Zionists, whose members came from all socio-economic ranks, stood for separatism; they were drawn to the new residential quarters, far from the city centre. The communists were likewise concentrated in these new "ghettoes". The communist cells that appeared undertook to represent the interests of the Jewish proletariat and underclass (*lumpen proletariat*). The distribution of the Jewish population among the political parties is reflected in the Jewish votes, by neighbourhood, cast in the 1928 elections for Salonica's Jewish Community Council: Zionists – 52 percent, communists – 28 percent, and moderates – 20 percent.[124]

These ideological divisions provoked new disputes in the Jewish community, mainly in the spheres of education and language,[125] and undermined creation of a uniform, effective front against institutional discrimination. One example of the increasing weakness of religious identity as a unifying factor was the failure of the struggle to preserve Saturday (*Shabbat*) as the Jewish day of rest. This issue pitted the economic–political interests of several Jewish entrepreneurs against those of the Jewish working class.[126]

The effects of Hellenisation became visible not only in the disappearance of the Jewish lifestyle that had once characterised Salonica's centre, but also in the neutralisation of the Jews' capacity to protest as a community against the new discriminatory measures.[127] On the other hand, the increasing economic competition between Jews and Greeks stimulated reconsolidation of Jewish solidarity now based less on ethnic identity than on professional and socio-economic status. Already in 1909, a Jewish teacher employed by the Alliance reported:

The Greeks who have not brought themselves to accept the Jews as leaders of commercial activity in Macedonia and in Salonica, and the Jews who feel that their interests are threatened, all continue to work in silence. The Jews are organising; the merchants now know what the dangers are and they have formed coalitions. They have founded the "Cercle Commercial Israélite" (May 1909), which works to protect the interests of the Jewish merchants.[128]

This association included about 200 Jewish merchants, mainly wholesalers.[129] The intense competition between Jewish and Greek traders and artisans sparked the creation of the Club des Intimes by the Jewish middle class in 1907; its purpose was to provide relief and charity for the community's members, but more importantly to support the acquisition of the skills required integrating more effectively into the local economy. Following Salonica's annexation and the imposition of new ideologically oriented union rules (e.g., the requirement that cobblers belonging to the union not work on Sunday), the Club des Intimes established the Federation of Jewish Corporations, a revised version of the Union of Jewish Professional Associations. From 1919 on, the Federation gradually extended the number of its member corporations from seven (tailors, cobblers, pastry cooks, wagon drivers, barbers, stonecutters, and potters) to thirteen (builders, butchers, charcoal makers (*karvoneros*), manufacturers of (brown) paper bags (*bolsa di papel*), luggage manufacturers (*forseleros*), box manufacturers (*kasheros*), and coffee grinders (*kavedjis*) by 1920, and to twenty-one (upholsters, grocers, restaurateurs, brush manufacturers, carters, lighters and stevedores) by 1922. The mission of the Federation, which eventually included all established craft associations, was to protect Jewish interests in all spheres and at all levels. Nevertheless, in May 1922, on the eve of the Transfer, a few Greek and Turkish workers did join the corporations of carters, lighters, and stevedores, occupations dominated by the Jews.[130]

This Federation of small Jewish craftsmen, which depended, as a rule, on ethnic resources (e.g., cheap credit organised by the community), helped preserve ethnic solidarity within the Jewish economy. (In the following chapters we examine whether larger entrepreneurs, those who provided employment to co-religionists and helped expand the Jewish economy, were able to maintain the same level of solidarity.)

3.5.2 Community Organisation

External stress had operated as a reactive ethnic resource, reuniting the Jewish community around its institutions. Records regarding the Jewish community's budget for 1929 suggest orderly management and maintenance of its programs throughout the period in question.[131] Detailed statements of income and expenditures indicate support for associations providing relief and welfare as well as for educational and religious services. These allocations indicate that for the Jewish community investment in the creation and regeneration of social capital (see Chapter 1) impacted on the revival of internal solidarity.

Like other ethnic group associations, the Jewish community made every effort to preserve Jewish culture and reinforce the ethnic cohesion essential for the recruitment of Jewish workers to Jewish-owned enterprises. The community's organisational structure, in place since the Ottoman Regime, was thus preserved until the Nazi occupation, under Law 2456 of 1920 (see above).[132] Jewish community institutions operating within this framework provided jobs for their Jewish members within a sheltered public sector[133] while sustaining the community's viability and distinctiveness as an unassimilated ethnic community.[134] The Jewish community was, in effect, run like a business – understandable since its officials were businessmen, such as the banker–historian Joseph Nehama.[135]

3.5.3 Jewish Investments in Human Capital: Educational Opportunities

Until passage of the Greek Compulsory Education Law in 1929, education remained the exclusive responsibility of the Jewish community. Prior to the great fire of 1917, in addition to the nine schools run by the Alliance and the ten communal schools supervised by the same organisation, eight Jewish private schools operated in Salonica, often named after leading community figures, including H. Salem, Leon Gattegno (known as l'Ecole Franco-Allemande), Itzhak Altcheh, Haim Pinto, Itzhak Benardout, and Moise Kazes. The Alliance system (established between 1873 and 1910) included schools at all levels: kindergarten, elementary, gymnasium, secondary, and vocational.[136]

According to an official report (7 April 1930), the schools operated by the Jewish community and supported by the state include eight complete primary schools and nine single-teacher nursery schools with a total of about 2,800 pupils; Alliance educational institutions included five primary schools and two nursery schools with about 2,100 pupils; about 1,000 pupils attended the fourteen private schools, and there were two schools of commerce.[137]

A young Jewish person's opportunity to acquire formal education was directly linked to his or her family's socio-economic status. Jacques Strumza, whose family belonged to the middle class, received his education in Salonica during the 1920s. Later he wrote that

> During the same period, it was possible to divide the population into three major groups with respect to the educational institutions attended by their children. The first group, which included those with few means, studied in schools run by Alliance Israélite Universelle, where they learned Hebrew and French. The second group studied in schools run by the Jewish Community, where classes were conducted primarily in Hebrew and gradually in Greek. Children from the third group, the wealthy, were sent to the Altcheh School or to foreign schools . . . [138]

The Altcheh education system, established in 1880 by Jacob Isaac Altcheh, was transferred to its new home in another neighbourhood following the 1917 fire. Its students came primarily from the Jewish business elite, which wanted its children educated in private Jewish schools that stressed training for commercial occupations. The system included a primary school, a gymnasium, and a commercial high school.[139] An advertisement placed in the *Jewish Almanac* (1923) by the Jewish commercial high school Iscola di Comergio Leon Gattegno informed its readers that Jewish youth could study "*la kontabilità*" (bookkeeping), a profession in demand in commercial houses and local banks. To meet the rising need for trained personnel, Jewish commercial houses also arranged for professional training courses to be given to their employees; Saul Jos. Molho, for instance, offered typing courses to its personnel.[140]

Following the local fashion for multilingual education, the Leon Gattegno School, like the Iscola Pinto (primary school) and Hahinuh (primary school), advertised that it gave instruction in the following languages: Hebrew, Greek, French, and German or English, in addition to Judeo-Spanish.[141] Nevertheless, the superiority of French, the *lingua franca* in the East, remained intact. French was the language of instruction in the Alliance school and the other schools under its supervision as well as in several other private schools. French was even taught in the German Zionist School established by the Hilfsverein in 1910.[142]

This list of private Jewish schools would be incomplete without the Écoles Varsano, a girls' vocational school managed during the late 1920s by Mrs. Varsano and located in the prestigious Quartier des Campagnes.[143] Such vocational schools trained Jewish girls to follow a trade after completing their studies. For instance, in one workshop, operating since 1887, girls learned mainly needlework (sewing, embroidery, and millinery).[144]

The Jewish school system in Salonica thereby prepared its young students for entry into the economy as entrepreneurs, managers, as well as craftsmen and factory workers.[145]

3.6 Conclusions

Hellenisation, in all its dimensions – demographic (primarily spatial redistribution and changes in ethnic composition), cultural (linguistic, day of rest), and political (reduction of Jewish representation in parliament) – imposed new constraints on the Jewish minority of Salonica.

The cultural transformation symbolised in the designation of Greek as the compulsory language in all spheres of life also discriminated against Judeo-Spanish and French speakers by compelling them to transform their global business culture into a national business culture. At the same time, the consequent reduction in Jewish communal resources, mainly internal solidarity as well as the freedom to choose educational opportunities, influenced young people's choices of profession. The spatial redistribution according to socio-economic criteria may have reduced the cohesion between the entrepreneurial elites and the masses. Because their uprooting from the devastated city centre transformed them into potential emigrants, we can examine the Jewish entrepreneurial activity in Salonica during this period as a variant of migration-generated entrepreneurship.

4 | Jewish Entrepreneurship after the Incorporation of Salonica, 1912–1922

In 1913, the Union des Associations Israélites, which had visited the Jewish communities of the Balkan region, including Salonica, after the Balkan Wars, reported:

> Commercial and industrial conditions will be changed basically. The Jewish merchant and tradesman will find himself face to face with new demands and a new class of consumers . . . Jewish tradesmen will face competition from . . . Greeks more intense than ever before.[1]

This period, between the region's annexation by the Greek nation-state (1912) and the emergence of a Greek demographic majority just prior to the arrival of Greek refugees from Asia Minor (1922–1923), represents the "de-colonisation phase" of former Ottoman Macedonia, the stage at which Greece was integrated into the world-economy. Immigration in both directions, with Moslem refugees moving toward the Ottoman territories and Greek refugees entering Greece from the Balkans as well as former Ottoman territories, gradually effected demographic consolidation of the area's Greek population.[2] The political and juridical status of Salonica and its environs remained at stake; partition of the hinterland among new nation-states led to legal problems. The regular conduct of regional economic life was interrupted as the inefficient Turkish administrators working under foreign direction were replaced by inefficient Greeks.[3] Adding to the confusion was the fact that Turkish currency, law, and weights and measures continued to be used alongside their Greek equivalents for several years.[4] Salonica's economy nonetheless remained tied to the International Financial Commission (IFC), which represented Greece's Western creditors from 1897 until the country finished repaying its debts in 1920. Through the IFC, Greece continued to pay the new annexed territories' portion of the debt owed to the Ottoman Debt Administration.[5] Salonica became involved in the internal political chaos resulting from the national schism (1916–1917), when the Venizelos government, located in the city, pitted itself against the Royalist-supported government sitting in Athens.[6] Salonica's Jewish minority consequently found itself caught in a web of economic and political transitions that intensified the implications of its status as a "former" middleman minority (see section 1.3).

This chapter traces the initial transformations in Jewish entrepreneurial activity during this phase. It examines the impact of the interplay between changes in the group's external environment (e.g., market conditions, state policy, and competition between ethnic groups) and its internal environment (e.g., socio-demographic profile and group cohesiveness) on its entrepreneurial activity. Based on two complete lists of firms operating in Salonica at two points in time, 1912 and 1921, the chapter provides a macro-level overview of the shifts observed along the entire spectrum of the Jewish-owned economy from a comparative inter-ethnic perspective. At the same time, the chapter redefines the new borders of the Jewish-owned economy as they emerged during this period.

4.1 New Markets in the Wake of Greek Macedonia's Annexation

The geopolitical transformations experienced by Salonica following Macedonia's annexation (1912) created a new structure of opportunity for Jewish entrepreneurial activity due to the altered constraints. Partition of the hinterland created legal problems that hindered the conduct of business as the laws validating contracts, for example, shifted between the new sovereign powers.[7] An alternative to the Commercial Tribunal of Salonica – the only suitable court for litigating trade contracts in the former Ottoman Macedonia – had yet to be established. Meanwhile, merchants separated by the new borders were compelled to rely solely on each other's word. Due to the lack of an institutional framework to facilitate debt collection, Greek creditors, but especially Salonica's Jewish merchants, were unable to sue debtors now residing beyond the shifted Greek borders. The great losses incurred from unpaid loans were thus added to the credit restrictions imposed by the banks.[8] With the transfer of 65 percent of Macedonian's mainland territory to other national powers,[9] Salonica's entrepreneurs were separated from their rural customers, whose agricultural produce (about 75 percent) was distributed at home and abroad mainly by Jewish merchants.[10]

Jewish entrepreneurs thus suddenly found themselves operating within a protected regional market, part of a protected national market subordinated to the interests of the consolidating national economic centre, Greater Athens. While the new customs duties differentiated between goods produced within the new nation-state's borders and foreign sources of those same goods, Salonica's "city tax", included in the new import levy,[11] created a permanent regional protected market. New customs duties, collected by Salonican authorities, suppressed the transit trade and effectively nullified Salonica's competitive advantages over its rivals (e.g., Bourgas, Bulgaria's export port) in other emerging nation-states. The new 16.5 percent *ad valorem* import levies were considered high in comparison to those exacted in the neighbouring Balkans (14 percent) and certainly very high when compared to those in effect during the Ottoman regime (11 percent). The result was ineffective integration of this market as well as similar regional markets into the new national domestic market.[12] At the same time, Salonica's port, the most important Greek port operating on the Aegean coast, lost its regional status as the only port open to transit trade in favour of recently opened and less expensive Balkan ports.[13]

Changes in the regional as well as metropolitan market in this period added to these troubles. As a result of the Venizelos government's cooperation with the Allies during World War I, Salonica had managed to temporarily return to its former status as the Balkan's regional centre. Salonica's port served the Allied navies, the military hospitals established in Greek territory treated wounded Allied soldiers, and the new "military market" provided the supplies needed by Allied field units.[14] The customs tax exemptions awarded the Allies in return for financing the Greek war effort (France, for example, enjoyed these exemptions until mid-1918) stimulated imports by Allied nationals – including Jewish entrepreneurs holding French, Italian, Serbian, English, or even Belgian citizenship – who enjoyed similar economic privileges.[15] This cosmopolitan "military market" with its Western orientation provided a temporary alternative to the city's lost markets, whether located in the hinterland or in what were now enemy states (Germany, Austria, Bulgaria, and Turkey).[16] Simply stated, the Allied presence (1915–1918) stimulated internal demand (food, uniforms, coal, gasoline, gunpowder, etc.), especially in Salonica, the city where the Allies procured huge quantities of food and textiles. The Allied forces' exposure to Greek crops, particularly Macedonian tobacco, created demand for these products in their home countries. The US and the UK (1919) thus became prime export markets for New Greece's agricultural goods, natural resources, and semi-finished products.[17]

Hence, despite the serious war-induced shortage of labour and the scanty energy resources,[18] some industrial growth was observed throughout the region during the decade. The size of the secondary sector (manufacturing exclusive of primary processing) as a percentage of the national economy increased slightly, from 5 percent in 1912 to 6 percent in 1921. Other, associated causes also contributed to the sector's gradual growth during this period, specifically, the allied blockade of Old Greece (1916–1917), which increased the market for Greek industrial goods,[19] and efforts to reconstruct the city centre following the great fire of 1917, which required the production of building materials.[20] Only at the end of World War I was there substantial targeted investment in local industry, a process facilitated by the establishment of the Bank of Industry and the General Bank of Greece immediately following the end of the war. Both banks, founded by Greek industrialists, created new links between industry and banking.[21] These developments emerged in a policy vacuum due to the government's inability to consolidate a protectionist regime until after 1923, a situation attributed to the internal turmoil that continued to rage until 1926.[22]

As to regional infrastructure, Allied troop movements in the Macedonian arena likewise stimulated development during the period. With French and British aid, Greece completed the Salonica–Athens railroad (1916), a project that later facilitated the region's annexation.[23] The presence of Allied forces also increased demand for transport and freight services, particularly the loading and unloading of warships, which revived port activity. Merchants consequently made large profits and came to possess considerable capital.[24] The subsequent euphoria encouraged Salonican entrepreneurship throughout the World War I period, or at least until the re-emergence of the military conflict in Asia Minor (1919–1922).[25]

The trade legislation passed in 1919 demonstrated increasing government intervention in the local economy. Salonica's Chamber of Commerce, which until then had been a private organisation, was placed under the authority of the Ministry of Finance by being structurally subordinated to the Athens Chamber of Commerce.[26] Laws governing exports, currency, and exchange assisted the Chamber in exerting its control over all firms doing business in foreign countries.[27]

4.2 Changes in the Entrepreneurial Structure of Opportunities, 1912–1921

The inter-ethnic comparative research to be described provides an overview of the Jewish-owned economy during the first decade of Greek rule in Salonica, a phase coloured by increasing de-colonisation. The data were collected from two lists of firms. The first, derived from an official confidential 200-page report written in German, was compiled and issued by the Museum of Commerce (1915) under order of the Austro-Hungarian authorities. Based on Ottoman data, the list reflects the conditions in Salonica during the closing decade of Ottoman rule (1912).[28] The second list, adapted from the *Annuaire Commercial* published by Salonica's Chamber of Commerce and Industry in 1922 (Appendix 4.1), mirrors Salonica's business world for the year 1921, prior to the Greek defeat in Asia Minor and the mass arrival of Greek refugees (see Appendix 4.2 Table A, Note). Since the vast majority of firms (96 percent) were privately owned – many of them family firms – they have been analysed as if they were of similar size and of small-to-medium scale. According to the industry census of 1920, 90 percent (2,312 out of 2,566) of the enterprises in Salonica were of small scale (1–5 employees), and 8 percent (201 out of 2,566) were of medium scale (6–25 employees). Only a tiny minority (2 percent or 53 out of 2,566) were of large scale (more than 25 employees).[29] Data on the number and distribution of the firms, excluding peddlers and petty artisans (see section 3.5), enabled an empirical inter-ethnic comparative analysis of Salonica's entrepreneurial structure. Although consistent financial data that would support differentiation between various types of firm assets is still lacking, this analysis complies with the demands of the Kuznets approach, which addresses not only excep-tional individual cases but also, more importantly, the mass of small- and medium-size businesses which determine a group's economic profile.[30]

By comparing the distribution of Salonica's Jewish firms by economic branch, we obtain a picture of the transformations in entrepreneurial patterns resulting from shifts in the economic structure of opportunities (see Table 4.2). Calculation of a dissimi-larity index indicates an overall change of 27.3 percent in entrepreneurial options between 1912 and 1921.[31] The branches "trade in agricultural products" and "finance and commission trade" contributed most to these changes. Their transformations mirrored the impact of geopolitics on the region's economy, particularly in Salonica's now shrunken hinterland following its incorporation into the Greek nation-state. This situation was further aggravated by the fact that the cultivators remaining within its borders had yet to return to the land, abandoned in the wake of the Balkan wars. In contrast, the rise in "finance and commission trade" (foreign trade) resulted from the growing demand for imported goods throughout the region. Tradesmen and farmers enriched by catering to the military were now in need of additional financial services to meet their own rising demand for the imported civilian and luxury goods that entered through Salonica's port.[32] The slight contribution of the "metals" and "printing, paper and office equipment" derived from the increase in the number of firms importing electrical products and photographic equipment (e.g., cameras). These findings corroborate a report transmitted by the British Consul stationed in Salonica, in which he claims that no significant industrial development occurred during the war because of the energy and labour resources diverted to meeting the requirements of the military.[33]

How did the Port of Salonica, the anchor for the Jewish economy, respond to the

Table 4.2   Firms by Branch, Salonica 1912–1921 (in percentage)

Branch	1912	1921
Food and beverages	10.7	14.9
Chemicals	3.0	4.1
Construction materials	5.3	1.8
Energy and public utilities	1.7	1.2
Metal	4.5	2.2
Wood	3.1	1.2
Hides, leather, and footwear	6.1	6.1
Textiles	5.4	3.8
Clothing	10.5	9.8
Printing, paper, and office equipment	5.6	2.1
Tobacco	1.9	3.6
Domestic wares and furniture	4.4	3.3
Trade in agricultural products (incl. grain)	14.5	5.2
General wholesale and retail	4.2	9.1
Finance and commission trade	19.0	31.4
Total percentage	100.0	100.0
Total (N)	931	1301

Source: For 1912 adapted from *Austrian Report* 1915: 138–184. See Meron 2005b, Appendix A; for 1921, *Annuaire Commercial* 1922: 303–345.

Note: The firms were classified according to two variables: "Ethnic Origin": Jewish, Greek and Others, and "Economic Branch". Since the overwhelming majority (96 percent) of firms in the samples were privately owned (e.g., 673 out of 676 of the Jewish firms in 1921), identification of the ethnic origin of their owners was accomplished by analysis of firm names. Firms that could not be classified according to ethnic identity (e.g., hospitality services and hotels) were eliminated from the comparison. In order to construct a common database amenable to comparative research with respect to the economic branch (15 branches in all), we adopted the sector and branch categories appearing in the Greek Census of 1928, specifically: industry, commerce, finance and brokerage. Only branches found in both the *Austrian Report* 1915 and the *Annuaire Commercial* 1922 lists were included in the sample (e.g., barbers, which appeared in the Austrian Report but not in the *Annuaire Commercial* 1922, were excluded). To avoid inter-dependence, each firm was assigned to a single branch, based on its primary activity. The frequency distributions were calculated on the basis of the resulting two independent samples, one for 1912 (931 firms) and one for 1921 (1,301 firms).

fluctuations between Greek rule and a Western military presence? The customs duties revised throughout the first decade of Greek rule impacted considerably on port income. Duties grew from 1913 to 1916, yet froze in the war years due to the exemptions awarded to the Allies (1915–1918). Income from these duties rose again in 1919, partly in response to the revised exchange rates (see Appendix 4.2, Table A). The report prepared in 1922 by the director of Salonica's Chamber of Commerce indicates that in comparison with the other Balkan commercial centres, Salonica's commercial activities had expanded, a fact that compensated for the city's loss of the main portion of its internal transit trade. However, when we examine port activity for the years 1915 to 1920, we find that the total volume of trade did not return to its pre-war level (Appendix 4.2, Table B). This discrepancy may be explained by differences in the types of goods traded. Military transport trade (1916–1918) was characterised by high average tonnage, whereas commercial transit trade involved smaller vessels. The Sofia-

Table 4.3 Firms by Ethnic Origin, Salonica 1912–1921 (in percentage)

Ethnic Origin	1912	1921
Jewish	57.8	52.0
Greek	17.6	36.6
Turkish	8.2	3.4
Others	16.4	8.1
Total percentage	100	100
Total (N)	931	1301

Source: Data for 1912 adapted from Austrian Report 1915: 138–184; data for 1921 adapted from *Annuaire Commercial* 1922: 303–345.

Notes: See above note for Table 4.2. "Others" included Bulgarians, Armenians, and other foreigners as well as anonymous firms.

based correspondent of the *London Times* succinctly captured this trend in an article entitled "Salonique en Decadence: Ruine d'un Grand Port", published on 27 September 1922, in which he reports on the slowdown in port activity during the armed conflict in Asia Minor (1921–1922). This decline was long term and contributed significantly to Salonica's deteriorating regional economic stature.[34]

4.3 Reduced Jewish Domination of Entrepreneurial Activity

Table 4.3 shows that although the Greeks enlarged their numerical share in the city's population and their proportion in its business sector, Jewish entrepreneurs continued to dominate commerce throughout the period studied. The majority of Salonica's firms thus remained in Jewish hands. We should, however, note that because our calculations are based on minimal estimates of the proportion of Salonica's Greek population (46 percent; see Chapter 3, note 19), the Greek representation index is maximal, that is, the share might have been smaller in reality. Yet, the percentage of Jewish firms declined at the same time that the percentage of Greek firms doubled. Irrespective of the precise level of accuracy, these findings do hint at the Greek population's economic participation once they became the dominant majority.

These changes in the firms' ethnic composition indicate the extent to which the ethno-demographic transformations witnessed in Salonica and its Macedonian hinterland affected Jewish entrepreneurial strength. To ascertain just how much, representation indices were calculated for the city's main ethnic groups, the Jews and the Greeks. When comparing the results with each group's size relative to the metropolitan population (see Figure 4.3), we find that although demographic trends favoured the Greeks, Jewish entrepreneurs continued to dominate the city's business world throughout the de-colonisation phase, even after the 1917 fire.

The addresses of the Jewish companies confirm that a good proportion of Salonica's well-to-do Jewish entrepreneurs did relocate in the city centre after its reconstruction (see Appendix 4.1). The distribution by sector likewise confirms that the emigration of Italian Jews holding European citizenship[35] did precipitate the decline in the total number of Jewish entrepreneurs. Indeed, this exit, which began in 1911 during the Italian-Turkish war over Tripoli, continued throughout Salonica's

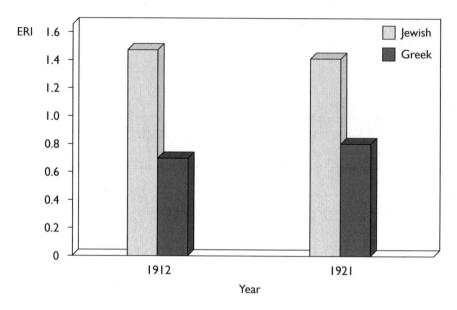

Figure 4.3   Ethnic Representation Indices in the Business Sector, Salonica, 1912–1921

Source: Adapted from Appendix 4.3.
Notes: Ethnic Representation Index = ERI = Ej/Pj, where Ej = the percentage of the business enterprises of a given ethnic group (j) out of the total number of enterprises constituting the sample in the city; and Pj = the percentage of the given ethnic group (j) out of the total city population. For population data by ethnic group, see Chapter 3.

incorporation into Greece. A series of commerce-related events – contraction of hinterland markets, disruption of the transit trade as a result of delays in allocating a free trade zone for Serbian commodities (including a separate Serbian Customs House),[36] abolition of the capitulations (December 1913), and replacement of Ottoman tariffs with higher Greek tariffs together with prohibition of property transfers (Decree 25 of January 1913) during the years immediately following the incorporation[37] – drove away foreign investors, including Jews, who feared the imminent nationalisation of their property. Although the cited legislation (Decree 25) was not enforced at this stage, it demonstrated intent; for this reason, its passage was sufficient to drive Italian Jewish entrepreneurs toward alternative and greener pastures.[38] These cosmopolitan merchants and bankers apparently anticipated the unfavourable repercussions of the contracting hinterland markets; they also rightly assumed that the New Greek nationalist administration would eventually impose discriminatory policies favouring their ethnic kinsmen.[39] And so, while the majority of Italian Jews left for Western countries,[40] others moved to Turkey, particularly Constantinople.[41]

Among the émigrés was Gino, son of the late Mario Fernandez, a member of the famous Italian entrepreneurial family, whose firm (established in 1915 by Mario) exported rawhide and sold insurance. Gino left for Paris in 1920, where he later became an executive in the automobile industry.[42] Others, like the Amar family members (merchants and professionals) requested visas from the French consulate in Salonica in 1919 and during the 1920s.[43] Although they relocated their company headquarters to their new country, these former Salonican residents maintained business ties with their native city through branches operated by local co-religionists, albeit at a lower level of activity. The firm Gino Mario Fernandez, mentioned above, retained its office in Salonica although they were no longer occupied with the export of hides; it was managed by Joseph Raphaël, who was authorised to sign for the firm according to a notary act.[44] Nefussy & Cie., a firm that sold metals and construction materials, was transformed into Albert Elie Nefussy following emigration of the founder's widow in 1917.[45]

During this period, Jewish émigrés were replaced by co-religionist immigrants from former Ottoman Macedonian towns, now under the control of Greece or other new Balkan states. The number of local Jewish entrepreneurs was therefore preserved: Jacques Nahmias and his son Joseph Nahmias, who came from Comotini (Greek Macedonia), established a partnership in 1922; Elie J. Nahmias, another son, joined the partnership in 1928 and eventually became its manager.[46] Jacob M. Nahmias, a Serbian subject, arrived from Monastir (Yugoslavia) to settle in Salonica in 1917 and opened a business for the sale of cotton and woollen textiles.[47] Liaou Camhi, also a Serb from Monastir, settled in Salonica (1917) and operated a grocery.[48] Two other former residents of Monastir, the brothers-in-law Elie Isac Massoth and Joseph Nahmias, established the trading house of Nahmias and Massoth in 1917.[49] Isac and Joseph Beja emigrated from Tikvech (Serbia, Yugoslavia) to settle in Salonica in 1914 and set up a trading establishment (1918).[50] The founders of De Mayo & Rousso, a firm which sold ironwork and furniture accessories, both wholesale and retail, also resettled from Monastir,[51] as did Salomon Menahem Rousso, who arrived after the Balkan wars.[52]

In a few cases, members of the Jewish entrepreneurial elite returned to Salonica from abroad. An outstanding example was Saul J. Capon, who made a small fortune during the war. After re-establishing residence in Salonica in 1919, he doubled his fortune by purchasing a large stock of diverse articles from the Allied armies and then reselling them.[53]

A letter written to the American Consul Henry Morgenthau in 1924 reveals something of the shift in resources available for Jewish entrepreneurship in Salonica:

> For the well-to-do of the Jewish population of Salonica, who have always accepted heavy sacrifices in favour of the community and its institutions, are themselves absorbed in very serious economic problems. That which formed the rich class of our population has to a large extent emigrated as a consequence of the fire of 1917 or the economical situation of the town.[54]

The expanded Greek population entered every economic sector. Policemen, gendarmes, and judges and lawyers were intentionally brought to the city from the Peloponnesus and Crete after the Turks withdrew.[55] In addition, Greek immigrants of rural origin, whether from Ottoman provinces freed by the Greeks or from those remaining under Serbian, Bulgarian or Ottoman rule, flowed to the city in search of the well-paying jobs now available in the developing service sectors as well as in commerce and industry.[56]

These events point to the Greek majority developing what Kuznets (1960) termed a "normal" economic structure in Salonica. When compared with the economic characteristics exhibited by the city's Jewish economy, we find the latter demonstrating a relatively high rate of entrepreneurs compared with the Greek population. Such a structure indicates the evolution of a Jewish-owned economy, where self-employment served as a refuge from unemployment in the mainstream economy.

4.4 Jewish-owned Firm Structure in Majority–Minority Perspectives

Did the entry of Jews into the city from the surrounding Balkan states compensate for the loss of the city's Italian Jewry not only numerically but also economically? How were Jewish-owned firms distributed in terms of sectors?

An inter-ethnic analysis of sector structure (concentration) at two points in time – 1912, the eve of the Greek Era, and 1921, one year before the Greek defeat in Asia

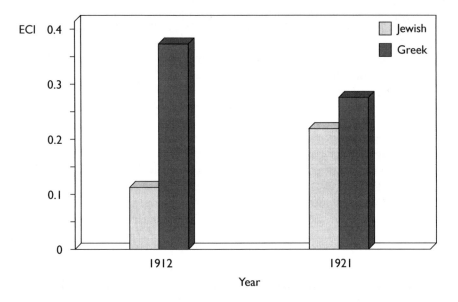

Figure 4.4   Entrepreneurial Concentration Index by Ethnic Origin, Salonica, 1912–1921

Source: adapted from Appendix 4.3

Notes: Entrepreneurial Concentration Index = $ECI_j = \sum_{i=1}^{15} |1 - Iij| * W_i$

$I_{ij} = O_{ij}/E_i$, where O_{ij} = the percentage of the enterprises in branch (i) out of the total number of enterprises of a given ethnic group (j); and E_i = the percentage of the enterprises in branch (i) out of the total number of enterprises in the entire sample. W_i = the relative portion ($W_i < 1$) of branch (i) in the entire sample ($\Sigma\Sigma A$ ij), where ΣAij = the distribution of the firms of a given ethnic group (j) by branch (i). This index refers to the entire sample and assumes that the total number of firms is not distributed equally between the fifteen branches. This index thus represents the weighted average of the absolute representational disparity (*1-I*) of a given ethnic group in the various branches. A hierarchic version of this index was used in the ethnic research focusing on Israeli society conducted by sociologists including S.N. Eisenstadt and Moshe Lissak. The index was introduced by Yaacov Nahon; see Nahon 1984.

The values of the Entrepreneurial Concentration Index range from 0 to 1, 0 for total equal dispersion and 1 for total concentration. The higher the index, the greater is the concentration, meaning ethnic participation in a small number of branches.

Minor – leads to the conclusion that Jewish firms remained scattered among all of the fifteen branches selected for study. Although the sectoral spread of Jewish firms continued to be broader than that of Greek firms, the distribution of Jewish firms by branch narrowed whereas that of the Greek firms broadened (see Figure 4.4). The distribution of Greeks among the entrepreneurial branches changed by 33.2 percent between 1912 and 1921 whereas the parallel distribution of Jews changed by only 20.3 percent. Total branch segregation (Jews versus Greeks) rose from 18.9 percent in 1912 to 24.4 percent in 1921.[57]

These same findings reflect the growing tendency of Jewish entrepreneurial branch structure to resemble other minority economies. This trend was complemented by Greek entrepreneurial branch structure in the region's primary economy, which began to acquire a majority-group coloration. As Table A, Appendix 4.4 indicates, Jewish representation rose especially in: construction materials, printing and office equipment, domestic wares, trade in agriculture products, and general trade; it fell in food and beverages, tobacco, and finance and commission trade. Simultaneously, Greek entrepreneurs, now in the majority, reinforced their positions in energy and public utilities, metal, tobacco, and finance and commission trade.

Turning to the large-scale trade in construction materials as an example of the financial strength of Jewish merchants, the proportion of Jewish importers and wholesalers was more than double (15 out of 24) relatively to that of Greek merchants (6 out of 24). Among the former we can discern several large-scale Jewish merchants of Livornese origin: Isac J. Abr[am] De Botton,[58] importers of iron and steel girders; galvanised or black metal plaques; zinc; iron pipes, window panes; cement, etc.; Mossery/[i] Raphael S. traders in windowpanes; cement, etc.,[59] and Nefousi, Moussafia & Cie., which replaced Ancienne Maison A. S. Mosseri and engaged in trade in construction materials: lead; nails, window panes; iron and cement from Greece and Europe, in addition to tin sheet metal[60] (Appendix 4.1, nos. 110, 114, 118).

The described changes in the relative representation of Jewish and Greek entrepreneurs in the respective branches (Appendix 4.4, Table A) indicate growing concentration in specific sub-branches. We now turn to an examination of how these ethnic niches developed between 1912 and 1921.

4.5 Transformations of Old Jewish Ethnic Niches

Were Jewish entrepreneurs able to sustain their ethnic niches during the first phase of Salonica's transition into part of the Greek nation-state? The empirical evidence provides support for the argument that while they survived during World War I, they did not necessarily survive after the war's end. The benefits of ethnic cohesion (see Chapter 3) explain why Jewish-owned businesses gravitated toward the respective niches. We nonetheless employed quantitative criteria to define an *ethnic entrepreneurial niche*, taken to mean an economic sub-branch controlled by an ethnic group whose entrepreneurs also own the respective firms.[61] To ascertain the presence of a niche, an ethnic group's representation in a sub-branch is compared with the same group's representation in the entire sample. An Ethnic Representation Index value of at least 1.2 was selected to indicate a "Jewish entrepreneurial niche",[62] i.e., at least 70 percent of the sub-branch's firms were Jewish-owned in comparison to 58 percent of total Jewish representation in the population for 1912 and 52 percent for 1921.[63]

Table 4.5 provides data describing three main trends in Jewish sub-branches, each of which demonstrates one of the business strategies adopted by Jewish entrepreneurs when confronting the new ethnic competition materialising in the emerging national economy: (1) continued control of the export of cash crops (opium and silkworm

Table 4.5 Transformations in Jewish Entrepreneurial Niches, Salonica 1912–1921

Group A

| | 1912 | | | 1921 | | |
| | T | J | ERI | T | J | JRI |
Sub-Branch	N	N	B/A	N	N	B/A
Banking	39	33	1.459	16	7	.841
Grain and flour	34	29	1.471	26	15	1.109
Colonial commodities	47	38	1.395	112	51	.876

Group B

| | 1912 | | | 1921 | | |
| | T | J | ERI | T | J | ERI |
Sub-branch	N	N	B/A	N	N	B/A
Silkworms and cocoons	13	11	1.459	4	3	1.442
Opium	10	7	1.207	2	2	1.923
Pharmaceuticals	13	9	1.193	15	10	1.282
Watches and jewellery	11	9	1.410	13	10	1.479
Glassware	8	8	1.724	17	16	1.810
Bones and rags	5	5	1.724	1	1	1.923

Group C

| | 1912 | | | 1921 | | |
| | T | J | ERI | T | J | ERI |
Sub-Branch	N	N	B/A	N	N	B/A
Cotton yarn (trade)	7	7	1.724	16	14	1.683
Jute: cordage and sacks	15	12	1.379	16	9	1.082
Raw wool and knitwear	14	10	1.231	5	3	1.154
Leather	8	7	1.509	24	15	1.202
Wood coal (charcoal)	8	8	1.724	0	0	.000
Glass, plates, and metals	17	16	1.629	21	14	1.282

Sources: Data for 1912 adapted from Austrian Report 1915: 138–184; data for 1921 adapted from *Annuaire Commercial* 1922: 303–345.

Notes: T = total firms (Jewish-owned and non-Jewish-owned firms) in a given sub-branch.

J = Jewish-owned firms in a given sub-branch.

A (J) = Percentage of Jewish-owned firms (J) in the entire sample for a given year (i), when i=1912; 1921. A(J_{1912}) = 58; A(J_{1921}) = 52 (see Table 4.3 above).

B = the percentage of Jewish-owned firms out of the total firms in a given sub-branch for a given year (i), when i = 1912; 1921.

ERI = B/A.

RI is greater than zero throughout; its value must be at least 1.2 to be defined as a Jewish entrepreneurial niche.

cocoons) to industries located in the core states, and import and distribution of manufactured luxuries in chain trade throughout Greece, particularly in Macedonia; (2)
discontinued control of local banking as well as trade in basic agricultural products
(grain and flour); and (3) a preference for commerce rather than manufacturing.

As Table 4.5 shows, Jewish participation in sub-branches belonging to the majority
economy (Group A) did weaken. Jewish entrepreneurs had dominated these sub-
branches during the period of European semi-colonialism, when Macedonia was under
Ottoman control.

4.5.1 Finance and Banking

Jewish participation in local banking gradually weakened. Jewish bankers had the
reputation of being highly professional, and Jewish banking before the Greek incorporation was considered a relatively stable sub-branch even when it suffered the
consequences of economic and political fluctuations (1906–1907; 1911).[64] As
mentioned, the decline in Jewish capital actually began with the emigration of foreign
(generally Italian) Jews, such as the Allatini family, founders of the Banque de
Salonique (section 2.4.2), who had previously controlled local banking.[65] This bank's
headquarters were relocated to Istanbul in 1909 although it maintained a branch in
Salonica until 1940.[66] Among the major reasons causing this outflow was the Balkan
Wars (1912–1913), which caused Jewish banks to collapse following defaults by their
Moslem borrowers (see section 4.1 above). As Moslems rarely held Greek citizenship
and no mechanism was in place to make legal proceedings possible, debts remained
unpaid. The decline in Jewish capital also resulted from the 1917 fire, as attested to by
the director of Salonica's Chamber of Commerce and Industry:

> Numerous merchants accumulated a significant amount of wealth and even became
> rich [during World War I]. If it had not been for the great fire – many of the victims
> being [Jewish] merchants – Salonica would have been the envy of its enemies.[67]

Concurrent with the exit of Jewish capital, private Greek capital entered Salonica. This
in-flow was the product of two events, one short-term, and the other long-term. The
short-term event was World War I, which, as previously noted, stimulated considerable private capital accumulation by local Greeks. The long-term event was the
increasing value of the remittances received from Greek immigrants working in the
West. These remittances rose from £1.7 million (1914) to £14.8 million (1919) to £22.6
million (1920) in less than one decade;[68] they partially continued to pour into Salonica
throughout the 1920s (see section 5). At the same time, the Greek elites began to assert
economic superiority in the region, at first symbolically, with the creation of new institutions. One of the first steps in this process was the establishment of a local branch of
the National Bank of Greece in Salonica immediately after the city's annexation
(1913).[69] The branch's opening was a tardy response to the preventive actions taken by
the Ottoman authorities, especially because the Greek National Bank had represented
the Greek elites active in Ottoman territories.[70] Other financial institutions having
headquarters in Athens soon imitated this move.

According to contemporary accounts, most Jewish businessmen used the local
Jewish banks, which together with local non-Jewish credit institutions almost
uniformly employed Jews.[71] The Jewish-owned Banque de Salonique SA was

considered the main institution providing financial services to local businesses;[72] the other local Jewish-owned banks were small in comparison to the non-Jewish institutions such as the Commercial Bank of Greece SA[73] or the Banque d'Athènes SA (Greek and French capital).[74] Yet, local Jewish-owned banks such as the Banque Amar SA[75] were not included among the official list of seventeen banks operating in Greece in 1921.[76]

4.5.2 Trade in Basic Staples: Grain and Flour, Colonial Commodities

Much as in the banking sector, Jewish entrepreneurs lost control of the grain and flour industry following the massive entry of Greek entrepreneurs into the sector. For instance, the Allatini family's sale of its shares in The Commercial and Industrial Company of Salonica, Ltd.[77] – the most technically advanced flour mill in the region – to Greek entrepreneurs in 1921[78] symbolised the transfer of control of this vital sector from Jewish merchants to the new dominant Greek elites. The sale of this family-controlled business coincided with the Greek nation-state's post-war promotion of national agricultural self-sufficiency. The government's emerging interventionist policy, with its readiness to employ protective tariffs and domestic price supports to guarantee wheat production, was a by-product of the suffering induced by the Allied blockade in 1916–1917, an event that brought home the consequences of heavy reliance on imported staples.[79] These policies were supported by the creation of a large new class of smallholders following the land redistribution that began in 1917. This new potentially Venizelist electorate was in need of financial benefits to ensure its support.

Jewish abandonment of industries thought likely targets for government protection was reflected in the merger of the Olympos Brewery (section 2.4.3) with the Greek-owned Naoussa Brewery in 1920, later registered as Olympos-Naoussa in the Salonican Chamber of Commerce and Industry by 1922. The merger was in fact, part of the final stage in the inter-ethnic competition initiated by the Greek-owned Brasserie Naoussa, Fabrique de Glaces et Halles Frigorifiques Géorgiadès et Cie., established in 1911 by four Greek entrepreneurs, who hoped to divert Greek consumers away from the Jewish-owned Olympos beer producer (section 8.3.1 below).[80]

In the face of these trends and the growing strength of Greek entrepreneurs, it is not surprising that Jewish control of the import and distribution of colonial goods (primarily basic commodities such as sugar, rice, coffee, and tea), the main imports reaching Salonica's port, also decreased. Appendix 4.1 nevertheless shows the continuing operation of established Jewish-owned firms in all phases of colonial commodities trade. Consider Peloussof Abram & Rousso (est. 1899); while engaged in beeswax and soap wholesale/retail trade, it broadened its commercial activities to purchasing and trade representation of firms in the province of Salonica (no. 52).[81] Another firm, Perahia Simon & Cie (no. 53), imported colonial commodities for local consumers but also for export to its branch in Skopje (Serbia, Yugoslavia);[82] Mahel Fratteli (est. 1910) added oil to its marketing products (no. 37).

As might be anticipated, this sector's ownership structure, which reflected the city's protected ethnic markets, was easily affected by demographic changes. The re-distribution of Jewish consumers to neighbourhoods lying in the city's outskirts, coupled with the gradual entry of Greek consumers into the city, strengthened the position of Greek vendors in their historical competition with Jewish merchants. In 1912, there was just one trading cooperative for colonial goods, apparently initiated by Jewish merchants although open to vendors belonging to other ethnic groups; by 1921, there were five, with the four new Greek-owned cooperatives[83] and closed to non-Greek merchants.[84] This change confirms that Jewish trade in colonial commodities, although still viable, had been circumscribed and now tended to reflect the size of the protected Jewish ethnic consumer market.[85] It also attests to the success of the Greek consumer co-operatives in their attempts to improve the competitive strength of firms owned by the increasingly dominant Greek population.[86]

It should be note that the described contraction of the Jewish economy charac-terised the end of the first decade of the Greek rule in Salonica (1921). Nevertheless, new entrepreneurial options did open before the Jews during the decade framing World War I, concomitant with the Allied stationing on Greek soil; this was particularly true regarding trade in consumer goods. The Commercial and Industrial Company of Salonica, Ltd., prospered during World War I (it was then managed by Moise Morpurgo), when it became the main supplier of flour and bread to the Allied armies stationed in Macedonia.[87] A firm owned by the Abravanel family (est. 1880) was another of the military's suppliers. This firm was engaged in a wide range of large-scale commercial ventures, including import/export and insurance representation. Abravanel furnished the Allied armies with colonial commodities and cereals as well as spirits: wines, brandy (*eau-de-vie*), and alcoholic beverages (Appendix 4.1, no. 72).[88] Other major firms supplying the Allies were Abastado Haim & Cie. (Appendix 4.1, nos. 496) and Nehama Albert & C/[k]/ohen (food, colonial commodities and cereals;[89] Appendix 4.1, no. 633), and Juda & Salmona, whose warehouses in Macedonia and Thrace stored condensed milk imported from the Anglo-Dutch Milk and Food Co. and Vlaardigen (Northern Holland)[90] (Appendix 4.1, no. 592). However, these successes were only temporary; the armistice would prove disastrous for Jewish busi-ness for it eliminated its main source of income, which came from supplying the various armies.[91] As shown previously, this interim was insufficient to alter overall trends in either specific sectors or regional and national economic development that would materialise by 1921.

4.5.3 Large-Scale Trade: Export of Primary Commodities and Import and Distribution of Luxury Goods and Pharmaceuticals

Jewish traders continued to control the export of cash crops, particularly opium and silkworm cocoons, directed at the pharmaceutical industry and textile industry, respec-tively, in the Western core states. Moreover, they were able to retain if not strengthen their economic power in these sub-branches mainly due to the absence of competitors having the financial capacity to respond to growing international and local demand for these goods.

The opium exported from Salonica's port in 1921 represented only about 0.8 percent of all primary exports destined for Germany, the US, England, Spain, Italy, Holland, and France that left its docks. This crop, which was also part of the transit trade, had declined from its 1910–1912 level due to the hinterland's contraction.[92] The pressure created by reduced supply encouraged what had been a minor transit trade, which also eliminated the non-specialists in the opium trade, i.e., traders in agricul-tural products for whom opium was a secondary commodity. As a result, the Scialoms become the principal players in the opium trade. This family-owned commercial network, which consisted of two established commercial houses – Fils de Jacob

Scialom (Appendix 4.1, no. 378)[93] established in 1820, and Albert Scialom & Cie.[94] (Appendix 4.1, no. 377) established in 1865 by Moise Scialom – managed to continue its domination of the opium trade through horizontal and vertical integration. These firms, which mainly exported opium and saffron, operated as middlemen between Serb growers (from whom they purchased the crop before it was even planted), Greek port officials, and industrialists in the core states. At the same time, these merchants helped create markets in Salonica for Western manufactured products, including imported pharmaceuticals, electrical products, and photographic equipment. These goods were distributed by the family's commercial branches throughout the Macedonian market. Jacob Scialom distributed pharmaceuticals as well as photographic articles (Appendix 4.1, no. 105); Samuel A. Scialom (Appendix 4.1, no. 359) operated as an agent in the countryside, while Albert Scialom (Appendix 4.1, no. 660) and David Scialom (Appendix 4.1, no. 661), located in Salonica, served as representatives of Western firms. Because of this structure, the Scialom network succeeded in penetrating the entire chain of international commerce associated with this product. The telegraph address of Scialom Albert et Cie. – PAX – not only hints at the family's ties to the Livornese branch of the family,[95] but also alludes to the Scialom family's international business connections.[96]

A different but perhaps related feature of the Jewish economy influenced the control wielded by Jewish merchants over trade in watches and jewellery as well as in glassware, including crystal. These sub-branches appealed to the Jewish entrepreneurs' strong preference for investing in precious and portable goods. Their partiality for liquid assets reflected the instability of their economic status as members of a minority. As the exclusive representative of Western firms such as Longines, Omega, and La Maison Christofle & Cie. de Paris, Salonica's Jewish jewellery importers (Appendix 4.1, nos. 348, 349, 352) became well known throughout Greece.[97] They located their shops in the urban centre – on Liberty Square, for example – locations from which they dominated the jewellery and watch trade in the metropolis through horizontal integration.[98]

Domination of the trade in luxury items for the home not only reinforces the assumption pertaining to the financial ability of the Jewish entrepreneurial elite, it also indicates their easy access to the city's affluent clientele, particularly indigenous Jews. Abravanel & Benveniste supplied imported glassware, porcelain, lamps, enamel as well as tinware and gramophones; Benr[o]ubi Haim engaged in wholesale and retail items, including glassware, pottery, porcelain, cutlery[99] (Appendix 4.1, nos. 329, 333). Such consumption patterns provide additional evidence of the Western and modern lifestyle enjoyed by the Jewish elites.

As to the remaining group on Table 4.5, Group C, this category is comprised of sub-branches whose histories shed light on the patterns of Jewish industrial participation as they emerged in wake of the said transformations.

4.5.4 Semi-Raw Materials and Manufacturing

The emerging Jewish concentration in commerce in cotton yarn alludes to their integration pattern in manufacturing. During the final days of the Ottoman Empire, the city's Jewish-owned spinning mills began to close due to their inability to compete with Greek-owned mills, which were located in the hinterland.[100] After the annexation, the Greek-owned mills organised into a cartel (1913) and extended their control over cotton production.[101] In 1919, the Greek-owned firm Pierrakos Oikonomopoulos et Cie. purchased the sole Jewish cotton-spinning mill in Salonica, Nouvelle Filature, Société Ottomane Anonyme de Salonique (section 2.4.3). The only other Jewish-owned spinning mill operating during that period, Sides & Co., had been destroyed in the 1917 fire.[102] Jewish urban entrepreneurs subsequently increased their preference for knitting cotton socks in small plants using fine imported cotton yarn.[103] International connections were apparently more useful for acquiring imported high-quality semi-raw materials than for making large long-term capital investments. These conditions supported the Jews' integration into the final stages of manufacturing, proximate to dealings with merchants and end-users.

It appears that the attempts made by Venizelos to prohibit the import of produc-tion-quality cotton – ginned and unginned cotton thread (straight or twisted) and coloured cotton fabrics (ginghams, drills, etc.) – or, alternatively, to impose protective tariffs on these products (1919), were meant to protect Salonica's Greek manufacturers against competition from foreign firms and domestic Jewish firms alike. He did not persist with these tactics, however, due to what may have been political constraints: It is quite likely that Venizelos' capitulation to the importers' protests, which led to the law's cancellation after a few short months,[104] derived primarily from his need to gain Jewish electoral support in the 1920 elections.[105]

The only textile niche dominated by Jews was "jute: sacking and cordage manu-facturing and trade", but why? Jewish industrialists preferred imported raw jute fibres cultivated in India to raw cotton cultivated in Greek Macedonia. With Greeks control-ling the local cotton weaving industry, Torres and Misrahi, the main shareholders in Nouvelle Filature Société Ottomane Anonyme de Salonique (section 2.4.3) sold their firm's shares in a cotton mill to the Greek firm Pierrakos Oikonomopoulos et Cie. (see above) once they found they were unable to compete with their Greek rivals.[106] Torres concurrently expanded his sack and cordage factory (see Appendix 4.1, no. 216), which was based on jute, the cheapest fibre used in weaving next to cotton. Because the manu-facture of products from jute fibres was not considered part of the native Greek economy, no tariffs were imposed.[107] The only Greek competitor in this industry was a firm manufacturing ropes made from hemp (*chanvre*).[108] Torres was thus able to operate efficiently in a branch where Greek industrialists were, in effect, simply absent. Since the Torres family also traded in colonial commodities and provincial agricultural products (see Appendix 4.1, nos. 34, 360), their jute operations could be vertically inte-grated. Sacking and cordage manufacture supported all commercial activities: sacks and strings for packing (colonial commodities, grain and flour, tobacco, etc.) and cordage for shipping. The jute factory Jutificio Elie A. Torres manufactured all kinds of jute products, the major ones being coarse fabric (*Hessians*), sacks, packing mate-rial for tobacco (*emballages*), and tarpaulins. It maintained a network of agents that operated in major markets in Greece (Volos, Kavalla, and Drama), as well as in Constantinople and throughout the Balkans (Sofia, Philippople, Haskovo, Belgrade, and Skopje).[109]

As for wool, a regional ethnic division of this industry between Jews and Greeks was already in effect before the incorporation of Macedonia. While Greek factories located in provincial towns such as Naoussa[110] consumed the greater part of Macedonia's considerable raw wool to manufacture clothing – principally socks for the peasantry, coarse cloth and khaki for the army – Jewish merchants remained prominent in the "export of raw wool" (see Appendix 4.1, nos. 192, 193, 202) and the import of fine wool from Italy, France, and the US.[111] Dominance in the importing of semi-raw wool enabled Jewish entrepreneurs to vertically integrate into the manufacture of flannels (see Appendix 4.1, no. 193; also section 5.6).[112]

Similarly, Jewish merchants retained their leading place in the lumber market.[113] Jewish firms (Appendix 4.1, nos. 138–144) were prominent (seven out of twelve firms) in the "wood for construction" sub-branch. As in other Jewish agricultural trade niches, the principle sources of timber, largely for construction, were foreign, mainly Romania and Yugoslavia. This industry was consequently considered part of the transit trade.[114] The wood coal (charcoal) trade, while present in the 1912 list,[115] was absent as a separate sub-category from the 1921 list. Yet, the fact that the Association of Wood Coal Merchants (1921) elected a Jewish president and a Jewish secretary to lead the association indicated the lasting Jewish control of this sub-branch.[116] Hence, the constantly expanding demand for wood coal to fuel Allied military transport trains during World War I[117] was met by local Jewish merchants, including those holding European citizenship. Due to their success, the sub-branch continued to be Jewish after the Allies departed. A similar continuity was observed in the concentration of Jewish merchants in the import and distribution of construction materials, an industry that grew directly in response to the rising demand for building materials after the 1917 fire.

Finally, Jewish traders kept their position in the former rags [and bones][118] trade (Appendix 4.1, no. 399), which included waste collection from the city and its hinterland.[119] The export of hide and textile industry by-products to industrialists in Germany, Austro-Hungary, England, Italy, and France[120] created a subsidiary source of income having minimum costs.[121]

4.6 New Jewish Entrepreneurial Niches

A comparison of the new Jewish entrepreneurial sub-branches that emerged after Salonica's annexation to the Greek nation-state with the Greek industries that developed contemporaneously confirms the trends just described (Table 4.6a). The new Jewish niches were characterised by trade in commodities, ranging from the import and distribution of new imported technologies (typewriters, photographic and cinematographic equipment) (Appendix 4.1, nos. 301–307) to trade in wax for candle manufacture (Appendix 4, no. 81) to supply finished products for local consumption.[122] The new niches demonstrated the Jewish entrepreneurs' preference for trade in finished products sold directly to individual consumers in the competitive market. When viewed in the context of consolidating nation-states, such markets were considered "blind" to group identity and devoid of discrimination.

The entrepreneurs in niches such as importing typewriters also attempted to be entrenched within the niche through adding auxiliary product lines increasing their economic efficiency to better act against the majority competition. Saul J. Molho (Appendix 4.1, no. 303), while concentrating in the installation and repair of electrical items as well as the sale and repair of typewriters, added typing courses in all languages.[123] The firm was thus able to penetrate a new and growing niche, increase its profits and thus improve its chances for survival (Illustrations 10 and 11).

Greek entrepreneurs, in contrast, strengthened their hold on local manufacturing, including spinning and weaving, tanning, the manufacture of machinery, as well as baked goods and sweets (see Table 4.6b). Except for sweets production, these sub-

Table 4.6a   New Jewish Entrepreneurial Niches, Salonica 1921

Sub-Branch	T	J	B(J)	ERI=B/A
Commodities trade	118	95	80.5	1.548
Dried legumes and fruits, oil	23	17	73.9	1.421
Office and photographic equipment	7	7	100	1.923
Wax	1	1	100	1.923
Oilcloth	3	3	100	1.923
Electrical items	8	7	87.5	1.683
Furniture and home equipment	13	9	69.2	1.331

Sources: Adapted from *Annuaire Commercial* 1922: 303–345.
Notes: T = total firms (Jewish-owned and non-Jewish-owned firms) in a given sub-branch.
J = Jewish-owned firms in a given sub-branch.
A(J) = Percentage of Jewish-owned firms (J) in the entire sample for 1921=52.
(See Table 4.3 above)
B(J) = the percentage of Jewish-owned firms out of total firms in a given sub-branch in 1921.
ERI = B/A.
ERI is greater than zero throughout; its value must be at least 1.2 to be defined as a Jewish entrepreneurial niche.

branches were linked to the processing of raw materials, sizeable and long-term fixed capital investments in relatively large-scale plants, industries typically controlled by dominant, i.e., non-minority entrepreneurs. One exception in this list is the art of tanning, considered a Greek speciality dating back to the Ottoman guilds. Not surprisingly, the only fur suppliers and leather tanneries active in Salonica were Greek-owned.[124] Jewish entrepreneurs entered the leather industry in two alternative ways: the first, through export of skins from the hinterland and import [of processed] leather to Salonica; the second, using the imported semi-raw materials required for producing leather footwear and accessories. The established Jewish-owned firm of Florentin Samuel (est. 1898)[125] (no. 175), like Fils de Jacob [E.] Fransès, imported leather, linings (*crépines*) [*sic*] to Salonica and exported rough hides from the city's hinterland[126] (no. 176); the Aroesti family's firms (no. 146, 517) were engaged in the import/export of hides, leather, and cotton from the hinterland in addition to the large-scale production of footwear.[127] Calderon & Aroesti (est. 1911) previously a supplier of boots to the Ottoman army[128] now operated a shoe factory (no. 186).

4.7 Conclusion

By delineating the borders of the Jewish-owned economy as well as its structure, we have shown that Salonica's transition from a member of the Ottoman Empire to part of the Greek nation-state stimulated changes in the Jewish economy, which narrowed and became more concentrated. The spatial redistribution of the Jewish minority helped sustain some of the established Jewish consumer sub-branches within the protected Jewish market. At the same time, branches rooted in international Jewish relational networks were able to sustain themselves as Jewish branches and even add new sub-branches.

Even if we are unable to provide unequivocal empirical proof, we can conclude with

Table 4.6b   Greek Entrepreneurial Industries, Salonica 1921

Sub-Branch	T	G	B(G)	ERI=B/A
Cotton yarn: Spinning and weaving	10	9	90	2.432
Bakery and sweets	24	18	75	2.027
Tanning: furs and skins	7	6	85.7	2.317
Machinery	4	4	100.0	2.703

Sources: Adapted from *Annuaire Commercial* 1922: 303–345.

Notes: T = total firms (Jewish-owned and non-Jewish-owned firms) in a given sub-branch.

J = Jewish-owned firms in a given sub-branch.

A(G) = Percentage of Greek-owned firms (G) in the entire sample for 1921=37 (see Table 4.3 above).

B(G) = the percentage of Jewish-owned firms out of total firms in a given sub-branch in 1921.

ERI = B/A.

ERI is greater than zero throughout; its value must be at least 1.2 to be defined as a Greek entrepreneurial niche.

a good measure of confidence that in light of the data analysed above, the weakening of the Italian Jewish entrepreneurial foundations in Macedonia's capital seriously depleted the total capital held by the remaining segment of Jewish entrepreneurs. This depletion forced a shift to small- to medium-sized firms requiring minimal fixed and long-term investments, typical minority enterprises.

Like other middleman minorities in societies undergoing de-colonisation (see section 1.3), the Jews vacated economic sectors that would become the core of the developing national economy. The latter gradually came to be occupied by the dominant ethnic majority in the emerging nation-state.

In the next chapter we examine whether these trends in the Jewish economy were sustained after the Transfer initiated the radical transformations in Salonica's demography.

5 | Macro-Level Restructuring of the Jewish-Owned Economy, 1923–1929

The post-colonial phase in which Salonica and its environs were gradually integrated into the modern world-system as part of the Greek nation-state, began with the entry into the city of more than 100,000 Greek Orthodox refugees from the former Ottoman territories (see section 3.1). This change in the local population's ethnic composition and size, as prescribed by the Lausanne Agreement (30 January 1923), was a fundamental factor influencing Jewish entrepreneurial activity in Salonica. Beginning in the summer of 1922, with the resettlement of Jewish "refugees" from the great fire (1917) still in progress, the repatriation of these Greek refugees forced Salonica's Jewish entrepreneurs to confront new sources of competition from a group that had access to "repatriation resources",[1] that is, especially easy and cheap credit together with official vocational training, resources denied to the Jewish population in the increasingly nationalist milieu.

This chapter accompanies Chapter 4 in providing a comprehensive overview of the most significant areas of Jewish entrepreneurial activity between the Transfer and the global economic crisis that erupted in October 1929.[2] Its aim is to portray the subsequent changes in both the branch structure and scope of the Jewish-owned economy. We first map the Jewish-owned economy's new boundaries (sections 5.2, 5.3 and 5.4), which we follow with illustrations of the trends in labour-intensive industries. This examination will delve into whether the increasing national-level discrimination against Jewish workers, together with Jewish emigration, impacted on the recruitment of Jewish workers to the Jewish-owned economy. The absence of detailed consistent firm data as well as official occupational breakdowns of employees by branch and ethnic affiliation (religion and/or language)[3] has placed barriers to the conduct of such evaluations. In consideration of these constraints, we have used the partial data available to describe as faithfully as possible the trends that characterised those labour-intensive sectors favoured by Salonica's Jewish workers: the port (section 5.3.5), the tobacco industry (section 5.5), and the emerging clothing industry (section 5.6). The first two sectors, while sensitive to discrimination, were also subject to shifts in international demand, which in this period meant declining prices for Greek tobacco beginning in the mid-1920s, an event that reduced the port's employment opportunities as demand for shipping fell. This analysis will thus set the stage for the in-depth analysis of micro data to be conducted in Chapters 7, 8 and 9.

5.1 New Entrepreneurial Structure of Opportunities

In the following pages we survey the main trends that impacted on the structure of opportunities for Salonica's entrepreneurs. To understand the new constraints as well as the entrepreneurial opportunities now before the city's Jewish entrepreneurs, we first map their participation in the major markets still available to them: the Macedonian overland transit trade, the internal Greek market including the Macedonian regional and metropolitan markets, as well as the Central Greece market.

5.1.1 Diminishing Transit Trade

The transit trade fed Salonica's port. However, official policy against continuity of the Balkan regional trade prompted degeneration of that trade. Instead of compensating Salonica and its port for the subsequent loss of revenue, the Greek government delayed the allocation of Balkan free trade zones.[4] A Greek Free Zone was established in 1914; yet, only in 1926, following an agreement signed by the Greek dictator, General Pangalos, was the zone opened. Only then could goods be efficiently transported to Belgrade, Yugoslavia by means of a train that tied Salonica's port to its destination. The Yugoslav free trade zone occupied a separate space in the port's customs area. Within this fenced-off space, goods could be brought solely for storage and trans-shipment without being required to pay customs duties.[5] However, the democratic governments that succeeded the Pangalos dictatorship cancelled this agreement, claiming that it impinged on Greek sovereignty over Salonica's port. It thus took over a decade for the Yugoslav free trade zone to actually function (1927).[6] Yet, despite the obvious benefits of such trade, other Balkan states, especially Bulgaria and Albania, were prevented from participating until as late as 1929, allegedly because no suitable rail infrastructure had been constructed.[7] The cost of rail development was, in fact simply an excuse used by the Greek authorities to rationalise the lack of progress.[8] A more germane explanation for the neglect was the Greek government's fear of concentrating a militant work force (in tobacco and coal) along its borders.[9] Reconstruction of this segment of the transit trade was consequently obstructed.[10]

The Greek government preferred a policy aimed at upgrading Piraeus and transforming it into a major national centre of international trade. To do so, a segment of port land was allocated to the construction of a military port, under the control and management of the Greek navy.[11] As to the Port of Salonica, government policy regarding Piraeus's main competitor involved cutting its ties to the hinterland markets that nourished it. According to testimony provided years later by a government official in the Port of Piraeus,

> National politics plays a heavy role in the day-to-day operations of the port. Greece can and must have only one national port – primary in all activities; and this port is Piraeus. Thessaloniki [sic] must not be allowed to grow to the point that it will draw traffic from Piraeus.[12]

This neglect ignored the Salonican port's greater efficiency in transporting passengers from the Balkans and central Europe to the south-eastern Mediterranean and to the Far East, via the Suez Canal,[13] as well as in distributing commodities destined for the Middle East, North Africa, and the Eastern Mediterranean.[14] Salonica's water transport facilities were also superior to those of Piraeus in terms of their ability to cater to international commerce.[15] The decision to develop Piraeus in favour of Salonica thus negatively affected trade agreement negotiations between Greece and foreign states, especially the new Balkan nation-states.[16] As a result, Salonica's port fell from its earlier leading position, to eventually becoming second to Piraeus in terms of import volume, and third (1924) in terms of exports (tobacco, hides, wool opium, wax, and cotton cloth).[17]

5.1.2 Expansion and Decentralisation of Greek Macedonia's Consumer Markets

Expansion of Macedonia's internal consumer market after 1922 was spurred by the arrival of the 638,253 Greek refugees (section 3.1, note 22), a number exceeding the 357,294 Muslims and Bulgarians who had been forced to emigrate within the framework of the population exchange agreement.[18] This population growth appears to have somewhat compensated Salonica for the loss of its hinterland consumer markets, especially with regard to imports. The same exchange likewise stimulated urbanisation, especially in Macedonia, where the urban population doubled (see Appendix 3.1, Table B). However, the distribution of refugees among Macedonia's small towns reduced rural dependence on Salonica and its port.[19] That is, with decentralisation of the urban population and the rise of rural regional centres supplying services formerly available only in the city, especially transport services, the hinterland market open to Salonican merchants and requiring port services gradually diminished. At the same time, the rising concentration of internal demand within "Old Greece", the area surrounding Athens and the port city of Piraeus, reflected the state's bias toward the new geographic centre of the emerging national economy[20] (see Appendix 3.1, Table B, note 4). In short, the spatial dimension of the government's refugee resettlement policy provoked the shrinkage of regional consumer markets formerly available to Salonica's entrepreneurs.

Alternatively, rising local demand for cheap basic products, another outcome of the mass entry of Greek refugees, the burgeoning tobacco industry, and the drachma's declining value did positively impact on the flow of goods through the port. The volume of imported cargo containing inexpensive goods increased by 36 percent between 1923 and 1924, while the value of those imports increased by 32 percent.[21] At the same time, the expanded domestic market for cheap consumer goods stimulated local production. The number of bakeries in Salonica, which produced basic products such as bread, grew from 184 in 1921 to 287 by 1928.[22]

5.1.3 Greek Industrial Policy and the Regional Effect

Official absorption policies nonetheless created new opportunities for entrepreneurs in Greece's metropolitan centres. The absence of public job-creation programs for urban refugees, a policy rooted in the Greek government's anti-labour bias, together with an abundance of cheap refugee – especially female – labour in the cities exerted downward pressure on wages, a condition ripe for private initiatives.[23] These trends were supported by Greek protectionist policies (1926), which shielded local producers together with local labour from foreign competition.[24] The scale of protection increased from 1923 to 1937, as seen in the shift from revenue-seeking to import-substitution duties, with the average tariff rising from 22–30 percent of the value of imported industrial goods to 35–40 percent in just over a decade. In 1928, protection of domestic manufacturers was increased by means of the high tariffs placed on previously exempt items (e.g., agricultural machinery) as well as on semi-raw materials (e.g., wool yarn and wood pulp). At the same time, existing duties on manufactured goods were doubled.[25] This policy is considered the main reason for the increase in Greek industrial production between the wars.[26] In addition, subsidies for industrial investment were introduced together with highly elaborated property rights.[27] The inflationary trends present in the Greek post-war economy (1922–1928), accompanied by the continuous decline in the drachma's value, further encouraged industrial expansion, which began in the 1920s.[28] Reorganisation of the banking system, stimulated by new requirements for the receipt of foreign loans, led to the creation of the Central Bank of Greece in 1927, which opened its doors in May 1928 (see section 6.1).[29]

Greek industrial policy included features specially targeted at Macedonia's urban centres. Government policy during the 1920s placed a priority on agriculture rather than on industry, a preference mirrored in the official settlement programs meant to channel refugees to rural areas. The policy had several purposes. On the declarative level, it was meant to prevent labour market pressure caused by competition between similarly skilled indigenous and refugee workers; it was also intended to increase agricultural production to meet the growing population's needs. Yet, its primary, undeclared motive was to quash the emerging militant urban industrial proletariat, especially in the recently annexed territories of Macedonia and Western Thrace.[30] Encouragement of agriculture at the expense of industry was supported by National Bank of Greece provision of easy rural credit in the said territories. By 1927, credit to industry constituted only 34 percent of all short-term lending approved by the five major Greek banks.[31]

This altered structure attracted both indigenous and refugee entrepreneurs who were eager to take advantage of the new opportunities. Did Jewish entrepreneurs benefit from this new environment? How did the entry of a refugee entrepreneurial force affect competition in the local market, especially for Jewish entrepreneurs?

5.2 Redrawing the Boundaries of the Jewish-Owned Economy

The available data on the number of Jewish-owned firms in Salonica are inconsistent but do indicate that the percentage of Jewish enterprises fell steadily from more than 50 percent in 1922 (section 4.2) to 21 percent in the mid-1920s,[32] figures approaching the new proportion of the Jewish component within Salonica's population (see section 3.1). It thus appears that the continued departure of Jewish businessmen contributed to the diminution of Jewish entrepreneurial strength remaining in Salonica.[33]

A review of the human capital and entrepreneurial skills of the Greek refugees who had reached Salonica leads to the conclusion that Salonica's repatriated Greeks did not perfectly replace the emigrating well-to-do Jewish entrepreneurs. According to a survey conducted by the League of Nations in 1926, about two-thirds of the Greek refugees arriving in Salonica from Turkey had been businessmen or professionals in their former homes; only one-third were labourers.[34] By 1926, before any compensation had been paid to the refugees, 25 percent (300 out of 1,200) of the members of Salonica's Chamber of Commerce and Industry were refugees, compared with not less than 14 percent (1,000 out of 7,000) in the Athens Chamber of Commerce and Industry.[35] Yet, a comparative analysis of the geographic origins of the refugees (in the absence of reliable data associating occupations with origins) indicates that the entrepreneurial resources brought by refugees to Salonica were less than those they brought to Athens. Whereas Athens and Piraeus absorbed the bulk of urban refugees (about 90 percent) coming from the developed coastal cities of Asia Minor, including Constantinople, only two-thirds of the refugees absorbed by Salonica belonged to this group. The remaining third came from border areas, mainly Eastern Thrace, an area characterised by small towns, or from rural communities in the Pontus and the Caucasus, areas known to be meagre in human and real capital (Appendix 3.1, Table C).[36]

The following figures support these trends: Whereas refugees represented only about 15 percent (12 out of 82) of the members of the Union of Macedonian Industrialists (large-scale firms), they made up about 40 percent (2,700 out of 6,700) of the members of the Chamber of Arts and Crafts (micro- and small-scale firms). In consequence, the average refugee entrepreneur in Salonica competed only with indigenous craftsmen or small and micro-scale traders having very modest entrepreneurial resources. The discriminatory attitude adopted by the National Bank of Greece exacerbated this relative dilution of resources: only 3 percent of all funds available for distribution to urban refugees in compensation for their assets left in Turkey were allotted to Salonica's refugees.[37] This amount was clearly inadequate for financing refugee entrepreneurial efforts in the city.

Reductions in the supply of Jewish entrepreneurial strength in the face of modest growth in the supply of refugee entrepreneurial skills and capital increased the interethnic competition but facilitated the recruitment of Jewish workers by Jewish employers. Although the relative and absolute numbers of Jewish firms had declined even before the Great Depression, the scope of the Jewish-owned economy appears to have remained considerable.

But did the branch distribution of the Jewish economy also change? The list of firms prepared by the former Salonican Jewish journalist Sam Lévy and published in his *Guide Sam* 1930 (see the Introduction) provides only a partial list of the 11,355 businesses operating in Salonica in 1930,[38] with just the city's major registered firms described in any depth. Although this list is biased toward Jewish firms and is in other respects an imperfect source for systematic statistical inter-ethnic or intra-ethnic comparison, it does provide sufficient information to form a general picture of the trends marking the Jewish-owned economy's development.[39] Hence, *Guide Sam* can assist us in redrawing of its boundaries following the period's radical demographic transformations. We have therefore relied on *Guide Sam* when preparing our overview from a minority–majority comparative perspective (see Appendix 5).[40]

Because the changes observed in the internal distribution of Jewish firms among the industrial branches reflected transformations in regional economic opportunities, it is difficult to perform a systematic inter-branch comparison of these firms for the period 1921–1930.[41] Yet, the data appearing in Appendix 5 strengthen our conclusion that the place of Jews among the major entrepreneurs supplying the military demand was indeed temporary, influenced as it was by the presence of the Allied armies (section 4.1). The same data consequently validate our hypothesis that the first decade of Greek rule was a transition period, from European semi-colonialism to nation-statehood. Nonetheless, the 1920s, especially 1922 on, saw the consolidation of the minority's entrepreneurship patterns. Jewish entrepreneurs were almost entirely absent from centres of large-scale business activity connected to the public sector;[42] that is, they took no or little part in entrepreneurial activity linked to state demand, such as the supply of military equipment, or the contracting of public works projects. Quite apparent, however, was (1) an increasing Jewish presence in the commodities trade coupled with a decreasing presence in large-scale commerce and commission trade (section 5.3); and (2) a deepening Jewish presence in the clothing industry, from manufacture to trade, together with declining participation in the labour-intensive manufacture of textiles (section 5.6) as well as production of tobacco and cigarettes (section 5.5), a sector that had entered the mainstream economy. These trends can be considered to characterise ethnic entrepreneurship (see Chapter 1).

5.3 Large-Scale Commerce, Finance and Commission Trade

Despite contrary trends in other sectors, Jewish businessmen indeed remained prominent in foreign trade during the 1920s. Table 5.3a provides data indicating the still significant presence of Jewish-owned firms in finance as well as trade support services (insurance, etc.) linked to the port.

Table 5.3a Jewish-owned Firms in Banking, Large-Scale Commerce and Commission Trade, Salonica 1929

Sub-Branch	Number of Jewish Firms	Total Firms in sub-branch	Percentage of Jewish Firms in sub-branch
Banks, bankers, exchange agents	8	23	35
Maritime agencies	7	38	18
Forwarding agents	5	6	83
Insurance companies	24	55	44
Appraisers*	4	7	57
Commission representation	60	125	48
Advertising and publicity**	1	2	50
Information office**	1	–	100
Real estate	4	5	80

Source: Adapted from *Guide Sam* 1930: 901–935; for the list of names of the Jewish-owned firms, see Appendix 5.
* Also included in insurance agencies.
** Also included in commission representation.
Notes:
1. Since firms co-owned by non-Jewish and Jewish partners were not included as "Jewish firms" in these calculations, the percentage of Jewish firms is minimal.
2. The data for categories 1, 3, and 5 were derived by *Guide Sam* from the following official sources: The Syndicate of the Insurance Companies in Salonica (*Guide Sam* 1930: 901); the Chambre Maritime de Salonique, which furnished a list of maritime agencies (ibid.: 903); and the Syndicate of Commission Representatives of Salonica (ibid.: 929–931). We may consequently assume that these data were unbiased.

5.3.1 Banking

Although Jewish commercial banks exercised less financial power than did the major Greek financial institutions,[43] the Jewish-owned Banque Amar and Banque Union, located in Salonica, as well as the local branch of Banque de Salonique (see section 4.5, above), continued to play a central role in the transit trade as well as in international commerce for Jewish as well as Greek merchants. Banque Amar and Banque Union provided a range of bank services and exchange, issued checks and letters of credit, and maintained representatives in the principal cities of Europe and America. Like other commercial banks, they offered warehousing for commodities in transit and paid duties.[44] We can hear the voices of Jewish entrepreneurs echoing in their correspondence with bank officials.[45]

5.3.2 Commercial Representation

Established Jewish-owned firms remaining in Salonica throughout the 1920s continued their commercial representation activity (e.g., Juda & Salmona (est. 1884) a partnership included I. S. Juda, I. S. Salmona, and Jos. Tiano, general commission agents specialising in the import of colonial commodities;[46] see Appendix 5, no. 609; section 4.1).

Jewish merchants continued to hold their prominent presence mainly within commercial niches in large-scale foreign trade, including the import of jewellery and watches (60 percent, or 6 out of 10 firms) as well as glassware (68 percent, or 26 out of 38 firms) (Appendix 5, nos. 464–469 and nos. 470–495, respectively), which required large-scale financial abilities (see section 4.5.3). These firms retained their locations in the city's best commercial sites, where they could attract affluent consumers. Fils de Haim R. Botton, whose shop was well located in Palait Zenith situated in the intersection of Venizelos and Metropole roads, in the city centre, were now the exclusive representatives of the Zenith watch factory for the whole of Greece.[47]

Jewish entrepreneurs represented the vanguard with respect to entry into the outdoor advertising industry, led by the Jewish-Italian entrepreneur Sam E. Modiano (Appendix 5, no. 619); in fact, the only "Office of Commercial Information for the Entire World" advertised was the Jewish-owned Nahmias A. S. (Appendix 5, no. 624).[48] Yet, the presence of Jewish "information" offices was not new.[49] Such agencies had been involved in the relocation of Macedonian emigrants, which included the extension of credit to finance departures, since the last decade of the Ottoman presence. Jewish shipping agents, bankers, and commercial representatives, mainly of Italian origin, were actively involved in this branch. Their information networks enabled them to keep track of the emigrants who had taken loans and concurrently realise the large profits to be made by supplying such services.[50]

The *Nos Annonceurs* column published in *Guide Sam* was created to provide commercial intelligence for Jewish émigré merchants in France. Suppliers of this information were local Jewish commercial representatives, Jewish-owned banks and non-Jewish-owned firms that employed Jews. Thus, the Salonica branch of Socombel (Société Commerciale Hellénique des Pétroles, SA),[51] which dealt with petroleum and petroleum by-products, and included Jewish businessmen on its board of directors,[52] became an important source of information. A new network was thereby created that would connect Salonican Jews in their new countries with their colleagues in the Old Diaspora.

5.3.3 Maritime Transportation and Auxiliary Services

The Jewish share in maritime agencies was tiny since the shipping industry in Greece was known for its "Greekness".[53] However, Jews still dominated international commercial services. Jews were prominent among those Salonican forwarding agents who represented foreign shipping companies, arranged cargo insurance, and saw to matters of storage and transport. The long-established firm of Amariglio, Tazartes & Revah (Appendix 4.1, no. 508; Appendix 5, no. 552) was engaged in various activities related to international transport: forwarding and customs agencies; consignment and transit. They also represented the Intercontinentale SA de Transports et Communications in Salonica. Its branches spanned from Old Greece (Larissa, Volo, and Athens) to New Greece (Guevgueli), crossed Balkan national boundaries in Yugoslavia (Tsaribrod, Skopje, Nisch, and Belgrade) and Bulgaria (Sofia), and reached Central European capitals (Vienna and Budapest).[54] Such networks expressed the dream of Jewish entrepreneurs regarding the return of Greek Salonica to its former status as the Balkan and central Europe *entrepôt*.

Several Jewish entrepreneurs who dominated the large-scale commission firms were often heavily involved in the insurance industry, which was frequently integral to the conduct of international trade. Among Jewish representatives of foreign insurers, only a small number were authorised to conduct damage appraisals (Table 5.3a). Molho Frères (founded in 1865) participated in numerous spheres, being vertically and horizontally integrated into large-scale international transport services. The list of firm activities is rather long. They acted as maritime agents, insurers, forwarding agents, chartered (*d'affrètements*) brokers, importers, coal merchants, American Express Co. correspondents, general representatives of "La Suisse" (transport and fire insurance); intermediate commissars of the Comités des Assureurs Maritimes, France, together with other insurance companies and groups of insurers, dispatchers, and remuneration agents[55] (see Appendix 4.1, no. 618; Appendix 5, no. 556). An indication of the firm's prominence is found in the only report available from the Port of Salonica and the first report from a Greek port to be cited by the International Union of Marine Insurance in 1927: "Messrs. *Molho Frères* write us. . . . "[56]

Jewish entrepreneurs also steadily penetrated into private life insurance, an industry characteristic of advanced capitalism. For instance, Asséo [M] Isac represented the French life insurance firm La Nationale de Paris, SA, in New Greece (Appendix 5, no. 585). By 1928, Isac Asséo and his father could transform their agency into a *société anonyme* (SA).[57]

Non-Greek citizenship remained an advantage in the local insurance industry due to its international character, expressed in the local dependence on reinsurers outside Greece. Moise Morpurgo, of the famous Jewish family from Trieste, the capital of insurance in Central Europe (section 2.4.3) thus served as the president of the Syndicate des Companies d'Assurance until 1925; he was then replaced by another Jewish businessman, also an Italian citizen. Modiano officially led the insurance syndicate, which was, in *Guide Sam*'s words, "*contrôlée par notre représentant M.S. E. Modiano*".[58] For similar reasons, it appears that Nicolas Manos, elected Salonica's mayor in 1929,[59] recruited Daniel Allalouf, the former Head of Services for the Banque d'Orient, Salonica, as early as 1917 to "assist" Maison Nicolas Manos (est. 1896), Commercial Representations and Insurance Company, to prosper.[60] Despite the intensifying demographic Hellenisation, Daniel Allalouf became a partner in Nicolas Manos & Co. in 1924, indicating that Manos, who belonged to the Greek political and commercial elite, recognised Allalouf's proficiency in industry affairs.

The continued relative prominence of Jewish merchants in the large-scale commercial services industry supports our claim that refugee entrepreneurs were imperfect substitutes for the Jewish entrepreneurial elites in Salonica. An alternative explanation is that the Greek elites who had been occupied in international trade in Constantinople and Izmir were attracted to Greater Athens, the resurging centre of Hellenic national stature, rather than Salonica. The expansion of the Greek mercantile fleet, partially due to the tax benefits decreed by the Greek government to encourage investment in shipping,[61] strengthened the standing of Piraeus as the national alternative for the former Greek port of Izmir.[62] Salonica simultaneously lost its place on the Greek shipping map[63] and ceased to be Greece's main hub for the distribution of goods to Central Europe and the Balkans.[64] The accumulated effect of all of these transformations could be seen in Piraeus[65] as described by Charles Eddy in 1931:

> Of greatest importance is the great expansion of the commerce of Piraeus, which is now a more important port than Constantinople, taking rank in the Mediterranean after Marseilles and Genoa; and connected with this is the creation of large industrial establishments in Piraeus. Without the competition of Constantinople and Smyrna to face, the city of Athens–Piraeus is supreme in the Greek world. . . .[66]

One example of the local efforts to revive and expand the international export trade was the Salonica International Fair, inaugurated in October of 1926. According to the British Consul, this "first attempt on the part of the Greeks to advertise their national industries was undoubtedly crowned with a considerable measure of success". Yet, apart from Russia and Bulgaria, which were officially represented, other countries, including the UK as well as the US, Germany, Italy, and France, were poorly represented. However, the greatest disappointment of the organising committee was the failure to generate the wished-for support, especially from foreign industrial circles maintaining offices in Athens.[67]

5.3.4 The Transit Trade

Table 5.3b indicates that Jewish merchants still dominated (1929) the export trade in crops, which was bound to the transit trade. Once the volume of transit trade contracted, Jewish merchants in Salonica were affected.

Jewish traders in traditional products such as silk cocoons and opium remained dependent on their former Serbian producers,[68] now located beyond Greece's borders. Jewish domination of the export of silk cocoons from Serbia was soon undermined by the Greeks. In contrast with local Jewish merchants (and their colleagues throughout the Balkans) who paid farmers to raise silkworms and then sold the cocoons to foreign mills, Greek merchants could take advantage of the presence of skilled Greek refugees from Broussa, the silk industry's centre. These refugees were vertically integrated throughout the industry, from the agricultural phase (raising cocoons), to the indus-

Table 5.3b   Jewish Firms Trading in Agricultural Products, Salonica 1929

Sub-Branch	Jewish Firms (N)	Total Firms (N)	Percentage of Jewish Firms
Locally grown products*	5	27	18
Cereals	12	15	80
Cereals and Flour	7	24	30
Opium (export)	3	3	100
Silk cocoons (export)	4	7	57
Dried fruits and legumes	18	24	75
Oils	13	70	19
Timber	17	40	42
Hides and Leather	58	95	61
Skins (*peaux*)	7	7	100

Source: Adapted from *Guide Sam* 1930: 903–935; for the list of names of the Jewish-owned firms, see Appendix 5.
* Many firms, which might have been placed in this category, were already included under cereals.
Notes: Based on data derived from the original commodity-based categories of *Guide Sam* 1930. Compare with Appendix 5. See also note 1 for Table 5.3a.

trial phase (spinning and weaving).[69] Indicative of the decline of the Jewish presence in this sector and the shift of its business abroad is the emigration of Joseph, Salomon S. Mordoh's heir (Appendix 5, no. 522), to Milan, the Italian silk centre.[70] Joseph left the firm's affairs to his brothers-in-law, Mallah and Yacoel, who remained in Salonica.[71]

Nonetheless, major established Jewish merchants such as the Scialoms (Appendix 5, nos. 519 and 520) and Abram Joseph Bensoussan [*sic*] (Appendix 5, nos. 500 and 501) continued to enjoy a virtual monopoly over primary agricultural exports (such as opium and cereals) from the Yugoslav interior; yet, they also ceased their activities in 1929.[72] According to *Guide Sam*, the firm Fils de Jacob Scialom continued to export opium from Constantinople.[73] As to the Bensussans, a new firm bearing the family name (Appendix 5, no. 173) indicates the family's shifting commercial activities, in this case to the automobile business: They opened a local branch of Fiat. During the 1930s, Réné J[oseph] Bensussan (one of Joseph's sons), representing the new generation, extended the firm's activities to importing automobile spare parts from Belgium,[74] a new growth niche.

Similarly, since the exploitation of Macedonia's rich forests became limited after the war,[75] the trade in timber remained integrated into the transit trade, conducted by rail from Belgrade directly to the Port of Salonica. Salonica's timber suppliers were Yugoslav firms, Jewish and non-Jewish, such as A. Sciaky, Bois de Construction, Sarajevo and Bosnia, Yugoslavia, and Dioničarsko društvo za Eksploatacÿu drua – Société Anonyme d'Exploitation Forestière, Zagreb. Yet, Jewish timber merchants from Salonica ceased to dominate this branch after the growing demand for construction materials needed to build housing for the uprooted refugees stimulated competition from Greek refugee merchants (section 8.3.4).

Another sector in which the transit trade with Yugoslavia continued was semi-raw materials for industry, especially cotton yarn and hides. Following the opening of the Yugoslav free zone, about 85 percent of exported Greek manufactured cotton yarn was absorbed by Serbia.[76] The only registered Jewish firm specialising in the raw cotton and wool trade[77] in the Macedonian hinterland,[78] Elie [S.] Pinhas & Cie. (Appendix 5, no. 273), had gone bankrupt and was dissolved by 1929.[79] Warehouses for storing hides and leather waiting to be forwarded in the Free Zone were operated by two other Jewish firms, Aroesti (Appendix 5, no. 211) and Salvator E. Florentin.[80]

The transit trade was mostly affected by the administrative barriers between the national borders of both Greece and Yugoslavia. The British Consul thus summarised the difficulties facing merchants active in the transit trade:

> Since the transit trade had been declining as a result of the constant difficulties put in the way of transit dealers [who were mostly Jews] at the Customs House; by the fluctuations of exchange; the establishment of a free zone at the port of Salonica, i.e., declaring the Serbo-Greek frontier open, Yugoslavia will be given a free zone with Customs control at Salonica and facilities for the transit of sealed wagons over the railway connecting the port with Yugoslavia. The balance of exports over imports is on the side of Serbia, whose cereals, livestock and opium are more than equivalent to the yarns and general merchandise crossing the frontier from Greece.[81]

Jewish commercial representatives also served as middlemen between the Western producers and Jewish as well as Greek merchants, who imported goods destined for Serbia *via* the transit trade. The following example shows how this trade was practiced. The Greek-owned firm D. N. Tsolekas & Frère was assisted by Jewish middlemen when conducting its transit trade in hides.[82] The seal of Samuel Ghedalia Yeni (Appendix 5, no. 255), the commercial representative in Salonica of the French producer Les Tanneries Lyonnaises,[83] was imprinted on the detailed bill of lading for tanned skins destined for Serbia (Yugoslavia) presents evidence of the involvement of a Greek importer. Similarly, Yeni was mentioned in other drafts, including certificates of origin, freightage, and freight insurance, sent to other hide importers, both Greek and Jewish[84] (see Chapter 7). The stamp of the port administration on the delivery notice [of Tsolekas], in French (*"Exempté du Timbre – Article 8, loi du 31 Décembre 1924"*),[85] indicates the profits to be made by the transit trade operating within the cross-border free zone.

Two factors enabled Jewish merchants to maintain horizontal control of the transit trade with Yugoslavia: They were familiar with the Serbian growers thanks to their historical commercial relations and they were thought to be free of Greek nationalism. The Jewish merchant, stable in his practices and devoid of any political ambitions, was considered an appropriate representative of Serbian interests. The transit trade within the framework of these nation-states increased the need for mediation: Jewish traders stood between Serbian agricultural producers and the Salonican port's Greek administration on the one hand, and between Serbian growers and industrialists in the West on the other hand. As middlemen whose loyalty to both sides derived solely from economic interests, Jews could serve all parties. Thus, they subsequently continued to create markets for Serbian agricultural goods (hides, opium, and silk cocoons) in the core states as well as distributing the core states' industrial products throughout Serbia.[86]

During the transition between the old and new frameworks, Jewish entrepreneurs were thus able to strengthen their hold on niches associated with the Serbian transit trade. There is evidence that Jewish merchants tended to take on Greek and Serbian partners (Appendix 5, nos. 651, 653, 656) to facilitate the cross-border commercial activities. Yet, Jewish transit traders were supported mainly by Ladino-speaking commercial networks cutting across the new borders. These networks were consolidated in the course of time through marriage between Salonica's Jews and their Serb co-religionists.[87] Established Jewish commercial houses such as Sciaky, Russo, and Scialom,[88] kept branches on both sides of the border; they were thus able to continue to import and export agricultural products between Greece and Yugoslavia. These same networks helped create a market in Yugoslavia for Western manufactured goods, including luxuries as well as metal products.[89] Evidence for this development is found in correspondence kept in the archives of the Jewish commercial bank, Banque Union (see section 7.2 below) in Salonica, whose officials functioned as middlemen. For their part, Jewish middlemen enjoyed an exemption from stamp taxes, which made the transit trade, even with its decreased volume, still profitable.

5.3.5 Jewish-Owned Manual Port Services

Reduction in the scope of Jewish international trade, the decline of Salonica's port as a national gateway, and the influx of Greek refugees all whittled away at Jewish control over the supply of cargo services in the port.[90] These services, although considered part of the semi-public sector because they were divided between loading and unloading goods (e.g., the custom's porters), were paid for by the port as well as by private entrepreneurs, with funds channelled through contractors and workers. Although this sector belonged to the Jewish-controlled economy, mainly due to the participation of ethnic labour rather than to the scope of ethnic entrepreneurship, we nonetheless review this sector in order to better understand its impact on the scope of the Jewish-owned economy.

While the marginal participation of Greeks in Jewish associations of port cargo workers before the radical demographic transformations provides evidence for Jewish domination of this sector (see section 3.5.1), the following factors exerted a negative impact on that domination after 1922. First, in contrast with the previous decade of chronic labour shortages resulting from the emigration of the Macedonian peasantry as well as military mobilisation,[91] the mass entry of skilled and semi-skilled Greek refugees increased competition for manual jobs in the port.[92] Since shipping was part of the Greek economic legacy,[93] these new migrants were thought to be perfect substitutes for Jewish workers. Second, the preference of Greek ship owners for Greek port workers following Salonica's incorporation into the Greek nation-state was part of the employment pattern that came to dominating the industry. Internal cohesion on the basis of kinship and national, cultural, and linguistic commonalities were the basis of the international maritime industry's "Greekness". Despite the increasing trade unionism, this communality engendered close relations between crew, masters, and ship owners on sea and ashore, helped to increase the industry's efficiency and reduced labour costs while maintaining high levels of productivity.[94] It should therefore not be surprising that Greek ship owners preferred Greek porters and dock workers to Salonica's Ladino-speaking Jewish labourers.

While such ethnic priorities, which were justified by internal cohesion, were firmly established, in the eyes of Jewish observers, this preference exposed the dark side of national discrimination. Ben-Zvi described the situation during his visit to Salonica in 1914:

As several Jewish seamen told me: "We make our living from the ships landing on Salonica's shores – whether Austrian, Russian, French, or whatever – but from the scores of Greek ships docking, we can't earn a single penny. The first thing they ask us is if we are Jewish; but we're not given to denying our people."[95]

Third and finally, rationalisation of lightering methods following construction of the port's new wharf resulted in the reduced demand for manual workers.[96] Molho Frères (Appendix 5, no. 556) reported (1927) to the editorial board of the Review of the International Union of Marine Insurance, Berlin on the impending changes in the discharge of this work:

Goods are discharged into lighters, a total fleet of 200 units in good condition being available. Every lighter is able to carry from 25 to 150 tons, and the whole fleet can carry about 7,000 tons of all classes of goods, so that discharging operations can always be promptly carried out, the more so, since the goods rarely remain in the lighters for more than 24 hours and are then stored in one of the 43 transit sheds or bonded warehouses of the free zone. . . . Furthermore, a large warehouse is under construction which will be several stories high on completion and belongs to the *Société Anonyme des Magasins Généraux de Gréce* [Anonymous Company of General Warehouses of Greece]. Owing to lack of space, the quays having a total length of only 1300 yards, it is not possible for every vessel to come alongside the quay. However, great extensions are planned and when they have been carried out all vessels will be able to do so. Lighters will then only be used for carrying goods not stored in warehouses, i.e., for inflammable cargo, timber, railway building materials, grain in bulk, etc. . . . [97]

Transfer of the port's management from French to a Greek firm, accomplished through establishment of the Salonica Port Fund (1930),[98] facilitated the replacement of Jewish workers with Greek refugees. Upon the new wharf's opening in 1932, Jewish stevedores suddenly found themselves unemployed. Construction of the new wharf reduced the port's dependence on lighters. Ships could now easily unload their goods directly onto the docks, for quick, direct transfer to warehouses located on the wharf. Barge work was diminishing in any case, as Haim Refael documents. Refael's grandfather, Haim Gilidi, had owned thirteen freight barges and employed about sixty to seventy stevedores until the mid-1930s, when he went bankrupt.[99] Gilidi's fate was the same as that of the majority of Jewish barge owners and contractors who owed their livelihood to Salonica's port.[100] The emigration of Jewish port workers to Palestine during the first half of the 1930s provides evidence of their shrinking employment options in the port.[101]

5.4 Industry

Although Jewish businessmen took part in many of the same industries favoured by Greek businessmen, the manner of their participation differed. They tended to enter these industries at their commercial stages. An analysis of the respective sub-branches (Table 5.4a) indicates intensification of the trends observed prior to the entry of the Greek refugees (see Chapter 4). Most of the food industry was overwhelmingly Greek,

Table 5.4a Jewish-owned Firms in Industrial Branches, Salonica 1929

Branch	Sub-Branch	Jewish Firms (N)	Total Firms (N)	Percentage of Jewish Firms
Food and Beverages	Flour mills	0	4	0
	Breweries	0	2	0
	Ice (producing)	0	5	0
	Locums (prod.)	0	5	0
	Butter and Cheese	5	40	12
	Wine and spirits	7	15	47
	Colonial commodities	46	100	46
Chemicals	Wax and paraffin	3	0	100
	Soap production	7	11	64
	Paints and Varnish	3	5	60
	Droguistes	13	19	68
Construction Materials	Cement (prod.)	0	1	0
	Bricks and tiles	1	2	50
	Marble cutting	1	2	50
	Ceramic	1	6	17
	Window glass and mirrors	0	3	0
	Sanitary items	6	8	75
Metals	Agricultural machines	3	18	17
	Mechanical workshops	1	9	11
	Arms and hunting equipment	2	9	22
	Automobiles and accessories	2	14	14
Metals	Tools, small metalwares and hardware (*quincailleries*)	40	51	78
	Blades (*fers*) and metals	23	35	66
	Electrical accessories	22	58	38
Tanning and Footwear	Footwear	2	9	22
	Tanneries	1	10	10
	Furriers	1	11	9
Wood	Firewood (*bois de chauffage*)	10	24	42
	Timber	17	40	42
	Furniture (workshops)	6	11	54
	Upholsters	3	3	100

Source: Adapted from *Guide Sam* 1930: 903–935; for the list of names of the Jewish-owned firms, see Appendix 5.

Notes: See notes for Tables 5.3a, 5.3b above.

Compare this to Appendix 5, which generally classified each Jewish-owned firm only once, according to its main activity. This table details the activities of the Jewish and, by default, non-Jewish firms in each sub-branch (excluding duplicate categories such as "cheese" and "cheese and butter", which were combined into one category without repetitions). The same firms may therefore have been included in more than one sub-branch.

excluding the trade and manufacture of wine and spirits, where Jews were rather inten-sively involved.[102] Wine production in particular attracted Jewish entrepreneurs given that Jews were traditionally prohibited from using wine (especially for libations) produced by gentiles.

Jewish involvement in the commercial activity linked to the food industry was long term. Although driven from flour mill ownership (section 4.5.2; Table 5.4a),[103] they remained over-represented in the cereal and flour trade (including imports) (Table 5.3b) due to the local shortages of this basic commodity emerging as the domestic consumer market grew. Among the prominent Jewish firms engaged in commerce in cereals was Fils de David Hasson, a partnership established by the founder's sons following David's retirement in 1924.[104] Similarly, Jewish wholesalers and importers, as owners of almost half of the businesses dealing in colonial products (46 out of the 100 businesses) directed at the domestic market, continued to be over-represented in the large-scale trade in staples (rise, tea, coffee, and sugar).[105]

From a macro-level perspective, comparison of the Jewish-owned economy with Greek entrepreneurial ventures in the leading growth industries (food, chemicals, and metals) indicates that although Jewish entrepreneurs were also active in these sectors, they concentrated in narrow, specialised niches and stayed away from branches domi-nated by the ethnic majority (Table 5.4a). In consequence, we find only a few Jewish entrepreneurs in the growing construction industry, including the production of construction materials.[106] Jewish entrepreneurs were thus conspicuously absent from the cement industry, and their presence in the trade of timber for construction was gradually reduced. The only Jewish-owned factory for mosaic tiles and bricks, owned by Modiano Frères (Appendix 5, no. 83), while still operating in 1929, was abandoned in the beginning of 1931.[107] However, Jewish merchants continued to dominate the trade in sanitation items, which generally consisted of imported fixtures required only at the final phase of the construction and generally sold directly to the end-consumer.

In keeping with the tendency to enter at the commercial phases of an industry, Jewish entrepreneurs were heavily concentrated in the ownership of shops selling building materials (*droguistes*) as well as in the wholesale and retail marketing of small tools and metalware. Relying on contemporary statistics, Roupa and Hekimoglou maintain that a plant or workshop, especially if it dealt with machine repairs and machinery, would open weekly.[108]

It thus appears that the entry of the refugees helped consolidate Greek dominance in traditional industries (e.g., tanning and furs), which had consequences for Jewish entrepreneurs and small businessmen present in or dependent on these branches. Consider Jewish footwear manufacturers; they faced increasing competition from their new rivals in the supply of inputs. The Jews' relative share (about 20 percent) of production, still done in small workshops was well-suited to their new proportion in Salonica's population. Boycotting of Jewish traders intensified in the second half of the 1920s, and may be a result of the ethnic division of the consumer market between Jewish and Greek cobblers; the existence of a separate union for Jewish cobblers supports this possibility.[109] A similar pattern seems to have characterised wood home furniture manufacturing. Vertical integration linked production crafts (carpentry, upholstery) to create a Jewish niche aimed at responding to Jewish demand; these establishments were characterised by modest fixed capital investments and traditional low-level technologies.

The expanding paper and printing industry seems to have retained its Jewish

Table 5.4b   Jewish-owned Firms in Printing and Paper, Salonica 1929

Sub-Branch	Jewish Firms* (N)	Total Firms (N)	Percentage of Jewish Firms
Bookshops	4	9	44
Office equipment	1	1	100
Stationary	29	60	48
Typography	1	1	100
Typewriters	2	2	100
Gramophones	2	6	33
Films	4	4	100

Source: Adapted from *Guide Sam* 1930: 903–935.
Notes: See notes for Tables 5.3a, 5.3b and 5.4a above.

colouration until the very end of the Jewish presence in Salonica (see sections 8.3.5; 10.2). Jewish entrepreneurs were preponderant in this light industry's new technology-related niches, which required the import of modern equipment such as typewriters. These entrepreneurs simultaneously entered the entertainment industry through the import of gramophones and movies.[110] Abravanel & Benveniste (section 4.5.3) (Appendix 5, no. 444), became the sole concessionaires for the whole of Greece of recordings in Greek, Turkish, and Spanish (operas, orchestras, dances),[111] supplying the market's multicultural demand. This exclusivity helped the firm integrate into the growing entertainment consumption niche.

In the next two sections, we discuss the two labour-intensive sectors that had the greatest impact on the scope of the Jewish-owned economy: tobacco (section 5.5) and clothing (section 5.6).

5.5 Jewish-Owned Tobacco Processing and Cigarette Plants

During the 1920s, tobacco processing in Salonica became a mainstream mercantile industry, operating within the fiscal framework of Greek state monopolies as of July 1914. Under the enforced regime, the government exerted strict fiscal control over every phase of production, from purchase of the cultivated leaves until their export or, alternatively, local cigarette manufacturing. Regulation diminished profits for merchants and manufacturers alike, causing a decline in the number of private ciga-rette manufacturers active in Salonica to a mere four.[112] The fiscal regime nonetheless affected Jews differently than it did Greeks. While the *Régie*, the former regime, repre-sented the interests of the Ottoman Empire's Western debtors and their economic rationality and left every phase of the industry open to all, the new Greek policy, espe-cially after 1922, was to express the "national taste for discrimination" and institute discriminatory regulation. This meant that the state began to realise its power to legally monopolise the tobacco leaf processing and cigarette manufacturing.[113] More partic-ularly, Jewish-owned factories, similar to other private-owned factories, came to suffer from surveillance by Greek fiscal agencies. The new brand of officials was committed not only to their direct employer, the government, but also to the chauvinistic policies that dictated the protection of Greek competitors' interests (sections 8.1; 8.3).

Table 5.5 Jewish-owned Firms in the Tobacco Industry, Salonica 1929

Sub-Branch	Jewish Firms (N)	Total Firms (N)	Percentage of Jewish Firms
Tobacco	4	44	9
Cigarette manufacturing	1	11	9

Source: Adapted from *Guide Sam* 1930: 933.
Note: Data without iterations. See note 1 for Table 5.3a above.

In the period following the Transfer, the focus of Greece's export economy shifted from the currants cultivated in the Peloponnesus for export to Britain toward tobacco for export to Germany, more than two-thirds of which was produced in Macedonia and Western Thrace.[114] Although the number of Jewish-owned tobacco plants was relatively small in comparison to non-Jewish-owned firms (see Table 5.5),[115] Jewish merchants were well integrated in the commercial networks constructed between the local producers and Weimar's cigarette industry.[116]

Several Salonican Jewish businessmen entered the tobacco industry following the transfer of the *Dönmes* (section 2.1) together with other Muslims to Turkey, which had presented an opportunity to take over *Dönme*-owned tobacco firms.[117] In one instance, the Jewish businessman Leon Recanati was appointed a trustee of a large tobacco plant owned by one of his old friends, a member of the *Dönmes*. This step helped the owner avoid a hurried sale of the firm at a below-value price. When the owner decided to end his business activities in Greece, he sold the plant to Recanati.[118]

Similar transfers of tobacco enterprises from Muslims to Jews occurred in the tobacco towns in the Macedonian periphery, such as Drama. Following the exit of Muslims from that city, Jewish entrepreneurs bought tobacco firms in addition to houses and shops in the city and its periphery (especially in Horisti, Prosotsani, and Doxato). Nevertheless, the fact that several important Christian–Jewish business partnerships (e.g., the Savopoulos & Benveniste tobacco dealership) were formed straight away in Drama[119] reflects two structural features of the contemporary Greek national economy: the need to have a Greek partner in order to operate smoothly in this mainstream industry (see sections 8.3, 8.4, 9.2, 9.5, and 10.1), and the availability of cheap refugee labour during the first half of the 1920s. Savopoulos & Benveniste also had branches in Salonica and in Kavalla.[120] In the latter, an important tobacco town, the firm operated beside another Jewish-Christian owned firm, Valstaris & Capsuto,[121] as well as alongside the old Jewish-owned tobacco mercantile firms of Jacques M. Benveniste and Aron Tsimino.[122]

According to *Guide Sam*, the information network connecting the Salonican Jews with their co-religionists in Macedonia's tobacco industry included Jewish-owned tobacco firms in Salonica (Appendix 5, nos. 450–454), among them Isaac M. Benveniste, the major Jewish tobacco merchant located in Kavalla.[123] Several Jewish tobacco merchants from Germany created joint ventures with Jewish tobacco merchants from Kavalla. We thus find the old firm of Mayer N. & Co. Ltd. (est. 1919) headquartered in Kavalla,[124] while L. H. Benveniste & Jaffe maintained its offices in Hamburg at the same time that it operated warehouses for the manipulation of leaf in Kavalla and Smyrna, under the name Tabacs d'Orient.[125] Similarly, Hermann Spierer & Cie., which was engaged with Tabacs d'Orient en feuilles, maintained headquarters in Dresden, Germany and *entrepôts* for the manipulated leaves in Trieste (Free Zone) and Geneva. Kavalla was its base in Greek Macedonia, with tobacco manipulation plants scattered throughout Salonica, Drama, Serres, Xanthie, Volo, and Samos[126] (see section 8.1).

The labour-intensive nature of the tobacco industry also had repercussions for the scope of the Jewish economy in general and the Jewish-owned economy in particular. Jewish tobacco workers were employed in Jewish- and non-Jewish-owned tobacco warehouses in Salonica, including firms associated with German-owned cigarette companies.[127] Before the arrival of the Greek refugees and their accelerated entry into the cultivation, processing, and marketing of tobacco, the tobacco industry represented a significant part of Salonica's Jewish-controlled economy.[128] The industry's workforce was overwhelmingly Jewish, although some evidence does indicate that Greek employers systematically replaced their Jewish or Muslim workers with Greek-speaking refugees after 1913.[129]

The persistence of Jewish labour in tobacco processing, cigarette manufacture, and cigarette paper production continued during the first decade of Greek rule in Salonica (1912–1921) due to the industry's continuous and rapid growth. This trend was supported by the chronic under-supply of labour caused by conscription into the Greek army, especially during the war years. Jewish control of those industries prior to 1920 was not solely numerical: Jews also dominated the Tobacco Workers Syndicate (which determined hiring, work conditions, etc.)[130] as well as the association representing workers employed in cigarette paper manufacture.[131] However, Jewish tobacco workers lost their control over hiring before the arrival of the Greek refugees, when the National Federation of Tobacco Workers (KOE, or Kapnergatike Homospondia Hellados) took over Salonica's local unions (1921).[132]

Jewish numerical control of Salonica's tobacco labour market ceased following the mass entry of the Greek refugees. According to an undated official report, Jewish male and female tobacco workers numbered more than 5,000; together with Greek refugees from Turkey and Asia Minor, they led the tobacco workers syndicate.[133] Nevertheless, based on official statistics prepared by TARK (the tobacco workers' unemployment and pension fund),[134] together with an onomastic analysis of registered tobacco workers, Dagkas concluded that the total number of Jewish workers in the tobacco industry in Salonica, Kavalla, and Drama, the main tobacco manipulation and processing centres, was 3,156 in 1928;[135] these represented only 5.5 percent of total tobacco workers (3,156 out of 56,819) for that year. The gender distribution of this workforce was 44.4 percent male (1,401 out of 3,156) and 55.6 percent female (1,755 out of 3,156).[136]

Although the geographical proximity to the tobacco factories of the post-fire residential enclaves might have strengthened Jewish involvement in Salonica's industry,[137] their new rivals, the refugees, had even greater advantages. The refugees came equipped with skills that made them suitable as both production workers and tobacco cultivators.[138] This convergence of skills became more important following introduction of the new bale-packing method, which enabled the same workers to be vertically integrated into tobacco processing, beginning with cultivation.[139] The industry's draw was also due to the achievements of its large, well-organised and militant labour union. Benefits included a 30 percent increase in wages (1922–1924) as well as improved working conditions, such as an eight-hour day, and the creation of an unemployment relief fund.[140] Women were attracted to this industry not least because it had social benefits. The freedom achieved by the industry's female workers was symbolised in their picketing beside male workers during strikes even though the union continued to support strict gender segregation by occupation. Female tobacco workers were treated like suffragettes and thought to exercise considerable control over their own lives.[141]

The relatively early introduction of new standardised and simplified methods of tobacco leaf manipulation during the second half of the 1920s helped feminise the industry's Jewish labour force.[142] Because the new methods did not require separation of different quality leaf,[143] they resulted in standard quality bales and thus abolished the traditional gender hierarchy effective in the industry.[144] Increased female together with decreased male participation acted to lower salaries: the men who had previously been responsible for high-quality tobacco leaf manipulation and rewarded accordingly, by relatively high wages when compared to those of females, were no longer needed. Both males and females thus came to be employed in the same jobs. Between 1927 and 1932, about one-third of the male tobacco workers became unemployed.[145] Following the industry crisis (sections 6.1 and 8.1), demand for female labour was eventually reduced.[146]

Feminisation of the Jewish workforce in cigarette production had nevertheless gained grounds before the Transfer.[147] The Jewish-owned factory Nahmias & Cie. (Appendix 5, no. 451), mechanised by 1919, employed female Jewish workers.[148] However, during the 1920s, cigarette production became a female refugee sector concentrated in Greater Athens; post-war Greek industrial policy had caused the transfer (1925) of the majority (about 64 percent) of cigarette factories from Northern Greece (New Greece) to Greater Athens.[149] As a government monopoly, cigarette production was more amenable to the creation of new vacancies, particularly for refugee females. Although the move to Piraeus and its outskirts overtly exploited female refugee skills, availability, and low wage demands, which reduced unemployment in Greater Athens, its motives were predominantly political: reduction of industrial employment in Salonica to weaken the period's most militant labour union, the National Federation of Tobacco Workers. Simultaneously, the policy diminished the Jewish-owned cigarette industry's place within Salonica's Jewish-owned economy. While the Salonica Cigarette Co., which employed Jewish workers, closed in 1928,[150] the factory owned by the Arditti family (Appendix 5, no. 454) in Xanthi (Western Thrace), one of the six main cigarette factories operating in Macedonia and Thrace, kept its considerable position in the branch throughout the 1920s.[151]

State-supported suppression of unionisation and labour militancy through the reduction of male employment also accelerated feminisation. Prior to the June 1928 elections, Venizelos had adopted a pro-labour platform reflected in his support of tobacco strikers. However, once in power, the government began to view organised labour as a threat. Striking workers were branded "communists", that is, enemies of the state. In a series of measures begun with the passage of the Idionymon Act in 1929, which penalised strikers in order to protect the state from subversive activities,[152] together with dissolution of the National Federation of Tobacco Workers and its affiliates in 1930, Venizelos finally institutionalised his anti-labour stance.[153] This process motivated a series of strikes, such as that in the Benveniste warehouse in Kavalla (1933).[154] Jewish-owned tobacco processing plants, with their diminishing size, thus gradually lost their weight in the Jewish-owned economy.

5.6 Jewish-Owned Clothing Enterprises

Jewish entrepreneurs avoided entering the long-established spinning and weaving industry, which had become the nation's chief industry, especially in Macedonia.[155] Instead, they became prominent in the growing clothing industry, another labour-intensive sector (see Table 5.6b). This trend, strengthened by the new availability of masses of unskilled or semi-skilled cheap female refugee labour, supported their entry into new industrial niches such as carpet weaving, which was vertically expanded by another new niche, carpet retailing in the local and the international market.[156] Although establishment of the largest carpet plants within the privileged Greater Athens (especially Piraeus) complied with the government's industrial location policy,[157] the geographical clustering of skilled refugee workers from Smyrna in the new colony of Toumba, situated at the eastern fringe of Salonica, promoted carpet industry niching in the deprived metropolis.[158]

The inferior environmental conditions of the textile plants, where workers worked long hours for meagre pay (typical of textile labour), were ignored due to the Greek government's anti-labour bias; yet the same policy inadvertently supported the growth of private ownership.[159] Government channelling of female refugees (generally through the RSC) to textiles rather than to tobacco (which also helped suppress tobacco labour activism along the northern borders),[160] made it easier for Greek textile entrepreneurs, especially if they were refugees, to recruit abundant numbers of compliant, female refugee primary breadwinners.[161] Growth in the textile industry thereby compensated for the lack of employment opportunities for women in the metropolitan market. The local and international philanthropic organisations that provided training in the weaving crafts to unskilled women and girls indirectly encouraged these developments.[162]

In contrast to their low representation in textiles, Jewish entrepreneurs increased their presence in the clothing industry, which was still in its infancy.[163] Between 1925 and 1927, ready-made garment production in Salonica represented no more than 4–6 percent of total local production.[164] While Greek entrepreneurs were busy establishing and rationalising the spinning and weaving industry in Salonica and its rural environs, Jews and Turks in the city had put the available infrastructure (including commercial distribution of sewing machines) to use in the manufactured clothing industry before

Table 5.6a   Jewish-owned Textiles Enterprises, Salonica 1929

Sub-Branch	Jewish firms (N)	Total firms (N)	Percentage of Jewish Firms
Raw cotton (trade)	1	3	33
Spinning mills	0	8	0
Yarn *(fils, files)*: Cotton, wool (trade)	15	16	94
Canvas (coarse fabrics); jute weaving	1	1	100
Jute, sacks (trade)	16	19	84
Dye works	1	1	100

Source: Adapted from *Guide Sam* 1930: 903–935.

Note: Based on data derived from the original commodity-based categories of *Guide Sam* 1930. See also note 1 for Table 5.3a above.

Table 5.6b   Jewish-Owned Clothing Enterprises, Salonica 1929

Sub-Branch	Jewish firms (N)	Total firms (N)	Percentage of Jewish Firms
Knitting and sewing machines	1	1	100
Knitting/hosiery manufacturing	3	3	100
Embroidery, Lingerie (manufacturing)	3	6	50
Confection	1	1	100
Seamstress	1	1	100
Tailor	0	1	0
Hats	1	4	25
Drapery	20	27	74
Tissues (fabrics) trade	33	45	73
Haberdashery and hosiery (trade)	29	35	83
Nouveautés	25	44	57
Modes	11	46	24

Source: Adapted from *Guide Sam* 1930: 923, 925, 935.
Note: Based on data derived from the original commodity-based categories of *Guide Sam* 1930. Compare with Appendix 5. See also note 1 for Table 5.3a above.

the Transfer.[165] In 1912, undergarment manufacturing in Salonica employed about fifty to sixty workers in six non-Greek-owned plants for flannels, in addition to another six non-Greek-owned plants for knitting socks, stockings, and undergarments, which employed another almost seventy workers.[166]

Salonica's expanding consumer market, which erupted with the arrival of the refugees, increased the demand for cheap basic clothing.[167] In tandem, the exit of Turkish entrepreneurs – experts in the clothing trade – created additional vacancies to be filled by Greeks, refugees, and Jews. In 1925, Greek entrepreneurs also entered the knitting, embroidery, shirts, socks, and stockings industries.[168] Yet, Jewish entrepreneurs remained densely concentrated in specialised niches in the clothing industry.

Table 5.6b shows that parallel to the traditional production of made-to-measure clothing supplied by tailors and seamstresses, the new mass clothing production developed within two main sub-branches: (1) ready-made confection for men and children (but not for women); and (2) hosiery (*bonneterie*) and, by extension, socks and stockings but also shawls and woollen or cotton undergarments.[169]

In Greece of the 1920s, undergarments rather than outerwear was democratised, much as it had been in the French apparel industry during the "bourgeois century", when clothing manufacture moved overwhelmingly from domestic to commodity production.[170] In our case, the refugee-driven demand for cheap and standardised undergarments was met by small-to-medium-scale factories (sections 8.4; 9.5) that sold their goods in the open market, directly to the consumer. Advertising helped generate local demand for these innovative commodities.[171] For Jewish entrepreneurs, this structure allowed them to deepen their penetration into this type of trade because it enabled them to sidestep overt discrimination in the larger, Greek-owned textile industry.

Greece, like many other new states, was able to introduce the mass production of undergarments, especially from knitted materials, once the price of new, imported machinery fell.[172] Knitwear production in Greece during the 1920s was important enough to warrant comments by Mr. Turner, the British Consul, who reported in 1928 that about six factories, which ran on 160 horsepower machinery, had been constructed during that year for the manufacture of "tricotage" (knitting, knitted goods).[173] Correspondence from the early 1930s between a German factory furnishing needles and other spare parts for knitting machines and their customers in Salonica, both Jewish and Greek, alludes to the expectation of continued growth in this branch of the local economy.[174]

Beginning in the first decade of the century, Jewish entrepreneurs had entered the ready-made clothing industry as suppliers of manufacturing equipment,[175] a repetition of the pattern established by Greek businessmen in the agricultural machinery industry, which was targeted at Greek farmers (see Table 5.4a). The Jewish-owned firm Veritas (Appendix 5, no. 292) was founded by Ino Benmayor before 1922 (Appendix 4.1, nos. 533, 534);[176] by 1929, it dominated commerce in knitting and sewing machines and replaced the departing Turkish-owned firms. Tables 5.6a and 5.6b indicate that Jewish businessmen not only continued to supply the technological infrastructure needed for the Jewish clothing industry, they also maintained their domination in trade in cotton and woollen thread, draperies, tissues, and haberdashery, the industry's essential inputs.[177]

Jewish-owned firms operating in this industry were often classified in overlapping merchandise categories – *Nouveautés*;[178] *Draperies*; *Merceries* [sic], and *Bonneteries* [sic][179] – Abravanel Ascer & Cie. (Appendix 4.1, no. 217, classified under *Nouveautés*) sold (wholesale and retail) woollens, silks, and cotton cloth;[180] the established firm of Jessua Mercado & Fils (no. 250, classified under *Merceries*), involved in the whole-sale/retail sale of linen drapery, silk, woollens, and cotton cloth, advertised its store as *Maison de Nouveautés.*[181] Both firms declared a policy of "*Prix défiant toute concur-ance* [sic]".[182] The goods sold by other firms, similarly classified in the *Annuaire Commercial 1922* under "*Merceries*", illuminate the types of inputs supplied by Jewish firms to the clothing industry: Florentin Saporta & Serero (no. 246), sold wholesale, manufactured and imported articles such as cotton cloth, velvet, satin, mules, etc. from England, France, and Italy;[183] Sides Yachiel & Cie. (no. 272) advertised itself as *Maison de Draperie* (wholesale and retail);[184] Errera G[edalia] A. Fils de & Cie Ltd. (Appendix 4.1, no. 243), a leading department store, was replaced after 1922 by Matalon G. & Cie. (Appendix 5, no. 314), which engaged in wholesale and retail sale of buckles, hosiery, haberdashery, trimmings, jewels, ironworks, oilskin clothes/cloth (waterproof fabrics), perfumes, ribbons, and lace.[185] While its owners emphasised the Parisian source of the selected merchandise, meant to imply their trendiness, the advertisement also declared its marketing policy: "*prix fixes*".[186] Beyond adopting the Western marketing practices prevalent in European department stores, the firm attracted an upperclass clientele, whose members were more concerned with symbols of prestige than with cost. Jewish merchants thus adapted to the demands and character of the developing clothing industry.

Organisation of the ready-made confection industry (sewing) as well as the hosiery industry (knitwear) continued to be led by department stores,[187] which employed the putting-out system (manufacture by subcontractors). Galleries Trias (Appendix 5, no. 392)[188] adopted this system. In addition to selling stockings (*bas de soie*), hats, and shoes, it was thus able to arrange for the mass production of ready-made garments for men and children, including undergarments, flannels, men's cotton shirts, and men's accessories,[189] items generally produced by female workers although not targeted at women buyers. Vertical integration from production to commercial distribution significantly reduced the firm's financial risks.

In awareness of this sector's growth potential, Jewish entrepreneurs established firms of various sizes to produce undergarments, which placed them into competition with the established manufacturers. These Jewish businessmen were attracted by the sector's stable mass demand and guaranteed income, which contrasted with the still unstable consolidating national market.[190] Moreover, heavy tariffs on imported cotton goods, especially after 1926, stimulated local production of undergarments by Jews and Greeks alike. Jewish entrepreneurs were in effect beginning to drift away from volatile international commerce in clothing products toward local, steady production. A list can in fact be constructed of several prominent Jewish entrepreneurs who either changed sectors or established new firms in the clothing industry parallel to their existing interests. For instance, the exit of G/J [di] S Modiano (established in 1908) from the maritime agency business was followed by its entry into the "highly successful" (knitted) stocking manufacturing branch in 1926; Jacques and Humbert S. Modiano of Modiano Frères, the brick producers,[191] likewise entered the industry. During this same period, Daniel S. Modiano continued managing his father's fire insurance portfolio while establishing (1927) a firm producing (sewing) and selling men's shirts.[192] At the same time, the veteran firm of Maison Samuel A. Florentin (est. 1870) continued to operate a knitting factory producing stockings and hosiery (*bas, bonneterie*).[193] Similarly, Fils d'Isac M. Nissim, a firm engaged in *bonneterie* and *nouveautés* since its establishment (1882) by Isac M. Nissim and through its transformation into a partnership (1928) by Haïm Nissim, his son, was thus able to survive the local and international economic upheavals.[194]

Personal linen and clothing accessories were also produced in small sewing workshops. Table 5.6b shows that the workshops making *broderies* and *lingeries* were equally distributed between Jewish and Greek owners. The embroidery crafts, which provided employment to about 40 percent of the refugee women,[195] also gave employment to orphans (*ouvroir des orphelins*), who were readily integrated into Salonica's "sewing rooms".[196] Equipped with considerable lace-making and embroidery skills,[197] female refugees succeeded in penetrating this local Jewish niche.[198]

5.6.1 Recruitment of Female Workers: The Ethnic Dimension

The growing demand for ready-made undergarments increased the scope of mass production marked by intensive female labour. Confection was increasingly characterised by an assembly-line mode of production, which meant that workers required only minimal skills in order to find employment in this industry. Yet, throughout the 1920s, Jewish entrepreneurs still seem to have had an advantage over their Greek competitors thanks to their ability to recruit skilled Jewish female workers for their new ventures. Jewish girls had acquired sewing, embroidery, and ironing skills through formal and informal training since the late nineteenth century. Expert Jewish seamstresses and milliners taught these skills in Jewish schools belonging to the Alliance network or, alternatively, in Alliance-organised workshops as well as at the seamstresses' homes. These vocational training arrangements continued to operate after the great fire (1917) once the Jewish educational frameworks were reconstructed[199] (section 3.5.3). For example, the Atelier Couture, which was established in the Jacob Cazès community school under the auspices of Jewish women belonging to the Benot Israel philanthropic organisation, trained young girls in sewing (including lingerie) and embroidery on fourteen sewing machines. In 1924, knitting was added to the curriculum.[200] On the declaration of skills declared by sixty-four other female candidates for emigration to Mandatory Palestine, about 86 percent (55 out of 64) declared occupations linked to the clothing industry (see Table 9.5b below). In one such handwritten declaration, the young Daisy Broudo (1932), whose family belonged to the *petite bourgeoisie*, described her studies in the Jewish community schools. She took lower-level courses in Jacob Cazès and upper-level courses in Talmud Tora Hagadol, in addition to classes in Hebrew, Greek, and French. She also explained why Jewish girls from Salonica sought jobs in the needle trades during the 1920s:

> I learned the sewing and embroidering craft at School. My family is not included among the wealthy families; we consequently live in a Jewish neighbourhood in the periphery. My father works a lot to make a living. My eldest sister is a dressmaker and I help her.[201]

In contrast, mass training in sewing skills among Greek girls was relatively backward. Whereas Jewish girls were attracted to sewing and knitting, indigenous Greek girls were attracted by the spinning and weaving industries; refugee females tended to be untrained due to the war's interference with their education. Only after the conclusion of the Greek–Turkish War in 1922 did young Greek women perceive the profession of seamstress (*couturière*) as an employment option. Although Born & Co., which represented the Singer Sewing Corp., was registered with Salonica's Chamber of Commerce before the arrival of the Greek refugees,[202] the firm organised a massive apprenticeship program after both local and international philanthropic and relief associations had found it difficult to put a suitable training infrastructure in place. Born & Co. began its training operations in 1925. By employing modern marketing methods throughout the province, this firm managed to inspire many girls and women, mainly in Greek Macedonia, to seek instruction on the use of Singer sewing machines.[203] It thus prepared the necessary infrastructure for sewing to become an occupation open to female Greek workers.[204]

Returning to the question of employment by Jewish entrepreneurs, we must ask why, given the flood of Greek female labour following the Transfer, they chose to hire skilled Jewish female workers? In the previous decade, the scarcity of skilled labour made hiring such employees very costly.[205] But in the 1920s, the flood of immigrant labour created downward pressure on salaries and an oversupply of inexpensive, semi-skilled female workers. This made it even more difficult for Jewish females belonging to the lower middle class, who were now living in the new neighbourhoods constructed in Salonica's outlying quarters, to find work outside the tobacco industry or domestic service. The number of knitting and sewing workshops, although increasing, was fewer than those established in the spinning and weaving industry; hence, fewer places of employment were available for the expert skills possessed by Jewish females. In addition, the industry's Jewish entrepreneurs continued using the putting-out system.[206] In Salonica's overcrowded metropolitan labour market, this situation intensified the "national taste for discrimination" among Jewish and Greek employers. Jewish entrepreneurs thus became more interested in recruiting loyal, skilled Jewish female workers.

Cultural factors also help to explain why Jewish entrepreneurs were reticent to recruit repatriated Greek women to work in clothing industry workshops, even under conditions of mass production (e.g., in hosiery and confection): (1) modesty was common to both Jewish and Greek girls, who avoided working under employers belonging to a different ethnic group;[207] (2) the "family wage" concept,[208] common in both societies, kept married women at home while it exploited the availability of younger and unmarried females;[209] (3) linguistic barriers between the Greek-speaking refugees and the Ladino-speaking Jewish entrepreneurs, prior to the issuance of the compulsory education edict (1929), placed further obstacles; and (4) a common religion, shared by employers and employees, made it possible for Jewish women and girls to observe the Sabbath and holidays without endangering their employment. The same could be said for Greek entrepreneurs and labourers.

Data about worker ethnicity are usually absent from official documents. Yet, the above-mentioned considerations lead us to the conclusion that at least during the 1920s, internal cohesion was still considered an important factor in Jewish hiring practices (see section 9.5 below).

5.6.2 The Spatial Dimension: "Hidden" Jewish Female Entrepreneurs

In contrast to the mass production of undergarments in sewing workshops, *haute couture*[210] production focused on seamstresses working at home. Jewish seamstresses often engaged in sewing made-to-measure clothing and lingerie that included decorated embroidered home wear (bathrobes and nightgowns) targeted at an older and wealthier clientele. Another market was based on Jewish consumer demands for the lingerie to be given by the bride's father as a supplement to her dowry (in Ladino: *ashugar*), which seamstresses began preparing while the potential bride was still a child. The *ashugar* included the dresses, undergarments, and bedding to be brought by the bride to her husband's house; these were sewn and embroidered by the bride and her mother, with the assistance of friends and relatives as well as paid professional seamstresses.[211]

Home-based firms were generally not registered in Greece's Chambers of Commerce and Industry. *Haute couture*, which required various sewing skills considered exclusively female, was a major haven for Jewish females who preferred self-employment. Seamstresses (and tailors alike) were thought to earn more than did clerks in commercial enterprises.[212] As the economy developed, the occupation of seamstress began to be considered a worthwhile and effective escape for the middle-class Jewess from the gender discrimination practiced in the poorly paid clothing workshops. Yet, married female entrepreneurs even in this exclusively female-oriented branch continued to adapt themselves to the traditional entrepreneurial space allotted to women, the home;[213] they tended to refrain from entering the larger space covered by the Chamber of Commerce and Industry, which was still occupied by men. The only *couturière* mentioned in *Guide Sam* was Miss Elvire Florentine (Appendix 5, no. 373), an unmarried Jewess and the sole player in this male arena.[214]

Jewish seamstresses enjoyed several advantages essential for easy access to opportunities in *haute couture*. First, Jewesses could take advantage of the working space available in their homes, a resource lacked by urban female refugees due to delays in the resettlement program (see Chapter 3). Second, they already belonged to the solid social and information networks that could facilitate access to an affluent female clientele. Although the spatial dispersion of the Jewish minority after the 1917 fire reduced opportunities to find employment within ethnic enclaves, it did not interfere with the resurgence of former client networks. Jewish seamstresses were thus able to continue to serve those Christian[215] and Turkish clients whose families had remained in the city after the Transfer[216] in addition to their Jewish clientele. In contrast, recently arrived refugee women suffered from restricted social networks and their homes were geographically distant from indigenous well-to-do Greek neighbourhoods.[217] Jewish seamstresses also had easier access to inputs including imported cotton tissue from Italy[218] and fine woollens from England,[219] which were obtained from co-ethnic merchants.

5.7 Conclusion: Adaptation and Adjustment

On the eve of the Great Depression, Jewish entrepreneurs functioned as minority group entrepreneurs, recruiting Jewish workers and utilising Jewish information networks. While the relative and absolute number of Jewish firms had begun to decline before the slump and continued to do so after the wave of Greek refugee repatriation, the revised entrepreneurial structure continued to be narrow and concentrated relative to the Greek structure. Yet, the relative scope of the Jewish-owned economy appeared to broaden as the occupational opportunities in the national labour market diminished for Jewish workers, male and female.

Jewish entrepreneurs were able to extend their retail operations by distributing innovative imported manufactured goods, for which there was ample demand. At the same time, they refrained from entering those developing mainstream industrial sectors that benefited from government stimulation programs – chemicals, machinery and textiles – which grew from 36 percent to 56 percent of the total production between 1921 and 1939.[220] These technology-intensive industries required high fixed-capital investments that could be acquired only with government and institutional funding, assistance available only to indigenous Greeks favoured by the authorities, or to refugee entrepreneurs supported by the repatriation funds.

The industries selected for entry by the Jews, such as clothing manufacture and tobacco processing, required modest investments in technology and a work force consisting largely of cheap female labour. This trend increased after the emigration of prominent and wealthy Jewish entrepreneurs, mainly of Italian origin. Other factors also supported Jewish entrepreneurs involved in these industries. In the clothing industry, for example, participants were mainly small-scale private producers and individual consumers, with trade conducted in the open market, free of institutional constraints and latent institutional discrimination. The vertical integration that Jews introduced, from importing manufacturing equipment to distributing goods to the final consumer, helped protect these smaller firms from financial shocks. The heavy representation of Jewish entrepreneurs in the growing clothing industry during the 1920s paralleled the arrival of their co-ethnics in Paris. As Morin describes the main Parisian street where Jewish merchants were concentrated, *le Sentier* (1920–1939), it became *"une petite agora"* full of Jewish Salonican boutiques specialising in *bonneterie*.[221]

As the structure of opportunities changed, Jewish entrepreneurs, like any entrepreneur wishing to survive in turbulent environments, increasingly nurtured their information networks to improve their response capacities. Sam Lévy apparently understood the importance of information for he published successive issues of his *Guide Sam* throughout the 1920s. The comprehensive list of *Nos Annonceurs* redefined the borders of the Jewish Sephardic networks because it effectively delineated the boundaries of that portion of the Jewish commercial network operating from Athens, the Greek capital and centre of the new Greek national economy; Salonica, the traditional but anachronistic centre of "New Greece"; and the town of Kavalla, internal Macedonia's major urban centre, and second in size only to Salonica[222] (see Map 1).

Unlike the era of Ottoman rule, when open borders encouraged trade, the new nationalism circumscribed commercial opportunities. In order to survive and even flourish, Jewish entrepreneurs would now be much more dependent on their individual capacities to create or recreate international commercial networks based on trust, that is, on ethnic cohesion. During the 1930s, when protectionism was at its strongest, these Jewish networks offered a way to do business even in the face of the new constraints.

PART THREE

Jewish Entrepreneurial Response
and the Jewish Economy during
the 1930s

6

New Externalities and Impoverished Jewish Collective Resources, 1930–1938

Various transformations, some interrelated, in the internal as well as external frameworks of the Jewish economy in Salonica generated new conditions for Jewish entrepreneurs throughout the decade. The 1930s began with the gradual disengagement of Greece from the Western European capitalist world-system, with the arbitrary imposition of new restrictions on foreign trade in September 1931; it climaxed with Prime Minister Eleftherios Venizelos' declaration that Greece would default[1] on its foreign debt and the suspension of commercial debts to foreign creditors in April 1932.[2] These events created a new environment for Jewish entrepreneurs in Salonica, whose business affairs were based mainly on the port economy (see Chapters 2, 4, and 5). For the Jews, this era (especially the period between 30 January 1933 and April 1938) ended with the Nazi occupation of Austria and its incorporation into the German economy (see Chapter 10). In the interim, the riots in Salonica's Campbell Quarter (June 1931) accelerated Jewish emigration – primarily to Mandatory Palestine – which previously had only been a trickle.

The year 1930 also marked a turning point in the Jewish community's internal affairs. This was the year that Article 16 of Law 2456, dated 27 July 1920, prohibiting Jewish residents holding foreign citizenship from voting or being elected to Jewish communal institutions, came into effect (section 3.2).[3] This prohibition resulted in the exclusion of prominent community leaders – such as the Modiano family, originally from Italy – from participation in communal life, which further weakened internal solidarity. This distancing of wealthier from poorer families by eliminating opportunities for contact within the framework of public service had a particularly dramatic effect because it occurred at a time of increasing depletion of demographic resources due to mass Jewish emigration.

In this chapter we survey the changes in political and economic policy made by the successive Greek governments, which created new conditions for Salonica's Jewish entrepreneurs. This survey is followed by an examination of the availability of the political resources – the official as well as unofficial relationships maintained with the Greek administration – needed for Jewish entrepreneurs to flourish in the consolidating autarky. We close with an evaluation of the influence of these external factors on the Jewish community's collective resources – demographic, social, and material – during this period.

6.1 De-Globalisation and Consolidation of the Greek Autarky

The international financial crisis that began with the collapse of the New York Stock Exchange on 24 October 1929 affected Greek financial markets primarily through the collapse of foreign exchange rates, severe deterioration in the balance of payments, and drastic reductions in foreign trade. Yet, an in-depth analysis reveals that the budgetary woes afflicting Greece were, in essence, the long-term outcomes of Greece's involvement in World War I, specifically, its participation in the Turkish conflict and the resettlement of Greek refugees returning from Ottoman territories.[4] The country's increased borrowing from foreign lenders at high interest rates eventually caused widespread defaults, a situation that motivated the Greek government's suspension of free foreign exchange and subsequently led to the collapse of the open international order.[5] By 1933, the nominal value of Greek national production had already exceeded the 1928 level.[6] If we also consider the increased income from shipping and emigrants' remittances,[7] we can state that Greece's recovery began in that year.[8]

6.1.1 Greek Economic Responses to the Financial Crisis

Faced with long-term obligations to foreign creditors and the fact that debt clearance was the major precondition for the borrowing necessary to finance refugee resettlement programs,[9] Venizelos led an unremitting "battle for the drachma" (1929–1932).[10] The drachma's instability was felt by the beginning of 1928, when it became fully convertible against the gold standard.[11] The Bank of Greece – the new autonomous financial institution established in 1928 to fulfil one of the preconditions for the extension of international loans (section 5.1.3) – had been drained of its currency and gold reserves by 1931.[12] The government's policy of raising interest rates on bank loans in order to curtail local demand and encourage savings reduced the marginal profits of domestic enterprises at the same time that it discouraged expansion of their operations. Ordinary individuals and entrepreneurs alike attempted to protect their savings from the threat of devaluation by purchasing foreign currency in the open market.[13] This policy plunged the domestic market further into the abyss. Industrial output, which had begun falling in 1929, reached its trough in 1932.[14]

In September 1931, following devaluation of the British pound, the Bank of Greece was forced to absorb weighty losses given that about one-quarter of its reserves had been held in sterling.[15] The government and the central bank placed the banking system under strict control by means of corrective measures passed on 28 September and 8 October. The Bank of Greece obtained a legal monopoly over the conduct of foreign exchange transactions in order to abolish open trade in foreign currencies. Greek commercial banks were consequently prohibited from accepting deposits and making advances or loans in those currencies. The sale of foreign currency was permitted only in the case of "essential" imports. Exporters were obliged to surrender their earnings to the central bank and to receive their value in drachmas at the official rate. The export of capital was also forbidden: All foreign exchange accounts held by Greek residents were frozen.[16]

Simultaneously, in order to prop up the drachma, Venizelos linked the drachma to the US dollar, which was still attached to the gold standard at the official exchange rate of GRD 77.05 = $1 (September 1931).[17] In response to these measures, a flourishing black market developed, which led to further deterioration in the drachma's official exchange rate, from GRD 86 = $1 (October 1931) to GRD 111 = $1 (March 1932) and finally to GRD 120 = $1 (April 1932). Simultaneously, reserves fell from 53.6 percent (September 1931) to 20.7 percent (August 1932), well below the legal minimum. In order to halt these trends, Greece finally abandoned the gold exchange standard (27 April 1932) and fixed the drachma's value at 51.20 percent of its stabilisation parity (May 1932).[18] In May of that year, the government declared a debt moratorium and suspended payments – completely for amortisation instalments, partly for interest payments – to its foreign lenders. Law 5422 (26 April 1932), which came into force in 27 April 1932, deepened the state's control over foreign currency flows by declaring that foreign currency could be sold only for legitimate commercial purposes. In May 1932, Law 5426 introduced sweeping import restrictions and obligatory deposits of export earnings while granting extremely broad discretionary powers to the Minister for the National Economy. The Bank of Greece thereby became the state's chief regulator of foreign exchange and, in consequence, the nation's main commercial bank. At the same time, established commercial banks faced liquidity problems.[19] The smaller Jewish-owned commercial banks, such as Banque Union and Banque Amar, consequently lost their relative freedom regarding international transactions (see Chapter 7). Access to the opportunities created under the new regime of restrictions in international trade came to depend on the acquisition of special import licenses, now required as part of the quota system.

6.1.2 New Entrepreneurial Opportunities within the Consolidating Greek Autarky

The international isolation that the default imposed on Greece, even temporarily, together with the "freshly imported ideas" from Europe of aggravated chauvinism, xenophobia, self-congratulation, and self-reliance eventually impacted on Greece's internal economy. The result was adoption of a defensive autarky characterised by increased state intervention.[20] In addition to the decline in state income together with the collapse of international trade and the soaring unemployment plaguing Macedonia's ports, remittances sent home by Greek migrants working abroad also shrank.[21] Yet, these structural transformations stimulated the emergence of new entrepreneurial opportunities in industry as well as internal trade.

6.1.2.1 The Transition from Export-Oriented to Self-Sufficient Agriculture
The Depression hastened the radical transition of Greek agriculture from export-oriented semi-luxury crops, mainly tobacco (to Germany) and currants (to Britain), to staples destined for the domestic market. Government aspirations for agricultural self-sufficiency in the face of growing prospects of another world war led to the discouragement of tobacco farming and the encouragement of grain farming. Measures aimed at restraining labour militancy in the tobacco sector prompted attempts to weaken growers through legislation limiting Macedonian tobacco planting to dry regions (1929) inappropriate for such crops, as well as a refusal to suspend tobacco growers' debts. By early 1927, high tariffs had been imposed on wheat and grain imports. Establishment of the Central Committee for the Protection of Domestic Wheat (KEPES), which implemented controls on wheat and flour prices, ensured implementation of the government's promise that local farmers would receive prices equivalent to those obtained by importers.[22]

Among the other steps taken was the establishment in 1929 of the Agricultural Bank to provide loans to farmers at reduced interest rates as well as government suspension of cereal farmers' debts to private lenders for five years, beginning in 1930.[23] Although this last measure created problems for lenders (1930–1935) by reducing consumption in villages, it set the foundations for the rural economic recovery that became visible by 1936. The introduction of new crop rotation systems and expanded cultivation of the north's irrigated fields assisted farmers who had been negatively affected by the land shortages caused by land reform and natural disasters. Taken together, these steps spurred the planting of grain,[24] resulting in improved wheat yields by 1933. The rural consumer market was consequently revitalised. Similarly, expansion of agricultural production of industrial inputs, particularly cotton, stimulated the textile industry and rejuvenated domestic markets.[25]

6.1.2.2 Industrial Growth: Substitutes for Imported Manufactured Goods

The collapse of international trade paved the way for local industrial development. Sectoral protectionism (the high protective tariffs and quotas mentioned above) restricted imports and supported a shift to local production of consumables as well as of durable goods. The lowered standard of living, together with the drachma's stabilisation, increased the problem of unemployment but kept salaries low. Macedonia's unskilled labour market, especially in the volatile tobacco industry, was flooded with unemployed small farmers, agricultural labourers, and industrial workers as early as 1926, making labour plentiful and cheap.[26] These conditions set the stage for new opportunities for industrial entrepreneurship.

During the 1930s, not only tariff protection, but also the increasing availability of credit accelerated industrial activity. Following establishment of the Central Bank of Greece, which catered to government enterprises, and the Agricultural Bank of Greece, which became the sole institution providing credit to farmers, the National Bank of Greece became a purely commercial entity and thus an important supplier of industrial credit. Over the decade, the percentage of the National Bank's loans to industry rose to 71 percent. However, this lending was geographically concentrated in the Athens–Piraeus area (70 percent), mainly in the chemical (35.3 percent) and food (47.5) industries,[27] mirroring government policy limiting industrial credit to New Greece, including metropolitan Salonica and its environs (section 5.1.3).

Greece therefore enjoyed high rates of growth in the 1920s and especially during the 1930s despite the hardships. While industrial output fell from 1929 to 1932, the early and strong devaluation of the drachma stimulated the industrial sector's robust recovery from the Great Depression. Excluding public utilities, two industries dominated overall industrial production in terms of total value added: textiles, with 27 percent, and foodstuffs, with 26 percent. Chemicals followed with 19 percent. These three industries represented about 75 percent of total manufacturing production.[28]

The chemical industry in Greece offered profitable new opportunities in armament production beginning in the mid-1930s to eventually fulfil the Metaxas regime's objective of self-sufficiency in munitions. New opportunities likewise opened in other industries supplying the Greek military, such textile factories that produced uniforms and blankets.[29]

Local industrial development from the mid-1930s onwards was also tied to the trade agreements signed by the Greek government with the Nazis. These agreements did not, however, restrain German efforts to contain Greek industrial competition, despite Greek attempts to stress the significance of the country's metal and chemical industries for its own defence.[30]

Government-initiated public works projects – such as the draining of the swamps west of Salonica – created numerous opportunities for the participation of private sub-contractors after the government adopted Keynesian policies of intervention and increased public spending to curb unemployment.[31] These new opportunities were apparently open to Jewish entrepreneurs as well (see section 6.2)

6.1.3 Changing Opportunities in Foreign Trade

Of all the regional economies functioning in Greece, the Macedonian economy suffered the most from the worldwide depression due to the region's dependence on tobacco exports. Declining international demand, especially by its main client, Germany (section 5.5), for high-quality Greek tobacco led to a 50 percent decline in the price of Macedonian tobacco, from GRD 34 per kilogram in 1928 to GRD 17.6 in 1931. This reduction in income negatively affected the region's agricultural, industrial, trading, and labour markets, especially in Salonica and Kavalla, the centres of Macedonia's tobacco trade.[32]

Domestic demand declined still further. The collapse of tobacco exports on the one hand and the reduced imports of consumer goods and grains on the other – the latter resulting from recently imposed quotas and protective tariffs – explain the 42 percent decline in the value of exports shipped from Salonica's port and the 49 percent decline in the value of imports arriving at the same port between 1929 and 1933.[33] With the significant decline in Salonica's port activity when compared with that of Piraeus (Appendix 6, Table A), Salonica's Jewish economy, which heavily depended on the port, suffered considerably.

While the worldwide economic slump diminished the scope of opportunities in foreign trade, the new restrictions on international transactions (quotas, clearing agreements) led to a re-structuring of that trade, a process that further reduced the opportunities open to Jewish entrepreneurs well into the 1930s.

Despite the Balkan Pact signed in 1934, two of the pact's partners, Greece and Yugoslavia (the others being Turkey and Romania) did not achieve trade interdependence even though they shared a common border. Trade with Bulgaria, which remained outside the pact, likewise declined precipitously between 1928 and 1938.[34] All of these trends reduced the scope of commercial activity linked to Salonica's port as well as diminishing the transit trade, in which Jewish merchants were experts.

By 1933, Greece had extended import controls by increasing protective tariffs. While instituting quotas, especially on imported luxury items, livestock, and machinery, imports of wheat, coal, and raw materials were unaffected.[35] The shortage of foreign currency stimulated the use of bilateral full or partial clearing arrangements[36] together with individual barter agreements, which required special licenses. These "individual clearing agreements" were preferred or, in some cases, permitted by the authorities only if the importer had pre-arranged barter clauses attached to his account. These agreements represented a compromise between the state's need to protect its foreign currency reserves and the individual merchants' need to maintain their autonomy. As the practice was discouraged by the Ministry for the National Economy, private clearings never became widespread,[37] although they were approved for favoured entrepreneurs who traded mainly with Germany (see Chapter 8).

Germany, as a debtor state also suffering foreign currency shortages,[38] was much more suitable as a trading partner than were other countries, such as Britain. Moreover, Germany was prevented from benefiting directly from its growing import-derived assets in Greece (1929–1933) due to Greek currency export prohibitions. A clearing agreement was consequently signed between the Central Bank of Greece and the German Reichsbank in August 1932,[39] thus permitting German purchases of Greek tobacco against reductions in German assets. However, Greece had begun to be integrated into the Nazi trading area as of 1934. Following implementation of the New Plan (*Neuer Plan*) devised by Hitler's Economic Minister Hjalmar Schacht,[40] Germany became Greece's principal foreign market, which led to the recovery of the declining Greek tobacco exports to Germany by the spring of 1934. Germany absorbed about half of Greek tobacco in addition to fresh fruit, wine, and minerals; in return, Germany supplied Greece with major finished industrial products, especially ironware, steel items, and coal.[41] Greek exports to Germany exceeded German exports to Greece, resulting in the accumulation of credits in Greece's favour (34.5 RM million in 1936).[42] Enforcing the Nazi regime's unique trade policies,[43] Germany purchased Greek agricultural products above world market prices, paid for in Reichsmarks accumulated in frozen accounts that could be used only to purchase German goods, especially armaments, usually at non-competitive prices.[44] As fear of the impending depreciation of the Reichsmark grew, Greece attempted to use its accumulated trade credits as guarantees for loans which it hoped to acquire in the international market, a plan torpedoed by Britain.[45]

During the international economic recovery from mid-1936 to August 1937, Greece experienced rising sales of her products in the international market. This led to restricting exports to Germany. As a result, an agreement was signed on 1 October 1937, effective immediately, to regulate Greek–German trade exchanges and create a basis for future trade in arms, especially in hard currency.[46] However, following Germany's attempt to manipulate raw tobacco prices, Metaxas instructed (5 December 1937) Greek growers to either limit the area under cultivation or produce crops saleable in markets other than Germany. The 11 percent decrease in tobacco prices during the years 1937 and 1938 proved him right. It should be noted that after Germany became Greece's main market for Macedonian tobacco, the Greek economy's key export, trade had become subject to German demands that Greece increase import of its goods. During the Metaxas era, the government repeatedly revised its regulations regarding the acreage dedicated to this product's cultivation. These regulations were meant to re-establish government control over tobacco prices and to prevent fluctuations in the affiliated labour and product markets as well as minimise German interference in the Greek economy.[47] Yet, the scope of trade was such that in 1938, Vandeleur Robinson, a British national working with the League of Nations Union and presumably active in political intelligence,[48] warned Britain of Germany's impending control over the Greek economy, especially over Salonica's port.[49]

Germany's new status as Greece's main international trading partner (the destination of 38.6 percent of her exports and the source of 29 percent of imports),[50] together with the intensification of the arms trade during the Metaxas regime, appear to have influenced the scope and character of the opportunities opening up in this sphere for Jewish entrepreneurs. These opportunities were also affected by the Jews' declining influence on German politics between the two world wars.

6.2 Political Resources: Jewish–Greek Relations

The 1930s encompassed, in effect, two sub-periods in the relations between the Greek authorities and the Jews. Stated simply, relationships between the Greek government and the Jews of Salonica continued to be determined throughout the decade by the Jews' position on Greek internal politics, that is, whether they rejected Venizelism. The fact was that the Jews tended to endorse anti-Venizelists.[51]

During the first sub-era, which lasted until 1935, power alternated between Venizelist and anti-Venizelist governments. Venizelists ruled between 1928, when Venizelos was re-elected prime minister, until November 1932, when Panayis Tsaldaris of the (anti-Venizelist) Popular Party and the Royalists captured the government. The years between 1932 and 1935 were characterised by political instability, with two Venizelist *coups d'état* attempted to prevent Royalists from returning to power (6 March 1933 and 1 March 1935). In the meantime, the Royalists gradually increased their power in Parliament and became its largest party in January 1936. In June 1935, the Royalist General George Kondylis formed a government that enabled him to re-establish the monarchy, which he did by returning George II to the Greek throne in November 1935. The second sub-period began on 4 August 1936, when General Ioannis Metaxas,[52] with the king's consent, abolished the constitution and established himself as dictator.[53]

6.2.1 Official Greek Attitudes toward Salonica's Jews

Successive interwar Greek governments, Venizelist and anti-Venizelist, shared a perception that Salonica's Sephardic Jews often refused to assimilate into the Greek body politic. This impression cast the Jews in a suspicious light with regard to their political loyalties, especially in connection with territorial consolidation.[54] During his second tenure as prime minister, Venizelos treated the largely non-assimilationist Jewish population of Salonica as a national minority despite its official status as a religious minority. Venizelos based his claims on the Jews' rich past as Ottoman subjects as well as their Zionist activities, which he continued to critique even two years after being ousted from office (1934).

> The Jews of Salonica follow a national Jewish policy. They are not Greeks and do not feel as such. . . . The Salonican Jews are not Greek patriots but Jewish patriots. They are closer to the Turks than to us.[55]

Jews were not only accused of lacking Greek patriotism, but were also portrayed as supporting communism, which was assumed to threaten Greek Macedonian territorial integrity.[56] These feelings intensified after the tobacco crisis (late 1920s) and the consequent disbanding of the trade unions (1930) (section 5.5), many of whose activists were Jews.[57]

Suspicion continued to generate Hellenisation legislation, often targeted at Salonica's Jewish population. Law 4837 (17 July 1930) introduced amendments to Law 2456 of 1920 (section 3.2). Whereas Law 4837 re-defined Jewish communities as exclusively religious organisations, including "all persons of Jewish faith residing permanently in the seat of the community, [who] are *ipso jure* deemed members of the Jewish Community",[58] Articles 2 and 4 granted eligibility for election to the

Community Assembly (the supreme authority of each community), community councils (elected from among Community Assembly members) and the post of each Jewish community's chief Rabbi only to Greek citizens.[59] This law expressed, in effect, partial Hellenisation of the Jewish Community's administration. While it excluded Jewish foreign nationals from the Community affairs, it increased Greek supervision of Jewish communal institutions, which had become more dependent on the Greek authorities and government funding. Petitions addressed to the government to grant Greek citizenship to Jewish community officials who were not Greek nationals expressed this dependence (see section 6.3).

Hellenisation in the sphere of education was also increased through legislation. The 1936 education law broadened the 1929 Greek compulsory education law by subjecting foreign schools as well as schools run by minorities to the jurisdiction of the Inspector General. Greek was now declared the universal language of instruction. Government officials likewise increased the number of hours of instruction in the Greek language, history, and culture. Law 818 (1937) and Law 2029 (1939) required all faculty members, including those teaching in minority schools, to be examined as to their competence in the Greek language. The supposed reluctance of Jewish teachers to learn Greek was perceived by Metaxist officials as an expression of "anti-Hellenic sentiments" and possible disloyalty to the state.[60]

During this entire period, daily Jewish life was conducted in an atmosphere suffused with politically tainted suspicion. The Greek Internal Intelligence Service, situated in the Foreign Ministry, operated through Macedonia's official Press Bureau to monitor Salonica's Jewish press.[61] The bureau served as the main interface between the non-Greek Jewish press and the authorities in Salonica and Athens. By means of the bureau, the government kept a watchful eye on the community's newspapers and journals while ceaselessly complaining about their linguistic policy (articles were written mainly in Ladino and French, the two languages also spoken in the home). The community managed to retain its cultural freedom in the short term, but its resistance to linguistic assimilation created a reservoir of explosive resentment.[62]

The fact that the Jews were inhabitants of the "new territories" and provided a sizeable group of organised workers also attracted the watchful eye of the Greek police. Since Salonica's police force was understaffed, it relied on informers. The Venizelist head of internal security, previously an officer in the Cretan Gendarmerie, not only recruited loyal staff from his home island but also introduced traditional Ottoman methods, which rested on a large network of spies.[63] Based on evidence collected during the riots in Salonica's Campbell Quarter (28–30 June 1931),[64] where many Jews resided, as well as on documents in the Historical Archive of the Greek Ministry of Foreign Affairs (HAMFA),[65] we can conclude that police treatment of the Jews was tinged by tacit but clear discrimination and hostility.

6.2.2 Public Attitudes toward the Jews

Venizelists purposefully enflamed mass antipathy toward the Jews of Salonica. Aggressive nationalists in Salonica incorporated anti-Semitism into their broader anti-communist program to promote the city's ethnic (i.e., Jewish) cleansing, an objective seen as acceptable after the Transfer. The Greek press, a major shaper of public opinion, often avidly participated in this campaign. The leading Venizelist newspaper in Salonica – *Makedonia* – was rabidly anti-Jewish and had important contacts with the Nazi regime as early as 1933.[66]

Because the majority of Jewish newspapers in Salonica were published in Ladino or French,[67] the Greek authorities, like the general public, were denied access to the internal Jewish discourse that might have quelled or mitigated their suspicions. As it was, the Greek public was forced to rely on selective or distorted reports printed in Greek dailies for information on the Jewish community.[68]

Anti-Semitic sentiments were further fuelled by anti-communist nationalist organisations whose members were mainly Greek refugees and Venizelist loyalists. The refugees had become frustrated and critical by the expropriation of their abandoned property, made possible through part of the Ankara agreement signed by Venizelos.[69] For these reasons, in addition to the intensifying competition between Jews and refugees over jobs and housing in Salonica from the late 1920s on, the anti-Semitic propaganda spread by the Greek press fell on receptive ears.

Awareness of the international networks of Sephardic Jewish families in the Balkans also fed doubts about the Jewish community's patriotism. The public was especially sensitive to the presence of Jews in Bulgaria because a Bulgarian revolutionary movement had declared its intentions to establish an independent Macedonian state. When a representative of Salonica's Jews attended the 1930 convention of the Maccabi Club in Sophia, the Venizelist newspaper *Makedonia* used that occasion to accuse him of participating in a meeting of the Bulgarian Macedonian Revolutionary Committee, likewise being held in Sophia. Active cooperation between *Makedonia* and the Venizelist Ethniki Enosis Ellas (EEE, National Union of Greece) reached its peak 28–30 June 1931, when a Greek anti-Semitic nationalist mob rioted in suburban Salonica's Jewish neighbourhoods while simultaneously waging a pogrom in the city's Campbell Quarter.[70] The Venizelos government's implicit support of the agitation, demonstrated by its acquittal of the riots' instigators (allegedly due to a lack of evidence), transformed Salonica's Jews into scapegoats for the public's anger at the party's failure to provide jobs for its unemployed supporters. And so, the Jewish working class was used as a shock absorber. The official anti-communist stance, mixed with xenophobia, made it acceptable to distinguish the unemployed according to their ethnic identity, irrespective of the common fate. This ploy enabled the party to maintain its rule.[71] The 1931 riots thus exacerbated the tension between non-Jews and Jews in Salonica, which remained severe into the Metaxas era.

One can readily conclude from this analysis that Jewish entrepreneurs suffered from a dearth of political resources during the Venizelist era, as they were treated as political rivals and a national minority. The description of Jewish businessmen as "resourceful and full of wiles",[72] found in *To Fos*, the Greek newspaper supported by the Populist Party (1932), suggests the universality of this attitude. Anti-Semitism and poor policies were thus successfully disguised as protection of the national economy from internal enemies. A leaflet circulated (20 October 1932) by the Pan-Hellenic Anti-Communist and Humanitarian Union, which was dedicated "to supporting the national economy", instructed its readers to avoid patronising Jewish businesses.

> Do not go into shops, which are not Greek. . . . Do not employ foreigners in your business. . . . Always prefer Greek products. . . . Greeks, never forget that every drachma you give to foreign workers or spend in shops not owned by Greeks and

Christians leaves the country for ever! . . . Let the watchword for all of us be: Greek money only for Greek products and to Greek shops![73]

6.2.3 Anti-Venizelism, 1933–1938

Beginning in 1933, with the rise to power of the anti-Venizelist Popular Party, but especially with the establishment of the Metaxas dictatorship in 1936, the Jews of Salonica enjoyed a temporary respite. Metaxas (1936–1941) prohibited anti-Semitic propaganda and dissolved the ultra-nationalist organisation, the EEE, which had undisputed links to the Nazis; the EEE was eventually outlawed.[74] The new anti-Venizelist regime was committed to its loyal Jewish supporters, whom it considered "more Greek" than the refugees. One expression of this commitment was the dissolution of the Jewish electoral college in 1932.[75] Furthermore, following the election of the anti-Venizelist Nicolas Manos – "the Jews' Mayor" – in 1934, Jewish relations with Salonica's municipal authorities improved still further.[76]

Despite its rightist leanings, the Metaxas government did not legislate any racial laws against the Jews. This behaviour contrasts sharply with that of the Mussolini regime in Italy, which adopted legislation prohibiting marriage between Semites and Aryans on 17 November 1938 and imposed severe civil and economic restrictions on the Jews' activities. As Pierron concluded, "In Greece nothing similar had happened and the Hellenic Jews continued enjoying the rights they got according to the liberal constitution until the German occupation."[77]

Yet Metaxas did pass legislation allowing expropriation of the old Jewish cemetery for construction of an extension of Salonica's Aristotle University,[78] which had been planned during the Venizelos regime. Moreover, when confronted with the dispute between the Jewish community and the tax authorities over the accumulated arrears in communal property tax payments, the Metaxas government decided to grant a tax exemption only on the buildings used for schooling but ignored the hardships of other communal institutions.[79] These decisions indicate that during the second half of the 1930s, the political resources available to the Jewish community, including its Jewish entrepreneurs, had improved only slightly.

6.2.4 Jews in Greek International Relations

Throughout the late 1930s, the consuls representing Italy, the UK, and other European states intensified intelligence collection aimed at protecting their respective interests. Unlike his colleagues from other countries, the German consul stationed in Salonica included the "Jewish Question" among the Third Reich's interests. During the Weimar Republic (1919–1933), Germany's attitude toward the Jews was clearly motivated by economic interests; hence, the good reputation enjoyed by Jewish firms in Salonica was carefully noted. In the months leading up to World War I, Jewish sympathies in Salonica usually sided with the "central powers" (Germany and Austria). The small German-speaking colony in the city engaged in economic cooperation with Sephardic Jewish businessmen (section 2.4.1); the Jewish students at the German school were also among the most excellent. The small German colony in Salonica, like the Jewish population, had reservations about the "new Greek Administration".[80] Nevertheless, immediately following Hitler's rise to power in late January 1933, Germany adopted a different stance toward Greece's Jews, who now found themselves caught in a maze of international relations reminiscent of the intrigue surrounding the "Macedonian problem".[81]

Germany's relationship with the Greek government was therefore influenced by the latter's treatment of Salonica's Jews. Internal alliances among politicians nonetheless caused inconsistencies in Greece's dealings with Nazi Germany. Although Venizelism was associated with support for the Allies against Germany, the party was identified with extreme anti-Semitism during World War I.[82] When the Jewish press attacked Nazism's racist policy and Jewish merchants initiated demonstrations and boycotts of German goods, the Panayis Tsaldaris government (November 1932–January 1933) chose to prohibit these actions. Tsaldaris was in effect succumbing to pressure from anti-Semitic elements, but particularly from the powerful tobacco lobby[83] (see section 8.1). Later, the German Reich would approve of Metaxas' authoritarian regime and its anti-communist measures, although the amicable relations between the prime minister and Greece's Jewish community remained troubling for the Germans.

Metaxas' policies were guided throughout by the need to protect Greek national interests in the face of the Third Reich's threats. Motivated by fears of a Nazi takeover, Metaxas began to reinforce Greece's ties with the UK beginning in 1938.[84] Germany and the UK alike were then operating intelligence-gathering networks in Greece. While people such as Vandeleur Robinson (section 6.1.3 above) served UK interests, German intelligence activities targeted on Salonica's Jews were openly conducted after Fritz Schönberg was appointed Consul General in Salonica (January 1938) (section 10.2).

6.3 Impoverishing Demographic Resources

The 1930s saw Jewish demographic resources depleted due to the increased unemployment in Greek labour markets, especially in the tobacco industry and the port.[85] Internal trends, such as demands for Hellenisation of Jewish education, rising Greek nationalism and anti-Semitism gradually came to stimulate Jewish emigration.

At a time when France (1932) was raising immigration barriers to "protect the national work force",[86] restrictions on Jewish immigration to Palestine were being lifted (1932–1936). The British Mandate's new immigration policy was now to be based on the "economic absorptive capacity" of two separate economies, one Jewish, the other Arab, unlike previous policy, which treated the two sectors as a single unit. This revision meant that the British authorities had consented to demands made by Zionist institutions on the basis of the flow of Jewish capital and the repeated Arab riots against the Jewish population. By 1935, the British authorities had increased the number of six-month residence quotas to their maximum level; in addition, the proportion of immigrants lacking assets (i.e., labourers) covered by these quotas was raised as well.[87]

During his campaign to attract Jewish capital and entrepreneurs to Eretz Yisra'el while on a visit to Salonica in late 1932, the Jewish Agency's (JA) envoy suggested that potential migrants take advantage of the new opportunities opening up in Palestine's growing new port of Haifa, "which possesses a hinterland entirely in Jewish hands". There was also discussion of the idea of establishing a tobacco industry there that would employ the skilled as well as unskilled labourers who had been ejected from Salonica's declining tobacco plants.[88] Emigration to British Mandatory Palestine therefore became a promising option for all unemployed Jews, including those previously active in the Jewish-owned economy.[89] For their part, the Greek authorities, fearing increasing unemployment in the wake of the departure of Jewish entrepreneurs,[90] sought ways to offset the influence of pro-emigration articles appearing in the Jewish press. These articles took the position that "emigration is the only source of salvation" from the intense economic misery of Salonica. In response, articles authored by Greek officials claimed that Jewish emigrants would encounter difficulties similar to those found in Greece in their foreign destinations, primarily in Europe and the Middle East,[91] but to no avail.

Although it is difficult to estimate the exact impact of the immigration to Mandatory Palestine on the number of entrepreneurs and labourers among Salonica's Jewish population, official sources provide data from which we can extrapolate estimates of those remaining. According to municipal registries, Salonica's Jewish community numbered 52,300 in 1935, of which 47,289 were Greek citizens and 5,011 foreigners.[92] Subtracting the 5,651 registered migrants (a minimal figure) to Mandatory Palestine during 1932–1938[93] from the 47,289 Jewish Greek nationals leaves us with about 40,000 Jews,[94] primarily Greek citizens, residing in Salonica by 1939.[95] A similar estimation was later sent by Schönberg to the Foreign Office in Berlin: "Today [i.e., 1938] it is [the Jewish segment of Salonica's population] estimated at 40,000, that is, about 17% of the total population."[96] The data were accompanied by information regarding "several large Jewish households that have recently moved from Salonica to Athens" in response to the local bans against conducting business with Jewish traders and the full-scale commercial boycotts that were increasingly common by the late 1930s.[97] Put briefly, the Jewish community supplied decreasing numbers of Jewish entrepreneurs and labourers to the Jewish as well as to the Greek economy during the 1930s. These population movements reduced the number of Jewish taxpayers, contracted the Jewish consumer market, and intensified community impoverishment.[98]

6.4 Sustaining Jewish Community Institutions

Demographic losses resulted in shrinking the size of institutional and communal financial resources. The reduced number of Jewish taxpayers directly depleted the community's financial resources, which were based on income from the direct tax (the *pecha*). As the Jewish market shrank, so did its purchasing power. The community's income also shrank as collection of the Purchase Tax, the *gabella* (or *gabelle* in French), an indirect tax imposed on kosher meat sales,[99] plunged. Meat consumption had declined as Jewish purchasing power, together with absolute population, fell. In 1932, considered the nadir of the economic depression, bread consumption increased among Salonica's residents by 15% in comparison with 1930, a figure that corroborated the impression that bread was replacing meat as the dominant ingredient in the population's diet.[100] At the same time, the community's income from fees collected for the issuance of certificates (birth, death, etc.) increased three-fold, from GRD 30,000 (1933) to GRD 90,000 (1934), to remain at about the same level (GRD 85,000) two years later,[101] a trend coinciding with the intensifying emigration. These trends added to the community's budgetary burden, which had swelled due to the increasing need for assistance.[102] Based on Salonica's Jewish press (August 1933), the Director of the Salonica Press Bureau reported on the state of the community to the Ministry of Foreign Affairs as follows:

The impoverished condition of the Jewish population and the exceptional circumstances in which the community finds itself has prevented it from granting aid to the
many members of the lower classes afflicted by misfortune and misery.[103]

As the community's sources of income dried up, debts related to the operation of
community institutions grew. The Jewish community therefore found it difficult to
independently meet its budget. According to the Jewish newspaper *Le Progrès* (16 July
1933), the budget for the current fiscal year showed a deficit of 250,000 drachmas,
which they hoped to balance by introducing measures such as a 10 percent reduction
in the salaries paid to community employees. These employees eventually rejected the
measure and recommended other ways for raising the needed funds.[104]

Emigration thus negatively impacted on the Jewish public sector, which had served
as a sheltered labour market for community members.[105] Unlike the national public
sector, which could initiate public works projects for the purpose of job provision
(section 8.2.5), the Jewish community found it difficult to maintain its former level of
activity. The especially burdensome growth in salary-related expenses was likewise
influenced by new legislation, requiring the payment of social security taxes for
community employees.[106]

Hence, we can conclude that in addition to the Jewish community's accumulated
debts (including their progressively growing interest costs) as well as losses from the
fluctuations in the financial system, the wave of emigration during the mid-1930s also
caused the deterioration of the Jewish communal infrastructure (see Chapter 3). A
review of community budgets for 1933 and 1934 indicates that Jewish institutions
continued to be active and well-supported by local and international Zionist organisations in those years.[107] In addition, after 1930, the municipal subsidy, which was
dependent on the good will of Salonica's mayor and its municipal council, doubled.[108]
Yet, the reduced allocations for communal associations in the proposed budget for
1934 would negatively impact on the regeneration of the social capital essential
for community vitality during the late 1930s.[109]

6.5 Internal Solidarity

Throughout the 1930s, forced Hellenisation began to influence the contours of Jewish
identity while it created cracks in internal solidarity. The Jewish community's lengthy
struggle to create a unified stance following Salonica's incorporation into the Greek
nation-state reached a watershed during the trial (1932), held in the city of Veria, of
those responsible for the Campbell Quarter pogrom (1931). According to one contemporary, it was Greek–Jewish relations that were actually on trial.[110] From this point
forward, the Jewish community split into two main factions. The first supported
Zionism; it saw Jewish residence in Salonica as a temporary condition prior to the
creation of a Jewish national homeland. The second faction supported assimilation;
its advocates wanted to merge into the Greek body politic even if it meant surrendering
the benefits attached to their legal and political status as a religious minority.[111]

In general, this division coincided with the Jews' residential patterns. The Zionist
faction was concentrated in the poorer Jewish neighbourhoods located in the
periphery, while the assimilationists, who belonged to the upper-middle class, were
scattered throughout the regenerated urban centre (see Map 2). Their desire to remain

in Salonica necessitated assimilation; this group therefore attempted to strengthen its "Greekness".[112] Jewish community fragmentation was mirrored in the 1930 and 1934 elections to the General Assembly of the Jewish Community. While the Zionists (represented by two parties) increased their presence at the expense of the communists and the Moderates in October 1930,[113] mass migration to Mandatory Palestine reduced their numbers in Greece, resulting in a slight improvement in the Moderates' position by 1934.[114] The two main camps also reflected the internal split regarding the preferred language of instruction. While the Zionists advocated teaching in modern Hebrew in order to prepare young Jews to make a living once they arrived in Palestine, the Moderates, inspired by the principles of the Alliance Israélite Universelle, believed in eliminating all differences, excluding religion, which might distinguish Salonica's Jews from their Greek neighbours. They believed that although the Jewish community should not cease to take an interest in the Jewish nation in general and in the Jews in Palestine in particular, they focused on their individual futures and adjustment to local conditions so as to live in complete harmony and absolute equality with their Greek neighbours.[115] Hence, the Moderates wished to retain Hebrew as a holy language to be used only in religious contexts, with Greek the dominant language in community-run schools. They likewise believed that other foreign languages, particularly French, should be taught to their children. As fluency in foreign languages was considered a prerequisite for conducting business outside the borders of Greece, they continued to educate their children in foreign schools even after the government declared that it would cover all the tuition in the Jewish–Greek schools under its jurisdiction.[116] According to an account given (1941) by André Havard, former director of the Lycée Française (1935–1940), Jews made up the majority of the school's pupils while its Jewish alumni continued to follow the institution's direction throughout their lives. Havard consequently tried to "*supprimer le monopole Israélite de l'influence intellectuelle française*".[117]

Hellenisation of the day of rest created an additional rift in the community. The debate over compliance with the official day of rest, Sunday, reflected differences already apparent between Sabbath observant and non-observant Jewish small businessmen, partly rooted in commercial interests. In April 1934, P. Dragoumis, Governor General of Macedonia, made it clear that the national day of rest, Sunday, was to be imposed only in designated commercial sub-sectors, such as groceries. The majority of grocery owners and their employees insisted on this move in order to diminish competition between Christians and Jews given that most Jewish grocers had already ceased to observe the Jewish Sabbath (Saturday). On the other hand, because "Jewish butchers are closed all day on Saturday for specific religious reasons and the introduction of a complete day of rest on Sunday would have been financially damaging to them", a plea made by Christian butchers and their employees to force Jewish butchers to close their shops on Sunday was rejected by the Greek authorities.[118] Obviously, these demands reflected the different consumer segments served: grocers had customers from both ethnic groups, whereas butchers served only their co-ethnic market, i.e., Jews purchased only kosher meat and only from Jewish butchers.

Internal solidarity was also threatened by the Hellenisation of the Jewish communal administration (see section 6.2) for it clearly interfered with the community's autonomy. For example, the success of efforts to find suitable candidates for crucial leadership positions came to depend on the willingness of Greek authorities to grant citizenship to nominees, who were often foreign nationals.[119] To illustrate how these factors impacted on communal life, we need only mention that the position of Chief Rabbi remained empty for a full decade (1923–1933) after the departure of Rabbi Bentzion Uziel to Mandatory Palestine in 1923, because the local rabbis were ineligible for the post due to their Serbian citizenship. The appointment of Rabbi Koretz, a Polish citizen and former resident of Berlin,[120] to this position (20 August 1933) only aggravated the internal rifts, because Koretz was accused by the Zionists of being assimilationist and therefore viewed as a divisive force by numerous community members.[121]

As previously mentioned, the Greek government's reluctance to grant citizenship to foreign Jews also depleted the ranks of the Jewish community's formal leadership. Without the sanction of citizenship, the upper-middle class pillars of the Jewish community, who tended to hold foreign citizenship, could not be elected to head the community's internal institutions.[122] Members of the Modiano family, who were Italian citizens, were thus excluded from participating in public life. Social solidarity suffered as this situation nurtured alienation between the Jewish elite and the Jewish masses. Evidence for the growing schism is found in the articles written by Eliyahu Veissi in *El Messagero*, the community's Ladino newspaper (see also section 10.2). In 1936, Veissi wrote,

> We should therefore protest against the shameful behaviour of our major business-men (Moises Gattegno, Abraham Maissa, and others) who told the delegation of officials who had come to collect the community tax [*pecha*] to supply the community's needs, that they refuse to pay, and that they no longer belong to the community.[123]

Yet, Jewish foreign national entrepreneurs like [first name unknown] Tazartes, of the firm Amariglio, Tazartes & Revah (Appendix 4.1, no. 508; Appendix 5, no. 552), who held Italian citizenship, continued to be engaged in philanthropic activity in the Jewish community. On the eve of World War II he served as head of *Matanoth Laévionim*, which provided hot meals for needy children.[124] Although the gap between Jewish elite entrepreneurs and Jewish small businessmen broadened during the 1930s, Jewish businessmen remained dependent on each other, in contrast with the growing alienation between Jewish entrepreneurs and the Greek officials. René Molho, a former Jewish resident of the city, described the situation in these terms:

> This is a matter of survival in the Jewish community, for it is the practice among merchants to borrow money or enter into agreements with one another on the basis of one's word or a handshake. No documents are used. Because the Greek language is foreign to most Jews, they avoid the regular courts altogether, but apart from this they prefer to keep their problems "in the family".[125]

6.6 Conclusion

Suspended convertibility (1932) ended the period of relatively free foreign exchange in Greece while marking the beginning of extreme protectionism and extensive state inter-vention in financial affairs. Following government imposition of restrictions on imports by means of quotas, tariffs, and clearing agreements, entrepreneurial oppor-tunities in international commerce diminished. At the same time, new entrepreneurial opportunities were created in the local market. While new conditions were created for Jewish entrepreneurship, dwindling Jewish ethnic resources impacted on the number, scope and character of the opportunities available to Jewish entrepreneurs. As for the international market, reduced trade between Greece and the countries to which it was financially indebted (especially England), in tandem with the official ties to Nazi Germany's economy instituted along with the New Plan (*Neuer Plan*) in 1934, effectively reduced the entrepreneurial opportunities in foreign trade open to Jews.

It is therefore appropriate to ask at this point whether the Jewish entrepreneurs remaining in Salonica continued to be committed to recruiting Jewish labourers and sustaining the Jewish economy. The dearth of youthful workers in the wake of mass emigration to Palestine and the West on one hand, and the declining wealth of those who remained on the other, directly affected the character of Jewish entrepreneurship. While small-scale entrepreneurial activity barely maintained itself with the help of meagre community resources, middle- and large-scale entrepreneurship continued and even increased, based on the personal wealth of the entrepreneurs. This group of entrepreneurs tended to belong to the moderate and pragmatic segment of Salonica's Jewish community, which indeed affected their attitudes toward the Jewish economy, as we shall see. In the coming chapters, we thus explore the short-term (Chapter 7) as well as long-term (Chapters 8 and 9) consequences of these transformations for Jewish entrepreneurship. To what extent did aggressive Hellenisation impact on Jewish entrepreneurial patterns? Did Jewish entrepreneurs assimilate into the Greek business world? To what extent did the boundaries of the Jewish-owned economy crumble in the face of the Greek national economy?

7

Confronting the Economic Crisis, 1930–1933

The worldwide financial crisis stimulated de-globalisation while simultaneously contributing to the consolidation of the Greek autarky. The rate of Jewish – and Greek – bankruptcies began to increase in 1929, but many of these firms were re-established during the 1934–1937 Greek economic recovery (see Chapter 8). Measures such as the devaluation of the drachma (1928–1932), the weakening of domestic customer bases, and introduction of new regulations governing foreign exchange transactions[1] (see section 6.1) further constrained bank activities together with possibilities for firm survival. Since September 1931, Banque Union, like other Greek commercial banks, was thus denied authorisation to conduct foreign currency exchanges and became subject to Central Bank of Greece supervision.[2] This meant that Banque Union could no longer act independently when expediting foreign currency payments to its clients' foreign suppliers.[3]

Contemporary sources may provide some explanation for why Jewish (and non-Jewish) entrepreneurs continued to use Banque Union despite its considerably weakened status.[4] A German document found in the Banque's surviving archive expresses its management's alienation from Greek banking authorities. Under the heading "Unimportant", the Nazi official authoring the report briefly describes the contents of the French–Greek correspondence from 1935, which was originally attached:

> Letter to the Foreign Exchange Commission of the Central Bank of Greece about Banque Union. In reference to Banque Union foreign exchange smuggling, your innocence will be proved.[5]

Unfortunately the respective documents are missing from the file. Yet, the German's comment hints at the Jewish-owned bank's attempts to bypass the new regulations, which included prohibitions against transferring local and foreign capital abroad.

Based on available fragmented correspondence, we can obtain a partial understanding of how foreign commercial debt was managed. Although the correspondence relates to Jewish and Greek clients alike, we focus on Jewish entrepreneurs, firms, and commercial agents. This correspondence, covering the relatively brief but important period from June to October 1932, allows a glimpse at the short-term responses of Jewish entrepreneurs to the new government regulations. The settlement of foreign debts through clearing agreements, realisation of frozen Jewish emigrant assets, adaptation reorganisation of import–export activity, in addition to the long-term impact of the financial crisis on the scope of the Jewish-owned economy, will all be discussed in later sections.

7.1 Formal Arrangements for the Payment of Foreign Commercial Debts

As one of the leading Jewish-owned private commercial banking institutions in Salonica, Banque Union correspondence and other documents can be assumed to reveal the process of foreign commercial debt management rather accurately. Private correspondence between Banque Union officials and a client living in Marseille expresses the Banque's embarrassment in the face of French creditors' uncertainty and the lack of confidence in Greek businessmen. In the case in question, Jacques Gattegno, who lived in Marseille, had asked Albert Nehama, manager of the Banque Union in Salonica, and his brother Joseph Nehama, manager of Banque de Salonique, to inform him about the effective exchange rates of the drachma against the French franc (GRD 580 = approximately FRF 100).

> [H]oping the Lausanne Conference will influence "your" currency positively; we would like to have your precise [calculation] at what price the Drh [sic] will be converted into Francs, at the official rate of 300 DRH [sic] for 100 FR [sic] or at the free market [rate].[6]

The parties involved appear to have had different interests. Whereas the Nehama brothers were concerned over how the 1932 Lausanne Conference would affect Greek government efforts to obtain a satisfactory solution for Greece's creditors,[7] Gattegno, in Marseille, was interested mainly in the measures adopted to deal with commercial debt. According to Gattegno, all banking institutions were involved in the negotiations meant to arrive at satisfactory arrangements for the payment of debts to French commercial creditors:

> Not only do the Minister of Commerce and the Foreign Office, but also the Paris Chamber of Commerce, inform us that very active discussions are taking place between France and Greece and that there is good reason to assume that an agreement will be reached to the satisfaction of French debt holders.[8]

The anxiety felt by French creditors regarding the payment of Greek debts was reflected later in a story related by Gattegno, which involves a claim made by one of his French colleagues regarding the success he had had in cashing in a substantial part of the debt, in British sterling, due him from Greece only eight days before. Gattegno also asked the Nehama brothers for their opinion regarding the possibility, raised by his colleague, of receiving payment through the "compensation" or clearing system, i.e., by sending Greek goods abroad and thereby avoiding any foreign exchange flows.[9]

Interestingly, the archival documents make mention of the considerable confusion caused by the Greek regulations that suspended foreign debts contracted prior to 26–27 April 1932. Foreign commercial creditors were forced to plead with Banque Union representatives to devise a method that would allow them to redeem the debts incurred by private firms. In reference to a debt owed by the Jewish merchants Samuel Salem & Fils (see Appendix 5: Sub-branches 5b and 5c), Nollesche Werke, a German producer of machinery, small metal wares (i.e., agraffes [a piano part], hooks, steel pins, and nails) as well as chemical products, complained in a letter (12 June 1932) that they had not received any information regarding the new Greek legislation. They were interested in exploring the possibility of obtaining the amount outstanding through a clearing arrangement. In a prompt reply, handwritten on the incoming letter, a bank official wrote:

> [t]he new provisions of the latter law does allow for the settlement of debts to foreign countries, contracted before April 27, so the settlement will take place under the Act of April 27 no. 5422 (which establishes the settlement of debts at 10 percent each semester).[10]

Suspended claims would be settled according to Greek law – ten payments, one every six months – a schedule determined by the details of the clearing agreement that Greece had concluded with the foreign supplier. In the absence of a clearing agreement, arrears would be collected in foreign currency.

7.2 Settling Commercial Debts in Practice

In this section we survey some of the solutions proposed by foreign creditors, based on the scope of their country's clearing agreement with Greece.[11] We should note at the outset that the Greek Ministry of the National Economy was accused of placing barriers in the way of merchants seeking to arrange private barter deals. Although Law 5426 encouraged such steps, the ministry frequently intervened by closely scrutinising the respective invoices.[12] Yet, difficulties encountered by foreign suppliers intent on collecting debts from their Greek customers indicated the growing need for commercial representatives when conducting business with Greek, including Jewish, entrepreneurs.[13] In numerous cases, the transfer of accounts to commercial agencies could ensure debt collection.

7.2.1 Creditors from Countries Having Full Clearing Agreements

7.2.1.1 German Creditors
While fully aware of the clearing arrangement that Germany, as a creditor nation, had devised to confront Greece's default, the German footwear machine manufacturer, Nollesche Werke, Weissenfels, proposed the following method to circumvent the legal prohibitions on capital transfers to its Greek debtors: firstly, payment of 10 percent of the sum immediately according to Greek law; secondly, "clearance" of the remainder by means of a "private" clearing agreement, i.e., paying the Greek firm's debt to its German supplier through (another) German cigarette producer against Greek

tobacco; and finally, the German cigarette producer would pay the amount due to the original German creditor (Nollesche Werke, Weissenfels):

> We might get our money through another German trading house that has a debt to pay in your country, [in exchange] for tobacco, for example . . . [W]e have heard that Reemtsma, the German cigarette manufacturer, does business with your country; one could, perhaps, obtain the money through this merchant house [i.e., Reemtsma]".[14]

Another example of a private clearing agreement concluded with a German creditor – in this case the German metalware producer Vincenz Werner, Merzdorf – involved the demand that Banque Union pay the amounts owed to the company by their Greek clients against exported fruit.[15] A different German creditor, Storchwerke (paint brush and roller manufacturers), proposed a barter transaction: supplying German-manufactured products in exchange for Greek tobacco.[16] Yet, in the case of D. Khyder,[17] a Jewish merchant holding Egyptian citizenship who represented several German manufacturers, his clients agreed to suspend their draft without protest.[18]

Greek Jewish merchants were frequently able to create markets for German manufactured goods, such as surgical glass instruments[19] and pharmaceuticals, with the assistance of their co-religionists living in the Weimar Republic.[20] However, when the foreign suppliers were themselves Jews, internal communal solidarity provided the framework for a series of secret financial arrangements that often flouted government regulations. For example, according to an invoice (dated 19 July 1932) issued by the Jewish manufacturer Clement Cohen of Chemnitz, Germany, two parcels of flowered embroidered stockings for women were expedited through Dresden-Guevgheli to Banque Union in the name of Haim Mano. The latter, who enjoyed a discount of 5 percent, was to redeem the bill for FRF 1,910 by a check payable on a bank in Paris. However, a letter dated 15 August 1932, written in response to a letter from Banque Union, indicates that Clement Cohen had attempted to use his ethnic connections to bypass the new regulations. He, Cohen, explained to Banque Union officials that he understood from their letter that following the clearing agreement between Greece and Germany, payment of German bills of lading would be expedited on the basis of product exchanges. Thus, bills of lading were to be cashed in drachmas, providing him with credit in a closed account with the Bank of Greece. Cohen, situated in Germany, had realised that the regulations made it doubtful that he would ever be reimbursed for the goods shipped. Hence, he refused to continue to operate in this way. The only compromise proposed by the Greek debtor was a two-month delay in payment by means of a pre-dated check. In Cohen's words,

> [b]ut if I understood correctly I can not touch my money; that will probably not be reimbursed. In these circumstances I think needless to say that I refuse categorically to agree, and I beg you to issue the said documents to Mr. Mano against a draft for the said amount FRF 1910 – payable after 2 months.[21]

7.2.1.2 Italian and Belgian Creditors
Although Italy had completed a full clearing agreement with Greece, problems similar to those arising with German suppliers afflicted commercial relations with Italian firms

as well. For example, the Italian Company IAFA inquired about the possibility of collecting payment through its Greek agent, who proposed four quarterly instalments, in drachmas, at fixed sums. This solution raised new issues, to which Banque Union officials responded, again in instructions hand-written in the margins of IAFA's letter: "According to which exchange rate was the calculation performed [unclear]. Which interest rate would the blocked drachma earn? (3%) Could the foreign firm dispose of drachmas by purchases made in Greece?"[22] This correspondence reveals that the drachma's new exchange rates had intensified the uncertainty meant to be resolved by the clearing agreements.

Since the Bank of Greece lacked the resources to cover the exchange rate losses incurred by commercial banks following abandonment of the gold standard, it ordered the compulsory conversion of all foreign exchange liabilities into drachmas at a rate of GRD 100 = $1 (the regulation was introduced in late July 1932).[23] Following devaluation of the US dollar and its abandonment of the gold standard in March 1933,[24] the drachma was again linked to gold standard currencies – the Swiss Franc (SWF) and the French Franc (FRF). After the devaluation and collapse of the Gold Bloc in September 1936, the drachma was linked to the British pound sterling once more.[25] This instability created the setting for the inquiry forwarded by the Swiss firm Graemiger Frères SA, asking whether the drachma's exchange rate vis-à-vis the Swiss franc, originally set at GRD 100 = SWF 1, had stabilised, risen, or fallen. In this case, a Banque Union official wrote, in his own hand, "30 le fs. [*sic*] environ".[26]

Similarly, the Solin, Yugoslavia branch of the Italian firm Spalato, Société Anonyme des Ciments Portland, delivered the matured bank drafts (in US dollars) given them by Maison David J. Magrisso (Appendix 5, no. 612) in payment for delivery of 2,000 sacks and 2,000 barrels of cement through its export agent in Trieste. All the drafts required Bank of Greece permission to complete the currency transfer. Since Banque Union had extended guarantees to Magrisso, the Italian firm asked the bank to expedite Magrisso's debt, which amounted to £833.07, converted into dollars as follows: $3.60 = £1, or $3,000 plus interest, from the date of payment in sterling. Against remittance of the new drafts in dollars, the bank was to return the original drafts, held in sterling, to Magrisso. On 12 August 1932, Spalato confirmed receipt of the payment in dollars, duly endorsed by Magrisso to the order of Spalato.[27]

Despite the clearing arrangements, no records could be found among Banque Union documents regarding the proper procedures for settling debts with Italian suppliers; hence, confusion was common. For instance, with respect to two drafts drawn on Zakkai & Co.,[28] the drawees had acquired authorisation from the National Bank of Greece to pay these drafts.[29] Yet, a draft sent by an Italian exporter to the hat manufacturer Makedoniki Pilopiia (Appendix 5, no. 652), delivered to Banque Union for payment with instruction to forward the draft to its Greek agent in Salonica, Nico Igino Malinco, was not handled smoothly, with the bank protesting payment for freight charges.[30] In another instance, an Italian paper producer had a similar experience when expediting payment for bales of cigarette paper, shipped by boat from Trieste to Salonica's port for forwarding to the Greek-owned firms Handaris & Kaplanides and Tsacassianos & Sophianopoulos. Banque Union instructed the Italian firm to deliver the documents against payment by check, this time in Zurich, for invoices specified in Swiss Francs.[31]

Payments between Belgian creditors and Greek debtors followed the pattern established with Italy. Belgian suppliers, after establishing full clearing arrangements with

Greece, tried to collect their Greek debts against foreign exchange. According to a telegram delivered to Banque Union, Verheyden & Biemans, a construction materials exporter, remitted – without charge – three drafts to its commercial representative in Salonica, Joseph Attas.[32]

7.2.1.3 French Creditors

Although full-clearing agreements had been finalised between France and Greece, French creditors often attempted to obtain cash for their delivered goods or propose various debt arrangements to their Greek debtors. The French metal producer Usines Spindler SA asked Banque Union to cover the costs of a shipment of its products to Dimitsa Frères (located in Salonica), amounting to FRF 2,489.90, through the sale of the merchandise contained in three of the crates. In order to complete the sale to other Salonica metal trading houses (the Greek-owned Iliados Frères as well as to the Jewish-owned David Fais; Salomon Yacar, and Yacar E. Ovadia), they empowered the bank to discount the price of the goods by about 30 percent. Banque Union's handwritten response stated that they preferred a larger discount (50 percent) in order to rid themselves of the unpaid-for merchandise.[33]

A different compromise was negotiated following non-payment of three drafts on the account of Jacob Menahem for five boxes of wooden pulleys sent from Marseille to Is. Nahmias. In this case, the French company requested that the previous three drafts be cancelled, to be replaced by three new drafts for FRF 703.05 each, which covered only the goods' nominal value. On a copy of the request, three handwritten payment dates can be seen: 13 July, (date unclear – O.M.) August, and 30 September 1932.[34]

After the failure of the Greek commercial representative Horras to pay his bill, a French aromatic goods producer succeeded in receiving a check through Banque Saul Amar & Cie., Paris, as the result of instructions from Banque Union.[35] Similarly, Banque Union paid a Greek client's suspended debts to the French tannery Les Tanneries Lyonnaises, also through Banque Saul Amar & Cie., Paris. The delayed payment of the original bill for delivery of tinted young goat hides (*chevreaux*), dated in November, carried an annual interest rate of 8 percent.[36] Les Tanneries Lyonnaises confirmed the instructions to suspend the drafts, without protest, which their representative in Salonica, Samuel Ghedalia Yeni (Appendix 5, no. 255), had received from Banque Union.[37]

7.2.2 Creditors from Countries Enjoying "Partial Clearing" Agreements

Agreements signed between Hungary and Greece represented a type of partial clearing arrangement. These agreements allowed imports of selected goods through barter transactions exclusively, while other imports of identical provenance could be paid for in foreign exchange.[38] The following example shows that rawhide was included among the latter goods. The Hungarian rawhide exporter Bern, Fried & Sohne agreed to an eight-day remission of the final payment of the $240 debt contracted by a Greek merchant, Yoaniddes. Through the intervention of the Jewish-owned Salonican Maison Aroesti, the Greek-owned firm paid $40 in advance for the bale of rawhide it had purchased.[39]

A special type of "partial clearing" agreement was negotiated with Yugoslavia (September 1932), Turkey (May 1933), and Romania (September 1933), facilitated through special cash vouchers (*bons de caisse*) issued by the Central Bank of Greece.[40] Yet, the debt arrangements between Greek debtors and Balkans creditors appear to have resembled arrangements made with other countries. To illustrate this pattern, consider the case of a Yugoslav timber supplier who had shipped sawed planks of coniferous wood first by wagon and then by rail from Zagreb to Salonica; he demanded a single payment, by check made out to a New York bank. The debtor, the Greek firm Zacharidis, was later able to negotiate a rescheduled payment of "up to four monthly payments".[41]

7.2.3 Creditors in Countries without Clearing Agreements

7.2.3.1 British Creditors

In the following extract, the British Consul advises British creditors (1937) that their government had not completed a clearing agreement with Greece:

> [A] Moratorium Law was passed and all commercial debts owed by a Greek person or firm became payable in ten half-yearly instalments, interest on the outstanding amounts being calculated at the mean between the official rate of the Bank of Greece and that of the country of which the creditor was a national. The payments under the Moratorium, though somewhat behind hand, are proceeding normally and the Bank of Greece grants exchange without difficulty for all debts that have been declared in conformity with the law.[42]

The same consul also reported on the debt repayment arrangements that had been finalised with British creditors. In line with British government policy, which did not countenance clearing agreements with Greece,[43] and individual Balkan suppliers, British textile manufacturers generally opted for rescheduling of payments, now quoted in drachmas, by their Greek clients. They also made greater use of agents located in Salonica when collecting debts.

Increased used of agents and intermediaries when paying debts to British creditors often compelled Jewish entrepreneurs to sell firm assets. The trading house of Mentech S. Arama (est. 1921), which was engaged in commerce in men's confection and drapery, was one firm that had to comply with this arrangement (1931–1932).[44] Although able to reschedule their payments with their suppliers, mainly British mills (e.g., J. & S. Rhodes, Ltd.) through a Jewish Salonican agent, Hector Capuano,[45] Arama was forced to sell the firm's building, located on the fashionable Rue Solomou, in order to meet the new schedule, at least until the firm's business had improved in 1935.[46] Another British supplier, A. & S. Henry Co., Ltd., through its liquidator Charles Semon & Co., appealed to Banque Union with a request to collect the unpaid bills accumulated by Beja & Saltiel.[47] Similarly, S. Selka, a Jewish-owned milling firm located in Bradford, England, instructed Banque Union as follows when attempting to collect payment from a Greek (Anghelos A. Anghelides) as well as a Jewish (Albert I. Benveniste) client:

> In case of non-payment [by check to London], please refer to Leon Castro in Salonica, who is empowered to instruct you how to act in all matters arising out of the law "sur la Protection de la Monnaie Nationale", and also to instruct you whether a bill is to be protested or not.[48]

In another case, a British creditor instructed Banque Union that if Albert I. Benveniste should refuse to pay his bill, his goods were to be warehoused on acceptance. The bank was then to refer to their local representative, Sam A. Gattegno.[49]

Acting on behalf of their British clients, British banks appealed to Banque Union to return bills to them (after consultation with their representative in Salonica) together with the required Act of Protest should the bills remain unpaid at maturity. In addition to postcards containing the bills' order numbers (without names) sent to Banque Union,[50] the letters of instruction referred to the Jewish Salonican drawees (e.g., Carasso Frères and Saltiel & Fils), with British firms listed as drawers.[51] Regarding banks located in the British colonies – e.g., the National Bank of India, Ltd. in Aden – although the receipt of documentary bills drawn on Salonica was approved, they declared that their head office in London was the source authorised to make the suitable arrangements with Banque Union officials.[52]

7.2.3.2 Dutch Creditors

Because the Netherlands had no clearing arrangements with Greece, Dutch firms acted in much the same manner as their British counterparts. So, for example, a Dutch suede-dressing firm in Tilburg deferred a debt dating from February 1932 for merchandise stored in the Banque Union warehouse in the Free Zone by order of their Jewish agent, E. Aroesti & Cie.[53] The supplier instructed Banque Union to transmit all of the instructions for total or partial delivery of these goods to the mentioned agent. At the same time, the Dutch exporter submitted an invoice made out to Salvator E. Florentin "*de v[otre]/v[ille]* . . . delivered against cashing the amount indicated, which you will remit by a check on New York". On 13 August, the factory confirmed receipt of the check.[54] That is, due to the absence of clearing agreements, Dutch firms often resorted to third-country financial institutions to arrange for payment of Greek debts (see section 7.4).

In the following sub-chapters (7.3 and 7.4) we explore some of the arrangements devised to cope with – and sometimes circumvent – the foreign exchange restrictions that threatened the viability of individual entrepreneurs and entire industries. Although our examples come primarily from the world of Jewish entrepreneurship, the same methods were used throughout the Greek business world during this period.

7.3 Settlement of Debts by Unfreezing Accounts

Despite the prohibition on the transfer of foreign capital out of the country legislated years earlier, orderly regulation and control of foreign exchange flows were practiced only after 1932. The freezing of accounts was particularly troublesome, as the following memorandum prepared by the British consul reveals:

> In April 1932, all monies lying to the credit of foreigners in Greek banks became blocked and could only be utilised by the owners for the purchase of property in Greece or for payment of taxes. All monies [being] the property of a foreign subject or firm not resident in the country also became blocked automatically if placed on Bank Account after that date. . . . Recently the Greek government permitted Egyptian nationals and Greek residents in Egypt access to blocked monies if they came to Greece as visitors and expended the money in this country. The accounts are not transferable, however, and may only be released to the actual owner. On represen-

tations being made to the relevant Greek authorities a similar concession has now
been made to persons or firms established in the United Kingdom.[55]

The uncertainty felt by foreign suppliers, including Jews who had immigrated from
Salonica to France, threatened to decimate the international Jewish commercial and
financial networks. Among those hurt by the currency regulations were the creditors
of those Jewish émigré entrepreneurs who had not yet realised their assets and whose
funds remained in closed accounts. Hence, only the transfer of those accounts to the
émigrés' commercial representatives in Salonica enabled their creditors to collect and
thus close outstanding accounts.

In a series of memoranda sent by Henry Mason, Ltd., Worsted Spinners and
Manufacturers in Shipley, northern England, the fabric supplier informed Banque
Union that they had instructed their British bank to accept on their behalf GRD 12,000
deposited in their name in a blocked account held by Matarasso & Rousso.[56]
Instructions sent by the British bank stated as follows:

> We beg to return herewith the above-mentioned bill [made out to Matarasso &
> Rousso], together with a letter of authority from our customers [i.e., Henry Mason]
> addressed to you and shall be glad if, upon completion of the transfer from Blocked
> Account of the GRD 12,000 mentioned, to our order, you will kindly deliver the
> relevant bill and protest herewith to the drawee [i.e., Matarasso & Rousso], free of
> payment against receipt.[57]

Fearing passage of new regulations that would retard payment, the British bank
made the following additional request to Banque Union in a telegram dated 18 July
1932: "... until such time as the Drachmae [*sic*] are definitely under our control, subject
to your laws, the bill must be retained in your hands".[58] A later cable, dated 3 August
1932, instructed Banque Union to deliver the bill, free of payment, to Mason's agent,
D. S. Recanati, against his receipt, endorsing the bill over to him.[59] It seems that the
Italian firm Gaetano Lanza SA, Milan, applied the same method with respect to other
drafts drawn on Matarasso & Rousso.[60]

7.4 Adjusting to New Conditions: Foreign Trade Transactions

How did Jewish entrepreneurs respond to the new foreign trade regulations? In this
section we discuss transactions made immediately after the new regulations came into
effect, a period that coincided with the final days of Germany's Weimar Republic. The
following examples are of new transactions executed a bit later, immediately after the
suspension of Greek commercial debts in April 1932. They have been chosen to illustrate the range of financial strategies adopted by Jewish merchants active in this sector.

The credit crunch caused by local bank fears regarding the issuance of new letters
of credit impeded international trade but especially the transit trade. A case in point is
the September 1932 clearing agreement signed with Yugoslavia, which anchored the
transit trade in special cash vouchers issued by the Bank of Greece (see above, section
7.2.2). A Yugoslav exporter would obtain such a voucher, which was made out upon
payment of the corresponding amount in drachmas, to be drawn in exchange for
convertible notes to be used exclusively when paying for Greek goods having an

equivalent value and imported into Yugoslavia. The Yugoslav Central Bank would then exchange these notes for dinars.[61] This system further complicated the conduct of the transit trade to Yugoslavia via Salonica and led to increased dependence on co-ethnic trustees on both sides of the border, especially among Jews.

In a letter dated 12 July 1932, addressed to Banque Union and written in French by Ing. Albert Gattegno in the name of Technokommerz, an agency representing foreign engineering firms in Skopje, Gattegno attempted to obtain a letter of credit for his British supplier.

> During my last visit at your offices I spoke with the honourable A. Nehama [the Banque Union manager] about a transaction I was about to finish, for which I would need to open a credit account in favour of my correspondents. It indeed concerns a consignment of pipes to be sent from England or Germany in transit through Salonica (possibly in one or more shipments) during this coming September. I would like to open an irrevocable letter of credit[62] in favour of the sender of the goods for an amount of £500 to £600, plus or minus, or for an equivalent value in Swiss francs. This procedure should be conducted in my name and the name of a third party that I will provide later, and at my risk. Mr. D. Jahiel of Athens will be the guarantor. It goes without saying that as soon as you are in possession of the shipping documents regarding this consignment, I will arrange to retrieve those documents from your offices or elsewhere, through your correspondents, against payment of the value in addition to your costs and commission. To expedite my business, based on your promise of help . . . and after having given you my trust, I would greatly be obliged if you would let me know at the earliest convenience if you are ready to open this credit account by sending me the required documents for my signature.[63]

This letter apparently refers to the case of a Jewish importer from Skopje, Yugoslavia, who was interested in maintaining his transit trade business within the framework of the new Greek international trade regulations. To this end, he was attempting to arrange for a loan from the Banque Union in Salonica. To qualify for the loan, he was required to transmit the name of his co-religionist guarantor, located in Athens.

Trade with the Weimar Republic was conducted through barter transactions, that is, against $500 (30 September 1932) for imported oriental tobacco, $500 (15 October 1932) worth of woollen cloth would be exchanged.[64] Otherwise, the transaction was fixed in drachmas: Hermann Seeber, a German producer of thermometers and glass instruments, in an arrangement with Banque Union, agreed to deliver its products against their value of 130.60 RM in drachmas (RM = Reichsmark = Goldmark = 1/2790 kg. of fine gold, 26 July 1932), as per government directives.[65] Similarly, the German firm of Leonhardt & Martini (as it was known at the time) informed Banque Union that they had sent two parcels of chemicals (zinc stearate, titanium oxide, and magnesium carbonate) to the bank's address and requested that the bank deliver the merchandise, against payment, to their Greek representative, Horras. They also requested that the bank transfer to them the equivalent in drachmas of the sum 43.75 RM. While payment was to be forwarded to their address in Hanover, the commercial bill of lading was to be delivered to Horras, together with all the necessary information, including the certificate of origin approved by Hanover's Chamber of Commerce and demanded by Salonica's Chamber of Commerce.[66]

In order to bypass the clearing procedures, transactions were often conducted through American banks (section 7.2.2). Chininfabrik Braunschweig Buchler & Co., a German pharmaceuticals manufacturer (of quinine, etc.), might post a parcel to Banque Union containing codeine and papaverine for the Jewish pharmacist Pinhas Angel against payment of $15. To avoid the clearing, they requested that the bank transfer the payment, by check, to New York after deduction of the bank's expenses.[67] The German firm also directed the bank to its representative in Salonica, in this case the Jewish merchant Bernard Landau (see section 8.3), should any difficulties arise.[68]

Although Belgium had a clearing agreement with Greece, Belgian auto parts suppliers still instructed Banque Union to deliver an invoice payable in US dollars in the form of an approved bank check. The six packages in question, which contained brake linings, were intended for the Jewish drawee, Réné J. Bensussan.[69]

Partial clearing agreements made ordinary transactions infinitely easier to expedite. The same could be said when there were no agreements held. As an illustration of the first case, a Hungarian exporter of ironware completed a transaction for metal hoop rings destined for a Salonican firm, Georges Floyennides, first through Lloyds Triestino, via Trieste, and then through the Greek firm's direct Jewish representative, Léon Recanati, against payment by a check sent directly to its account in Zurich.[70] Regarding the second, an American manufacturer of dipped and moulded rubber goods sent a draft drawn on Yakar & Ovadia. The draft covered a shipment of five cartons of rubber toy balloons, which were consigned to Banque Union. The manufacturer asked Banque Union to deliver the shipment upon acceptance of the enclosed draft and the collection of payment on their behalf.[71]

7.5 Emigration, Liquidation and Firm Relocation

The new regulations accelerated emigration which obviously initiated ownership changes, including liquidation of partnerships; for example, Carasso & Varsano liquidated in 1932 following Carasso's settlement in British Mandatory Palestine, whereas his partner, Varsano, settled in Paris.[72] The firm of Joseph Francès (or alternatively spelled Francès, est. 1888) had a similar fate. The company operated a building materials store (*droguerie*) and later sold cotton yarn and cheap cotton fabrics (*cabot*) (Appendix 5, no. 266); in the beginning of 1931, it still was in commercial collaboration with Isac Nahmias and Albert Gattegno. Following the departure of Joseph Francès for London, the firm was dissolved. Francès's now former collaborators, Isac Nahmias and Albert Gattegno then set up a partnership in the same sector (Appendix 8, no. 136).[73] Expanded regulation of foreign currency and thus of international trade increased the importance of personal contacts (today's "networking") with the authorities.[74] These resources tended to be more readily available to entrepreneurs belonging to the majority ethnic group – indigenous Greeks – than to Jews. After considering the rising constraints imposed by the economic and political environment, several Jewish entrepreneurs chose to immigrate to traditional destinations in the West (see Chapter 3), where they hoped to relocate their businesses.

As one might anticipate, they found it difficult to transfer their assets to their new homelands. One approach to overcoming these constraints was to maintain business ties with current or former partners, family members and others. Consider Vital Albert Cohen, originally from Old Greece, who founded (1908–1910) the confection and hosiery-trading house of Vital Cohen & Cie., with a partner, Isac A. Gattegno.

Following Gattegno's emigration in 1930, the firm was dissolved, with Cohen, as sole owner reopening the business under the new name of Vital Cohen (Appendix 8, no. 143),[75] (see also section 9.1). For Jewish émigré entrepreneurs who had no partners, firm management was often transferred to trusted individuals who acted as their agents after being given the power of attorney. In a "Note pour la Banque Amar SA", Vita Amar informed the institution that in addition to managing his own import–export agency, he was also occupied with the liquidation of the inheritance left by the late David Elia Torres, who had settled in Manchester – the British textile centre – while leaving his property in Salonica.[76]

To facilitate the liquidation and transfer of their assets from Greece to France, Jewish businessmen often delayed naturalisation in their new homes while retaining their Greek addresses[77] (section 3.4). The few available letters written by Jewish émigrés to Banque Union probably meant to obtain confirmation of their Salonica addresses (no such letters were found addressed to non-Jewish Greek clients)[78] prior to their becoming French citizens hint at the forms of assistance that Banque Union provided these clients with respect to the realisation and eventual transfer of their Greek assets. The cited correspondence between bank officials and the firm of J. Gattegno indicates that Banque Union continued to manage either all or part of Gattegno's assets as well as commercial affairs. Accordingly, J. Gattegno regularly received letters from Banque Union, on the 18th and 27th of each month. In the final letter he was told that his storehouse, which had been abandoned by Papaditriou et Ergas (importers of hides from the hinterland),[79] had been rented to Mr. Samuel G. Yeni (another importer of hides active in the transit trade, section 5.3.4) for an amount of GRD 10,500 for one year only, payable semi-annually. In reply, Gattegno wrote,

> We thank you for this service and believe that this rental was made for one year. It is understood that at the end of the period, our freedom of action will be reinstated. We have no doubt that you took all the necessary steps regarding the payment of income tax in such manner that we may be proportionally credited for the diminishing returns from the rent.[80]

Although Jacques Gattegno had immigrated to Marseilles before 1930, he delayed his official exit from the Salonica business. An advertisement in *Guide Sam* (1930: 214) lists the firm's branches in Marseille (J. Gattegno, 35 Rue Pavillon, Marseille, Importation-Exportation-Commission, Cuirs et Peaux [skins and leather]) as well as Salonica (Moché, Gattegno et Cie. Fondée en 1885, 12 Rue Salamine) (Appendix 5, no. 242). It appears that by July 1932, Gattegno had become interested in dissolving the Salonica partnership and transferring his holdings through Banque Union, which intervened with the Greek authorities on Gattegno's behalf. Assuming that Gattegno had yet to be naturalised as a French citizen,[81] the validated residence certificate mentioned in the letter pertains to his Greek address. Otherwise, as a foreigner in Greece, he was prohibited from taking such actions. To be sure, these financial constraints apparently affected all émigrés, not just entrepreneurs. For instance, the dental surgeon I. H. Covo, then living at 107 Rue Lafayette, Paris, declared the following in reply to a Banque Union request: "Herewith is the certificate of residence demanded . . . I think it will be valid . . . for the prospective remissions".[82]

In light of these circumstances, it appears that the return of an isolated number of émigrés to Salonica in 1932 was designed to enable realisation of their assets as well as to prevent the freezing of their accounts. Consider Haim Marcos, a former exchange broker who returned to Salonica from Paris in 1932. In Paris, Marcos had operated a store dealing in the wholesale and semi-wholesale trade in small metal goods (*quincailleries*). In Salonica, he was entrusted with managing the enterprise of his friend Haim Mechoulam. The firm of Mechoulam had suspended payments (1931) and concluded arrangements with his creditors in return for payment of 40 to 60 percent of his debts. But, because some creditors had not accepted this arrangement, the firm could not work under its proper name if it wished to comply with the law; it was thus forced to operate under a pseudonym – which Marcos provided.[83]

Many of the Jewish entrepreneurs who were unable to transfer their capital prior to the inauguration of the new regulations frequently chose to act as silent partners in active Salonican firms. They also often transferred the power of attorney needed to manage their affairs to relatives and other trusted individuals. These strategies benefited the émigrés as well as those who remained in the city. First and foremost, it enabled the émigrés to protect their assets; second, it prevented the government from blocking their capital accounts because the funds were now treated as belonging to foreigners. For instance, a long-established drapery shop, Mano & Co. (est. 1885), was transformed into a *société en commandite* (1932), with its partners listed as Gracia Moise Bourla née Mano – who retained her maiden name, Mano, solely to perpetuate the company's name – as well as Aron J. Yacar and Elie Semtov Saltiel. Mathius Joseph Carasso, who had settled in Milan where he now operated a vast hosiery shop (*bonneterie*), also acted as a silent partner in Mano & Co. To protect his holdings, he conferred a power of attorney upon Joseph Broudo.[84] In another case, following the emigration of one of the Mahel brothers to Paris, the old firm of Fratelli Mahel (Appendix 5, no. 22) was dissolved, leaving Salomon Mahel of Mahel Rousso & Cie. to manage what remained of the business.[85]

Alternatively, by leaving family members or business partners behind in Salonica, émigrés could exploit their residence in another country to expand their commercial networks or at least continue to finance their Salonican firms. Evidence of this pattern is found among the Salonican émigrés in France, where local Jewish entrepreneurs often assisted those recently arrived from Salonica. For instance, David Bloch, a well-known and respected local businessman,[86] had been a partner in the French firm of Fernandez & Bloch, established when Gino Fernandez immigrated to Paris in 1920 (the partnership was dissolved only in 1936).[87] Importantly for us, even after Fernandez emigrated, his company, bearing his full name, remained registered with Salonica's Chamber of Commerce (1937) as dealers in insurance and exporters of rawhide. The firm's Patras branch (Old Greece) was managed by Maurice Bayonna, a local Jewish businessman.[88]

Some Jewish firms from Salonica invested in Jewish firms abroad to protect their financial future. Maison Fils de David Hasson, which maintained a branch in Marseilles, received assistance from the above-mentioned David Bloch, who held 40 percent in the firm branch bearing his name, which he himself managed.[89]

Capital transfers – despite the new strictures – to foreign partners were often executed to finance the expansion of commercial networks. For instance, Albert Saporta (Appendix 5, no. 370; Appendix 8, no. 228), a textile wholesaler still living in Salonica, transformed his company (est. 1904) into a mixed-liabilities corporation during the 1930s. His silent partner was the Salonican Salomon S. Yeni, who had settled in Paris (year unknown) to promote the export of French textiles to Salonica.[90]

Beginning in April 1932, Jewish banks began to protect their income from transactions made outside of Greece. The commissions collected by Banque Union were usually deposited by foreign suppliers in their local banks, which provided Greek banks with a mechanism for bypassing the new regulations. In the Magrisso transaction, for example, Spalato, the Italian exporter, confirmed a deposit of the commission and port expenses due to Banque Union in Banca Commerciale Italiana of Milan, where they would remain until Banque Union claimed them.[91] In another case, a Belgian supplier proposed that Banque Union require its foreign clients to remit their expenses and fees to a local Belgian bank.[92] This cooperation between foreign banks and Jewish banks in Greece apparently continued until the late 1930s.

7.6 Shifting Jewish Business to the Old-New Homeland

The second major foreign destination chosen by Salonica's emigrating entrepreneurs was Eretz Yisra'el, still under the control of the British Mandate. The Recanati family is a case in point. Harry Recanati, whose father Leon had owned a large tobacco plant in Salonica (section 5.5), described his decision to immigrate (1933) to Mandatory Palestine in these words:

> Devaluation of the drachma and the behaviour of the Greek tax and regulatory authorities with respect to foreign currency made life for an honest businessman extremely difficult. In order to smooth things over, they had to either activate their connections with people in high places [higher authorities] or find favour in official eyes by some other means. My father, a man of character, could not bow to these demands even though he did have powerful friends. He preferred life in a country with a stable economy and an honest government. We therefore decided to move to Palestine [in 1935] where some of our family had already settled.[93]

After his decision was made, Recanati faced the quandary of how to transfer his financial assets to Palestine. He chose to assign local Jews remaining in Greece the task of managing their funds and acting on their behalf in other arenas, too. To quote Harry Recanati:

> More than three years were required for my father to liquidate his business assets and find others to fill the public offices he held . . . excellent associates fortunately surrounded him as well as some good friends, who helped him complete this project. This was especially true of Asher Malah, the only Jew sitting in the Greek senate, and Edwin Saltiel, Greece's honorary Consul to Japan. . . . [94]

The transfer of wealth that sometimes accompanied emigration was not necessarily completed in one step. Many entrepreneurs, like Leon Recanati, were forced to shift their properties and wealth in stages, after first establishing a branch in their destination country. Only after the bulk of their funds and moveable properties had arrived in their new country did the owners actually leave Salonica. Consider the long-established trading house of Saporta Frères (est. 1918) (Appendix 5, no. 171), which was dissolved in 1932 following the retirement of Elie Saporta, who settled in Palestine. Samuel Saporta, a brother, also settled in Palestine in 1932, leaving the remaining partner, their brother Isac (Appendix 8, no. 88), to manage the company. Once in Palestine, Samuel operated a shop selling electrical appliances while simultaneously investing in Mandatory Palestine's budding construction industry.[95]

Other members of the Saporta family conducted their business in a similar way. The firm of Société pour la Commerce du Bois, Iomtov Is Saporta (Appendix 5, no. 197; see also Appendix 8, no. 107), had established an active branch in British Mandatory Palestine by 1933, under the name of Fils de Yomtov Saporta & Cie. Albert Benveniste, a relative, joined them as an equal partner. While Isac Saporta (son of I(Y)omtov Saporta) directed the branch in Palestine, his brother Meir Saporta directed the branch in Salonica.[96]

Jewish shipping firms were prodded into transferring their activities from Salonica to the coastal ports of Mandatory Palestine in response to severe competition from the state-supported Greek shipping industry. The fate of Salonica's Jewish marine transport industry was decided by the emigration of Jewish port workers to Palestine.[97] Beginning in 1932, Allalouf & Co.,[98] shippers and insurance agents, maintained branches in Tel Aviv, Jaffa, and Haifa, which were managed by Elie Allalouf, with a commercial department directed by Isac Cohen. Elie Allalouf and Sam Maïssa also purchased several plots of land near Tel Aviv. In 1937, with two-thirds of the maritime, aviation, and insurance trade captured by Allalouf & Co. partners working in Palestine, the firm had achieved *"une place enviable dans les milieux de la branche"*.[99] Similarly, the Jewish-owned firm of Revah, Mattia & Co. (est. 1932), which was engaged in international transport, customs, export, sales, and consignments for Yugoslav trading houses, also gradually extended its activity toward Mandatory Palestine[100] even though its business was satisfactory thanks to the expertise of its senior management.[101]

European financial institutions continued to seek information, for their own purposes, about these Jewish émigrés to British Mandatory Palestine. Banque Union thus began to receive information requests from foreign banks regarding the financial viability and honesty of Jewish businessmen who had emigrated from Salonica and wished to act as business representatives in their new homeland.[102] The Anglo-Palestine Bank, Ltd. in Jaffa would forward these requests, stamped "confidential", to Banque Union, Salonique [*sic*]. Also requested was detailed information, including "means and financial standing", of businessmen such as Mr. Jacques Abram Beja of Tel Aviv, formerly of Salonica.[103] The Dresdner Bank sought precise information on K. D. Angel while promising to keep the information confidential and suggesting that it would give Banque Union information in return.[104] Similarly, the Swiss Dairy Industries Association requested that Banque Union provide information on the financial status of the Salonican trading house Lewis Is. Nahmias, and asked whether it could recommend a serious and energetic agent for this transnational (Greece–Palestine) firm.[105]

7.7 Transforming the Jewish-Owned Economy in Salonica

With the international economic recession and the local financial crisis came a stream of delayed payments, bankruptcies, and firm liquidations.[106] Small businesses closed, one after the other, although others opened. According to Salonica's commercial guide (Christodoulou, 1936), 649 bankruptcies were officially declared while 1,000 new businesses were formed during the years 1929–1934.[107] Among the well-known Jewish companies that closed their doors were Alcalay & Juda (Appendix 5, no. 89), dissolved in April 1931,[108] and Israël & Vidal Tiano (est. 1922) (Appendix 5, no. 151), dissolved by mutual agreement in late 1931, with Vidal subsequently becoming the firm's sole owner–manager (*pour son propre compte*).[109] The partnership of Naar Moise & Abram (est. 1910) was dissolved in 1932 after declaring bankruptcy.[110] Another partnership, Francès & Menache (est. 1928) was liquidated in 1935 due to losses suffered by its partners, Abram Menache and Azriel Francès.[111] Fratelli Mahel (Appendix 5, no. 22), one of the local market's largest and most respected traders in oils and fats since 1910, suffered great losses due to its inability to cope with the intensifying competition. After losing the greater part of its massive capital reserves, the firm was dissolved in late 1932.[112]

Emigration to Mandatory Palestine therefore intensified two structural trends already observable in Salonica: dissolution and reduction in the scope of the firm's activities. For instance, following the emigration of the Saltiel brothers to Palestine, Saltiel Fréres & Cohen (see Appendix 5, no. 297) was dissolved, with the remaining partner, Saltiel S. Cohen (1932), continuing to operate the firm on a much reduced scale, selling draperies in a small shop until 1935–1936. After economic recovery began to be felt in 1936, Cohen joined the firm of A. Arianoutsos & Co. (see Appendix 8, no. 170), a men's clothing manufacturer. By 1937 he could again open a large store selling wholesale and retail draperies.[113]

Similar changes in management awaited the partnership of Fils de Moise Saltiel (Appendix 5, no. 367) following Jacob Saltiel's emigration to Palestine in 1934. The remaining partners, Joseph and Isac Saltiel (Appendix 8, no. 226), continued to conduct the firm's business, with great success.[114] In contrast, Altcheh & Co., Nouveautes, a firm dealing in the retail sale of wool, cotton and silk cloth originally owned by Bension and Isac Altcheh, was dissolved in 1932 following Isac's emigration to Mandatory Palestine.[115] Aron Florentin & Co., established in 1924 (or 1927) by Aron Florentin and his brother Isac (who served as a silent partner) was dissolved in 1933 when Isac, a Yugoslav citizen, departed for Tel Aviv. Aron, a Greek subject, continued to run the firm single-handedly.[116] Sefiha & Benveniste, established in 1928, was dissolved in 1931 following Benveniste's [first name not available] emigration to Palestine. However, the firm was reconstituted as Sefiha Frères (Appendix 8, no. 79) in 1932.[117]

Emigration of a partner was therefore one mechanism employed to sustain a firm's operations, even if it involved limiting its scope. Another method used was to sustain partnerships as sole proprietorships while adding silent partners from the Salonican Jewish Diaspora (see section 9.2). Isac Abram de Mayo, a textile wholesaler, became the sole owner of Fils d'Abram de Mayo (1926–1932) (Appendix 8, no. 218), a mixed liability firm (*société en commandite*), following dissolution of his partnership (1932). Among the firm's original owners were de Mayo's brothers and two silent partners (*commanditaires*): Moise Acher of Milan and Zaharia Vital of Patras.[118]

Still another approach to firm survival under conditions of absent ownership is represented by Humbert Scialom & Hassid (Appendix 8, no. 78). Although the exact date of Humbert Scialom's departure is unknown, we do know that he lived abroad during the 1930s and that his business interests (export of medicinal opium) in Salonica were managed by his partner, Asher Hassid.[119] In another instance, after settling in Milan, Joseph Mordoh, son of the late silkworm cocoon exporter Salomon Mordoh, handed over the management of his affairs to his brothers-in-law, Yacoel and Mallah, who lived in Salonica. Only Aron Mallah had the authority to act as a signatory (Appendix 8, no. 269).[120] In like manner, Salomon Nehama (Appendix 8, no. 318), who had immigrated to Paris in 1932, left his brother Samuel to direct the Salonica branch of his firm, which was involved in commission representation. Only after Salomon's retirement did Samuel list the firm under his own name and take full responsibility for its operation.[121]

Nevertheless, because the economic recession was international in scope, a number of Jewish entrepreneurs were forced to return to Greece, especially to Salonica, or to settle elsewhere. Consider Haim Saltiel, who had settled in France but returned in 1935 in order to establish a new partnership including his daughter, Ms. Esther Haim Saltiel (Appendix 8, no. 227).[122] Yet, difficulties in concluding business in Salonica prevented Jewish businessmen from realising their emigration plans. After returning from Palestine, where he had thought he might finally settle, Pepo Menahem concluded some business in colonial goods with the firm Isac & Charles Saias (Appendix 8, no. 11), which closed due to losses. Menachem was later unable to dispose of his rolling capital in order to conclude his affairs; he was then forced to live off the rent from his fixed property holdings, including a building shared with the firm Moise et Albert Isac Navarro (Appendix 8, no. 53).[123]

With the reduction in the number of Jewish entrepreneurs and enterprises remaining in Salonica, a shortage of Jewish commercial credit began to be felt. Small Jewish-owned lending enterprises faced difficulties in mobilising capital due to this shortage, made more serious by the restructuring of the Greek banking industry. Several firms therefore resorted to partnerships as one method for increasing efficiency as well as expanding resources. The Salem brothers, Haim, Joseph, and Salomon, operated a very small-scale banking institution (Appendix 8, no. 282). The firm's decrease in revenues was due to the termination of its membership in the Union des Banques and its inability to obtain a license to conduct exchange transactions.[124] Under similar circumstances, Ipalliliki Micropistossis, owned by Albert Jacob Houlli (Appendix 8, no. 280), was compelled to add a subdivision for selling drapery and use the revenues to increase its capital designated for its small credit agency (*un bureau de petit crédit*). According to the Notary's Act, the associates could deduct only a very small part of their profits as salaries, with the remaining profits transferred to the firm's capital.[125] In the same fashion, Oikos Mikropistosseos, Ouziel & Hazan (Appendix 8, no. 281), reconstituted in 1935, engaged in small-scale loans (*petit crédit*) and insurance, with one set of activities supporting the other.[126]

The growing shortage in credit for Jewish businessmen threatened the survival of micro-scale Jewish entrepreneurs (e.g., peddlers, small shopkeepers, and craftsmen) in particular. In response, a new source of cheap credit for these businesses, as well as unemployed workers, was established through cooperation between the Jewish community and international Zionist organisations. After recognising the growing problem, the Zionist publicist Shimon Bourla (whose brothers, Menachem and Moise Bourla, were leaders in maritime transport) urged Jewish community leaders in late 1929 to create a fund for small-scale loans (*caise de petits prêts*),[127] to be made available at reasonable rates. The fund, once established, was not registered as a legal entity (*juridical corpus*). According to an internal statute, it was controlled by the Jewish community, which had the right to appoint its board of directors. In 1938, seven out of the nine board members were appointed by the Jewish community.[128]

Lending capital for micro-scale business thus soon grew. The two factors leading to this surprising event were, first, the Jewish elite's response to Shimon Bourla's campaign; and second, the reviving international social solidarity, fostered by Zionist institutions, between Jews living in the core states and Jews living in peripheral countries. The fund's seed money, equalling GRD 75,000, was donated by Salonica's Jewish community, with another GRD 100,000 collected through a special appeal. However, the fund could increase the number of loans and their size only in direct proportion to the contributions received from a Jewish-American organisation, the American Joint Reconstruction Foundation (hereinafter the Foundation) was established by the American Jewish Joint Distribution Committee (Joint or JDC) and the Jewish Colonization Association (JCA)[129] after World War I to help finance and develop co-operation between Jews from various countries, especially those in Eastern Europe. Moshe Ossoskin, who was the general manager of the Foundation in Romania and responsible for its activities in the six Balkan states, visited Salonica, probably at the beginning of 1938. He documented the fact that the Salonica fund had received two loans of GRD 412,500 each (in 1933 and 1936) from the Foundation. In addition, in March 1936, the community's *caise de petits prêts* purchased majority shares in the Salonica–Palestine Society (Société Anonyme Salonique–Palestine), which later ceased its activities. Its active and passive resources were also dedicated to the Fund for Small Loans.[130]

The list of loans approved during 1930–1937 indicate that the average loan was for more than GRD 2,000 before 1933 but grew to about GRD 3,000 after additional contributions were received in 1933. The great majority were short term, to be repaid in weekly or bi-weekly payments. In very few cases were the loans repaid in one lump sum, adjusted to current value (see Table 7.7a).

The extension of small inexpensive loans also enabled unemployed Jewish workers with liquidity constraints to re-enter the same labour market as small-scale entrepreneurs.[131] Once the prospects of self-employment appeared, they were motivated by "push" factors to broaden the Jewish-owned economy by opening micro-enterprises (see Table 7.7b). The rise in the number of loans as well as their value between 1930 and 1937 indicate the positive effect the fund had on the Jewish-owned economy. The Jewish-owned economy during the mid-1930s was therefore able to expand. The entry

Table 7.7a   Confirmed Loans, Salonica 1930–1937

Year	Number of Loans	Total Value in Greek Drachmas	Average Value of Loan
1930	558	1,148,000	2,057.3
1931	764	1,477,525	1,933.9
1932	768	1,519,100	1,978.0
1933	903	2,339,100	2,590.4
1934	1,003	3,103,900	3,094.6
1935	1,062	3,526,300	3,320.4
1936	1,414	5,261,500	3,721.0
1937	1,721	6,021,400	3,498.8

Source: Adapted from Ossoskin 1967: 214.

Note: The data for 1929, which is excluded here, relates to only the second half of December and thus includes only 33 loans for the sum total of GRD 82,000.

Table 7.7b   Distribution of Loans by Occupation and Value, Salonica 1937

Occupation	Percentage of Total Number of Loans Extended	Percentage of Total Sum Borrowed
Traders	36	52.2
Craftsmen	26	23.2
Hawkers	18	10.7
Professionals	3	2.5
Others	17	11.4
Total	100	100

Source: Adapted from Ossoskin 1967: 214.

of new small-scale entrepreneurs more than compensated for the loss in numbers of the medium- to large-scale entrepreneurs who had emigrated. Nevertheless, given their origins in the working class, these new entrepreneurs were unable to compensate for the loss in practiced entrepreneurial skills.

In the following chapters, we turn to the entrepreneurial structural patterns adopted by larger Jewish firms, those that turned to Jewish banks for credit. Information on the ability of these firms to repay their outstanding debts will provide the foundations for our examination of the changing Jewish firm structure (Chapter 8) and business management patterns (Chapter 9).

8 | Recovery and Survival within the Consolidating Greek Autarky, 1934–1937

With the onset of de-globalisation in trade and capital movements in April 1932, new opportunities for entrepreneurial ventures were created. Government restrictions on imports, high tariffs, and the rapid devaluation of the drachma drove up the prices of imported goods, which stimulated industrial and agricultural production of their substitutes. Within the evolving closed economy, the stimulation of wheat cultivation benefited peasants, particularly smallholders. Rising demand for mass consumption goods likewise stimulated domestic manufacturing. Moreover, the expansion of cultivated areas dedicated to the domestic equivalents of imported produce somewhat balanced the decline in export crops (tobacco and currants).[1] Hence, while the new opportunities in the consolidating Greek autarky were based on intensified state intervention, the new opportunities in the foreign trade passing through Salonica's port (see Chapters 2, 4, and 5) were connected to Germany's emergence as Greece's primary trading partner. With respect to the former, Jewish entrepreneurs found themselves in an inferior position due to their reduced ties with national economic elites; as to the latter, the Jewish economy was placed in a vulnerable position. Weimar Germany's transition to Nazi Germany (30 January 1933) temporally coincided with the Greek economy's budding recovery.

The year 1934 thus seemed to mark a turning point: "Primavera" signs were observed in the Salonican business world,[2] and Germany became Greece's main trading partner (section 6.1.3). Based on micro data culled from surviving Banque Amar records (see Introduction), this chapter, which covers the time span between 1934 and 1937 or, more accurately, March 1938, the date of Germany's annexation of Austria (*Anschluss*) (section 10.2), explores the long-term Jewish entrepreneurial response to the new conditions. These included transformation of the Jewish-owned economy's sectoral structure and its market orientation on the national as well as the international level. Unlike the Jewish small tradesmen who relied primarily on ethnic resources (section 7.7), entrepreneurs listed with the city's Chamber of Commerce and Industry[3] enjoyed access to substantially greater credit through commercial banks, including Banque Amar, against suitable collateral.

This chapter, which focuses on the Jewish firms still operating in the city, either in their original or reconstituted form[4] (see sections 7.5 and 7.7), also addresses the question of whether anti-Semitism was used as a competitive strategy much as it had been in Germany (1933–1937) before the "Aryanisation" of Jewish enterprises (i.e., the transfer of Jewish assets into the hands of either Christian Germans or the state).[5] It likewise explores the effects on Jewish entrepreneurial activity of the increasingly close connections between the Greek and the German economies. We therefore focus here on two interrelated aspects of Jewish entrepreneurship: entrepreneurial strategy and branch structure. We argue that international economic trends and the Greek economy's recovery affected Jewish entrepreneurs not only as members of a minority within an emerging nation-state but also as Jews.

8.1 An Inter-Ethnic Comparative Overview: The Tobacco Industry

Taken together, the Jewish and Greek firms listed in Banque Amar's archive comprised about 22 percent (606 out of 2,726) of all the firms registered with Salonica's Chamber of Commerce and Industry in 1938.[6] Nevertheless, the Jewish firms mainly listed for 1935–1937 (Appendix 8) reached about 35 percent (328 out of 935) of Jewish firms registered with the Chamber of Commerce in 1938 (935 out of 2,726) (section 9.1).[7] We can therefore be confident that this "natural" sample represents Salonica's registered Jewish firms for the late 1930s fairly accurately.[8]

However, only 16 percent (278 out of 1684) of the Greek firms registered with Salonica's Chamber of Commerce and Industry had dealings with Banque Amar, far below the proportion of Greek firms registered with Salonica's Chamber of Commerce and Industry (62 percent, or 1684 out of 2,726).[9] We can consequently conclude that the bank's Greek clientele, again if treated as a "natural" sample, may not have been representative. Whereas Jewish firms were inherently over-represented among the Jewish Banque Amar's clients, Greek firms were inherently under-represented for the same reason. It can also be assumed that the number of Greek entrepreneurs who turned to Jewish banks was lower because the Greeks had other sources of credit. Just as importantly, efficient communal information networks provided Jewish banks with more accurate information about the solvency of their Jewish clients as opposed to potential Greek clients. In an environment of liquidity constraints, this represented an important advantage to lenders as well as borrowers (see section 9.3 below). These circumstances explain the prominence of Jewish firms in our sources and, consequently, our database. Still, the common denominator between the Jewish and the Greek firms found in the sample was their registration with the Chamber of Commerce and Industry of Salonica during the 1930s just as it was for the 1920s (see Appendices 4.1 and 5). This fact enabled us to derive the structural characteristics of Jewish and Greek firms in isolation from the changes in branch structure during the same period, even if it somewhat reduces the desired level of statistical reliability.

The distributions of Jewish and Greek firms by branch were found to be rather similar.[10] Yet, comparing the computed representation indices of Jewish as well as of Greek entrepreneurs – given the appropriate statistical and empirical reservations – (Table 8.1) does shed some light on the structural aspects of Jewish entrepreneurship from a minority–majority perspective.

When comparing Jewish and Greek branch structure in the 1930s, one difference is particularly salient: the severe under-representation of Jewish tobacco firms, a process that marked the final decline of Jewish entrepreneurial activity in the tobacco

Table 8.1 Jewish-owned Firms (*N* =328) and Greek-owned Firms (*N* =278) by Branch (13), 1935–1937

Branch	N = 606		Percentage in Branch (B)		ERI (B/A)	
	J	G	J	G	J	G
Food and beverages	25	23	52.1	47.9	.962	1.045
Chemicals and pharmaceuticals	24	18	57.1	42.9	1.056	.934
Construction materials	5	7	41.7	58.3	.770	1.272
Metals, ironware, and metalwares	37	29	56.1	43.9	1.036	.958
Wood	16	19	45.7	54.3	.845	1.183
Hides, leather, and footwear	23	25	47.9	52.1	.885	1.135
Textiles	10	8	55.6	44.4	1.026	.969
Clothing and home textiles	92	70	56.8	43.2	1.049	.942
Printing, paper, and office equipment	19	7	73.1	26.9	1.350	.587
Tobacco	2	14	12.5	87.5	.231	1.907
Domestic wares and luxuries	7	5	58.3	41.7	1.078	.908
Trade in agricultural products	19	13	59.4	40.6	1.097	.886
Banking and large-scale commerce	49	40	55.1	44.9	1.017	.980

Source: See in Appendix 8.
Notes: J = Jewish-owned firms; G = Greek-owned firms.
A = Percentage ethnic firms (J,G) in the sample. A(J) = 54.1; A(G) = 45.9.
B = Percentage of ethnic-owned firms in a given branch.
Ethnic Representation Index (ERI) = B/A.
ERI = 1 indicates full-representation; ERI < 1 indicates under-representation; ERI > 1 indicates over-representation.

industry by the decade's end (see Table 8.1). Tobacco completed its transformation into an exclusively Greek industry as the state's economy recovered.[11] While the majority of Greek tobacco firms improved their status, only two Jewish tobacco merchants remained in the industry (nos. 252, 253); according to Banque Amar documents, one firm dealt with surplus cheap tobacco leaf (*tabacs en dechets*)[12] while the other dealt with the more expensive tobacco leaf (*tabacs en feilles*). Whereas the former was a small-scale exporter, sending goods to Switzerland and Arabia,[13] the latter was a large-scale endeavour, having signed contracts with Germany's leading tobacco firm,[14] Reemtsma of Hamburg.[15]

The co-operation between the Jewish firm Raphaël Jakob Varsano & Co. (no. 253) and Reemtsma would appear to be a continuation of clearing agreements in effect during the last days of the Weimar Republic,[16] when Reemtsma was prepared to accept a quantity of Greek tobacco against a reduction of German assets in Greece (section 7.2.1.1).[17] However, it can be argued that the steady exit of Jewish entrepreneurs from the Greek tobacco industry was closely tied to the Nazis' rise to power in January 1933; the industry's subordination to the Third Reich's economic policies frightened many Jews. The Hitlerian threat decided the fate of tobacco entrepreneurs such as Léon Recanati just when their businesses began to prosper. While on a business trip to pre-Nazi Germany, Recanati had witnessed one of Hitler's appearances before the masses, staged in a major Dresden square. As Recanati's son, Harry, later testified,

> What he heard made my father rather anxious; he told himself that if Hitler ever obtained the reins of government, the results would be disastrous for Europe and for the Jewish people. The idea of migrating from Greece began to mature in his mind.[18]

Announcement of Germany's New Plan on 24 September 1934 (section 6.1.3) led to a substantial increase in the value of Greek tobacco exports. However, Germany simultaneously threatened to condition its continued purchases of Greek tobacco on Greek orders for German industrial products.[19] Following Greece's passage of a special law (19 April 1935) favouring German imports and a final agreement on a private clearing system between Germany's Dresdner Bank and the National Bank of Greece, Reemtsma offered to buy a consignment of Greek tobacco for a total value of about five million Reichsmarks. This transaction was tied to Greek orders for German goods valued at twice that amount.[20]

The Greek tobacco industry consequently deepened its dependence on German clients, which prevented implementation of the Greek government's previous decision (20 February 1936) to cease accumulating credits in Germany by refraining from giving guarantees.[21] On 1 March 1936, the Greek government not only nullified this decision, it also increased the import quota from Germany. With the appointment of Metaxas as Minister of War (5 March 1936) and the later establishment of his dictatorship (August 1936), Greek–German commercial relations began to focus on the export of Greek tobacco to Germany, balanced primarily by the import of German-produced arms.[22]

The Greek–German trade negotiations (spring 1936) became subject to heavy pressure from Greek tobacco merchants (see below) but also from workers, who initiated strikes throughout northern Greece – but especially in Salonica – of intensity never before witnessed in the country. The Greek government's decision to increase imports from Germany was an urgent measure meant to re-stabilise the tobacco market, an act considered necessary for restoring social and political order.[23] The German cigarette firms, concerned about the fate of their considerable stockpiles of tobacco, stored in Macedonian warehouses, prodded the German press to publish false reports about the prominence of Jews among Salonica's tobacco labour activists. Such propaganda was meant to show that the communists, sworn enemies of the Third Reich, had penetrated deep into Greek labour organisations.[24]

Concurrent with the Greek unrest, German factories began conditioning their orders on the results of inspections of raw inputs. In the case of tobacco, such inspections could take place only after the leaf had been cured in Salonica's warehouses, some two months after their purchase from the growers. As tobacco is particularly sensitive to climatic conditions and thus given to decay, any increase in inspections brought the threat of order cancellations.[25] In 1936, German inspectors spread their gaze to tobacco industry workers. By May 1936, German tobacco companies (e.g., Buchler and Fal) demanded that the Union of Tobacco Workers not assign Jewish workers to the firm's Greek factories. Long-term business relationships, such as that maintained between Raphaël Jakob Varsano & Co. and Reemtsma, were thus jeopardised.[26] Other Jewish tobacco merchants were gradually excluded from or marginalised in the industry. Moreover, their disadvantages relative to Greek majority traders may have helped convince them to exit this increasingly risky sector (see section 10.2)

Although there was no evidence of official persecution of Jewish tobacco entrepreneurs in the surviving Banque Amar archive, the increasing presence of Greek entrepreneurs in the tobacco industry appears to reflect the reversed trend observed among Jewish entrepreneurs. A review of Banque Amar records relating to the thirteen Greek tobacco firms registered there indicates that these firms usually exported prime tobacco leaf to German cigarette manufacturers.[27] By utilising multiple private Greek–German clearing agreements, Greek merchants, especially members of the refugee elite, already considered important agents of German commercial interests in the pre-World War I Ottoman Empire, were able to continue supporting Germany's interests in the Orient, this time with the new nation-state.[28]

Contracts were brokered by agents who were either related by family or shared residence in the entrepreneurs' home towns or villages. These ties ensured the cohesion of the newly created international networks that bound Salonica to Germany. Ermokratis Khristoforidis, originally from Constantinople, was one of those agents. He had engaged in the tobacco trade in London and Hamburg during 1923–1929 as part of his family's business network. Following the tobacco crisis, during which he suffered great losses, he returned (1931) to Salonica.[29] However, after the clearing agreement with Germany was instituted, he again left for Hamburg, where he worked as an agent for a German firm while retaining an autonomous office in Salonica.[30] Another well-to-do merchant, Antigonos Hadjigeorgiou, whose firm had also suffered heavy losses, especially between 1930 and1933, similarly improved his business after 1934, as explained by an anonymous witness.

> The position of this firm as with all the other tobacco merchants, in the few years from 1930 to 1933, was poor and inspired no confidence. However, thanks to lucrative deals the firm has secured in 1933 and 1934 the situation has improved significantly. Yet it can still not be considered quite successful, as this would depend on the demand from tobacco buyers abroad.[31]

We should note that the term "abroad", when used by tobacco merchants, usually meant Germany, particularly Hamburg.

Greek tobacco firms subsequently prospered. Panagopoulos Frères was engaged in purchasing tobacco leaf in the name of German companies.[32] Stelios Voivodas, originally from Arginion (Old Greece), who had lived in Hamburg at some point, became a major wholesaler of tobacco leaf, which he sold primarily to Reemtsma[33] (see section 10.2).

Greek tobacco merchants eventually became the industry's leaders. For instance, Georges Hadjigeorgiou, originally from east Macedonia (probably a relative of the above-mentioned Antigonos Hadjigeorgiou), became president of the Ligue des Bureaux de Protection du Tabac.[34] Theodoros Arzoglou, chairman of the local tobacco merchants club, was engaged in purchasing tobacco leaf in the name of his son-in-law, Omiros Pissanis, whose firm had been operating out of Hamburg for many years. The two merchants also shared a common birthplace, Pontus (north-eastern Anatolia, along the southern coast of the Black Sea).[35] The majority of Greek tobacco merchants also took advantage of the clearing agreements to purchase industrial goods from German producers, which were paid for in shipments of tobacco leaf.[36]

It should therefore come as no surprise that the Greek tobacco traders' lobby did not permit Salonica's Jews, who were appalled by the German government's new racial and anti-Semitic policies, to threaten their commercial ties with Nazi Germany.[37] Beginning in 1934, Greek tobacco firms began to approach Germany's Ministry of

Foreign Affairs directly, denouncing the continued trade and cooperation of "German Christian enterprises" with their Jewish partners in Salonica. The Greek firms quite openly offered their own services as a substitute for the ties they hoped would soon be severed.[38]

Irrespective of any commercial clearing arrangements, the German tobacco market became pivotal to the continued existence of the Greek industry, because it offset changes in international demand for aromatic, high-grade and therefore expensive Greek tobacco. In the 1930s, the high taxes imposed on cigarettes and other tobacco products simply collapsed demand for this product.[39] In Egypt, imposition of a tariff, coupled with British smokers' preferences for Virginia-type American tobacco,[40] led to the drop of tobacco exports from Greece to their Greek compatriots distributors in Egypt by the mid-1920s.[41] The Greek merchant Constantin Moscoff, of Russian origin, whose head office was located in Alexandria, exported tobacco leaf to Egypt's cigarette producers through his branch in Salonica. He also owned a tobacco warehouse where he employed a large number of male and female workers in tobacco leaf manipulation. As 1929 approached, he was a partner in the established firm Moscoff & Sedenko.[42] Despite suffering serious losses, he continued to conduct his business independently after 1931. Moscoff was able to balance these losses with lucrative deals signed in 1936 with an English cigarette company in Egypt[43] (probably the Eastern Tobacco Company) for the production of the new "blended cigarette" (Virginia mixed with Greek leaf).[44]

In order to understand the difficulties burdening Jewish tobacco merchants during this period, we first describe how this trade was conducted among Greek firms. Our example is that of George Ch. Christoforides, a tobacco merchant originally from Constantinople, whose commercial activities spread from Brussels to Salonica, via Paris. When in Brussels, Christoforides was engaged in *"transactions en tabacs sur lesquelles il a eu des hauts et des bas"*. After settling in Salonica in 1935, he collaborated closely with the technical director of the Compagnie Internationale de l'Industrie des Tabacs, a Parisian firm. Christoforides also purchased small bales of inferior tobacco leaf, probably for French or Belgium monopolies, with the support of his brother, Dimos Christoforides, a tannery owner, who provided him with guarantees for the required bank loans. These tobacco parcels were regularly pledged to the National Bank of Greece, with the pledges cashed after the goods were exported.[45]

When confronted with such a web of internal interests and external events, Jewish entrepreneurs found themselves in a subordinate position when competing with Greek business elites.[46] Not being on the National Bank's list of preferred clients meant that Jewish tobacco merchants were more likely to encounter difficulties in obtaining the large-scale credit that enabled the payment of advances to growers, a fundamental requirement for the conduct of international trade in this industry. If we use the previous case as an example, we see that in order to purchase raw tobacco leaf, the wholesaler would receive credit from a bank against the goods, which were treated as security. This arrangement held until the tobacco leaf was sorted and sold to foreign cigarette manufacturers, hopefully at a profit. Payments were then assigned to the bank to serve as security within the framework of the tobacco merchant's long-term credit account. However, should a cigarette manufacturer find it difficult to pay the requested amount, perhaps because the price received was below the raw tobacco's estimated value (sometimes caused by rejection of some portion of the raw product), the tobacco merchant would remain with unsold goods and a debt to the bank. Much of this process depended on the ties maintained between merchants and Greek bank officials within the framework of reciprocal trust. In light of the increasing alienation between Jewish entrepreneurs and Greek bank officials as nationalism intensified, Jewish tobacco merchants, already in an inferior position, found themselves financially stifled and unable to conduct such transactions. The mid-1930s therefore saw the demise of the few Jewish firms still operating in the tobacco industry.

8.2 Reorganising Commercial Activity: New Market Orientations

The global depression, together with the Greek economy's decline, left considerable stocks of merchandise in the hands of merchants just at the time when import restrictions were coming into effect. The timing of these events proved to be felicitous for some firms. Marked discounts, awarded by the firms' foreign creditors, enabled many firms to settle old debts, a measure that improved their viability.[47] Hananel E. Naar & Co. (no. 243) was one such firm, which after its reconstitution in the stationery and office supplies industry, it was noted, "The business is functioning well as a the consequence of the added value of the stock of goods held at the time of the dissolution of the former partnership."[48]

This recovery, notwithstanding, increasing government intervention in the import–export sector, made the success of local and international commerce dependent on access to the Ministry of National Economy. Access was necessary to ensure the acquisition of import entitlements and the orderly flow of private barter transactions, now jeopardised by Greece's new pro-German trade orientation. This section therefore focuses on the adaptations Jewish merchants introduced to contend with the new orientation toward international trade as well as the escalating anti-Jewish stance in commerce (see chapter 6). Table 8.2 provides a statistical introduction to Jewish commerce by sub-branch, excluding textiles and clothing (see section 8.4), which constituted the largest proportion of Jewish businessmen.

8.2.1 Horizontal Control in Traditional Jewish Commercial Sub-Branches

The continued Jewish domination of the import, wholesale, and retail sale of luxuries (Table 8.2a) as well as small metal products and stationery (Tables 8.3b, e) did more than mirror traditional Jewish preferences for trade in finished products sold to private consumers (see Chapter 4). It also reflected the Jews' access to different types of capital. For instance, Jewish firms retained their traditional control over the luxury item sub-branch as a direct result of their ability to recruit the capital necessary to obtain import and distribution entitlements. Jewish importers of home glassware (no. 257), lenses as well as precision measuring equipment (no. 256) sustained this Jewish niche by recruiting family contacts as well as Jewish bank credit. In one case, Haim Jacob Benrubi and his cousin Haim Samuel Benrubi (no. 257; Illustration 9),[49] in association with Abravanel & Benveniste (glassware)[50] as well as Asséo Frères & Fils (no. 255), were able to obtain a mortgage from Banque de Salonique for the purpose of establishing a new partnership, the Société Anonyme EFEK.[51] The new firm, which concentrated on import and commerce in enamelware and cutlery, operated as a conglomerate. An added benefit to this structure was the firms' ability to recruit the additional capital needed to obtain exclusive entitlements, a distinct asset in a tiny

Table 8.2a Jewish-owned Firms (*N* = 7) and Greek-owned Firms (*N* =5) in Domestic Wares and Luxuries, 1935–1937

Sub-Branch	N = 12		Percentage in Sub-Branch (B)		ERI (B/A)	
	J	G	J	G	J	G
Furniture trade	1	3	25.0	75.0	.429	1.800
Glassware	5	1	83.3	16.7	1.429	.400
Jewellery and watches	1	1	50.0	50.0	.857	1.200

Source: See in Appendix 8.
Notes: J = Jewish-owned firms; G = Greek-owned firms.
A = Percentage ethnic firms (J,G) in the branch: A(J) = 58.3; A(G) = 41.7.
B = Percentage of ethnic-owned firms in a given sub-branch.
Ethnic Representation Index (ERI) = B/A.
ERI = 1 indicates full-representation; ERI < 1 indicates under-representation; ERI > 1 indicates over-representation.

Table 8.2b Jewish-owned Firms (*N* = 19) and Greek-owned Firms (*N* = 13) Trading in Agricultural Products, 1935–1937

Sub-Branch	N = 32		Percentage in Sub-Branch (B)		ERI (B/A)	
	J	G	J	G	J	G
Locally grown produce	2	6	25.0	75.0	.421	1.846
Grain and flour	6	4	60.0	40.0	1.011	.985
Silk cocoons (export)	1	0	100.0	.0	1.684	.000
Dried fruits, fresh fruits, legumes, oil	10	3	76.9	23.1	1.296	.568

Source: See Appendix 8.
Notes: See Table 8.2a above.
A(J) = 59.4; A(G) = 40.6

Table 8.2c Jewish-owned Firms (*N* = 49) and Greek-owned Firms (*N* = 40) in Finance and Commission, 1935–1937

Sub-Branch	N = 89		Percentage in Sub-Branch (B)		ERI (B/A)	
	J	G	J	G	J	G
Banking	3	2	60.0	40.0	1.090	.890
General and large-scale commerce	42	33	56.0	44.0	1.017	.979
Construction of public utilities	4	5	44.4	55.6	.807	1.236

Source: See in Appendix 8.
Notes: See Table 8.2a above.
A(J) = 55.1; A(G) = 44.9

competitive market threatened by rising prices.[52] While the original firm, Benrubi, was considered "*comme une de plus importantes Maisons de la Branche en notre ville*", the new partnership was described as "*la plus importante Maison de verrerie de Salonique et même du Pays*".[53] It was sufficiently successful to establish branches in Athens as well as Piraeus.[54] These branches, like other long-established Jewish firms, were able to cope with competition by constructing complex, horizontally integrated family-based commercial networks.

Yet, some private Jewish firms – such as Eliezer & Chimchi – did continue to trade in glassware, crystal, enamelware, and related goods without entering into any mergers. Abram Eliezer and Abram Chimchi, who had previously worked with Haim J. Benrubi as silent partners (*commanditaire*) (no. 259), left to open their own firm following Haim Benrubi's resignation in 1932. Their success (1933) was based on their ability to arrange for sufficient capital (*disposant de moyens suffisants*) to acquire import entitlements.[55]

Who competed with the above-mentioned Jewish glassware merchants? The only Greek glass firm registered with Banque Amar was N[icolas] Constantinides (est. 1926), which operated two stores in this sector. Yet, its estimated capital was far below that of the Benrubi merger (see Appendix 8).[56] We can therefore conclude that Jewish firms continued to control the trade in home luxuries throughout the 1930s.

Expansion through the acquisition of exclusive rights to national commercial representation of foreign firms helped several Jewish importers who already dominated Salonica's regional market to turn toward Old Greece's developing markets. This strategy facilitated entry into new industries where Greek rivals were not yet present. The springboard for this activity was the introduction of foreign producers, new to the local market, among which were firms belonging to the American rubber industry. For example, Eletan SA (no. 89), headquartered in Athens but with a branch in Salonica, maintained shops for the sale of automobile spare parts. The firm was the exclusive representative for the American tyre manufacturer Goodrich, to which it also provided warehouse services (*représentants-entrepositaires*) sufficient for the entire Greek tyre market.[57]

Jewish merchants who had qualified for import entitlements such as those awarded to the firm of H. A. Altshey (no. 287), which dealt in top-quality inputs for the textile industry: wool and cotton yarn, skins, furs, carpets, tissues, chemical products, colonial goods (e.g., sugar, coffee), general merchandise, and electrical goods, among others.[58] When found in a situation of financial stress, several Jewish merchants, like Greek importers,[59] sold their entitlements for profit.[60] For example, Aélion & Hassid (no. 196), a family partnership engaged in the wholesale trade of cotton and wool cloth, was forced to suspend its debt payments in 1932.[61] According to an agreement with its creditors, a liquidator was appointed to arrange for the sale of their stock. However, in order to ensure the firm's continuation, the family sold some of its import entitlements for cash: "On the basis of the compromise reached, this realisation, with the addition of the funds acquired from the sale of a portion of the import entitlements, enabled not only the payment of credit arrears . . . [but] also it enabled leaving several disposable bundles of goods."[62] The firm's situation subsequently improved considerably.[63]

8.2.2 Traditional Markets

Although one might assume that the vast majority of the imported goods came from states that had full clearing agreements with Greece (i.e., Czechoslovakia, Germany, Italy, and Belgium), this was not the case. Clearing arrangements did not prevent imports from states lacking full (e.g., the UK and the US) or even partial clearing agreements (e.g., Hungary). The following examples provide evidence for this phenomenon.[64]

After adopting a name taken from Greek mythology – Hermes – for their organisational umbrella, the two partnerships of S. Benveniste, H. Pardo & Co. (no. 293) and H. Pardo & M. Carasso (no. 296) continued to engage in commission representation, import–export, and customs clearing, all from the same address on Stoa Davidetto. The firm of H. Pardo & M. Carasso represented several foreign firms located in Hungary (leather, essence oils), Denmark (textiles, *caoutchouc*), England (nautical supplies), Japan (cotton and silk cloth, etc.), Italy (aniline chemicals), and Czechoslovakia (office furniture). This firm, like a small number of other Jewish firms, continued to import goods from Germany (industrial tools, asbestos building materials, electrical supplies, paints, minerals, and cement) while exporting leather to Germany and textiles (*mélange* wool) to Belgium[65] even after individual Jews joined the Jewish press in attacking Germany's racism (January 1933) while advocating a boycott of German goods.[66]

8.2.3 The Transit Trade

Partition of the Macedonian hinterland among the surrounding new nation-states placed political boundaries between Jewish Sephardic families yet motivated the creation of new networks compatible with the restructuring of the Jewish Diaspora. During the 1930s, Jewish entrepreneurs in Salonica benefited from these networks when coping with the emerging difficulties.

What gave Salonica's Jewish firms an advantage over other Greek firms participating in the transit trade was the ease with which they could operate under a range of legal statuses and national identities and thus avoid clearing restrictions. Supporting this structural flexibility was the Sephardic Diaspora, consisting of branches of the same family planted in cities spread throughout the Balkans.

Although transit trade opportunities declined between the wars due to the autarky-oriented policies of the Balkan economies, Jewish entrepreneurs occupied in this trade, especially those holding Yugoslav citizenship, succeeded in sustaining at least some of their activities by adopting a transnational organisational structure. Now separated from their coreligionists by the new national borders, Jewish businessmen became even more desirous for relationships in which trust was valued, as in extended family firms.

The specific mechanism that facilitated this circumvention of the clearing restrictions, already in use by 1932 (see section 7.4), was a set of intricate but legal accounting procedures: Salonican mother firms would "balance" their export profits against the import costs of their branches. Consider the firm Sabetay Daniel Asséo, the name of the Uskub (Skopje, Yugoslavia)[67] branch of the long-established Salonican firm David S. Asséo; it fulfilled the following function:

> For tax reasons the firm operated with two different names in Salonica and in Uskub. In Salonica it concerned itself with the export of cotton yarn to its office in Uskub, while the Uskub office sent dried legumes, etc. to Salonica."[68]

Hence, while its Uskub branch was involved mainly in automobile repair work, the Salonica firm used the same Uskub address to export cotton thread to Yugoslavia while channelling imported dried legumes to Salonica.[69] In this way, the Salonica firm created two seemingly independent firms, one in Greece and one in Yugoslavia. Greek branches purchasing imported Yugoslavian goods would export Greek goods, with the costs balanced among the branches. This family-owned chain thus created "internal clearing" arrangements and thereby circumvented the new trade barriers.

In a similar fashion, the head office of the Salonica branch of Salomon Pinhas Pardo was formally located in Monastir (Yugoslavia), where the firm's founders, the brothers Dario, Moise and Isac Pardo, Yugoslav citizens, owned property. The fourth Pardo brother, Salomon, resided in Salonica, where his home served as the address of the Greek branch for tax purposes.[70] In another case, the old Salonican trading firm Albert Elie Nefussy maintained a branch in Uskub listed as Haim Salem – the name of the Nefussy brothers' brother-in-law. The Nefussy firm was never openly listed as a branch in the records maintained by Salem. The brothers were consequently able to avoid responsibility for the contracts signed by their brother-in-law.[71] Another Salonica firm, Isac A. Aroesti, had branches in Monastir and Skopje that were structurally connected.[72] In 1933, the firm Menachem Rousso & Fils, which had been dissolved in 1926, was reconstituted; it then established an independent branch in Monastir, directed by Menachem Rousso and his fourth son Jacob.[73] These and other less common strategies exploited family ties to create Jewish Sephardic commercial networks capable of compensating for the lack of economic cooperation between the Balkan autarkies.

Jewish international partnerships and their branches could therefore continue to conduct transit trade in traditional agricultural goods as well as in items as diverse as silk cocoons, hides, and wood, although at lower volumes. Whereas Joseph Mordoh's brothers-in-law, Mallah and Yacoel, continued managing the firm's silk cocoon business from Salonica,[74] Joseph Mordoh's son Salomon, who had managed the firm's Serbian branch, immigrated to Milan, Europe's silk centre. Salomon Mordoh now set up a new firm to help compensate for declining trade in these traditional goods. Partnerships also proved to be important in the hide and leather trade, a branch with significant Jewish participation. The merger of the Scialom brothers' firm with Asher Hassid in 1930 enabled the survival of a lively commercial relationship between suppliers of raw skins in the periphery and leather traders and manufacturers in the centre. Whereas Humbert Scialom resided abroad most of the year, his partner Asher Hassid directed the company in his absence.[75] Isaac Scialom had previously worked together with his brother Avram in the leather and hides trade, which included exporting goods to Skopje. Following his brother's emigration in the early 1930s, Isaac continued to work independently although on a smaller scale.[76]

8.2.4 New Opportunities in Finance and the Commission Trade

Jewish entrepreneurs quickly learned to adapt themselves to developments in Greece's consolidating internal markets. Regeneration of agricultural production had revived the consumer market for manufactured goods and for real estate in Greek Macedonia's hinterland (section 6.1). This made it possible for firms that had experienced cash flow difficulties during the economic crisis to recover some of their losses by liquidating their rural properties. For instance, the haberdashery and semi-wholesalers firm of Nissim Frères found their finances to be severely restricted throughout the crisis due to its inability to liquidate assets located in the interior. However, by 1937, the company was reported to have recovered: "Since then, the firm recaptured its place [in the market and] has continued to conduct its affairs on a proper footing and regularise its debt payments."[77]

New opportunities likewise opened up for commission agents prepared to work in the interior. A network of Jewish agents began to spread throughout the country in order to gather the information crucial for the entry of Jewish firms into new commercial relationships with non-Jewish growers and craftsmen in the periphery. The sizeable capital accumulated by one such firm, Fils de Levy Simha, can be seen as a measure of its success in the changing economic environment.[78]

As their connections with the interior grew, Jewish entrepreneurs began to play a more significant role in the funding of agricultural exports. Their participation became more crucial as the clearing agreements with Germany increasingly restricted the availability of capital to this as in other sectors. Thanks to their extensive commercial networks, Jewish entrepreneurs could help Macedonian farmers avoid compulsory clearances by routing their produce through Old Greece and then into markets free of such agreements, such as those of Egypt, Mandatory Palestine, and Britain.[79] Similar arrangements were used by merchants belonging to the Jewish as well as the Greek diasporas in the Middle East's developing cities.[80]

As part of these networks, Jewish firms in Salonica were able to add moneylending to their roles as middlemen between producers and customers in Old and New Greece. Jewish traders would thus extend cash advances to Greek growers and producers while ensuring delivery of the goods to buyers, to whom they also extended credit. Moise Massarano & Fils (no. 278), for example, despatched consignments of fresh fruits and vegetables to exporters in Old Greece and Egypt. The firm was financially responsible to a Greek exporter, acting as a principal (*commettant*), due to the fact that the transacted was based on credit.[81] The Jewish firm would make cash purchases of goods from producers using funds borrowed from a bank, and then sell the goods – on credit – to the exporters. This arrangement made Moise Massarano & Fils liable for these sums until all the debts were repaid. Although quite risky financially, this strategy forged interdependence between Jewish financiers (acting as middlemen) and Greek growers/exporters. These same Jewish middlemen gradually established themselves as actors capable of helping local producers evade the high-risk trade conducted with Greece's clearing agreement partners.

Jewish merchants from Salonica, latecomers to the markets in Old Greece, also began to act as "bankers" in the 1930s, financing vegetable and fruit cultivation while extending credit to an established group of Greek dealers; they in effect purchased crops prior to planting (an arrangement similar to purchasing futures). Such financial services served to channel their interests in the direction of fresh fruit and vegetable cultivation, a risk-laden industry deterring the participation of other traders. The firm of Fils d'Isac S. Saltiel (no. 319), for example, was involved in commercial representation, which included the export of indigenous products to Serbia and Hungary. The Saltiels, who had reputations as "gifted with initiative" (*doués d'initiative*), were highly skilled entrepreneurs; they extended their business by maintaining a collaborative arrangement with the Greek firm Dimitracopoulos & Xenakis, exporters of seed onions for planting.[82]

One can thus conclude that Salonica's Jewish businessmen filled the vacuum left by Greek merchants who, more attracted to the profitable new opportunities created by trade between Greece and Germany (section 8.1), exited from less-profitable niches.

8.2.5 Large-Scale Entrepreneurship: Public Infrastructure

As a numerically negligible group in this industry, Jewish contractors concentrated their business in the Jewish sector, where they had easy access to private and communal construction projects. Elie Modiano (no. 326), an Italian national and the Jewish engineer most frequently mentioned in Banque Amar documents, built buildings and shops for private Jewish clients[83] as well as the Jewish community's Kazes School.[84] Opportunities in the private sector were especially prevalent during the 1920s, when reconstruction of Salonica city's centre was under way. By the 1930s, however, the same Jewish contractors found demand drying up. The credit squeeze, coupled with a reduced Jewish consumer market as Jews continued to emigrate, forced Jewish contractors to intensify their attempts to penetrate the burgeoning public sector, traditionally closed to them. Government-initiated infrastructure projects had multiple objectives, ranging from the improvement of internal transportation and reclamation of agricultural acreage (e.g., draining Macedonia's swamps) for rural refugee resettlement to job creation for the growing numbers of unemployed. This last goal was held to be important for avoiding exposure to radical communism in the cities where labourers were gathering.[85]

Jews were consequently under-represented in the construction industry (see Table 8.2c) during the 1930s. The barriers facing Jewish contractors in the public sector included favouritism and outright corruption. By utilising these means, Greek contractors obtained access to highly profitable projects. E. Guikas, a civil and mechanical engineer who had earned his diploma in the Polytechnion in Athens was also a member of Salonica's Municipal Council. His firm received, among other things, several of the contracts associated with the Vardar Valley reclamation project, which had been contracted to the US firm of Monks-Ulen & Co. in 1928. Monks-Ulen had been commissioned to construct a dam on the Strymon River in the environs of Katerini (Greek Macedonia), the city where Guikas had been born.[86] The Guikas case thus illustrates the close connection that existed between the local political authorities, ethnicity, and economic power.[87]

The increasingly close ties between wealthy Greeks and the authorities effectively blocked whatever access to Jewish minority entrepreneurs (and foreigner entrepreneurs) might have had to opportunities opening up in infrastructure projects and construction. Lacking such political connections, Jewish contractors tried to obtain contracts on the basis of their professional expertise, generally as engineers,[88] and access to investment capital. Jews who were foreign nationals found their situation to be even more difficult, especially when competing in government tenders. While in semi-colonial Ottoman Macedonia the Jewish engineer–contractor Elie Modiano had planned and participated in various public sector projects like the office complex (*bureau*) and the warehouses (*entrepôts*) of Salonica's Customs House (1910) as well as several bridges in Salonica's periphery,[89] he had to hide himself behind a firm created purely to enter bids for government tenders for the construction of public utilities.

Technique Hellenique de Defense Fluviale SA (no. 328) was established in 1931 for the purpose of providing maintenance services to the hydraulic installations situated along Macedonia's rivers: "The company in question works exclusively with the state, given that all the rivers are state property."[90] The nationalities of this firm's owners point to the constraints to be overcome. The figure driving this venture, Elie Modiano, had become an associate of an Italian industrialist from Bologna (name unknown, perhaps a Jew) for the purpose of financing the corporation. While these two partners acted as the guarantors, Constantin Anguélakis, the former mayor of Salonica, joined to provide the necessary political "assurances". Like other foreign entrepreneurs,[91] Modiano, turned to a local Greek political figure who was well-liked by the Greek business community and who had access to the state bureaucracy that was otherwise closed to foreigners.

Another piece of the new corporation was owned by Errera Frères.[92] Cooperation between the Jewish Modiano and the Jewish Errera brothers, expert hydraulic engineers who also held Italian citizenship, began in 1928 when they founded, as equal partners, the firm of Elie Modiano & Errera Frerès (no. 327). This was a merger of convenience, designed to facilitate each partner's independent participation in state tenders for canal projects. This merger was able to compete because it had established vertical control over all the project's phases, from engineering and planning through the production of trellises (*treillage*) and commercial representation of small-scale technical input firms. Its financing was secured primarily through the Modiano family.[93]

At a certain point, the state stopped respecting its commitments to its foreign contractors,[94] which led to heavy losses for the firm, almost to the point of bankruptcy. As a Banque Amar official wrote with respect to Elie J. Modiano that

> his financial situation is a bit difficult lately because he has yet to receive significant sums [of money] from the government for the work he has already completed. Nevertheless, the aforementioned contract entailed borrowing, backed by the guaranties provided by his father, a major proprietor of buildings whose fortune is valued at about £50,000.[95]

The pattern illustrated by the Modiano-Errera case was repeated with other non-Greek-owned firms (including European, British, and American firms supported by Greek Diaspora entrepreneurs).[96] One can only conclude that the local Greek entrepreneurial elites controlled the state's capital resources, which they reallocated among themselves. The Greek state had become, in effect, a "client" of entrepreneurial patronage.[97] In the following sections of this chapter, we indicate how this environment forced Jewish entrepreneurs to channel their activities into the private sector almost exclusively.

8.3 Food, Chemicals, Metals, Wood, and Paper: New Industrial Entrepreneurial Strategies within a Protected Economy

The industrial growth materialising during the 1930s, especially in the decade's second half, has frequently been attributed to the Greek government's protectionist policies. Among the steps taken was the amendment (in 1937) to the tariff of 1926, as described by S. R. Jordan (1937), the British consul stationed in Athens:

> Through the customs tariff the Government affords a large measure of protection to the local industries. This assistance has, in many cases, been increased recently by the many trade restrictions in force, which have prevented the importation of similar

or competing articles, and there are no indications of any radical change in the existing position.[98]

Protectionist tariff policies do more than bolster local production; they also make it more profitable. As a general introduction to the influence of this policy on local Jewish entrepreneurs, we offer some examples. We should note before plunging into the details that many of these policies were not intentionally prejudicial to Jewish businessmen. Nevertheless, the dominant commercial networks functioned as pressure groups trying to induce concessions and benefits from the state. These Greek networks controlled competition by establishing associations and formulating industrial policy.[99]

In 1931, the firm Isac Carasso & Co. (est. 1918, no. 166), which carried on an active trade in clothing accessories, purchased a factory manufacturing tinder (*amadou*), laces for corsets, rubber bands, wicks for lamps, etc. By increasing its manufacturing capacity, the firm increased its profits: "Operate any business satisfactorily with the help of [tariff] protection . . . and any industry can be viable."[100] Pepo Moïse Perahia (no. 238), who reconstituted (1936) his late father's firm, Moïse Perahia & Fils, paper and carton wholesalers, boldly appealed directly to the Metaxas government for tariff protection "*pour donner à l'affaire un plus grand essor*" (in order to help the business to develop greatly). The young Perahia took himself to Athens where, upon his arrival, he submitted a memorandum to the Minister of the National Economy, suggesting that the Ministry increase the countervailing duties on imported goods that were competing with his product line (typewriter ribbons, carton, and carbon papers). His colleagues in the community of Jewish businessmen were convinced that this demand would be seriously considered because the Metaxas government was intent on protecting and encouraging industries capable of competing with foreign suppliers.[101]

Tariff protection stimulated manufacturing by making it easier to expand the production of local consumer goods. However, taking advantage of this opportunity represented only one element among the Jewish organisational strategies, which focused on deepening the vertical integration of their businesses. In the following pages we show how the restructuring of Jewish entrepreneurial strategies supported the Jewish presence in the period's prominent new industries.[102]

8.3.1 Food

Food, considered the fastest growing industry in the consolidating Greek autarky, symbolised, perhaps more than any other industry, the rising level of concentration in the domestic market.[103] Assuming over-representation of Jewish firms within the industry sample and the consequent bias (see section 8.1), we focus on the modification of Jewish entrepreneurship in this branch from a minority–majority perspective, that is, from a comparison with Greek entrepreneurial patterns.

The new niches created by Greek entrepreneurs extended the boundaries of the local food industry but exerted no influence on the position of the Jews already active in that industry. Greek refugees – repatriated entrepreneurs – equipped with pre-migratory skills introduced new but narrow niches based on their acquired skills in, for example, rice sorting and scouring.[104] For the same reasons, repatriated Greek entrepreneurs, now settled in the Macedonian periphery developed fish salting and preserving companies.[105]

Table 8.3a Jewish-owned Firms (*N* = 25) and Greek-owned Firms (*N* = 23) in the Food Industry, 1935–1937

Sub-Branch	*N* = 48		Percentage in Sub-Branch (B)		ERI (B/A)	
	J	G	J	G	J	G
Groceries	4	0	100.0	.0	1.920	.000
Colonial commodities	8	9	47.1	52.9	.904	1.105
Production of sweets and bakery products	3	5	37.5	62.5	.720	1.304
Wine, alcoholic, and sparkling beverages	7	5	58.3	41.7	1.120	.870
Dairy products	0	2	.0	100.0	.000	2.087
Preserves and salted fish	3	2	60.0	40.0	1.152	.835

Source: See in Appendix 8.
Notes: See Table 8.2a above.
A(J) = 52.1; A(G) = 47.9

The several large-scale refugee-owned firms transplanted from Asia Minor to Greek Macedonia exemplified the joint restructuring of indigenous Greek firms. Repatriated Greeks cooperated to recreate the food industry in Salonica and its hinterland, along the lines of a minority–majority branch structure. Georgiades Frères, owned by the brothers Yordanis and Pandelis, originally from Salonica, established a complex network of partnerships based on family ties, in the best tradition of Greek entrepreneurship as it developed in the Hellenic diaspora. The firm concentrated on the production and distribution of spirits, a government-supported monopoly usually dominated by the majority entrepreneurs.[106] The Georgiades Frères holdings in the food industry were extensive. They included shares in a brewery (Société Anonyme des Brasseries FIX); five refrigeration warehouses for the cold storage of fruit, located in Alexandroupolis, Xanthie, Drama, Serres, and Larissa; and Flours Mils [*sic*] SA.[107] Their concern grew through collaboration with Coniordou Frerès, a firm that had relocated to Salonica from Constantinople in 1925. Coniordou Frerès was engaged in wholesale commerce in wines and spirits as well as in shipping; it was considered "*une des plus importantes Maisons de la Branche en notre ville*" (one of the most important firms of the branch in our city). The modernised Proteus factory, owned by the partnership of Georgiades & Coniordou (equal parts), was founded in 1928 and produced spirits, wine, vinegar, carbonic acid, and related items.[108] These products were manufactured from currant surpluses, created when currant exports to Britain fell by 23 percent between 1922 and 1929, as world market preferences shifted to cheaper raisins from Australia and California. At this time, currant growers, mainly from southern Greece, were organised within the Autonomous Currant Organisation (ASO, est. 1924), a combined co-operative organisation and cartel, which came under state control during the 1930s through the intervention of the National Bank of Greece.[109] It could be concluded that the Greek concern, Georgiades Frères, founded in 1908,[110] had completed the gradual replacement of the Jewish-owned Allatini Fratelli (section 4.5.2), a concern that had dominated agricultural trade in the Macedonian interior during the Ottoman era (section 2.4). It soon became apparent that Greek-owned ventures, whether owned by the majority veterans or refugees, would be replacing Jewish-owned firms dealing in staples, a trend that symbolised the consolidating self-sufficient autarchy.

The only route remaining for Jewish entrepreneurs to compete with Greek entrepreneurs was increasing efficiency, especially vertical efficiency, usually introduced through the integration of small enterprises or partnerships (Appendix 8, sub-branches 1c and 13b). According to several unrelated bits of information, the process seems to have been implemented as follows: Jewish entrepreneurs would act as bankers, taking on the risk of financing local growers. The core of this form of financing lay in purchasing a crop before it was even planted. Such control over the crop facilitated the entry of the Jewish entrepreneurs into manufacturing. For instance, Jewish merchants entered the growing sub-branch of flour production at the grain-threshing stage, the first steps after planting and reaping by the growers, from whom they bought the crop (probably in advance). One such firm was Aron Gavios (no. 265), which bought outright and independently operated a threshing machine.[111] Another firm, Marco Matarasso Romani & Co. (no. 267) initiated commercial activity in wheat after it began operating a flour mill, with flour considered a semi-finished good;[112] purchase of the mill allowed the firm to begin pasta production.

Jewish entrepreneurs also vertically integrated into the pasta production. In 1926, the Jewish-owned Beraha & Cie.[113] a pasta producer, together with three Greek-owned pasta-producing firms formed a large merger Société Anonyme Industrielle de Pâtes Alimentaires (AVEZ).[114] The merger's aim was to control internal competition: "to incorporate all the pasta factories and bring an end to their competition."[115] The merger was led mainly by C. Micas Fréres, which maintained a similar pasta-producing plant in Constantinople. George C. Micas, managing director of the Salonica merger, was also the partner in another pasta concern in Constantinople, owned by C. Micas Fils. Although the respective Banque Amar document makes no mention of Beraha & Cie. as one of the merger's partners, the document notes that by 1936, the AVEZ board included a Jewish director, one Joseph Haim.[116] This notation confirms the continuing involvement of Jewish entrepreneurs in Greece's significant basic food industry (see section 9.2.2 below). This large factory's prosperity during the 1930s, but especially in 1933–1937,[117] could also explain why Fils de David Hasson (no. 266), a veteran firm occupied in the sale of cereals (in addition to raw skins), managed to expand its interests by establishing a new pasta-producing firm, Hermes SA, in 1935. Despite its Hellenic name, this relatively small factory exhibited a significant Jewish identity, expressed in the makeup of its board of directors (section 9.2.2).[118]

Merger with a Greek firm was a technique used in the beverage sector. Moise Moissi expanded his involvement in the sparkling beverage sector by merging with the Greek firm Diamopoulos & Cie. (est. 1929). Previously, each of the three partners in the new company, now called Nektar, had operated separately. After the merger, all three managed the concern, which owned a factory generally employing about eight workers.[119]

One early example of such Greek–Jewish cooperation was the conglomerate Pliancas, Kastritsis (also spelled Castritsis) & Co. (no. 15). This group (each partner held an equal share) managed the following companies: G. A. Pliancas & Co., Georges M. Papadopoulos, Pepo I. Sedicario, and Kastritsis & Levy (Appendix 4.1, no. 685) as well as a confectionery production facility, all from their offices in Rue Aphroditis, Vardar. In addition, the firm maintained two stores selling its products exclusively, one in the building housing its offices in Vardar, and one in Kavalla. The partners were well known and very active in the branch. This large, successful partnership further expanded its business by entering into another partnership (in mid-1936) with the confectioners VIRON, Société Vassiliades & Floras, which ran an even larger factory.[120] Each stage of the expansion apparently represented a step in the cartelisation of the regional confectionery (sweets) industry and its protection from competition by new or larger local producers.

Two major competitors in this industry were the Greek-owned Société Floca Frères (est. 1895) and Chocolaterie Démétre Floca (est. 1924). The two merged in 1934 into the giant Chocolaterie Floca SA, which exported its products throughout the Balkans and Egypt. This firm employed 220 production workers and eight sales representatives.[121] Unfortunately, we lack similar information about Pliancas, Kastritsis & Co. In order to gain an impression of the difference in the scope of their business, we should note that the estimated value of Floca's immovable property was about GRD 25,000,000, while Pliancas, Kastritsis & Co. held an estimated GRD 3,300,000.[122]

8.3.2 The Metal Industry[123]

From the 1920s on, when the Greek iron and metal industry was in its infancy, [124] firms had begun to increasingly shift away from the repair to the manufacture of agricultural machinery, nails, safes, beds, copper articles, and electrical wire.[125] Expanding agricultural production in rural Macedonia following consolidation of the Greek autarky also stimulated the growth of commercial opportunities in the trade of agricultural machinery and other equipment.

Jewish entrepreneurs, however, continued to be under-represented in this branch due to the weakness of their ties with the newly settled Greeks. In contrast, Greek-owned companies were able to establish branches throughout Macedonia. For instance, Gheorgiki Eteria Thrakis & Makedonias SA, producers of agricultural tools and importers of agricultural machinery, maintained a branch in Xanthie and an agency in Komotini,[126] whereas only a few Jewish machine shops managed to reconstitute themselves during the recovery. One such firm was Leon A. Juda (no. 56), which had acquired the assets and liabilities of the defunct (April 1931) firm of Alcalay & Juda (Appendix 5, no. 89) at an apt moment. Juda was then able to register his firm as engaging in the manufacture and sale of agricultural equipment rather than as a simple workshop.[127]

The developing metal industry was sufficiently broad and active to allow the creation of ethnic niches in association with different metals: copper belonged to the Greek refugees and iron to the Armenians. Anastassios Kazgandjoglou, a Greek refugee entrepreneur, utilised his pre-migratory skills to participate in the trade in copper.[128] The established Armenian firm of D. Hovaghimian & Co. maintained foundries (*fers à repasser*) for the production of iron pipes and metal inputs for infrastructure projects (rail, telegraph, electricity, etc.).[129] After the severe local competition drove him out of the fabrics trade and foreign exchange, his pre-migration occupation in Turkey, the Armenian refugee Agop Keklikian shifted to the production of horseshoes and similar iron products. Supported by his brother-in-law Mardiros Mardikian, considered a skilled foundry craftsman, he was able to enter the emerging Armenian niche.[130]

As to Jewish firms in this industry, they were concentrated in the manufacture of

Table 8.3b Jewish-owned Firms (*N* = 37) and Greek-owned Firms (*N* = 29) in the Metal Industry, 1935–1937

Sub-Branch	N = 66		Percentage in Sub-Branch (B)		ERI (B/A)	
	J	G	J	G	J	G
Machinery	3	10	23.1	76.9	.412	1.751
Nails and wire	2	0	100.0	.0	1.784	.000
Manufacture and trade in small metal products, hardware (*quincaillerie*)	23	9	71.9	28.1	1.282	.640
Manufacture of metal furniture	3	0	100.0	.0	1.784	.000
Tinware	2	0	100.0	.0	1.784	.000
Ironware	0	2	.0	100.0	.000	2.276
Copperware	0	1	.0	100.0	.000	2.276
Electric appliances	1	2	33.3	66.7	.595	1.517
Automobile accessories	3	5	37.5	62.5	.669	1.422

Source: See in Appendix 8.
Notes: See Table 8.2a above.
A(J) = 56.1; A(G) = 43.9

metal household goods aimed at the mass consumer market and sold on the open market to private customers: furniture made of iron and bronze, small metal products and notions (toys, locks, pins, nails, etc.), as well as tinwork. Jewish entrepreneurs thus came to be over-represented in these narrow niches within this light industry. Following the expansion of Macedonia's canned goods industry, stimulated by the influx of refugees, Jewish entrepreneurs were able to extend their presence by responding to the increasing demand for tin canning. Moise Benrubi (no. 64) was one of the major figures in tin can production[131] whereas Ouziel & Menaché (no. 86), which produced and sold tin boxes and cans, became the leading firm in this sector in Salonica as well as nationally.[132]

Jewish entrepreneurs also spearheaded the growth of metal bed manufacture in the 1930s. The privately owned firm Joseph Sabetay Saadi (no. 84) had produced and sold beds having iron frames and metal springs since 1916. Within two years, the firm's estimated capital grew from GRD 800,000 (1935) to GRD 1,500,000 (1937).[133]

Investments were made in efficiency measures and modernisation throughout the industry. One case in point was Galeries Modernes – S. Zadok (also spelled Sadock, Zadock) & Cie. (no. 85),[134] which electrified its factory for the production of beds, exported to Egypt, Palestine, Morocco, and Albania. This firm also sold its products (wholesale and retail) through a huge showroom owned by Victor Zadok, one of the partners. When even this successful and financially healthy firm found it difficult to survive in the relatively small domestic market,[135] it, like other firms, turned to markets outside Greece. Firms entering the export market would take advantage of their ties with the commercial and family networks woven by Jewish emigrants outside Salonica. Another such firm was Revah, Levy & Co. (no. 83), which was registered with Salonica's Chamber of Commerce as a wholesaler and retailer of ironware and furniture. To improve its business, the firm established commercial ties with Salonican immigrants in Mandatory Palestine.[136]

Once economic conditions had deteriorated, Salonica's Jewish firms preferred to cooperate instead of compete with one another, a strategy that helped them maintain their dominant position in the small metalwares market. Benjamin J. Benforado (after dissolution of Benforado & Francès in 1935) (no. 63) joined Pepo Yacoël & Co. (no. 82) that, *inter alia*, represented a German knife manufacturer, Solingen. These partners were also equal partners in A. Ménaché & Co. (no. 70), a hardware store (*quincaillerie*).[137] Abram D. Ménaché himself had suffered sufficient losses in this sector to require liquidation of his holdings in his partnership with Azriel Francès (1928–1935). Nehama Mallah, who represented Pepo Yacoël & Co., counselled his partner to refrain from trade in weapons and shotguns with Solingen. Thus, Pepo Yacoël & Co. – "*n'est pas intéressée dans le département armes et fusils de chasse*" – which meant limiting its commercial operation to wholesale, semi-wholesale, and retail sale of phonographs, pocket electric flashlights, razor blades, lighters, penknives, and so forth.[138] We can therefore conclude that although Jewish entrepreneurs refrained from trading in German-produced arms, a trade that would be monopolised by Greek merchants and was sensitive to fluctuations in Greek politics,[139] they nevertheless continued to develop markets for other German products.

Jewish entrepreneurs also increased their activity in the manufacture of substitutes for German imports. Old and highly reputable Jewish firms such as Alvo Frères (no. 58) had already extended their operations from wholesale commerce in ironware (*ferronerie* [*sic*]) and hardware (*quincaillerie*), which for them ranged from health and beauty products (*articles de santé*, e.g., metal combs, tweezers, etc.), to the manufacture of barbed wire and similar goods in 1931.[140]

Concurrently, Jewish firms established conglomerate-like companies, based on the understanding that larger partnerships facilitated the capital recruitment necessary to ensure a firm's competitive strength. The changes undergone by the firm owned by the Navarro Brothers (no. 53) are a fine example of this trend. The firm was originally involved solely in the large-scale trade of metals used in construction. They diversified their activities by becoming stockholders in Clouterie et Tréfilerie Macédonienne SA (no. 59), a nail and wire producer. Their wares, however, were sold exclusively in Greece. The firm was considered "*une de plus importante Maison de la Branche dans notre ville*" (a most important firm in this branch in our city) and "*la marche de l'affaire est plus que satisfaisante*" (the progress of the business is more than satisfactory).[141] Among the prominent Jewish industrialists sitting on the expanded firm's board of directors were Isac Bensussan (technical director) and Haim Bensussan (administrative director); other sitting members included Isac Angel (of Angel & Saltiel, no. 38); Maurice Navarro (of A & M Navarro, no. 53);[142] Albert I. Navarro (of M & A Navarro); Joseph A. [I.] Hassid; Elie J. Bensussan and Benico H. Angel (of Benico and Isac Angel & Cie., no. 119). The firm's subsidiaries included major metal merchants such as Joseph Isac Hassid & Frères (no. 50), which re-invested the huge profits made by the sale of their old stock during a period of rising prices for metal wares, hence we are told, "Their businesses are in good condition and they have realised excellent profits because of the stock they hold and the rising prices of the metals."[143]

For several shareholders this firm provided an opportunity to invest in a business having no connection to their own entrepreneurial specialisation. And so firms unrelated to the iron and metals industry saw investment by means of partnerships in metal industry firms to be an excellent opportunity. The firm of Angel & Saltiel, retailers of chemicals, paints, and herbs, together with Benico & Isac Angel & Cie., wholesalers of treated hides (see section 9.6) and suppliers of raw materials to shoe manufacturers, were partners in a corporation that manufactured nails and wire.[144] The firm Clouterie et Tréfilerie Macédonienne SA also had unofficial interests in another nail factory, Paris, Flogenides & Hassid. The latter Jewish–Greek partnership included Salvator Hassid, son of one of their partners (Moise I. Hassid), who had joined this initiative in mid-1936.[145] These Jewish-owned firms (nos. 58 and 59) employed at least seventy workers and twenty-four managerial employees, indicating that nail production was still a niche dominated by Jews during the period in question.[146]

Another firm taking this tack was Dario Joseph Assael, which was active in construction prior to 1925. After accumulating a considerable fortune, its owners began to import (1932) wire (cords of black melted steel for springs) from Germany.[147] However, in 1937, this firm shifted to the manufacture and sale of metal items such as metal buttons for army uniforms, mechanical toys, cutlery, and the like.[148] This transition from importing to manufacturing demonstrated the type of new opportunities opening up in the wake of Metaxas' policy, which saw development of the local metal industry as one part of a comprehensive plan to upgrade the Greek army.[149]

Over-representation of Greek entrepreneurs in the sale of electrical appliances (Table 8.3b) hints at the rapid replacement of Jewish businessmen by Greek rivals following to the strengthening of links between Germany and Greece.[150] The strong position in international trade held by German firms such as AEG and Siemens was based on their technical advantages, protected by patents and licenses. Siemens controlled a significant portion of world trade in these products, which was regulated by an international cartel agreement between 1929 and 1939.[151] Such imports could consequently be linked to private clearings, which were more accessible for majority entrepreneurs.

8.3.3 Chemicals and Mining[152]

New entrepreneurial opportunities also appeared in the chemical industry, which was tied to mining but also considered essential to the defence of the country.[153] The main stimulus for the mining industry's development in the mid-1930s was Germany's rapidly progressing military industry. Expansion of Greek mining activities after passage of the Four-Year Plan for rearming Germany (see section 6.1.3) stimulated the export of metals and minerals such as talc, iron, nickel, copper, bauxite, and chrome to Germany.[154] The British Consul in Salonica commented on the profitability of these ventures during 1936:

> The mining industry in Greece is making considerable headway and the export of base metals is increasing each year. The Customs returns show that there has been a further considerable increase in the exports of minerals during this year.[155]

Between 1926 and 1938, exports of minerals grew about fivefold, from 169,904 tons in 1926 to 959,083 tons in 1938, while exports of metals more than doubled, from 5,040 tons in 1926, to 12,202 tons in 1938. Most mines were small-scale enterprises using primitive technologies and modest batch furnaces that had a limited daily output. Because operators, whether contractors or lessees, had to pay rent, they generally refrained from investing in installations or equipment.[156] When the credit available to

Jewish entrepreneurs became scarce, those interested in taking advantage of opportunities in the sector did so through the acquisition of a Greek partner. A Jewish commercial agent, Vita Amar (no. 288) commented on the apparently growing Jewish participation in strip mining in 1935, saying, "The mining business, which is becoming more profitable day by day, is occupying all my attention. I am very busy." As Banque Amar files provide no evidence of direct Jewish involvement in the export of minerals to Germany, Vita Amar comments that Jewish businesses were open to financing such transactions in the role of silent partners.[157]

Jewish entrepreneurs might adopt these models when deepening their interests in the wholesale distribution of small-scale metalwares, or the production of chalks and crayons for slates (writing tablets). By introducing a Greek partner from the quarrying industry who would supply raw white limestone, firms like Pepo Yacoël (also spelled Jacoël) & Co. (no. 82) could extend their metal business into this sub-sector. And so, in 1933, Pepo Yacoël & Co., together with a Greek partner well known in the industry, opened a factory for chalk production in Betchinars (see Map 2).[158] Since Pepo Yacoël & Co., together with Benjamin Benforado, was also a partner in Maison Haim Mattia (est. 1934; no. 29), which engaged in the commercial representation and production of chalk and crayons for writing and painting slates,[159] we can conclude that vertical integration, from manufacture through distribution, enabled these firms to expand control over their markets. The sources support this conclusion. One of the firm's partners was known to frequently visit Athens and other localities in Greece for the purpose of selling the firm's products, which ranged from electric appliances and metal products to chalk and crayons.[160] What made vertical integration and mergers crucial, especially in the chalk industry, was Greek control over the supply of primary raw materials (chalk and magnesium silicate) that, like the quarries from which they were gathered, were considered national resources. It was therefore a major achievement for Jews to gain access to these resources even if it involved doing so through an anonymous Greek partner.

Table 8.3c shows that within the consolidated Greek autarky, Greek entrepreneurs dominated production of chemical products (lime, paints, etc.) for the developing construction industry. As the rate of construction rose in Salonica's urban periphery,

Table 8.3c   Jewish-owned Firms (N = 24) and Greek-owned (N = 18) Firms in the Chemical Industry, 1935–1937

Sub-Branch	N = 42		Percentage in Sub-Branch (B)		ERI (B/A)	
	J	G	J	G	J	G
Production of paints, dyes, varnish, oils	0	6	.0	100.0	.000	2.333
Manufacturing of paraffin and talc	4	0	100.0	.0	1.750	.000
Soap	4	2	66.7	33.3	1.167	.778
Aromatic productions	3	0	100.0	.0	1.750	.000
Drogueries and pharmacies	13	10	56.5	41.7	.989	1.014

Source: See in Appendix 8.
Notes: See Table 8.2a above.
A(J) = 57.1; A(G) = 42.9

local Greek entrepreneurs attempted to control competition in the lime industry by merging eleven small firms, all located in Asvestohori, one of Salonica's northern suburbs, into one large firm, Eteria Asvestopiis "ENOSSIS" (1931). ENOSSIS operated three whitewash (*chaux*) factories, one in Athens and two in Asvestohori, with a fourth factory just beginning to function in Salonica.[161]

While Greek entrepreneurs were able to control lime, paint, and dyestuff manufacture (Table 8.3c) due to their easy access to natural resources, Jewish entrepreneurs concentrated on importing pharmaceuticals as well as manufacturing perfumery and home wax products whose raw materials were less subject to ethnic constraints. Like their brethren in the metals branch, these Jewish merchants vertically integrated the industry's commercial and manufacturing stages. Acquisition of exclusive representation for all of Greece expanded the circle of their potential clients and made it possible for the branch to survive the economic crisis.[162] To illustrate, Pepo Is. Joseph & Co. (no. 45) had become the exclusive representative in Salonica of the French pharmaceutical firm Comar & Co., Paris (Laboratories Clin); by July 1932, the firm then expanded its representation activities throughout Greece. It consequently set up a branch in Athens, managed by Pepo Joseph.[163]

Yet, in 1935, the Greek medical industry, supported by the Greek Ministries of Economy and Foreign Affairs, together with the German Dresdner Bank, rebelled against the cartel formed by Dutch, French, British, and Swiss suppliers in the quinine industry and gained permission to import quinine from Germany.[164] This change in the market introduces the interesting case of Bernard Landau, a Jew born in Germany but holding Greek citizenship, who was even able to expand his commission agency (no. 32), which represented German pharmaceutical, chemical and quinine producers (see section 7.4) into the manufacture of refined products belonging to this branch.[165] He operated a small factory producing soap and perfumery items in what appears to have been a silent partnership with the German perfume manufacturer Drall de Hamburg. The strict confidentiality of this arrangement[166] hints at the rare willingness of German producers to take a Jewish partner outside Germany. It appears, however, one of the resources provided by Landau that made cooperation feasible was commercial information on local firms. We may also wonder if this entrepreneur, who had already worked for the Germans during World War I, was not also providing intelligence (it is not known to whom) during the mid-1930s, when the Third Reich began watching Salonica's Jewish community (section 6.2.4). If such was the case, we can readily understand why bank documents referring to Landau carried the words "*Strictement Confidentielle*", hinting at bank officials' suspicions.[167]

Other Jewish entrepreneurs concentrated in the talc (magnesium silicate powder) and paraffin (including soap) industries. These industries relied on simple, traditional technologies, with manufacturing conducted in old factories; little additional investment in capital goods was ever required.[168] Joseph Menahem Hassid (no. 306), in addition to running a commercial representation agency, also operated a talc production facility together with a Greek partner (Mr. Papacosta), under the firm name of Société Industrielle Hellénique de Talc.[169] Adding a Greek partner enabled him, like other Jewish entrepreneurs, to obtain supplies of minerals such as magnesium silicate, a raw material mined in Greek quarries and considered a national resource.

For similar reasons Salonica's Jewish entrepreneurs were also attracted to the production of paraffin, soap, and wax, by-products of the oils and fats industry. Importantly, these industries were free of ties to German trade. Although Jews had been active in the paraffin and wax trade in Macedonia since the 1920s (sections 4.6 and 5.4), any attempt to expand into Old Greece, especially Athens–Piraeus, required formal connections with Greek businessmen, that is, the presence of some level of Greek ownership. The bank documents related to the paraffin manufacturing factory jointly owned by Nahama B. Capon & Co., Henri Asséo, and the Greek Theodore Gheorgacopoulos (no. 27) illustrate this need for a Greek presence. Gheorga-copoulos's minor share of stock demonstrates that his main contribution to the firm was access to the Piraeus market. The firm's contractual terms alluded to the increased efficiency of the manufacturing process to be installed in the existing facilities, at minimal cost: the factory, land, and installations were to be rented free of charge, the owners waived receipt of a salary, and the firm's capital was to be liquidated every September following annually realised profits. Such cost reductions maximised profits. Gheorgacopoulos, Asséo & Capon was thus able to realise net profits of GRD 800,000, or more than a quarter of the initial invested capital of GRD 3,000,000, between 10 September and 31 December 1935.[170]

The capital distribution of the firm's major partner, Nahama B. Capon & Cie. (no. 26) indicated an attempt to dominate paraffin manufacture within the Greek metro-politan market. While about 58 percent (or GRD 3,500,000 out of 6,000,000) of that capital covered a shop with a factory on its upper floor and another small factory producing bougies and night lights (*veilleuse*) near the Hirsch Hospital in Salonica. The remaining 42 percent (or GRD 2,500,000 out of 6,000,000) was divided between the Gheorgacopoulos, Asséo & Capon paraffin factory (GRD 1,500,000) and Maison Gheorgacopoulos, Asséo & Capon of Piraeus (GRD 1,000,000).[171]

Such a partnership structure reinforces our original hypothesis that beyond its purely financial aspects, Jewish–Greek partnerships were created mainly to provide Jewish entrepreneurs with the legal leverage needed to penetrate the huge retail market developing in Piraeus, the new centre of urban demand. This example also indicates the direction taken by Salonica's Jewish entrepreneurs – following the trail of burgeoning demand by expanding beyond New Greek and Macedonian markets to those in Old Greece. Vertical integration throughout the commercial phase could be observed when commercial firms, such as Abram Pelossof & Amariglio (oils, soap, and paraffin) (no. 10), established a branch in Piraeus (1932).[172]

Mergers also drove the Hellenisation of Jewish entrepreneurial activity in the soap industry. A. S. Léon, S. J. Léon, Juda J. Léon, and the Yacou (also spelled Jacou) brothers merged their interests into one corporation, Macedonienne pour l'Industrie de Savon SA (no. 33), on 22 March 1929.[173] This successful enterprise eventually attracted other small-scale chemicals manufacturers such as Hassid & Cuenca (no. 31), which invested about GRD 100,000 in the firm.[174] The firm's evolution into a conglom-erate enabled Jewish as well as Greek entrepreneurs to compete with new local and foreign initiatives and thus maintain control over the domestic market. This strategy was aided by locating factories in the city's outskirts, a measure meant to broaden the circle of customers by making products easily available to hinterland consumers. Moise Jacob Hassid (no. 30), a highly reputable Jewish soap manufacturer, adopted this policy, as attested by the company's slogan: "Its excellent products are sold even in the countryside."[175] Yet, such steps were only secondary to cartelisation, the main strategy applied in industries exhibiting a sizeable Jewish presence.

Jewish merchants already active in the import of finished metal products also began to shift to new, still relatively neglected sectors based on developments in the celluloid market, which geared almost exclusively toward the private consumer.[176] Isac David Tiano (no. 168), who had left (1925) his job in the Bills of Lading Department at Banque de Salonique, began an official partnership with David Pessah, together operating a warehouse (*magazin*) for storing metals, ironwork, and so forth. Beside his partnership in the new company, which retained the name David Pessah, Tiano independently ("*pour son propre compte*") established (1932) a workshop for the production of articles made of celluloid, such as combs.[177] Similarly, Industrie Hellenique [*sic*] de Matieres [*sic*] Plastiques, Cuenca & Cie., produced plastic goods, which were distributed by the Jewish merchant emporium "Hermes", owned by S. Benveniste and H. Pardo (no. 293).[178]

It appears that entry into this new, growing niche was more successful than attempts to enter the rubber industry, which required larger investments. The chemicals industry in general and the polymer industry in particular were controlled by Greeks. These factories produced products for the military, meaning that the state was their main customer.[179] Entry into such an industry by small businessmen was almost surely doomed to failure, especially if they were Jews who had no connections in the government. This proved to be the case for Albert Ammir (no. 289), who was the principal interest holder in the dissolved firm of EVEM (the Greek acronym for the Société pour l'Industrie du Caoutchouc de Macédoine, est. 1930), a rubber products manufacturer. In order to indemnify his long-term partners, Ammir established a new partnership with his brother-in-law Michaïl, who resided in Drama (Greek Macedonia). Thanks to the liquid capital that Michaïl brought with him, the new firm was able to recruit the necessary technical personnel and proceed with the planned structural transformation of the bankrupt firm. But these efforts were insufficient to save the company, which limited itself to selling the merchandise held in stock following its failure.[180]

8.3.4 Wood Industry

The pattern observed in the metal industry appeared to be repeated in the wood industry. Table 8.3d illustrates Jewish over-representation in the wood furniture industry in tandem with the loss to Greek entrepreneurs of the Jews' historical domination of the timber trade. Although the former required modest capital and relatively simple traditional technologies, with products sold directly to end customers, timber, like minerals, was considered a national resource. The changing ethnic control of the sector may have been motivated by timber's place in the construction industry, which was frequently the object of government intervention in connection with the urban and rural reconstruction projects undertaken during the 1930s, especially in Macedonia. State restrictions on the import of timber undermined traditional Jewish domination of supply, a domination previously attributed to the Jews' advantages in the transit trade (see section 8.2). At the same time, state protectionism made timber, now mainly of local origin, available exclusively to favoured entrepreneurs. By 1937, as one informant wrote, the Greek-owned firm Kokou & Co. (est. 1912, all three partners of Salonican origin) had prospered considerably as the result of state policy: "Business in the [local] timber sector was able to realise great profits during recent years following the restrictions imposed by the state on imported timber."[181]

As the following case shows, Greek timber merchants also benefited from the kinship ties that enabled them to recruit the credit essential while nurturing favourable

Table 8.3d   Jewish-owned Firms (*N* = 16) and Greek-owned Firms (*N* = 19) in the Wood Industry, 1935–1937

Sub-Branch	*N* = 35		Percentage in Sub-Branch (B)		ERI (B/A)	
	J	G	J	G	J	G
Wood for construction	7	13	35.0	65.0	.766	1.197
Furniture	9	5	64.3	35.7	1.406	.658
Wood coal (charcoal)	0	1	.0	100.0	.000	1.842

Source: See in Appendix 8.
Notes: See Table 8.2a above.
A(J)=45.7; A(G)=54.3

relations with Greece's government-controlled construction authorities. The recovery of the Greek timber merchant, Alexander Zaharides (also spelled Zacharidis) (originally from Constantinople but a resident of Salonica as of 1927), was attributed to a loan provided by his brother Jean Zaharides, then the Directeur de la Colonisation de la Macédoine and later a most enterprising Salonican businessman (*"un de plus serieux entrepreneurs de notre ville"*, one of the most serious entrepreneurs in our city), which allowed him to overcome his difficulties in repaying his Serbian suppliers (1930–1932) (see section 7.2.2).[182]

While the lucrative timber trade attracted Greek refugee entrepreneurs, the major Jewish firms in the industry did manage, on occasion, to maintain their status. The long-established firms belonging to the extended Saltiel family even prospered. With expansion of the partnership by means of additional partners, Moise Saltiel Fils & Cie. (no. 106) came to be considered *"la plus importante de la branche à Salonique"* (the largest in the industry in Salonica), honest, solvent, and reliable. Among its various properties, the firm possessed three warehouses, one in the Nea Xyladikia quarter, another on land contiguous to the warehouse owned by the Société pour le Commerce de Bois Iomtov Is. Saporta (no. 107), and a third close to Betchinar (see Map 2). The expansion provided an opportunity to increase the firm's efficiency through deepening vertical integration, which now covered all the stages from large-scale commerce in wood for construction to the manufacturing of finished wood products for the home. The new subsidiary, operated by Isac Moise Saltiel, included a shop with a workshop producing wooden window frames and glass windowpanes, both lucrative growing industries at the time.[183]

Tariff protection similarly stimulated new business in wood for home consumption. The local Jewish-owned business Beja Frères (no. 94), which operated a shop and two factories producing mirrors, window glass, whistles, toys, and snuffboxes, among other items, grew in profitability. According to an informant, "The operation of their affairs is normal, with a tendency toward improvement due to the state protection given to all enterprises recognised as viable."[184]

The expansion of Jewish home carpentry in Salonica and intensification of vertical integration explain the 1934 relocation from Athens to Salonica of M. I. Barouh (no. 93), a small firm supplying wood for furniture manufacture. M. I. Barouh operated the local sub-branch of the Athens' branch of the international firm Winter, which supplied semi-raw materials for carpenters in Salonica.[185] Similarly, the sub-branch run by Yahiel Jacob Alevy (no. 92), a commercial representative dealing in imported walnut wood, apparently from Yugoslavia via Salonica, was considered to be too small to operate as an independent branch, like the one managed by his father Jacob.[186] Both firms had participated in small-scale production, mainly carpentry. Their owners also shared a common country of origin, Yugoslavia, which might hint at a shift from the large-scale transactions of wood for construction to small-scale transactions of wood for carpentry. Their membership in transnational networks may also have given them a relative advantage in the trade.

8.3.5 Paper, Stationery, and Mass Communications

The same trends characterising the other sectors mentioned here were also to be observed in the printing and paper industry. Hence, in the wake of intensifying competition, manufacturing was added to commercial activities. Jewish entrepreneurs actively initiated horizontal as well as vertical integration in paper. As Table 8.3e shows, six Jewish firms were active in this branch as opposed to only three Greek firms.[187]

Jews were also among the principal shareholders of the Société Anonyme Hellénique de Papeterie Aighion, a paper mill. The wealthy Haïm Benveniste (no. 234), a major shareholder, specialised in marketing this mill's products. Yet, he also imported newsprint, which was considered a cheap semi-raw input for the production of wrapping paper as well as office stationery.[188] Newsprint was generally produced from the fibres extracted from various softwood trees by a mechanical milling process, without the addition of the chemicals often used to remove lignin from pulp. Due to its relatively low cost and high strength, this type of paper was favoured by publishers and printers.

With intensifying competition cutting into profits, efficiency measures were introduced here as well. A major source of savings was reduction in the cost of inputs, which motivated the shift to cheap imported semi-raw materials. Profit maximization was achieved through the local production of alternatives to imported finished items. Errico Jakob Arones (no. 233), a Jewish entrepreneur of Salonican origin, was able to save his firm by importing cheap newsprint as well as cellulose for local paper production.[189]

Jewish producers of wrapping paper generally worked in small family workshops.

Table 8.3e Jewish-owned Firms (N = 19) and Greek-owned Firms (N = 7) in the Paper Industry, 1935–1937

Sub-Branch	N = 26		Percentage in Sub-Branch (B)		ERI (B/A)	
	J	G	J	G	J	G
Paper importing and manufacturing	6	3	66.7	33.3	.912	1.238
Office equipment; bookstores	9	2	81.8	18.2	1.120	.675
Typewriters and radios	1	0	100.0	.0	1.368	.000
Cinema	3	2	60.0	40.0	.821	1.486

Source: See in Appendix 8.
Notes: See Table 8.2a above.
A(J) = 73.1; A(G) = 26.9

Consider Pepo Moise Perahia (no. 238), a firm established by the late Moïse Perahia, who extended his business from the wholesale trade in paper and cartons to the manufacture of substitutes for imported stationery and paper products.[190] Another firm active in the industry, Abram J. Juda (no. 237), lithographers, joined forces with Salomon Cohen (no. 232), the firm owned by Juda's brother-in-law, which manufactured office registers.[191] This partnership reflected more than diversification – it provided evidence of the Jewish preference for vertically integrated firms with trusted kinsmen and co-religionists.

The Jewish concentration in wrapping paper and stationery production also reflected the evolving shift away from the manufacture of cigarette paper, a branch now subject to state surveillance after its official declaration as a state monopoly. Since 1926, in an effort to aid the tobacco industry, the state used its legal power to authorise the exclusive right of import, possession and sale of paper bobbins by the cigarette industry.[192] While Greek-owned companies such as Handaris & Kaplanides and Tsacassianos & Sophianopoulos easily obtained licenses to import bales of cigarette paper,[193] Abram Hassid (no. 236), a Jewish cigarette paper manufacturer, preferred to exit from this sector in 1931. Hassid was motivated by three factors: his desire to escape the tight control and what was in effect surveillance of Jewish producers by the Greek authorities once this product became a government monopoly;[194] the international tobacco crisis that threatened solvency; and in all probability the wish to avoid any connection with the tobacco industry, which was now tied to Nazi Germany. Hassid therefore turned to the production of office stationery. His business acumen apparently helped his business survive the increasingly troublesome constraints imposed on the industry, "as a result of the strong competition currently in existence in the branch as well as the general crisis. . . . "[195] Hence, the firm's estimated capital was able to grow from GRD 750,000 in 1935 to GRD 1,500,000 in 1937.[196]

The paper industry was, of course, intimately connected with the major means of mass communication – the press. Yet, contrary to their often-desperate straits in the print paper industry (see sections 6.2 and 10.2) Jewish entrepreneurs flourished in the mass media through the horizontal entry into related branches. While indigenous Greeks operated the Dionyssia (est. 1930),[197] and Ylissia (est. 1932)[198] cinemas, Benico Segura (no. 251) and Elie Attas, co-director and proprietor, respectively, of the Jewish *Independent* newspaper, worked in association with Salonica's two most popular cinemas, the Alcazar and Pantheon. Attas, the wealthier of the two investors,[199] financed the two cinemas and managed to integrate the firm into the vertically structured mass communication industry, which covered everything from publishing newspapers to importing movies, including newsreels.

By obtaining rights for the exclusive representation of American film companies, Jews were able to penetrate new branches of the entertainment industry, which were still "open to all".[200] As of 1919, Saby Nissim Mallah (no. 250) acted as the exclusive representative of Fox Films, Athens.[201] Some firms, like that of Jacques Yacoel (no. 248), entered the branch by sharing representation of the European firm Philips (distribution of radios and accessories) with the Greek firm Telloglou.[202]

* * *

This review of Jewish entrepreneurial activity in light industries was meant to demonstrate the realisation of historical trends developing throughout the world in addition to those representing responses to the transformations in the Greek political and economic environment. Light industry in the 1930s required low-level, periodic investments but also the avoidance of friction with the increasing mechanisms of government control. Participation in these industries also reflected a preference for liquidity that has been found to characterise minority entrepreneurship in general. Liquidity considerations would become increasingly important after the government blocked the accounts held by foreign residents and by émigrés, such as the Jews who sought to escape the local political constraints by immigrating to Europe and Mandatory Palestine.

The clothing industry provides another excellent example of these patterns. It was also characterised by a high level of liquidity together with low capital investments and unsophisticated, portable technologies, such as the sewing machine. What made this industry unique, however, was its reliance on a labour force composed primarily of women.

8.4 Textiles and the Ready-Made Clothing Industry

Salonica's local textile industry, already dominated by local Greek entrepreneurs, was not inviting to Jewish entrepreneurs, especially after the government introduced its protection policy (Table 8.4a). As an alternative, Jews chose to deepen their presence in the clothing industry by continuing to import the necessary inputs, such as yarns and other semi-finished raw materials (Table 8.4b). Recruitment of Jewish workers in labour-intensive clothing manufacture was more directly affected by the state of the Jewish economy, which we discuss in section 9.5.

8.4.1 Continued Import of Clothing Inputs

Although local firms producing cotton cloth benefited from protective tariffs, a contemporary Jewish observer noted that the wholesale trade in imported cotton cloth remained profitable: "Business has been good for all merchants in the branch. In recent years, profits have been very healthy."[203] The British Consul aptly summarised this

Table 8.4a   Jewish-owned Firms (N = 10) and Greek-owned Firms (N = 8) in the Textile Industry, 1935–1937

Sub-Branch	N = 18		Percentage in Sub-Branch (B)		ERI (B/A)	
	J	G	J	G	J	G
Spinning and weaving cotton	0	7	.0	100.0	.000	2.250
Carpets	0	1	.0	100.0	.000	2.250
Jute, sacks, nets, and ropes	3	0	100.0	.0	1.800	.000
Trade in cotton and wool yarn	6	0	100.0	.0	1.800	.000
Oilcloth	1	0	100.0	.0	1.800	.000

Source: See in Appendix 8.
Notes: See Table 8.2a above.
A(J) = 55.6; A(G) = 44.4

Table 8.4b Jewish-owned Firms (*N* = 92) and Greek-owned Firms (*N* = 70) in the Clothing Industry, 1935–1937

Sub-Branch	*N* = 162		Percentage in Sub-Branch (B)		ERI (B/A)	
	J	G	J	G	J	G
Sewing machines; knitting machines; hosiery	12	17	41.4	58.6	.729	1.357
Confection: Ready-made garments	12	4	75.0	25.0	1.321	.579
Clothing accessories: Manufacturing	4	5	44.4	55.6	.783	1.286
Hats	7	3	70.0	30.0	1.233	.694
Trade in haberdashery and novelty goods (*nouveautés*)	20	17	54.1	45.9	.952	1.063
Trade in fabrics and draperies	37	22	62.7	37.3	1.104	.863
Mattresses	0	1	.0	100.0	.000	2.314

Source: See in Appendix 8.
Notes: See Table 8.2a above.
A(J) = 56.8; A(G) = 43.2

situation: "Nevertheless, the importation of textiles and textile materials is still the largest item in the Greek customs returns and it is to correct this state of affairs that the Government affords protection and assistance to this growing industry."[204]

Salonica, one of the industry's centres, benefited especially from the rising value of the local output, produced by the rapidly developing spinning and weaving industry. Yet, the presence of cotton yarn (Table 8.4a) and fine fabric (Table 8.4b) importers, Jewish and Greek alike (Table 8.4), is explained by the near absence of local production of fine yarns comparable in quality to imported goods. Locally manufactured cotton cloth was generally produced of cheap coarse yarns, destined for consumption by the country's peasants, labourers, and the military.[205] As long as the tariffs protecting the local fine cotton cloth industry were relatively low – when compared with the high protective tariffs on imported coarse yarn – the sector remained profitable. However, because the few existing Greek producers of fine yarns were successful in pressuring the government to impose restrictions on the import of new technologies (e.g., electric looms), expansion of the local fine yarn industry remained stalled. While a setback to overall industrial development, the same restrictions were effective in enabling the few established fine yarn producers who had installed modern equipment prior to 1932 to maintain their almost monopolistic power.[206]

Jewish importers were therefore able to continue to import semi-finished inputs from Britain, a country that had not signed any clearing agreements with Greece. Maison Mario Lezer Salmona (no. 190), for example, continued to represent the Glasgow commercial agent charged with distributing Coats sewing threads until the firm's demise with Mario's death in 1937.[207] For similar reasons, Jewish firms importing knitted goods and cloth from Britain, items targeted at the urban or wealthier sectors of society, were able to survive. S[alomon]. A. Mordoh (no. 313) represented, *inter alia*, Manchester City Mills (a cotton cloth producer), M. I. Florentin, Manchester (an English exporter of British textiles), other English and even German firms.[208] In the notions branch of the industry, firms like Salomon Menahem Rousso (no. 188), commercial representatives, were able to maintain shops for semi-wholesale and retail sale of imported buttons and costume jewellery.[209] Drapers such as the Sidés brothers chose to extend their presence in the branch by investing in the Anonymous Company for Trading in Woollen Fabrics, Albion[210] (Illustration 7). This Greek name for Great Britain alluded to these fabrics' origin while obfuscating its Jewish ownership.

Analogous conditions prevailed in the highly protected silk industry. The local industry, brought to Greece by refugee entrepreneurs coming from Broussa, the former Ottoman silk centre,[211] increased silk floss production more than threefold between 1922 and 1930.[212] A sign of the seriousness with which contravention of the protection policy was viewed is revealed in the following case. A note found among the mass of documents located in Banque Amar indicates that in 1930, the Saltiel brothers (due to the lack of given names, the specific individuals cannot be identified) had been implicated in contraband shipments of silk floss. After being found guilty, the brothers were imprisoned and their firm heavily fined.[213] Jewish merchants such as Haim Isac Nissim Succ. (no. 186) and "HERMES", H. Pardo & M. Carasso (no. 296), nonetheless continued to import silk stuffs from Japan.[214]

Jewish firms continued to supply woollen and cotton yarn inputs to local hosiery and knitted goods manufacturers. Fils de Jacob Saltiel & Broudo (no. 191) therefore managed to achieve a relatively important place in this branch.[215] At the same time, the old Jewish trading house Veritas (no. 141), kept operating by Ino Benmayor, the firm's remaining partner after the emigration of Bension Cohen to Paris in 1931 and Joseph A. Molho to Brussels in 1932,[216] continued to import new technologies targeted primarily to Jewish hosiery and clothing manufacturers.

8.4.2 Niching: Distribution of Local Cheap Coarse Cotton Goods

The introduction of weighty protective tariffs on imported textiles, especially cotton cloth, in addition to exchange rate differences, placed a heavy burden on the recovery of Jewish importers of cotton cloth and forced Jewish merchants to shift to the purchase and distribution of inexpensive textiles of local manufacture, in order to survive. These goods would then be sold in the mass market developing in Salonica's hinterland in conjunction with the agriculture's rehabilitation. This was apparently the reason why Raphaël Simtov Asséo, after about twenty years of collaboration with Maison Affias Frères,[217] decided to establish a new partnership, Asséo & Capuano (no. 171) in 1934, which would sell (wholesale and semi-wholesale) textiles and *fichus* (the traditional triangular shawl worn by peasant women) throughout the surrounding villages.[218] Juda Noah & Fils (est. 1923) (no. 222) likewise engaged in wholesale and retail trade "of lower quality fabrics for use by the labouring classes".[219]

8.4.3 Textile Manufacture: Cotton Ginning and Fishing Nets

Like entrepreneurs active in other branches, Jewish merchants adopted vertical integration of clothing manufacture with merchandising and sales as a survival strategy. The decisions made by the old Jewish firm of Elie [S.] Pinhas & Cie. (no. 137) demonstrate this trend. Upon the firm's reconstitution in 1933 (it had been dissolved in 1929; see section 5.6), it was listed with Salonica's Chamber of Commerce under the category of "industry". Its new activities indicated a shift away from commerce in raw (apparently unginned) cotton throughout the countryside to a vertically integrated industrial enterprise involved in every stage of production, from cotton ginning to commerce in raw cotton. The main reason for the re-entry and restructuring appears to have been the firm's attempt to fill the vast demand for local substitutes for the now-restricted import of quality textiles that, coupled with the high tariffs imposed on imported coarse yarn in 1932, had created serious shortages. The slow rise in raw cotton prices after 1933, together with the availability of low-cost labour following the fall in real wages, provided additional incentives for entry into cotton manufacturing. Exploding demand for indigenous raw cotton also prompted increased cultivation: Between 1933 and 1937, the cultivated area doubled and the unginned cotton crop quadrupled; local annual industrial consumption of ginned cotton rose from 5,610 tons in 1922 to 21,843 tones in 1935.[220] New vacancies were thus created for gin operators in companies such as Elie Pinhas & Cie.,[221] which employed seasonal workers and had invested about GRD 700,000 in machinery as well as in merchandise.[222]

The case of Saltiel & Elie Angel & Fils (no. 139; est. 1929) illustrates a somewhat different structural transformation. The original firm, Saltiel & Elie Angel (est. 1895), had begun operations by importing and then selling cotton yarns at wholesale (Appendix 5, no. 207). The expanded firm, established in 1929[223] when Angel's sons joined the business, entered a new growth industry: the manufacture and sale of fishing nets and related equipment:[224] This move also benefited Jewish-owned jute and rope manufacturers, whose products were used to make fishing nets. The firm's financial strength indicates that this transition was profitable.[225] "This firm has enlarged its scope, and consequently production, in response to demand."[226]

8.4.4 Mass-Produced Clothing: Hosiery and Confection

Together with the spinning and weaving industries, identified with the mainstream economy, the clothing industry, especially the relatively new ready-made garment (confection) industry, experienced rapid growth throughout the mid-1930s. However, a comparison of the value of clothing (including footwear) produced in 1934 (GRD 56,300) with that of spun and woven articles (GRD 3,328,605),[227] unambiguously testifies to the fact that during this period the industry, which welcomed Greek and Jewish entrepreneurs, was in its formative stages. Unlike the situation in other sectors, the protective tariff policy had not spurred creation of a major industrial sector capable of keeping pace with demand.[228] One sign of the economic rationalisation demanded by this situation was the strategy adopted by Moise I. Mordoh (no. 149), a former partner in the dissolved (1931) firm of Bitran & Mordoh, who opened an independent wholesale hosiery establishment in tandem with a nearby workshop for the manufacture of inexpensive knitted goods. According to Banque Amar records, "During the past two years firm's affairs have been excellent due to the restrictions introduced by the state on the importation of similar articles from abroad."[229]

8.4.4.1 Knitted Goods
The mergers formed between Jewish and Greek knitting mills throughout the 1930s indicate how much the knitting industry had ceased to be a Jewish niche. Although Banque Amar archives generally reveal a smaller number of Greek firms than Jewish firms (see above 8.1), the Greek hosiery manufacturing firms were greater in number than the Jewish firms active in the industry (see Table 8.4). Ethnic ownership *per se* was not, however, the sole factor that differentiated between firms. More significantly,

ethnic ownership indicated structural differences. Whereas Jewish production was based on small workshops attached to stores selling the finished goods, Greek firms and Greek–Jewish mergers (relying on Jewish capital and female refugee labour; see Table 8.4) established factories in the dense residential districts populated primarily by Greek refugees (section 9.5 below).

Indeed, within the hosiery sector, situating a workshop close to a store standardised and rationalised the mode of production and increased profits while it took advantage of the protective tariff policy. The number of such vertically structured concerns founded by Jewish businessmen consequently multiplied. Alfred (aka Abram) Guelermann (also spelled Kuelermann, no. 146), a Polish national who arrived in Salonica in 1928, soon became a partner in Sam Sarfati (also spelled Sarfatty) & Co. (no. 152) after contributing GRD 300,000 to the enterprise. In 1935, he opened a second hosiery factory bearing his wife's name, Rosa. After the dissolution of the partnership with Sarfati (see below), Alfred took over the R. Guelermann factory (no. 146) and merged the two firms under his own name – A. Guelermann – in September 1937.[230]

Still another route taken by Jewish entrepreneurs in the hosiery sector, which paralleled trends in the metal industry, was expansion of production by purchasing stock issued by Jewish corporations. While Daniel S. Modiano (no. 161) continued to manufacture and sell ready-made men's shirts,[231] Modiano Frères, following the death of G. di S. Modiano in May 1931 expanded the firm's business by transforming it (May 1935) into Makedoniki Kaltsopiia SA (no. 148). The property owned by this new corporation included a building containing a new factory located in the Harilaos suburb; it had two floors and was equipped with state-of-the-art machinery for the manufacture of women's luxury hosiery (*bas grand luxe*). The factory was considered one of the most advanced in Macedonia.[232]

This pattern was repeated in the case of Sam A. Sarfati, but within the framework of a Jewish–Greek merger. Sarfati dissolved his original partnership (Sam Sarfati & Co., est. 1933) with Alfred Guelermann in September 1936 in order to participate in a new merger, Fabriques Réunies de Bas et Chaussettes de Sal/Que, SA (no. 144), which incorporated an additional three Greek-owned factories for the purpose of controlling internal competition: "These companies [SAs] have merged to end the competition existing between them."[233] Sarfati's workshop, which was attached to his hosiery shop in the city's commercial quarter, was consequently integrated into the new corporation. The merger's installation, located in the Harilaos quarter (section 9.5.1) represented, together with its shop, only a portion of Sarfati's investments: he also had interests in another hosiery manufacturing corporation, SA Vergopoulos, which made a profit of GRD 250,000 annually.[234]

Another case of expansion through creation of a Jewish–Greek partnership was that of Papadimitriou & Assael (no. 150), which operated one of the largest hosiery factories in Salonica ("*une importante fabrique de bas et chaussettes de notre ville*"). This merger (1936) revived the operations of two dissolved firms – Assael & Lazarides and Papadimitriou Frères – each of which had owned a hosiery factory. Given that Levi Tazartes, a commercial representative for foreign fabric firms, had interests (1935) in Assael & Lazarides amounting to GRD 100,000, Tazartes became a silent partner (1937) when the new firm came into being.[235]

To conclude, while Greeks were able to increase their presence in hosiery manufacturing thanks to their access to cheap refugee female labour (Table 8.4b), Jewish entrepreneurs remained involved in small-medium scale vertically structured firms, that is, hosiery workshops attached to stores. Simultaneously, they expanded their activities into the new, rapidly growing mass production of clothing.

8.4.4.2 Confection

Jewish entrepreneurs active in the growing ready-made clothing market also adopted the strategy of operating a workshop close to the owner's retail establishment. Such an arrangement contributed to cutting costs by exploiting the same premises for the full range of production and sales activities. Tchico & Bitran (no. 163) operated a store and atelier for the manufacture of men's and infants' clothing. In addition to the two to four salespeople employed in its store, it also employed several tailors in its atelier. The firm was considered the largest in its branch.[236] Just as frequently, manufacturing represented a separate line of a store's activities. A major example of this arrangement was Semtov Saltiel, a sister firm of the Jewish retailers Saltiel & Guilidi (no. 162), which maintained a workshop producing men's shirts within its store.[237] In their campaign against insolvency, several fabric importers vertically expanded their activities into related, already established firms. Barouh S. Venezia (no. 164), with its sizable resources, operated a store for the retail sale of draperies and tailoring equipment as well as a workshop for ready-made clothing.[238] This trade thus became a fortress of Jewish businessmen in Salonica on account of the fabrics and draperies trade, which gradually shrank due to the high tariffs and the high interest rates attached to the loans often required for large-scale purchases of goods.[239]

The increasing Jewish presence in the ready-made clothing industry was also felt in the manufacture of notions. Experienced Jewish importers had clear advantages over local producers, not the least of which involved the expertise needed to identify new vacancies created by the dearth of imported goods following the introduction of protective tariffs. The firm of Moise Paladino Fils & Cie (no. 167) thus maintained a workshop producing tourniquets in the basement of its haberdashery and hosiery store. According to one informant, "The business was invigorated due to the application of restrictions on imported products that have no local substitutes. Everyone knows that tourniquets were imported from abroad before the restrictions."[240]

It should therefore come as no surprise that Simon Molho (no. 184), who had previously been the owner of a workshop producing and selling furniture, decided to apply his skills to the clothing sector. And so, he opened a store for the sale of tailors' supplies in 1920.[241]

8.4.4.3 Hats

The attempt of Jewish entrepreneurs to control competition in the local millinery market motivated complex business partnerships with Greek hat manufacturers. Moscovitch Frères and Isac Jacob Francès, which had bought (1925) the established firm of Maison Trilor, Dalendas & Haniotis, formed a mixed liability company together with Mario Moscovitch, Leon Haim Moscovitch, Isac Jacob Francès, Serafim L. Serafimides (a silent partner), and Haim and Salomon Isac Levy (silent partners). The new firm, together with Salonica's largest Jewish hat manufacturer, Makedoniki Pilopiia Moscovitch, Francès & Cie. (no. 175), quietly acquired control over the labyrinthine network of hat producers in the city. The factory for caps and hats had belonged to Moscovitch Frères and Isac Jacob Francès, whereas the store in Rue

Egnatia, Makedoniki Pilopiia, was owned exclusively by Moscovitch Frères.[242] This firm also had interests in A. Arianoutsos & Co. (no. 170),[243] another mixed liability company (*société en commandite*) producing hats that had absorbed (January 1936) the business formerly maintained by N.K. Arianoutsos, a branch of the already dissolved (1933) Athenian corporation of the same name. The new firm's partners included Antonios Arianoutsos, who resided in Athens; Saltiel S. Cohen, a textile merchant and former partner of the dissolved firm Saltiel & [S.] Cohen (Appendix 5, no. 297); Makedoniki Pilopiia Moscovitch, Francès & Cie. (no. 175); and lastly, Albert de Majo, a silent partner who contributed GRD 150,000. This partnership also operated a store selling hosiery, hats, men's wear, capeskin (sheepskin leather), fine leather goods, and footwear, with an atelier run by the Greek tailor Panayotides for the production of custom-made men's suits. By preserving the original Greek name of the Jewish–Greek partnerships, the partners were able to hide their true identities, a device adopted to evade economic discrimination. Moreover, the reputation of Saltiel [S] Cohen was such that his participation appeared to ensure the firm's success.[244] Cohen, who owned 33 percent of the partnership, was able to rebuild his commercial empire by opening a vast store for the wholesale and retail trade in draperies in early 1937, after his partner's (in Saltiel & Cohen) emigration to British Mandatory Palestine.[245]

Banque Amar records indicate that only two other Greek hat manufacturers – Constantin Zografakis (est. worth: GRD 300,000)[246] and Seraphimides Frères (est. worth: GRD 300,000),[247] with the latter incorporated into the Saltiel partnership – were operating in the city at the time. Based on its expertise in women's hat decoration, another firm, the Jewish-owned Jacob Gabriel Alevy (no. 169),[248] was able to horizontally and vertically dominate that sector.

8.4.4.4 Footwear and Leather

During the 1930s, increasing demand for footwear and leather goods in Germany and France, countries that had full clearing agreements with Greece, prompted the extension of Jewish entrepreneurial activity to tanning, fed by their access to raw materials. Samuel Avayou & Frères (no. 116), which maintained a modernised tannery in addition to a retail store, realised substantial profits during 1936 due to the strong demand for rough leather in particular.[249] Ammir & Mevorah (no. 115) likewise ran a tannery in addition to a chain of stores selling raw leather for shoe soles as well as tanned sheep leather for other shoe parts. The firm procured locally produced rough leather and exported part of its production.[250]

A survival tactic adopted by the sector's Jewish firms was the giving of down payments to Greek tanners to ensure the supply of raw materials. In a similar fashion, Jewish entrepreneurs acted as agents – *commission pour compte* – connecting the cobblers spread throughout the Greek Islands with leather goods consignees (receivers) in Greece. Sabetay I. Nehama (no. 126) made advance payments to its consignees for the dispatched goods produced by the craftsmen. The arrangement proved to be quite satisfactory for all parties, as indicated by the considerable increase in dispatches.[251]

Jewish footwear firms that had already responded to rising demand following the post-Transfer resettlement of Greek refugees in rural Macedonia now began to extend their businesses to the peasantry. Market opportunities were sufficiently promising to entice small shopkeepers, such as Liaou Camhi (no. 123), who left the grocery business to open a store (1924) for the sale of cheap footwear (e.g., sandals) to farmers.[252]

Table 8.4c Jewish-owned Firms (*N* = 23) and Greek-owned Firms (*N* = 25) in the Footwear and Leather Goods Industry, 1935–1937

Sub-Branch	*N* = 48		Percentage in Sub-Branch (B)		ERI (B/A)	
	J	G	J	G	J	G
Trade in rawhide	7	10	41.2	58.8	.859	1.129
Tanning	2	1	66.7	33.3	1.391	.640
Footwear and leather goods	14	14	50.0	50.0	1.043	.960

Source: See in Appendix 8.
Notes: See Table 8.2a above.
A(J) = 47.9; A(G) = 52.1

Yet, Jewish industrialists continued to manufacture and sell fashionable shoes. The old firm Moise Cohen (est. 1896), known as the "*Grande cordonnerie à l'Elegance*" (the "Great Shoemaker of Elegance")[253] (Appendix 5, no. 259) during the 1920s, was officially dissolved in 1932 and re-established under the name of Cohen Frères (no. 124). The renamed firm engaged in confection and the sale of all types (*en général*) of shoes and remained a major shoe producer in the city ("*leur Maison devenue une des principales cordonneries de notre ville*").[254]

Vertical integration of Jewish-owned firms in the industry also affected sector structure. The well-known firm of Benico & Isac Angel & Cie. (no.119), which supplied processed leather and accessories for cobblers, also held a 60 percent interest in J. Cazassis & Cie., a shoelace and accessories factory (i.e., *amadou* – tinder).[255]

8.5 Sector Structure and Jewish Networks

Minority–majority relations as they developed within the framework of the autarky-centred policy adopted by the Greek government altered the structure of opportunities available to Jewish entrepreneurs during the 1930s. The increasingly strident competition waged between Jewish and Greek merchants spread beyond the micro level of small-scale trade to entire industries. In contrast with Greek merchants who expanded their business with Germany based on "individual clearing agreements" as well as on the formula "tobacco against arms", Jewish entrepreneurs withdrew from industries (e.g., tobacco) that were tied to the Nazi economy. The branch structure that had previously characterised the Jewish economy consequently narrowed and became more concentrated.

As the 1930s progressed, Jews thus distanced themselves from three sectors of entrepreneurial activity: those dominated by Greek entrepreneurs, those in which government was a major client (e.g., infrastructure), and those tied to trade with Nazi Germany. Instead, they directed their energies to industries like clothing, which belonged to the private sector and were thus less sensitive to national-level ethnic discrimination. An undated official report states that Jews were absent from commerce in currants (a leading export crop) and mercantile armament.[256] While the former was second only to tobacco as a key agricultural export from Old Greece, and was thus dominated by Greek merchants,[257] the latter was monopolised by its main customer, the state. The commerce in arms was thus channelled to the Greek merchants who were linked to the administration through political or social networks. These networks also functioned as pressure groups attempting to obtain concessions and benefits for their members, which culminated in controlling market competition and designing industrial policy.[258]

While Jews did integrate into the Greek national economy, they were crowded into intermediate commerce, in niches that were not susceptible to the influence of evolving government monopolies.[259] This state of affairs marked the second Venizelos government (1928–1932) in particular, when links between politics and business were bolstered to ensure the smooth adaptation of the institutional framework to the needs of an emerging autarky.[260] Networks of Greek government favourites blocked the entry of outsiders, including Jews, into the profitable sectors like construction and heavy industry. Throughout the 1930s, several scandals revealed the high degree of collusion between the political administration and economic power.[261] While indigenous and refugee Greek businessmen had easy – if not always legal – access to government contracts,[262] Jewish businessmen sought Greek political intermediaries in order to smooth their access to those same opportunities.

During the 1930s, entrenchment in vacant niches and traditional Jewish niches intensified. Jewish networks, based on common culture and family relations, collaborated in order to obtain the capital required to compete with non-Jewish rivals. The latter, usually clients of the National Bank of Greece, met this challenge by seeking this financing institution's help in supporting cartelisation and creating barriers to entry.[263]

Reduction of costs through the introduction of efficiency measures was commonly employed as a survival tactic by Jewish entrepreneurs as it increased business while reducing the need for middlemen. As indicated previously, the most common method was to integrate commerce with production. Another tactic was to manufacture local substitutes for expensive imports after protective tariffs were introduced. Trade in final consumer goods, that is, items sold directly to the end consumer in the open, competitive, and "colour-blind" market, was also stressed. Such merchandise included, *inter alia*, office equipment and paper products, the production and sale of which could rest solely on Jewish expertise.[264] A significant number of small Jewish corner shops (*Kinkaylería y Bonetería*) (see Illustrations 4 and 5) that sold items ranging from small metalwares, notions, and underclothing were able to remain in operation during the mid-1930s because their stock was manufactured by the shop's owner, which reduced external costs. This also explains why the clothing industry, which traditionally attracted immigrant workers, became a major new outlet for Jewish entrepreneurship. Trade in commodities likewise allowed Jewish merchants to overcome increasing competition and economic chauvinism through aggressive price cutting (sometimes to the point of bankruptcy). This policy confirmed the rural clientele's belief "that one can [still] buy more cheaply in Jewish stores"[265] while it encouraged much of the urban clientele, even after hearing the call to boycott Jewish shopkeepers, to secretly continue purchasing goods from Jewish shops.[266]

With the credit crunch, Jewish entrepreneurs also returned to act as bankers to Greek agriculture producers, either by advancing funds to cultivators and purchasing crops before they were planted, or through other arrangements. In this way, Jewish entrepreneurs regained significant control over the supply of agricultural commodities.

International family-based networks also ensured a flow of information that might lead to the identification of new profitable opportunities and their financial realisation.[267] The rich experience accumulated by Jewish importers of clothing, semi-finished goods (fabrics, sewing threads, etc.), and varied accessories enabled them to be among the first to identify the new industrial niches created following the enactment of protective taxes. Long-standing ties with European manufacturers and distributors provided Salonica's Jewish entrepreneurs with access to industrial intelligence, which they shared with co-religionists. Jewish businessmen were thus among the first to produce and sell local substitutes for imported goods.

Jewish commercial networks nevertheless began to acquire a "Hellenic" coloration. Networks established between Greece and Egypt began to make greater use of Greek diaspora as middlemen, who connected the developing Egyptian market, then under British colonial rule, with the Greek market.[268] At the same time, commercial ties were strengthened with the Salonican Jewish Diaspora located in France and Britain as well as in a new location – Mandatory Palestine. Signs of developing business relations with American producers also appeared.

The members of these networks became more and more dependent on each other, whether through vertical integration or expanding networks. Consider Moise S. Abastado (no. 138), Salonica's exclusive wholesaler of the jute articles produced by the Jewish firm of Jutificio Torrès SA.[269] Abastado was assured of his supply of colonial commodities by other firms, such as David & Joseph Abastado (no. 5), previously associated with the wholesaler Maison Haim D. Abastado (Appendix 5, no.1). All these individuals belonged to one extended family.[270]

Intensification of internal dependence was also adopted in the competitive tobacco industry. Raphaël Jakob Varsano, the senior partner in the tobacco merchants Raphaël Jakob Varsano & Co. (no. 253), and the brother-in-law of Elie Torrès,[271] was also a member of the board of Torrès SA.[272] Like Varsano, Salomon Is. Amariglio was occupied mainly in the sale of sacks and cords for use in the tobacco trade, together with small-scale trading in cheap tobacco leaf.[273] This linkage ensured the Jewish entrepreneur a supply of sacks required to ship his bales of tobacco leaf at minimal cost as they were bought directly from the producer.

Yet, as the next chapter will show, these methods were limited in their effect. During periods of unemployment, the adoption of new organisational methods, often resting on community solidarity, were necessary for business survival. This observation applied especially to the worker recruitment that impacted on the Jewish economy.

9 | Jewish Entrepreneurial Patterns and the Jewish Economy

In this chapter we identify the reciprocities linking Jewish entrepreneurship with the Jewish economy as it changed during the 1930s. Based on micro data derived from the archive kept by the Jewish-owned Banque Amar, this chapter traces Jewish-owned businesses from their establishment, usually on the basis of family and ethnic resources (9.1). We explore the various organisational and managerial strategies adopted by individual firms to survive (9.2 and 9.6) but also how they preserved places of employment for their co-religionists during rising unemployment (9.5). The information culled from Banque Amar sources will help us identify the types of business know-how, the private (9.3 and 9.4) as well as the ethnic resources available to Jewish entrepreneurs (9.6), in addition to the long-term trends that characterised Salonica's Jewish-owned economy.

9.1 Self-Employment and Family Firm Formation

In 1938, the proportion of Jewish firms out of all firms registered in Salonica's Chamber of Commerce and Industry was still higher than the proportion of Jews in the city's population: now 35 percent (935 out of 2,726) and less than 25 percent, respectively (see section 6.3). The proportion of these firms was sizeable when compared with the proportion of Greek firms: Greek firms represented only 62 percent (1,684 out of 2,726 firms) of all registered firms,[1] well below the proportion of Greeks (at least 75 percent) in Salonica's population.

Even if we assume that all ethnic segments experienced a post-slump boom in new firm creation commensurate with their shares in the population, the significant number of Jewish firms formed during the 1930s (see Appendix 8) appears to have stemmed from another source: the lack of alternative employment; that is, self-employment was not necessarily volitional.[2] Stated differently, these new entrepreneurs appear to have been influenced primarily by negative "push" factors that drove them towards self-employment as a shelter against discrimination or, alternatively, unemployment in the recession-blighted mainstream economy. Yet, as Chapter 8 indicated, self-employment's "pull" factors – whether in partnerships or single ventures – also offered opportunities for success.

The case of Joseph S. Djahon (no. 303)[3] illustrates how self-employment served as a solution to uncertainty. Djahon had acquired skills in foreign trade during long training in several Greek-owned financial institutions. He held the position of Director of Foreign Exchange at a local bank until 1927, followed by a position in a major commercial firm. By 1929 he had been appointed cashier (*caissier*) of the Greek head-quarters of the Swiss firm Compagnie Générale Financière des Tabacs SA, a post that he retained until 1935. It seems that Djahon turned to self-employment following his dismissal from the tobacco firm. He opened an office for the general commercial representation of companies dealing in textiles, chemicals, metals, and raw materials (*matières premières*) while taking advantage of his long familiarity with the firms active in these branches. His financial connections extended throughout the internal Greek market and to Belgium as well.[4] The story of Joseph R. Hazan (no. 174) also reflects such a "push" factor. Hazan, an employee of S. Matalon until 1920 and then a partner in Calderon & Hazan (1920–1930), joined the firm of Abram Florentin upon the dissolution of his previous partnership. After Florentin retired (1934), Hazan opened a small shop of his own.[5]

The history of Fils d'Azriel Francès reflects the pattern of venture formation in response to unemployment rather than changes in family firm structure. Its roots were laid in 1920, with the creation of the partnership of Arditti, Benforado & Hanen, dealers in hardware (*quincailleries*) and haberdashery (Appendix 5, no. 97). Upon Hanen's retirement in 1930, recruitment of a new partner led to a change in the firm's name to Arditti, Benforado & Francès. This firm remained intact until Arditti retired in 1933, leaving the two remaining partners, Benjamin Benforado and Azriel Francès, to sustain the firm (Benforado & Francès) until its dissolution in April 1935 (see section 8.3). Jacques and Henri Francès, Azriel's sons and former employees of the dissolved firms Benforado & Francès and Mechulam & Matarasso, thereupon formed a new partnership in May 1935, with their father's participation.[6] The new firm retained Azriel as the "senior" partner while his sons prepared to lead the firm, evidently in order to take advantage of his experience as well as his resources, primarily real estate holdings, to be used as security for bank loans.

The case of Lezer Angel also illustrates how the new generation of Jewish entre-preneurs appreciated such advantages. The senior Angel was not required to contribute any money for his share in the footwear manufacturing partnership established by his nephews, Benico and Isac. For the privilege of participating in the firm's profits, he provided his intimate knowledge of the market, information networks, and expertise, reflected in the following comment: "His nephews awarded him with this privilege because they appreciated his collaboration, considering his acquaintance with the branch."[7]

Individually owned Jewish firms (115 out of 328 firms) were, in fact, often the products of failed or dissolved partnerships (see section 7.3). One such firm was Franco, Mattia & Choël (est. 1925), which was dissolved in 1932 following disagreements between the partners. Abram M. Mattia then opened a store, which he registered as a private company, for the sale of the same sweets that had been sold by his former partnership.[8] Family firms as well were not protected from internal disruptions, some of which were based on inter-generational conflicts or disputes with a deceased partner's survivors. Following disagreements between two brothers-in-law over the management of its Uskub (Skopje, Yugoslavia) branch, Nahmias & Massot was dissolved in 1935. Joseph Mordohai Nahmias then assumed sole ownership of the firm while his eldest son took over management of the Uskub branch.[9]

Although institutions for training in commercial occupations were available in Salonica (see sections 3.5.3; 6.4 and 6.5), the path to entrepreneurship for most Jews began with an initial apprenticeship or employment in a family firm or, alternatively, a different Jewish-owned firm, all of which served as incubators for nascent Jewish entrepreneurs. Thus, before becoming a self-employed commercial representative (1933), Dario Pinhas managed the real estate assets of the Jacob Sidés family.[10] Similarly, before Moise Pinto and Daniel Barzilai (no. 151) opened their own establishment (1936), they were employed by the Salonican firm Ino Benmayor, Maison VERITAS (no. 141).[11] Samuel Sion, too, worked as a bookkeeper for Gabriel E. Nissim (no. 244) prior to establishing his own firm.[12]

One aspect of this incubation process encompassed the role played by established firms. Marcel Abram de Mayo (1934) was known throughout the draperies branch thanks to his experience working for Fils d'Abram de Mayo & Co.;[13] Raphael Asséo could easily establish a firm of his own due to the contacts he had made while working in an older firm, located at the same address where " . . . for about twenty years, Mr. Asséo was employed at the firm of Affias Frères where he acquired great experience of the business sector".[14] In like manner, Salvator J. Varsano was engaged in the commission sale and representation of small hardware (*quincaillerie*) firms at Maison Mosserie (ironware) before establishing his own firm (1931).[15] Hands-on training could shape an employee's career track within a firm, often to the position of partner, as when the owner of the veteran firm Haim Moché (no. 160) established a partnership with his former employee, Joseph Angel.[16]

In the cosmopolitan atmosphere characterising the Ottoman period and shortly thereafter, Jewish entrepreneurs often completed their commercial apprenticeship in non-Jewish firms, leaving only after they had acquired sufficient experience and an international network of contacts. Moïse S. Francès (no. 305), who later became an important commercial representative, acquired his skills while a senior employee in several banks in Salonica, including a stint as chief accountant with the power to act (*fondé de pouvoirs*) on behalf of the Franco-Serb Bank.[17]

While the employment of family members, mainly sons, enabled a firm owner to train his successors,[18] recruitment of relatives could achieve the same results – the prevention of an enterprise's closing. Such was the case of the firm owned by Henry Mardoché following his emigration to Paris (about 1933). Henry's father Hanania, together with his two brothers Joseph and Jacques, who had declared interests in the original firm, simply kept it running.[19] In July 1935, the brothers established a partnership, Mardoché Frères (no. 147). Their firm operated a store for the sale of hosiery with the long-distance cooperation of Henry. Mardoché Frères also utilised cheap family credit to expand into production by establishing a network of workshops for the manufacture of stockings and socks (*bas et chaussettes*). This they did by dipping into their father's funds, a fortune estimated at GRD 5,000,000–6,000,000, for which they paid moderate interest.[20]

Yet, the dissolution of Jewish partnerships did not represent a death knell to the industry of which they were a part; on the contrary, dissolution even spurred growth by giving former partners a second chance to express their managerial talent. The reorganisation of Fils de Samuel Florentin (est. 1870) following the retirement (1937) of Joseph Florentin (32 percent ownership), into the new solely owned firm of Salomon S. Florentin (no. 145), resulted in the expansion of its knitting operations. Its workforce subsequently grew from twenty female workers and four administrative employees to about thirty-five female workers and six administrative employees; its capital also grew, from GRD 700,000 to about GRD 800,000–1,000,000 during that same year.[21]

9.2 Patterns of Business Organisation: The Ethnic Dimension

Many Jewish-owned firms retained their status as private companies by introducing family members or other co-religionists into managerial and/or proprietary positions. Appendix 8 provides data regarding the frequency of Jewish family partnerships. Such small-scale enterprises, characterised by individual ownership or intra-ethnic partnerships primarily with co-ethnic relatives, were not unique to Jewish entrepreneurship. The family firm prevailed among all the ethnic communities involved in Salonica's commercial life as the Ottoman Balkans presence drew to a close. This pattern was not just a response to the delay in Turkish legislation regarding joint-stock companies.[22] The high frequency of family firms resulted mainly from the distrust that reigned between the different ethnic segments in the Balkans, but especially in Macedonia, a product of the lengthy Ottoman occupation. Traditional loyalties were thereby strengthened, with trust transformed into a strategic asset. Participation in inter-ethnic partnerships in general and in modern forms of business enterprise, rooted in major capital investments and especially in trust between "blood strangers", was therefore negligible[23] (see sections 2.2 and 2.4). The desire to establish trust relations as a protection against uncertainty increased after the Greek annexation of Macedonia. Merchants separated by the new geopolitical borders were likewise legally separated from the Commercial Tribunal of Salonica, the court authorised to decide disputes based on contracts signed (or negotiated) before the Balkan Wars, when merchants had to rely on each other's word of honour (section 4.1).[24]

To grasp the conduct and organisational strategies of Jewish-owned family firms in the context of the inter-war Greek nation-state, we compare the similarities and differences in the experiences of Greek-owned family firms with those of Jewish-owned family firms. As previously mentioned, Jewish entrepreneurs were more vulnerable than Greek entrepreneurs, who belonged to the dominant majority, due to their meagre contacts within the Greek administration well into the 1930s. Like Harry Recanati (see section 7.6), Dr. Zvi Zohar, the Jewish National Fund (Keren Hakayemet) representative in Prague in 1939, was also able to describe the alienated relations between Jewish entrepreneurs and the Greek authorities:

> With the cancellation of parliament [4 August 1936], the [Jewish] delegation was also cancelled. Despite our attempts . . . it is no more. Hasty contacts could initiate a conversation among former [Jewish] representatives with senior administrators, yet the lower ranks go their own way and inform on us, and so forth, which helps them. . . . [25]

In response to the new conditions, the number of inter-ethnic joint ventures, especially between Jews and Greeks, grew steadily.[26] By the first decade of Greek rule, Jewish–Greek partnerships amounted at least to twelve out of the seventeen (70 percent) of the new ethnic-mixed ventures formed in 1921, or the majority of inter-ethnic partnerships involving Jews (see Appendix 4.1, Jewish-Gentile Joint Ventures). Jewish entrepreneurs usually took Greek partners in order to penetrate Greek-dominated industries, such as halva (Middle East confection) production (see Appendix 4.1, Jewish-Gentile Joint Ventures, no. 2), to assure the Jewish partner of an adequate supply of the sesame seed cultivated by Greek growers near Salonica.[27] Similarly, a joint venture facilitated access to the Greek tanning niche for Jewish traders in hides (see Appendix 4.1, Jewish-Gentile Joint Ventures, no.1). The survival motive was even stronger in the sensitive foreign trade sector. There, evidence indicates that Jewish traders, some of whom, like David Hasson (see below section, 8.3), who spoke Greek and Turkish, mediated between the Ottoman and Greek bureaucracies in order to expedite the speedy release of goods arriving at Salonica's port immediately after the Greek occupation.[28]

More importantly, it appears that the increase in the number of Jewish–Greek commercial partnerships, with Greeks assigned the task of middlemen in dealings with government authorities inside as well as outside the port, demonstrates a well-known strategy adopted by minority businessmen operating in new nation-states.[29] This conclusion is supported by the *Annual Report* of Salonica's Chamber of Commerce, which lists the majority of registered customs agents as Greeks.[30] Yet, the low rate of Jewish–Greek partnerships found in 1921 (only 12 out of 1,301 firms) indicates a lack of interest in such arrangements on the part of Greek entrepreneurs, behaviour that resulted from Greek awareness of their new majority status and political superiority. The attachment of Greek partners to Jewish firms increased in the 1930s for similar reasons, aided by increasing competition (see section 8.3.3).

Most partnerships adopted one of three legal structures. The most frequent was that of the straightforward partnership (*société en nom collectif*), where the partner's responsibility was unlimited (i.e., sources of debt payment were not limited to the firm's capital). Unlimited liability was inseparable from the culture of family firms (see section 9.1) because it was based on trust relations between the partners, who were assumed to be drawn from the extended family or at least co-religionists. The unlimited liability family firm seemed to be the most suitable response to the market failures of the late 1920s and overt discrimination within the Greek nation-state,[31] because it minimised exposure of their business activities before the hostile Greek authorities.[32]

The remaining partnerships were distributed between mixed liability (*société en commandite*) and limited liability (*société anonyme*, or SA) firms. The first category included partnerships where only some shareholders had unlimited liability (i.e., direct responsibility for the firm's debts), with the remaining partners considered silent partners, liable for the amount of capital specified in their partnership agreement. The second category entailed the partners' liability only for the firm's capital, meaning that creditors could not seize the partners' personal assets for repayment of the firm's debts.

9.2.1 Mixed-Liability Firms and Silent Partners

The legal restructuring of straightforward partnerships into mixed liability firms was quite appealing during the credit-short 1930s because this model supported capital recruitment (see section 7.7). For instance, the addition of Maïr S. Amariglio as a silent partner in Hananel E. Naar & Co. (no. 243) in 1932 essentially "reconstituted" the bankrupted firm (Appendix 5, no. 432),[33] as noted by an observer:

> Since the creation of the new mixed liability company, business has been good, following the improved value of the merchandise in comparison to its value at the

time of the old partnership's dissolution. Also, because the firm Hananel E. Naar & Co. was founded with a silent partner, the money to ensure proper running of the business is now available . . . In 1935 the firm turned a net profit of almost 20 percent.[34]

Silent partners could also support expansion of a firm's commercial contacts. The mixed liability firm of Fils d'Abram de Mayo & Co. (est. 1926; dissolved 1932) had two silent partners: Moise Acher of Milan and Zaharia Vital of Patras. Acher and Vital appear to have assisted the firm's penetration into Milanese as well as Old Greece markets.[35] Heightened competition, too, functioned as an incentive for the recruitment of silent partners even though it did not always serve its purposes. Despite the presence of Haim Saltiel, Jacob Joseph's brother-in-law, as a silent partner (*commanditaire*) in Jacob Joseph & Cohen, Maison "Camelia" (no. 156), this vast retail establishment (sale of hosiery and confection) could not accelerate its development due to its inability to overtake its competition, which had much greater capital at its disposal.[36]

Silent partners were not, however, required to be businessmen acquainted with the firm's industrial branch. Dr. Moïse S. Matalon, a physician, was a silent partner in a branch of Israel & Arditti (sellers of agricultural and industrial machinery) concurrent with his son-in-law's employment there. Retiring before the firm's formal dissolution, Dr. Matalon became owner of M. S. Matalon, a firm of commercial agents operating in the same branch. Lazar Sephiha, his son-in-law, who was considered quite competent by others in the sector, directed the business under a special power of attorney.[37]

The taking on of silent partners when facing bankruptcy was necessitated by the terms of the Greek bankruptcy law. This law, which was based on the ancient Roman principle treating bankruptcy as an act of fraud, dominated Greek law until the late 1930s. The debtor's property, present and future, was subject to immediate seizure and redistribution; the debtor could be imprisoned and deprived of all civil and property rights. This law required the bankrupt party to settle all his debts prior to recovering his right to manage his property and business (in contrast with other legal systems that restored the right to trade after some period of time, irrespective of the settlement of debts). This requirement compelled the bankrupt party to liquidate his assets, which were often sold at far below their value given the relatively limited Greek market. This meant that the law could prevent the recovery of Jewish- as well as Greek-owned firms. These severe sanctions depressed entrepreneurial initiative among all groups,[38] but especially among the Jews, due to their lack of contacts within the Greek administration.

9.2.2 SA Firms and Mixed Ethnic Ownership

While the mixed liability format was linked to Jewish partnerships in particular, incorporation was a format more prevalent among inter-ethnic partnerships, which usually involved Jews and Greeks. Generally speaking, the legal system effectively restrained the development of large-scale corporations between the wars; traditional values and institutions obstructed the introduction of new organisational structures and business developments, while the inefficient administration of justice posed a barrier against new initiatives.[39]

Yet, the proportion of Greek-controlled corporations in Greece remained low in comparison to Western states[40] in part due to the Greek diaspora's respect for its legacy of mercantile-type family capitalism. This legacy determined the character of business organisation in Greece in the 1870s, a period when the rate of repatriation in mainland Greece by the Greek diaspora increased significantly.[41]

In 1921, only 3 out of 676 Jewish-owned firms listed with the Salonica Chamber of Commerce were clearly anonymous corporations (henceforth SAs).[42] The small number of joint-stock companies can be attributed to the Greek legal system's backwardness; the first Law of Joint-Stock Companies was passed only in 1920. Yet, this law had several defects that limited its effectiveness. For instance, it afforded inadequate protection to minority stockholders, which forced family-controlled firms to divert any savings they might compile away from corporate ventures. Moreover, in order to establish a joint-stock company, the initiators were required to obtain a license and explicit approval from the Minister of the National Economy (or from the Council of Ministers in the case of insurance or real estate) before registering the company's charter.[43] This arbitrary system obviously slowed corporate development for those entrepreneurs who were unable to informally oil the wheels of government. As a result, very few joint-stock companies were established in Macedonia during the 1920s,[44] especially in Salonica, because the urban leadership suffered from a paucity of representatives among the wielders of economic and political power in Athens.[45]

During the 1930s, the number of Jewish partnerships opting for transformation into SAs nonetheless increased. This trend should be seen in the context of the accelerating industrialisation observed in the growing Greek autarky (see sections 8.2, 8.3, and 8.4) together with the Jewish-owned economy.[46] Expansion of a firm's capital through incorporation was found to provide the means for surviving the intensifying competition at the same time that it supported firm dominance if not monopolistic control of its areas of activity (e.g., import entitlements, see section 8.2). Six of the nine SAs established with Jewish shareholders during the 1930s included industrial firms (in food, chemicals, iron, clothing, and construction); the remainder were commercial firms (draperies, transportation, automobile tyres; see Appendix 8).[47] Only six (other) out of the 264 Greek-owned firms listed in Banque Amar records were SAs. According to the surviving documents, these firms were distributed among the following industrial branches: food (2), utilities and metals (2), and textiles and clothing (2).[48]

The number of Greek SAs listed in the Banque's archive was relatively small when compared to the number of Jewish anonymous corporations listed, for obvious reasons. Yet, it is worth noting that throughout the 1930s, despite the rise in SA creation, the number of Greek SAs in the Salonica area remained small in comparison with the number registered in Greater Athens. Among the 1,502 SAs registered in interwar Greece (1922–1939), most of the new SAs located in Athens[49] included companies in capital-intensive sectors such as arms, which were linked to state and political power. In comparison, Salonica's firms, whether Jewish- or Greek-owned, were situated in the disadvantaged new territories and thus suffered from the shortage of capital resources essential for establishing joint-stock companies. The National Bank of Greece, the nation's major bank and source of credit, on its part, focused on serving the industries established in the centre, that is, the Athens–Piraeus area, rather than the periphery, including Salonica.[50] Salonica's Jewish entrepreneurs therefore suffered the dual burdens of ethnic and geopolitical discrimination when attempting to obtain the credit necessary for participation in corporate ventures, even in the industries favoured by the National Bank: chemicals (fertilisers) and infrastructure (construction, electricity, and railways).

In order to better understand the economic and structural dynamics, we should note that all SAs, Jewish and Greek alike, were actually run like private corporations, irrespective of their legal definition. The Jewish-owned Alain Hassid & Co. (est. 1927) was transformed into an SA following *"décret No. 17829 du 16-4-34 paru dans le Journal Officiel No. 93 du 24-4-34, pour raisons fiscales, sans perdre pour cela son caractère privé* (decree N. 17829 of 16 April 1934 appeared in the Official Journal No. 93 of 24 April 1934, for fiscal reasons, without losing its private character)."[51] For instance, even though a board of directors managed each firm, stockholders were not "anonymous". That is, SAs in Greece were far removed from the public joint-stock companies and corporations operating in Western Europe, and would wait for some time before becoming the prevalent form of business organisation, as it had elsewhere.[52]

With respect to Jewish SAs, we can summarise their features (despite their inconsistent listing in Appendix 8) as follows. First, Jewish shareholders appeared to have been related in most cases (nos. 13, 33, 59, 89, 148, and 201). Second, a firm's board of directors generally consisted of shareholders, whose effective power reflected their relative shareholdings, meaning that management was equated with ownership. Third, the time horizons, as noted in their charters, of two out of the nine Jewish SAs ranged from twenty to twenty-five years (nos. 32 and 201), a shorter period than that required for Greek SAs in Salonica (thirty or fifty years).[53] Fourth, the nominal capital of these SAs ranged from GRD 500,000 up to at least GRD 5,600,000 (compared with Greek SAs worth a maximum of GRD 25 million). And fifth, share denominations grew from GRD 100 to GRD 5,000, while the total number of shares for Jewish SAs rose from 500 to 30,000, resembling Greek SAs.[54]

For Jewish entrepreneurs in Salonica, the establishment of joint-stock companies with stockholders spread throughout the country was especially advantageous because it facilitated the expansion of their regional operations to nationwide networks, meaning that they were now able to gear their activities toward the developing national market and locate their headquarters in Athens or Salonica or both. Several firms adopted such a solution; witness the case of Eletan SA (see section 8.2). Another instance was that of Agetra SA (no. 284): Rodolphe Mazlliah, a stockholder who apparently was a Jewish resident of Athens, helped extend the Salonican firm's activities to Greater Athens.[55]

Nevertheless, realisation of the SA structure as a form of risk management did differ between Jewish and Greek companies, observed primarily in the ethnic composition of the shareholders as well as the proportional distribution of firm shares. While most Greek SAs registered with Banque Amar were almost entirely Greek from the perspective of their shareholders' ethnic identity, Jewish SAs often sold shares to non-Jewish holders as well. Excluding Makedoniki Kaltsopiia SA (no. 148), the shares of which were owned exclusively by the Modiano family, all of whom were Italian citizens, the other eight SAs had ethnically mixed owners: four included minor Greek shareholders (nos. 13, 201, 284, and 328); one included Belgian partners (no. 89); and three were mergers: one purely Jewish merger (no. 59) and two with Jewish–Greek equal ownership (nos. 33 and 144).

The same principle applied to the SA's board of directors: the ethnic affiliation of the board's members hinted at the firm's ethnic ownership. Applying the criterion suggested by Robert Tignor for determining whether a joint-stock company was run primarily by a national – or, in this case, ethnic – group or by a nationally mixed group (i.e., examination of its board of directors), assuming that "ownership and management were merged",[56] one can classify the nine Jewish SAs as follows: five were predominantly Jewish-run firms (nos. 13, 59, 148, 201, and 284), two Jewish–Greek firms (nos.33 and 144), and two Jewish-European firms (nos. 89 and 328). The participation of a Western partner was usually meant to expand the capital basis required to implement a project (see for example no. 328), or to facilitate the marketing of Greek goods overseas and vice versa, as in the case of Eletan SA (no. 89): Eletan's board of directors consisted of prominent Jewish and foreign founders, all of whom were experienced financiers.[57] At the same time, the Greek Société Anonyme Industrielle de Pâtes Alimentaires (AVEZ), which included a Jewish director among its board of directors (section 8.3.1), apparently sustained the moderate ethnic mix of its ownership into 1936.[58]

Comparing the corporate legislation in Greece with that of other new nation-states, such as Egypt (1920–1950), where operating joint-stock companies were required to have at least two Egyptian directors, the Greek Company Act is different in that it did not stipulate the presence of any Greek directors. However, Greece's Law of Joint-Stock Companies (1920), which initially required a royal decree for the establishment of a corporation – a function later shifted to the Minister of the National Economy (see above)[59] – motivated the recruitment of Greek shareholders to facilitate access to government bureaucracy. These bureaucratic barriers appear to be the most likely reasons for Abram Benveniste SA (no. 201) to have listed a Greek partner who held only 0.2 percent of the company (1 out of 500 shares).[60] Based on a written source, we can conclude that this strategy was effective: "At the time of the firm's incorporation, the estimate its merchandise in store was valued below its cost price for fiscal (tax) reasons."[61]

Similarly, in the case of Hermes SA (no. 13), all five members of the board were Jews with the exclusion of Nico Manolis, who was also a partner in the firm of Manolis Frères.[62] It was the Greek partner who would petition for the firm's license rather than the Jewish members of the board.

Hence, toward the end of the 1930s, Jewish entrepreneurs began more forcefully to recruit Greek partners (see Chapter 8), even minor partners, who might facilitate contacts (networking) with the Greek authorities and oil the bureaucratic machinery necessary for obtaining licenses and thereby, we may assume, easing access to Greek lending institutions.[63] This step was considered imperative for Jewish firm survival, as Harry Recanati was to confirm.[64]

As the previous discussion has shown, Jewish entrepreneurs in general, and those from Salonica in particular, remained outside Greek family- or community-based business networks, which were frequently interrelated; they also faced difficulties in acquiring bank credit (from Jewish and Greek banks alike) during the 1930s (section 9.3 below). The attempt to remain solvent inhibited risk-taking in the form of bank loans and continued to influence Jewish entrepreneurial behaviour throughout this period of tight credit. Sam Saporta (no. 229), whose firm dealt in wholesale fabrics, principally cotton, generally refused to take loans. However, while this policy kept his firm solvent, his caution handicapped possibilities for expansion.[65] Finding themselves blocked from entering industrial branches requiring large-scale fixed investments (see section 8.3) as well as large periodic investments (section 8.1 above), Jewish entrepreneurs apparently became reluctant to expand existing family firms and preferred the private firm or partnership type of structure. This may also explain why, despite its benefits, the joint-stock company remained the choice of only a minority within Jewish entrepreneurial circles.

This discussion cannot conclude without mentioning the role that different firm structures played in the still vital international business networks maintained between Salonican Jewish expatriate businessmen and their former compatriots (see Chapter 7). Within the de-globalising Greek environment of the late 1930s, these Jewish émigrés attempted to provide new international business opportunities for their co-ethnic colleagues in Greece through participation in transnational networks. The core of this border-crossing network was typically a partnership, with senior partners and head-quarters registered in the émigré's host country and small sub-branches situated mainly in Greece. The transplanted familial firm network was thus able to connect the Salonica Diaspora with the new French, Italian, British, or American Diaspora.[66]

One such firm was the holding company owned by the Nahmias family. The firm's roots were set in July 1928, when Elie J. Nahmias became an equal partner with his father Jacques and his brother Joseph in the Salonican Maison Jacques Nahmias & Fils (no. 314). After Jacques died in 1932, Joseph settled in Paris [n.d.], where he founded the French firm of Société Petrofrance SA in 1934, with capital reserves of FF 1 million. The main shareholders were the same two brothers, with other members of Jacques' family holding the remaining shares. The firm's board of directors included Paul Huyman (President) and Joseph J. Nahmias (Administrator Delegate), by now a French subject, with Elie J. Nahmias, a Spanish subject who resided in Salonica, acting as the branch manager. (Banking services were provided to the firm by Banque Française et Italienne pour l'Amérique du Sud, Paris.) This firm operated as a multi-national agency selling petrol as well as fire and maritime insurance. It provided services in Greece, the Dodecanese islands, Albania, and Southern Yugoslavia for firms such as La Steoua Romana (petrol); London Guarantee & Accident Company, Ltd., and Standard Marine Insurance Co., Ltd. of Liverpool. Its estimated capital worth of GRD 10 million covered the total capital and fixed assets held by all the enterprises belonging to the extended Nahmias family. Real estate was registered in the names of various family members, who also owned property in Alexandrople, Komotini, and Xanthie (Northern Greece).[67] It appears that these Salonican emigrants formed a business network resembling a global entity whose transnational operations were controlled by the firm's headquarters abroad. This structure enabled easy entry into Greek markets for the firm's Balkan as well as British clients by means of a firm's local branch. Simultaneously, it provided access to new opportunities in the international market for local Jewish middlemen in addition to access to breaches in the law that might enable them to bypass prohibitions against moving capital out of Greece.[68]

9.3 Individual Resources: Honesty, Competence, and Solvency

Although supported by ethnic credit (see Chapters 7 and 8), Jewish firms were still required to play according to the rules dominating their commercial environment, where one's business reputation depended on three main characteristics: honesty, competence, and solvency.[69] Therefore, before making a loan, Banque Amar repeatedly investigated the "*moralité*" of a firm owner's behaviour, together with the firm's solvency on one hand and business track record on the other: The company [*Fils de Sam. Florentin*] enjoys a very good reputation locally. The aforementioned is well-known, very honest, active, and punctual in their commitments."[70]

Firms with international ties also needed an international reputation like that enjoyed by Maison Jacques Nahmias & Fils: "The company enjoys a very good reputation in Greece and abroad. It is considered to be first-rate, solvent and, according to a number of opinions, merits full trust."[71]

David Molho, a respected Jewish businessman and Greek citizen, owned a huge amount of property and had a reputation for liquidity ("He was respected by all. He never used bank credit."[72]), two factors that undoubtedly led to his being appointed to several consular posts by foreign governments, including Honorary Consul of Finland in Salonica.[73]

As the credit crunch continued, and the capital reserves of even the strong Banque de Salonique, considered by Christodoulou (1936) to be the city's most important bank – at least when compared to other Jewish-owned banks – fell to about half, from FRF 30,000,000 in the 1920s to FRF 15,000,000 in 1934,[74] it surprised no one that all local banks began to check the solvency of the entrepreneurs who requested loans even more meticulously. Greek banks of all sizes, like Banque Amar, were officially committed to objective evaluation criteria yet granted loans at the discretion of their owners or chief executives. The latter were assisted in their decisions by information acquired about a client's reliability by the "intelligence bureaux".[75] Jewish firms, including those who could provide a mortgage as collateral and who were therefore formally eligible for a business loan, nevertheless had too many reasons to avoid exposure to Greek bank inquiries. Jews were rarely represented on a bank's board; they could therefore not ensure access to credit, as could their Greek peers. The position of director of the board was particularly important for the benefits it included, such as detailed information about the solvency of other Greek entrepreneurs as well as industrial intelligence, which reached the hands of the banks' "good clients", that is, the Jews' Greek competitors.[76] This was especially true during the 1930s, when the National Bank of Greece pursued a policy of cartelisation in order to rationalise industry and minimise competition between its industrial clients.[77]

Greek antagonism and suspicion regarding the Jews on one hand, and the consequence shortage of information regarding Jewish firms on the other, thus placed additional barriers to Jewish access to Greek-owned banking institutions and increased their dependence on Jewish banks.[78] The firm of Isac S. Saltiel (no. 279), for example, apparently used Jewish bank credit to overcome shortages in cash flow,[79] which often prevented firms from reimbursing foreign suppliers. Such was the case of Moise Sciaky & Frères: "Business turnover is relatively restricted . . . the firm has not disposed of any rolling capital because it has not yet repaid its debts abroad."[80]

Jewish banks naturally found it easier to obtain confidential information about solvency if the client was Jewish than if he were Greek.[81] One source of information used by Banque Amar was the firm of M. J. Bourla (commission agent; commercial representation), which would forward assessments such as the following about the Salonican firms I. Raphael & Benveniste and Moise Benveniste (16 June 1937):

> Based on information collected from authorised sources, capital is assumed to be that shown. This is not the opinion of Mr Samuelides [the notary] who assured me that the capital of both companies exceeds 3000 lstg. . . .[82]

Through his own network of contacts, Bourla was likewise able to provide information about Jewish entrepreneurs who had relocated to Athens. In a report based on two confidential sources attached to a letter sent to Banque Amar, Bourla wrote:

Included [is] the requested report on the Erricou J. Arone business in Athens. My correspondent in this city used two different sources for his survey, including information differ [sic] them. It is your responsibility to determine your decision, taking into account all the details provided.[83]

Such information generally determined the fate of the loan requests. The firm Maison Daniel Marcos (no. 277) was considered impudent in its dealings, with a tendency toward commercial intrigue. The informant consequently recommended that Banque Amar handle this firm with caution and demand extensive guarantees. This information was repeated by three sources, as noted in a document dated September 1937: "He is portrayed as a rather difficult character and prone to chicanery. Thereby, [it is] well [to] lay down conditions in dealing [with him]."[84] Similarly, Fils de Moise Saltiel (no. 226), considered one of the top firms engaged in the import and wholesale distribution of cotton cloth, had not settled all its foreign debts. According to the document: "It is not to its credit [i.e., of the firm], as other less important firms have already paid their debts. It is having difficulties and consequently our source of information recommends caution."[85]

Assessment of solvency in particular required access to private information due to overt firm policies. The wealthiest Jewish businesses, such as Salomon Mordoh, rarely used bank credit; instead, they depended on the capital gains from their real estate and other assets (see section 7.7).[86] The firm of Saltiel & Elie Angel & Fils (no. 139; fishing nets) belonged to the same category.[87] Isac Saporta ran his firm (no. 88) according to the same rule: "*La firme fait rarement usage des crédits*" (The firm rarely makes use of credit).[88] Yet, we should be wary of statements regarding a firm's avoidance of specifically bank credit. When shortfalls occurred, they had access to alternative sources of financial support, garnered from family-based networks and other local Jewish entrepreneurs, arrangements that were based on mutual trust. We must therefore assume that the comments referring to the non-utilisation of bank credit found in Banque Amar records applied solely to a firm's relations particularly with this bank.

Despite the reluctance of Greek-owned banks to extend credit, as mentioned above, Jewish entrepreneurs did turn to various non-Jewish-owned banks, including the National Bank of Greece. For example, Fils de David Hasson (no. 266) worked with Banca Commerciale Italiana & Greca – its current account in credit; the firm's capital was estimated at GRD 6,000,000.[89] Furthermore, during the late 1930s, wealthy Jews did take mortgages from the National Bank of Greece to finance real estate purchases. For instance, the firm of Haim Salem & Frères (no. 128), together with Haim Salem's widow Esther, had private fixed assets mortgaged to the National Bank of Greece in the amount of GRD 40,000 (the property's value was estimated to be GRD 400,000);[90] Nissim Gheledi (no. 274) had a mortgage valued at GRD 600,000 from the same source, with collateral based on a building whose worth was estimated at GRD 2,000,000.[91]

Finally, we cannot ignore the importance of "self-capital" – cash. Jewish entrepreneurs continued to be firm believers in liquid capital. For obvious reasons, the practice was not officially documented, yet contemporary witnesses affirmed that the keeping of gold coins was very popular among Salonica's Jews. As a well-known entrepreneur remarked: "They kept gold coins [sovereigns] in barrels",[92] conveniently stocked for ready transfer from Greece to any destination abroad, including British Mandatory Palestine.[93] During economic and security crises, demand for gold (considered a real asset) would rise due to its use as an economic shelter to protect the true value of assets.

Gold bullion was considered a safe investment, as gold was a scarce natural resource. According to evidence given by Holocaust survivors, the Nazi military commander of Salonica knew that Jews were wont to invest their money in gold coins as well as jewellery. He would therefore arrest Jews and set the price of their redemption in sacks full of coins.[94]

This attitude was especially fitting given the state of the Greek economy and trade policy immediately after Salonica's incorporation (see section 4.1) and attempts to block the transfer of funds abroad. Since the par value of gold currency was (more or less) equal to its nominal monetary value, gold was commonly used in large-scale, international transactions.[95] The relatively heavy presence of Jews in international trade simply supported the preference for keeping their resources transportable.

9.4 Firm Capital

The capital invested in a firm generally consisted of buildings, machinery, and raw materials; it was declared at minimum value for tax purposes. According to a decree dated 3 March 1922:

> Individuals resident in Greece before January 1922 are taxed on houses, land and other property, properties resulting from business in Greece. . . . The rate of taxation is on a sliding scale, varying from 2 to 20 percent, according to the total value of the property, which is calculated at twelve times the annual rent.[96]

The arbitrary application of this scale by Greek fiscal authorities was motivated by the "possibility of hardship in the method of assessment of the capital for taxation"[97] but also by growing Greek nationalism, which reached full bloom during the period in question. This atmosphere negatively affected the administration's attitudes towards Jews and explains much of the defensive stance adopted by Jewish entrepreneurs in their confrontations with Greek tax authorities. It had in fact become common knowledge that whereas the tax-paying Greek refugees who had arrived after 1922 received tax benefits, Jewish taxpayers were objects of tax discrimination. In the words of Joseph Nehama, "The Hellenic regime instituted direct taxation – a tax on income – and this led to an irritating inquisition, which was carried out, it would seem, with excessive zeal where Jewish taxpayers were concerned. . . . "[98]

Banque Amar records clearly document attempts made by Jewish entrepreneurs to distance themselves from direct contact with the tax authorities, whenever possible, by lowering the firm's declared capital worth, as in the case of Mano & Co. (no. 217):

> According to the notary, the capital invested in the contract amounted to GRD 370,000. This sum has been fixed due to fiscal considerations, but the partners also have quite substantial personal liquid assets.[99]

Figures 9.4a and 9.4b show the distribution of Jewish and Greek firms that turned to Banque Amar by their declared nominal assets. Businesses considered to be of small scale by bank officials were those with nominal assets estimated at less than GRD 100,000; the firm owned by Victor Almosnino (no. 239) was valued at a mere GRD 50,000,[100] as was the firm S. Damkou & M. Beraha (no. 302),[101] compared with

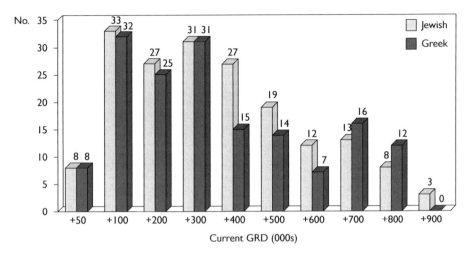

Figure 9.4a Jewish-owned Firms (*N* = 181) and Greek-owned Firms (*N* = 160), by Nominal Assets, Salonica, 1935–1937

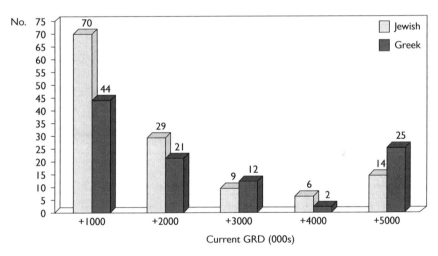

Figure 9.4b Jewish-owned Firms (*N* = 128) and Greek-owned Firms (*N* = 104), by Nominal Assets, Salonica, 1935–1937

Source: Adapted from CAHJP Gr/Sa FO 346.
Note: Estimates of the value of nominal assets were available for only 309 (out of 328) Jewish-owned firms and 264 (out of 278) Greek-owned firms.

Elie Sarfatti & Ovadia Ezratti (also spelled Ezratty, no. 77), with assets valued at a bit more than GRD 100,000 and *"affaires de seconde importance dans la branche"* (affairs of secondary importance in the sector).[102] The remaining firms, the majority, having nominal assets valued up to GRD 100,000 were often classified according to their nominal assets in thousands of current drachmas: low-medium (100–300), medium-high (400–900), high (1,000–4,000), and very high (5,000+).

As Figures 9.4a and 9.4b show, the distribution of Jewish as opposed to Greek firms differed significantly at almost all asset levels.[103] In other words, while Greek-owned firms of low-to-medium size (100–300) as well as very large size (5000+) were greater in number when compared to Jewish-owned firms. Among the latter, the rate of the medium-to-high firms (400–900 and 1,000–4,000, respectively), was higher than in the equivalent Greek sample. The bank's records (see Appendix 8) indicate that the assets of almost 60 percent of the Jewish firms as well as 60 percent of the Greek firms were valued at less than GRD 1 million (Figure 9.4a). While about 41 percent (128 out of 309) of the Jewish firms were valued at GRD 1,000,000 or more, only 39 percent (104 out of 264) of the Greek firms belonged to this category (Figure 9.4a). While the distribution was similar among the lowest layers, about 3 percent of Jewish and Greek entrepreneurs had about GRD 50,000 in assets. In contrast, the rate of Greek firms belonging to the wealthiest layer (9.5 percent or 25 out of 264) was twice the rate of Jewish firms (about 4.5 percent or 14 out of 309), with capital greater than GRD 5,000,000 (Figure 9.4b). Based on these findings, we can conclude that the distribution of nominal assets among the Jewish firms that sought loans from Banque Amar was more egalitarian than the distribution among the Greek firms that sought loans from the same source.

An important question to be raised at this point is whether the differences in the distribution of business capital between the two ethnic groups were affected by branch structure. Unfortunately, the categorical structure of the two distributions does not

Table 9.4 Branch Distribution of Major Jewish-owned and Greek-owned Firms Having Nominal Assets Exceeding GRD Million (Current Values)

Branch	No. of Firms (I) Jewish N	Greek N	Total No. of Firms in Branch (II) Jewish N	Greek N	Percentage of Firms in Branch (I/II)*100 Jewish N	Greek N
Food and beverages	5	12	24	22	20.8	54.5
Chemicals	11	6	24	18	45.8	33.3
Construction materials	5	3	5	6	100	50
Metals	14	5	35	24	40	20.8
Wood	6	5	15	19	40	26.3
Hides, leather and footwear	7	8	23	25	30.4	32.0
Textiles	8	5	10	8	80	62.5
Clothing	39	27	91	70	42.9	38.6
Printing, paper and office equipment	8	3	19	7	42.1	42.9
Tobacco	1	10	2	13	50	76.9
Luxury products	3	1	8	5	37.5	20.0
Agricultural products	3	5	17	12	17.6	41.7
Banking and large-scale commercial activities	18	14	36	35	50	40.0
Total	128	104	309	264	41.4	39.4

Source: See Figures 9.4a, 9.4b.

Note: Total includes only those firms in the original sample for which capital was assessed.

permit statistical testing of the relationship between branch affiliation and value for either Jewish or Greek firms. Tests of validity on branches, including the composite branches, were also inconclusive.[104] Table 9.4 provides a partial response to this question by allowing us to identify those branches in which firms valued at more than GRD 1 million (high assets) were active.

Yet, an exploration of the ethnicity of the wealthiest layer of firms, by branch or business domain, may provide indications of the relations between the owner's ethnicity (Jewish or Greek) and the structural patterns of entrepreneurship. The fourteen Jewish firms having capital above GRD 5,000,000 belonged to the following branches: trade in luxury goods and agricultural products (5), metals and wood (4), clothing and fishing nets (4), and chemicals (1) (see Appendix 8). In contrast, the twenty-five Greek firms of comparable worth were distributed among these branches: tobacco (5), food (5), inland transit trade (1), trade in agricultural products (1), engineering and construction of public utilities (2), commercial representation (2), hides (3), textiles (2), clothing (2), chemicals (1), and commerce in construction materials (1).

Among the wealthiest Greek entrepreneurs we find Panayotis G. Kyrtsis (textiles), whose fortune was estimated at more than £60,000 (or about GRD 32,355,600). Kyrtsis, together with his brother Kyros, were partners in G. Kyrtsis Fils, a firm maintaining large-scale spinning and weaving factories.[105] Another wealthy Greek firm was Théodore Hadjiparaskévas, which sold fashion accessories and had twenty employees; its capital was estimated at GRD 5,000,000.[106] The long-established firm of N. Krallis & Fils had been active in the wholesale selling of chemicals since 1896; its capital was estimated at GRD 5,000,000 (GRD 3,000,000 in stock and GRD 2,000,000 in real estate).[107] Eteria Asvestopiias "Enosis", a Greek partnership operating in the lime industry, employed eighty workers; its worth was estimated at GRD 10,000,000;[108] Chocolaterie Floca SA, with nominal assets of GRD 25,000,000, employed about 220 workers;[109] Alexandre P. Karapanayotis, a firm exporting hides and originally located in Adrianople,[110] was valued at GRD 5,000,000, whereas A. D. Serefas, another firm active in the leather industry, claimed assets (including real estate) estimated at about GRD 4,000,000;[111] and the tannery Dimos Christoforides, with assets valued at about GRD 6,000,000, employed about seventy workers. Tobacco merchants represented a particularly wealthy group of entrepreneurs (see section 8.1): Antigonos Hadjigeorgiou had capital estimated at GRD 12,000,000, Ermokratis Khristoforidis GRD 18,000,000; Constantin Moscoff (est. 1924) GRD 24,266,700 (or £45,000);[112] Stelios Voivodas GRD 22,000,000–27,500,000 (or £40,000–50,000).[113]

Although their nominal assets did not exceed GRD 5,000,000 (per firm), we cannot ignore the Greek firms that were involved in the growing large-scale trade in arms with Germany, a profitable domain that was blocked to Jewish businessmen (Table 9.4). G. Gregoriadés Frères, which sold life and fire insurance in addition to acting as commercial representatives for munitions manufacturers, acted as the exclusive representative of the German arms manufacturer Krupp Industries[114] and of Ruston & Hornsby, a British industrial equipment manufacturer. G. Gregoriadés Frères declared their estimated worth to be GRD 1,617,780 (or £3,000). A related phenomenon was the apparent centrality of Greek arms merchants in Greek political life. Stavros Gregoriadés was (1936) President of the Comité de la Zone Franche de Salonique, President of Syllogue Commercial, and financial advisor to the Bank of Greece and the National Bank of Greece.[115] In fact, Greek middlemen working with the National

Bank of Greece promoted the interests of German industry in exchange for percentage commissions. These same middlemen, acting in the bank's name, also tried to negotiate as many contracts as possible through private clearing accounts.[116]

The documents therefore indicate that during the 1930s, the Greek economy's most profitable branches were controlled by the Greek entrepreneurial elite and effectively closed to Jewish entrepreneurs. For instance, Jews were now excluded from the tobacco industry, where their co-religionists had formerly represented the greater part of the work force. As might be expected, they were also excluded from the arms trade with Germany (see section 8.1). Jews consequently found themselves confined to narrow niches in the developing textile industry (jute and sack manufacture, section 8.4);[117] commerce in luxury goods (section 8.2), manufacture of small metal products and hardware (*quincaillerie*, section 8.3), and trade in wood for construction, what had traditionally been conducted within the framework of the transit trade.

Other bank documents indicate that the wealthiest Jewish firm-owners, as mentioned earlier (see section 9.3), were also rare users of Banque Amar credit. Interestingly, Yomtov Yacoel, who was well-acquainted with the socio-economic conditions of the community's members due to his tenure as the Salonica Jewish community's legal advisor from the 1920s until the Nazi occupation, wrote in his diary (1943) that "the richest Jewish families were Italian or Spanish citizens".[118] This statement raises a major question regarding minorities and migrants participating in a host economy: Is there any relationship between the level of capital worth and the entrepreneur's citizenship in differing socio-political contexts? That is, could foreign citizenship be an asset for ethnic firm owners in a budding nation-state (see section 6.5), just as it had been in the political environment existing prior to Salonica's annexation to the emerging Greek nation-state (see Chapter 2)?

The main part of Banque Amar's clientele therefore appears to have consisted of Jewish Greek citizens and non-Jewish Greek citizens (see also section 3.2). Foreign Jewish entrepreneurs (in addition to the Yugoslav nationals mentioned above) included the following, classified by nationality: among the Spanish subjects we can count Abram Elie Francès (no. 157), Salomon Moché of S. Moché & Co. (no. 112), the partners in the firms Botton, Saias & Co. (no. 177),[119] Fils de J M Francès (no. 208), Salomon Hassid & Frères (no. 213), Daniel S. Saltiel & Fils (no. 104), Joseph & Abram Samuel Saltiel (no. 103), Sidés Frères (no. 231), Sam A. Saporta (no. 229), and Albert D. Saporta (no. 228).[120] Italian nationals included Barouh S. Venezia (no. 164), Joseph J. Tiano (no. 323), and Elie Modiano (no. 327) as well as other members of the Modiano family. Léon A. Juda (no. 56) was a British national.[121]

Although not all foreign Jewish businessmen belonged to the wealthiest layer of Salonica's Jewish entrepreneurs, there is no doubt that they formed an important part of the upper level of its Jewish business elite (see Chapter 2). The total assets of the fifty-two wealthy families belonging to Salonica's Italian "colony of the Jewish race" in 1942 were estimated at GRD 400 million in pre-war values.[122] This wealth was referred to by the manager of Salonica's Chamber of Commerce and Industry in a remark quoted by the German consul in Salonica (1940):

> According to an estimate by the director of the Chamber of Commerce, 33 percent of the business firms are [Italian] Jewish while [their share within the] distribution of capital is estimated at about 50 percent.[123]

According to an estimate transmitted by the Italian consul in 1942, the industrial property belonging to the Italian Jewish firm Makedoniki Kaltsopiia SA (no. 148) was valued at GRD 12,000,000, double that shown on our list (see Appendix 8), while that of Elie Modiano was GRD 16,000,000, also higher than the figure on our list.[124] These figures lend further credibility to our stated assumption that the nominal assets noted in Banque Amar documents are minimum values.

What, then, were the benefits that foreign citizenship granted to participants in the consolidating national Greek economy? Perhaps the first and most important advantage was the protection of foreign consulates, especially after the June 1931 Campbell riots.[125] It appears that consular protection was likewise available when faced with the increasing arbitrariness of Greek officials during the national economy's consolidation. Holding foreign citizenship also gave Jewish merchants an advantage by helping them avoid the interference with commercial activity provoked by compulsory military service[126] while it eased entry into increasingly restricted international trade. Although foreign citizenship was considered a burden for Jews wishing to invest in real estate in New Greece[127] (see also section 4.3), it remained a meaningful and important asset, considered part of the Jewish entrepreneur's human capital even after the state's cancellation of the capitulations. We can conclude that holding foreign citizenship meant that these Jews could be considered as "sojourners", "temporary residents", and thus better prepared than their "Greek" Jewish peers when new options materialised.[128]

9.5 Worker Mobilisation: Gender and Ethnicity

The emigration of Jewish businessmen during the 1920s and 1930s induced a cumulative reduction in potential jobs openings for Jewish manual labourers as well as commercial clerks, thus adding to the growing Jewish unemployment.[129] Competition between veteran Greeks, refugees, and the Jews thus intensified as the labour market shrank. To forestall further decline in job availabilities, the Greek government opposed the emigration of Jewish entrepreneurs during the early 1930s (see section 6.3). In December 1932, a Greek civil servant noted, "Emigration would not be in our interests . . . for it was the rich and the enterprising who tended to leave first, causing unemployment to worsen."[130] These trends were also the subject of comment in 1939:

> Despite the absence of official, overt anti-Semitism . . . the [Greek] authorities are pushing Greeks into every corner of the economy in order to expand the employment options available to their countrymen, especially in those territories that were once under foreign rule [i.e., New Greece]. . . . [131]

Increasing unemployment generally facilitated the recruitment of workers in the mainstream labour markets during the late 1930s, which made it possible for entrepreneurs to cut costs by taking advantage of the escalating availability of increasingly cheap unskilled and semi-skilled labour and forestalled the substantial investments required for mechanisation of their business. While the Greek nation-state was preoccupied with creating employment for its non-Jewish Greek citizens through the initiation of new public works projects (see section 6.1.2.2), Jewish entrepreneurs were able to recruit Jewish fellow workers due to their inferior position in the shrinking mainstream labour market. Trust and a shared culture – a common religion and

Table 9.5a Jewish-owned Workshops and Their Jewish Workers, Salonica 1936

Branch	Sub-branch	Workshops	Workers
Food and beverages	Wines and mineral water bottlers	28	70
	Bread bakers	23	75
	Coffee bean roasters	23	23
	Pastry bakers	2	20
	Cookie bakers	2	30
	Halva and sweets production	5	10
	Subtotal	83	228
Chemicals	Bee and mosquito repellents	1	2
	Chemicals	3	5
	Nickel plating	2	15
	Glass housewares manufacture	2	5
	Tin products manufacture	6	6
	Subtotal	14	33
Construction	Plumbers	71	200
	Marble cutting and polishing (stonemasonry)	11	50
	Lime and whitewash production	1	7
	Shingles manufacture	5	30
	Slate processing	2	10
	Subtotal	90	297
Metals	Engravers	14	25
	Marine (seamen's) equipment manufacture	2	4
	Cart and wagon builders	1	3
	Blacksmiths	33	70
	Cooking utensil repairing	2	6
	Bed frame manufacture	10	60
	Hydraulic equipment manufacture	2	4
	Travel equipment manufacture	3	10
	Garages – auto repair	2	6
	Electricians	0	30
	Knife and scissor sharpening	5	15
	Machinery repair	4	0
	Iron nail and wire manufacture	2	80
	Subtotal	80	313
Wood	Chair manufacture	33	80
	Wooden clog manufacture	5	5
	Shoe last producers	19	30
	Chest and suitcase manufacture	36	60
	Brush manufacture	7	40
	Basket and crate making	4	5
	Broom manufacture	9	44
	Mechanized sawmills	2	2
	Subtotal	115	264

Branch	Sub-branch	Workshops	Workers
Leather and footwear	Shoe manufacture	166	275
	Furriers	1	0
	Saddle makers	7	15
	Subtotal	174	290
Textiles	Knitwear manufacture	19	120
	Fabric dying workshops	18	70
	Subtotal	37	190
Clothing and home textiles	Tailors	90	350
	Cotton shirts manufacture	7	60
	Hat manufacture	43	160
	Hat cleaners	9	10
	Embroiderers	10	15
	Upholsterers	15	70
	Curtain and screen manufacture	2	10
	Blanket makers	33	130
	Subtotal	209	805
Jewellery and watches	Goldsmiths	10	17
	Watchmakers	5	11
	Subtotal	15	28
Printing and paper	Book printing	11	35
	Carton manufacture	6	15
	Bookbinders	3	3
	Sign makers	7	10
	Subtotal	27	63
	Total	844	2511

Source: Adapted from Mentesh Bessantchi [1936] (1986): 209–210.
Note: An error appears to have entered the jewellery industry list compiled by Bessantchi; specifically, the number of workers is less than the number of workshops. To correct the error, I have replaced the number of workers indicated by Bessantchi with the number of active workshops.

language, Ladino[132] – reduced the risk to be borne by Jewish employers while it increased what Arcadius Kahan has called "psychological income". This type of income was accrued whether the employer acted out of reasons of familiarity, cultural affinity, or what he considered "good deeds," even if this practice simultaneously decreased his operational costs[133] and might otherwise be considered an act of self-interest. It can be assumed that the reduction in costs achieved by employing Greek labour on the Jewish day of rest during the late 1930s was not a decisive factor for Jewish entrepreneurs.[134]

Appendix 8 provides partial data indicating how the structure of Jewish firms affected the scope of their workforce. The sources available do not, however, provide verifiable data regarding the ethnic origins of employees (unskilled and semi-skilled) retained by Jewish firms. By comparing and complementing these data with information collected from other historical sources, we can obtain a portrait of the segment of Jewish labour employed within the Jewish-owned economy. Assuming that small firms employed primarily family members or fellow Jews (see section 9.1), and excluding the Jewish-owned tobacco firms (nos. 252 and 253) for which we lack employment data, we focus on textile, clothing, and metal production, sectors that had relatively large, labour-intensive systems of production. For instance, the Jewish firm of Saltiel & Elie Angel & Fils (no. 263), in response to increasing demand for fishing nets and equipment,[135] apparently employed thirty Jewish men and women in its factories, which were located in heavily populated Jewish residential areas (Rue Miaoulis and Rue Comninon).[136] The nail factory belonging to Alvo Frères (no. 58) also employed thirty male and female workers; it was managed by a German foreman and located in the Xyladica Quarter, close to the Zadok factory. The latter metal furniture factory owned by Zadok (no. 85), located in the same quarter near the railway station, employed about thirty men and women.[137] The Clouterie et Tréfilerie Macedonienne SA plants (nails and wire) were equipped with modern machines operated with the energy supplied by two electrical generators, one of 125 horsepower and the other of 30 horsepower; altogether, the firm employed an average of forty workers.[138]

If we compare the data in Appendix 8 with those in Table 9.5a, taken from a comprehensive survey of the Jewish workforce employed in Salonica's Jewish workshops during 1936 as conducted by the Jewish journalist Mentesh Bessantchi, we can identify some industry trends. The two datasets appear to be quite compatible regarding the metals industry. The accuracy of Bessantchi's observations is demonstrated by the data for the two Jewish factories producing nails and wire (nos. 58 and 59), which were ranked second (and third) among all the Greek firms active in this industry.[139] A different picture emerges in the labour-intensive clothing industry (primarily knitwear and shirt manufacture), which employed primarily female labour. No correlation was found between the data shown in Appendix 8 and the Bessantchi data, with the latter indicating far fewer Jewish female workers.

9.5.1 Female Employment

Given the intensifying urban unemployment, and assuming that Jewish female labour did not impose additional costs upon Jewish employers, the data available (see Appendix 8) raise doubts as to whether Jewish entrepreneurs, especially in the clothing industry, were committed to Jewish female workers; alternatively, we can ask if a shortage in Jewish female workers had developed.

Following the continued emigration to the West from the very start of Greek rule in Salonica, and the mass emigration to Mandatory Palestine between 1932 and 1936, the Jewish community faced the loss of a sizeable proportion of Salonica's Jewish entrepreneurs but, not less importantly, the loss of large numbers of Jewish workers. The departure of sizeable numbers of Jewish skilled or semi-skilled female workers, most of whom specialised in the needle trades, forecast the emerging shortage. According to a 1933 list of applicants for immigration, half of the females (55 out of 110), representing 86 percent (55 out of 64) of all applicants with declared occupations, had been engaged in the needle trades (see Table 9.5b). In addition, the small number of formerly employed women among the prisoners who arrived at Auschwitz in 1943 – Aure Recanati has gathered and published a list of their names – only strengthens this conclusion.[140]

Based on these data, we can argue that there was an ethnic division of labour within the labour-intensive clothing industry: While Jewish-owned workshops attached to

Table 9.5b Salonican Jewish Female Clothing Industry Workers: Applicants for Emigration to Mandatory Palestine, 1933

Occupation	N	%
Seamstress	37	67
Shirtmaker	9	16
Embroiderer	5	9
Footwear	2	4
Socks	1	2
Milliner	1	2
Total	55	100

Source: Adapted from CZA S6/2535, 14 September 1933, a list of Salonicans who applied to emigrate. *Note:* Only **64** out of the 110 female applicants (**86** percent) declared an occupation. Among these women, 55 worked in the clothing industry, 3 listed themselves as carton producers (including boxes), 2 as clerks, 2 as *chaises*, 1 as a teacher, and 1 as a pastry cook. Among the 46 with "undeclared" occupations were 38 pioneers (persons destined to establish *kibbutzim* and *moshavim* in unsettled areas of Israel) in addition to 8 women with no occupation.

Jewish-owned stores employed Jewish female labour, large-scale Jewish-owned factories as well as Jewish–Greek partnerships depended on the female Greek refugees who had arrived during the 1920s. The Jewish-owned firm of Vital Albert Cohen (no. 143) can serve as an example for the former; it employed fifteen apparently Jewish male and female workers (Illustration no. 8) in its raincoat manufacturing workshop. The establishment of factories of Jewish or ethnically mixed ownership in refugee neighbourhoods can be counted among the latter. By creating jobs for Greek refugee females, Jewish entrepreneurs compensated for the loss of unskilled Jewish female workers; jobs requiring higher levels of skill were usually kept open to the Jewish women who could meet the manufacturer's needs. In addition, such locations eliminated the need to transport manual labours to distant factory sites. A further motive for establishing manufacturing sites in the periphery was the apparent pressure it applied to grant their owners the licenses needed to form corporations.[141] Yet, we cannot unequivocally determine whether ethnically mixed employment in plants having ethnically mixed ownership was viable. Cultural barriers (see section 5.6) often proved to be too strong.

Consider the Jewish-owned hosiery-knitting firm of Makedoniki Kaltsopiia SA. Since the total number of Jewish workers employed in Salonica's knitwear industry (1936) was about 120 (see Table 9.5a), it can be assumed that not all of this factory's eighty-five manual and skilled employees were Jewish. The character of the neighbourhood in which the factory was located – the Harilaos quarter, populated mainly by working-class Greek refugees during the 1930s, with a small population of Jewish labourers[142] – supports this assumption.[143] We can therefore conclude that a geographically linked ethnic division of labour did emerge.[144] And so, while the Makedoniki Kaltsopiia store in the city's centre hired Jewish male and female salespersons, with Jewish females working in the attached workshop, the new factories built in the working class quarters lying in Salonica's outskirts employed local Greek refugee labour.

In like manner, the new factory built by the Jewish–Greek partnership L'Union des Fabriques de Bas SA (no. 144) was also located in the Harilaos quarter. At the same time, Sam Sarfati, the Jewish partner, continued to employ Jewish females in the workshop operating in the basement of his flagship store (no. 152).[145] With Greek manufacturers adopting a similar location strategy, the Harilaos quarter soon gained prominence as a centre for Greek-owned knitting, sock, and stocking factories, such as Ladas & Djadjas and Société "Melissa" (eighty workers and twelve white-collar employees).[146]

Job creation was also one of the factors motivating the award of government tenders to Jewish engineering firms, such as Elie Modiano (no. 326; see section 8.2.5) and Moché (no. 325). The infrastructure projects initiated in Macedonia absorbed thousands of the Greek labourers ejected from the shrinking tobacco industry.[147] From the perspective of Jewish contractors such as Jacques Juda Moché, winning a tender did not interfere with his firm's policy of retaining trusted and loyal co-religionists in clerical and administrative positions in offices located in Salonica as well as Athens.[148]

To conclude, if we exclude the tobacco industry, in which the Jewish workforce was scattered among Jewish-owned as well as non-Jewish-owned factories (see section 8.2), it can be argued that the increasing shortage of jobs in the mainstream labour markets on the one hand, and the shortage of Jewish female workers on the other, affected the ethnic structure of employment. Jewish-owned enterprises, which were usually of small size and dominated by men, were able to recruit Jewish male workers, especially when increasing national and ethnic discrimination aggravated the job shortage. Yet, in the clothing industry, it was the size and the location of the plants that affected the ethnic origin of labour force. In workshops attached to Jewish-owned clothing stores, Jewish females were employed, while in large-scale clothing factories, usually under mixed ethnic Jewish–Greek ownership and situated in working class refugee neighbourhoods, Greek refugee females were also recruited.

9.6 Jewish Networks and Increasing Efficiency Strategies

The family business thus became the cornerstone of the ramified, internally dependent Jewish entrepreneurial networks, where trust represented a strategic asset. An examination of the kinship ties that linked the partners in the majority of Jewish firms corroborates the prevalence of this strategy (see Appendix 8). This structure also helped reduce financial costs while it prevented confiscation of the owners' private assets by the tax authorities. The main tactic used to achieve this end, which was particularly useful for avoiding foreclosures, was registration of the firm in the name of the owner's wife or children.[149] And so, David Sarrano registered his house in his wife's name[150] whereas Salomon S. Sciaky, a partner in Moise Sciaky & Frères (no. 100), listed his home in the *cadastre* (the official land registry) as follows: half in the name of his wife Estherina and half in the name of his son Samuel.[151] Because the firm was in debt, this seemed a convenient way to forestall confiscation. In yet another case, the fixed assets of Léon Josué Amaraggi (no. 51), a very profitable firm, were located on part of a plot at Rue Valaoritou No. 2, bought from Abravanel & Benveniste. Amaraggi constructed *"une grande baraque en maçonnerie"* (a large brick-built shed) and a warehouse on this plot, which he registered in his wife's name.[152]

Homes, which often represented part of a wife's dowry, were also recruited to this cause. Joseph Ruben (also spelled Rubin), Paul Ruben, and Mentech Tchénio, the

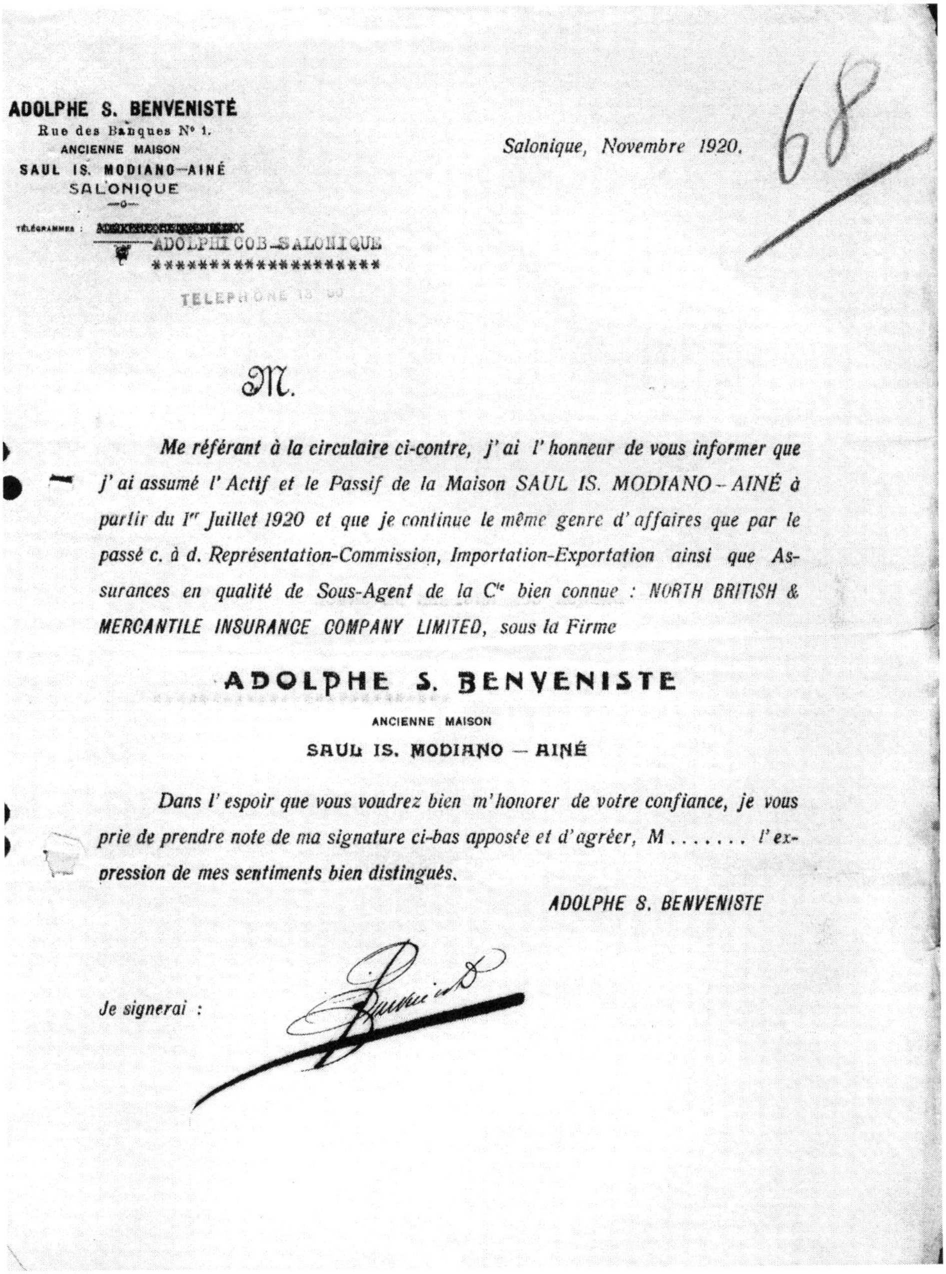

ADOLPHE S. BENVENISTE
Rue des Banques Nº 1.
ANCIENNE MAISON
SAUL IS. MODIANO—AINÉ
SALONIQUE
—o—

Salonique, Novembre 1920.

TÉLÉGRAMMES : ~~ADRESSE TÉLÉGRAPHIQUE~~
ADOLPHICOB-SALONIQUE
* *

TELEPHONE 15 00

𝕸.

Me référant à la circulaire ci-contre, j'ai l'honneur de vous informer que j'ai assumé l'Actif et le Passif de la Maison SAUL IS. MODIANO - AINÉ à partir du Ier Juillet 1920 et que je continue le même genre d'affaires que par le passé c. à d. Représentation-Commission, Importation-Exportation ainsi que Assurances en qualité de Sous-Agent de la Cie bien connue : NORTH BRITISH & MERCANTILE INSURANCE COMPANY LIMITED, sous la Firme

ADOLPHE S. BENVENISTE

ANCIENNE MAISON
SAUL IS. MODIANO — AINÉ

Dans l'espoir que vous voudrez bien m'honorer de votre confiance, je vous prie de prendre note de ma signature ci-bas apposée et d'agréer, M . . . . l'expression de mes sentiments bien distingués.

ADOLPHE S. BENVENISTE

Je signerai :

Illustration 1 The firm of Adolph S. Benveniste assumes the assets and liabilities (*l'actif* et *le passif*) of Maison Saul IS. Modiano–Ainé (export–import, insurance representative) on 1 July 1920 (Appendix 4.1, no. 540; Appendix 5, no. 596)

(Courtesy of the Yannis Megas Archive, Salonica)

Illustration 2   Share certificate issued by Banque Amar SA in January 1920
(Courtesy of the Yannis Megas Archive, Salonica)

Illustration 3   Share certificate issued by Banque Union SA in July 1926
(Courtesy of the Yannis Megas Archive, Salonica)

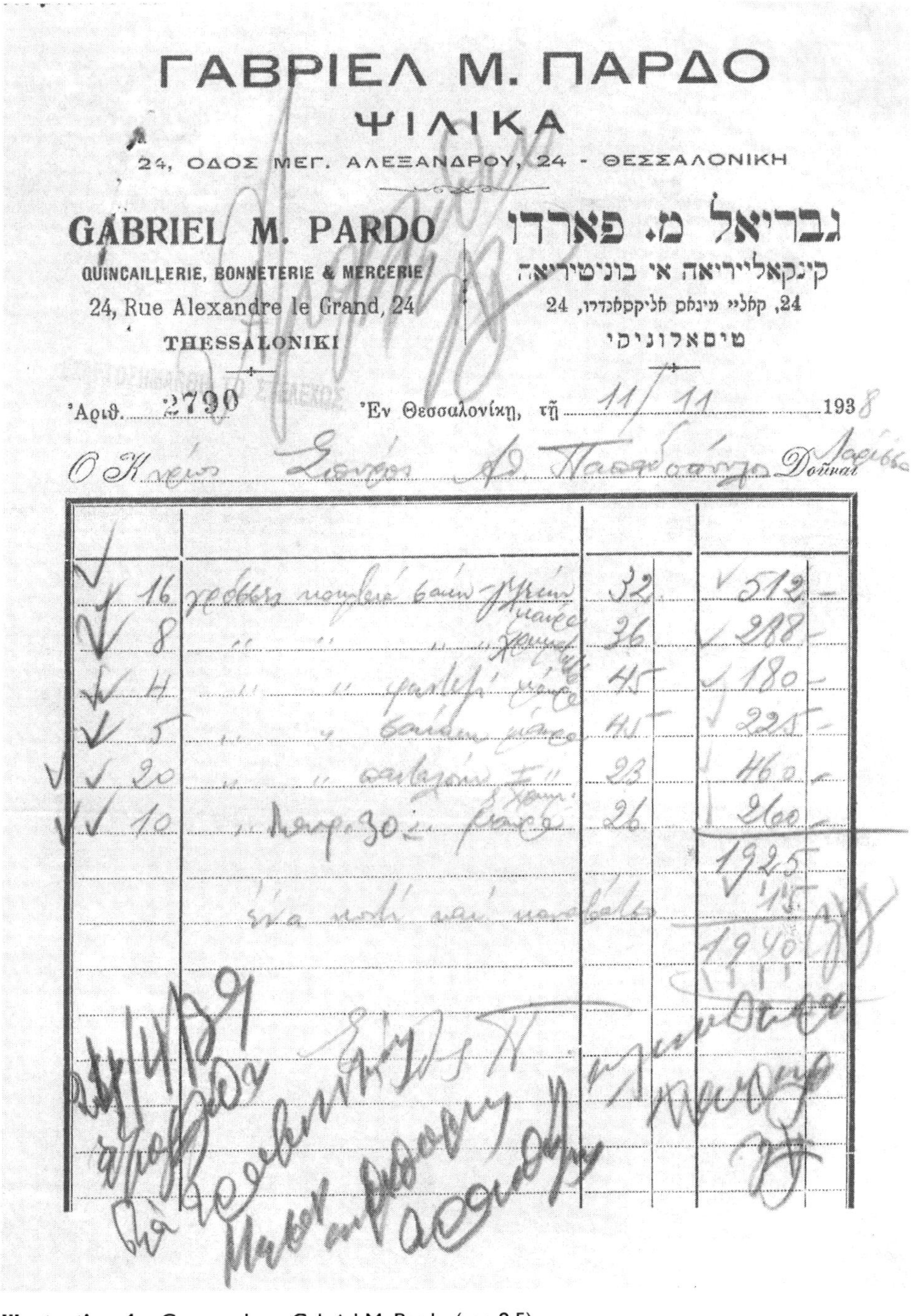

ΓΑΒΡΙΕΛ Μ. ΠΑΡΔΟ

ΨΙΛΙΚΑ

24, ΟΔΟΣ ΜΕΓ. ΑΛΕΞΑΝΔΡΟΥ, 24 - ΘΕΣΣΑΛΟΝΙΚΗ

GABRIEL M. PARDO

QUINCAILLERIE, BONNETERIE & MERCERIE

24, Rue Alexandre le Grand, 24

THESSALONIKI

גבריאל מ. פארדו

קינקאלייריאה אי בונטיריאה

24, קאלי אינאם אליקסאנדרו, 24

טיסאלוניקי

Ἀριθ. 2790 Ἐν Θεσσαλονίκῃ, τῇ 11/11 1938

Ὁ Κ. ... Δοῦναι

16	...	32	512
8	...	36	288
4	...	45	180
5	...	45	225
20	...	23	460
10	...	26	260
			1925
			15
			1940

Illustration 4 Corner shop, Gabriel M. Pardo (see 8.5)

(Courtesy of the Yannis Megas Archive, Salonica)

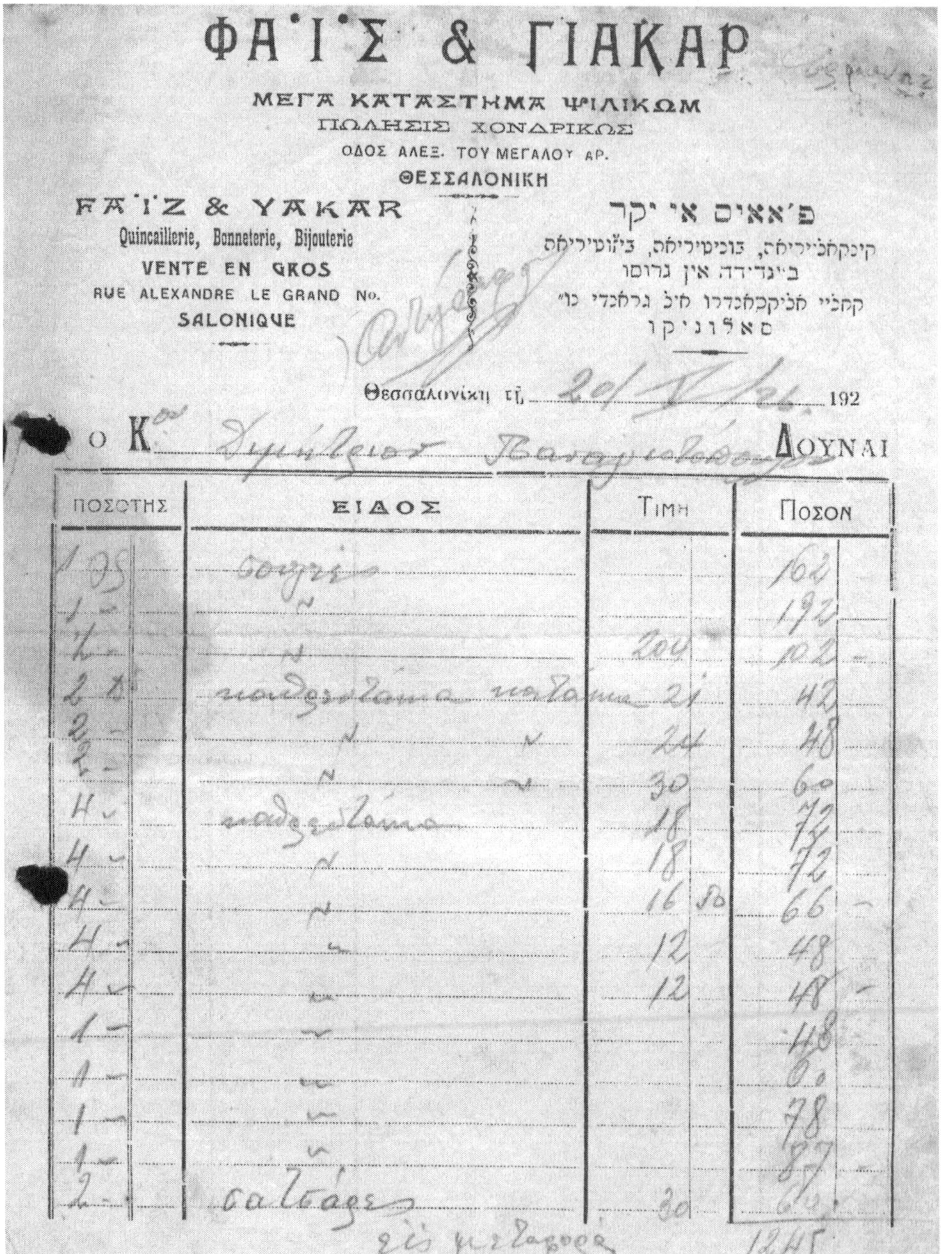

Illustration 5 Fais & Yakar, a corner shop established in 1919 and dissolved in 1926 (see 8.5; Appendix 8, no. 43)

(Courtesy of the Yannis Megas Archive, Salonica)

Illustration 6   The firm of Angel & Saltiel (est. 1906) was engaged in the sale of chemicals, including dyes (Appendix 8, no. 38)

(Courtesy of the Yannis Megas Archive, Salonica)

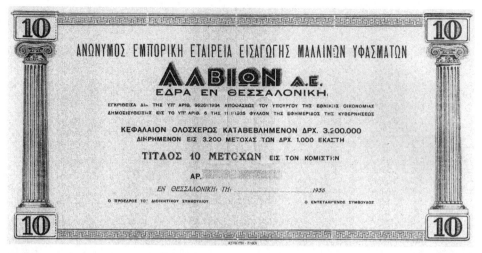

Illustration 7   Share certificate issued by Albion SA, traders in woollen fabrics apparently imported from Britain; the firm's shareholders included the Jewish drapery merchants Sidés Frères (Appendix 8, no. 231; see 8.4)

(Courtesy of the Yannis Megas Archive, Salonica)

Illustration 8   Garment manufacturer Vital Cohen – "Home of the Raincoat" – store and workshop, 1937 (Appendix 8, no. 143)

(Courtesy of the Yannis Megas Archive, Salonica)

Illustration 9 Haim Benrubi (est. 1919) considered Salonica's largest glassware and porcelain importer/distributor (Appendix 8, no. 257)

(Courtesy of the Yannis Megas Archive, Salonica)

Illustration 10 S. Molho, selling typewriters (Appendix 5, no. 443)

(Courtesy of the Yannis Megas Archive, Salonica)

Illustration 11   S. Molho, the typists' classroom above the shop on Rue Egnatia 47 (Appendix 5, no. 443)

(Courtesy of the Yannis Megas Archive, Salonica)

Illustration 12   A delegation from the Polish aviation company LOT in the Allalouf & Co. offices, 24 April 1934 (see 7.6; Appendix 8, no. 285)

(Courtesy of the Jacky Allalouf Archive, Tel Aviv, Israel)

three partners of Ruben Fils & Tchénio (no. 246), registered all their properties in their wives' names. Clearly indicated in the relevant Banque Amar document was that Paul, the youngest of the three partners, had obtained his real estate holdings through *"la dot de sa femme"* (his wife's dowry).[153] If two or more buildings were owned, the properties could be divided between the couple. And so, the less expensive house owned by Joseph Mordohai Nahmias was registered in his name while the more expensive house owned was registered in his wife's name.[154] Such practices were considered legitimate because the dowry was perceived as representing the support given by the bride's family for her husband's entrepreneurial ventures: "Maurice Dav. Sasson has no fortune other than the dowry, which he will receive from his intended, [a member of the] Saltiel(s), to finance him."[155] The Saltiels themselves had acquired some of their personal property by the same method.[156]

We close this discussion by returning to a strategy already mentioned, one practiced since the Ottoman period (see Chapter 2) – marriage as a method for extending the family network of trust and strengthening business alliances. For instance, in 1936, it was announced that the widow of Isac Lezer Florentin, a partner in Yomtov, Franco & Cie., would replace her late husband as a partner. The informant added that the Yomtov and Franco families had become related by marriage when Franco's son became engaged to Yomtov's sister.[157]

We should remember that marriage was a particularly efficient arrangement especially during economic crises. Local and international Jewish networks of interlocking families eased access to cheap co-ethnic credit and enabled Jewish entrepreneurs to survive in periods of tight capital, overt anti-Semitism, and increasing market competition, and might even give these entrepreneurs an advantage over non-Jewish entrepreneurs. Joseph Samuel Paladino (no. 187), the owner of a haberdashery shop,[158] had limited means and was thus unable to invest capital in his firm. He did, however, receive a loan of GRD 100,000 in the form of a mortgage on his home from his brother Moise Paladino.[159] Relatives often provided family members with business loans in the form of mortgages on their personal property but at minimal rates of interest. Consider Raphaël David Bendavid (no. 102), the son of David Isac (Bendavid is not listed as his family name), who owned two warehouses; he took out a mortgage of GRD 150,000 on the first from Joseph Sarfati, and a mortgage of GRD 163,635 on the second from Samuel Benuziglio.[160] Although we do not know whether Sarfati or Benuziglio were directly related to Raphael, both were Jews.

From another perspective, investing in a business owned by co-religionists but belonging to an unrelated branch also increased entrepreneurial interdependence. The following example demonstrates this type of Jewish network. In 1931, Gabriel E. Nissim (no. 238), became an associate partner (28 percent) in Maison Simon J. Perahia & Co. (see Appendix 5, no. 36, colonial commodities) while simultaneously functioning in the same role (at a cost of GRD 400,000) for Maison Florentin & Ezratti (no branch mentioned).[161] In another case, Benico & Isac Angel & Cie. (no. 119), a firm in the leather industry, also invested in the metals branch through participation in the anonymous partnership Clouterie et Tréfilerie Macédonienne SA (no. 59), producers of nails and wire.[162]

The spatial spread of Jewish-owned businesses also supported the consolidation of Jewish networks. Based on the addresses of Jewish-owned businesses located in Salonica during the mid-1930s (see Appendix 8; Map 2), one may conclude that Jewish owners chose their store locations in order to control competition within a geographic area (see section 8.3). Yet, these efforts of Jewish businessmen to horizontally integrate were not always successful, as in the case of the attempt to officially merge two geographically proximate textile shops belonging to Isac Raphael and his son-in-law Haim I. Benveniste (no. 223), and Moise Isac Benveniste (brother of Haim) (no. 203) in 1935; the firm was forced to dissolve in 1937.[163]

Jewish entrepreneurs attempted to enlarge their incomes by adding a secondary occupation. For example, Ino Jakob Matalon (see above), who had resided in Vienna for many years, participated in the liquidation of Elie Florentin & Cie. upon his return to Salonica in 1928. As a sideline, Matalon ran a small-scale commercial enterprise selling fabrics. To reduce his overhead Matalon allowed two other modest traders from the same branch to operate from his shop.[164] Thus, integrating themselves into Jewish networks enabled firm owners to increase efficiency, which was essential for business survival. Shared purchase or use of property also strengthened internal dependence among Jewish entrepreneurs concomitant with the introduction of efficiency measures.

Haim M. Mano, another small-scale wholesaler of women's lingerie and accessories, began to share his premises with Leon Bissardo, who sold thread.[165] When the firm Nahama B. Capon (nos. 26 and 27) found itself in similar circumstances, it reduced operational costs as follows: the firm eliminated all personnel costs, excluding a domestic worker, by having all the paperwork done by the associates themselves, who maintained *"une vie modeste et sont très économes"* (a modest and frugal lifestyle).[166]

9.7 Conclusion

During the 1930s, the entrepreneurial patterns adopted by Jewish businessmen reflected Greece's transition from a *laissez-faire* to an autarkic economy, infused by state intervention designed to promote policies directed at economic self-sufficiency. New conditions for international trade included increased tariffs on imports, quotas and bilateral clearing agreements. These measures sent shock waves through the Jewish economy, which had historically relied on international trade. These and other measures intensified the dependence of the Jewish economy on government officials and agencies, relationships that Jews had rigorously attempted to avoid but became necessities for those remaining in Salonica during the 1930s.

Cooperation between Jews – for the most part Greek citizens who had undergone Hellenisation – and non-Jewish Greeks generally benefited the larger society, with the business structures creating or maintaining places of employment in the private as well as the public sector. These benefits did not, however, prevent the mutual suspicion that poisoned relations between the two groups. The Greek business elite's blatantly preferential status in the new nation-state often forced Jewish entrepreneurs to adopt patterns typical of minority economies.

By the second half of the 1930s, those Jewish entrepreneurs who chose to remain in Salonica found themselves increasingly dependent on private as opposed to ethnic resources. The demographic dilution of Salonica's Jewish population, the weakening of the community's internal solidarity, together with the credit crunch hampered commercial activities rather pervasively. Establishment of limited liability corporations supported efforts to avoid bankruptcy but did not ensure adequate recruitment of Jewish labour. At this juncture in the development of the Greek autarky, the con-flation of several socio-political as well as economic processes thus drove the Jewish economy to become confined to the Jewish entrepreneurial sector. During this twilight of the Jewish economy in Salonica, further shocks were felt after Greece's entry into World War II. In the final chapter, we trace the final stages of the Jewish economy's demise.

10 | Epilogue

The Jewish economy of Salonica diminished between the city's experience of the first phases of globalisation and the conclusion of de-globalisation in Greek trade and capital movement. The integration of the Jewish economy into the autarkic national economy, operating regionally within an atmosphere of Balkanisation (i.e., separate, non-cooperative national economies preventing the exchange of mutual benefits), brought into stark relief the Jews' *de facto* civil inferiority, which negatively impacted their position within Greek national economy.

This concluding chapter will summarise this story in two main sections. In the first, new theoretical insights will be presented, based on comparative perspectives in the context of the de-globalisation phase of the world economy. In the second section, the tragic demise of the Jewish economy of Salonica is portrayed, closing on the eve of the Italian offensive through Albania on 28 October 1940, the event that marked Greece's entry into World War II.[1]

10.1 Jewish Entrepreneurship and the Jewish Economy in a Comparative Perspective

The empirical findings detailed in this book have shed light on the reciprocities maintained between Jewish entrepreneurship and the scope of the ethnic economy at every stage of de-globalisation. In contrast with the de-colonisation phase, the chronic shortages that characterised the mainstream labour market, mainly because of the recruitment of Greek males into the army, helped preserve the Jewish control over labour in the tobacco branch and likewise, in overland and maritime transportation services (see Chapter 4). During the post-colonial phase the number of "former" middleman minority entrepreneurs increased as a result of "push" factors: increasing cheap labour supply following the mass entry of Greek refugees (1923) (see Chapter 5). The ethnic-owned economy, as a hedge against national discrimination, consequently broadened in scope. As long as national discrimination increased, the scope of the Jewish-owned economy approached that of the whole Jewish economy as Jewish control of workers in the tobacco industry and transportation services in the port shrank.[2]

Concurrently, linguistic and cultural barriers blocked the entry of non-Jewish Greeks, especially females, into the Jewish-owned economy. Thus, the accumulation of Jewish workers into the Jewish-owned economy was sustained. During the 1930s, Salonica's Jewish-owned economy withered. Along with the registered entrepreneurs, who were the subject of Chapters 7–9, Jewish micro level businessmen ran small shops and stalls that mainly catered to their co-religionists, while many others slipped into indigence.[3] Only a small number of Jews worked outside the Jewish-owned economy.

Greek nation-statehood likewise impacted on the structure of the Jewish economy. We should recall the privileged status that Jewish entrepreneurs enjoyed in the semi-colonial period had enabled them to operate in the formal sector, generally blocked to minority businessmen.[4] Despite the fact that registered Jewish entrepreneurs, the subject of the empirical research of this book, continued to conduct their business in the formal sector during the consolidation of the Greek state following the Transfer. Also the intensified entrepreneurial patterns characterised the informal sector, including preferences for sectors with easy entry, family-based ownership, small-scale enterprises, and competitive markets that are neither state-regulated nor subsidised. Already by the first decade of Greek rule in Salonica, and especially after World War I, new trends were beginning to affect the Jewish-owned economy's sectoral structure, namely the gradual exit from essential branches such as cereals and flour, together with entrenchment in commerce in commodities and the clothing industries, two sectors that typified migrant and minority economies. In order to cope with the risk and uncertainty attendant on their inferior political status, Jewish-owned firms increased their concentration in a smaller number of branches and niches. Simultaneously, these entrepreneurs sought to increase the efficiency of their still operating firms (see Chapters 8 and 9).

As Macedonia and its capital Salonica became almost totally Greek and the Jewish population lost thousands of émigrés, the remaining Jewish entrepreneurial elites functioned as immigrants. When attempting to integrate into the national Greek business sphere, they found themselves divided between two contradictory trends: the Hellenisation policies enforced by the Greek state encouraged these Jewish businessmen to attempt integration into the national economy on the one hand, whereas rejection of the Greek nation-state's suspicious treatment, replicated by its business elites (see below 10.2), motivated avoidance of the Greek administration on the other. Consequently, the multi-dimension complicated integration process of the Jewish entrepreneurs reflected the tension between de-globalisation and globalisation.

Their response patterns reflected their desire to adapt to the national economy as follows: 1. They continued to be members in Salonica's Chamber of Commerce and Industry and participated in local businessmen's social circles.[5] 2. They attempted to appeal to the potential growing Greek clientele following the Transfer by adopting Greek business cultural patterns (i.e., business acculturation) such as marketing strategies, including giving Greek names (e.g., Hermes, Albion) to their firms. 3. They gradually shifted the language of advertising and publicity from mainly French and even Ladino (with Hebrew letters), prevalent at the beginning of the 1920s,[6] to Greek during the 1930s.[7] 4. They adapted their business operations to the Greek national market, including the location of additional branches in Athens in order to broaden the range of Jewish businesses from Salonica – the old Jewish entrepreneurial centre – to the national Greek capital. Their emigration objectives during the 1930s came to include the Greek national centre – Athens – which demonstrated their internalisation of the geopolitical transformations. 5. They officially registered their businesses before state officials in Greek.[8] 6. They created joint ventures with Greek partners (see below). 7. They also created places of work for the increasing numbers of unemployed refugees to demonstrate solidarity as Greek citizens (see Chapters 8 and 9).

At the same time, the discriminatory treatment imposed upon them prompted these Jewish businessmen to develop their enterprises by broadening local Jewish partnerships and through Jewish networking, which bound together Jewish entrepreneurs from Old and New Greece (see Chapters 7, 8, and 9) in order to contend with Greek competition. Yet, while these networks mainly emphasised "reactive ethnic cohesiveness" (section 1.3), they were undeniably incapable of repairing the cumulative effect of Greek market failures on the overall Jewish economy. Although discrimination against the Jews had neither a legal basis nor any constitutional justification, the documentation that stemmed from Jewish entrepreneurial activity corroborates how much the Jews suffered from the pressures applied by the Greek administration.

Adoption of typical ethnic entrepreneurial strategies that could also be interpreted as "business assimilation resistance" usually assisted immigrant entrepreneurs who identified flourishing economic niches (or enclaves) in which to develop their enterprises. These strategies not only maintained the actors' original socio-economic status, but also might even have helped them to prosper without surrendering their ethnic cultural practices or associations, as observed in advanced Western economies.[9] Indeed, such practices could have made it possible for the former middleman minority's entrepreneurs in Salonica to survive. In addition, by adopting transnational entrepreneurial patterns, extending their Jewish networks to include the newly established Salonican émigré concentrations in the Balkans, the West, and British Mandatory Palestine, Salonica's Jewish entrepreneurs exhibited a preference for investing within fellow Jewish immigrant communities rather than vainly attempting to invest in the Greek market.[10]

Preservation of French as the language of business as well as the *lingua franca* of the local elites (see above) was a major sign of this global perspective.[11] The use of French was eminently practical as it facilitated the cross-border transfer of information essential for the management of business and commerce. Furthermore, contacts and trade between Jewish businessmen from Hellenistic Salonica and their co-religionists in the new Balkan states as well as in France continued to be conducted in Judéo-Fragnol, the Jewish-Spanish dialect heavily laced with French.[12] This common linguistic variation, which had formerly united the Jewish entrepreneurs operating within the multinational context of Ottoman Macedonia, now helped to cement Jewish cross-border networks, essential for coping with the new autarkic Balkan markets.[13]

While the Jewish economy, Jewish entrepreneurship, and the Jewish-owned economy were interrelated, they were all linked to the modern world-system and were integrated into the Europe-dominated world economy. Hence, application of world-economy perspectives are essential for analysis of the uniformity as well as the variety of the Salonican Jewish economy from the patterns set by non-Jewish former middleman minorities on one hand and the Jewish economies established in other new European nation-states during the same period on the other. In contrast with the pre-nation-state era, when cross-cultural trade was predicated on, as well as generated by, familiarity among strangers, making religious coexistence feasible,[14] the transition into the modern world-system was accompanied by discrimination against minority entrepreneurs as emerging nation-states competed with one another.

The findings of the research described in this book enabled us to deduce the entre-preneurial patterns of "former" native-born middleman minorities as well as the structural characteristics of the ethnic economy while stressing their adaptive capaci-ties within the historical context of the newborn and autarkic nation-states in the late nineteenth and early twentieth centuries. Starting with the middleman minorities orig-inally driven by geopolitical transformations and thus "compelled" to migrate to newborn nation-states, the process revived their mobility. For those remaining, they faced a situation that deprived them of their political connections with the ruling administration, ties now only available to native-born and repatriated immigrants belonging to the majority. Native-born former middleman minority members thus became part of an ethnic-national minority, compelled to confront homogeneity enforcing policies, especially following World War I.

The transformations undergone in Jewish entrepreneurial patterns in Salonica points to the common denominator of all Jewish communities active in Europe before the Holocaust – the "great art of flexibility and the capacity to adjust to new situa-tions".[15] This characteristic was also found among "former" middleman minorities like the Chinese in Thailand following the *coup d'état* of 1932, where this community of businessmen repeatedly demonstrated "this ability, to adapt their businesses to strik-ingly different contexts".[16]

Jewish entrepreneurial patterns in this period also came to strongly resemble Jewish entrepreneurship in new European nation-states (e.g., Hungary) and the Ottoman Empire's successor states (e.g., Iraq). The experience of similar forms of economic nationalism forced their co-religionists, like Salonica's Jews, to increase efficiency, cut costs, and deepen their operations without enlarging the business' basic capital, steps that intensified concentration. However, it also encouraged them to avoid entry into sectors controlled by the national majority's entrepreneurial and political elites, espe-cially the public sector and its commercial satellites. Further constriction of their sectoral structure ensued.[17] As we have shown, an enduring sense of alienation in addi-tion to fears of discrimination from the Greek elite ensured that the presence of Jewish contractors in tenders for public utilities and infrastructure would be negligible (section 8.2.5). The Greek nation-state was, in effect, replicating a process typical of the transition experiences by new Asian and African ethnic states, where essential commodities and services were the first sectors to come under national control.[18]

The new Turkish Republic likewise applied a Turkification policy after its estab-lishment in 1923.[19] Thus, adaptation to the nation-state framework was required of Jews who remained in Greek Salonica as well as by their fellow Jews who chose to migrate to Istanbul. As a contemporary Jewish witness wrote,

The rise of narrow nationalism in Turkey and in Greece and a movement in both countries to favour the majority nationalities have cut deeply into the economic exis-tence of the Jews, and have created Jewish questions where they did not exist before.[20]

The institutional reorganisation of Jewish-owned firms and businesses within the New Greek nation-state signified the limits within which Jewish entrepreneurs could preserve established forms of production, the most prominent being the "family firm". Although they were an indigenous minority, their entrepreneurial patterns were gener-ally similar to those labelled pseudo-middleman minorities in the advanced capitalist economies of the Western hemisphere (see Chapter 1). The family business, the common pattern of business organisation observed among ethnic groups in advanced capitalist economies, was especially prominent among minorities operating in hostile national environments with turbulent markets. This business model's advantages included features of ethnic solidarity, such as trust, readily available partners and credit, as well as the ability to mobilise cheap yet loyal ethnic labour. Family members were therefore preferred as partners ("core loyalties"), followed by members of broader circles within the ethnic group.[21]

Transformation from a middleman minority into an ethnic–national minority lacking useful political contacts also affected their entrepreneurial strategies. These entrepreneurs, considered loyal to the ruling elites during the semi-colonial phase, tended to form coalitions with those in power.[22] Suspicious treatment from the Greek ruling elites made such alliances improbable. Jewish business elites proposed straight-forward business integration without social structural assimilation in contrast with former Asian middleman elites such as the Chinese during Thailand's transition from European semi-colonialism to independent statehood, whose strategic mechanism for merging with the new ruling entrepreneurial elites was intermarriage.[23] In Salonica, the Greek majority and the Jewish minority alike rejected this commonly used minority strategy even though intermarriage with Greeks could easily have afforded Jewish entrepreneurs access to special government concessions. Yet, although mixed marriages between Jews and Greeks did increase during the 1930s (see below), their numbers remained negligible. Jews, like Orthodox Greeks and Muslim Turks in the multi-ethnic Balkan environment, continued to be treated like permanent non-assim-ilated groups.[24] Under such circumstances, minority entrepreneurs maintained a distinct status and adopted common strategies suited to the post-colonisation phase, which entailed the establishment of joint ventures with the new national ruling elites. Such enterprises, expressing "business assimilation" patterns, enabled Jewish entre-preneurs to overcome the Greek authorities' discrimination and alienation. Jewish entrepreneurs attempted to increase joint ventures with Greek partners (section 9.2).[25]

Creation of mixed ethnic joint ventures or the participation of majority managers effectively modified the imposition of hostile national administrative practices. The presence of Greek minor partners in firms whose capital was controlled and managed by Jews pointed to a major difference between majority and minority entrepreneur-ship in the Greek nation-state; it likewise reflected the similarity in the context of other emerging nation-states whose both ethnic majorities and minorities were intent on avoiding assimilation. To illustrate, consider how the Greek entrepreneurs in transi-tional Ottoman Smyrna were able to rescue their industrial machinery by taking Muslims as partners; they were thus able to stave off Turkish attempts to requisition the Greek-owned tanneries as soon as the Greco-Turkish War broke out (1921).[26] Following formation of the Turkish Republic in October 1923, foreign corporations often acquired Turkish silent partners – such as deputies sitting in the new Parliament – whose primary role it was to legitimate the enterprise and provide them with crucial ties to the new regime even if they presumably shared in the profits.[27]

Ideally, these adaptive strategies would have demanded the reinforcement of alliances with what remained of the powerful veteran Greek elites or, alternatively, the forging of new alliances with the emerging refugee entrepreneurs. In the nationalistic climate, however, such an objective was nearly impossible. State intervention in the economy was becoming more intense and Greek networks were becoming impenetrable to "foreigners", that is, non-Christian Greeks, including Greek Jews. Openings for Jewish entrepreneurs in the Greek state consequently fell below the number available during the Ottoman regime because the Greek majority had a legacy of a cohesive trading diaspora.[28] Within such a context, dominant networks functioned as pressure groups aimed at trying to induce concessions and benefits from the state and directing market competition by establishing what could be called "lobbyist" associations and by the proposing of industrial policies.[29]

Although former middleman minorities in emerging nation-states shared entrepreneurial patterns with the Jews of Salonica, a tragic end was in store only for the Jewish economies surviving in Europe in the late 1930s. The factor that differentiated between these Jewish minorities and the other former middleman minorities in the post-colonial phase was the unique institutional discrimination, overt and covert, directed against the Jews prior to the Holocaust. Among all types of ethnic-based discrimination, nationalistic economic policies based on anti-Semitic discrimination, even when implicit, were considered to have been the most extreme due to the accumulated historical hatred, which was much more damaging than individual discrimination against minorities and immigrants in advanced capitalist labour markets.[30]

In closing this book, we therefore turn to a summary of the events that transpired in the two years preceding the demise of Salonica's Jewish economy. Our survey supports the argument that continued attempts to increase the enforced Hellenisation of Jewish society in Salonica (see Chapter 6) during the late 1930s only aimed at demonstrating Jewish disloyalty and, *ipso facto*, providing an excuse for Greek economic chauvinism.

10.2 The Demise, 1938–1940

The documents surviving in the Bank Amar archive provide scant evidence for the entrepreneurial activity in Salonica between 1938 and 1940, and for good reason. This period began with Germany's incorporation of the Austrian economy into its economy, including the iron ore mines necessary for steel and arms production, and closed with Greece being swallowed up by World War II. This incorporation thus predicted the demise of Jewish entrepreneurship.

Following the Anschluss, in March 1938, Austrian clearing agreements were merged with the German system (14 April 1938).[31] Despite the absence of racial legislation in Greece, the economic interdependence between the expanding Nazi economy and the Greek economy spelled the destruction of the Jewish economy. Economic nationalism was subsequently radicalised as part of the effort "to remodel the European market to make the German race the most economically advantaged in Europe".[32] Expropriation became a matter of official Nazi policy, especially after November 1938, when it was decided that over 100,000 Jewish businesses in Germany should be closed down, nationalised, or transferred to private German ownership. This expropriation was ruthlessly and systematically carried out among the Jewish population of Occupied Europe after 1939.[33]

The Germans had planned that Greece would be included within the German autarky, with Jewish businesses in Salonica to be expropriated as well (section 6.2). Jewish-owned enterprises thus ceased to function as protected labour markets for co-ethnic workers. Earlier, Germany's efforts to impose its racial policy on its Greek business partners had effectively ousted the Jewish presence from the tobacco industry. The Greek family business Voivodas (see section 8.1) lost the custom of the German tobacco giant Reemtsma after the German vice-consul in Volos lodged a complaint that the family employed a Jew in its plant.[34] Enforcement of German sanctions against Greek-owned companies that employed Jews resulted not only in excluding Jewish employees but also in delegitimising the Jewish economy. The formula "Greek tobacco imports in exchange for German arms" not only excluded the Jewish-owned tobacco industry, it also promised high profits to collaborating Greek industrialists. Jewish merchants who had been working for the Austrian tobacco monopoly,[35] which now found itself under monopolistic German control, discovered that their contracts had been voided; they were thus forced to seek out new customers. Because German consumers continued to import Greek tobacco, the tobacco industry, which was sensitive to changes in German–Greek trade relations,[36] actually became closer to Jewish entrepreneurs and workers alike. The small number of Jews claiming their occupation as tobacco workers on the eve of their transport to the death camps in 1943 confirms this trend.[37]

Even though Greece had not passed any legislation making it illegal for Jews to participate in trade or act as company directors, as the German Bundestag had done, Greece's increasing economic dependence on Germany threatened the Jewish economy. Jews who held key positions in public firms representing German interests in Salonica thus found themselves in danger. For instance, Dario Modiano, together with Charles Heitmann, served as conjoint delegates in the management of John Campbell Succ. S.A., which represented German and Yugoslav shipping companies in addition to providing *commissaire d'avarie* (damage surveyor) services to almost all German insurance companies.[38]

The appearance of the names of Jewish entrepreneurs who had created markets for German goods, such as the Asséo brothers (glassware) and Dario Assael (general imported German wares) on the lists of prisoners arriving in Auschwitz[39] succinctly illustrates the fate of the Jewish entrepreneurs who remained in Salonica and who are among the subjects of this book.

Government implemented ethnic discrimination in the labour market also went past the stage of competition once it was anchored in law.

> A law was recently passed stating that every economic and public institution was to hire a specified percentage of veterans of the Greek army. Because there are no Jews among this group of candidates, all the Jewish banks and institutions are obligated to employ Greek clerks. Hence, even the offices of the Jewish community in Salonica had to accept a Greek Christian employee.[40]

Dr. Zvi Zohar was incorrect in his assessment that Jewish males did not serve in the Greek army.[41] However, the placement of a Greek Christian employee into the Jewish community's offices,[42] considered a protected Jewish labour market, hinted at the changes to come. The following example shows to what extremes nationalist economic discrimination was taken:

> A few days ago, during the qualifying exams taken by candidates for a position in the National Bank of Greece branch in Salonica, two Jews obtained outstanding grades. After the exams, when it was discovered that they were Jews, they were informed

that they had not been accepted. They appealed to the central management [which overturned the decision], but it was obvious that this would be the last time that such assistance would be received.[43]

Increasing Greek government intervention was also felt in private firms. According to testimony given by Jacky Allalouf (of Allalouf and Co.), the attempts of the Greek authorities to transfer representation of the Polish airline company LOT from a Jewish family firm to a local Greek firm failed only because of the airline's refusal to comply with their plans.[44]

As intensifying economic difficulties strained efforts to earn a living in the anti-Jewish atmosphere, Jewish communal resources degenerated. This may partially explain the decline in the number of Jewish firms registered in the local Chamber of Commerce and Industry. Between 1924 and 1938, the number of Jewish companies (935) had declined by 580, whereas the number of Greek firms had increased slightly, to 1,684, and Armenian firms by 40.[45] As noted by the German consul in November 1938,

> The numerical decline in local Jewry also means a decrease in its financial power and its overall economic impact. This is because financially powerful elements in particular have immigrated to Western Europe, while the numerically larger group immigrating to Palestine consists of a larger [proportion] of middle class and poor elements.[46]

German intelligence activities targeting Salonica's Jews became overt after Fritz Schönberg was appointed consul general in Salonica (January 1938). Schönberg openly stated that in his view, the Jews' support for Zionism undermined any change in Metaxas' true attitude toward them. According to Schönberg, Metaxas did not really consider the Jews to be an integral part of the Greek people. The "Jewish problem" in Greece was different from that in Germany, and was focused in Salonica, the centre of what was considered Jewish separatism.

> Only one substantial Jewish colony, where the Jews live together, exists in this country. . . . In this colony, the Jewish spirit and the Jewish customs have been preserved. There has been no assimilation with the Greeks. Out of the four Jewish newspapers published in Salonika [sic], two are in French, one in Ladino, and one is in Greek . . . No racial mingling between Jews and the Greek host nation takes place in Salonika because of its special position. The Greek state is *de facto*, if not in the legal sense, inclined toward anti-Semitism. The Orthodox Church plays a major role in this true anti-Semitic inclination by forbidding intermarriage with Jews . . . conversions to the Orthodox Church are rare. A feeling of foreignness exists between the Jews and the Greeks that [is similar to that which] National Socialist Germany aims to achieve through its Jewish policy.[47]

The following event, described by the German consul in Salonica, indicates the increasing discrimination against Jews in Greek courts:

> This morning, two Jews on a tram were beaten up until they bled because they were speaking Ladino and reading the Jewish newspaper, *Le Progrès*, which was

demonstratively torn up. One of the Greek attackers on the tram was arrested and taken to court. During the proceedings, the son of the wholesale merchant Karamaounas appeared as a defence witness and swore that the detainee was innocent. The judge rejected [the accusations made by] the Jews, explaining that he believed the testimony of the Greek witnesses. He told them to look for the "real" attacker.[48]

Schönberg also related that the Greek masses, like their government, tended to exhibit anti-Semitic attitudes. When spying on Greek society, the German consul attempted to find cracks in Jewish–Greek relations. After recognising the increasing economic competition, Schönberg wrote (11 November 1938) that the Greek people had "matured" sufficiently for implementation of an anti-Jewish policy.

As I am repeatedly given to understand through my conversations with Greeks, the protective racial measures of Germany and Italy have been received here with great understanding and full acceptance. Regret is often expressed that the Greek government has not yet decided to implement similar measures.[49]

As an example of his deductions he pointed to the local Ethniki Etaireia (National Society), an anti-Venizelist organisation with national–socialist tendencies that was expanding throughout Greece. Although the organisation's main task was to support the Metaxas government as well as fight communism, Schönberg argued that Ethniki Etaireia forces had apparently received secret instructions from the government to operate more intensely against the Jews: "The numerous Freemasons in the Ethniki Etaireia, who are trying to block anti-Semitic activity, are the main supporters of this tendency toward camouflage."[50] The German consul argued, "[T]he boycott of Jewish stores that is already being imposed quite openly by Greek customers in the Macedonian cities could be attributed to the covert agitation of the Ethniki Etaireia. Recently, as I hear, this boycott also spread to the rural population."[51]

The contemporary testimony of a Jewish traveller to Salonica appears to confirm the German consul's report. During his visit in 1940, Yaacov Tshernovitz, envoy of the Keren Hakayemet branch in Sofia, Bulgaria, described the Metaxas regime as a "fairly soft dictatorship which is usually comfortable for the Jews. However, this regime is making efforts to Hellenise the population, especially the Judeo-Spanish-speaking community of Salonica."[52] Tshernovitz went on to stress the severe official Greek censorship of private letters as well as of local Jewish journals (two in French and one in Judeo-Spanish), which resulted in the publication of articles praising Metaxas and his administration. He also described the secret police that followed him everywhere.[53] He likewise noted that the Greek perception of the Jews as a non-assimilated national minority supported discrimination. The poverty that rapidly spread among the majority of Jews and the decline in employment opportunities open to Jews further weakened the community's internal solidarity. In this way he confirmed the findings of the survey conducted by the same Dr. Zohar mentioned above. According to Zohar, although Jewish communal institutions continued to operate independently even under the Metaxas dictatorship, Jewish communal resources were no longer renewable.

Although assimilationists do not have control here as in other communities, no war has broken out between assimilationists and Zionists. . . . Nonetheless, the community has no constructive direction, no thoughts about the future, and no initiative. People's ideas are divided with respect to the preservation of Jewish culture, or the younger generation's spirit. It should therefore come as no surprise, for example, that it has been impossible to recruit any energetic young people to become a community representative. Moreover, despite all the invitations and searches, no suitable person, who is interested in participating in the community's government, has been located. The community therefore continues to exist in a state of inertia; it apathetically maintains its educational institutions, the rabbinate, the little social assistance it still provides, and so forth. There is no vitality to be found here, no confrontation of ideas or power. [54]

Although racial legislation was absent in Greece of the 1930s, the tightening economic relations between the Greek and Nazi economies impacted the Jewish economy negatively, similarly to how Hungarian Jewry was affected at the beginning of the 1940s.[55] These events apparently widened the economic differences within the Jewish community and increased inequality in both income and wealth. While established Jewish industrialists and merchants remained members of the Salonica Chamber of Commerce, Jewish micro traders as well as Jewish workers who were experiencing exacerbating competition from both indigenous and refugee competitors were deprived of their livelihood. The intensifying Jewish pauperism on the eve of Greece's going to war[56] and the widening economic gaps appear to be the subject of Dr. Zohar's comment when he stated that "knowledgeable individuals" from the Jewish community had attempted to refute "the popular opinion about the declining economic circumstances of Salonica's Jews".

The Greek authorities' *de facto* discrimination, which was supported by economic interests strongly linked to the German war industry, left the Jewish economy in a hopeless state long before the Nazi occupation. Again in the words of Dr. Zohar: "Although no anti-Jewish laws have been passed, and the central government has not yet instituted an anti-Jewish climate, slowly, day by day, while taking advantage of the Jews' internal weakness, havoc is being wrought."[57] Zohar's description, summarised in the Sabbath Index,[58] reveals the weakness not only of religious life but also of the Jewish economy.

We are well aware of how much the laws regarding the duty of observing Sunday [i.e., as the Christian day of rest] affect the religious life of parts of the Jewish community in other states. However, nothing resembles what has occurred in Salonica. Economic life flourishes on Saturday [the Jewish Sabbath] in all the Jewish quarters; all the shops are open, all the institutions operate, every labourer, every porter, every merchant – everyone is busy at his trade or craft. As to those who observe the Sabbath and lock their business, they can be counted on one hand. A story is told about Jack or Harry who, because they observe the Sabbath, labour in their workshop, or their shop, until very late on weekdays in order to make up for the income lost on Saturday.[59]

Yomtov Yacoel, the legal advisor to the Jewish community of Salonica, perhaps intentionally, described Jewish-Christian relations in Salonica during the two preceding decades when providing the background to his detailed description of German activities against Jewish businessmen. According to his diary, written in 1943,

Salonika [sic] was not totally free of passionate anti-Semites who, for ideological reasons of business competition (the majority among them), would countenance with pleasure the elimination of Jews from the city. . . . [S]tarting in the summer of 1942, certain German authorities began activities of an anti-Semitic character . . . initially turned against the Jewish movie house businesses and by using force reaching even to imprisonment of the owners obliged them to transfer – by notarial acts, no less – their businesses to Christians . . . proceeded in sealing at first and then removing the inventory of all the Jewish paper wholesalers and printing houses . . . appointed Greek journalists beholden to it to a special office, which under the ostensibly legal management of paper supplies proceeded to the looting of these substantial Jewish assets . . . expulsion of fifteen [Jewish] shop owners (fruit vendors, grocers, butchers, etc.) from the main market . . . and the installation in their place of Christian vegetable vendors who had been evicted from another place in the city. This method, which proved successful in the case of these tradesmen, whetted the appetite of other competitors of the Jews. There followed more regular interventions by Germans arbitrarily expelling Jewish owners from centrally located commercial stores and installing in them Christian businessmen intimate with the Germans or others who paid handsomely for the goodwill of intermediaries close to them. Finally, the municipality itself . . . found it expedient to take a decision concerning the changing of the names of a few city streets long named after prominent Jews notable for their civic-minded activities. This decision of the municipality was carried out and caused the justified resignation of the only representative of the Jewish element at the city council.[60]

The description transmitted by Yacoel, one of the leading figures charged with administrating the Jewish community prior to the German occupation, portrays how, in retrospect, evidence of a nationalist economic discrimination, in its overt and covert form, could be identified. Traces of this perspective had been visible among Greek officials as well as economic competitors since the 1920s. The destruction of the Jewish business world was completed by the Nazis in Auschwitz. Among the victims was Yomtov Yacoel, who was found and arrested while hiding in an apartment in Athens. This book is a memorial to the Salonican Jewish entrepreneurs and their Jewish employees who were murdered during the Holocaust.[61]

Appendices

Appendix 2

Table A Population of Salonica by Ethno-Religious Groupings, 1710s–1810s

Year	Jews	Greeks	Turks	Others	Total	Percentage of Jews
1714	30,000	10,000	25,000		65,000	46
1734	20,000	9,000	10,000		40,000	c. 50
1777	25,000	15,000	25,000	100	70,000	36
1788	23,000	20,000	37,000		80,000	29
1800	12,000	16,000	30,000	2,000	60,000	20
1806	13,000	15,000	35,000		65,000	20
1816	15,000	8,000	30,000		53,000	28

Source: Moutsopoulos 1981: 22–23.
Note: The "Others" are foreigners, primarily of European origin. The figures in the "Total" column do not necessarily reflect the sum of all ethnic components, but rather the "total" figures in the original sources. Stoianovich (1960: 247) provides more systematic, consistent data, indicating that the Jewish population was 18,000 in 1783 and 12,000 in 1792.

Table B Population of Salonica by Ethno-Religious Group, 1880–1914

Year	Jews	Greeks	Turks	Others	Total	Percentage of Jews
1880	50,000	15,000	20,000		85,000	59
1883	50,000	18,000	28,000		96,150	52
1901	60,000	20,000	25,000	15,000	120,000	50
1910	65,000	35,000	30,000	2,200	132,000	49
1912	81,000	27,000	33,000	9,000	150,000	54
1914	95,200	30,600	34,000	10,200	170,000	56

Source: For 1880, 1883, 1910: Moutsopoulos 1981: 22–23; for 1901, 1914: Dumont 1979: 34; for 1912: M. Molho 1986: 17.
Note: The "Others" are foreigners, primarily of European origin. The figures in the "Total" column do not necessarily reflect the sum of all ethnic components, but rather the "total" figures in the original sources.

Appendix 3

Table A The Urban Population in Macedonia Following the Transfer, 1920–1928

Urban Center	1920	1928	Change in Percentage
Salonica	170,321	236,524	38.9
Veria	13,349	14,589	9.3
Katerini	6,540	10,138	55.0
Naussa	8,468	10,250	21.0
Drama	15,263	29,339	92.2
Kavalla	22,939	49,980	117.9
Kozani	10,334	12,702	22.9
Edessa	9,441	13,115	38.9
Serres	14,486	29,640	104.6
Florina	12,513	10,585	-15.4
Kastoria	6,280	10,308	64.1
Total	289,934	427,170	47.3

Source: Adapted from Greek Census of 1928, vol. I, Table 11*.
Note: These census data were available for each *ville*, which is defined as a population center with at least 10,000 people.

Table B Distribution of the Greek Metropolitan Population in 1928 by Place of Birth (in percentages)

Birthplace	Local	Greece	Refugees Before 1922	After 1922	Total %	No.
Salonica	36.0	16.2	8.2	39.6	100.0	244,680
Athens	28.7	43.1	2.2	26.0	100.0	459,211
Piraeus	27.4	32.4	2.6	37.6	100.0	251,659

Source: Adapted from Greek Census of 1928, vol. 4, Tables 1e, 3*; Annuaire Statistique de la Grèce (1930), Table 13b.

Notes: 1. The "veteran population" (V) is defined here as complementing the "refugee population" (R) in the total population (T). "Persons who arrived after 1922" are included in the census category "refugees" (97,025). Consequently: V = T − R. In Salonica in 1928, V = 147,655 and R = 97,025.
2. Because refugees were defined by the Lausanne Treaty as Greek Orthodox, the negligible number of Jewish refugees from Turkey was not mentioned.
3. The veteran population was distributed between "born in Salonica" (88,050) and "born in Greece" (39,589), and also included the population categorized as "born abroad" but who arrived before 1922 (20,016).
3. Adding together the two sub-categories of "born abroad" (those born abroad and who came to Greece before 1922, and those born abroad and who came after 1922) the sum is 117,041. Consequently, many more than the 100,000 Greek immigrants might actually have been refugees.
4. Between 1920 and 1928, the population of Athens grew from 317,209 to 459,211, of which the increase of 119,420 were refugees; Piraeus expanded from 135,833 to 251,659, of which 94,683 were refugees; Salonica likewise grew from 174,390 in 1920 to 244,680 in 1928, of which the increase included 97,025 refugees. See Greek Census of 1928, vol. I, Tab. 11*.

Table C Distribution of the Refugee Metropolitan Population (1928) by Gender and Country of Origin (in percentages)

Country of Origin	Salonica		Athens		Piraeus	
	Males	Females	Males	Females	Males	Females
Asia Minor	57.6	57.8	78.0	81.3	78.9	81.1
Thrace and Pontus	31.3	32.8	9.8	9.5	10.8	10.6
Constantinople	7.6	6.4	10.0	7.5	7.7	6.3
Russia	1.5	.4	.9	.7	1.1	.9
Others	1.9	2.5	1.3	1.0	1.5	1.1
Total percentage	100.0	100.0	100.0	100.0	100.0	100.0
Total number	44,122	52,903	51,951	67,469	43,135	51,548

Source: Adapted from Greek Census of 1928, vol. 1, Table IIe, pp. 461–62 (Salonica), p. 455 (Athens), p. 456 (Piraeus).

Note: "Others" includes people from the Caucasus, Balkan States, and Cyprus, a minor component since their numbers were negligible.

Appendix 4.1 Jewish Firms in Salonica, 1921

1. Food and Beverages

1a. Groceries

No.	Name	Address	Notes
1	Carasso Inio A.	——	
2	Catan Haim & Cie	——	
3	Cohen & Massarano	Alex. le Grand 42	
4	Escapa & Levy	Alex. le Grand 36	
5	Hagouel	Egnatias 289	
6	Hanen Simon & Saporta	Catouni 2	
7	Leon Juda & Aelion Joseph	Lycourgo 15	
8	Litsi & Halegoua	Alex. le Grand 43	
9	Mizan Eliezer A.	Olgas 13	
10	Pardo Pinhas D.	Hiou 27	
11	Pinhas Salomon & Cie	[Rue Platéa Embouriou 1][1]	Chocolate, sweets, jams
12	Roubin I. & Saoul I.	——	
13	Saltiel Jacob A.	Alex. le Grand 37	
14	Sasson & Benforado	Alex. le Grand 71	
15	Soures & Carasso	Alex. le Grand 45	

1b. Colonial Commodities – Coffee, Sugar, Rice, and Spices

No.	Name	Address	Notes
16	Abastado Haim D.	Hiou 25	
17	Abastado Salomon D.	Catouni	
18	Aelion Sam & Cie	Orvilou 10	
19	Angel & Sciaky	Egyptou 50	
20	Angel Juda & Cie[2]	Catouni [3]	[Import]
21	Ascher & Venezia	Lycourgou 13	
22	Beja, Sion & Revah[3]	Katouni	
23	Beraha Joseph Abram[4]	Edessis	
24	Carasso Haim David	Alexandre le Grand 33	

No.	Name	Address	Notes
25	Carasso Moise Haim	Alexandre le Grand 27	
26	Coenca Frères Abram & Fils	Rong. Han 116	
27	Cohen & Saias	Catouni	
28	Cohen Yomtov Joseph	Katouni 2	
29	Errera Isaac Guedalia	——————	
30	Gattegno Salomon D.	Egyptou 42	
31	Hassid Joseph Isac et Frères	Alexandre le Grand 37	
32	Hassid Samuel E.[5]	Mazi Han 8	
33	Karasso & Zarahia	Catouni 6–8	
34	Kohen & Torres	Orvilou 6	
35	Leon Raphael S.	Monastiriou 41	
36	Litsi & Yahiel	Alexandre le Grand 32	
37	Mahel Frères (Fratteli)	Zafiraki 29	Oil
38	Mano Jacob Saltiel	Alexandre le Grand 23	
39	Mano Michel A. & Cie	Zafiraki 18	
40	Massarano Frères[6]	Orvilou 11	[Import]
41	Menachem Victor	Tourpali Han 12	
42	Menahem Pepo J.	Zafiraki 20	
43	Menahem Pepo S.	Franque 43	
44	Menahem Salomon & Fils[7]	[Rue Edessis Passage Kyrtsi] [Rue Franque][8]	[Import/export]
45	Mizan Isaac Abram	Egyptou 39	
46	Mordoh & Saltiel	Peristeriou 8	
47	Mordoh Isaac S.	———	
48	Nahmias Jacques S.	Orvilou 4	
49	Navarro Emmanuel Isaac[9]	[Egyptou 59]	And olive oil
50	Navarro Isaac Emmanuel[10]	Egyptou 52, Telegraph. ISAKINO NAVARRO	
51	Navarro Leon E.	Egypto 59	
52	Peloussof Abram & Rousso[11]	Salaminos [20]	
53	Perahia Simon & Cie[12]	Alexandre le Grand 46	import/export;
54	Saias & Cohen[13]	[Katouni 7, Telegraph. SAIAS-COHEN]	[Import, consignation]
55	Salem Richard Daniel[14]	Franque 43 [Telegraph. address: RICHEM]	Consignation
56	Saltiel & Koenca	Alexandre le Grand 54	
57	Saltiel Isakino		Cooperative
58	Saltiel Sabi Samuel	Allatini Han 6	
59	Saporta Samuel A.	Egyptou 34	
60	Saul Vidal & Co.[15]	Plat. Emboriou [Alex. le Grand 37]	
61	Sevy Avram	Platia Emborio	
62	Stroumza Pinhas & Cie	Vaiou 21	
63	Uziel David M.[16]	Zafiraki [25]	
64	Yachiel Manouel	Tsimiski 2	
65	Yoel Joseph Samuel	Catouni	
66	Zaharia Moise et Cie	Egyptou 55	

1c. Production of Sweets and Bakery Products – Confectionaries

67	Almosnino Haim[17]	Franque 37 [Vas. Georgiou 84]	Pastry shop
68	Ammiras & Levy	Alex. le Grand 65	Pastry shop
69	Perahia & Cie	Karatasso 7	Macaroni

No.	Name	Address	Notes
70	Perahia Ilias	Tsimiski	Pastry shop

I d. Production and Distribution of Dairy Products

71	Carasso (Karasso) Frerès[18]	Alex. le Grand 32	Wholesaler of white cheese, *kashkaval*, local and American butter

I e. Production and Trade in Wine and Alcoholic Beverages

72	Abravanel Jacob	Salaminos [telegraph Jacob Abravanel]	
73	Amariglio Samuel D.	Hiou 14	Beverage factory
74	Angel Aelion et Cie	Vas. Iracliou 6	Trade in wine and alcoholic beverage
75	Benveniste David Intov	Ast. Proestou 12	
76	Coenca Veisi & Cie	Countouriotou 27	Beverage factory
77	Florentin Joseph & Frères	Hermou 24	
78	Menaham Joseph E.	Egnatias 179	Spirits
79	Rousso Aelion & Cie	Egnatias 206	Beverage factory
80	Uziel Daniel M.	Max Harden 9	

2. Chemicals and Pharmaceuticals

81	Capon Nahama & Cie	S I Alex. le Grand 45	Wax

2a. Paints, Varnish, and Ink

82	Amaraggi & Salmona	Vas. Iracliou 59	
83	Hassid Samuel H. & Fils	Orvilou 6	Red powder and chemicals
84	Yomtov Elie	Alex. le Grand 89	Chemicals

2b. Soap Production

85	Arditti Juda & Fils[19]	Ol. Diamandi 49. Telegraph: SAPOUNDJI- ARDITTI	Flour milling and colonial commodities too
86	Ezratty & Pelossof (*3)	Egyptou	Colonial commodities
87	Hassid & Koenca	Alex. le Grand	Soap manuf.
88	Hassid Moise[20]	[Zafiraki 21b]	Soap manuf.
89	Hazan & Molho[21]	Zafiraki 16	Oil; colonial products
90	Leon Samuel & Yomtov (Into)	Zafiraki 27	[Huge] soap manuf.[22]
91	Levy & Hassid	Zafiraki 20	
92	Saltiel Isac & Cie	Catouni 2	Cottonseed oil, butter
93	Saporta Yinto M.	Egyptou 45	Mineral oil
94	Simha Lazare	Monastiriou 32	Soap manuf.
95	Stroumza Mayo & Cie	Victor Hugo 12	Soap factory

2c. Pharmaceuticals and Photographic Articles (see also 10b below)

96	Angel Pinchas J.	Alex. le Grand 107	Pharmacy
97	Benveniste Menteche A.	Vas. Iracliou	Photographic articles
98	Benveniste Sam I.	Vas. Iracliou 7	Pharmacy
99	Cohen Gabriel S.	Alex. le Grand 44	Pharmacy
100	Cougno & Bueno	V. Georgiou 77	Photographic works; pharmacy

No.	Name	Address	Notes
101	Francès Nathan	Egyptou 31	Chemicals production
102	Francès Samuel E.	Orvilou 9	Pharmacy
103	Matalon David I.	Edessis [Verias 4][23]	Pharmacy (and wholesale)
104	Nahmias V.	Franque 34	Pharmacy
105	Scialom Jacob I.	Vas. Iracliou 4	Photographic articles

3. Construction Materials

3a. Production and Trade in Construction Materials (Including Metals)

106	Aboav Isac I. & Cie	Egyptou 12	Metals
107	Alvo Frères	Franque 41	Metals
108	Amaradji Jesua Fils de	Ol. Diamanti 56	Cement production
109	Benveniste Gattegno & Cie	Egyptou 9	Metals
110	Botton De Isac J.[24]	Zafiraki [22]	Metals
111	Covo Juda S.	Franque 45	Metals, leather
112	David Israel & Tiano Isac	V. Hugo 2, Alex. le Grand 59	Metals
113	Hassid Joseph & Frères	Al. le Grand 7	Metals
114	Mossery (Mosseri) Raphael S. [25]	Ol. Diamanti	Metals
115	Nahman & Bendavid	Alex. le Grand 69	Metals
116	Navarro Leon I.	Alex. le Grand 38	Metals
117	Navarro Samuel I.	Ol. Diamanti 73	Metals
118	Nefousi, Moussafia & Cie[26] [Ancienne Maison A. S. Mosseri]	Pindou 4	Metals
119	Nissim & Guilidia	Monastiriou 23	Metals
120	Salem & Alvo	Alex. le Grand 55	Metals

4. Energy and Public Utilities

4a. Electricity, Gas, and Water
4b. Petrol, Salt, Coal, and Matches

121	Almosnino Gabriel	Franque 36	Coal merchant
122	Amariglio Isac	Zafiraki 14	Salt and petrol
123	Asséo David S.	Lycourgou 6	Salt merchant
124	Parente Avram Haim	Zafiraki 24	Petrol vendor
125	Saltiel Salomon Fils de	Rodopis 3	Salt traders

5. Metal

5a. Minerals
5b. Metal Industry (Machinery Production)

126	Sarfatti Menahem

5c. Metalwares

127	Bivas Samuel Avram	Zafiraki 8	Motor vehicle equipment and repair (carosserie) [sic]
128	Juda Fils de Sabetay	Alex. le Grand 13	Marine equipment

No.	Name	Address	Notes

5d. Machinery

129	Alcalay & Juda[27]	Egyptou 27	Agricultural machinery
130	Israel I. & Arditty I.	Condouriotou	Machinery representatives

5e. Electrical Products

131	Cohen & Pardo	Leondos Sofou 9	
132	Cohen I. & Perahia A.	L. Sofou 13 B	
133	Kaki Emil Isac	Leofor. Nikis 21	
134	Nahama Dan.	v. Hugo 8	
135	Nahmias E. & Yacoel V.	Hermou 84	
136	Sevy Frères & Aelion Frères	Max Harden 1	

6. Wood

137	Serrero Isac M.	Leontos Sofou 7	Brush factory[28]

6a. Wood Coal (Charcoal)
6b. Furniture (see 12a below)
6c. Wood for Construction

138	Mallah Aaron & Cie	Top Hané	
139	Saltiel Daniel & Simtov	Vassileos Georgiou	
140	Saltiel David Isac Fils de	Top Hané	
141	Saltiel Joseph & Avram	26 Octovriou 11	
142	Saltiel Moise & Cie	Vass. Georgiou 16	
143	Saporta Into I.	Leoforos Octovriou 26	
144	Vaena Moise	Leoforos Stratou	

7. Hides, Leather, and Footwear

7a. Trade in Hides – Import, Wholesale, and Retail

145	Amir & Mevorah (*2)	Egnatia 5	Retailer
146	Aroesty & Frères	———	Import from the hinterland
147	Avahiou Samuel & Frères	Lycourgou 6	Import from the hinterland
148	Avayou Samuel & Co.	Lycourgou 6	
149	Cohen Moise A.	———	Retailer
150	Cougno & Revah	———	Import from the hinterland
151	Ezratty & Cougno (*2)	Plat. Morihovou	Importer
152	Gattegno Moche & Co. (*2)[29]	Salaminos 12 [POB 92] Telegraph. MOGAT	Hides and leather export/import
153	Gavios [Isac] Aaron (*2)	Ol. Diamandi 14	Import from the hinterland
154	Hagouel Haim	———	Retailer
155	Hasson David	———	Import from the hinterland
156	Magriso Joseph	———	Import from the hinterland
157	Mevorah Moise	———	Retailer

No.	Name	Address	Notes
158	Modiano Abram S.	Ermou 12	Broker
159	Rophel Iz[a]ia & Cie	———	Importer
160	Saltiel Benico	———	Importer
161	Saltiel David (*2)	Zafiraki 19	Import from the hinterland
162	Sarfatty Barouh	———	Exporter
163	Sarfatty Solomon (*2)	Sofocliou 29	Import from the hinterland
164	Serrero Davicos	Countouriotou	Consignment of cattle
165	Tiano Elie Moise (*2)	Karatasou 11	
166	Tiano Moise (*2)	Salaminos	Import from the hinterland
167	Yacoel & Cie (*2)	Doxis 9	Exporter

7b. Leather Trade

No.	Name	Address	Notes
168	Acher Isac	Victor Hugo 2	
169	Angel Isac Joseph	Alexandre le Grand 54	
170	Arama Juda	Alexandre le Grand 44	
171	Ascer Moise & Fils	Victor Hugo 5	
172	Asséo Isac M.	Colombou 10	
173	Covo & Angel	Edessis 4	
174	Florentin Isac & Elie	Ol. Diamandi 25	
175	Florentin Samuel I. / [Z.][30]	Victor Hugo 5	
176	Fransès Fils de Jacob [E.][31]	Syngrou 8	
177	Fransès Jessua	Victor Hugo 12	
178	Hanen Juda I. & Cie	———	
179	Marcozi Abram E.	Alexandre le Grand 107b	
180	Salem Haim Frères	Egnatia 179	
181	Sarfatty Baruch Joseph	Thassou 5	
182	Simon & Angel	———	

7c. Leather Products and Footwear

No.	Name	Address	Notes
183	Altcheh Eli	Reine Olga 4	Cobbler
184	Angel Abram Salomon (*2)	Vas. Iracliou 5	
185	Angel Samuel I. (*2)	Vas. Iracliou 52	
186	Calderon & Aroesti	Esopou 1	Shoe factory
187	Cohen Moise & Frères	Hermou 27	Cobbler

8. Textiles

8a. Oilcloth

No.	Name	Address	Notes
188	Basso Samuel A.	Mazi Han 2	
189	Haim Abram E.	Cité Saul	
190	Perahia Fils Joseph	Alex. le Grand 107	Tarpaulins

8b. Wool: Raw Material and Knitwear Production

No.	Name	Address	Notes
191	Beja Fils de David & Cie	———	Sale of raw wool and grains
192	Cohen Abram	———	

No.	Name	Address	Notes
193	Revah (Tevah) Isac Joseph & Cie[32]	Colocotroni [13]	Knitwear factory [flannel underwear]

8c. Trade in Cotton Yarn

194	Albelda Avram D.	Victor Hugo 3	
195	Florentin Yomtov & Franco	Egnatias 98	
196	Frances Joseph S.	Victor Hugo	Yarn and chemicals
197	Hassid Abram Fils de	Eminiet Han 3	
198	Hassid David	Victor Hugo	
199	Moise Aron & Strumza	Vas. Iracliou 2	
200	Nahama Salomon Yomtov[33]	Franque 49 [47]	
201	Nehama Salomon Joseph	Victor Hugo	
202	Pinhas Salomon Elie[34]	[Zafiraki 17]	Cotton and wool
203	Salem & Levy	Victor Hugo	
204	Salmona Marios	Vas. Iracliou	
205	Salomon G. et Cie	Tsimiski	Yarn and ropes
206	Saltiel & Angel Elie[35]	Salaminos 20	
207	Trabout Juda A.	Egyptou 17	

8d. Cotton: Spinning and Weaving
8e. Jute, Sacks, and Ropes

208	Benadon Ilias		
209	Benadon Simtov & Cie	Zafiraki 14	
210	Benardout Joseph	Egyptou	
211	Berissi Isac	————	
212	Berissi Jacob & Cie	Orviliou 10	
213	Hassid Isac	A. le Grand 46	Ropes
214	Perahia Moise & Cie	Egyptou 46	
215	Sciaky Levi H.	A. le Grand 36	Sacks
216	Torrès E. Jutificio & Cie[36]	[POB 37, Telegram: Torrès]	Jute weaving and sacs manufacturing

9. Clothing

9a. Linen Drapery and Novelty Goods (Nouveautés)

217	Abravanel Ascer & Cie[37]	Ermou 22	
218	Botton de Joseph M.	Egnatia 73	
219	Confortes & Carasso	Ractivan 5	
220	Gattegno Haim M.	Victor Hugo 42	Ladies' fashions
221	Israel Ascer M.	Vas. Iracliou 4	
222	Malah (Mallah) Fils de . N[ehama] A	Voulgaroctonou [2]	Firm est. 1870, woollens, silks; cotton cloth, tissue.[38]
223	Matarasso, Saragoussi & Rousso[39]	Place de la Liberté [1]	
224	Mordoh I. N.	Franque 39	
225	Nahmias Joseph Salomon	Alex. le Grand 155	
226	Nahmias Moise	Hermou 27	
227	Nissim Isac Fils de	————	
228	Noah Juda S.	Menexe 14	
229	Paladino Isac	Ermou 20	

No.	Name	Address	Notes
230	Perahia Moise A.	Colombo 65	
231	Sciaky & Yomtov	Cité Saul 29	

9b. Haberdashery (Merceries) and Hosiery

No.	Name	Address	Notes
232	Alcalay Nissim & Cie	Catholicon 14	
233	Altchech & Tazartes	Alex. le Grand 76	
234	Altcheh Haim M.	Alex. le Grand 1	
235	Assael, Attas & Catan	Vas. Iracliou 7	
236	Basso David	Syngrou 4	
237	Benmayor Samuel E.	Bedesten [Ermou] 49	
238	Benssusan Mentech		
239	Benveniste Mair & Frères	Place de la Liberté	Manufacturer and agent woollens, silk stuffs, cotton cloth[40]
240	Beraha Avram H.	Alex. le Grand 101	Cotton threads
241	Cohen Isaac A.	Djalmi Han 5	Flannels
242	Cohen Juda M.	Yeniston 7	
243	Errera G[edalia] A. Fils de & Cie Ltd.[41]	Pas. St. Minas	
244	Ezratty Hasday	Ermou 19	
245	Faiz & Yakar	Alex. le Grand 76	
246	Florentin Saporta & Serero[42]	Catholicon 9	
247	Halegoua David & Salomon	Her. Cité Saul	
248	Hassid Haim & Albert	Al. le Grand 66b	
249	Hassid Samuel H.	Kolomvou 2	
250	Jessua Mercado & Fils[43]	Ermou 22	
251	Juda P. & Cie	Franque 28	
252	Kohen Avram G.	——	
253	Kohen Joseph I.	Al. le Grand 97	
254	Levy Isaac	Tahidromiou 4	
255	Levy Joseph & Elie A.	Colomvou 61	
256	Levy Moise E.	Alex. le Grand 76	
257	Modiano Haim	——	Agent
258	Mordoh Haim David	Saoul Han	
259	Nahmias & Massoth	[Syngrou 12]	Cotton threads[44]
260	Nahmias Elie Samuel	Vas. Iracliou 4	
261	Nissim Daniel & Frères	Kasmirdji Han	
262	Paladino Moise S.	Alex. le Grand 80	
263	Pardo Moise G.	Syngrou 12	
264	Pessah Isac M.	Arap Han	
265	Raphael & Benveniste	Vas. Iracliou 50 [–51]	Wholesale/retail of draperies and clothing[45]
266	Raphael & Botton	Egnatia 168	
267	Raphael & Nahmias	Ermou 29	
268	Salem Levy	Egnatias 83	
269	Saltiel Serrero & Tazartes	Catouni 10	
270	Saporta, Amiras & Cie	Alex. le Grand 46	
271	Sefiha Samuel	Catholicon 10	Handkerchiefs
272	Sides Yachiel & Cie[46]	[Victor Hugo 5]	Manufacturer's agent
273	Tchenio Mair & Cie	Al. le Grand 107	
274	Yacoel Moise & Levy Hanen	Pas. St. Minas 16	

No.	Name	Address	Notes
275	Yakar Leon	Egnatias 42	
276	Yeni Gedalia	Colombo 33	

9c. Hats and Shawls

No.	Name	Address	Notes
277	Acouni Joseph Jacob	Egnatias 319	Ladies' hats
278	Levy & Fransès	Egnatias 88	Military
279	Moscovitch Haim	V. Constantinos	Civil and military
280	Recanati Nissim S.	Alex. le Grand 4	Men's hats

9d. Mercantile Tailors and Confection

No.	Name	Address	Notes
281	Abram & Fransès Isac	Colombo 33	
282	Allalouf Jacob M.	Alex. le Grand 107	Confection/Manufacturing
283	Cohen Frères	Vas. Iracliou	
284	Errera Isac D.	Franque	
285	Fransès & Allalouf	Menexe 11	
286	Saltiel Jacob M.	Colombo 69	
287	Venezia Barouh	Franque 37	Tailor
288	Ventoura Marios E.	Colombo 26	Tailor

10. Printing, Paper, and Office Equipment
10a. Printing, Bookshops, Paper, Lithographies

No.	Name	Address	Notes
289	Angel Isac Salomon (*3)	Franque 23	Cardboard packing, lithographs
290	Asséo Jacques & Juda	Salaminos 21	
291	Benveniste Haim & Albert	Fokeas 4	
292	Covo Frères	L. Sofou 9	
293	Errera David	Ermou 5	
294	Gattegno David Jacob	Colomvou	Printers
295	Hassid Abram Haim	Tsimiski 6	
296	Mallah Nissim E.	Voulgaroctonou 55	
297	Mesoulam & Mattarsso	Franque 9	
298	Modiano Into S.	Tsimiski 2	
299	Molho Mair	Condouriotou 36	
300	Nissim Gabriel Elie	Al. le Grand 50	

10b. Office Equipment and Photography

No.	Name	Address	Notes
301	Barzilai Albert[47]	Franque 87	Stationery, office supplies and furniture, typewriters
302	Cougno Salvator M.	Vas. Iracliou 7	Photographic equipment
303	Molho Saul [J.]	Egnatia 121 [Rue des Banques 5, Telephone no. 6][48]	Wholesale/retail typewriters
304	Naar Haim (*2)	Countouriotou 13	Cinematographic equipment
305	Naar Hananel	Edessis [6][49]	Stationery
306	Naar Isac Salomon	Leof. Nikis 89	Cinematography equipment
307	Pardo Aron et Joseph (*2)	Victor Hugo / Syngrou	Film, photographic/ cinematographic equipment

11. Tobacco: Tobacco Trade and Cigarette Production
11a. Tobacco Trade and Cigarette Production

No.	Name	Address	Notes
308	Algava Jacob M.	Leo. Sofou 10	Merchant
309	Amiel Saul I.	Velissariou 14	Merchant
310	Bensussan Samuel	Syngrou 6	Merchant
311	Florentin Mair & Cie	Odisseos 19	Merchant
312	Karasso & Cie	Em. Papa 6	Cigarette paper
313	Nahmias Avram & Cie	Arap Han 11	Merchant
314	Revah & Mathia	Salaminos 13	Consignor of tobacco
315	Salem & Amariglio	Tsimiski 2	Cigarette paper
316	Sides Isac A.	Trapezis 5	Merchant

11b. Cigarettes and Tobacco Sellers

317	Barouh Guedalia S.	Alex. le Grand 13	
318	Mechoulam Frères & Cie	Egnatias 17	
319	Nadjari Juda	Tour Blanch	

12. Domestic Wares and Furniture

12a. Furniture Trade

320	Bitti Haim	Alex. le Grand 17	Upholsterer
321	Cohen & Handali	Hermou 11	
322	Cohen Joseph J.	Hermou 13	
323	Molho Saul & Chimchi	Egnatia 121	Pianos
324	Nahmias Samuel Fils de	Franque 32	
325	Revah, Zadok Levy & Cie	Egnatia 153	
326	Sadi Joseph	Hermou 15	Antiques
327	Saltiel & Handali	Colomvou 71–73	
328	Sciaky Moise & Cie	Catholicon 14	Carpenter

12b. Wallpaper
12c. Glasswares

329	Abravanel & Benveniste[50]	Vas. Iracliou 7 [Cité Saul]	
330	Abravanel David	Vas. Iracliou 56	
331	Abravanel Moise, Ezratty & Cie	Iracliou 7	
332	Amaradji Baruh & Moise	Iracliou 59–61	Colours
333	Benrubi (Benroubi) Haim[51]	Franque 31 [Leontos Sofou 11, branch on Nikis 18 in Piraeus]	
334	Benveniste & Asséo	Iracliou	
335	Benveniste & Mossé	Vas. Iracliou 49	
336	Castro Aggi & Leon	Menexe 31	Bottles (empty)
337	Chimchi Eliezer & Cie	Franque 45	
338	Cohen Moise S.	Colombo 26	Lamps
337	Modiano & Benrubi	Gastou 6	
340	Saal Sabetay Simtov	Vas. Iracliou	
341	Saltiel Isac M.	Franque 45	
342	Saltiel Jacob Abram	Vas. Iracliou 60	
343	Saltiel Mentech Sabetay	Franque 40	
344	Soustiel Diadohi Sabetay	Vas. Iracliou 4	

12d. Jewellery and Watches

No.	Name	Address	Notes
345	Aelion Levy & Sam	Ermou 1	
346	Asséo Moise J.	Franque 37	
347	Botton Isakino	Place de la Liberté 2	
348	Bourla S.[52]	Place de la Liberté 1	
349	Gattegno M. & Cie[53]	Ermou 23	
350	Hasson Samuel	Menexé 9	
351	Mallah Aron & Cie	Ermou 48	
352	Mallah Frères[54]	[Ermou 78]	
353	Pelossof Joseph & Sevy	Victor Hugo 12	
354	Salem Moise Jacob	Egnatias 147	Watchmaking

13. Trade in Agriculture Products, including Grain

13a. General Agents in the Hinterland

355	Bueno & Sasson	——	
356	Kaki Leon & Bensussan René	Salaminos 1	Representation
357	Marcou Frères	Al. le Grand 20	
358	Saltiel V. et Saporta	——	Indigenous products
359	Scialom Samuel A.	Loudias 1	
360	Torres Albert	Countourioti 17	Indigenous products
361	Varsano Nahoum Fils	Hiou 16	Indigenous products

13b. Grain and Flour

362	Aboav & Mordoh	Salaminos 5	
363	Ascer & Stromza	Salaminos 9	
364	Beja Pepo David	Egnatia 217 [Zafiraki 21]	Import/export[55]
365	Bendavid Abram L.	Zafiraki 5	
366	Benjamin Moise E. (*2)	Countouriotou 13	Silk cocoons, too
367	Bensussan I. & A.	——	Export of indigenous products
368	Cazes Jacob	Zafiraki 18	
369	Hanen Levy & Beja Moise (*2)[56]	Platia Morihovo	All kinds of flour
370	Juda Leon J.	Zafiraki 12	Flour and colonial commodities; import/export[57]
371	Mordoh Salomon & Cie	Coundourioti 11	
372	Nefoussi David Elie Fils	Salaminos 5	
373	Pinhas Haim Elie (*2)	Countouriotou	Silk cocoons, too
374	Rousso Haim & Cie	Zafiraki	
375	Saporta Semtov Fils de	Salaminos 6	
376	Sidès & Cie	Salaminos 13	

13c. Opium (Export)

377	Scialom Albert & Cie[58]	Victor Hugo Telegraph:PAX	Export opium, saffron.
378	Scialom Fils de Jacob[59]	——	Export opium

13d. Silk Cocoons (Export)

379	Benjamin & Saporta	Contouriotou	Cereals, too
380	Saporta Isac A.	Emm. Papa	Grains, too

No.	Name	Address	Notes
381	Yacoel Juda I.	Leont. Sofou 10	Grains, too

13e. Dried Fruits, Fresh Fruits, Legumes, and Oil

No.	Name	Address	Notes
382	Altcheh David A.	Alexandre le Grand 24	
383	Amiel Isac A.	Nikis 27	
384	Broudo Salomon	Nikis 29	
385	Cohen Moise	Voulgaroctonou	
386	Errera Isac Moise	Zafiraki 27	
387	Gilidi Nissim	Alexandre le Grand 22	
388	Houli David I.	——	
389	Israel Guedalia S.	Alexandre le Grand 33	
390	Juda Haim	Egyptou 57	
391	Juda Isac & Cie	Alexandre le Grand 14	
392	Levy David S.	Ol. Diamandi 58	
393	Marcos Abram & Cie	Egnatias 220	
394	Marko Moise & Cie	Alexandre le Grand 16	
395	Saltiel Abram & Fils	——	
396	Tevah Haim & Cie	Alexandre le Grand 26	
397	Yachiel Barouh I.	Nikis 28	
398	Yhaskel Jacob & Cie	Alexandre le Grand 17	

14. General Wholesale and Retail

14a. Rags

No.	Name	Address	Notes
399	Nissim & Beja Isac	Odisseos	

14b. Manufacturers' Agents

No.	Name	Address	Notes
400	Aélion & Hasid	——	
401	Aelion Fils de Joseph	Franque 8	
402	Aelion Isac & Cie	Catholicon 5	
403	Alvo & Nahmias	Aelion Han 17	
404	Angel Jessua & Cie	Syngrou 6	
405	Arouh Juda H.	Hermou 29	
406	Assael Moise	Franque 14	Tissue material
407	Attias Semtov Fils de	——	
408	Baruch Avram Elie	——	Consignor, too
409	Bayona August	Edessis 5	Consignor, too
410	Bendavid & Abravanel	Hermou (*Bedestin*)	
411	Benousiglio & Sadok	Colomvou 22	
412	Bensussan Jacob Fils de	Trapezis	
413	Benveniste Albert I.	Victor Hugo 3	
414	Benveniste Daniel P.	Alexandre le Grand	
415	Benveniste David M. Fils	Cité Saoul	
416	Benveniste Haim & Jacob	Hermou 24	
417	Bivas Juda & Cie	Egnatias 31	Haberdashery
418	Botton & Saias	Catholicon 12	
419	Bourla Isac D.	Trapezis 4	
420	Calderon (Kalderon) Ilias S.	Syngrou 3	
421	Camhi Frères	Cité Saoul	
422	Carasso & Modiano	Alexandre le Grand	

No.	Name	Address	Notes
423	Carasso Isac & Cie	——	
424	Carasso Salomon	Syngrou 1	
425	Cohen & Benveniste	——	
426	Cohen, Amon & Cie	Franque 40	
427	Cohen Haim & Cie	Catholicon 15	
428	Cohen Mentech M.	Cité Saoul	
429	De Mayo Abram S. & Fils	Cité Saoul	
430	Ergas Albert Moise	Egnatias 74	
431	Ezratty Isac Sol.	Ath. Diacou 32	
432	Florentin Liaou E.	Syngrou 1	
433	Franco Baruch & Cie	——	
434	Fransès & Bourla	Syngrou 2	
435	Fransès Fils de J. M.	Syngrou	
436	Fransès Joseph M. Fils de	Colomvou 29	
437	Fransès Moise S.	——	
438	Hanen & Modiano	——	
439	Hanen Frères & Cougno	Hermou 14	
440	Hassid Frères & Cie	Trapezis 4	
441	Hassid Haim A.	Egyptou 44	
442	Hassid J. Albert & Cie	Verrias 6	
443	Hassid Lazar & Cie	Verias 9	Cotton tissue
444	Israel & Salmona	Victor Hugo 3	
445	Israel Abram I.	Kazmirdji Han	
446	Jessua & Beraha	——	
447	Joseph Jacob & Cohen	Hermou 61	
448	Juda Felix & Cie	Trapezis 5	
449	Levy Elie	Alexandre le Grand 62	
450	Levy Moise M.	Catholicon 8	
451	Mallah Moise S.	Catholicon 10	
452	Mallah Samuel	Djamli Han 7	
453	Matalon & Altchech	Franque 36	
454	Matalon Sabetay[60]	Franque 36	
455	Misrahi Aron A.	Vas. Iracliou 4	Commission merchant
456	Modiano & Florentin	Victor Hugo 8	
457	Mordoh Hassid & Cie	——	
458	Mosse & Broudo	Hermou 29 (*Bedestin*)	
459	Nahmias Benjamin & Cie	Vas. Iracliou 7	
460	Nahmias Jacob	Cité Saoul	Retail manufacture
461	Nahmias Nissim I.	Trapezis	
462	Negrim & Scialom	Franque 38	
463	Nissim Sabetay & Fils	——	
464	Ovadia Eliezer	Tahidromiou	
465	Pardo Avram & Cie	Catholicon 10	
466	Perahia Aron & Cie	Syngrou	
467	Perahia Sam	Syngrou 3	
468	Rousso Menahem & De Mayo	Catholicon 10	
469	Salem Isac & Cie	Alex. le Grand 83	
470	Salmona Isac & Cie	Syngrou 2	
471	Saltiel Abram & Isac	Colomvou 33	
472	Saltiel Abram S.	Ermou 11	
473	Saltiel Haim M.	Trapezis 2	

No.	Name	Address	Notes
474	Saltiel Joseph M. & Cohen	Colomvou 31	
475	Saltiel Moise Fils de	Catholicon 16	
476	Saltiel Semtov	Kalderon Han 3	
477	Saltiel Semtov & Cie	Victor Hugo	
478	Saporta & Salmona	Franque 45	
479	Saporta Albert D.	Catholicon 14	
480	Sarfatty & Amariglio	Verrias	
481	Sarrano & Hassid	Catholicon 10	
482	Sarrano David S.	Alex. le Grand 103	
483	Sarrano Saltiel Jacob	Alex. le Grand 89	
484	Sasson Joseph & Salomon	Trapezis 4	
485	Sasson Moise I.	Makedonias 57	
486	Scialom & Allalouf	Colomvou 31	
487	Serrero & Arditty	Léontos Sofou 6	
488	Simha Haim I.	——	
489	Tazartes Juda Mair	Ol. Diamandi 56	
490	Uziel & Assael	Franque 45	
491	Uziel Jacob	Kibar Ali Han 9	Consignor, too
492	Yacoel & Nahmias	Tsimiski 9	
493	Yacoel & Sarah	Hermou (*bedestin*)	
494	Yoel & Bendavid	Dimosthenis 91	

15. Finance and Commission

15a. Large-Scale Commerce: International Traders and Commission Agents

No.	Name	Address	Notes
495	Abastado Elie Moise	Salaminos 10	Representative
496	Abastado Haim & Cie	Langada	
497	Abravanel L.	Lycourgou 11	Broker
498	Abravanel Sam I.	26 Octobre 4	Rep.
499	Aelion Elie I.	Meandrou 29	Broker
500	Alfandori Joseph & Haim	Zafiraki 25	Mandatary
501	Altcheh Isac	Alex. le Grand 63	Broker
502	Alvo Pepo A.[61]	Franque 31	Commerce representative [*hosiery*; hardware; metals; glass; stationery, etc.]
503	Amar B. Biniamin	Vas. Iracliou	Representative
504	Amar Elie & Cie	Victor Hugo	Representative
505	Amar Felix & Cie	——	Representative
506	Amar Frères	Allatini Han	Commission agent
507	Amar Henri	Tassou 6	Representative
508	Amariglio & Tazartes & Revah & Cie[62]	[Franque 38 Mazi Han 3–4]	
509	Amiel Joseph	Nikis 41	Representative
510	Angel & Matalon	Salaminos 1	Representative
511	Angel Abram	Kassandro 100	Broker
512	Arama David M.	Artimiou 30	Broker
513	Arditti Sam	Rue des Banques	Representative
514	Arditty Haim I. Fils	Stoa Tiano 13	Broker
514	Arditty Jacob & Cie	Etablis. du Port	Foreign trade

No.	Name	Address	Notes
516	Aroesti Egisto & Co.	Rogotti 116	Representative
517	Aroesti Haim & Frères[63]	Ol. Diamanti [10]	
518	Aron Jacob	Victor Hugo 75	Representative
519	Arouh Simtov A.	Ipodromou 35	Broker
520	Assael Emmanuel N.	Edessis 8	Broker
521	Assael Marc [Jos.] & Cie[64]	Teldji Han 10	Commission agent [reps.]
522	Assael Marcos I.	Franque, Al. Han	Commission agent
523	Asséo Elie S.	Contouriotou 11	Commission agent
524	Asséo Joseph A.	Ol. Diamandi 44	Broker
525	Asséo Leon D.	Cité Hadji Osman 15	Commission agent
526	Asséo Moise & Albert[65]	Salamine 2 [Passage] Kirtsi 1–3	Representative [Import/export; commission agent]
527	Asséo Ovadia E.	——	Commission agent
528	Attas Moise	Alex. le Grand 31	Broker
529	Barzilay Moise I.	Yeni Djami 14	Broker
530	Benadon Saul D.	Victor Hugo 10	Commission agent
531	Benforado Albert I.	Doxis 9	Commission agent
532	Benjamin Bros	Franque 31	
533	Benmayor Ino	Allatini Han	Broker
534	Benmayor Molho & Cohen[66] [Veritas sewing machine reps.]	Allatini Han 55 [Franque 29]	Commission agent
535	Beno[u]siglio (Benousiglio) Leon/[Elia] (*2)	Tourpali Han	Commission agent
536	Bensussan & Sidès	Aelion Han	Representative
537	Benveniste & Cie (*2)	——	Import/export
538	Benveniste & Gattegno	Catholicon 10	Commercial reps.
539	Benveniste Abram M.	Aelion Han	Broker
540	Benveniste Adolph	Banque 1	Representative
541	Benveniste Albert Z/.I	Victor Hugo 3	Commodities
542	Beraha Albert	Hiou 14	Commission agent
543	Beraha Maurice	Orvilou 4	Representative
544	Bitti Salomon	Syngrou	Commission agent
545	Botton A.S. de	Franque 24	Commission agent
546	Botton de & Sides S.	Ipodromiou	Broker
547	Broudo Isaac M.	Italias 23	Broker
548	Broudo Salomon M.	Evzonon	Broker
549	Calderon (Kalderon) Ilias M./S (*2)	Syngrou 3	Military supplies
550	Calamaro Leon	Kirtsi Han 10	Representative
551	Capoano Moise	Tsimiski 15	Broker
552	Carasso David R.	Egyptou 44	Exporter
553	Carasso Iosef G.	Baron Hirch	Consignor
554	Carasso Leon E.	Kirtsi Han 17	Broker
555	Coenca Guedalia M.	Vic. Hugo 225	Broker
556	Coenca Simon	——	Representative
557	Cohen & Varsano	Franque 36	Broker
558	Cohen Aron H.	Yildiz Han	Import/export
559	Cohen David T.	Pas. St. mina 22	Commission agent
560	Cohen Haim I.	Catholicon 5	Broker
561	Cohen Juda Liaou	——	Broker: hides, wool

No.	Name	Address	Notes
562	Cohen Moise D. & Cie	Egyptou 1	Forwarding agent; commission agent; import/export; maritime insurance broker[67]
563	Cohen Salomon I. (*2)	Katouni 2	Commission agent
564	Cohen Vidal & Cie	L. Nikis 18	Commission agent
565	Cohen Z.	Rue des Banques	Export
566	Confortes Elie A.	Victor Hugo 2	Broker
567	Covo Mario	Lycourgo 8	Representative
568	Ergas & Saltiel	Egnatias 14	Investments
569	Ergas Haim M.	——	Commission agent
570	Ergas Moise Joseph	Salaminos 2	Import/export
571	Errera Louis	Velissariou 20	Representative
572	Ezratty Moise G.	St. Nicolas 134	Broker
573	Ezratty Salomon	Verrias 11	Commission agent
574	Faradji (Faraggi) Moise[68]	Victor Hugo [Telegraph: FARAGGI]	Commission agent – consignment
575	Faraggi Frères	Egnatias 55	Com. with Serbia
576	Fernandez Djino [M]. (*3)	Allatini Han	Rep. hides import
577	Florentin Abram	Istira	Commission agent
578	Florentin I. Fils	Franque Cité Oriental	Commission agent
579	Fransès Richard	Victor Hugo 12	Representative
580	Gattegno Jacob	Leont. Sofou 11	Commission agent
581	Gattegno Moise	Colocotroni 15	Broker
582	Gattegno Vidal	Gatsou 10	Commission agent
583	Gormezano Nahoum & Cie		
584	Haguel Mochon	Miaouli	Public crier
585	Hassid & Sides	Edessis 10	Commission agent
586	Hassid A.M. & Cie	Edessis 6	Representative
587	Hassid Acher & Co.	Catholique 15	Representative
588	Hassid Isac S. & Fils	Victor Hugo 2	Commission agent
589	Hasson Aron A.	Colombou 55	Broker
590	Hasson David Abram	Doxis	Commission agent
591	Hasson Sam P.	Edessis	Commission agent
592	Juda & Salmona[69]	[Teldjis Han]	[Import/export representatives: dairy product
593	Juda Leon & Cie (*2)	Victor Hugo 8	Insurance
594	Landeau Bernard	Leond. Sofou 1	Representative
595	Lando & Benveniste	Leond. Sofou 1	Import/export
596	Levy Salomon Elie	Syngrou 10	Representative
597	Levy Salomon M.	Kavtandoglou 6	Broker
598	Levy Saul & Cie	Trapezis 1	Commission agent
599	Levy Simha	Egyptou 47	Commission agent
600	Lo(m)bel Jacques	——	
601	Magrizo Haim	Ol. Diamanti	Representative
602	Mallah E. & Cie	Voulgaroctonou 55	Cinematography firm representative
603	Mallah Veissi	Trapezis 6	Broker
604	Mano Yessua I.	Orvilou 1	Import/export

No.	Name	Address	Notes
605	Matalon Dario		
606	Matalon Frères	Salaminos 2	Ship owner
607	Matarasso & Safarano Bureau Hel		
608	Menaché & Confortes[70]	Edessa 3	[commission agent; representation; consignation]
609	Modiano Abram I.	Velissariou 46	Broker
610	Modiano Elie	Hermou 29	Engineer
611	Modiano Henry & Cie	——	Representative
612	Modiano Hugo R.	——	Representative
613	Modiano Isac Frères & Fils		
614	Modiano Péon E.	Allatini Han 8	Representative
615	Modiano Samuel & Fils	Lombardo Han	Import/export
616	Modiano Yomtov Joseph Isac	Emieh Han	Representative
617	Molho David Barouh	Kirtsi Han 18	Representative
618	Molho Frères (*2)	Anglias [7] [POB 31, Telegr. MOLHOM]	Sea and land transport; maritime agents.[71]
619	Molho Joseph M.[72]	Franque 39 [Office: Jean Dragoumis 39, Telegraph. MOLHO Rongoli Han]	Import/export, transit trade.
620	Molho Saul Salomon	Tsimiski 6	Commission agent
621	Mordoh Sam	Allatini 33	Import/export
622	Mosseri Albert H.	Allatini Han	Representative
623	Na/[e]/hama Moise & Fils	——	Consignor by rail; commission agent[73]
624	Nahama Jacob D.	Anglias 5	Ships
625	Nahama Joj.	Salaminos 2	Commission agent
626	Nahama Salvator	Averof 15	Maritime agent
627	Nahmias & Bitran	Victor Hugo 3	Commission agent
628	Nahmias & Modiano	Ermou 84	Commission agent
629	Nahmias Zaharia	Egnatias 56	Commission agent
630	Nahoum & Bensussan	Catouni 2	Import on commission
631	Nahoum Leon D.	Kibar Ali Han	Representative
632	Nehama & Sasson	Salaminos 2	Insurance
633	Nehama Albert & Cohen (Kohen)[74]	Countoriotou 28	Military supplies
634	Nehama Isac Moise	Lycourgo 8	Consignor of commodities
635	Nissim & Levy		
636	Nissim Fils	Anglias 5	Maritime agent
637	Pardo Isac D.	Catholicon 10	Consignor to Serbia
638	Perez(i) Mentes & Fils	——	Import/export
639	Recanati & Molho	Anglias	Maritime agent
640	Recanati Avram M. & Cie	Aelion Han 16	Representative
641	Recanati Leon	Banque 1	Representative
642	Recanati (Recanaty) David [S.][75]	L. Sofou 49	Representative: hemp cloth, strings and sacks
643	Rousso Menachenm	Syngrou Araphan	Broker
644	Rousso Moise Matatia	Caldéron Han 4	Hinterland representative
645	Rousso Simon E.	Botsari 3	Broker
646	Sadi Salomon	Djamli Han 15	Representative
647	Salem Frères	Zafiraki 16	Import/export

No.	Name	Address	Notes
648	Salem Joseph Isac	————	Commission agent
649	Salmona Moise I.	Thassou 2	Commission agent
650	Saltiel Abram M.	Sakelariou 23	Broker
651	Saltiel Fils d'Isac [S.][76]	[Katolicon 6?]	Consignation; commission agent; import/export
652	Saltiel Frères		
653	Saporta & Naar	Averof	Maritime agent
654	Saporta Albert I.	Vas. Iracliou 29	Commission agent
655	Saporta H.S.	Mazi Han 17	Commission agent
656	Saporta Leon	Franque Cité Oriental	Commission agent
657	Saul Frères	Trapezis 10	
658	Sciaky Aron & Isac	——	
659	Sciaky V. & Cie	——	Commission agent
660	Scialom Albert	——	Representative
661	Scialom David	Kirtsi Han 4	Representative
662	Sévy A. & Cie	Salaminos 1	Commission agent
663	Tiano Henri	Victor Hugo 8	Representative
6664	Trabout Jacob M.	Platonos 42	Broker
665	Uziel Leon M.	Max Harden 9	Representative
666	Varsano & Cohen	Djamli Han 41	Import/export
667	Yacar Mercado	Peristeriou 1	
668	Yahiel Isac J.	Colomvou 22	Commission agent
669	Yeny Samuel Guedalia	Plata Emporio	Broker

15b. Finance: Banking

670	Amar Banque *Société anonyme*[77]	——	All bank and exchange operations
671	Banque de Salonique Ltd.	——	
672	Benveniste Fils de Jacob	Trapezis 4	
673	Mosseri & Cie Banque[78]	Trapezis 15	Also representatives of fire insurance firm "La Baloise"
674	Perahia Hananel J.	Ermou 27	Exchange
675	Salem Haim & Joseph Salomon[79]	Allatini Han 11	Members of the Syndicate des Banques
676	Simha Frères & Cie	Syngrou 6	

Jewish-Gentile Joint Ventures[80]

	Firm	Ethnicities	Address	Notes
677	Angelos Armenis & Nahmias	Jewish–Greek	——	Broker
678	Brentas Ant. & Jahon Aron	Jewish–Greek	Verrias 8	Export to Serbia
679	Capoano & Marocco	Jewish- "Other"	Allatini Han 49	Representatives
680	Dobrovolski & Livada	Jewish-Serb	Verias Tourpali Han	Insurance
681	Emmanoulides & Benjonanas	Jewish–Greek	Lombardo Han	Commission agent
682	Fotiou Antonos & Karasso	Jewish–Greek	Egyptou 28	Foreign trade
683	Gattegno, Nastos et Cie	Jewish–Greek	Pl. Emboriou	Consignors

	Firm	Ethnicities	Address	Notes
684	Haim, Boueno, Anagnostou et Benveniste	Jewish–Greek	Ol. Diamanti 36	Commission agent
685	Kastritsis N. & Levy	Jewish–Greek	Edessis 3	Halva and sesame oil manufacture
686	Ouziel (Uziel), Fotiades & Gattengo	Jewish–Greek	——	Consignors
687	Papadimitriou & Ergas (*2)	Jewish–Greek	——	Importers of hides from the interior
688	Salamonesco & Segura	Jewish-Roman	Teldji Han 10	Import/export
689	Sidros & Arditti	Jewish–Greek	Gionbrou Han 2	
690	Uziel, Tsoumanis & Haim[81]	Jewish–Greek	Catouni [1]	Commission agent
691	Xenakis S. & Eliakim (Eliaguim)I[82]	Jewish–Greek	Salaminos [1, first floor]	Forwarding and customs agents
692	Yeni et Vock	Jewish-German	Franque 22	Commission agents
693	Yoel Sam & Karleman	Jewish-German	Leondos Sofou 14	Musical instruments Importer/ exporter

Source: Adapted from *Annuaire Commercial* 1922: 303-345
Notes
See Table 4.2, notes.
The processed list contains 676 Jewish firms with an additional 17 firms of mixed ethnic ownership, all located in Salonica in 1921. (The *Annuaire* was published during 1922). Hence the list effectively provides a natural sample composed of commercial and industrial enterprises for 1921, prior to the massive entry of the Greek refugees.

1   *Annuaire Commercial* 1922: 346.
2   *Annuaire Commercial* 1922: 177.
3   According to pictures from 1926, 1933, and 1939, this company was also famous for its alcoholic beverages. Yair Ben-Ya'akov (February 2003).
4   *Annuaire Commercial* 1922: 13.
5   *Annuaire Commercial* 1922: 177. Samuel S. Hassid & Cie, Colonial Commodities, Passage Kyrtsi 6.
6   *Annuaire Commercial* 1922: 174.
7   *Annuaire Commercial* 1922: 349.
8   According to a different advertisement. See *Annuaire Commercial* 1922: 43.
9   *Annuaire Commercial* 1922: 119.
10   *Annuaire Commercial* 1922: 26, 119.
11   The firm advertised its telegraph address in Greek. *Annuaire Commercial* 1922: 33.
12   *Annuaire Commercial* 1922: 50.
13   *Annuaire Commercial* 1922: 24.
14   *Annuaire Commercial* 1922: 175.
15   *Annuaire Commercial* 1922: 7.
16   *Annuaire Commercial* 1922: 46.
17   *Annuaire Commercial* 1922: 172.
18   *Annuaire Commercial* 1922: 44.
19   *Annuaire Commercial* 1922: 180.
20   *Annuaire Commercial* 1922: 298.

21   *Annuaire Commercial* 1922: 298.
22   *Annuaire Commercial* 1922: 295.
23   *Annuaire Commercial* 1922: 184. The advertisement deals with wholesaling and ware-housing of chemicals and pharmaceuticals, which explained the different addresses.
24   *Annuaire Commercial* 1922: 242.
25   *Annuaire Commercial* 1922: 166.
26   *Annuaire Commercial* 1922: 35.
27   *Annuaire Commercial* 1922: 99.
28   According to I. Emmanuel (1972: 156), this Jewish firm received a Certificate of Distinction and later a gold medal during the exhibition (1909) arranged by the Alumni of Alliance Israélite Universelle.
29   *Annuaire Commercial* 1922: 31.
30   *Annuaire Commercial* 1922: 174.
31   *Annuaire Commercial* 1922: 122.
32   Identified with Isac Tebah & Cie. *Annuaire Commercial* 1922, p. 189.
33   *Annuaire Commercial* 1922, p. 99.
34   *Annuaire Commercial* 1922, p. 8.
35   See also *Annuaire Commercial* 1922: 97: Angel & Saltiel (spices, colours, and chemicals), Victor Hugo 3.
36   *Annuaire Commercial* 1922: 293.
37   *Annuaire Commercial* 1922: 173.
38   *Annuaire Commercial* 1922: 126.
39   *Annuaire Commercial* 1922: 125.
40   *Annuaire Commercial* 1922: 125.
41   *Annuaire Commercial* 1922: 108.
42   *Annuaire Commercial* 1922: 109.
43   *Annuaire Commercial* 1922: 240.
44   *Annuaire Commercial* 1922: 6.
45   *Annuaire Commercial* 1922: 291.
46   *Annuaire Commercial* 1922: 127.
47   *Annuaire Commercial* 1922: 124.
48   *Annuaire Commercial* 1922: 242.
49   *Annuaire Commercial* 1922: 123.
50   *Annuaire Commercial* 1922: 121.
31   *Annuaire Commercial* 1922: 236.
52   *Annuaire Commercial* 1922: 237.
53   *Annuaire Commercial* 1922: 118.
54   *Annuaire Commercial* 1922: 118.
55   *Annuaire Commercial* 1922: 183.
56   *Annuaire Commercial* 1922: 47.
57   *Annuaire Commercial* 1922: 104.
58   *Annuaire Commercial* 1922: 29.
59   *Annuaire Commercial* 1922: 11.
60   *Annuaire Commercial* 1922: 190.
61   *Annuaire Commercial* 1922: 98.
62   *Annuaire Commercial* 1922: 30.
63   *Annuaire Commercial* 1922: 18.
64   *Annuaire Commercial* 1922: 346.
65   *Annuaire Commercial* 1922: 45.
66   *Annuaire Commercial* 1922: 128.
67   *Annuaire Commercial* 1922: 38.
68   *Annuaire Commercial* 1922: 5.
69   *Annuaire Commercial* 1922: 231.
70   *Annuaire Commercial* 1922: 98.
71   *Annuaire Commercial* 1922: 290.
72   *Annuaire Commercial* 1922: 27.
73   *Annuaire Commercial* 1922: 188.

74 *Annuaire Commercial* 1922: 121.
75 *Annuaire Commercial* 1922: 174.
76 *Annuaire Commercial* 1922: 185.
77 *Annuaire Commercial* 1922: 115. The advertisement did not mention that the bank issued stock as an anonymous company in 1920.
78 *Annuaire Commercial* 1922: 146.
79 *Annuaire Commercial* 1922: 114.
80 Other inter-ethnic joint ventures included Mantsi, Dedi et Nikita (match manufacturing); Pateranovitch, Nastis & Hadji (trade in leather); Abot Jules & A. Kosmopulos (maritime agents); Piperkovitch, Karatas & Nascos (export to Serbia); Pavlovits & Anastassiades (import/export).
81 *Annuaire Commercial* 1922: 41.
82 *Annuaire Commercial* 1922: 291.

Appendix 4.2

Table A Fluctuations in International Trade in the Port of Salonica (1913–1921). Based on Customs Duties Collected (indexed duties, base year: 1913)

Year	Sum in GRD	Indexed Duties
1913	10,910,331	100.0
1914	10,805,562	99.0
1915	13,128,818	120.3
1916	13,101,018	120.1
1917	11,178,803	102.5
1918	11,324,067	103.8
1919	23,795,846	218.1
1920	39,243,421	359.7
1921	28,799,663	264.0

Adapted from: *Annuaire Commercial* 1922: 92.
Note: The data for 1921 encompassed only the first eight months of that year. The Index expresses the change in percentages between 1913 (the base year) and the following year.

Table B Movement of International Trade in the Port of Salonica (1915–1920)

Year	Entries			Exits		
	No. of Vessels	Total Tonnage	Average Tonnage per Vessel	No. of Vessels	Total Tonnage	Average Tonnage per Vessel
1915	388	492,305	1268.8	368	517,679	1406.7
1916	62	113,196	1825.7	35	72,254	2064.4
1917	55	75,383	1370.6	27	40,774	1510.1
1918	69	47,923	694.5	19	18,530	975.3
1919	262	441,405	1684.8	241	359,526	1491.8
1920	281	472,117	1680.1	249	438,506	1761.1

Source: Adapted from *Annuaire Commercial* 1922: 92–94.
Note: The average tonnage per vessel was calculated as a ratio of total cargo handled in the respective year to the number of vessels docking in that year.

Appendix 4.3

Table A   Jewish-owned Firms and Greek-owned Firms by Branch (Salonica, 1912, 1921)

	1912			1921		
Branch	Jewish	Greek	Total	Jewish	Greek	Total
Food and beverages	61	27	100	80	104	194
Chemicals	17	5	28	25	24	53
Construction materials	31	11	49	15	6	24
Energy and public utilities	8	1	16	5	6	16
Metal	15	5	42	11	15	29
Wood	20	5	29	8	4	15
Hides, leather, and footwear	28	18	57	43	30	79
Textiles	34	8	50	29	16	50
Clothing	48	10	98	72	32	128
Printing, paper, and office equipment	26	8	52	19	8	27
Tobacco	10	2	18	12	25	47
Domestic wares and furniture	30	3	41	35	5	43
Trade in agriculture products (incl. grain)	77	34	135	44	24	68
General wholesale and retail	24	2	39	96	13	119
Finance and commission trade	109	25	177	182	164	409
Total firms per ethnic group	538	164	931	676	476	1301

Source: Adapted from: For 1912: *Austrian Report* 1915: 138–184; For 1921: *Annuaire Commercial* 1922: 303–345.
Note: Total = Number of firms in a given branch (included "Turkish" and "Others").

Appendix 4.4

Table A Representation Indices of Jewish-owned Firms (*N* = 538; 676) and Greek-owned Firms (*N* = 164; 476) by Branch (15) (Salonica, 1912, 1921)

Branch	1912		1921	
	J	G	J	G
Food and beverages	1.060	1.523	.794	1.465
Chemicals	.993	1.209	.908	1.238
Construction materials	1.099	1.267	1.203	.683
Energy and public utilities	.868	.353	.601	1.025
Metals	.579	.672	.730	1.414
Wood	1.198	.973	1.026	.729
Hides, leather, and footwear	.853	1.782	1.048	1.038
Textiles	1.181	.903	1.116	.875
Clothing	.851	.576	1.083	.683
Printing, paper, and office equip.	.868	.868	1.354	.810
Tobacco	.965	.627	.491	1.454
Domestic wares	1.271	.413	1.566	.318
Trade in agriculture products	.991	1.421	1.245	.965
General Trade	1.069	.289	1.553	.299
Finance and commission trade	1.070	.797	.856	1.096

Source: Adapted from Appendix 4.3

Notes: J = Jewish-owned firms; G=Greek-owned firms.

Ethnic Representation Index by Branch (ERI) = $I_{ij} = O_{ij}/E_i$

Where O_{ij} = percentage of the firms in the branch (i) out of the total sum of firms of a given ethnic group (j); E_i = percentage of the firms in the branch (i) out of the total sum of firms in the entire sample.

The ERI value is greater than 0. An ERI of 1 implies full representation; an ERI < 1 implies under-representation; and an ERI > 1 implies over-representation.

Appendix 5   Jewish Firms in Salonica, 1929

1. Food and Beverages

1a. Groceries
1b. Colonial Commodities

No.	Name	Address	Notes
1	Abastado Haim D.	3 rue Saint-Minas	
2	Abastado Salomon D.	Rue Zafiraki	
3	Altech & Saltiel	6 rue Orvilou	
4	Angel & Haguel	1 Place Morihovo	
5	Angel Juda & Cie	3 place Commerce	
6	Asséo Benjamin	49 rue Egypte	
7	Asséo Elie S. (*2)	3 rue Saint-Minas	Dry fruits and legumes; colonial commodities and oils; import-export[1]
8	Beraha Joseph & Cie	7 rue Edessis	
9	Carasso & Zaraya	Place du Commerce	
10	Coenca & Saltiel	44 rue Egypte	
11	Coenca A. Frères & Fils	Rue Heracliou	
12	Cohen Frères	Rue Zafiraki	
13	Cohen Isaac & Fils	Rue Alexandre le Grand	
14	Cohen Yomtov	Rue O-Diamandi	
15	Gattegno Salomon	42 rue Egypte	
16	Hanen Saporta Soures	Rue Katouni	
17	Hassid Samuel & Cie	6 Kirtsi Han	
18	Jahiel Jacob	17 rue Alex. le Grand	
19	Katan, Florentin & Cie	5 Peristeriou	
20	Levy Abram	2 Place du Sibi	
21	Levy David L.	Rue O.-Diamandi	
22	Mahel Frères (*3)	29 rue Zafirakis	Locally grown produce and oils
23	Maimon Nissim	6 rue Zafirakis	
24	Mano Michel & Cie (*2)	18 rue Zafirakis	And oils
25	Marco Frères	20 rue Alexandre le Grand	
26	Menahem P.	15 rue Zafirakis	
27	Mijan Isaac A. A.	39 rue Egypte	
28	Morde/o/h S. I.	8 Peristeriou	
29	Nadjari Bueno	Rue Alexandre le Grand	
30	Nahama Moise & Fils	3 rue Licourgo	
31	Nahmias Raphael	5 rue Salamine	
32	Navarro Isaac E.	52 rue Egypte	
33	Navarro Leon & Haim	52 rue Egypte	
34	Ouziel David M.	25 rue Zafirakis	
35	Pelossof & Rousso	20 rue Salamine	
36	Perahia Simon	B.P. 246	
37	Saias & Franses	2 rue Orvilou	
38	Saias Isaac & Fils	7 rue Katouni	
39	Saltiel & Coenca	54 Alex. le Grand	
40	Saltiel Jacob H.	37 Alex. le Grand	

No.	Name	Address	Notes
41	Saul Vidal & Cie	37 Alex. le Grand	
42	Stroumza, Pinhas & Cie (*2)	21 Vaghio/ Valou	Oils
43	Torrès Cohen & Cie	6 rue Orvillou	

1d. Production and Distribution of Dairy Products
44	Carasso Frères (*2)	38 Alex. le Grand	Butter and cheese
45	Cohen Jac. & Cie	18 Alex. le Grand	Cheese
46	Cohen Jacob L.	14 Alex. le Grand	Butter and cheese
47	Massarano Frères (*2)	11 rue Orvilou	Butter, cheese, and oils
48	Pinhas Isaac	10 rue Chio	Butter and cheese
49	Scapa & Levy	34 rue Alex. le Grand	Cheese

1e. Production and Trade in Wine and Alcoholic Beverages
50	Abravanel Jacob	2 rue Salamine	
51	Amariglio S.D. & Fils	65 rue Singrou	
52	Angel, Aelion & Cie	6 rue Eracliou	
53	Beja Nissim I & Co	Rue Thassos	
54	Benvenist David	Rue Tsimiski	
55	Menahem Joseph	179 rue Egnatia	
56	Ouziel Daniel M.	Rue Tsimiski	

2. Chemicals

2a. Paints, Varnish, Wax, and Paraffin
57	Amaraggi & Salmona	Rue Askitou	Paints and varnish
58	Amiel	Rue Roi-Georges	Wax and paraffine
59	Asséo Jacques et Juda	6 rue Veria	Wax and paraffine
60	Capon Nahama	Rue Ermou	Wax and paraffine
61	Cohen Isaac	3 rue Catouni	Colours and varnish
62	Fransès Nathan	Rue Chio	Colours and varnish

2b. Soap Production
63	Arditti Juda & Fils (*2)	49 rue Diamandi	Cereals and flour
64	Carasso Moise & Cie	7 rue Alexandre le Grand	
65	Hassid Moise	22 rue Zafiraki	
66	Leon Yomtov Isaac	28 rue Zafiraki	
67	Mayo, Stroumza	12 Victor Hugo	
68	Pelossof Joseph	4 rue Aphrodite	
69	Simha Lazare	32 rue Monastir	

2c. Chemicals (Droguiste)
70	Aelion Vidal	21 rue Askitou	Chemical products
71	Altcheh Isaac	Rue Askitou	
72	Angel Mair	Rue Comnimon	
73	Angel & Saltiel	3 rue Victor Hugo	
74	Benveniste Sam	Rue Solomou	
75	Counio Isac & Salvator	Pl. Commerce	
76	Florentin, Yomtov & Franco	Ermou	
77	Franses Nathan	Bazar Central	
78	Matalon David	4 rue Verria	

No.	Name	Address	Notes
79	Pinhas Joseph & Angel	Rue Ermou	
80	Yomtov Elie	Nouveau Bazar	

3. Construction Materials

3a. Production and Trade in Construction Materials

81	Mallah Nissim S.	Rue Boulgarochtono	Marble cutting
82	Leon Raoul & Cie		*Briqueteries*
83	Modiano Frères	Rue de la Republique	Ceramique

3b. Trade in Finished Products for Construction

84	Alvo Frères (*3)	Rue Alexandre le Grand	Sanitary wares; *fers et metaux; quincailleries*
85	Cohen Isaac & Frères	Rue Comninou	Sanitary wares
86	Jacoel Victor J.	Rue Tsimisky	Sanitary wares
87	Nahmias & Barnaba	Rue Saint-Minas	Sanitary wares
88	Pardo Haim	Rue Tsimiski	Sanitary wares

5. Metal

5a. Metal Industry (Machinery)

89	Alcalay & Juda (*3)	27 rue Egypte	Electricity and electric accessories; hardware; agricultural machinery
90	Israel Leon J.	26 rue Condouriotis	Agricultural machinery
91	Navarro Maurice & Albert (successors of Isac J. Navarro, established 1855)[2]	8 Victor Hugo	Metals
92	Tiano Frères (*4)	34 rue Olimpio-Diamandi	Electrical equipment; fine machinery; agricultural machines; mechanical workshop

5b. Ironsmith Wares, Hardware (Quincailleries), Blades, and Metalware

93	Aboav Isaac & Cie	19 rue Zafirakis	Iron and metals
94	Alvo & Bendavid	70 rue Egnatia	Iron and metals
95	Amarglio & Mallah	27 rue Venizelos	*Quincailleries*
96	Angel & Safan	7 rue Langada	Iron and metals
97	Arditti & Benforado & Hanen (*2)	Rue Alexandre le Grand	*Quincailleries* and haberdashery
98	Arditti & Bessantchi	71 rue Egnatia	*Quincailleries*
99	Barouh Salomon	5 passage Carasso	*Quincailleries*
100	Barzilai & Nahmias	28 rue Venizelos	*Quincailleries*
101	Beja Frères	20 rue Venizelos	*Quincailleries*
102	Beja Sam & Isaac	Rue Odysseos	Iron and metals
103	Benforado Abram	Rue Ermou	*Quincailleries*
104	Benveniste Gattegno & Fils	Rue Alexandre le Grand	Iron and metals
105	Benveniste Joseph Isaac	Rue Alexandre le Grand	*Quincailleries*
106	Beressi Jessua	12 rue Leondo-Soufou	*Quincailleries*
107	Botton Isaac	22 Zafiraki	Iron and metals

No.	Name	Address	Notes
108	Carasso Salomon	28 rue Caripi	*Quincailleries*
109	Castro Samuel	Besisten	*Quincailleries*
110	Cohen Albert I.	27 rue Venizelos	*Quincailleries*
111	Cohen Hananel	1 passage Carasso	*Quincailleries*
112	Cohen Samuel & Cie	29 Alexandre le Grand	Iron and metals
113	Confortes Menahem	37 Alexandre le Grand	*Quincailleries*
114	Covo Juda	45 rue Franque	Iron and metals
115	Danielides & Guillidi	1 rue Venizelos	*Quincailleries*
116	Errera Albert, Juda	35 rue Analipseos	*Quincailleries*
117	Fais David	Alexandre le Grand	*Quincailleries*
118	Fransès Samuel S.	9 rue Orvilou	Iron and metals
119	Gheledi Abram	23 Monastiriou	Iron and metals
120	Lazare & Hanoca	Sainte-Sophie	Iron and metals
121	Hassid Haim & Albert	49 Egnatia	Iron and metals
122	Hassid Haim & Albert	6 Alexandre le Grand	*Quincaillerie*
123	Hassid Hananel I.	9 passage Carasso	*Quincailleries*
124	Hassid J. & Frères	51 Diamandi	*Quincailleries*
125	Hazan Frères (*2)	74 rue Egnatia	Rifles and hunting equipment
126	Iehaskel Vidal	29 rue Venizelos	*Quincailleries*
127	Israel Acher M.	4 rue Eracliou	*Quincailleries*
128	Levy Samuel Juda	Pas. Saint-Minas	*Quincailleries*
129	Matarasso & Angel	39 rue Venizelos	*Quincailleries*
130	Matarasso Salomon	62 rue Colombo	*Quincailleries*
131	Menache Abram D.	69 rue Singrou	Rifles and hunting equipment
132	Molho Rouben S.	Rue Ermou	*Quincailleries*
133	Montekio Aron	50 rue Egnatia	*Quincailleries*
134	Mordoh Haim	17 rue Ploutarho	*Quincailleries*
135	Mosséri Raphael	37 rue O.-Diamandi	Iron and metals
136	Nahmias Ghélidia	205 Hippodr	*Quincailleries*
137	Navarro M. & A.	Rue Egypte	Iron and metals
138	Nissim Frères	3 rue Tahidromos	*Quincailleries*
139	Paladino Joseph & Fils	105 Venizelos	*Quincailleries*
140	Paladino Moise Frères	80 Alexandre le Grand	*Quincailleries*
141	Pardo Haim G. & Fils	10 Alexandre le Grand	*Quincailleries*
142	Revah, Zadoc (Zadok), Levy & Cie (*2) / Galeries Modernes	30 Venizelos	Electrical appliances; iron and metals
143	Rubein (Ruben), Tchenio & Nehama	Rue Tsimiski	*Quincailleries*
144	Salem & Menasse	47 rue Egnatia	Iron and metals
145	Salem Frères	Rue Colombo	*Quincailleries*
146	Salem Levy	Cité Saul	*Quincailleries*
147	Saltiel Salomon	11 rue Alexandre el Grand	*Quincailleries*
148	Saporta David	32 rue Alexandre le Grand	Iron and metals
149	Sasson Albert S.	41 passage Sasson	*Quincailleries*
150	Tiano David (*2)	34 rue Alexandre le Grand	*Quincailleries*; electrical appliances
151	Tiano I[srael] & V[idal] (*3)	3 rue Victor Hugo	*Quincailleries*; *fers et metaux*; electrical appliances

No.	Name	Address	Notes
152	Tiano Ino	39 rue Egnatia	Foundry
153	Tiano Ino (*2)	67 rue Alexandre le Grand	Store: *Quincailleries*; electrical appliances
154	Venezia Joseph	39 rue Alexandre le Grand	Iron and metals
155	Zakai Frères	Rue Diamandi	Iron and metals

5c. Electrical Equipment and Materials

No.	Name	Address	Notes
156	Alba Frères	13 rue Franque	
157	Alvo J. & I.	172 rue Egnatia	
158	Benveniste Gattegno	9 rue Egypte	
158	Chimchi Frères	13 rue Egypte	
160	Cohen Is & Frères	3 rue Comninos	
161	Cohen Samuel	48 Alexandre le Grand	
162	Hassid H.A.	Rue Egnatia	
163	Israel & Arditi	26 Condouriotis	
164	Matalon Frères	Rue Tsimiski	
165	Matarasso & Jacoel	184 Egnatia	
166	Menahem Jacob	15 L. Sofou	
167	Nahama & Aelion	Rue Tsimiski	
168	Navarro Albert	38 Aleandre le Grand	
169	Pardo Haim D.	24 rue Tsimiski (POB 276)	Heaters; electrical appliances[3]
170	Salem & Menasse (*2)	67 Egnatia	
171	Saporta Frères	29 rue Comninos	

5d. Automobiles and Accessories

No.	Name	Address	Notes
172	Assael R. (Studebaker)	Rue Tsimiski	
173	Bensussan (Fiat)	Rue Melas	

6. Wood

6a. Firewood (Bois de Chauffage)

No.	Name	Address
174	Angel Daniel & Cie	81 Nikis
175	Bèraha Liaou	Asile-des-Enfants
176	Cohen J.M.	84 Roi-Georges
177	Cohen Mentech	Rue Italias
178	Cohen Mochon	Yeni-Djami
179	Eshkenazi Aron	Roi-Georges
180	Grakas Samuel	Asile-des-Enfants
181	Hanen Jacques	78 rue Nikis
182	Joseph Abram	Pédion-Aris
183	Joseph Sabetai	32 Roi-Georges

6b. Wood for Construction

No.	Name	Address
184	Botton Elie	Rue Egnatia
185	Cohen A	Vis-à-vis Tophane
186	David Isaac Fils	Rue 26-octobre
187	Esformès Aaron	Arrêt Aminis
188	Hasson Frères	Rue Santarosa
189	Jessua David	Rue Tophane

No.	Name	Address	Notes
190	Mallah A. & Cie	Rue 26-Octobre	
191	Marcos & Mordoh	Rue Roi-Georges	
192	Nefussy Samuel	Rue Roi-Georges	
19	Saltiel Daniel	4b rue Gimnastiriou[4]	
194	Saltiel J. & A.	Rue du 26-Octobre	
195	Saltiel Moise & Fils	16 rue Roi-Georges	
196	Saltiel Sinto	4 rue Gimnastiriou	
197	Saporta Yomtov [Is.][5]	Rue du 26-Octobre	
198	Sformes D. & Fils	Rue Def. Nationale	
199	Vaennas Moise	Rue du 26 Octobre	

7. Hides, Leather, and Footwear

7a. Trade in Hides and Leather – Import, Wholesale, and Retail

No.	Name	Address	Notes
200	Abastado & Moch.[e]	8 place du Sibi	
201	Acher Isaac M.	22 rue Colombo	
202	Acher Moise Fils	10 rue Verrias	
203	Algava Jacob	Rue Monastiriou	
204	Almosnino Salomon (*3)	3 place du Sibi / 3 pl. du Commerce / Emb.	Processed hides
205	Angel A. David	18 rue Egnatia	
206	Angel Abram S.	1 rue Edessis	
207	Angel Isaac J.	5 rue Verrias	
208	Angel Samuel Fils	52 rue Heracliou	
209	Arama & Saltiel	44 rue Alexandre le Grand	
210	Arama Juda	150 Egnatia	
211	Aroesti Haim Frères	16 rue Diamandi	Leather
212	Ascher & Saltiel	3 rue Victor-Hugo	
213	Assael Israel	206 rue Egnatia	
214	Assael Sabetai S.	14 rue Menexe	
215	Asséo & Angle	4 rue Halkeon	
216	Asséo M. Isaac/ I. *2	10 rue Colombo	Leather
217	Beja David M.	Rue Solomou	
218	Beja Matteo M. & Fils	83 Roi-Georges	
219	Beja Nissim	139 Egnatia	
220	Benousiglio Levy	14 rue Victor-Hugo	
221	Benveniste & Cie	27 Aya Triada	
222	Beraha Jacob	180 rue Egnatia	
223	Beraha Joseph	74 rue Venizelos	
224	Berressi Sabetai	Rue Perdicas	
225	Chimchi Acher	3 rue Veria	
226	Covo & Angel	4 rue Edessis	
227	Covo Juda	15 rue Solomou	
228	Cuenca Salomon M.	215 rue Egnatia	
229	Ezratti & Counio	Place Morihovo	
230	Fils de David Haim	Salonique	
231	Florentin Is. Elie	Rue des Postes	
232	Florentin Isaac	8 Djamli Han	
233	Florentin Jacob & Cie	Rue Heracliou	
234	Florentin Samuel	5 rue Victor-Hugo	

No.	Name	Address	Notes
235	Franses Fils de Jacob	8 rue Singrou	
236	Franses Jessua	12 rue Victor-Hugo	
237	Franses Richard	19 rue Komnimon	
238	Haim Jacques	Rue Solomou	
239	Hasson Fils de David (*2)	3 rue Doxis	Leather; cereals export; *peaux brutes*; opium[6]
240	Jacoel & Cie	Istira	Raw leather[7]
241	Kunio Joseph	40 rue Diamandi	
242	Moché Gattegno & Cie (*2)	12 rue Salamine	Leather
243	Modiano Michel	19 rue Victor-Hugo	
244	Moise Salomon	157 Egnatia	
245	Perez Sabetai M.	8 rue Victor-Hugo	
246	Pesah Abram	170 rue Egnatia	
247	Salem Haim & Florentin	171 rue Egnatia	
248	Salmona Moise	2 rue Thassou	
249	Saltiel Isaac	Rue Solomou	
250	Saragoussi Barouh	Rue Perdicas	
251	Saragoussi Isaac	Rue Solomou	
252	Sarfati Abram	180 Egnatia	
253	Sarfati Salomon (*2)	5 rue Thasson	
254	Talvi & Nahmas	184 Egnatia	
255	Yeni Samuel Ghedalia	B.P. 2	
256	Ezrati Abram		Leather

7b. Tanneries
257   Sarfati & Ammir   Rue Diamandi

7c. Furriers
258   Arditi Juda & Fils (*2)   Rue Colombo   Furs

7d. Leather Products and Footwear
259   Cohen Moise & Frères (*2)   15 rue Venizelos   Footwear; shoe repairs[8]

8. Textiles

8a. Dye Works
260   Benveniste Frères   Rue Leondo-Sofou

8b. Yarn (fils, files): Cotton, Wool Trade

261	Albenda Abram	3 Victor Hugo
262	Allalouf Frères	Rue Comninon
263	Angel Elie	5 Comninon
264	Angel J. & Fils	13 Ermou
265	Angel S & Fils	8 Ermou
266	Franses Joseph	Rue Edessis
267	Hassid Files de A.	2 Edessis
268	Levy Aaron	3 Victor Hugo
269	Modiano A.	12 Victor Hugo
270	Modiano Leon	8 Allatini Han
271	Nahama Y.S.	Rue Victor Hugo

No.	Name	Address	Notes
272	Nahmias & Massot	Rue Doxis	
273	Pinhas Elie & Cie (*2)	Rue Zafiraki	Trade in raw cotton, too
274	Salmona Mario	Stoa Modiano	
275	Zaharia Em.	Rue Orvilou	

8e. Jute, Sacks, and Ropes

No.	Name	Address	Notes
276	Abastado Moise S.	Allatini Han	
277	Benadon Moise	5 rue Loudia	
278	Benadou Dario & Sinto	7 et 8 Licurgo	
279	Benardouth Joseph	Rue Egypte	
280	Beraha Moise & Cie	Rue Egypte	
281	Beressi Isaac H.	14 Proestou	
282	Beressi Jacob & Cie	1 rue Orvilou	
283	Florentin Sabetai	Rue Diamandi	
284	Hassid Haim	6 rue Orvilou	
285	Hassid Isaac	Rue Egypte	
286	Hassid Samuel	Rue Diamandi	
287	Jutificio Torrès & Co. (*3) / Torrès Elie & Cie	Pas. Davideto	Sacks and jutes; canvas
288	Mazliah Joseph	Rue Alexandre le Grand	
289	Mazliah Lazare	Rue Alexandre le Grand	
290	Recanati David	9 rue L.-Sofou	
291	Sciaky Levy Haim	Rue Alexandre le Grand	

9. Clothing

9a. Knitting Machines and Hosiery Manufacture

No.	Name	Address	Notes
292	Benmayor, Molho & Cohen (*2) / établissements "Veritas"[9]	36 Egnatia	Knitting and sewing machines; accessories and spare parts
293	Modiano G. di S. (*2)	Stoa Cazes / 2 rue Salamine	Hosiery manufacture
294	Modiano H.S. (*3)	42 av. Reine-Olga	Hosiery manufacture; trade in haberdashery & hosiery[10]
295	Jacob Joseph & Cohen (*4)	19 Venizelos	Trade in haberdashery and hosiery; draperies

9b. Embroidery, Lingerie (Manufacture)

No.	Name	Address	Notes
296	Franses & Allalouf	Rue Alexandre le Grand	Lingerie
297	Saltiel & Cohen	31 rue Colombo	
298	Saltiel Jacob Moise	69 rue Colombo	

9c. Haberdashery (Merceries) and Hosiery (Bonneterie)

No.	Name	Address	Notes
299	Alcalai Nissim	14 rue Capodistria	
300	Alcheh Haim A.	Rue Egnatia	
301	Basso David	4 rue Singrou	
302	Benahmias Joseph S.	105 Alexandre le Grand	
303	Bivas Juda & Cie	31 rue Egnatia	
304	Cohen Juda Mercado	7 rue Enidje	
305	Cohen Moise & Sam	26 rue Colombo	

No.	Name	Address	Notes
306	David Samuel H.	2 rue Colombo	
307	Fais & Yacar	Rue Venizelos	
308	Gattegno & Calderon	Rue Venizelos	
309	Halegua David & Salomon	Cité Saul	
310	Hassid Haim & A.	96 rue Alexandre le Grand	
311	Israel Acher M.	4 rue Eracliou	
312	Levy Isaac Behor	4 rue Tahidromos	
313	Levy Moise Elie	76 rue Alexandre le Grand	
314	Matalon G. & Cie	[11] Rue Saint-Minas	Formerly Fils de G. Errera & Co., Ltd. [11]
315	Menache Abram D.	102 rue Egnatia	
316	Nahmias Elie & S.	4 rue Eracliou	
317	Pessah Isaac M.	Rue Singrou	
318	Raphael & Botton	138 rue Egnatia	
319	Raphael & Nahmias	29 rue Venizelos	
320	Slatiel & Serrero	10 rue Catouni	
321	Tchenio Fils de Mair (*2)	3 rue Ermou	Established 1876[12]
322	Yacar Leon	42 rue Egnatia	
323	Yeni Ghedalia A.	3 rue Colombo	

9d. Drapery

No.	Name	Address	Notes
324	Benveniste Abram M	1 rue Ermou	English draperies
325	Bourla Isaac	Rue des Banques	
326	Carasso Frères	Rue Saint-Minas	
327	Cohen Vitali & Co.	Rue Venizelos	
328	Frances & Bourla	1 rue Ermou	*Maison de draperies*; wholesale and retail[13]
329	Frances Abram & Isac (*2)	Rue Ermou / [Casmirdji Han]	
330	Gordon Frères	6 rue Alexandre le Grand	
331	Hassid Frères	6 rue des Banques	
332	Jacoel & Nahmias	9 rue Saint-Minas	*Maison de draperies*[14]
333	Leoni Vincenzo	Rue des Banques	
334	Nahma [sic] Frères	Rue Alexandre le Grand	
335	Perahia & Co.	8 rue Syngrou	
336	Raphael & Benveniste	Vas. Eracliou	
337	Raphael I. & Benveniste	Palais Cazes	
338	Saltiel Frères & Co.	Rue Alexandre le Grand	
339	Scialom & Allaluf	31 rue Colombo	
340	Scialom, Saltiel & Co.	Rue des Banques	
341	Sides Frères	Rue Franque	

9e. Trade in Fabrics

No.	Name	Address	Notes
342	Abastado R. & Cie	Rue Victor Hugo	
343	Aelion & Hassid	Rue Ermou	
344	Botton & Saias	Rue Ermou	
345	Camhi Abram	Rue Syngrou	
346	Camhi, Pitchon & Co.	Rue Ermou	
347	Carasso & Co.	Rue des Banques	
348	Carasso & Modiano	Rue Ermou	
349	Cohen	Rue Vas. Eracliou	

No.	Name	Address	Notes
350	Cohen Haim	Rue Ermou	
351	Florentin & Co.	1 rue Singrou	
352	Florentin & Saporta	Rue Syngrou	
353	Franco, Barouh & Co.	Rue Venizelos	
354	Hassid Albert & Cie	6 rue Verrias	
355	Hassid Haim A.	Rue Victor Hugo	
356	Hassid Jacob & Joseph	Rue Ermou	
357	Hassid, Mordoh & Cie	3 Singrou	
358	Jessua & Florentin	Rue Syngrou	
359	Jessua Frères	Rue Singrou	
360	Mizrahi Aaron & Avram	Rue Eracliou	
361	Modiano & Amariglio	Rue Ermou	
362	Modiano 24& Florentin	Rue Victor Hugo	
363	Nahmias & Mordoh	Rue Singrou	
364	Nahmias Nissim	Rue Ermou	
365	Ovadia Eliezer	Rue Ermou	
366	Rousso & Fils	Rue Singrou	
367	Saltiel Fils de Moise	10 Catholique	
368	Saltiel Haim	4 rue Ermou	
369	Saltiel Semtob & Co.	Rue Victor Hugo	
370	Saporta Albert	Rue Ermou	
371	Sarfati & Amariglio	Rue Solomou	
372	Sarfati & Errera	Passage Hassid	

9f. Couture

373	Florentin Elvire (Mademoiselle)	8 rue Tricoupis	*Couturière*[15]

9g. Hats

374	Recanati Nissim	Rue Catouni	

9h. General Fashion Houses (Modes & Nouveatues)

No.	Name	Address	Notes
375	Akouni Joseph	309 Egnatia	*Modes*
376	Akouni Samuel	217 Egnatia	*Modes*
377	Arouh & Frères	Rue Venizelos	
378	Bitran Am[n]ir & Cie	7 cité Saul	
379	Botton Moise Abram	73 rue Egnatia	
380	Camhi Nahmias Benjamin	Passage Carasso	
381	Castro Vital	10 Aya-Triada	*Modes*
382	Cohen Haim	98 Egnatia	*Modes*
383	Cohen Isaac A.	6 rue Singrou	
384	Florentin M.	12 Metropole	*Modes*
385	Hanen & Abastado	7 rue Eracliou	
386	Hazan Leon	Place du Kapan	
387	Israel Ascher M.	4 rue Eracliou	
388	Lévy & Fransès	92 Egnatia	
389	Levy Moise, Hanen	Rue Alexandre le Grand	
390	Mallah, Barouh Franco & Cie	Rue Ven	
391	Matarasso & Molho	8 rue Ermou	*Modes*

No.	Name	Address	Notes
392	Matarasso, Saragoussi & Rousso (*3) / Galeries Trias[16]	19 rue Venizelos	Haberdashery & hosiery; draperies;
393	Menache Agnel & Cie	21 pas Carasso	
394	Molho & Broudo	28 cité Saul	
395	Molho Isaac	76 Roi-Georges	*Modes*
396	Mordoh Jacob	Rue Venizelos	
397	Moskovitz Haim	28 Def. Nationale	*Modes*
398	Nahmias & Cie	29 rue Venizelos	
399	Nahmias & Massot	17 rue Miaoulis	
400	Nahmias Moise	10 rue Metropole	
401	Nissim Isaac M.	19 rue Venizelos	
402	Paladino Isaac	20 rue Ermou	
403	Perahia Léon	6 rue Republique	*Modes*
404	Sakidouti Nissim M.	19 rue Venizelos	
405	Salomon Fils de Rophel	7 Eracliou	
406	Saltiel Sinto	59 Roi-Georges	*Modes*
407	Tchenio Rouben	13 rue Tsimitski	
408	Zarahia Moise & Cie	44 rue Venizelos	

10. Printing, Paper, and Office Equipment

10a. Bookshops

409	Chimchi R.	19 rue Tsimiski	
410	Manou Elia	Rue Franque	
411	Molho Mair	9 rue Tsimiski	
412	Naar Ovadia	Rue Ermou	

10b. Printing, Stationery, Office Equipment, Paper, and Lithographs

413	Covo Frères (*2)	8 rue Vassileou-Heraclio	Typo-lith. items
414	Abastado Haim	Rue Catouni	
415	Abravanel Moise	Rue Egnatia	
416	Angel Isaac Salomon	23 rue Franque	
417	Asséo Jacques & Juda (*2)	6 rue Verria	Wax and paraffin
418	Barou Frères	31 rue Aminis	
419	Barzilai Isakino	Rue de banques	Office equipment
420	Benoziglio J.	Rue Spandoni	
421	Benveniste Haim & Albert	Rue Fokeas/Phokeas 4 A branch in Athens[17]	Paper and carton
422	Bezes Benito	12 rue Askitou	
423	Cohen & Zaharia	Rue L. Sofou	
424	Cohen Daniel	Rue Leondo-Sorou	
425	Cohen Sformes & Cie	Mais acuarone	
426	Gattegno David	Rue L. Sofou	
427	Hanen & Soures	Rue Catouni	
428	Hassid Haim Abram	Rue Saint-Minas	
429	Mechoullam & Matarasso	Catouni	
430	Modiano Yomtov	Rue Roi-Georges	
431	Molho Mair	Rue Metropole	
432	Naar Hananel	Rue Saint-Minas	
433	Nahmias & Saltiel	Rue Alexandre le Grand	

No.	Name	Address	Notes
434	Nissim Eliaou	Immeuble Naar	
435	Nissim Gabriel	50 Alexandre le Grand	
436	Perahia Fils Joseph	Alexandre le Grand	
437	Perahia Fils Moise	Rue L. Sofou	
438	Sasson Mair	Rue Egnatia	
439	Serero & Perahia	Bazar Central	
440	Simos & Tiano	Rue Condouriotis	
441	Uziel Haim	Istira	

10c. Typewriters

442	Jacoel Victor J. (*2)	31 rue Tsimisky	Radiophones
443	Molho Saul Jos	Rue Egnatia	

10d. Gramophones

444	Abravanel & Benveniste	26 Venizelos	
445	Jacoel Pepo	Stoa Amerikaniki	

10e. Cinema

446	Allalouf Sam	Cine Palace	
447	Cohen Aron	Cinema Pathe	
448	Mallah Sabi	Messageries Maritimes	
449	Naar Isaac	Cine Moderne	

11. Tobacco: Tobacco Trade and Cigarette Production

11a. Tobacco Trade

450	Florentin Mair	15 rue Pericles	
451	Nahmias & Cie	4 rue Zafiraki	
452	Nahmias A. & Joseph	Rue Ste-Sophie	
453	Ouziel & Nathan	41 rue Antigoni	

11b. Cigarettes: Production and Trade

454	Arditty David	Rue Voulgaroctone	Cigarette manufacture

12. Domestic Wares

12a. Furniture – Wood, Iron, and Bronze

455	Benjamin Benusiglio & Cie	[16] Rue Venizelos[18]	Upholsterers; furniture tissues and articles; wholesale and retail
456	Cohen Jacob G.	13 rue Tsimitski	Furniture atelier
457	Nahmias fils de Sam	Rue Tsimiski	Furniture (wood) atelier
458	Nathan Abram & Frères (*3)	Rue Tsimisky [17][19]	Upholsterer-decorateurs
459	Revah Zadoc & Levy	Rue Venizelos	Furniture (iron) atelier
460	Saadi Joseph Sam	15 rue Ermou	Furniture (iron) atelier
461	Saltiel & Handali	73 rue Colombo	Furniture atelier
462	Sciaky Moise & Frères	Rue Venizelos [18][20]	Tissues and furniture (production and trade); upholsterer

12b. Musical Instruments[21]

No.	Name	Address	Notes
463	Yoel Samuel	82 Roi Georges	

12c. Jewellery and Watches

No.	Name	Address	Notes
464	Botton fils de Haim R.	Palais Zenith (Venizelos/ Metropole roads)[22]	
465	Bourla S.	Palais Bourla	
466	Garti Salomon	Rue Tsimisky	
467	Mallah Frères	Rue Venizelos	
468	Salem Moise & Cie	Rue Egnatia	
469	Sevy Jacques	Rue Venizelos	

12d. Glassware (Verreries)

No.	Name	Address	Notes
470	Abravanel & Benveniste	7 Eracliou	
470	Abravanel & Zaraya	Rue Eracliou	
472	Abravanel David	Rue Eracliou	
473	Abravanel Moise	27 rue Ermou	
474	Aelion David	Rue Egnatia	
475	Azaria Barouh	9 rue Haleko	
476	Beja Juda	56 rue Eracliou	
477	Benrubi Haim	Rue Capoudistriou	
478	Benveniste & Asseo	62 Eracliou	
479	Benveniste & Moche	Rue Eracliou	
480	Botton Samuel	223 rue Egnatia	
481	Chimchi E.	59 rue Egnatia	
482	Crispin & Pinhas	2 rue Halkeo	
483	Crispin Frères	249 Egnatia	
484	Ezratti & Abravanel	Rue Eracliou	
485	Halegua & Botton	Rue Eracliou	
486	Levy B. & Cie	60 rue Eracliou	
487	Modiano & Benrubi	Rue Franque	
488	Rosa Isaac	Rue Venizelos	
489	Salem Frères	Rue Colombo	
490	Saltiel Sinto	Rue Tramouchi	
491	Saporta & Jacoel	2 rue Dragoumis	
492	Soulam Haim	Rue Colombo	
493	Soustiel Sabetai	4 rue Eracliou	
494	Soustiel Salomon	6 rue Eracliou	
495	Varsano Albert	Rue Xevriou	

13. Trade in Agriculture Products

13a. Locally Grown Products

No.	Name	Address	Notes
496	Marcos Moise & Cie	5 rue Velissariou	
497	Yacoel & Cie	9 rue Doxis	

13b. Cereals and Flour

No.	Name	Address	Notes
498	Beja Fils de D. & Cie	4 Yenissou	
499	Beja Salvator & Peppo	21 Zafiraki	Colonial commodities; pasta (*pâtes alimentaires*)

No.	Name	Address	Notes
500	Bensoussan Abr. Jos	Rue Istira	Trade in cereals
501	Bensoussan J. & A.	1 rue Doxis	Cereals
502	Cattan, Florentin & Cie	6 Salamine	
503	Confortès & Navarro	Rue Salamine	Cereals
504	Counné Frères	1 rue Vermiou	Cereals
505	Hasson Fils de David (*2)	2 rue Doxis, 3 rue Doxis	Opium
506	Levy & Moise Hanen	1 Orvilou	
507	Nefoussi Fils de David	5 rue Salamine	Trade in cereals
508	Nefussi Lezer D.	15 Salamine	Cereals
509	Nehama, Coehn & Cie		Trade in cereals
510	Pinhas Haim	3 rue Condouriotis	Cereals
511	Rousso Joseph	Rue Salamine	Cereals
512	Saias & Fransès	2 Salamine	
513	Saporta Abram	10 Gataou	Cereals
514	Saporta Joseph	6 Salamine	Cereals
515	Scialom Samuel (*2)	1 rue Loudia	Locally grown produce
516	Sides & Cie	Rue Salamine	Trade in cereals
517	Stroumza & Acher	9 rue Salamine	Trade in cereals
518	Torrès Albert (*2)	17 Condouriotis	Locally grown cereal products

13c. Opium (Export)

519	Scialom Fils de Jacob	Rue Franque	
520	Scialom Albert Moise	Pas Kirtzi	

13d. Silk Cocoons (Export)

521	Benjamin & Saporta (*2)	13 Condour	And cereals
522	Mordoh Salomon (*2)	11 rue Dragoumis / Codouriotis	And cereals
523	Saporta Isaac A.	4 rue Em. Pappas	
524	Yacoel Juda J.	28 rue Solomou	

13e. Dried Fruit and Legumes

525	Altcheh David	24 rue Alex. le Grand	
526	Broudo Salomon	Rue Nikis	
527	Cohen Moise	Rue Voulgarochtonos	
528	Errera Isaac M.	27 rue Zafirakis	
529	Gheledi Nissim	22 rue Alex. le Grand	
530	Houlli David	Rue Alex. le Grand	
531	Ilia Isaac	Rue Defense-Nationale	
532	Juda Haim S. & Cie	Rue Alex. le Grand	
533	Levy David S.	58 rue O.-Diamandi	
534	Mano & Sion	32 rue Alex. le Grand	
535	Marcos Abram & Cie	22 rue Egnatia	
536	Salomon Isaac A.	5 rue Tsimitski	
537	Saltiel Isaac & Cie	5 rue O-Diamandi	
538	Saporta Sabetai	Rue Alexandre le Grand	
539	Tevah & Juda	9 rue Franque	
540	Tevah Haim & Cie	26 rue Alexandre le Grand	
541	Yahiel A./Barouh I.	Rue Alexandre le Grand	

13f. Oils

No.	Name	Address	Notes
542	Amariglio S. & Fils	Rue Diamandi	
543	Beja & Pinhas	Rue Licourgo	
544	Buenu & Sasso/u/[sic][n]	Rue Licourgo	
545	Hassid & Uziel	26 Zafiraki	
546	Hassid Moise	21 Zafiraki	
547	Leon Juda	13 Licurgo	
548	Saltiel Is. & Cie	42 Diamandi	
549	Sèvi Abram	6 Peristeriou	
550	Stroumza J. & Cie	10 Orvilou	

15. Finance and Commission

15a. Large-Scale Commerce: International Traders and Commission Agents
15a1. Maritime Agencies, Forwarding Agents, and Maritime Insurance

551	Allalouf & Cie	2 rue Salamine	*Commissaires d'avaries*
552	Amariglio, Tazartes & Revah	Eracliou [6]/BP 275; tel. 10-94	Forwarding agents; consignment; transit.[23]
553	Carasso & Benaroya	Alexandre le Grand	Maritime agents
554	Coehn Moise & Cie	1 rue Egypte	Forwarding agents
555	Hassid Allain & Cie	B.P. 174	Forwarding agents
556	Molho Frères (*3)	7 rue Votsis (Immeuble [24] Molho)	Maritime agents, forwarding agents, *commissaires d'avaries*
557	Molho Joseph M.	30 Condourioti	Consignments, import/export[25]

15a2. Insurance

558	Banque Benveniste (Guardian Eastern)		Rue des Banques
559	Fernandez Dino & Fils (*2) (Cornhil Ins. Comp. Ltd.)	Stoa Davidetto	Commercial representatives
560	Franses Elie (Danube)	35–36 Palais Kitriki	
561	Fernandez Gino (Northern)	Allatini Han	
562	Haim Gattegno (Helvetia)	2 rue Salamine	
563	Maissa B. (Assicurazioni Generali, established 1831)	33 rue Franque (Banque Ottoman building)[26]	Regional headquarters for fire and transport insurance
564	Nahmias Jacques & Fils (London Guarante & Accident)	8 rue Eracliou	
565	Perahia Jacques (Neuchateloise)	Ermou & Alex. le Grand	
566	Loebel & Arditti (Nippon Fire Insurance)	Stoa Altcheh	Commercial representatives
567	Mordoh S.M. (chief representative of Victoria de Berlin S.S., General Insurance)	Rue Tsimiski [Palais Mordoh]	National headquarters[27]
568	Morpurgo M.M. (North British & Mercantile Insurance Cy Ltd.)	Rue Tsimiski [25, Immeuble Morpurgo]	General regional agent (Macedonia) fire and transport[28]

No.	Name	Address	Notes
569	Morpurgo George ("Assicurazioni Generali" de Trieste)	Rue Tsimiski [25, Immeuble Morpurgo]	Regional Headquarters for Macedonia and Western Thrace[29]
570	Mosseri / Baloise (Banque Union S.A.)	6 rue Ermou	
571	Nehama Mario Im. (*2)	3 rue Nikis	Agents maritimes, commissaires d'avaries
572	Raphael Maurice	2 rue Tsimiski	Maritime agents
573	Recanati M.	5 rue Votsis	Maritime agents
574	Saporta S. & Co.	3 rue Votsis	Maritime agents
575	Sasson Max	Palais Uziel	Commissaires d'avaries

15a3. Real Estate

No.	Name	Address	Notes
576	Amar Vita	Rue Vassil. Eracliou	
577	Barzilai Nathan	Passage Davidetto	
578	Perahia Gabriel & Cie	Rue Ermou	
579	Saporta & Barzilai	1 rue des Banques	
580	Saporta & Barzilai	Rue Venizelos	

15a4. Commercial Representatives

No.	Name	Address	Notes
581	Abravanel S.	25 rue Colombo	
582	Amir Albert	23 rue Alexandre le Grand	
583	Arditi Sam	Rue de la Banque	
584	Asséo David	5 rue Ermou	
585	Asséo Isaac	6 rue Victor Hugo	
586	Asséo Leon	10 rue Colombo	
587	Asséo M. et A.	Kirtsi Han	
588	Asséo Ovadia	Teldji Han	
589	Attas Moise	11 rue Licurgo	
590	Benadon S.D.	12 rue Victor Hugo	
591	Benardout Albert	4 rue Veria	
592	Benieche Joseph	26 Turpali Han	
593	Benousiglio L.	2 rue Edessis	
594	Bensussan Saul	Banque de Salonique	
595	Benveniste & Cie	4 rue Edessis	
596	Benveniste Ad.	1 rue des Banques	
597	Bourla & Abastado	53 Han Allatini	Import/export, consignment, insurance[30]
598	Capuano Hector	Kirtsi Han	
599	Carasso Albert & Cie	Banque Salonique	
600	Cazes Isaac	Levant City	
601	Cohen Aron	Davidetto Han	
602	Cohen David	7 cite Castoria	
603	Covo Mario	30-32 Allatini Han	
604	Ezratti Salomon	11 rue Veria	
605	Fischmann & Cie	6 rue Ermou	
606	Guerchon Frères	34 rue Ermou	
607	Hassid Acher	5 Ermou B.P. 205	
608	Jahiel Isaac I. & Fils	(B.P. 111)[31]	Established 1878
609	Juda & Salmona (*2)	Rue Katouni / B.P. 56	Colonial commodities

No.	Name	Address	Notes
610	Landeau Bernard	I rue L. Sofou	
611	Maalalel & Cie	Stoa Iris	
612	Magrisso David	Levant City	
613	Menache & Conforte	3 Edessis	
614	Moche & Uziel	S10 rue Veria	
615	Modiano & Cie	Stoa Partenon	
616	Modiano Faccino	25 Partenon	
617	Modiano Henri	4 rue Veria	
618	Modiano Iomtov	Banque Salonique	
619	Modiano Sam E. (*2)	2 Franguinis	Advertising, publicity
620	Molho A. & Cie	II Catouni / POB 278[32]	General trading company
621	Naar Jules	7 rue Tsimiski	
622	Nahama Joseph	7 L-Sophou	
623	Nahmias & Cie	42 Venizelos	
624	Nahmias A. S.	42 rue Venizelos (POB 290)[33]	Commercial information
625	Pedossof & Amariglio	20 rue Salamine	
626	Perez Levy H.	Rue Harrapourris	
627	Recanati David	B.P. 161	
628	Recanati Joseph Fils	Stoa Partenon	
629	Sadi & Sarfati	Stoa Yoniki	
630	Saltiel Bénico[34]	10 Véria	
631	Saltiel Isac & Fils	4 Ermou	
632	Saporta David & A.	23 Alexandre le Grand	
633	Saporta Isaac I.	I Sigrou	
634	Saporta Leon M.	19 Tsimiski	
635	Sciaky Isaac	Stoa Commerciale	
636	Stroumza Pascha	7 rue L. Sofou	
637	Tiano Moise	14 rue Venizelos	
638	Varsano Jacques	5 rue Eracleou	

15b. Finance: Banking

No.	Name	Address	Notes
639	Matalon Arditti	Stoa Bensussan	Exchange agents
640	Matarasso Aron	3 rue Egnatia	Exchange agents
641	Beraha Charles	Mazi Han	Banking and bourse operations[35]
642	Banque Amar (S.A.)	Han Bensussan/ [I rue Ermou][36]	Banking
643	Banque Benveniste (Guardian Easten)	Rue de Banques	Insurance
644	Banque de Salonique	Rue des Banques	Banking
645	Banque Union	6 rue Ermou	Banking
646	Salem Haim & Joseph	Allatini Han	Banking

Jewish-Gentile Joint Ventures

No.	Name	Address	Notes
647	Assael & Taxidi	Sainte-Sophie	Electrical appliances
648	Abram & Marcosis	Rue Salomon	Hides & leather
649	Benveniste & Sirris	Rue du 26-Octobre	Wood for construction

No.	Name	Address	Notes
650	Jenny & Vock (*2)	22 rue Franque	*Commissaires d'avaries,* commercial representatives
651	Condoyanis & Benveniste	I rue Fokeas	Maritime agents
652	Makedoniki Pilopia	Rue Egnatia	Est. in 1925. Fashion hats; *modes*
653	Nahmias & Fotiades	9 rue Doxis	Forwarding agents; colonial commodities
654	Whittall & Saltiel Ltd.[37] (*3) (Alliance de Londres, Sun)	5 rue Anglias/ Votsis	Import of colonial commodities; export of opium; maritime and insurance agents; commercial representatives
655	A. Y. Cazati & Mano (*Phénix Français*)	8 rue Victor Hugo	Insurance
656	Dobrowolsky & Livada (Royal)	Teldji Han	Insurance
657	Saltiel, Seropian, Collins & Cie (Atlas Assurances Cy Ltd.)	14 rue Venizelos	Insurance, national headquarters[38]
658	SA Pâtes Alimentaires "Aves" [*sic*] / AVEZ	No address	Beraha & Cie.; G. Mikas; Kouskouras & Mokas; Hadjiyannis & Verrou[39]

Source: Guide Sam 1930: 901–935.

Notes: Because the survey was not scientifically planned and lacked mutually exclusive, systematic classification by branch, recurring firm names introduced statistical bias into the original list. In order to generate an independent sample suitable for comparative analysis with Appendix 4.1, we applied the following rules:

Branch classification was performed according to the system developed for Appendix 4.1 (see Table 4.2, notes). Only those branches found in Appendix 4.1 were included in the processed list based on *Guide Sam* 1930. Thus, a number of branches were deleted in the current appendix (5): hospitality retail services including hotels, brasseries (restaurants serving alcoholic beverages) as well as private retail services, e.g., bathhouses (only one existed, owned by Barouh A. Ouziel).

To avoid interdependence, each firm was assigned to a single branch, based on its primary activity, as long as the firm's address was identical. The number of repetitions is indicated in brackets. Repetitions appear only when different locations were given, such as for a workshop/factory and a retail outlet. In addition, because a connection had to be established between a firm's geographic distribution and its business activity, we listed each with a separate location. In any case, the number of repetitions is minor.

The absence of the branch "manufactured products distribution" (category no. 14, Appendix 4.1) in *Guide Sam* 1930 may have resulted from the altered economic structure of opportunity in Macedonia after the radical change in the region's ethnic make-up. Yet, that absence explains part of the growth in the clothing branch.

As this list included only the Jewish-owned firms whose owners were variously linked to the local Jewish community, it excluded a number of firms owned by Jews who were considered to be foreign nationals. It remains unclear as to whether their owners were truly part of the local Jewish community or, alternatively, actually belonged to the European investors community (e.g., Hermann Spierer & Cie.; see also section 5.5).

This revised list contains 646 Jewish firms with an additional 12 firms of mixed ethnic ownership located in Salonica in 1929 (*Guide Sam* was published during 1930).

1   *Guide Sam* 1930: 946.
2   *Guide Sam* 1930: 920.
3   *Guide Sam* 1930: 914.
4   *Guide Sam* 1930: 932.
5   *Guide Sam* 1930: 932.
6   *Guide Sam* 1930: 918.
7   *Guide Sam* 1930: 922.
8   *Guide Sam* 1930: 940.
9   *Guide Sam* 1930: 922.
10 *Guide Sam* 1930: 920.
11 *Guide Sam* 1930: 908.
12 *Guide Sam* 1930: 912.
13 *Guide Sam* 1930: 922.
14 *Guide Sam* 1930: 924.
15 *Guide Sam* 1930: 916.
16 *Guide Sam* 1930: 913.
17 *Guide Sam* 1930: 944.
18 *Guide Sam* 1930: 916.
19 *Guide Sam* 1930: 910.
20 *Guide Sam* 1930: 932.
21 Excluded: Bader Hermann, 6 Rue Fokas; Carlmann, Rue du Roi-Georges.
22 *Guide Sam* 1930: 928.
23 *Guide Sam* 1930: 888.
24 *Guide Sam* 1930: 900.
25 *Guide Sam* 1930: 910.
26 *Guide Sam* 1930: 928.
27 *Guide Sam* 1930: 930.
28 *Guide Sam* 1930: 930.
29 *Guide Sam* 1930: 930.
30 *Guide Sam* 1930: 912.
31 *Guide Sam* 1930: 918. BP = Boite Postale = POB.
32 *Guide Sam* 1930: 910.
33 *Guide Sam* 1930: 914.
34 *Guide Sam* 1930: 946.
35 *Guide Sam* 1930: 924.
36 *Guide Sam* 1930: 904.
37 *Guide Sam* 1930: 930.
38 *Guide Sam* 1930: 920.
39 Beraha & Cie., previously Florentin & Beraha, (Roupa and Hekimoglou 2004: 346, note 32). Dagkas (2003: 265) based on Georgoulis, who related to Florentin & Beraha.

Appendix 6

Table A   The Ports of Salonica and Piraeus: Foreign Trade (in tons; index: 100 = 1931)

Year	Salonica	Piraeus
1931 (base year)	100	100
1932	87	95
1933	58.7	65.4

Source: Adapted from DOT 1934: 28.

Appendix 8 Jewish Firms in Salonica (1935–1937)

I. Food and Beverage

1a. Groceries

No.	Name	Address	Partners	Economic Activity	Capital (GRD)	Employees
1	Cattan, Florentin & Co. (1917)	Rue Pindou 4	Haim Sabetay Cattan, Haim Moise Sevy, Elie Moise Florentin	Foodstuffs	400,000	
2	Charles Cuenca	Rue Odisseus 7	Charles Cuenca's brothers	Wholesale and semi-wholesale grocery items, specialising in provincial trade	400,000	
3	Simon Hanen (1928)	Rue Saint Minas, Stoa Rozis		Foodstuffs, tea, wrapping paper	150,000	1 employee, 1 assistant (his brother)
4	Yacar Frères (n.d)	Rue Vaiou 21 (add'l branch in Doyran)	Jacques Yacar, Albert Yacar	Colonial commodities; chemical products	200,000	

1b. Colonial Commodities – Coffee, Sugar, Rice, and Spices

No.	Name	Address	Partners	Economic Activity	Capital (GRD)	Employees
5	David & Joseph Abastado (1929)	Immeuble Rozi 3	David Abastado, Joseph Abastado	Wholesale trade in colonial commodities	1,200,000	2
6	Abram M. Angel (1910)	Rue Egypte 24	Angel (son)	Colonial commodities and edibles	350,000	
7	Angel Frères (1930)	Rue Egypte 59	Salomon and Moise Haim Angel	Colonial commodities and dried legumes	400,000	
8	Juda Abram Angel [before 1931]	Rue Edessa 5		Colonial commodities	500,000	
9	Albert J. Menahem [n.d.]	Rue Alexandre le Grand 18		Commercial representation, especially of colonial commodities	None	

#	Company (year)	Address	Partners/Management	Activity	Capital	
10	Abram Pelossof & Amariglio (1928)	Rue Verria 6, (1932 branch in Piraeus)	Abram I. Pelossof, Albert S. Amariglio, Jo. Abram Pelossof	General commerce in oil, paraffin; soap, colonial commodities, etc.	2,000,000	
11	Charles Is. Saias (1930)			Commission, representation, imports; colonial commodities	2,157,040 (£4,000)	
12	Moise Zaraja & Co. (1920)	Rue Zafiraki 8	Moise Zaraja, Moise Moche	Sale of colonial commodities, halva	150,000	

Ic. Production of Sweets and Bakery Products (Confectionaries)

#	Company (year)	Address	Partners/Management	Activity	Capital	
13	"Hermes" SA Pâtes Alimentaires* (1935)		President: David Hasson; Vice-President: Albert Hasson; General Director: Salvator Béja; Secretary: Moise Levy; Member: Isac Amariglio; Member: Nico Manolis of Maison Manolis Frères	Pasta production	600,000 (GRD 500 x 1,200 shares) was the part of Fils de David Hasson	3
14	Abram M. Mattia (1932)	Rue Vassileos Heracliou 5		Sale of sweets	400,000	
15	Pliancas, Kastritsis (Castritsis) & Co. Societe "MEZAP"* (1926)	Rue Katouni	Main partners: Georges A. Pliancas, Georges M. y Papadopoulos, Pepo I. Sedicario, Nicolas Th. Castritsis, Mordochai N. Lev	Manufacture of confections	3,300,000	

Ie. Production and Trade in Wine and Alcoholic Beverages

#	Company (year)	Address	Partners/Management	Activity	Capital	
16	Samuel Amariglio D. and Fils (1934)	Rue Orvilou 5	Mario B. Molho (brother-in-law)	Production and sale of wines and liqueurs	500,000	
17	Attas & Sephiha (1919)	Monastiriou 14	Joseph Isac Attas, Nissim Juda Sephiha	Beverage and spirit production	400,000	2
18	Beja & Revah (1918)	Rue St. Minas 1	Joseph S. Beja and Albert J. Revah	Conserves, wines, liqueurs, etc.	300,000	2

No.	Name	Address	Partners	Economic Activity	Capital (GRD)	Employees
19	Jacob I. Benveniste [c. 1934]	Rue Asteriou Proestor 12		Sale of wines and spirits	2,200,000 (£4,000)	13
20	Bernardouth & Venezia (1937)	Rue Alexandre le Grand	Pepo Bernardouth, Isac Venezia	Wines, liqueurs, etc.	300,000	1
21	Diamopoulos & Cie.* (1929) - Nektar	Afroditis 6	Including Moise Moisis	Sparkling beverages	250,000	
22	Joseph Mevorah Florentin	Olympos Diamantis 41		Wholesale wines and spirits	500,000	

1d. Preserves and Salted Fish

No.	Name	Address	Partners	Economic Activity	Capital (GRD)	Employees
23	J. Scapa Frères (n.d)	Rue Catouni	Salomon J. Scapa, Joseph (Salomon's son), Joseph Jessue Scapa (Salomon's nephew)	Curing (*salaison*)	250,000	
24	Sevy & Aelion (1927)	Rue Franque 14	Joseph Levy, Leon Aelion	Sale of wines and spirits; production and sale of preserved and salted fish	250,000–300,000	
25	Sion & Levy (1929)[1]	Rue Tsimiski 1	Joseph Sion, Jacques Levy	Sale of colonial commodities, building materials (*droguerie*), and preserves	250,000	

2. Chemicals and Pharmaceuticals

2a. Chemical Production: Paints, Varnish, Wax, Paraffin, and Talc

No.	Name	Address	Partners	Economic Activity	Capital (GRD)	Employees
26	Nahama B. Capon & Cie.		Nahama Capon (24.5%), Isaac Capon (23.5%), Hazday Capon (22.5%), Haim Capon (16%), Salomon Perahia (13.5%)	Manufacture of paraffin, bougies and veilleuses	6,000,000	1
27	Gheorgacopoulos, Asseo & Capon* (n.d)	None	Nahama B. Capon & Co. (50%), Henri Asseo (33%), Theodore Gheorgacopoulos (17%)	Manufacture of paraffin	3,000,000	

				Activity		
28	"Société Industrielle Hellénique de Talc"*	No address available	Joseph Menahem Hassid; Papacosta	Talc production	150,000	
29	Maison Haim Mattia (1934)	No address available	Benjamin Benforado; Pepo Yacoel & Co.	Production of chalk and pencils for slate (craie et crayons pour ardoises)	n.d.	

2b. Soap Production

30	Moise J. Hassid (1920)	Store: Rue Zafirakias 29; Factory: Rue Tantalou 22		Manufacture and sale of soap	1,000,000	
31	Hassid & Cuenca (1913)	Stores: Rue Alexandre le Grand 13 / Rue Catouni 13; Factory: Aphrodite 25	Sabetay Hassid, Avram Cuenca	Manufacture and commerce in caustic soda and soap	500,000–600,000	
32	Bernard Landau (1921)	Rue Paicou, Immeuble de Majo		Manufacture of soap and perfume	1,500,000[2]	
33	SA Macedonienne pour l'Industrie de Savon* (1929)	Store: Rue Lycourgo 11; Factory: Rue Octobre 26	Main partners: Abram Sam Leon (4,950 out of 30,000); Juda Isac Leon (4,950 out of 30,000); Vassilio I. Jacou (Yacou) (3,750 out of 30,000); Vassilio G. Jacou (Yacou) (5,625 out of 30,000)	Manufacture and sale of soap	3,000,000 (GRD 100 × 30,000)	8 employee-; 30 workers (f & m)

2c. Aromatic Products: Trade and Manufacturing

34	Ezra P. Barzilai (1932)	Rue Victor Hugo 9		Essences	250,000-300,000	
35	Isac G. Cohen (1919)	Rue Victor Hugo 6		Wholesale and retail sale of essences, cork and oak, flytraps, etc.	250,000	1
36	Jacques Cohen[3] (1922)	Rue Victor Hugo 6	None	Sale of essences, couchons, perfumery items, bottles, flacons	200,000	1

2d. Chemicals, Pharmaceuticals and Photographic Articles (Drogueries)

37	Isac Aron Altcheh (1920)	Rue Comninon 33		Chemical products	500,000	

No.	Name	Address	Partners	Economic Activity	Capital (GRD)	Employees
38	Angel & Saltiel (1906)	Rue Victor Hugo 3	Raphael D. Angel & Isac J. Saltiel (brothers-in-law)	Chemical products, spices, dyes, etc.	2,000,000	1
39	Assa I Marc J. (1916)	Rue Franque 36		*Quincaillerie*, shoe polish, other polishing and waxing materials	1,000,000	1
40	Cougno Isac (1935)	Place du Commerce, Palais Kitriki	Isac Cougno exclusively	Wholesale trade in chemical products, pharmaceuticals, including special pharmaceuticals	700,000	6 (incl. 1 son and 2 daughters)
41	Counio Salvator (1915)	Rue Roi Constantin 15		Photographic accessories, pharmaceuticals	2,500,000	
42	Dassa Elie M. (1931)	Palais Mallah		Commercial representative: import of pharmaceuticals, marine articles, and paints	70–80,000	
43	Faiz David Joseph[4] (1926)	Rue Alex. le Grand 16		*Quincaillerie*, polishes, waxes, etc	1,500,000	
44	Francès (Franses) Nathan M. Fils de (June 1937)	Rue Egypte 31	Albert and Maurice N. Francés (sons of the late Nathan M.)	Chemical products (*droguerie*): import/export of spices; indigenous herbalist trade	300,000	
45	Joseph Pepo Is. & Co. (1927)	Rue Kapodistriou 3	Pepo Joseph, Robert Raphael	Pharmaceuticals produced by Comar & Co., Paris	700,000	
46	Jacques Nissim (1935)	Rue Edessis 7		Colours	40,000 at most	
47	Haim Isac Rousso (1932)	Rue Franque 30 [36]		General commerce, particularly in soaps, oils, paraphine, and *cabot*	1,500,000	Collaborators: Peppo Rousso (son); Lezer Elie Angel (nephew)

	(Firm/year)	Address	Owners/Partners	Activity	Value	Employees
48	Fils d'Elie A. Yomtov (1934)	Rue Edessis 3	Albert E., Margarite E. and Mathilde E. Yomtov; Isac Saragouss (an uncle and the children's guardian)	Wholesale and semi-wholesale trade in herbs, pharmaceuticals and colonial commodities	800,000	
49	Yomtov, Franco & Cie (1917)	Rue Franque 36, Allatini Han	Vidal David Iomtov, Menahem Sal. Franco, Esther Benveniste-Matsa (widow of the late Isac Lazar Florentin)	Droguerie and pharmaceuticals	600,000	4

3. Construction Materials

	(Firm/year)	Address	Owners/Partners	Activity	Value	Employees
50	Ascher J. Amaraggi (1931)	Rue Franque 22–24B		A store with a vast supply of wholesale and semi-wholesale trade in iron for construction, especially iron traders	2,500,000	1 bookkeeper and 4 labourers
51	Léon Josué Amaraggi (1931)	Rue Valaoritou 2		Construction materials and small ironworks (ferronnerie)	1,500,000	
52	Joseph Isac Hassid & Frères (1926)	Olympiou Diamanti 51	Joseph Isac, Moise and Salomon Hassid (brothers)	Wholesale in metals and iron for construction	8,250,000 (£15,000)	5
53	Maurice and Albert Isac Navarro (1924)	Rue Victor Hugo 3	Maurice Navarro, Asser Navarro (brothers)	Import/export of used and new metals, particularly copper	2,000,000	2
54	Albert Elie Nefussy (1922)	Rue Olympiou Diamanti 33	Albert and Lazare Nefussy (brothers)	Metals and construction materials	1,500,000	

5. Metals

5a. Machinery

	(Firm/year)	Address	Owners/Partners	Activity	Value	Employees
55	Jakob S. Angel (1891)	Store: Rue Solomou 53; Workshop: Askitou 21	Salomon and Salvator (sons)	Sale of tinware; production of stoves (poêles) and stove pipes	500,000	

No.	Name	Address	Partners	Economic Activity	Capital (GRD)	Employees
56	Léon A. Juda (1931)	Rue Egnatias 39		Commerce and manufacture of machines, tools, equipment	1,000,000	2
57	M. S. Matalon (~1906)	Rue Egnatias 21	Moise S. Matalon, Lazare Sephiha (son-in-law)	Sale of agricultural and industrial machinary; ironware, tools, etc.	1,348,150 (£2,500)	2

5b. Nail Factories and Wire Mills

No.	Name	Address	Partners	Economic Activity	Capital (GRD)	Employees
58	Alvo Frères (1912)	Store: Rue Alexandre le Grand 22; Factory: Xyladica	Joseph Alvo, Simon Alvo (brothers)	Wholesale ironworks and quincaillerie; manufacture of barbed wire (fils barbelés) and similar articles	11,863,720– 13,481,500/ (£22,000–£25,000)	Shop: 20 employees; factory: 30 workers (m & f)
59	Clouterie et Treflerie Macedonienne SA (1931)	Office: Rue Ermou 1; two plants: Rue Yeniston	Board of Directors: Isac Bensussan (technical director); Haim Bensussan (administrative director); Isac Angel; Maurice Navarro; Joseph A.[I] Hassid; Elie J. Bensussan; Benico H. Angel and Albert I. Navarro	Nail factory and wire mill	3,375,000	4 employees; 40 workers

5c. Manufacture and Trade in Small Metal Products and Hardware (Quincaillerie)

No.	Name	Address	Partners	Economic Activity	Capital (GRD)	Employees
60	Alvo & Bendavid (1925)	Rue Egnatias 70	Joseph Aron Alvo & Isac David Bendavid	Small ironworks	1,000,000	3
61	Leon Is. Angel (1927)	Rue Ioustinianou 12		Manufacture of pocket knives (canif), cutlery, etc	175,000	
62	Dario Joseph Assael (1925)	Rues Olympiou Diamanti - Navmahia Limnou	Pepo (plant manager) & Jacques (firm accountant) Assael (sons)	Manufacture of parts for suitcases and boxes; metal buttons for army uniforms; mechanical toys;	2,000,000	

Activity

No.	Name (year)	Address	Partners/Associates	Activity	Value	Workers
63	Benjamin Jakob Benforado (1935/6)	Rue Egnatias 38		Quincaillerie, cirages, etc.	1,000,000-1,200,000	
64	Moise Benrubi (1937)	Factory: Rue Odysseos 17		Manufacture of ironware (articles de ferronerie), e.g., locks	150,000	8
65	Levy Benusiglio (n.d)	Stoa Allatini 7		Manufacture of quincaillerie, locks	1,800,000	
66	Moise S. Beraha (1937)		Sabatay Sulyman Beraha, Moise Sabatay Beraha	Import of iron	300,000	
67	Salomon J Camhi & Co. (1929)	Rue Faicou/ Rue Syngrou, Stoa de Mayo	Salomon J. Camhi, Isac Mazliah	Manufacture of metal buttons	250,000	10-12 workers (f)
68	Saul J. Capon (1919)	Rue Egnatia 17		Sale of ironware (ferronerie), etc.	808,890 (£1,500)	2
69	Fils d'Azriel Frances (1935)	Rue Alexandre le Grand 28	Jacques Frances, Henri Frances (sons)	Small store for quincaillerie, etc.	250,000	
70	Ménaché & Cie (1935)	Rue Egnatia 44	Abram D. Ménaché, Nahama S. Mallah (representing the interests of Peppo Yacoël & Co.) [Benjamin Benforado]	Quincaillerie, hunting rifles and arms	600,000	4
71	Moise Meschoulam & Fils[5]	Rue Valaoritou 24		Wholesale and semi-wholesale of quincaillerie	500,000–600,000 (belonging to Haim Meschulam)	3
72	S. Modiano		Son	Commerce in metal products		
73	Juda M. Montekio (1916)	Rue Syngrou 8		Wholesale and retail of quincaillerie	300,000	2
74	Simon J. Nahmias (1931)	Rue Ermou 13	Simon, Elie, and Sam Nahmias (brothers)	Cutlery, hairdressing items, quincaillerie	400,000	
75	Daniel Naké (1937)	Rue Egnatia 45		Trade in quincaillerie	Less than 200,000	
76	Joseph Ovadia (before 1927)	Rue Valaoritou 20	[collaborator: his father]	Trade in quincaillerie	150,000	None

No.	Name	Address	Partners	Economic Activity	Capital (GRD)	Employees
77	Elie Sarfatti & Ovadia Ezratti (Ezratty) (1928)	Rue Monastiriou 80	Elie Sarfatti, Ovadia Ezratty	Retail trade in *quinciaillerie* and diverse construction materials	140-170,000	2
78	Humbert Scialom & Hassid (1930)	Rue Ermou 5	Humbert Schialom, Acher Hassid	Fabrics, metals and ironworks	10,000,000	
79	Sefiha Frères (1932)	Rue Valaoritou 31	Benjamin and Salomon Sefiha (brothers)	Semi-wholesale and retail sale of *quincaillerie*	300,000	1
80	Vidal I. Tiano (1931)	Rue Ermou 17	Vidal Tiano; Ino and Salvator Tiano (sons)	Ironware, cutlery, etc.	1,500,000	3
81	Salvator J. Varsano (1931)	Palais Aslanian		*Quincaillerie*	150,000	1
82	Peppo Yacoël (Jacoël) & Co. (1924)	Store: Rue Egnatias 38	Nahama Mallah (brother in law)	Greek representative of "Poker Play", Solingen (i.e., electric pocket flashlights, razor blades, lighters, penknives)	2,000,000	3

5d. Manufacture of Metal Furniture

No.	Name	Address	Partners	Economic Activity	Capital (GRD)	Employees
83	Revah, Levy & Co. (1926)	Rue Roi Constantin 18	Semtov. Revah, Joseph Levy, Isac Revah (silent partner, Barcelona)	Wholesale and retail of ironware and furniture supplies	800,000	4
84	Joseph Sabetay Saadi (1926)	Rue Ioustinianou 7		Production and sale of iron beds and bedsprings	1,500,000	2 sons (assistants)
85	Galeries Modernes S. Zadok (Sadock, Zadock) & Co. (1926)	Rue Tsimisky 23	Saltiel A. Zadok, Victor S. Zadok, Abram Revah, Pepo Florentin	Manufacture and sale (wholesale and retail) of iron and bronze furniture and beds	2,500,000 (or 1,617,780 = £3,000)	30

No.	Name	Address	Partners	Economic Activity	Capital (GRD)	Employees
86	Ouziel & Menache (1922)	Rue Asteriou Proestiou 6/8	Barouh Ouziel, Guedelia Menache	Manufacture and commerce in boxes and cans	1,500,000	
87	Salomon H. Roza (1882)	Rue Egnatias 17	Salomon Roza; collaborators: Isac Roza (son), Salomon Roza (grandson)	Tinware workshop	120,000	

5f. Electrical Appliances

No.	Name	Address	Partners	Economic Activity	Capital (GRD)	Employees
88	Isac Saporta (1934)	Rue Comninon 29	Isac Saporta, Samuel Saporta (brother, settled in Palestine in 1932)	Commerce in electrical appliances	450,000	4

5g. Automobile Asscessories

No.	Name	Address	Partners	Economic Activity	Capital (GRD)	Employees
89	Eletan SA. - Elliniki Eteria Antibrossopion An. Et. (est. August 1935)	Salonica & Athens	Board of Directors: President: Conrad Weynandt; Weynandt's wife Marie C. Weynandt; and the Jewish brothers Jacques Nahama, Director of the Athens office, and Albert Nahama, Director of the Salonica branch	Tyres and automobile accessories	1,000,000 (GRD 1,000 x 1,000)	2 in Salonica
90	Moise Soustiel & Co. (1935)	Rue Tsimiski 54	Moise Soustiel, Juda Cohen, Joseph Cohen, Lazare Perahia	Automobile accessories and spare parts	350,000[6]	2
91	Saltiel Venetsia [n.d.]	Odiseus 5		Automobile spare parts	80,000	

6. Wood

6a. Furniture: Manufacturing and Raw Materials

No.	Name	Address	Partners	Economic Activity	Capital (GRD)	Employees
92	Yahiel Jacob Alevy (1933)	Rue Vassileos Harecliou 10, Stoa Saal		Export of walnut wood	300,000 (belonging to his father)	

No.	Name	Address	Partners	Economic Activity	Capital (GRD)	Employees
93	M.I. Barouh (1934)	Rue Ioustinianou4		Commerce in wood for furniture	70,000	1
94	Beja Frères (1926)	Store: Rue Alexandre le Grand 14; two plants: Rue Virsodeption 6; Rue Navmahias Limnou	David and Joseph Beja (brothers)	Manufacture and sale of mirrors, window glass, whistles, toys, snuffboxes, etc.	400,000	2 employees; 30 workers (m & f)
95	Samuel S. Cohen (1913)	Rue Halkeon 11		Manufacture and sale of suitcases and trunks (malles)	75,000	4
96	Jacques Bohor Crispi (1921)	Rue Tsimiski 22		Manufacture and commerce in furniture	300,000	10
97	Mentech Jacob Frances (1900)	Nea Xyladika	2 sons	Mechanized sawmill	800,000	
98	Moche & Nahmias (1931)	Rue Valaouritou 33/39	Juda Jacob Moche, Haim David Nahmias	Wood and articles for furniture and cabinet making	1,000,000	
99	Levi Nahmias (1931)	Rue Valaouritou 22	Spyridon Franoudakis	Articles made of cork oak	150,000	
100	Moise Sciaky & Frères (1914)	Rue Roi Constantin 18	Moise, Ovadia, and Salomon Sciaky (brothers)	Furniture	1,000,000	2

6b. Wood for Construction

No.	Name	Address	Partners	Economic Activity	Capital (GRD)	Employees
101	Albert Iomtov Benveniste (1932)	Rue Promotheos 7	Mair [last name]	Timber	450,000	
102	David Isac & Fils (1925)	Rue Santa Rosa, Quartier Xyladika	Raphaël David Bendavid (son)	Wood for construction	400,000	
103	Joseph et Abram Samuel Saltiel (1908)	Rue Santa Roza 9, Quartier Xiladikia	Joseph Samuel and Abram Samuel Saltiel (brothers)	Wholesale trade in timber	750,000	
104	Daniel S. Saltiel & Fils (1930)	Xyladika Quarter	Semtov Saltiel (son)	Timber	2,000,000	
105	Joseph & Abram S. Saltiel (1914)	Rue Santarosa 9	Joseph Saltiel, Abram Samuel Saltiel	Timber	1,500,000	

No.	Name	Address	Owners/Partners	Activity	Value	
106	Moise Saltiel Fils & Co. (1924)	Nea Xyladikia Quartier	Semtov Moise Saltiel, Isac Moise Saltiel, Benico Semtov Saltiel, Albert Semtov Saltiel, Moise Isac Saltiel, and Moise Semtov Saltiel	Timber	6,000,000	
107	Société pour la commerce du bois, Iomtov Is. Saporta (1936)	Rues 26 Octobre and Langada 43	Iomtov Saporta, Isac Saporta, Mair Iomtov, and S. Iomtov Saporta (sons)	Commerce in wood	2,000,000 (2,400,000 in 1938)	

7. Hides, Leather, and Footwear
7a. Trade in Rawhide – Import, Wholesale, and Retail

No.	Name	Address	Owners/Partners	Activity	Value	
108	Sabetay S. Assael (1911)	Rue Solomou 36		Store for sale of tanned leather and skins	500,000	
109	Abram L. Chimchi (1928)	Rue Spandoni 29		Sale of tanned leather and skins; cobblers' articles	170,000	
110	Joseph Moise Cougno (1910)	Rue Salamine 15		Hides & leather	800,000	
111	Salomon M. Cuenca (1914)	Rue Spandoni 10	Solomon and Albert M. Cuenca (brothers)	Sale of leathers and skins	300,000– 350,000	—
112	S. Moché & Co. (1930)	Rue Salamine 12	Salomon Moché, Aron David Moché) (silent partner)	Export of raw skins	1,000,000	
113	Joseph Saltiel	Rue Solomou 77		Commerce in tanned skins	1,058,300 (£2,000)	
114	Isaac Scialoum (1932)			Commerce in raw hides and skins	100,000	—

7b. Tanning

No.	Name	Address	Owners/Partners	Activity	Value	
115	Ammir & Mevorah (1918)	Store: Rue Egnatias 2; Tannery: Abattoirs Quarter, near Betchinar	Joseph Ammir & Isac Mevorah	Tanning; sale of tanned sheep leather and raw hides for soles	2,000,000	

No.	Name	Address	Partners	Economic Activity	Capital (GRD)	Employees
116	Samuel Avayou & Frères (1907)	Store: Rue Verria 4; Tannery: Rue 26 Octobre	Vital Avayou (son); Moise, Juda and Elie Avayou (uncles)	Tannery	2,500,000	

7c. Leather Products and Footwear

No.	Name	Address	Partners	Economic Activity	Capital (GRD)	Employees
117	Elie Agoustari & Menahem (1925)	Rue Rapadopoulou 20	Elie Joseph Agoustari & Moise Haim Menahem	Cobbler's shop	300,000	
118	Salomon M. Almosnino (1915)	Rue Solomou 62		Hides and rough leather and articles for cobblers	700,000	2
119	Benico & Isac Angel & Cie[7] (1928)	Rue Edessa 4	Benico and Isac (nephews of the late David Angel) and Lezer Angel (David's brother)	Hides and leather goods; shoe repair supplies; interests in 2 other firms	2,000,000	3
120	David Abram Angel (1924)	Rue Solomou 56		Leather and cobblers' goods	100,000	
121	Isac M. Asséo & Co.* (Unknown)	Rue Spandoni 16	Heirs of Isac A. Asséo and Ioannis Noussias	Store for sale of tanned leather, skins and cobblers' goods	175,000	
122	Albert Joseph Benveniste	Rue Doxis 8	Albert and Moise Beneviste (brothers)	Export of catgut (boyaux)	3,000,000	
123	Liaou [Elie] Jacob] Camhi (1924)	Rue Monastiriou 11		Wholesale and retail sale of farmers sandals, slippers	200,000	1
124	Cohen Frères (1932)	Rue Roi Constantin 15	Samuel and Joseph Cohen (brothers)	Manufacture and trade in shoes	1,000,000	
125	Israel R. Errera (1931)			Wholesaler of shoes	400,000–450,000	
126	Sabetay I. Nehama (1931)	Rue Tsimisky 59	Albert (son)	Commission agent for trading houses in the Greek islands dealing in leather for cobblers	350,000	
127	Sabetay J. Nehama[8]	Rue Tsimisky 59	Jacques (son)	Commerce in hides and rough leather	600,000	

#	Firm (year)	Address	Partners	Activity	Value	Workers/Notes
128	Haim Salem & Frères[9] (1909)	Rue Egnatias 65	Haim and Moise-Joseph Salem (brothers), Esther Salem (widow of third brother, Guedalia)	Commerce in rough leather and cobblers' supplies	500,000	2
129	Isac Samuel Saragossi (1910)	Rue Solomou 31	Levy (son)	Leather and cobblers' supplies	750,000	1
130	Elie S. Sarfati (1915)	Rue Egnatia 46		Store and workshop for manufacture and sale of leather articles for travel	150,000	8 workers; also assisted by his sons

8. Textiles

8a. Oilcloth

#	Firm (year)	Address	Partners	Activity	Value	Workers/Notes
131	Samuel A. Basso (1917)	Rue Ermou		Commerce in oilcloth (toiles cirés)	400,000-500,000	2

8b. Trade in Cotton and Wool Yarn

#	Firm (year)	Address	Partners	Activity	Value	Workers/Notes
132	Dario A. Albelda (1917)	Rue Alex. le Grand 35		Cotton and wool yarn	1,000,000	2
133	Sons of Jakob Angel (1930)	Rue Ermou 35	Pepo and Albert Angel (sons)	Indigenous cotton yarn and textile fabrics	1,000,000	
134	David S. Asséo	Rue Valaoritou 33 (Francès Building)	Moise and David Asseo (brothers), Sabetay Daniel Asseo (nephew)	Export of cotton threads to Monastir (Uskub) and dried legumes to Salonica	3,000,000	
135	Joseph Mordohai Nahmias (1935)	Rue Syngrou 2		Cotton yarn	1,200,000	
136	Nahmias & Gattegno (1931)	Rue Verria 10	Isac M. Nahmias, Albert L. Gattegno	Cotton yarn and cabot[10]	1,000,000	2
137	Elie Pinhas & Cie (1933)	Rue Orphanidou 4	Elie S. Pinhas, Haim Elie Pinhas (silent partner)	Ginning and commerce in raw cotton	700,000	20 seasonal workers (f)

8c. *Jute, Sacks, Nets, and Ropes*

No.	Name	Address	Partners	Economic Activity	Capital (GRD)	Employees
138	Moise Sal. Abastado (1912)	Rue Franque 36, Stoa Allatini		Wholesale trade in jute articles: sacks, hessian, tobacco bands	3,000,000	
139	Saltiel & Elie Angel & Fils (1929)	Store: Rue Comninon 36; Factory: Rue Miaoulis 27	Saltiel and Elie Semtov Angel (brothers); Haim and Semtov Saltiel Angel's sons; Semtov and Isac Elie Angel's sons	Production and sale of fishing nets & equipment	10,000,000	30 workers (m & f); 1 office boy
140	Levy H. Sciaky (1919)	Rue St. Minas 6	Levy H. Sciaky, Samuel Alvo	Commerce in jute sacks, cords and strings	1,000,000	

9. Clothing and Home Textiles
9a. *Knitting Machines and Hosiery Manufacture*

No.	Name	Address	Partners	Economic Activity	Capital (GRD)	Employees
141	Ino Benmayor (1932)	Maison "Veritas", Rue Ermou 1		Sale of knitting and sewing machines; workshop for manufacture of gloves, stockings and socks	300,000	Shop: 3; Factory: 10 workers (f)
142	Benrubi & Jacob (1934)	Rue Valaoritou 20	Daniel Benrubi, Avram Jacob	Hosiery, knitware and textile fabrics	250,000	2
143	Vital Albert Cohen (1930)	Rue Roi Constantin 15		Shop and workshop: confection as well as hosiery for men, women and children; gabardine coats	1,500,000	15 workers (f & m)

				Activity		
144	Fabriques Reunies de bas et Chaussettes de Sal/Que S.A. (1/11/1936)	Factory: Harilaos quarter; Shop: Rue Alexandre le Grand 37	A fusion/merger of the following factories: A. Koroxenides & Co. (est. 1930); Sam Sarfati & Co. (est. 1925); Anastassiades & Dimopoulos (est. 1933); Lazarides & Frères (est. 1935)	Manufacture of underwear and socks	Sarfati's total interests amounted to GRD 1,128,000 out of 4,627,000	60 workers; 4 employees
145	Salomon S. Florentin (1937)	Rue Ermou 5		Manufacture and sale of knitted ware, socks and hosiery	800,000–1,000,000	35 workers (f); 6 employees
146	A. Guelermann (Kuelermann) (1936)	Rue Paicou 2, Stoa Hassid		Manufacture of hosiery and socks	400,000–500,000	1 employee; 10 workers
147	Mardoché Frères (1935)	Rue Ermou	Joseph and Jacques Mardoché (brothers)	Manufacture and commerce in hosiery	400,000	2
148	Makedoniki Kaltsopiia SA (Ex-Modiano Fréres) (5/1935)	Store: Rue Ermou 13; Factory: Harilaos quarter	Jacques Saül (3/5) and Humbert Saül (1/5) Modiano (brothers), the widow of Giuseppe Saül Modiano (1/5)	Manufacture of luxury hosiery	5,600,000	82 workers
149	Moise I. Mordoh (1931)	Corner of Rues Valaoritou & Syngrou		Manufacture and wholesale of diverse knitted articles (Bonneterie)	250,000–300,000	3 employees; 10 workers (f)
150	Papadimitriou & Assael* (1936)	Rue Tsimiski	Harilaos P. Papadimitriou, Raphael M. Assael	Manufacture of hosiery, socks, and handkerchiefs	1,500,000	25 workers (f); 2 employees
151	Pinto & Barzilai (1936)	Corner Valaoritou and Catholicon	Moise Pinto, Daniel Barzilai	Commerce in knitting machines and accessories	100,000–125,000	
152	Sam A. Sarfati (Sarfatty) (1936)	Stoa de Mayo 2	Sam Sarfati	Manufacture and commerce in stockings and socks	500,000	

9b. *Ready-Made Garments (Confection)*

No.	Name	Address	Partners	Economic Activity	Capital (GRD)	Employees
153	Joseph S. Angel (1937)			Manufacture and sale of wholesale shirts	189,000	
154	Mentech S. Arama (1921)	Rue Solomou 14		Commerce in confection and draperies for men	400,000	
155	Leon and Nissim Barzilai		Levy and Nissim (brothers)	Manufacture of shirts	300,000	
156	Jacob Joseph & Cohen "CAMELIA" (1894)	Rue Roi Constantin 30	Jacob Joseph, David Cohen, Haim Saltiel (brother-in-law of Jacob Joseph, silent partner)	Sale of ready-made clothing, including hosiery	1,000,000	12
157	Abram Elie Francés (1918)	Rue Valaoritou 26		Sale of ready-made clothing	600,000	3
158	Gattegno, Matalon & Saltiel (1917)	Rue Solomon 7	Jacob Gattegno, Salomon Matalon, Albert Saltiel	Manufacture, wholesale and retail trade in ready-made clothing for men and children	1,500,000	3
159	Haim I. Koen & Sons (1914)	Rue Ermou 7	Haim Koen; Leon, Meir and Moise Koen (sons)	Men's and children's clothing	250,000	
160	Haim J. Moche & Fils[11] (1937)	Rue Caripi [6]	Nissim Moche (son)	Atelier and sale of ready-made clothing	150,000–200,000	1
161	Daniel S. Modiano (1927)	Rue Papadopoulos 26		Manufacture and commerce in ready-made men's shirts; fire insurance	2,000,000	8 workers (f); 1 accountant
162	Saltiel & Guelidi (1932)	Rue Alexandre le Grand 26	Semtov I. Saltiel, Gabriel Guelidi	Commerce in flannels, socks and all types of hosiery	350,000–400,000 +150,000 (workshop for shirts)	
163	Tchico & Bitran (1922)	Rue Solomou 3	Albert Tchico, Albert Bitran	Atelier and sale of ready-made clothing for men and children	1,887,410-2,157,040 (£3,500–£4,000)	4 (1936); 2 (1937); several tailors

No.	Name	Address	Owners	Activity	Capital	Workers
164	Barouh S. Venezia (1917)	2 stores including workshop: Rue Alex. le Grand 10; Ermou 2	Barouh S. Venezia	Sale of draperies and tailors' supplies; workshop for confection	1,000,000	4

9c. Clothing Accessories: Manufacturing

No.	Name	Address	Owners	Activity	Capital	Workers
165	Bourla Frères (1928)	Store: Tsimiski corner Charles Diehl; Workshop: Evzonon 3	Albert, Leon and Nissim Bourla (brothers)	Store: Notions for women's clothing (buttons, etc.); atelier: plaiting, etc.	200,000	4 workers (f)
166	Isac Carasso & Co. (1918)	Rue Syngrou 5	Isac Carasso, Moise Levy, Oscar Hassid (M. Levy's son-in-law)	Manufacture of amadou, laces for corsets, rubber bands, wicks for lamps	1,000,000	
167	Moise Paladino Fils & Cie. (1936)	Rue Ermou 10	Moise S. Paladino, Sam M. Paladino (son), Sarah David Paladino (widow of M. Paladino)	Manufacture of balls (pelotes) of yarn, etc., tourniquets, etc.; sale of haberdashery and bonneterie	750,000	10-12 workers (f)
168	Isac David Tiano (1932)	Rue Valaoritou 29		Production of celluloid (plastic) articles: combs, bracelets, etc.	100,000	5 workers (f)

9d. Hats (Chapelleries) and Shawls

No.	Name	Address	Owners	Activity	Capital	Workers
169	Jacob Gabriel Alevy (1916)	Rue Vassileos Iracliou 10, Stoa Saal 12	Henry Alevy (son)	Decorations for hats	100,000	
170	A. Arianoutsos & Co. (1936)*	Rue Roi Constantin 5	Antonios Arianoutsos, Saltiel S. Cohen, Makedoniki Pilopiia and Albert de Majo (silent partner)	Sale of hats, fabrics for men's clothing, capeskin, hosiery, footwear, etc.; atelier for custom-made men's clothing	1,000,000	8

No.	Name	Address	Partners	Economic Activity	Capital (GRD)	Employees
171	Asséo & Capuano (2*) (1934)	Rue Ermou 1	Raphaël Simtov Asséo & Henry Nissim Capuano	Wholesale and retail of woollens and *fichus* for villagers	600,000	
172	Avram (Abram) Juda Cohen (1918/9)	Rue Capodistriou 2	Isac Cohen (son)	Wholesale of women's scarfs and handkerchiefs	250,000[12]	1
173	Hadjidakis & Arouh* (1927)	Rue Alex. le Grand 20	Christos Artemius Hadjidakis, Isac Juda Arouh	*Fichus* of cotton for women's clothing, scarves, and handkerchiefs	1,200,000	
174	Joseph R. Hazan (1934)	Rue Solomou 1		Women's scarfs and handkerchiefs, wool yarn	80,000	1 (son)
175	Makedoniki Pilopiïa Moscovitch, Francés & Cie. (1925)	Rue Egnatia 47	Mario Moscovitch, Leon Haim Moscovitch, Isac Jacob Francés; Haim Levy, Salomon Isac Levy and Serafim L. Serafimides (silent partners)	Manufacture and commerce in men's felt and straw hats, berets, etc.	1,500,000 + 600,000 (interest in Arianoutsous & Co.)	15 workers; 2 employees

9e. Trade in Haberdashery and Nouveautés

No.	Name	Address	Partners	Economic Activity	Capital (GRD)	Employees
176	David R. Basso (c. 1890)	Rue Alexandre le Grand 18		Haberdashery; wholesale of cotton sewing threads; export of hides, zinc, used metals and rags	4,000,000[13]	His 2 sons
177	Botton Saias & Co. (1926)	Corner of Rues Ermou-Roi Constantin 19	Juda H. de Botton, Haim J. de Botton, Isac S. Saias, Albert J. de Botton	Novelties for women	2,000,000	5
178	Samuel J. Hassid (1923/4)	Rue Valaoritou 20		Sale of hosiery, flannels and socks	300,000	1 + his brother (asst.)

				Activity		
179	Fils d'Ascher M. Israel & Co. (1935)	Rue Vassileos Heracleou 9	Moise and Baruch A. Israel (brothers) (60 percent); Aron Barzilai, Marcos Barzilai (brothers) (40 percent)	Wholesale and retail sale of wool and silk thread, haberdashery	1,500,000 (December 1936)- 2,000,000 (April 1936)	
180	Levy Frères[14] (1933)	Rue Egnatia 58	Haim J. and Salomon J. Levy (brothers)	Wholesale and retail trade in hats, caps and hosiery	450,000	3
181	Moise E. Levy (1919)	Rue Alexandre le Grand 20		Tailors' supplies	300,000	
182	Haim M. Mano (c.1927)	Rue Valaoritou 39		Wholesale trade in undergarments, women's scarves and handkerchiefs, etc.	100,000-125,000	2
183	Elie Isac Massoth[15] (1935)	Rue Syngrou 4, Passage Davidetto		Wholesale and semi-wholesale trade in threads, hosiery, parfumes, etc.	1,500,000	
184	Simon S. Molho (1920)	Rue Solomou 1A	Salomon and Samuel[12] Molho (sons)	Sale of tailors' supplies	700,000	
185	Nissim Frères (1924)	Rue Capodistriou 34	Barouh D. Nissim, Vital D. Nissim (son of the late Nissim D. Nissim)	Semi-wholesale trade in haberdashery	200,000	None
186	Haim Isac Nissim Succ. (1928)	Rue Ermou 17	Haim Nissim; Isac and David Nissim (Haim's sons)	Hosiery and novelties	1,000,000	10
187	Joseph Samuel Paladino (1933)	Rue Vassileos Heracleou 12	Leon Paladino (son)	Retail sale of cotton and woollen thread, haberdashery	300,000	
188	Salomon Menahem Rousso (c.1926)	Stoa Bezesteniou 9/10		Commercial representative; sale of semi-wholesale and retail trade in buttons and costume jewelry	500,000	2
189	Sadicario & Nahoum (1931)	Rue Solomou 5	Dario Sadicario (son of the late Salomon), Raphael Nahoum	Sale of ready-made garments for men and children	150,000-200,000	

No.	Name	Address	Partners	Economic Activity	Capital (GRD)	Employees
190	Mario Lezer Salmona [n.d.]	Rue St. Minas 4	Nissim Lezer Salmona, Salomon Abram Botton	Sewing threads	4,000,000 (incl. Istanbul branch)	
191	Fils de Jacob Saltiel & Broudo (1926)	Rue Vassileos Iracliou 11	Albert Jacob and Salomon Jacob Saltiel (sons); Isaac Sabetay Broudo (brother-in-law)	Silk and cotton yarn, wool for knitting, notions (threads, buttons) etc.	800,000–1,000,000	5
192	M. Saltiel & D. Serrero		Mordoche Jacob Saltiel, David Moise Serrero	Handkerchiefs	200,000	
193	Salomon Saltiel & Fils (1927)	Rue Ermou 12	Emmanuel Saltiel (son)	Wholesale and retail trade in tailors' supplies	1,200,000	
194	Fils de Mair A. Tchenio (1876)	Rue Ermou 3	Albert, Pepo, Moise Tchenio (sons of late Mair A. Tchenio)	Retail trade in woollen and silk threads, haberdashery	1,000,000	
195	Marc (Marco) Ventura & Co. (1933)	Rue Alexandre le Grand 18	Marc Ventura, Joseph Saltiel	Semi-wholesale and retail trade in standard drapery and tailoring supplies	500,000 (in 1936) –700,000	1

9f. Trade in Fabrics and Draperies

No.	Name	Address	Partners	Economic Activity	Capital (GRD)	Employees
196	Aelion & Hassid (–1908)	Rue Ermou 10	Mentech J. Hassid (dec.) & Moise J. Aelion (brothers-in-law)	Textile fabrics	600,000	3
197	Affias Frères (1936)	Rue Ermou 1	Samuel & Haim	Textile fabrics: cotton and wool	2,000,000	
198	Semtov Allalouf[16] (1917)	Rue Franque 36, Allatini Han	No partners after 1933	Draperies	500,000	1
199	J. Barzilai & W.V. Brand	Rue Saint Mina	J. Barzilai and W.V. Brand	Draperies	Very low capital	1 office boy
200	Isac & Joseph Beja (1927)	Rue Roi Constantin 24	Isac Beja, Joseph Beja (brothers)	Textile fabrics	450,000	3
201	Abram Benveniste SA (November, 1935)	Rue Saint Minas 10	Share holders: Abram Benveniste (345 of 500); Moise Benveniste (154 of 500); Alexandre Lascaris (1	Draperies	2,500,000 (500 × GRD 50,000)	

				Activity		
202	Daniel R. Benveniste (1900)	Rue Syngrou, Stoa Davidetto		Textile fabrics	1,000,000	
203	Moise Isac Benveniste (1937)	Rue Saint Minas No. 10, Immeuble Cazès		Draperies	1,000,000	3
204	Ovadia Menahem Bourla (1938)	Rue Alex. le Grand 17		Draperies	350,000	
205	Carasso Frères (1920)	Rue St. Minas 14	Isac Jacob and Michel Jacob Carasso (brothers)	Draperies	300,000	
206	Saltiel S. Cohen (1932)	Rue Saint Minas 10		Vast store for wholsale and retail draperies	2,200,000 (£4,000)	3
207	Moise S. Faiz & Co. (1936)	Rue Roi Constantin	Sarina, wife of Isac Saltiel, Moise Sam. Faiz	Retail trade in textile fabrics, silk and woollen cloths	800,000	6
208	Fils de J.M. Francès (1860)	Rue Alex. le Grand 29	Albert and Moise Francès (sons)	Wholesale and retail trade in draperies	5,000,000	4
209	Aron J. Florentin (1933)	Rue Kapodistriou 7		Wholesale trade in textile fabrics, cotton cloth	600,000	1
210	Hassid, Mordoh & Cie (1908)	Rue Syngrou 2	Salomon Hasid, Mair S. Hassid (son), Sabetai Mordoh	Wholesale trade in textile fabrics	1,200,000 (total)	
211	Fils d'Abram Hassid (1919)	Rue Ermou 1	Jakob and Leon Hassid (brothers)	Wholesale trade in cotton yarn and cloth	1,000,000	
212	Jacques Joseph Hassid (1936)	Rue Ermou 4		Textile fabrics: cotton and woollen cloth	1,000,000	2
213	Salomon Hassid & Frères (1933)	Rue Franque 36	Salomon, Marcel and Edgar Hassid (brothers)	Wholesale trade in textile fabrics: cotton and woollen cloths	1,500,000	
214	D. Khider (1924)	Palais Coffa 77/78		Woollen and drapery for men	400,000–500,000	1
215	Ino Jakob Matalon (~1928)	Rue Syngrou 9		Sale of textile fabrics	250,000	

No.	Name	Address	Partners	Economic Activity	Capital (GRD)	Employees
216	Salomon Modiano & Amariglio (1926)	Rue Ermou 8	Salomon A. Modiano, Isac S. Amariglio (brothers-in-law)	Wholesale and retail trade in cotton and woollen cloths	4,000,000	5
217	Mano & Co. (1932)	Rue Ermou 12	Gracia Moise Bourla née Mano; Aron J. Yacar, Elie Semtov Saltiel, Mathius Joseph Carasso (silent partner)	Draperies	370,000	3
218	Fils d'Abram de Mayo (1932)	Rue Syngrou 6		Wholesale trade in textile fabrics and draperies	1,375,000–1,650,000 (£2,500–£3,000)	2
219	Marcel A. De Mayo (1934)	Rue Solomou 22		Commerce in local and imported draperies	400,000	
220	Jacob M. Nahmias (1917)	Rue Ermou 11		Sale of textile fabrics: cottons and woollens	750,000	10 empl. incl. brother and son
221	Nahmias & Mordoh (1926)	Rue Syngrou 5	Semtov Nahmias, Albert Mordoh	Wholesale trade in cotton cloth	800,000	
222	Juda Noah & Fils (1923)	Rue Ermou 26	Raphael, Elie and Simantov Noah (sons)	Wholesale and retail trade in inferior textile fabrics	8,000,000 (incl. immovables)	3: his son-in-law and 2 other young sons
223	I. Raphael & Benveniste (April 1937)	Corner of Rues Alex le Grand and St. Minas	Isac Raphael, Haim I. Benveniste (son-in-law)	Retail trade in draperies	750,000	1
224	Menahem I. Rousso & Fils (1933)	Rue Syngrou 4, Passage Davidetto	Isac, Albert and Coutiel Rousso (sons)	Wholesale trade in cotton and woollen cloth	1,000,000 (Salonica) + 1,000,000 (Monastir)	
225	David R. Salem (1932)	Rue Ermou 3, Stoa Davidetto 1	Benico Menache (brother-in-law)	Semi-wholesale and retail trade in textile fabrics	300,000	
226	Fils de Moise Saltiel (1934)	Rue Catholikon 2	Joseph and Isac Saltiel (sons of late founder Moise)	Wholesale trade in textile fabrics, especially cotton cloth	1,200,000	5
227	Salomon Saltiel & Co. (1928)	Rue Ermou 4	Salomon Saltiel, Esther Haim Saltiel (sister-in-law)	Wholesale trade in cotton and woollen cloth	1,200,000	1

				Activity		
228	Albert D. Saporta (1930s)	Rue Ermou 5	Salomon S. Yeni (silent partner, Paris)	Wholesale trade in textile fabrics	808,890 (£1,500)	2
229	Sam A. Saporta (1919)	Rue Syngrou 5	Sam A. Saporta, Salomon M. Broudo	Wholesale trade in textile fabrics, principally cotton cloth	1,500,000	2
230	David S. Sarrano (~1907)	Rue Valaoritou 27	As of 1924, Joseph Saltiel Sarrano (nephew)	Wholesale and semi-wholesale trade in textile fabrics	400,000	
231	Sidés Frères (1927)	Rue Alex. le Grand 17	Daniel and Jacques Sides (sons of Joseph)	Draperies	500,000 (+1,152,000 shares in Albion)	
232	Levi Tazartes (1927)	Rue Roi Constantin 14		Commercial representation of imported textile fabric and thread manufacturers	550,000 (£1,000)	

10. Printing, Paper, and Office Equipment
10a. Paper Manufacturing: Paper, Carton, and Lithographs

				Activity		
233	Errico Jakob Arones (1930)	Rue Anthimou Gazi 11, Athens		Import of newspaper and cellulose for paper production	1,000,000–1,500,000	
234	Haim Benveniste (1933)	Rue Votsis 3	Albert and Haim Benveniste (brothers)	General commerce, particularly import of newsprint and producing paper	12,000,000	
235	Salomon J. Cohen (1922)	Rue Franque 3		Manufacture of envelopes, notebooks, and ledgers	700,000	20
236	Abram H. Hassid (1905)	Rue St. Minas 6		Manufacture and sale of stationery (ledgers, envelopes, etc.)	1,500,000	3; 10 workers
237	Abram J. Juda [n.d]	Rue Valaoritou 10;		Lithography	300,000	7 workers

No.	Name	Address	Partners	Economic Activity	Capital (GRD)	Employees
238	Pepo Moïse Perahia (E.B.G.Y) (1936)	Rue Franque 39; Factory: Daimonos 27	Isidore and Hananel Perahia (Pepo's brothers)	Manufacture of ribbons, carbon papers, etc.	1,000,000	

10b. Bookstores and Stationery

No.	Name	Address	Partners	Economic Activity	Capital (GRD)	Employees
239	Victor Almosnino [n.d.]	Vasileos Konstantinu, Aslanyan		Bookstore	50,000	
240	Beressi & Benrubi (1933)	Rue Catouni	Haim Beressi, Moise J. Benrubi	Stationery	400,000	2
241	Matarasso Frères (1933)	Rue Vassileos Heracliou	Juda and Henri Matarasso (brothers)	Wholesale and retail trade in stationery and office supplies	400,000	3
242	Barouh Mechoulam[6] (1933)	Rue St. Minas 6		Stationery	400-500,000	
243	Naar Hananel E. & Co. (1932)	Rue St. Minas 4	Maïr S. Amariglio (silent partner)	Semi-wholesale and retail trade in stationery and office supplies	Han. Em. Naar: 800,000; Em. Han. Naar: 400,000)	6
244	Nissim Gabriel E. (1907/1912)	Rue Vassileos Heracliou 9		Wholesale and retail trade in stationery, school and office supplies	700-800,000	Gabriel's young son Elie
245	Perahia & Arditty (1936)	Rue Ermou 13	Elie Perahia, Albert Arditty	Sale of stationery, office supply, jute doormats, oilcloth/linoleum	2,000,000	
246	Ruben (Rubin) Fils & Tchenio (1932)	Rue St. Minas 13	Joseph Ruben (father), Paul Ruben (son), Mentech Tchenio	Commerce in toys and school supplies	700,000 (1935); 600,000 (1937)	4
247	Samuel Sion (1932)	Stoa Alberga 5		Stationery	175,000	1

No.	Name	Address	Partners	Economic Activity	Capital (GRD)	Employees
248	Jacques Yacoel (1933)	Rue Tsimisky 24		Radios and accessories; typewriters; electrical appliances, etc.	450,000	

10d. Cinema

No.	Name	Address	Partners	Economic Activity	Capital (GRD)	Employees
249	Albert Levy, (Cinema Apollon)		Albert Levy and Elie B eneviste (replaced by his son-in-law Elie Pinhas)	Operation of Cinema Apollon	500,000[17]	
250	Saby Nissim Mallah (1925)	Rue Tsimisky 7		Exclusive representation of Fox Films, Athens	1,000,000	3
251	Benico Segura		Elie Attas	Operation of the Alcazar and Pantheon cinemas	2,700,000	

11. Tobacco: Tobacco Trade and Cigarette Production

No.	Name	Address	Partners	Economic Activity	Capital (GRD)	Employees
252	Salomon Is. Amariglio (1937)	Rue Vassileos Iracliou 6 / Rue Ermou 4	Salomon and David Amariglio (brothers)	Sale of sacks and stripping for tobacco and small-scale export of tobacco leaf leftovers (*déchets de tabacs*) to Switzerland and Arabia	300,000	
253	Raphael Jakob Varsano & Co. (1934)	Rue Syngrou 44	Abram Daniel Saporta	Bales of tobacco leafs	3,000,000	

12. Domestic Wares and Luxaries

12a. Furniture Trade

No.	Name	Address	Partners	Economic Activity	Capital (GRD)	Employees
254	Sam E. Haim (1934)	Rue Vassileos Heracliou 19	Abram E. Haim (brother)	Sale of furniture and linoleum	300,000	1

12b. Glassware

No.	Name	Address	Partners	Economic Activity	Capital (GRD)	Employees
255	Asséo Frères & Fils (1926)	Rues Alex. le Grand-Ermou	Mentech and Elie Asséo (brothers), Dario Mentech Asséo (son)	Wholesale and semi-wholesale trade in glassware, crystal, chandeliers, etc.	2,000,000	
256	Isac Israel Benrubi (1895)	Rues Spandoni 11 et Alex le Grand		Optician; glass articles and instruments: lunettes, barmometers, thermometers, batteries, electrical items	400,000	3
257	Haim J. Benrubi (1919)	Corner of Rues Paik/c/ou-Capodistriou	Haim J. Benrubi, Haim S. Benrubi (cousin)	Household utensils; glassware, crystal, porcelain, lamps, enamelware	4,000,000 (£8000)	10–12
258	Benveniste & Moché (1914)	Rue Vassileos Heracliou	Moise Jakob Benveniste, Jakob Aron Moche	Glassware	600,000	
259	Eliezer & Chimchi (1913)	Rue Alex. le Grand 33	Abram Eliezer, Abram Chimchi (brothers-in-law)	Glassware, crystal, enamelware, etc.	1,000,000	5

12c. Jewellery and Watches

No.	Name	Address	Partners	Economic Activity	Capital (GRD)	Employees
260	Jacques David Sasson (1924)	Rue Roi Constantin 33		Pearls and jewels	600,000	

13. Trade in Agriculture Products including Grain
13a. Locally Grown Produce

No.	Name	Address	Partners	Economic Activity	Capital (GRD)	Employees
261	Cuenca Leon (1929)	Rue Monastiriou 42	Various brothers	Commerce in foodstuffs with the interior	150,000[18]	2
262	Jacques Juda Saïas (1933)	Stoa Kyrtsis 3		Commercial representation and export of onion seeds	100,000	

No.	Name	Address	Partners	Economic Activity	Capital (GRD)	Employees
263	Fils de David Beja & Co. (1918)	Rue Yenitson 4	Salomon and Matheo David Beja (brothers), Abram Jacob Cohen	Cereals, raw wool, etc.	500,000	
264	Cuenca Frères (1937)	Rue Odysseos 7	Jacques and Moise Cuenca (brothers)	Cereals wholesaler	200,000	2
265	Aron Gavios (1934)		Albert Gavios, Jacob Rousso	Operation of a threshing machine		
266	Fils de David Hasson (1924)	Rue Doxis 3	Albert, Moise, Simon and Baruch Hasson (brothers)	Commerce in cereals and raw skins	6,000,000	
267	Marco Matarasso Romani & Co.		David Matarasso, Haim Romano, Elie Marius, Ovadia Bitran	Grain mill	1,000,000	
268	Sarfatti & Cohen (1933)	Rue Olympiou Diamanti 1	Liaou Sarfatti, Moise Cohen, Isac Cohen (son)	Semi-wholesale and retail trade in cereals	400,000	

13d. Silk Cocoons (Export)

No.	Name	Address	Partners	Economic Activity	Capital (GRD)	Employees
269	Salomon S. Mordoh Succ.[essors]	Rue Coundouriotis 11	Joseph Mordoh (son of the late Salomon), Milan. Local managers: Aron Mallah (power of attorney) and Yacoel (no first name; brothers-in-law)	Primarily of silk cocoons from Serbia	6,000,000	

13e. Dried Fruit, Legumes, Fresh Fruit, and Oil

No.	Name	Address	Partners	Economic Activity	Capital (GRD)	Employees
270	Fils de David Alcheh & Cie (1928)	Rue Catouni 12	Isaac D. Alcheh; Peppo David, and Samuel David Alcheh (brothers)	Commerce in legumes and dry fruits	600,000– 700,000	
271	Isac A. Aroesti (1930/31)	Rue Vaiou 25	Avram Aroesti (father, Monastir)	Legumes	400,000	
272	Abram Benrubi (1929)	Oporo Agora (Marché des fruits)	Abram Benrubi, Saltiel Roza, Mordoh Tchico	Legumes and fruits	350,000	
273	Moise Iomtov Cohen (1918)	Oporo Agora (Marché des fruits)		Legumes and fresh fruits	150,000	2

No.	Name	Address	Partners	Economic Activity	Capital (GRD)	Employees
274	Nissim Gheledi & Fils (1936)	Rue Egypte	Albert, Moise (sons)	Lemon, oranges, dry legumes	500,000	
275	Kassopoulos, Frances & Co. (1935)*	Rue Orvilou 13	Constantin Kassopoulos, Jacob Sa. Frances, Abram Frances, Eliezer H. Aelion, Samuel Ab. Esformes	Wholesale and retail trade in dried legumes, colonial commodities, etc.	200,000	
276	Fratelli Mahel (1910-1933)	(no address)	Raphael, Samuel and Salomon Mahel (brothers)	Oils and fats	Suffered losses: no remaining capital	
277	Daniel Marcos (*2) (1935)	Rue d'Egypto [38/37]	Dino Mano (minor partner)	Commerce in dried legumes	275,000	
278	Moise Massarano & Fils (1920)	Oporo Agora 1	Dario Massarano (son)	Commerce in fresh fruit and legumes to Old Greece and Egypt	300,000	
279	Isac S. Saltiel (1927)	Rue Olympiou Diamanti 53		Sale of dried fruit	250,000	

15. Banking and Large-Scale Commercial Activities

15a. Finance: Banking

No.	Name	Address	Partners	Economic Activity	Capital (GRD)	Employees
280	Ipalliiki Micropistossis, Albert Jacob Houlli (1936)	Rue Franque 36 (Stoa Allatini 18-19)	Albert Jacob Houlli, David Torres, Elie Camhi, Isac Jacob Houlli, Isac A. Bourla, Samuel Saltiel	Agency for small-scale loans (*un bureau de petit credit*) with a sale drapery dept.	525,000	
281	Oikos Micropistosseos Ouziel & Hazan (1935)	Rue Roi Constantin 11	Salomon Mair Ouziel, Joseph Aron Hazan	Small loans and insurance	300,000	
282	Haim et Joseph Salomon Salem (1902)	Rue Franque 36 (Stoa Allatini)	Haim Salem, Joseph Salomon Salem (brothers)	Very small-scale bankers	3,000,000	

15b. General and Large-Scale Commerce: International Traders and Commission Agents

No.	Name	Address	Partners	Economic Activity	Capital (GRD)	Employees
283	Fils de Salomon Abravanel (1900)			Commercial representation	Insufficient	

				Activity	
284	AGETRA, General Agency of Transport, Alain Hassid & Co., SA (1934–1936)	Rue Alexandre le Grand 23	Share holders: Alain Hassid (520 of 1,000); P.A. Palsoiogue [not clear] (10 of 1,000); Rodolphe Mazlliah (10 of 1,000); Nahman S. Saadi (360 of 1,000); Sabetay Nahman (100 of 1,000)	General transport agency	500,000 (1000 × GRD 500)
285	Allalouf & Co. (1922)	Rue Metropole 10	Elie and Nathan Allalouf (brothers), Sam Maissa	Maritime and aerial insurance agency; import–export, specialising in export of tobacco leaf leftovers (*tabacs en déchets*)	Estimated turnover: 800,000-1,000,000 8
286	Almosnino & Scapa (1931-32)	Rue Ermou	Isaac Almosnino & Israel Scapa	Additional offices in Larisse, Drama, Kavalla, and Athens	1,100,000–1,375,000 (£2,000–£2,500)
287	H.A. Altshey (1932)	Alexander the Great St. 5	Solely owned since 1927	Exclusive commercial representation, commission trade, import–export; consignment	More than necessary for guarantee
288	Vita B. Amar (1902)	Cité Saul		Liquidator; real estate; export–import	
289	Albert J. Ammir (1935)	Rue Franque 26	Albert Amir, Mr. Michail (brother-in-law); Dario Perahia	Commercial representation with offices in Athens and Tel-Aviv managed by Albert & Salomon Ammir	Sufficient for operation
290	S. Asséo & D. Leon (1924)	Rue Valaouritou 10	Semtov and Leon Asséo (brothers)	Broker: import–export of chemical products, paper, cigarettes, machines, etc.	1,500,000

No.	Name	Address	Partners	Economic Activity	Capital (GRD)	Employees
291	Leon E. Benusiglio (1911)	Edessis St. 2		Commercial representation of foreign firms for the metal (tinplates, galvanized steel, iron wire) and wood (timber) industries		
292	Albert D. Benveniste			Commercial insurance broker		
293	"Hermes" S. Benveniste, H. Pardo & Co. (1935)	Stoa Davidetto 16	S. Benveniste, H. Pardo	Commission, representation; import-export; customs agent for office equipment, electrical goods, chemical products, talc, hides and leather	100,000	
294	Paul Benahmias [n.d.]			Comercial representation	100,000	
295	Carasso & Vital Cohen (1936)	Emmeuble Cazes	Vital Cohen, Sam Carasso	Representation of maritime and air transport companies	100,000	3
296	"Hermes" H. Pardo & M. Carasso [n.d.]	Stoa Davidetto 16		Export-import, customs agent	300,000	
297	"Hermes" Société de transports internationaux (1937)	Stoa Albergas	Nahman Saadi, Sabi Saadi, Moise S. Molho (silent partner)	International transport	120,000 (Salonica) & 300,000 (Athens)	
298	Alber J. Cohen (1936)			Sales representation for hat manufacturers; insurance broker; export of hides	100,000	
299	Aron H. Cohen & Cie. (1919)	Rue Verria 4	Aron H. Cohen, David E. Arditty, Saul A. Pipano	Commercial representation; export agents	1,000,000	

				Activity		
301	Moise Is. Covo (1932)	Stoa Allatini 52		Commercial representative for his father Mario's small-scale business	100,000	—
302	S. Damkou & M. Beraha (1935)*	Rue C/K/atouni No. 3	Sotirios Dankou, Marcel Beraha	Commercial agents for textile fabrics and iron products		—
303	Joseph S. Djahon (1935)	Rue Agiou Minas 13		Commercial representation: textiles, chemicals, metals	1,400,000	
304	Jack Fisman	Koffa Building		Representatives		
305	Moïse S. Francès (2*) (n.d)	Rue Valaoritou 33, Stoa Frances 4		Commercial representation	222,780 ($2,000)[19]	
306	Joseph Menahem Hassid (1927)	Rue Franque 33, Palais de la Banque Ottomane		Commercial representation	1,000,000	—
307	Hazan & Florentin (1932)	Rue Valaoritou 31, Makedoniki Stoa	Hazan and Florentin (Florentin was the son-in-law of Hazan's late partner from Hazan & Guerchon, 1931)	Commercial representation	200,000	1 typist and 1 office boy
308	Ladopulos Nikolaos* (1922)	Stratu corner Ethnikis Aminis	Nikolaos Ladopulos, Renée Bensusan	Gas station, automobile spare parts	100,000	
309	Mano & Co. (1928)[20]	Stoa Tatti 5–8	Isac Mano, Mardoche Gallea (Isac Mano's maternal uncle)	Commission & commercial representation	Amply sufficient	—
310	Matsa Bros (1924)	Valaoritu 31, Makedoniki Stoa	Salomon & Ilia Matsa (brothers)	Representation	250,000	
311	Oscar E. Misrachi (1915)	13 Rue Salamine		Commercial agent in Greece and the Balkans: foodstuffs, salt, oils, textile fabrics	Sufficient	
312	David S. Molho (1903)	Rue Aristotelos 5		Appraiser (Commisairs d'avarie)	4,000,000	

No.	Name	Address	Partners	Economic Activity	Capital (GRD)	Employees
313	S[alomon]. A. Mordoh (1934)	Rue Catouni, Stoa Albergas	Salomon A. Mordoh	Representation of English, German and Yugoslav trading houses	Sufficient	
314	Maison Jacques Nahmias & Fils (1922)	Rue Alex. le Grand 33	Joseph and Elie J. Nahmias (sons of late Jacques)	Petroleum, benzine, fire and maritime insurance brokers	10,000,000 (incl. immovables)[21]	
315	Salomon Pinhas Pardo (1916)	Rue Victor Hugo	Yugoslav partners: Dario, Moise and Isac Pardo (brothers)	Commercial agents mainly of colonial goods destined to be sold to Monastir	2,157,040 (YUD 1,000,000)[22]	
316	Dario Pinhas (1933)	Palais Aslanian 36		Commission and representation	Sufficient	
317	Revah, Mattia & Co. (1932)	Rue Vassiléos Heracliou 8	Jacques J. Revah, Moise Barzilai Mattia, Joseph Jacques Hasson, David Isac Matalon and Soulema Isac Molho	International transport; customs; export, sales and consignment agents for Yugoslav trading houses	300,000	
318	S. A. Nehama (1932)	Rue Vassileos Heracliou 9	Samuel A. Nehama (Salomon's brother)	Commission representation	150,000	1
319	Fils d'Isac S. Saltiel (1915)	Rue Ermou 2	Saul and Sam Saltiel (sons of the late Isac)	Export-import; representation of indigenous products producers, from/to Serbia, Hungary	1,000,000	
320	Maurice Dav. Sassoon (1936)	Rue Tsimisky 7	Nico (David) Sassoon (son of the late Max)	Commercial representation, quincaillerie, stationery and haberdashery	300-350,000 (1,000,000 belonging to Maurice)	
321	Fils de Levy Simha	Rue Catouni 23	Nissim and Matheo Simha (sons)	Commission agents in the Macedonia interior (Serrès, Drama, Kavalla)	1,000,000	
322	Pascal M. Strouza (1928)	Rue Kaningos 23B		Comission and	Modest	

No.	Address	Owners / Partners	Activity	Capital	
323 Joseph J. Tiano[23] (1935)	Rue Catouni 7	Solely owned by Joseph Tiano after Juda's death and Salmona's retirement	Commercial representation for fabrics and colonial commodities	Considerable	
324 Samuel Ghedalia Yeni (1917)	Vassileos Heracliou	Ghedalia, Albert (brothers)	Commission and representation	2,800,000	2

15c. Construction Contractors

No.	Address	Owners / Partners	Activity	Capital	
325 Jacques Juda Moché (1936)	Head office: Athens; Salonica Branch: Rue Roi Constantin 14		Civil engineer and public works contractor	2,000,000	2 employees in Salonica; many in Athens
326 Elie J. Modiano (n.d.)	Rue Venizelos - Cité Saüll		Civil engineer: large buildings, roads & bridges	10,583,000 (£20,000)	(immovables)
327 Elie Modiano & Errera Frères (1928)	Rue Roi Constantin / Rue Venizelos - Cité Saüll	Elie Modiano (Jacob's son), Moise Errera (manager of the Salonica branch), and Joseph Errera (manager of the Athens branch)	Public utilities, especially hydraulic and canalisation projects	1,058,300 (£2,000)	3
328 S.A. Technique Hellénique de Defense Fluviale (1931)	Stoa Saül	Italian industrialist from Bologna; Elie J. Modiano; Errera Frères; Constantin Anguelakis	Construction of water infrastructure exclusively for the state	2,000,000 (mostly from the Italian investor and Elie Modiano)	

Source: CAHJP Gr/Sa [Thessaloniki] 346, BA [initials for Banque Amar] Salonica 1935–1938; Gr/Sa 370.

Notes: The table [above] contains a sample of the Jewish and some of the Jewish-Greek (marked with an asterisk) firms that applied to Banque Amar for loans during the period in question (1935–1937); they include a few firms which applied in 1938. If the firm applied for a loan more than once, we used the information contained in the last application, based on the assumption that this information represented the firm's then current conditions.

Except for a few small firms, such as Elie Sarfatti & Ovadia Ezratti (no. 77), Victor Almosnino (no. 239), and S. Damkou & M. Beraha, (no. 302), all of the Jewish firms were registered with Salonica's Chamber of Commerce and Industry.

Firms generally did not retain their original names over the years due to changes demanded by the dissolution of partnerships, the entry of new partners, or changes in the firm's status (from a private firm to a corporation), and so forth. These facts prevented construction of a list with the same level of coherence found in the appendices to Chapters 8 and 9 and also in the footnotes of this appendix.

Additional factors contributing to the inconsistencies include the macro-level transformations experienced by the various industrial branches and by commerce in general during the 1930s, especially at the level of sub-branches. We have tried to preserve the original branch structure and distribution as much as possible, given the firms' individual histories.

The appendices to Chapters 4 and 5 are based on complete listings of the firms registered with Salonica's Chamber of Commerce, while the current appendix consists of the applicants to Banque Amar for credit, and thus is inevitably less complete than the list of firms registered with the Chamber of Commerce (see the Introduction).

However, like the previous appendices, this list contains information on those medium- and large-scale firms sufficiently successful to allow them to request bank credit. What these firms had in common financially was their ability to provide sufficient collateral and guarantees, meaning that they were unlikely to turn to the Jewish community's fund, which provided loans to small borrowers (see section 7.7).

The following comments relate to the pertinent variables consistently listed in the documents:

1. Name of firm: Firms are listed alphabetically according to the owners' surnames as given in the Banque Amar records, even if the full name of the firm is different or the owners are not mentioned in alphabetical order within that name, e.g., S. Damkou & M. Beraha is listed under Damkou. Partners' names are listed as noted on the documents because the order of the names sometimes indicates the relative order of ownership. A firm's middle name generally indicates the name of the entrepreneur's father, which facilitates identification of cousins.

2. Year of establishment: This data appears in parentheses. The specific year noted is that of the firm in its then current format; earlier formations are ignored.

3. Address of firm: Unless otherwise indicated, all of the firms listed were located in Salonica.

4. Partners: Current partners are listed. In cases of mixed-liability partnerships, the denotation "silent partner" appears in parentheses. In cases of incorporation, the main shareholders also appear.

5. Economic activity: The firms are divided into branches. The activities listed are literal translations of the information found in Banque Amar records. Due to inconsistencies in the entries, which are often written in an ancient or local French dialect, the English translations may be incomplete or unclear. For this reason, the original French is often cited. Despite the structural transformations experienced by the respective industries during the 1930s, I attempted to preserve the sub-branch structure to allow for comparisons with the firms listed in Appendix 4 and 5. Even though branches 4 and 14 do not appear here, we preserved the original branch numbers for purposes of consistency.

6. Capital: This category represents the bank's assessment of the firm's worth. It includes capital investments in equipment (*machines et installations*), merchandise (*stock des merchandises*), raw materials, and sometimes real estate.

7. Real estate was excluded from Appendix 8 because property was not consistently registered as owned by the firm. As a rule, real estate was treated as private wealth, belonging to the firm's owners or their relatives, unless its value was included in the firm's estimated capital.

8. Currency: Unless otherwise indicated, all values are given in drachmas (GRD). When the currency specified in the sources was the pound sterling, the sums were converted into GRD using the relevant year's exchange rate, with the sterling or dollar sums appearing in parentheses (Mazower 1991, Appendix I, Table A1.3, p. 310).

9. Employees/Workers (E/W): Total number of employees or workers. The workers' gender – male or female – is indicated when available, but these data are not available for most companies. Yet, the source documents do differentiate between "employees" (usually those engaged in semi-skilled or professional labour

distribution of the respective position-holders.

10. Firms solely owned by Jews represent about one-third of the Jewish firms found in the registry maintained by Salonica's Chamber of Commerce and Industry. Given that the present list was not filtered by the Nazis, we assume that the data are unbiased. In order to generate an independent sample suitable for statistical analysis, I eliminated the recurring firms (those firms which had more than one record), which would have caused statistical dependency. When classification of firms was problematic, a footnote was added to explain the circumstances and to prove that it is not a recurring firm.

1. Previously Sion, Gattegno & Cie (1924).
2. Including two buildings, one in rue Coromila and the other in rue Valaoriyou. Bernard Landau BA/250 8/10/1936.
3. Although the details are similar, they may be two different firms, based on the differences in personal details. Jacques Cohen BA/254 23/10/1936; Isac G. Cohen BA/233 12/8/1936.
4. Previuosly Faiz & Yakar (est. 1919), dissolved in 1926.
5. After its debts were suspended (1932), the firm was forced to operate under the name of Haim Marcos, a family friend (see section 7.5).
6. Plus the capital invested in Cohen & Perahia.
7. Previously David Angel & Cie.
8. After suffering losses and a decline in his business, his address was changed to that of his son Jacques (commerce in leather and accessories for cobblers) (see BA/none Sabetay J. Nehama 7/1/1935).
9. The sources listed "le sieur Moise Joseph Salem". This firm was identified with another firm bearing the same name and the same address but established in 1918, a partnership between Haim Salem, Moise Salem, and Joseph Salem, having rolling capital of GRD 1,200,000; BA/none Haim Salem & Frères 12/12/1935 (see BA/4672 Haim Salem & Frères 12/4/1937). Compare also with Hekimoglou 2004: 203.
10. Cabot is inexpensive cloth made of 100 percent cotton, thin or thick, usually grey in colour.
11. Previously Haim Moche & Angel (est. June 1935) dissolved some time around July 1937; private capital estimated at GRD 300,000.
12. This amount was in addition to capital invested abroad, estimated at about GRD 50,000, obtained from the sale of a plot he possessed in Palestine. See BA/4849 Avram Juda Cohen 27/7/1937.
13. His estimated capital, after about forty years of work, including immovables and interest accounts. See BA/none 31/12/1935.
14. Previously Levy & Frances (1931).
15. Previously Nahmias & Massoth (est. 1917) by the two brothers-in-law, Joseph Nahmias and Elie Massoth, dissolved in 1935. See BA/4639 Elie Isac Massoth 31/03/1937.
16. Originally Allalouf & Bourla.
17. Including his wife's dowry.
18. In addition to the GRD 250,000 dowry provided by his wife and deposited in the Romanian gasoline firm as a guarantee for his purchases of petrol.
19. The exchange rate in 1937 was GRD 111.39 = $1. Mazower 1991, Appendix, Table A1.3, p. 310.
20. No relationship appears to exist with Mano & Co. (no. 214), given the total lack of agreement between the companies' details.
21. Total capital invested in all the family enterprises. See section 9.4.
22. The exchange rate in July 1936 was £1 = YUD 250, and £1 = GRD 539.26.
23. Previuosly Juda, Salmona & Tiano (1901).

Notes

Introduction

1   Dumont 1979.
2   Quataert 1993a: 177–194.
3   Quataert 1993b: 87–122; Quataert 1995: 59–74, 171–173.
4   Quataert 1993a: 189.
5   Kuznets 1960: 1624.
6   Roupa and Hekimoglou 2004: 2–3; Hekimoglou 2004: 2.
7   Light and Gold 2000.
8   *Guide Sam* 1930, p. 17. The Jewish Sam Lévy, the son of Saadi Lévy, also published the Salonican Jewish newspapers *La Epoka* and *Journale de Salonique* at the turn of the twentieth century.
9   Abravanel 1996: 501–503.
10 These Jewish-owned banks operated beside the other Jewish banking firms of Benveniste and Salem: see Hekimoglou 1997b: 153, n. 122.
11 Hekimoglou 1987; Mourghianni-Estela 1996: 598 n. 12.
12 YIVO, Greece, RG 207, FO. 156, *The Bankers' Almanac & Year Book, Banque Union SA*, Salonica. 13 July 1932; YIVO, Greece, RG 207, FO. 156, Union de Banques Suisses, Zurich, to Banque Union, SA, Salonica, 8 July 1932.
13 YIVO, Greece, RG 207, FO. 156, Plaza Hotel, Leicester Sq., London, to Banque Union, SA, Salonica, 9 August 1932.
14 See Hekimoglou 1987; Mourghianni-Estela 1996: 598 n. 12.
15 Following is the exact wording of the Nazi confirmation of the bank's seizure: "*Gefunden im Archivmaterial deir Judischen Bank Amar. Enhält. Vertrauliche Auskünfte über die Gründung Führung, Finanzen und Arbeiten der griechischen und judischen Firmen in der Stadt Salonik. 15 August 1941*" [*sic*]. Author's translation: "Found, in the archival material of the Jewish Bank Amar. Inventory of confidential information regarding the establishment, management, finances and employment of the Greek and Jewish firms in the city of Salonica."
16 Molho and Nehama 1965: 114; Nehama 1989: 251.
17 Between May and November of 1941, a special unit including more than thirty German officers and academics under the command of Alfred Rosenberg, the Nazi regime's chief ideologue, seized archival and cultural material owned by Greek Jewry; among these were the papers of financial institutions located in Salonica. The documents' destination: a new institution to be established in Frankfurt, by Hitler's order, for the exploration of the "Jewish question". Mazower 1993: 237–238.
18 All of the documents are found in Gr/Sa 346 (original Xerox, 775 pp.), while copies of a small portion are located in Gr/Sa 370.

19 Few documents including a debt's redemption date after 1938.

20 Megas 1993; Stavroulakis et al. 2006; Naar 2006.

21 Steven Gold (2004), based on visual sociology techniques, referred to the contribution of photography in conducting research on immigration.

Chapter I

1 Evidence to this effect is provided by Vidal Nahum, an entrepreneur born in Salonica and father of the sociologist Edgar Morin, in his statement found in Morin 1989: 16. Author's translation: "Saturday was a public holiday in Salonica, and the Muslims, Orthodox, and Bulgarians would all close their shops, because Saturdays were sacred . . . the customs, the post office, everything was closed." Morin 2009: 5. See also Dishon 2006.

2 The various definitions of minority group have three main characteristics in common: 1. Uniqueness or "ethnic boundaries", referring to a salient attribute (religion, language, nationality, etc.) that differentiates the group from the majority. 2. Exclusion and differential treatment by the majority (experienced in alienation and the denial of full participation in the dominant society), resulting from its inferior political status as a subordinate group. 3. An inclination toward *inclusion*, the creation of in-group solidarity attributable to the discrimination and prejudice suffered at the hands of the majority; also expressed as involuntary membership in groups that share common values. For various definitions of "ethnic minority" see Blalock 1967: 145; Rex 1970: 25; Krausz 1971: 10; Van Amersfoort 1982: 12; Banton 1983: 9.

3 This alternative approach to what might otherwise be considered neo-classical economic behaviour stresses non-economic factors such as the greater solidarity found among migrants, a feature that impacts on ethnic entrepreneurial patterns. See Gold 2005.

4 These include ethnic employers who employ non-ethnic workers, the latter being referred to as the "migrant economy". See Light, Bernard and Kim 1999.

5 Light and Gold 2000: 23–24.

6 Brezis and Temin 1999: 5.

7 Aldrich and Waldinger 1990.

8 See also Foreman-Peck 2005: 80–81.

9 Anthony D. Smith (1994: 383) defined "ethnic community" as "named human populations with shared ancestry, myths, historical memories and common cultural traits, associated with a homeland and having a sense of solidarity". In Smith's typology, a "demotic/vertical ethnic community", as opposed to an "aristocratic/lateral ethnic community", refers to the diffusion of solidarity throughout all social strata of an ethnic community, accompanied by group endogamy. See A. D. Smith 1986: 79–89.

10 Light and Gold (2000: 108–109) determined that "ethnic sources are created, maintained and reproduced as part of the collective lives of group members. Specific skills, outlooks, and rules for interaction are taught as parts of family and communal life. Maintaining in-group loyalty, co-ethnics join together in cooperative activities either to make up for their inability to access economic resources used by the mainstream society or simply because they value co-ethnic interaction". According to Light (1984: 201), reactive hostility, which deepens internal solidarity, can be included among ethnic resources as it motivates consolidation and improves ethnic institutional organisation.

11 On the contribution of ethnic communal institutions to internal solidarity, see Smith 1986: 22–31.

12 A recent analysis supports the hypothesis that liquidity constraints were an important determinant of self-employment among recent immigrants in Canada at the beginning of the twentieth century and explained the high rate of Jewish entrepreneurs in contrast with those of Christian affiliation (Minns and Rizov 2005).

13 Immigrant neighbourhoods, where immigrant businesses thrive and immigrants interact with the majority population, can foster group solidarity. Segregation within non-isolated urban spaces eases the immigrant entrepreneur's access to diverse (majority) clients with potentially higher incomes. Elmlund and Bohl 2006.

14 James Coleman defined "social capital" as "a variety of different entities with two elements

in common: they all consist of some aspect of social structure and they facilitate certain actions of actors . . . within the structure". Like other forms of capital, social capital is productive, making possible the achievement of objectives that might otherwise not be possible. Like physical capital and human capital, social capital is not completely fungible and may be specific to certain activities. See Coleman 1985: S98.

15   Bailey and Waldinger 1991.
16   The term "class resources" as used in relation to Asian immigrants in the US during the 1980s. Light (1984: 201–202) and Light and Gold (2000: 84) broadly defined "class resources" as "vocationally relevant cultural and material endowment of bourgeoisies . . . enable entrepreneurs to initiate and to run business firms in the formal sector . . . lack of distinctive ethnic or cultural character". Defining capital as "any store of value that assists production and productivity", they determined that all class resources, including financial capital, human capital, cultural capital and social capital, are essentially are forms of capital. Light and Gold 2000: 84–97. This term is also equivalent to "competitive resources" as used by Blalock in reference to the resources available to minority individuals by virtue of their possessions: personal skills, income, assets, etc. See Blalock 1967: 118.
17   Aldrich and Waldinger 1990; Waldinger 1993.
18   Casson and Godley 2005.
19   For the basic theory, see Aldrich and Waldinger 1990; for a comprehensive survey on ethnic entrepreneurship in the US, see Zhou 2004. The so-called mixed embeddedness approach, proposed by Kloosterman and Rath (2001) as well as Rath (2002), provides useful insights into ethnic entrepreneurial patterns. It acknowledges the significance of immigrants' concrete embeddedness in social networks for the analysis of economic transactions and recognizes that these relationships are more abstractly embedded in broader economic and political-institutional structures.
20   The general lack of entrepreneurial culture in nineteenth-century Utrecht left openings for German entrepreneurs (Schrover 2001). In contrast, Israel's vibrant entrepreneurial culture reduced the number of openings available for immigrant entrepreneurs from the former Soviet Union. That is, few under-served niches were available for starting a business (Razin and Scheinberg 2001). Assuming homogeneity among the Jewish migrants arriving in New York and London, Godley (2001) has shown that London's smaller share of entrepreneurs can be attributed to the absorption of anti-entrepreneurial values by these immigrants.
21   Phizacklea and Ram 1995.
22   Chiswick and Wenz 2006.
23   Light 2005.
24   Kuznets 19603. The so-called Kuznets Model has been applied to several Jewish communities, including Hungary of the 1930s (see Don 1990), Iraq of the 1930s–1940s (see Darvish 1987); and Argentina and other Latin America countries during the 1960s (see Syrquin 1985).
25   Aldrich and Waldinger 1990: 130–131.
26   Gopalkrishnan and Shapiro 1999.
27   Bonacich 1973.
28   Aldrich and Waldinger 1990; Anthias 1992: 74; Light 1984; Light and Gold 2000; Model 1993. Morawska 1996; Tsukashima 1991; Waldinger 1990, 1994, 1996.
29   Bonacich 1973.
30   Anker 1998:19.
31   Bailey and Waldinger 1991.
32   Kuznets 1960: 1601.
33   Already in1954, the late S. N. Eisenstadt (1954), while focusing on the nation-state as the framework for socio-political and economic behaviour of immigrants, argued that assimilation is not a one-dimensional process with a specific point of culmination but a multi-dimensional and changeable event that varies by institutional arena. Milton Gordon (1964), who examined the integration of immigrants in the US from the beginning of the twentieth century, defined two fundamental levels of adaptation. The first, cultural assimilation, involves immigrant absorption of the host society's cultural patterns (e.g., language) but without loss of the ethnic group's unique cultural elements. The second, structural assimilation is characterized by the institutional dispersion of immigrants and their descen-

dants among social organisations, including business organisations, until fusion into the host society. Gans (2007), following Gordon, studied the migration of groups to the US during the last decades of the twentieth century. He argued that while acculturation and assimilation are processes by which immigrants come to resemble non-immigrants, these processes do not ensure the immigrants' upward mobility.

34 The clothing industry in Germany is a good example of a case where group traits were not decisive. Strict rules and regulations imposed barriers mainly for Turkish and Greek immigrants interested in setting up clothing workshops in contemporary Germany and thus explain the absence of the respective ethnic niches in this branch of the garment industry. Immigrants were more attracted to the garment repair sub-sector because of the absence of constraints. The same can be said for the construction sector in the Netherlands. See Rath 2002.

35 Casson and Godley 2005: 46–50.

36 On the classic middlemen minorities model linked to colonial/patrimonial societies, see Shibutani and Kwan 1965: 168–198; Blalock 1967: 79–84; Armstrong 1976; and Van den Berghe 1981: 137–156. Compare with Robin Ward (1996: 237–238) who describes middleman minorities as a "wide range of minorities concentrated in intermediate niches in which they engage in trade and brokering but suffering hostility in doing so". On the expanded middleman minorities model to include such ethnic minorities with evidence to considerable inclination towards entrepreneurship due to the high degree of hostility they encounter in industrialized societies, see Bonacich 1973; Turner and Bonacich 1980; and Zenner 1982. Critics of the theory argue that it was incorrect to refer to the socio-economic behaviour of such minorities as "attributes" or "tendencies" while ignoring the unique circumstances motivating that behaviour. Those critics propose discerning between "classic middlemen minorities" in patrimonial frameworks and "pseudo-middlemen minorities" in industrialized societies. See Kashima 1982 ; Aldrich and Waldinger 1990; Kieval 1997; and Bonacich 1993. On middleman minority entrepreneurs, see Zhou 2004: 1041–1046.

37 For the "semi-colonial phase" characterised by the absence of direct European political control, as in Thailand from the middle of the nineteenth century until 1932 (establishment of the modern state), see Hamilton and Waters 1997.

38 Historical frameworks of this type display a multi-ethnic plural agrarian host society under colonialism/semi-colonialism, rigidly polarised between elites and masses, almost lacking a middle class and characterised by slow upward social mobility; new profitable entrepreneurial opportunities in international markets as well as in the colonial consumer market. On the Chinese in Southeast Asia at the turn of twentieth century, see Yambert 1981; on Pakistanis and Indians in East Africa, see Cable 1972 and Jain 1988; on the Lebanese in West Africa (up to the 1960s), see Leighton 1979.

39 Bonacich 1973; Turner and Bonacich 1980; Aldrich and Waldinger 1990: 125–126.

40 According to the literature, the classic concept of the middleman minority stresses the minority's vulnerability, a result of mass hostility. The minority's sponsors, the dominant elites, profit from this group's continuing political inferiority and disinterest in political power, behaviour generally anticipated from a dominant middle class. The middleman minority thus acts as a buffer between the ruling elites and the masses, a "scapegoat" for the elite's omissions during instances of social agitation. In return, the middleman minority continues to enjoy the privileges that support its entrepreneurial activity.

41 For the class attitude toward the middleman minority model, see: Jain 1988: 95–103.

42 This appears to be the solution Reid (1997:34–37) proposed to the "too broad" term applied by Bonacich. Instead, Reid proposes the usefulness of categorizing such groups under the heading "entrepreneurial minorities" when discussing historical state-oriented transitions.

43 Zhou 2004: 1041–1046.

44 Zhou 2004: 1043; Waldinger 1996; 2000.

45 Scott 1998.

46 The popular definition of the "first era of globalisation" (in contrast with the second era, which began in 1989) refers to the period extending from the mid-1800s (British colonialism) to the late 1920s. This era ended with a series of successive socio-political ruptures: World War I, the Russian Revolution, and the Great Depression. See Friedman 2000: xvi–xviii.

47 Here we refer to globalisation as a process incorporating a region into the modern world-

system. The "first era of globalisation" is equivalent to the "effective incorporation" stage (following "formal incorporation") of the modern world-system. In this phase, former patterns of production cease to dominate the incorporated region's economy. While the new "periphery" regularly produces a real economic surplus, it simultaneously becomes a potential consumer of manufactured goods imported from industrialised states in this world-system. See Chase-Dunn and Hall 1997: 272–273.

48 While colonisation promoted globalisation, accelerated the erosion of trade and migration barriers between countries as well as contributed to the emergence of a global mosaic of regional economies, decolonisation culminated in the establishment of nation-states that would compete with each other in the modern world-system. Bergesen and Shoenberg 1980; Boswel 1989; Chase-Dunn and Hall 1997: 204–206.

49 Immanuel Wallerstein defines a "world-system" as a multi-cultural network for the exchange of "necessities" (in contrast with "luxuries"). He distinguishes between two types of world-systems: Old World Empires (e.g., the Ottoman Empire) and the "Modern World-System" (or the "Capitalist World-Economy"). The latter is defined as an inter-societal division of labour that is politically structured as an inter-state system – a multi-centric system of unequal and competing states located along the core-periphery axis, with core states dominating peripheral states. Capitalism drives consolidation of the "Modern World-System", which is dominated by the Law of Value that prioritises ceaseless accumulation of capital. See Bergesen and Shoenberg 1980; Boswel 1989; Chase-Dunn and Hall 1997: 27–40, 204–206; Wallerstein 1974–1989; and Wallerstein 1993: 292–296.

50 Deutsch 19662: 101–104.

51 One essential element of the modern world-system is "the non-primordial characters of states, ethnic groups, and households, all of which are constantly created and recreated" (Wallerstein 1990, cited by Frank 1993: 203). A similar approach was formulated by Eisenstadt (1998: 17), who argued that the primordial components of the collective identity are re-created within each different historic context and subject to the influence of societal forces. Although primordial components are sustained as "ancient" features and treated as "natural" elements, they are ceaselessly rebuilt.

52 Smith 1992: 76 n.20. On the value of assets comprising "political resources" (including ethnic political organisations) to the ethnic economy, see Light and Gold 2000: 122–124.

53 Goldscheider and Zukerman 1984: 237–239.

54 Deutsch 19662: 101–104; Svennilson 1954: 36–38.

55 Discriminatory government policies against minorities have included prohibitions against owning land, forests, and natural resources; heavier taxation; trade restrictions; nationalization of essential industries at all levels of production (e.g., from cultivation and milling to distribution of cereals); restrictions on exports and imports; blocked employment opportunities in the public service excluding medical services. On government discrimination against the Chinese in the Philippines, see Eitzen 1968: 224–225; for similar legislation against the Chinese in independent Malaysia, see Banton 1983: 193–195.

56 Greenberg 1980: 142–147; Metzer 1978: 222–223.

57 Garry Becker (1971), who studied the phenomenon of competitive discrimination, coined the term "taste for discrimination", meaning the readiness of majority's employers to absorb the costs incurred from a preference (in his case racial) for dominant-group workers. See also Krueger 1963. On the institutional discrimination common to nation-states, considered more serious in its consequences than competitive discrimination, see Kahan 1986: 101.

58 On the circular process whereby the minority's exclusion and persecution by the majority results in the minority's internal strengthening, see Bonacich 1973.

59 "Small minority" was defined by Kuznets as an ethnic group whose population is less than 10 percent of the host country's total population. See Kuznets 1960: 1599–1600.

60 Darvish (1987) showed that although the Jewish minority in three of Iraq's main regions was an indigenous minority of non-recent origin, but that its economic behaviour strongly resembled that of the migration-generated minority described in the Kuznets model. Don (1997), who conducted an empirical application of the Kuznets model to the Jews of Hungary between the two World Wars, broadened the preliminary condition of being a

"new" ("recently arrived migrants") minority to include its "new emancipated status", i.e., its new legal status.

61 The concept "plural society" was originally formulated by Furnivall (1948) to describe societies in South Asia. According to a later version revised by M. G. Smith (1960), a "plural society" is a multi-ethnic society characterised by the existence of separate institutions (family, religion, etc.) for each ethnic segment but a common government for all. As a result, structural pluralism (or cultural pluralism) merely represents different points on the developmental continuum of societies exhibiting plural structures. For an exhaustive discussion, see Schermerhorn 1970: 122–58.

62 Banton 1983: 193–195.

63 They were suspected of remaining loyal to the previous regime and thus of being disloyal to the current regime, a type of fifth column. See Chirot 1997; Levine 1997; Van den Berghe, 1981.

64 Deutsch 1966: 101–104.

65 Jain 1988: 102; Yambert 1981: 189–193.

66 Light and Gold 2000.

67 Rath 2001.

68 In the context of the nation-state and immigrants, including native-born ethnic minorities, it appears that research pertaining to Turkish immigrants in contemporary Germany provides us with a more suitable comparative context. Diehl and Schnell (2006) argued that Turkish migrants try to compensate for their comparatively disadvantaged social status by revitalising ethnic cultural habits or homeland-oriented identifications. They are not content with Gans' discussion of acculturation (adopting the host-land culture) and assimilation (formation of inter-ethnic ties).

69 Compare Kloosterman and Rath 2001.

Chapter 2

1 Lewis 1984; Hacker 1993; Lowry 1986, 1994.

2 Hacker 1993: 27–30; A. Levi 1994: 6, 23–37; Lewis 1984: 50, 118, 122–123; Rozen 1993b: 66.

3 "Greek Jews" were considered to be the progeny of the ancient Byzantine community; see M. Molho 1967.

4 Avitsur 1971–1978; Braude 1983. See also Veinstein 1997.

5 During the 1580s, signs of the Empire's degeneration and disintegration began to appear. The first of its main causes was the expansion of tax farming, which shifted the Empire's control over its income to local leaders. The second was the transformation of international trade, particularly the diversion of primary trade routes from the Mediterranean Sea to the Atlantic Ocean (see Wallerstein 1989). Inflation, the increasing tax burden, and the expansion of capitations given to foreign merchants all forecast economic decline and the Empire's incipient demise; see Avigdor Levi 1994: 71–74; Bashan 1989.

6 As early as the first decade of the seventeenth century, Salonica's textile manufacturers had relocated to Manisa in Western Anatolia, now the preferred centre for the industry due to favourable special tax exemptions. See Gofman 1990.

7 Among the many of Jewish businessmen who migrated to Izmir after 1614 was the father of Sabbatai Tsevi, who established a family-owned commercial network that operated in cooperation with English businessmen; see Gofman 1990: 90–91. On the *Dönme* in Salonica see Benayahu 1971–1978; Baer 2004; Landau 2007.

8 Compare with Weiker 1992: 134. A similar estimate of 25,000–30,000 was given by a British missionary (1828), also reached by multiplication of the same number of males by five: see Emmanuel 1972: 123.

9 Ottoman Macedonia was not an independent administrative division but a network comprised of provinces and sub-provinces. The provinces of Skopje and Monastir the remained the region's principal provinces, together with the province of Salonica. The

Jewish population in the first two provinces would eventually come under Serbian rule. McCarthy 1990: 298; Svoronos 1991: 356.

10   Based on Ottoman census data; see: Karpat 1985:Tab I.8A, 133–7; 140–1; 144–5.

11   Issawi 1980: 82; Pamuk 1984; Kural Shaw 1993.

12   The "semi-colonial situation" is characterised by the absence of direct European political control, and could be observed, for example, in the case of Thailand from the middle of the nineteenth century until 1932, when the modern state was established. See Hamilton and Waters 1997.

13   Wallerstein et al. 1989; Pamuk 1987.

14   On Ottoman financial integration with Europe see Eldem 1999: 179–196.

15   Lewis 1961: 114–115; Shaw and Kural Shaw 1979: 138–141; Kural Shaw 1993.

16   Issawi 1982.

17   On the various regulations defining the rights associated with different kinds of land ownership and possession, issued between 1857 and 1863, see Shaw 1975: 441; for a detailed survey of the Ottoman reforms see Shaw and Kural Shaw 1979: 55–171.

18   The first railway line from Salonica to Mitrovic (1871–1874) joined up with the section of the line linking Salonica to Monastir (1891–1894) and on to Constantinople (1893–1896). For details see Gounaris 1993: 156–167; 1997.

19   Yerolympos and Colonas 1993; Anastassiadou 1997: Ch. 8 and 421–426.

20   Gounaris 1993: 156–167.

21   E.K. Shaw and Shaw 1977: 115–118; Jackson 1985; Karpat 1985: 11; 65–70; Gounaris 1997: 112–113; 119.

22   Todorov 1983: 334.

23   For detailed descriptions of these developments see Gounaris 1993: 172–190; idem 1997; idem 2001.

24   Jelavich and Jelavich 1977: 212–213; Gounaris 1989.

25   Stavrianos 1963: 72–86; see also Anastassiadou 1997: 97–103.

26   On the struggle for rule over Macedonia between the new Balkan states (Bulgaria, Serbia), Central Europe (Germany, Austria), and the western powers (Britain, France), see Dakin 1966; Jelavich and Jelavich 1977.

27   Sugar 1977: 48; Landau 1994; Landau 2004: 351–358.

28   The Young Turks waved the flag of Turkish nationalism. Much like the Christian national minorities in Macedonia, the Young Turks adhered to "a new unity based on the mighty and multitudinous Turkish race, stretching from the Aegean across Asia to the China Sea" (Lewis 1964: 84). The group's aspiration to establish a "national middle class" and "national economy" was eminently suitable to a modern nation-state (Wallerstein et al. 1987: 94–95). The location of a Turkish national government in Salonica intensified the regional conflict and provoked the Balkan nation-states to divide Macedonia among themselves and to complete its political-administrative incorporation into the modern world-system. On the Young Turks' regime in Salonica, see Anastassiadou 1997: 410–420, 427.

29   Ahmad 1982; R. Molho 1988.

30   Braude and Lewis 1982: 24; Stoianovich 1960: 244–248.

31   Armstrong 1976. For comparative research on Greeks and Jews in cosmopolitan Salonica and Odessa, see Vassilikou 2001.

32   Considered allies of the Ottoman "conqueror", Jews were consequently accused of conspiring in the murder of Constantinople's Greek Orthodox patriarch (1821) and subsequently persecuted inside as well as outside Greece. See Bashan 1985 (in Hebrew).

33   Y. Uziel 1967a: 54–55; Emmanuel 1972: 197–198; Dumont 1979: 62–70.

34   Expressions of this attitude included the study of Turkish. About 2,000 Salonican Jews joined the Turkish army, which provided them with kosher food; Jewish merchants also contributed funds to purchase equipment for the Turkish army. See *American Jewish Year Book*, 1910; Dumont 1979; Cooperman 1991: 286–290; Benbassa 1994: 462.

35   From the Archives of the Alliance Israélite Universelle, Grèce I.C.48. A letter written by the teacher M. Benghiat, Salonica, 1 December 1909, cited in Rodrigue 1993: 234.

36   Kansu 1997a: 206–207.

37   For the implementation of boycotts as manifestations of economic nationalism in this era,

see Levene 2001. The practice of ethnic boycotts quickly spread from the Greeks (who first boycotted Bulgarian businesses in 1907) to other communities; see Mazower, 2004: 270.

38   Ahmad 1982: 414, 427. See also Cooperman 1991.

39   From Archives of the AIU, Grèce I.C.48. Letter written by the teacher M. Benghiat, Salonica, 1 December 1909, cited in Rodrigue 1993: 234–235.

40   For Dr. Moise Allatini's report on the state of the Jewish community in mid-nineteenth-century Salonica, see Allatini 1875; See also Barnai 1986: 108; Lewis 1984: 171.

41   Dumont 1979: 37.

42   Landau 2004: 336.

43   Schwarzfuchs 1989; Quataert 1994: 98.

44   On the distinction between "orthodox" and "reactive" components in "ethnic resources", see Light 1984.

45   Dumont 1979: 33–72; Weill 1982; Rodrigue 1990a; Benbassa 1994; R. Molho 2005a.

46   Jewish elites encouraged other Jews to learn the Turkish language and thereby enhance their chances to take advantage of new opportunities. See Allatini 1875.

47   For a systematic detailed demographic survey based on the Ottoman official resources, see Meron 2008a.

48   Shaw 1991: 193, 204; Kerem 1993; McCarthy 1994: 375–397, 379.

49   Milano 1949: 185–189; Morin 1989: 24–26.

50   The Jewish community's rising income from the *gabelle* levy on kosher meat, transferred by butchers since the mid-nineteenth century until the end of the Ottoman rule, confirms this trend. See Nehama 1935–1978: 735; Michael Molho 1986: 17–16.

51   Following is Jewish population data for the province of Salonica: 1893: 37,206; 1896: 41,984; 1897: 43,423; 1906: 52,385. These figures are based on data published by Kemal H. Karpat 1985. For 1893 (year of completing census): Tab. I.8.A, pp. 134–137; for 1896: Tab. I.12, pp. 158–159; for 1897 (updated census data): Tab. I.13, pp. 160–161; for 1906 (the year the second census was completed): Tab. I.16.A, pp. 166–167. On the Jews' under-registration in the Ottoman census and the consequent difficulties in determining the group's size see, for example, McCarthy 1994: 375–397.

52   Salonica Province (*Vilâyet*) was constituted of three sub-provinces (*sancak*) named according to their main towns: Kavalla, Drama and Salonica. Salonica City belonged to the central district (Kaza) within the sub-province of Salonica. For a similar approach to the city's Jewish population data regarding the central district, see Weiker 1992: 138.

53   See Anastassiadou 1997: 95.

54   It could be assumed that the higher estimate, itself transmitted by the Jewish community, included foreign Jews. The latter were, however, registered separately in the Ottoman census (section 3.1). The lower estimate complies with that of Justin McCarthy (1990: Table 5), who corrected the Ottoman statistics for under-registration of women and children in the Selanik sub-province and then projected the figures for 1911; his final figure amounted at 60,252 Jews. For a comprehensive survey of the Jewish population estimates see, Meron 2008a: 31–35.

55   Adapting the concept of "plural society" (chapter 1, note 61), Braude and Lewis (1982: 1) hold that "the Ottoman Empire was a classic example of the plural society".

56   Risal [1914] (1917): 344.

57   This culture area contained descendants of Marranos (converted Jews) who either rejoined their brethren in the East or established new communities in Western Europe, in cities such as Bordeaux, Amsterdam, Hamburg, and London. See Benbassa and Rodrigue 1995: xvi–xxii.

58   *Beratli* were Ottoman subjects holding a *berat,* i.e., an edict issued by the Sultan endowing the bearer with the privileges associated with the status of "foreigner".

59   Jewish sub-ethnic acculturation had begun in the sixteenth century. See M. Molho 1967: 29; Rozen 1993c: 166; Schwarzfuchs 1995.

60   Morin 1989: 25.

61   At the beginning of the twentieth century, about 5,000 of Salonica's Greeks were in fact Greek citizens. See Gounaris 1997: 119. Ahmad 1982; Braude and Lewis 1982; Davison 1982; Issawi 1982; Lewis 1984: 61; Ezel Kural Shaw 1993.

62   Jews, Greeks, and Armenians served as dragomen and high secretaries in the consular repre-

sentations of the following states: Austro-Hungary, Germany, Persia, Britain, France, Belgium, Italy, Spain, Portugal, Denmark, and the US. See *Austrian Report* 1915: 194–198.

63 This decree was framed under the assumption that a large population was the main precondition for economic development as well as for strong defence against outside enemies; it was translated and published in the major European journals. The policy encouraged immigration from European countries for families with a minimum capital of 60 *mecidiye* (about 1,350 francs). In return for their allegiance to the Sultan, the settlers received, among other benefits, exemptions from all taxes and military service for a varying number of years, depending on their chosen place of residence. For instance, if they settled in Rumelia (including Macedonia), these exemptions were for six years. See Karpat 1985: 61–63.

64 The *Austrian Report* 1915 mentioned several foreign Jewish residents originally from central Europe, e.g., Edmund Maulwurf, considered one of the leaders of the Austro-Hungarian colony in Salonica. See *Austrian Report* 1915: 131.

65 The *francos* included Ottoman Jewish traders who had reached Italy within the framework of their commercial activities and had returned while enjoying "foreign protection": see Rodrigue 1994. The term, which derives from the Spanish verb *franquear*, reflects their original status as tax-exempt residents. Compare Grunhous 2008: 81 n. 8. French *protégés* in Salonica enjoyed the capitulations France had won from the Ottoman regime (1673), including freedom from the Sultan's legal authority. From the mid-eighteenth century, consular protection was granted by several European states (Austria, Britain, etc.) to Jewish merchants. See also Nehama 1935-1978: 240–284; Rozen 1993a; 1993b.

66 For the numerical assessment of the Italian migrants derived from Italian consulate records, see Milano 1949: 193–194. For a narrative on the decline of Livorno's Jewish traders since the close of the eighteenth century and their emigration to Salonica, see Trivellato 2009: 265–270.

67 Risal 1917 [1914]: 255.

68 Morin 1989: 25; for a translation, see Morin 2009: 13.

69 See Morin 1989: 28: "*Les 'Livournais' avaient continué à parler italien entre eux, utilisé l'italien dans leurs transactions et institué une école italienne, ce sont eux qui se font les propagateurs de la langue française. La culture italienne en ce XIXe siècle est du reste elle-même très Francophile et francophone.*" Author's translation: "The 'Livornese' have continued to speak Italian among themselves, the Italian used in their transactions, and have established an Italian school; it is they who are the propagators of the French language. Italian culture in the nineteenth century was itself and remained very Francophile and Francophone."

70 The Jewish entrepreneur Edmund Maulwurf was considered one of the leaders of the Austro-Hungarian colony in Salonica. See *Austrian Report* 1915: 131.

71 Local documents indicate that a small number of "recently arrived" Ashkenazi Jews, originally from Central Europe, were provided with religious services (e.g., burial) by Salonica's Sephardic community. See for example M. Molho 1975: *The Epitaphs* tombs nos. 1560, 1572, and 1618. As German Jews remained outside the larger Jewish collective, we include their firms under the general category of European-owned firms.

72 For a review of the evolution of the Ladino literary culture in the Ottoman Empire over the centuries, see Rodrigue 2002. Ladino had been, in the main, part of oral rather than written culture before the eighteenth century. On the development of Ladino newspapers during the second half of the nineteenth century, see Abrevaya-Stein 2002; idem 2004.

73 From Archives of the Alliance Israélite Universelle, Grèce I.C.48, a letter from the teacher M. Benghiat, Salonica, 1 December 1909, translated (from the French) and cited by Rodrigue 1993: 233.

74 Gounaris 1997: 115.

75 *Austrian Report* 1915: 127–130; Lampe and Jackson 1982: 309; Hekimoglou 1987: 62–63.

76 From Archives of the AIU, Grèce I.C.48, a letter from the teacher M. Benghiat, Salonica, 1 December 1909, translated and cited in Rodrigue 1993: 233.

77 For the history of the Jewish banking tradition in Italy since the late Middle Ages see, for example, Filippini 1989; Meron 1990; 1992; 1998.

78 Hekimoglou 1999.

79 The Banque de l'Orient was a branch of the Deutsche Orient Bank (founded in Constantinople in 1906). The Greek bank lent considerable sums but only to borrowers

who possessed capital or land resources worth more the value of the loan. See Hekimoglou 1999: 37.
80 Hekimoglou 1987: 73–74; Gounaris 1997: 170.
81 Salonica's dependence on Jewish capital in this period can be illustrated by the fact that during the Italo-Turkish War (1911), the city fell into financial crisis following the departure of the Italian Jewish banker Saul Modiano. See Hekimoglou 1997: 178; Gounaris 1997: 115–116.
82 According to another source, Saul Modiano's banking house had capital/reserves estimated at £250,000 in 1911. See Gounaris 1997: 116.
83 For the criteria governing our categorisation of the Jewish entrepreneurial elite in Salonica by sub-ethnicity, see Meron 2005b.
84 See also Meron 2005b. For their activities as economic intermediaries in the international mercantile trade conducted since the sixteenth century, see Rozen 1993: 65–113; Trivellato 2009.
85 Inter-generation accumulative capital is considered an advantage in business entrepreneurship. See Mathias 1997.
86 Quataert (1993: 189), who documented and analysed the industrial development of the entire Ottoman Empire, stated that Salonica was unique in that its industrial promoters were Jews. On the Allatini family, see S. Levy 1937; on the Allatini Group, see Roupa and Hekimoglou 2004: 372–374.
87 On the Jewish-owned cotton spinning mills in Salonica, see *Austrian Report* 1915: 56–57; the only two Jewish-owned cotton spinning mills used British equipment exclusively. Quataert 1993: 181–182.
88 The Allatini flour mill (a joint venture with a French partner, est. 1854) came into Allatini's ownership in 1882. The mill was destroyed in a fire in 1898. See *Austrian Report* 1915: 49.
89 Megas 1993: 87.
90 Torres's partners were Dino Fernandez and Eriko Mizrahi. The mill used jute fibre as raw material. See *Austrian Report* 1915: 66; Quataert 1993: 181; Roupa and Hekimoglou 2004: 548; for a photograph of this mill see: Megas 1993: 90.
91 See Sciaky 1946: 45–47.
92 Initial capital equalled FRF2 million; its board of directors included: André Bénac (president), W. V. Adler (Vienna), Jacques Bourget (Paris), Isac Fernandez, Eduard Julia (Paris), E Giraud, E. Malwarf, Josef Mizrahi, Theodor Motet (Paris), Em[manuel] Salem and Alfred Mizrahi (general director). *Austrian Report* 1915: 127; Quataert 1993: 178.
93 Quataert 1993: 189.
94 The other four were The Oriental Tobacco Trading Company, Ltd.; The Alston Tobacco Company, Inc.; The Export Tobacco Leaf Company; and Sebastiano Tani. Dagkas 2003: 122.
95 *Austrian Report* 1915: 67–68.
96 Quataert 1993: 182.
97 *Austrian Report* 1915: 67.
98 Moise Camondo (1860–1935) was the son of Nissim de Camondo (1830–1889) and Élise Fernandez (1840–1910). See Assouline 19992: 13.
99 See Assouline 19992: 177; Seni 2007.
100 According to Assouline (ibid.), Camondo's biographer, the Morpurgo family "*avait fait de Trieste la capitale des assurances dans l'Europe centrale*". Moise Morpurgo (Meron 2005b: Appendix A, firm no. 456) was an agent of the North British & Mercantile Co. (*Austrian Report* 1915: 179). See also Mourghianni-Estela 1996: 598, n. 13.
101 In Morin's (1989: 49) own words: "*C'est que la famille est une communauté très forte. . . . Ce réseau est souvent cosmopolite, comportant des frères, des oncles, des cousins à Livourne, à Alexandrie, à Usküp . . . et il s'élargit aux grandes villes d'Occident, notamment Vienne et Paris . . .*".
102 Meron 2005b.
103 See Sciaky 1946: 43.
104 See Sciaky 1946: 39.
105 Nehama 1935–1978: 240–284; Rozen 1993a; idem 1993b: 102–104.

106 As Edgar Morin phrased it: "*Les séfarades de Salonique et d'Istanbul se déidaignaient, ne se faisaient guère confiance et ne pouvaient songer à s'allier par le sang.*" See Morin 1989: 50.

107 Meron 2005b.

108 Meron 2005b: 190–192.

109 Meron 2005c.

110 A French company that farmed the state monopoly in tobacco (cultivation, harvesting, and sales) and cigarettes for the Ottoman state, it maintained factories for processing tobacco leaf in Salonica and the environs. See Pallis 1948: 6; Cooperman 1991: 195–196.

111 For contemporary testimonies, see Y. Uziel 1978: 82; on the ethnic division of labour in Salonican enterprises, see *Austrian Report* 1915: 73–56; and Quataert 1995: 66.

112 Dumont 1975, 1979; Quataert 1995, 2002.

113 An international organisation of Jewish societies that, with the American Committee as a founding member, was formed to unify the relief work in the Balkan countries. AJYB 1913: 188.

114 According to Nathan Mayer, the Jewish owner of several tobacco enterprises in Kavala, a tobacco industry centre in the province of Salonica, about 3,000–4,000 Jewish workers were engaged in the industry; see N. Mayer 1913: 38; and Quataert 2002.

115 Quataert 1995: 71–73.

116 Dumont 1980.

117 Dimitriadis 1983.

118 *American Jewish Year Book* 1913–1914: 203.

119 Broudo 1967: 243.

120 Ibid., 242–243.

121 For comprehensive empirical research on the Jewish economy in this period, see Meron 2005a; 2005b; 2005c; 2008a.

122 Seven out of twelve members of its Board of Directors were Jewish. See Georgios K. Christodoulou, cited in Gounaris 1997: 114.

123 According to the report written by delegates of the Union des Associations Israélites who visited Salonica in January 1913, the Jewish work force on the eve of the Greek annexation of Salonica consisted of 24,385 employed persons. Adapted from the *American Jewish Year Book* 1913–1914, 203.

124 See Svoronos 1991.

125 The lack of secular Ottoman state institutional education also dampened the possibility of using common Ottoman citizenship to unite all Ottoman subjects. See: Karpat 1985: 11; E. Kural Shaw 1993; Rodrigue 1995: 241-243.

126 Although Jews demographically dominated the city of Salonica, Jewish participation in the Salonica City Council was reduced to one representative (similar to other non-Muslim communities such as the Greeks and Bulgars). See Georgeon 1993; Anastassiadou 1997: 116–117; 425–426.

127 Baer 2007.

128 On the proportion of Muslims (including *Dönme*) in the entrepreneurial structure of Salonica, see Meron 2005a; Meron 2005c. Several firms were *Dönme*-owned. Among bankers: Kapandji Youssouf, Murteza fils Ihat et Idayet; grain merchants: Hamdy bey (Mayor of Salonica); fez producers: Ahmed Kapandji, Société Halil Sebbi et Cie., Société Anonyme Ottoman pour la Fabrication de Tissus et Fez (*Dönme*-Jewish partnership); textiles: Ipekdji Frères; tobacco: Hassan Ar[k]if [sic], Husein Moustapha Rachid. See *Austrian Report* 1915; also Cooperman 1991.

129 There were about 250 *Dönme* families out of 1,900 Muslim families: see Gounaris 1997: 117. For a higher estimate of about 10,000 souls, see Dumont 1984: 72. Compare with Georgeon 1993: 109.

130 Mayer [1913]: 38. This division of labour, typical in the Balkans and Asia Minor where the non-Muslim population was concentrated in urban centres, apparently struck Sussnitzki, too. Yet the pattern is less evident in other Middle Eastern Ottoman territories, where Muslims were a larger percentage of the population. Sussnitzki [1917] 1966; Gilbar 2003.

131 Abbot 1903: 20.

132 Quataert 1993a: 189; Marc Baer's (2007) estimate of the *Dönme*'s contribution to the glob-

alisation of Macedonia is excessive, especially when compared with that of the dominant Muslim elites.
133 See also Findley 1982; Cooperman 1991: 74–75; Rodrigue 1995.
134 Meron 2005b; 2006; 2010.
135 See Y. Uziel 1978: 31.
136 Some Salonican Jewish bankers owned *ciftliks*; Jacob Modiano, for example, owned fifteen estates. See Christov 1964: 105, 108, 116–117.
137 Although not winegrowers, Salonican Jews were involved in Macedonia's wine industry. See *Salonique, Ville-Mère en Israël* 1967: 237–238.
138 Greek fisheries, in contrast, operated in lakes of the Macedonian hinterland. On the Salonican Jewish fisheries see Baruch Uziel 1967; Isac Molho 1951: 36–37.
139 See Meron 2005a, 2005b, 2005c.
140 On the classic division of labour, see Chase-Dunn 1990: 121–148.
141 For a detailed analysis of Jewish entrepreneurship in Salonica during this period, see Meron 2005a; 2005b; 2005c.
142 From Archives of the Alliance Israélite Universelle, Grèce I.C.48, a letter of the teacher M. Benghiat, Salonica, 1 December 1909, cited in Rodrigue 1993: 233–234.
143 Pierron 1996: 75.
144 On the formal relationship between the port administration and the Albanian privileged customs porters who represented the Ottoman authorities, see Dagkas 2003: 561. For a contemporary description of Jewish port workers, see also Y. Uziel 1978: 15–22.
145 The Greek community in Salonica supported the new Greek state (Gounaris 1997: 118). The Ottoman regime was suspicious of all foreign governments with respect to their intentions regarding Salonica's port: there was concern that the port would be considered an extra-territorial entity and meet the same fate of China's ports. For this reason, it delayed opening the port. See Quataert, 1995: 59.
146 The daily wages of port workers (7s–8s, 1911) were considered among the highest ever paid in Macedonia. See Gounaris 1989: 145; Quataert 1995.
147 *Salonique, Ville-Mère en Israël* 1967: 237.
148 *American Jewish Year Book* 1911: 186.
149 From the Archives of the Alliance Israélite Universelle, Grèce I.C.51, letter written by J. Nehama, Salonica, 12 November 1912, cited in Rodrigue 1993: 237–238.

Chapter 3

1 Plaut 1996: 187.
2 The Jewish minority, unlike national minorities, did not claim a separate national identity. For the Greeks, "religion equals nationality. Because the Jews were obviously identifiable as a separate religious group, they were not, therefore, seen as members of the Greek ethnic body". On the Greek immigrants' ethnic identity, see Glaser 1976: 322–323.
3 The international protection of minorities originated at the Paris Peace Conference of 1919, when the Allied and Associated Powers compelled the new states of East Central Europe (Poland, Czechoslovakia, and Yugoslavia), states that had increased their territory (Romania and Greece), and states that had been defeated (Austria, Hungary, and Bulgaria) to sign agreements granting religious and political equality as well as some special rights to their minority peoples. See Fink 1995. For the Jews in this issue, see Levene 1993.
4 The Treaty of Lausanne decreed the population exchange between Turkey and Greece. This coerced transfer excluded Orthodox Christians in Constantinople and Muslims of Western Thrace. See Campbell and Sherrard 1968: 127–129; Hirschon 1989: 36–37; Barutciski 2003. For the treaty's original draft, concluded on 30 January 1923, see Hirschon, 2003: 282–287; for the final draft completed in July 1924, see <http://untreaty.un.org/unts/60001_120000/14/39/00027946.pdf>, accessed 19 January 2009.
5 Compare Kontogiorgi 2006: 7.
6 Mazower 2004: 303–304; on the publication of the 1913 census, see Dimitriades 1983.

7   The census data were apparently kept from official publication because they indicated Jewish pre-dominance in the city.
8   In this census, Bulgarians (6,263) and foreigners (4,364) are combined here into one category, "others" (7 percent); see Dimitriades 1983.
9   Florentin had not yet adopted Zionism as his national affiliation, yet he was influenced by the new population formula manifested in Macedonia, which bound national territorial claims with demographical strength. See CZAJ Z3/2, D. Florentin, Editor of *El Avenir* and Vice-President of Maccabi, Salonica to Prof. [Otto] Warburg, President of the Zionist Organization, Berlin, 15 December 1912; 17 December 1912. This confidential memorandum was also sent to Zionists associations in London, Paris, and Vienna. It supported the Austrian plan for internationalisation of Salonica, which would be managed by its Jewish population. See Gelber 1955; Molho 1988/1993; 1992.
10   *American Jewish Year Book* 1913: 191.
11   Author's translation of: "*Le Grec, le Deunmeh, le Turc, l'étranger, sont des minorités. Le gros de la population est composé de Juifs. Les Juifs sont tout ici, et la ville est juive de langue, d'aspect, de religion. Ils sont les maîtres incontestés du commerce, de la banque, de l'enseignement, du barreau. Le samedi tout chôme. Le jour du Grand Pardon, on ne voit personne dans les rues, les cafés sont déserts. . . . Le langue à tous [Juifs] est le castillan . . . et cette langue s'est imposée à toute la ville comme une sorte d'espéranto que le Grec. Le Turc, l'Albanais, le Bulgare, l'étranger baragouinent. Le conducteur de tramway turc, le garçon de café grec, le cireur de bottes tsigane vous interpelleront dans la langue de Cervantès quand ils concevront un doute sur votre nationalité.*" Risal [1914] (1917): 348–349.
12   "Old Greece" included the five regions: Central Greece and Eubée; Thessaly; Ionian Islands; Cyclades Islands, and the Peloponnesus. "New Greece" includes the provinces acquired by Greece after the Balkan Wars (1913): Macedonia; Epirus; some Aegean Islands (Lesbos, Chios and Samos, excluding Rhodes and the Dodecanese, which came into Italian possession in 1912 and were transferred to Greece only in 1947, following completion of an international postwar settlement); Crete and Western Thrace (Fleming 2008: 32–33).
13   For a comprehensive discussion of this issue see Meron 2008a.
14   On Salonica and its Jewish population during this era see Cooperman 1991; Levene 2001.
15   On the emigration of the Shaki [*sic*], Benusilio, Beraha, Ezratty, Gattegno, and Haim families to Naples in October 1917, see Varsano 1997: 95–102.
16   For example, see Morin 1989: 60–62.
17   For example, Jacques Nahmias and his son Joseph, originally from the North Eastern Greek city of Comotini, founded Maison Jacques Nahmias & Fils in 1922. CAHJP Gr/Sa FO 346 Maison Jacques Nahmias & Fils BA/4661 4/4/1937.
18   Delivanis 1980: 198–199; Koliopoulos and Veremis 2002: 169.
19   No data regarding population distribution by ethnicity is available for Macedonia in general or for Salonica in particular; see Pallis 1925. According to my retrospective calculations based, *inter alia*, on the 1928 Greek census, the Greek component in 1920 comprised about 46% of total population (170,321; Meron 2008a). According to Moutsopoulos (1981: 55), Greeks represented 51 percent of total population in 1920. The 1928 estimate is perhaps biased, influenced by the diplomatic struggle Venizelos conducted during the Paris peace conference, when Greece presented its claims for international recognition of its sovereignty over Salonica and the Macedonian hinterland.
20   On the great fire and subsequent reconstruction of Salonica's urban space see Hastaoglou-Martinidis 1997a, 1997b; Mazower 2004: 324–331; Yerolimpos 1993.
21   The forced population exchanges between Greece and Turkey in January 1923 only reinforced the already established trend. See also Meron 2008a.
22   Of the 1,221,849 refugees who reached Greece, 638,253 (52.2 percent) settled in Macedonia and came to represent 45.25 percent of the regional plain's population (1928). Western Thrace, resting on Greece's eastern borders, absorbed about a third of the refugees, who were allowed to remain there in accordance with the Lausanne Treaty. See Kayser and Thompson 1964: 204, and Mackridge 1997.
23   Following the Balkan Wars, Jews from Ottoman Macedonia's satellite towns, like Kavala, Serres (Greece), and Monastir (Serbia), emigrated to Salonica. See *American Jewish Year Book* 1913: 192–193.

24 Refugee Jews were mainly from urban locations in the Balkans (e.g., Monastir).
25 The Bulgarians left voluntarily, according to a reciprocal agreement calling for the migration of the "racial minorities" of both countries as well as liquidation of their properties. This contract was signed between Bulgaria and Greece immediately after the end of the Balkan Wars, at the Convention of Neuilly (14–27 November 1919). Vacalopoulos 1963: 136; Kontogiorgi 2006: 201; Greek Census 1928, I, Table 12*.
26 While Greater Athens became religiously homogeneous, with over 98 percent of its residents Greek Orthodox (448,161 out of 459,211) in Athens, and over 99 percent (248,047 out of 251,659) in Piraeus, the Jewish population in these cities was negligible (Athens: 1,578 out of 459,211; Piraeus: 167 out of 251,659). Adapted from Greek Census 1928 IV: Tab. 7*.
27 According to the 1928 Greek census, 98 percent (or 54,196 out of 55,250) of the Jewish population (*de facto*) in Salonica declared Judeo-Spanish as their mother tongue, while 91 percent or 172,841 out of the 189,430 non-Jews in the city declared Greek as their mother tongue. Adapted from Greek Census 1928 IV: Tab 13* IIE, 378–379.
28 "Metropolitan Greece" consisted of three major urban centres, each with a population exceeding 100,000.
29 While the former had experienced a century of living in a modern Western state (since 1830) and expressed pride in its capital Athens, the Greek refugees came principally from Asia Minor or Western Thrace, where they had developed their own collective identity as a religious community (*millet*) under Ottoman rule. They aspired to the restoration of the Byzantine capital Constantinople, with language differences (Turkish or demotic Greek) reinforcing their ethnic boundaries. See Hirschon 1989: 1–35; Hirschon 2003: 17–19; Mavrogordatos 1983: 182–225.
30 The Jewish population in Salonica represented 76 percent (55,250 out of 72,791) of the Jewish population in all of Greece and 83 percent (55,250 out of 66,461) of the Jews in New Greece. Adapted from Greek Census 1928 IV: Table 13*Iib, Iie, pp. 246–254; 378–379.
31 In contrast with Diaspora Jews returning to Israel, who saw themselves as exiles in their countries of origin and exhibited feelings of homecoming upon immigrating. On the Repatriated Diaspora in Israel see Ben-Rafael, Olshtain and Geijst 1998: 333.
32 Only 6 percent (4,039 out of 66,461) of the Jews of New Greece declared Greek as their mother tongue, with very few of these (731) from Salonica; compare with the majority among Jews of Old Greece (about 80 percent or 5,051 out of 6,330). Greek Census 1928 IV: Table 13*Iib, pp. 246–254.
33 Mavrogordatos 1983: 227.
34 Lewkowicz 2006: 46–47. Residential concentration of an ethnic minority within a nation-state can be considered a threat to the national integrity of the host state, e.g., the Muslim majority in Malaysia felt threatened by the Chinese minority, which was estimated to be about a third of the total population. See Smith 1976: 10–12; Chirot 1997: 21.
35 Mavrogordatos 1983: 257.
36 On Salonica during World War I, see Vaclopoulos 1963: 132–135.
37 R. Molho 1988: 394.
38 Shibi 1967: 208–210; for the law's articles see Constantopoulou and Veremis 1998: 103–110.
39 Eddy 1931: 35; Kritikos 2001. For similar assimilation policies implemented in other Balkan states, see Stoianovich 1994: 176–177.
40 Lewkowicz 2006: 46–47.
41 See Macartney 1934.
42 See Hastaoglou-Martinidis 1997b.
43 The law was passed after a marketing campaign initiated by Salonica's municipality and the local Chamber of Commerce and Industry. It was justified mainly by the demographic transformation that had transformed the Greek population into the dominant religious group in the city. See Constantopoulou and Veremis 1998: 146–147.
44 For the legislative aspects of the Hellenisation of the day of rest see Pierron 1996: 158–164.
45 Pierron 1996: 164.
46 Author's translation of: "*Le français est devenu ainsi la langue seconde de toute la population instruite. Il est employé dans tous les bureaux, dans toutes les administrations, pour la comptabilité, la correspondance, les relations de service; il sert dans les avis, les affiches. . . .*

Conférences, discours, comptes-rendus des sociétés financièrs, des associations, tout est fait en français. L'étranger qui serait sans contact avec le menu people et qui ne connaîtrait que les hôtels, les restaurants, les cafés, les bureaux des commerçants, les gens de la bonne société aurait l'illusion de vivre dans quelque ville de province de France." Risal [1914] 1917: 347–348.

47 Recanati 1972: 329.

48 The older generation met the challenge of linguistic assimilation through Judeo-Spanish translations of Greek books and attendance at lectures aimed at facilitating the absorption of Greek culture. See Ginio 2002: 247–254.

49 Hellenisation via education was significantly delayed to 1929 due to financier and economic difficulties. Vassilikou 2003: 106.

50 Rozen 2005a: 265–267.

51 Two expressions of this position were encouragement of the study of Turkish and volunteering for military service. About 2,000 Salonican Jews joined the Turkish army, which provided them with kosher food; Jewish merchants also contributed funds to purchase equipment for the Turkish army. See *American Jewish Year Book* 1910; Dumont 1979; Cooperman 1991: 286–290; Benbassa 1994: 462.

52 Ahmad 1982; Molho 1988; Benbassa 1994; Dumont 1994: 73; Mazower 2004. For the Zionist and socialist options in Salonica see Benbassa and Rodrigue 1995: 134–143, 154–158.

53 Joseph Nehama (1978:759-760): "*Le 26 octobre, à 11 heures du matin, les avant-gardes grecques apparaissent devant Salonique, tandis que de leur côté, Bulgares et Serbes avancent à marches forcées. L'armée grecque campe à Bechtchinar, Constantin à Tekeli. Enfin , les 27 et 28 octobre, la ville arbore le drapeau hellénique. Les Bulgares sont arrivés à la Melvi hané et veulent aussi entrer, mais les sept divisions grecques s'y opposent. Constantin s'installe à Salonique.*" According to the protocol "signed on 26 October 1912 (8 November 1912) between the Greek and the Turkish military authorities, Salonica was surrendered to Greece, in whose possession it was to remain until the making of peace". FO 371/1135 Greece, 14 November 1924. Thus citation explains why Richard Clogg (1986: 102) noted 9 November 1912 as the date when of the "capturing [of] Salonica", achieved in effect by the Greek army. Compare with Vacalopoulos 1963: 129–131.

54 Campbell and Sherrard 1968: 114; Clogg 1986: 102.

55 Campbell and Sherrard 1968: 119; Mavrogordatos 1983: 227–229.

56 For comprehensive research on Jewish integration within the Greek nation-state, see Molho 1989; Pierron 1996: 69–90; Mazower 2004: 402–420; Rozen 2005a: 166–181; 255–310.

57 Starr 1945: 329; Dumont 1980; Cooperman 1991: 230–235; Benbassa and Rodrigue 1995: 154–158.

58 In David Florentin's words, "*Salonique, capital d'une Macédoin autonome, conserverait au moins une partie de son commerce actuel.*" Author's translation: "Salonica, the capital of an autonomous Macedonia, would retain at least part of its current trade." CZA, Z3/2, D. Florentin to Central Zionist Organisation, Berlin 17 December 1912; see also *American Jewish Year Book* 1914: 196–197; Gelber 1955; R. Molho 1988, 1992.

59 In the framework of the capitulations between the Ottoman Empire and Spain, some Sephardic Jews had received the status of protected persons under Spanish consular rather than Ottoman jurisdiction. After the breakup of the Ottoman Empire, Spain offered these persons the opportunity to obtain full citizenship while remaining in their own countries. This was accomplished by a 1924 decree, which provided descents of Jews exiled from Spain in 1492 full-fledged Spanish citizenship by the mere formal application to a resident consul, to be completed by the end of 1930. Consequently, Jews who did not wish to become Greek citizens might become Spanish citizens. See *American Jewish Year Book* 1925: 76–77. According to R. Molho (1988: 395), 450 Jews held Austrian, 750 held Spanish, and 1,200 held Portuguese citizenship. For the Greek census data, see Meron 2008a: 43–45.

60 *American Jewish Year Book* 1914: 198.

61 *American Jewish Year Book* 1917: 282–283.

62 In fact, the Jews of Salonica first participated in the war during 1940–1941, along the Albanian frontier. See Moisis 1972a: 331. On Asher Moisis, see Salem 1999: 20–21.

63 Vassilikou 2003: 105.

64 Constantopoulou and Veremis 1998: Law 2456, article 16. On the indecision exhibited by foreign Jews regarding recruitment into the army of their "citizenship homeland" (e.g., Italy, France, Austria, Belgium, etc.) especially after the Allied armies were positioned in Macedonia during World War I, see: Morin 1989: 67–88.

65 On the intensifying rifts and subsequent crises between the two Greek political parties, see Mavrogordatos 1983: 273–302. On the Jewish vote, see idem: 239, 253, 280–288.

66 Mavrogordatos 1983: 231–236; Lewkowicz 2006: 48–49.

67 This behaviour contrasted with Jewish political activity during the Ottoman era, when the "compact voice" of a Jewish minority lacking any political aspirations supported the rule of the Muslim elite. Incorporation into the Greek nation-state thus altered the Jews' position. See Kansu 1997: 206–207.

68 Mavrogordatos 1983: 238–239.

69 On inter-war electoral engineering, which assigned higher weights to the preferred electoral regions found in Old Greece, see Mavrogordatos 1983: 351–353.

70 On this law, see Mavrogordatos 1983: 98.

71 About 52 percent (638,253 out of 1,221,849) of the refugees settled in Macedonia, to form about 45 percent of the region's total population by 1928. Similarly, about a third of Western Thrace's population, in addition to the Turks, were excluded from the Transfer. See Kayser and Thompson 1964: 204; Mackridge 1997; Kontogiorgi 2006.

72 Mavrogordatos 1983: 291–295; 351–353.

73 Lewkowicz 2006: 36–37; Carabott 1997; Alexandris 2003; Mackridge & Yannakakis 1997.

74 Kallis 2006: 37.

75 Cited in Mazower 2004: 409–410.

76 For a vivid description of the Jewish émigré embarrassment regarding the declaration of their national origins when in their new destinations (e.g., France), see Morin 1989: 67–88.

77 For a comprehensive survey of Jewish–Greek rivalry in Salonica during the 1910s, see Meron 2006.

78 According to the Treaty of Sèvres, the District of Smyrna was transferred to Greek authority in 1920.

79 Pierron 1996: 167–171.

80 Kallis 2006: 49–50.

81 Voutira 2003.

82 Hirschon 2003: 6. League of Nations (1926).

83 Freris 1986: 48, 63–67; Pentzopoulos 1962: 145–149.

84 Hastaoglou-Martinidis 1997b: 498–499; Mazower 2004: 351–355; 362–363.

85 Dagkas 2003; Marantzidis and Mavrodi 2004.

86 Mazower 1991: 137.

87 Kallis 2006: 36; Kritikos 2000: 205; Mavrogordatos 1983: 147–152, 255, 258–259; Mazower 1991: 128; 2004: 410–416.

88 Koliopoulos and Veremis 2004 [2002]: 132; Mavrogordatos 1983: 256–262.

89 Marantzidis and Mavrodi 2004.

90 Kallis 2006: 36.

91 Abatzopoulou 1997: 218; Vassilikou 2003: 111.

92 Vassilikou 2003: 112

93 Meron 2008a.

94 *American Jewish Year Book* 1912–1913: 207–210.

95 For details regarding these events, see Mazower 2004: 270.

96 Data derived by Devin Naar from Ellis Island passenger lists indicate that from 1909 to 1912, total Jewish emigration from Salonica to the US equalled 189, about half of the 362 immigrants (Jews and non-Jews) from Salonica to reach US shores. See Naar 2007: 443–47.

97 Nehama [1989]: 244.

98 *American Jewish Year Book* 1914: 197–198.

99 For an analysis of the Jewish emigration to the US as a "response to the new dynamics of the consolidating Greek nation-state", see Naar 2007. For data, see ibid: 445, Table 1.

100 Naar 2007: 460–462.

101 Naar 2007: 445, Table 1.

102 Hastaoglou-Martinidis 1997a, 1997b; Mazower 2004: 324–331; Yerolimpos 1993.

103 On the emigration of Jewish Italian families to Naples in October 1917, particularly of the families Isaac Shaki [*sic*], Benusilio, Beraha, Ezratty, Gattegno, and Haim, see Varsano 1997: 95–102.

104 The Jewish proprietors accused the Greek government of damaging their legitimate interests in the expropriated plots. See for example CZA Z4/1523, a report sent to Justice Louis D. Brandeis, President of the Zionist Organisation of America, on the condition of Salonica's Jews on 19 June 1919.

105 Rosen 2005: 174 quotes Luigi Villari, a contemporary, who documented (1922) the fire and wrote that the government's original decision was to evacuate the Jewish survivors to Old Greece, the islands and other countries. The Jews gave clear signals that they would refuse such a proposition. For more on the expropriation of Jewish property, see Constantopoulou and Veremis, 1998: 71–72; Yerolimpos 1993.

106 The plots were expropriated against a special, essentially worthless bond supporting former ownership claims. See Meron 2008a.

107 On emigration to France, see Aelion 1997.

108 See Meron 2008a.

109 Only 320 out of 1,876 Jews in Central Greece and Eubée, mainly including the Jews of Athens and Piraeus, declared Spanish as their mother tongue, compared with 1,403 out of 1,876 who declared Greek their mother tongue. See Greek Census 1928 IV: Table IIb, p. 247.

110 "*Marseille est une Salonique non pas séfarade, mais française. C'est aussi un grand port, où l'on peut pratiquer les mêmes activités qu'à Salonique. C'est à peu près le même climat méditerranéen. . . . C'est le même mode de vie . . .* " See Morin 1989: 90.

111 On the Naturalisation Act and the establishment of a federal naturalisation bureaucracy in the US in 1906, see Bloemraad 2006.

112 See M. Molho 1967: 24. There are no data available on the precise scope of emigration from Salonica by year, nor for the entire period. Nehama [1935] 1978: 707 estimated that there were a total of 15,000 migrants from Salonica to France. For micro-data on migrants from Salonica, see Rozen 2005a: Appendix 1.

113 This agency was instituted by the law on 11 August 1926. However, foreigners had been required to purchase, renew and carry an identity card since 1917. This card restricted the immigrant to specific geographical areas and determined the type of work the migrant could do. The law prohibited the employment of immigrants who lacked an identity card, thus transferring the enforcement of the law regarding identity cards to the employers. See Bonnet 1976: 145–150.

114 *Guide Sam* 1930: 140.

115 Morin 1989: 87–88, 148–149.

116 Risal [1914] 1917: 345, 347.

117 *Guide Sam* 1930: 139–141.

118 Morin 1989: 148.

119 Gil 1950: 28, Table 4.

120 Molho 2002.

121 On social conditions in Greece, see Mavrogordatos 1983.

122 See Elbaz 1967: 226–227; M. Molho 1986: 31.

123 Vacolopoulos 1972: 132–133.

124 Mavrogordatos, 1983: 255–257; see also Vassilikou 2003: 107–113.

125 For a comprehensive discussion of these topics, see Rozen 2005a.

126 "Surprisingly, it was the large store owners, the bankers and the rich, who had wanted to open their business on the Sabbath" (D. Recanati 1972: 348).

127 On the local and international struggle to preserve the Sabbath in Salonica, see Recanati 1972: 334–356; Constantopoulou and Veremis 1998: 146–147.

128 Archives of the Alliance Israélite Universelle, Grèce I. C. 48 M. Benghiat Salonica, 1 December 1909, cited in Rodrigue 1993: 235.

129 Y. Uziel 1967b: 128.

130 Two Turkish and one Jewish member controlled the barbers' corporation. See Angel and Levi, *Almanach Israélite* 5683 [1923]: 128–135; Emmanuel 1972: 198; Y. Uziel 1967b: 128–129.

131 For a comprehensive survey of the management of these institutions, see David (Daut) Levi

[1941] 1986: 127–148. For the adapted Jewish community budgets during 1928–1934 see Meron 2010 .
132 Shibi 1967: 208–210; Constantopoulou and Veremis 1998: 103–110.
133 For a similar case see Lewin-Epstein and Semyonov 1994: 625–627.
134 See Mavrogordatos 1983: 281.
135 D. Levi [1941] 1986.
136 Nehama 1978: 773; R. Molho 1997: 32–35. For a comprehensive survey of the Jewish education system, including its curricula, see R. Molho 2005a. For the detailed list of Jewish Schools in Salonica in 1912 see Ibid, p. 131, Table 1.
137 Constantopoulou and Veremis 1998: No. 44, p.154.
138 See Strumza 1995: 10. Translated from Hebrew by the author. Among the foreign schools was the Lycée Français.
139 Angel and Levi, *Almanach Israélite* 5683 [1923]: 179.
140 Angel and Levi, *Almanach Israélite* 5683 [1923]: 126. See also illustrations 10, 11.
141 Angel and Levi, *Almanach Israélite* 5683 [1923]: 176–177, 123.
142 R. Molho 2005a: 135.
143 *Guide Sam* 1930: 914.
144 R. Molho 2005b.
145 Opportunities to acquire training in the free professions depended primarily on private resources, and will be discussed separately outside this research. For Jewish professionals during the Ottoman Era, see Meron 2005b; for Jewish engineers, see Meron 2009 (unpublished paper).

Chapter 4

1 *American Jewish Year Book* 1913: 204–205.
2 Koliopoulos and Veremis 2004: 200–204; Kontogiorgi 2006.
3 Gounaris 1998.
4 Mazower 2004: 301–304.
5 Revenues from port levies were transferred to the IFC, which controlled state revenues from the customs duties collected in Greek ports as well as the taxes collected from state monopolies (e.g., cigarette paper, salt, gasoline, playing cards, stamps, and tobacco). DOT 1921; Botsas 1987: 213.
6 Petridis 1997: 133–135.
7 To illustrate, in a petition submitted to the British government, the Jewish merchant Jacob Sides asked which law validated the lease of its assets in Salonica. The lease contract was signed with the Oriental Railway Co. on 21 March 1910. FO 371/1135 Greece, 14 November 1924.
8 According to the report of the Union des Associations Israélites, "Many of the Turks and the Albanians have been exterminated, many have abandoned the country. Thousands of dollars owed by them to Jews can never be collected." *American Jewish Year Book* 1913: 205; see also R. Molho 1988; Gounaris 1998.
9 *Austrian Report* 1915: 12.
10 Lefeuvre-Méaulle 1916: 233.
11 A uniform 15 percent *ad valorem* levy was imposed on all imported items, with an additional 1.5 percent transferred to city coffers. "Transit goods" exempt from the city tax (*Austrian Report*, 1915: 13) included fifteen basic goods such as coffee, flour, sugar, alcohol, machinery, iron, coal, and salt among others. See Lefeuvre-Méuelle 1916: 234–235.
12 Division of the country into regional protected markets by means of a national network of toll stations and communal taxes were counted among the institutional obstacles to industrial development because they impeded the creation of a unified domestic market by helping to perpetuate barter and self-sufficiency. Louri and Pepelasis Minoglou 2002: 331.
13 Port activity experienced a sharp but temporary slowdown in 1914 as imports declined from an annual average of FRF 120 million during Ottoman rule to FRF 52 million by 1914;

exports declined from FRF 35–40 million to FRF 19 million in the same period. See Lefeuvre-Méuelle 1916: 234–238; *Annuaire Commercial* 1922: 90–92.

14 Mavrogordatos 1983: 280–288; Mazower 1991: 51–71; Vafopoulos 1993: 256–257.

15 Delivanis 1980: 196.

16 HMSO 1920: 25, 30; Delivanis 1980: 195–196.

17 According to a report prepared by the British Consul, the US absorbed Macedonia's entire opium export harvest and 60 percent of Greek tobacco while the UK absorbed 25 percent of tobacco exports. See HMSO 1920: 20–21.

18 Alternatively, a labour shortage indicates industry's growing pull on the labour market.

19 Louri and Pepelasis Minoglou 2002: 329.

20 Gounaris 1998.

21 The General Bank was absorbed by the Popular Bank of Greece in 1927 and the Bank of Industry failed in 1928. See Dritsas 1992: 206–207.

22 At the beginning of this period (1914), Venizelos granted tax breaks within the "new terri-tories" to prevent popular opposition to his regime. Despite the need to finance the war effort, his government refrained from introducing fiscal reforms in Salonica during the war years. His reasons were: (1) the internal weaknesses following the national divisions within Greece (1915–1917), and (2) his fear of profiteering as a result of shortages. See Mazower 1991: 56, 60–61.

23 Lampe and Jackson 1982: 347.

24 HMSO 1920: 15.

25 Lampe and Jackson 1982: 336–375.

26 Mavrogordatos 1983: 131, n. 58.

27 As the British Council describes it: "When a Greek firm wishes to export bills of exchange, or open credits in payment of merchandise to be imported, application has to be made to the Chamber of Commerce at Athens, which furnishes guarantees on behalf of the importing firm to the Ministry of Finance, who through the Exchange Control Committee, issues the necessary permit to authorise the sale of bills of exchange by the banks. Thus, the Greek importer is under the direct control of the chambers of commerce not only by the reason of the hold which they have at present over the importers, but also by virtue of their power to refuse to furnish guarantees on behalf of firms who do not comply with their regu-lations. It was stated further that the Greek Chamber of Commerce at Athens was considering the establishment of a 'black list' of defaulting merchants, both Greek and foreign. The entry of the name of the firm on this 'black list' would involve a general boycott of the firm in Greece and render it practically impossible for a firm so listed to do further trade in the country." See HMSO 1920: 23–24.

28 K und K. Österreichisches Handelsmuseum, *Salonik, Topographisch – Statistische Über-sichten*, Wien Dezember 1915 (II.41.821), (hereinafter: *Austrian Report* 1915). The compendium *Saloniker Firmen - Verzeichnis: Nach Branchen alphabetisch geordnet nach dem stande von 1913* (free translation: Index of Salonican firms in alphabetical order and branch, 1913), placed at the end of the report, was apparently compiled primarily from information gathered from the *Annuaire Oriental 1913* (The Ottoman Yearbook). For the reorganised list of Jewish firms, see Meron 2005b, Appendix A.

29 Grèce, Ministère de L'Economie Nationale, *Statistique Générale de la Grèce* (1927). *Recensement des Entreprises Industrielles au 18 Décembre 1920*, vol. D, *Nombre, personnel et force motrice des entreprises recensées en général*, Athens: Imprimerie National, Table 9.

30 Kuznets 1960: 1624.

31 $D = \frac{1}{2} |a_i - b_i|$, where a_i and b_i are the percentages of firms belonging to a given sector (i) in the entire firm sample structure in 1912 and 1921, respectively. The value of the Dissimilarity Index ranged from zero (total similarity) to 100 (no similarity).

32 HMSO 1920; Lampe and Jackson 1982: 347–348.

33 HMSO 1920.

34 *Annuaire Commercial* 1922: 90–92.

35 Meron 2005b.

36 Baxevanis 1963: 15–16; 70–71; draft of the "Convention Relative to Transit through Salonica Concluded between Greece and Serbia" had been completed by 1914: see *The American Journal of International Law* 13(4) (1919): 441–456.

37   Gounaris 1998; Hekimoglou 1997: 143.
38   For more on the emigration of Jewish bankers from Salonica to Paris, where they relocated their banks, see Aelion 1997. For more on the emigration of Italian Jewish families (e.g., the Shaki [*sic*], Benusilio, Beraha, Ezratty, Gattegno, and Haim families) from Salonica to Naples in October 1917, see Varsano 1997.
39   Delivanis 1980.
40   See Morin 1989: 59–67.
41   On the emigration of upper-class Jews to Turkey after the Greek incorporation see Nehama 1989: 244. According to the genealogical research conducted by Mario Modiano between 2000 and 2004, Italian Jews, e.g., Menachem Modiano, avoided confiscation and expulsion during the Italian-Turkish war (1911) by renouncing their Italian citizenship in favour of Turkish citizenship. After the incorporation, these Jews left for Constantinople.
42   In 1920, Gino Fernandez established a partnership in Paris under the name Fernandez & Bloch, which was eventually dissolved. On 15 May 1936, Gino, now domiciled in Paris, founded Fernandez & Derin, an SA that operated a factory producing automobile bodies (*carrosseries*). CAHJP Gr/Sa FO 346 Gino Mario Fernandez BA/4784 31/05/1937.
43   See <http://www.amarfamily.org/histories/visas.php>, accessed 15/10/2009.
44   CAHJP Gr/Sa FO 346 Gino Mario Fernandez BA/4784 31/05/1937.
45   Previously, Nefussy, Bivas & Cie. (1910–1917). CAHJP Gr/Sa FO 346 Albert Elie Nefussy BA/4616, 27/05/1939.
46   CAHJP Gr/Sa FO 346 Maison Jacques Nahmias & Fils BA/4661, 07/04/1937.
47   CAHJP Gr/Sa FO 346 Jacob M. Nahmias BA/4657, 07/04/1937.
48   CAHJP Gr/Sa FO 346 Liaou Camhi BA/406 1/6/1937; BA/77, 26/4/1935.
49   CAHJP Gr/Sa FO 346 Elie Isac Massoth BA/4639, 31/03/1937.
50   CAHJP Gr/Sa FO 346 Isac & Joseph Beja BA/410, 2/6/1937.
51   CAHJP Gr/Sa FO 346 Menahem Rousso & Fils. BA/none, 29/8/35; BA/4436, 12/11/36.
52   CAHJP Gr/Sa FO 346 Salomon Menahem Rousso BA/246, 10/09/1936.
53   CAHJP Gr/Sa FO 346 Saul J. Capon BA/131, 21/1/1936. For a similar case of a non-Jewish entrepreneur, see CAHJP Gr/Sa FO 346 D. Evanghelopoulos BA/394, 20/5/37.
54   Hastaoglou-Martinidis 1997: 164.
55   Mavrogordatos 1983: 280–282; Mazower, 2004: 302.
56   Delivanis 1980: 198–199.
57   In order to measure the similarity or entrepreneurial branch segregation of Jews as opposed to Greeks in 1921, we used the Duncan and Duncan (1955) dissimilarity index (D), calculated as the sum of the total averages of the positive percentage differences between the two firm distributions (Jewish and Greek) by economic sector, $D = \frac{1}{2} |ai - bi|$, where ai and bi are the percentages of firms belonging to a given branch (i) of the separate firm structures in 1912 and 1921, respectively. The values of the Dissimilarity Index range between zero (total similarity or no ethnic segregation) to 100 (no similarity or total ethnic segregation). The long-term (1912–1921) transformations in the two entrepreneurial structures by economic sector were similarly calculated.
58   *Annuaire Commercial* 1922: 242.
59   *Annuaire Commercial* 1922: 166.
60   *Annuaire Commercial* 1922: 35.
61   Kloosterman and Rath 2003; M. Schrover et al. 2006.
62   Razin and Light refer to "entrepreneurial niches" as resulting from the clustering of immigrants of the same nationality in specific industries rather than their fanning out in search of the best opportunities throughout the market. Cf. Light and Gold 2000: 18.
63   Although the commonly used ratio for determining a niche is over-representation of 1.5 (Wilson 2003: 438–439), the quantitative criterion for demonstrating a Jewish *niche* was set at about 1.2 due to data constraints. Cf. Wright and Ellis 2000: 588.
64   Hekimoglou 1997.
65   *Austrian Report* 1915: 50.
66   Gounaris 1997; Colonas 2002: 169; see also Chapter 10.
67   The French text reads: "*Un Grand nombre de ses commerçants augmentèrent considérablement leurs capitaux, plusieurs s'enrichirent, et si le malencontreux incendie ne survenait pas,*

dont les victimes furent nombreuses, Salonique aurait attiré la jalousie de ses ennemis."
Annuaire Commercial 1922: 94.

68 Mazower, 1991: 56.

69 Sfika 1990.

70 Theophanides 1991.

71 Toledano 1986: 204. Since the Greeks perceived Jewish bankers as cornerstones of the banking industry, Jews took part in the management of the local branch of the National Bank of Greece. See *Austrian Report* 1915: 127–130.

72 According to an advertisement, in addition to its Salonica branch, this bank, with headquarters located in Constantinople, also had branches in Kavalla as well as in Smyrna, Adrianople, and Samsoun; capital of [FR]F 30,000,000, regular reserves of [FR]F 2,057,533 and special reserves of [FR]F 8,000,000; see *Annuaire Commercial* 1922: 114. For the transformations experienced by the Banque de Salonique, see *Austrian Report* 1915: 127–130; and Mourghianni-Estela 1996: 598.

73 The Salonica branch at Verias 4 was only one of its several branches dispersed throughout Greece (in Piraeus, Patras, Corfu, Volos, etc.); it had capital amounting to only GRD 20,000,000 and reserves of GRD 10,123,920.45. See *Annuaire Commercial* 1922: 20.

74 The Banque d'Athènes SA held capital of GRD 48,000,000. It also operated through the Salonica office of the Near East Commercial Company, SA, with headquarters in Athens (capital: GRD 2,000,000), which dealt in commercial and maritime affairs. This company also had branches in Piraeus, Constantinople, and Smyrna. *Annuaire Commercial* 1922: 233.

75 According to an advertisement, this bank was licensed to conduct exchange operations; it listed capital of GRD 1,200,000, and reserves of GRD 517,312.65. See *Annuaire Commercial* 1922: 115; compare with section 5.4, Chapter 5.

76 DOT 1921:11.

77 See the illustration on this book's front cover.

78 Megas 1993: 89; Anna Mourghianni-Estela 1996: 595.

79 On the development of the self-sufficiency in cereals policy in Greece before the 1929 slump, see Mazower 1991: 88–91.

80 On the Greek-owned brewery, see *Austrian Report 1915*: 69; Quataert 1993: 187. This merger included the ice factory maintained by the Olympos brewery: see *Annuaire Commercial* 1922: 303; for a photograph of the brewery, see Megas 1993: 90.

81 *Annuaire Commercial* 1922: 33.

82 *Annuaire Commercial* 1922: 50.

83 The following firm names indicate the Greek initiative for "Coopératives en Denrées Coloniales": Christos Lampoudis, Georges D. Rompapas; Constantin Parashos, Thomas Xenos & Cie. See *Annuaire Commercial* 1922: 330–331.

84 *Salonique, Ville-Mère en Israël* 1967: 23.

85 The only similar Jewish cooperative was led by Isakino Saltiel. See Appendix 6.1, No. 57.

86 For more on consumer cooperatives in nation-states, see Deutsch 1966: 47–55.

87 Roupa and Hekimoglou 2004: 372–374.

88 *Annuaire Commercial* 1922: 178.

89 *Annuaire Commercial* 1922: 121.

90 *Annuaire Commercial* 1922: 231.

91 Compare with Morin 1989: 95.

92 This crop level reached 47,443 *okes* (1 *oke* = 1.28 kg) out of total agricultural exports of 5,825,008 *okes*. *Annuaire Commercial* 1922: 347–348. This quantity, equivalent to 56,887 kg, was below the 1911 and 1912 levels (82,000 kg and 132,000 kg, respectively), but above the 32,000 kg exported in 1913. See Eddy 1931: 11. For 1911–1913 data, see *Austrian Report* 1915: 78, 94.

93 *Annuaire Commercial* 1922: 11.

94 *Annuaire Commercial* 1922: 29.

95 In the nineteenth century some Livornese families changed their surnames from Salom to Salmon while others became Pacifici. See Sebag 2002.

96 Like opium, silk cocoons formed only a small percentage (2.6 percent) of total agriculture exports, but continued as a Jewish niche within the transit trade. They amounted to 149,564

okes out of total agricultural exports of 5,825,008 *okes*. See *Annuaire Commercial* 1922: 347–348.

97 Advertisements in the *Annuaire Commercial* 1922 shed light on the history of these merchant houses but also indicate the consumption patterns for luxuries: Bourla S., previously Maison M. & S. Bourla, successors of Is. & M. Bourla House of Confidence (est. 1850) [*sic*]; diamonds, pearls, precious stones; jewellers; watch making; silverware; gifts; representatives of La Maison Christofle & Cie de Paris; artefacts, gold and silver plate jewellery *Annuaire Commercial* 1922: 237; Gattegno M. & Cie., representative of Longines: watches, jewellery; silversmith and goldsmith; artefacts; Mallah Frères: Omega watches; silverware and jewellery; purchase, and reselling of jewellery and precious stones *Annuaire Commercial* 1922: 118; See also Appendix 4.1, nos. 345–354.

98 For contemporary testimony, see for example Toledano 1986: 203. On Jewish domination of the jewellery trade, see *Salonique, Ville-Mère en Israël* 1967: 237.

99 *Annuaire Commercial* 1922: 236.

100 The city's mills suffered from production costs that exceeded those of their competitors in the countryside due these reasons: 1. Energy costs, especially coal, compared to hydro-energy available in interior Macedonia; 2. Higher land values; 3. Higher labour costs (1913), which could be three times higher than in the countryside, especially due to labour market competition from the booming tobacco industry, and 4. Countryside mills could add lines of productions (grinding flour; weaving cotton) to increased income. See Quataert 1995: 64.

101 Quataert 1993: 182–183.

102 These mills were exempted from paying taxes to the Ottoman government in the late 1880s, a policy that helped improve their market position. See Quataert 1993: 181–182; Quataert 1995: 63; see also Mourghianni-Estela 1996: 595; Megas 1991: 94.

103 Imported refined cotton threads produced in Italy, England, and Austria with new technology not yet introduced in Salonica, were valued at (1913) FRF 912,403, and third in import value after sugar and flour (*Austrian Report* 1915: 85).

104 HMSO 1920: 13–14.

105 Venizelos supported the tobacco workers for similar reasons; see Starr 1945: 331–332; Avdela 1998: 432.

106 *Annuaire Commercial* 1922: 304.

107 Mazower 1991: Table 4.6.

108 The rope factory was owned by Iraklis Hadjimoula. See *Annuaire Commercial* 1922: 304.

109 *Annuaire Commercial* 1922: 293.

110 Lapavitsas 2006.

111 DOT 1921: 17. Only in 1930–1931 were Greek textile plants, including Helleniki Eriourgia ["Greek Wool Industry"] to acquire finishing and bleaching machines from Germany. See Papastefanaki 2004; 2007.

112 Indeed, several large knitting and flannel shirt plants operated in Salonica as early as the 1880s. See Quataert 1993: 180.

113 In 1912 the distribution of firms included in "wood and construction materials" by ethnic ownership was as follows: eight Jewish-owned firms, two Greek-owned firms, and three Turkish-owned firms. The firms exclusively engaged in "wood for construction trade" in 1912 included seven Jewish-owned firms: Mordoh Joseph, Rafael Avram, Estormez Daniel et Fils, Mallah Aron et Cie., Pelossof Joseph et Cie., Saltiel Daniel Semtov et Cie., Saltiel Moise & Cie. In addition to Navarro, the firm of Hane et Cie. was also engaged in "construction material". See Meron 2005b: Appendix A, nos. 146–152; 93.

114 DOT 1923: 19.

115 The firms engaged in "wood coal trade" in 1912 included eight Jewish-owned firms: Florentin Jacques, Nahman Isac, Nahman Ovadia, Haim Eilo et Cie., Almochnino Gabriel J., Almochnino Haim, Saltiel Juda et Perez, Hananel Eliakim. See Meron 2005b: Appendix A, nos. 133–140.

116 *Annuaire Commercial* 1922: 162–163.

117 HMSO 1920: 12.

118 See Meron 2005b: Appendix A, nos. 406–410.

119 See Meron 2005c.

120 For example, in 1912 the value of the bones exported to England and Austro-Hungary was

about FRF34,000; the rags exported to Germany, Austro-Hungary, England, Italy, and France were valued at FRF30,000. See *Austrian Report* 1915: 80.
121 On the trade in trash from textile or hide industry or second-hand goods, considered "Jewish", see Gross 1975: 266–269; Garncarska-Kadary 1985: 168.
122 Beeswax from Salonica was produced in considerable quantity but consumed locally in the manufacture of candles. An insignificant amount was exported (DOT 1921: 17).
123 *Annuaire Commercial* 1922: 242.
124 Tannery: Georguiou Frères et Cie.; fur tinting: Grigor Papasoglou et Cie.; furs: Thomas Yanoutas, Naoum Papageorgio, P. Mantopoulo et Fils and Papantina Frère et Zografos. *Annuaire Commercial* 1922: 303–304; 342.
125 *Annuaire Commercial* 1922: 174.
126 *Annuaire Commercial* 1922: 122.
127 *Annuaire Commercial* 1922: 18.
128 *Austrian Report* 1915: 70.

Chapter 5

1 These resources represented compensation to the refugees for their status as political evacuees who were prohibited from transferring assets from their former home countries. See Light and Gold 2000: 125.
2 On the brutal competition encountered by Jewish micro-scale entrepreneurs, see Mourghianni-Estela 1996: 596–597; Roupa and Hekimoglou 2004: 23–42; Hekimoglou 2004: 2–3; Mazower 2004: 326–328.
3 Disaggregating the census data (1928) on the occupational distribution of the Greek refugees who arrived in Salonica after 1922 allows us to derive the occupational patterns exhibited by Salonica's indigenous Greeks. The indigenous component of the population (which generally included Jews) was calculated by deducting the number of refugees from the appropriate total population segments. For the indicated trends among the Jewish employees (integrated among the indigenous employees) in the various branches and occupations, see Meron 1999; 2005d; 2008a; 2008b.
4 Eddy 1931: 116–120; Pentzopoulos 1962: 136–140; Hirschon 1989: 39–42; Hirschon 2003; Kritikos 2000.
5 See Baxevanis 1963: 13–16; 70–71.
6 Some researchers contend that the actual starting date of the Serbian free zone's activities was even later, that is, 1 January 1929. See Dagkas 2003: 351–353; Baxevanis 1963: 13–16; 76–80.
7 In 1929, about 4,120 wagons of imports to Yugoslavia and about 1,870 wagons from Yugoslavia passed through the Yugoslav free zone. Only 29 wagons of imports made their way to Bulgaria through Salonica's port while no Bulgarian exports arrived there. *Guide Sam* 1930: 889.
8 *Guide Sam* 1930: 889–891.
9 The Bulgarian regions of Doubnitza, which provided tobacco, and Perinn [or Pirin], which provided coal, were situated proximate to the Greek frontier. *Guide Sam* 1930: 889–891.
10 Roupa and Hekimoglou 2004: 25.
11 HSMO 1920: 28.
12 Baxevanis 1963: 24.
13 According to the British Consulate General, "Passenger traffic from Central and Eastern Europe towards the South-East [*sic*] basin of the Mediterranean would be much facilitated by the adoption the Salonica route. . . . " PRO FO371/9894 , Salonica, 7 July 1924.
14 Baxevanis 1963: 60.
15 Baxevanis 1963: 15.
16 Baxevanis 1963: 60; Petzopoulos 1962: 166.
17 Following Kavalla (ranked first in tobacco) and Patras (ranked second in red currants). These cities were ranked ninth and third, respectively, with respect to imports. See DOT 1925: 48; and Gounaris 1998.

18   Adapted from Greek Census 1928, vol. I, Tables 4*, 6*, 12*.
19   Official resettlement policy promoted the growth of a chain of Macedonian towns dedi-
      cated to furnishing urban services and markets as well as outlets for agricultural exports.
      See Eddy 1931: Chapter 6.
20   These factors contributed to the development of political-oriented population concentra-
      tions in the new "inheritance" states, such as Istanbul and its environs (see Keyder 1995).
      This trend was particularly remarkable when compared with the population concentrations
      observed in the capitals of the neighbouring Balkan states. For each 100 Greek residents
      (1928), 7.3 dwelt in Athens; this should be compared with the rates of 3.7 per 100 residents
      in Sofia, 4.4 in Bucharest, and 1.9 in Belgrade. Yet, the concentration rate in Greece was
      lower than that observed in Central European capitals such as Budapest (10.8) and Vienna
      (27.9) (Greek Census 1928, vol. 2, Table 26; see also Lampe and Jackson 1982).
21   For British Consul data, see DOT 1923–1924.
22   See the data in the CD attached to Dagkas 2003: table 111.
23   Christodoulaki 2001; Kritikos 2000.
24   According to the British Consulate's Commercial Secretary R. Turner, "This increase in
      the number of industrial enterprises was mainly due to private initiative." Turner added
      that " . . . realising the importance of better industrial development both from the economic
      and social point of view, [the Greek government] has taken various measures to encourage
      it. Apart from the measure of protection afforded under the tariff, special privileges have
      been granted to those prepared to start new industries such as duty-free importation of
      machinery and raw materials: the preservation in the first instance of Greek raw materials
      – e.g., hides – for home industry." DOT 1927: 25–26.
25   Calculating import duty as percentage of the sum of cargo, insurance, and freight costs,
      tariff levels on manufactured imports reached the following levels: soap, 215 percent;
      varnish, 70–100; tiles, 60–1000; bricks, 50–90; cement, 60–62; beer, 62; bottles, 47; shoe
      leather, 40–48; paint, 35–50; cotton thread, 20–35. Mazower 1991: 96, Table 4.6; see also
      Dameskenides 1974; Koliopoulos and Veremis 2004: 169–170.
26   Statistics for 1927 also show considerably increased foreign trade and local industrial
      production: DOT 1928: 24.
27   Louri and Pepelasis Minoglou 2002: 331.
28   Christodoulaki 2001.
29   Mazower 1991: 104-106.
30   Kontogiorgi 2003: 66.
31   Dritsas 1992: 208, 210, 216 note 11.
32   According to statistics supplied to the German consul by Salonica's Chamber of Industry
      and Commerce in 1924, there were 1,515 Jewish companies active out of a total of 3,400.
      Dublon-Knebel 2007: 76–78: Consul Schönberg, Salonica to FO, Berlin on the anti-Jewish
      atmosphere in Salonica and the activity of the *Ethniki Etaireia*, 30 November 1938;
      according to data derived from Routzounis & Mihaïlidis (1926), there were 1,470 Jewish-
      owned firms out of a total 7,000 in 1926. See Mourghianni-Estela 1996: 599.
33   According to Ioannis Skourtis (1992: 238) cited by Vassilikou 2003: 114, many Jewish-
      owned commercial houses as well as retail shops closed following the emigration of
      Salonican Jews to France in the 1920s.
34   The loss of Greek entrepreneurial know-how in Western Anatolia had deleterious effects
      on its economy. See Aktar 2003: 90.
35   League of Nations (1926) *Greek Refugee Settlement* (Geneva) also cited in Hekimoglou
      1997: 146; Aktar 2003: 82.
36   For the distribution of the refugees according their origin, see also Sandis 1973: 168–169;
      Kontogiorgi 2006: 93–97.
37   The property deserted by the Turks in "New Greece" had been transferred to the Greek
      government by the Refugee Settlement Commission (RSC) and from there to the National
      Bank of Greece. This institution held the property as collateral for government bonds. See
      Eddy 1931: 165; Pentzopoulos 1962: 145–149; Nehama 1978: 771.
38   The 1930 industrial census listed 11,355 businesses in Salonica, employing 37,368 persons.
      Of these, 4,175 (37 percent) were industries and craft workshops employing 20,646, with
      7,180 (63 percent) commercial concerns employing a total of 16,722 people. Whereas 57

percent of commercial enterprises employed only one person, 47 percent of all industries employed only two to five persons (Hekimoglou 1997: 146).

39 Similar sources are the commercial almanacs written by J. S. Modiano, which also classi-fied firms according to commodity-based categories.

40 Published in 1930, *Guide Sam*, edited by Sam Lévy, for the most part mirrored the commer-cial situation of 1929. However, review of the data reveals that it contains some firms that had been dissolved in 1929 (e.g., Scialom, est. 1865).

41 Roupa and Hekimoglou, who also based their research on local commercial guides, came to a similar conclusion. Salonica of 1928 was completely different from Salonica of 1912 from this perspective. See Roupa and Hekimoglou 2004: 34.

42 Military equipment suppliers (0 out of 2 firms); contractors (0 out of 3). See *Guide Sam* 1930.

43 Banque d'Athens, SA, established 1893; headquarters: Athens; branches: ninety-six in Greece, nine abroad (in the US, England, Egypt, and Cyprus); capital: GRD. 100,800,000; reserves: GRD 221,800,000 (*Guide Sam* 1930: 934). Banque d'Orient SA, also popular among Jewish merchants, offered, in addition, savings deposits, savings funds, and safe-deposit boxes; capital: Frs. 35,000,000; headquarters: Athens; branches: Salonica and Egypt (Alexandria, Cairo, and Zagazig), and others (*Guide Sam* 1930: 938).

44 The following Jewish banks had branches only in Salonica: Banque Benveniste SA (Illustration 1); Banque Amar SA (it was connected with Banque Saul Amar, Paris), Rue Ermou 1; in 1930 its capital was GRD 2,400,000; reserves GRD 9,735,184.15 (Illustration 2). Banque Union SA, Rue Hermès 6; capital £50,000; and reserves £3,750 (see *Guide Sam* 1930: 904, 938, 906) (Illustration 3). Compare with the comprehensive survey found in Hekimoglou 1987.

45 For example, Albert Gattegno, a Jewish merchant from Skopje, Yugoslavia, apprised Banque Union in Salonica of the receipt of a new bill (similar to an invoice) for £3,001 to cover the dispatch of imported goods. According to Banque Union instructions, Gattegno was to simultaneously transfer 5,052 Serbian *dinars* to the firm's account in Banque Franco-Serbe, Belgrade. See YIVO, Greece, RG 207, FO. 156, Engineer Albert Gattegno, Skopje to Banque Union, SA, Salonica, 13 July 1931. Banque Franco-Serbe had a branch in Salonica, located in the Ottoman Bank building. See *Guide Sam* 1930: 905.

46 *Annuaire Commercial* 1922: 231; *Guide Sam* 1930 : 946.

47 *Guide Sam* 1930: 928.

48 As advertised: "*Renseignements commerciaux sur le monde entier.*" *Guide Sam* 1930: 914.

49 The information offices were: Allatini Fratelli, Fernandez Dino, Jahiel Isac, Juda & Salmona, Modiano F. et Cie., Nahama F., and also the Jewish Partner of Jenni & Vock. In addition, there were three emigration offices: Modiano S.D. et Cie., Mosseri Albert H., and Nahum V. (the other four were not Jewish). See *Austro-Hungarian Report* 1915: 138–139. See also Meron 2005b: 187, n.38.

50 Political struggles between the national churches, both Greek and Bulgarian, regarding petitions made by emigrant farmers to their offices indicate the healthy profits to be made. The emigration of Macedonian farmers on one hand and the development of oceanic trans-port on the other stimulated the branch's growth. See Gounaris 1989: 143.

51 The firm's offices were located in the Altcheh Building at Vassile-Heracliou and Comninon 28 (see *Guide Sam* 1930: 926).

52 Hekimoglou 2004: 7.

53 See Harlaftis 1996: 207–225.

54 *Guide Sam* 1930: 888; in 1921, the firm's branches included Larissa in Old Greece and Skopje (*Uskop*), Nich [*sic*], and Belgrade in Yugoslavia. *Annuaire Commercial* 1922: 30.

55 *Guide Sam* 1930: 900.

56 See Frenzl 1927: 119.

57 *Guide Sam* 1930: 916; Roupa and Hekimoglou 2004: 35.

58 *Guide Sam* 1930: 901.

59 Roupa and Hekimoglou 2004: 36.

60 BA/212 25/06/1936.

61 Greece came to be ranked tenth in the world in tonnage transported by its commercial fleet

and third in tonnage *per capita* (Germany was ranked first, followed by Britain). See Mazower and Veremis 1993: 125.

62   Dritsas 2003. According to Betty Cunliffe-Owen, who joined her husband in Greece when he was engaged in the work of the Refugee Settlement Commission in various periods between 1923 and 1926: "Before 1913, 2,000,000 tons of shipping passed through Constantinople, and I think about 400,000 through Piraeus. Now the figures are practically reversed, and the Turks find, to their cost, that without the Greeks and Armenians to carry on the internal life and trade of the country, they have thrown themselves back centuries." Cunliffe-Owen 1927: 216.

63   During the period 1914–1938, the percentage of Greek shipping concerns with their headquarters in the port of Piraeus rose from 62 percent (1914) to 96 percent (1938). At the same time, the percentage of Greek shipping concerns active in Constantinople fell from 14 percent (1914) to zero (1938). In other ports, such as those located in Rumania, Russia/USSR, Marseilles, and Rotterdam, the corresponding percentages also fell, from 15 percent (1914) to 3 percent (1938). Greek shipping lanes spread from Piraeus to the Ionian Islands. See Harlaftis 1996: 272. Yet, Salonica and its port were barely appeared on their routes.

64   Baxevanis 1963: 60, 76–80.

65   During the consolidation of Greek territory, connections were re-established with Greeks in the geographic proximity who had adopted this new Mediterranean orientation. Greek solidarity subsequently re-emerged around the national capital and its port. The funds donated by Greek communities in the Levant to their relatives in Greece did more than strengthen the country's foreign reserves. These Greek businessmen and traders in Egypt virtually transformed Piraeus into their home port. The shift of the grain market from the Balkans and the USSR to Australia and the US, spurred by international competition, also pushed Greek commerce in new directions. Bostas 1987: 214–218.

66   Eddy 1931: 160–161.

67   DOT 1927: 32–33. See also Hekimoglou 1997; Mazower 2004: 372–375.

68   On the declining cultivation of these crops in Greek Macedonia, see Dagkas 2003: 214–215.

69   DOT 1925: 27. On the negative impact of the Greek exit on the Broussa's silk industry, see Keyder 1994.

70   *Guide Sam* 1930: 314.

71   CAHJP Gr/Sa FO 346, Salomon S. Mordoh Successors, BA/4817, 22/6/37.

72   Roupa and Hekimoglou 2004: 37.

73   Kodjamanoglou han, Stamboul T. St. 1640. *Guide Sam* 1930: 831.

74   YIVO, RJCS, Greece, RG 207, FO. 156, Corneliussen & Stahgold, SA, Automotive Manufactures' Representatives, Brussels, Belgium, to Banque Union, SA, Salonica, 22 and 28 July 1932.

75   Dagkas 2003: 216.

76   DOT 1927: 27; see also Roupa and Hekimoglou 2004: 29.

77   Since the Ottoman period with the exception of the large-scale spinning mills that dominated all phases of the industrial process, most spinning mills obtained cotton from local gins. Gin operators would provide farmers with cash advances, receive the cotton at harvest time, and then negotiate directly with mill owners. The cotton was then exported to Serbia. Wool was consumed locally, mainly in the production of knitted socks. DOT 1921: 16–17.

78   Pinhas & Cie.'s (1921) advertisements were written in Greek, like those of its Greek competitors, but unlike the majority of Jewish entrepreneurs, whose ads were generally written in French. An ad's language hinted at the ethnicity of the firm's potential clients: local Greek farmers and manufacturers. *Annuaire Commercial* 1922: 8. Compare with Hekimoglou 2004: 191.

79   CAHJP Gr/Sa Elie [S.] Pinhas & Cie. BA/4016 28/2/1936.

80   YIVO, RJCS, Greece, RG 207, FO. 156 N.V. Chroomlederfabriek "De Hinde", Tilburg, Holland, to Banque Union SA, Salonica, 20 July 1932.

81   DOT 1923: 20.

82   D. N. Tsolekas & Frère took over (1929) the affairs of the old trading house of P. J. Dellia & Co., (P. J. Dellia and Dimitrios Tsolekas) which had two branches abroad – in Nice (presumably Niš, Serbia) (directed by Emmanuel) and in Belgrade, Serbia (directed by his

son Panayotis E. Dellia) – in addition to the Salonica branch. The partnership of Dimitrios Tsolekas (2/3) and his brother Panayotis Tsolekas (1/3) was engaged in the wholesale trade in rawhide and tanned skins on a vast scale. CAHJP Gr/Sa D. N. Tsolekas & FrèreBA/311, 16/02/1937.

83 Les Tanneries Lyonnaises à Oullins was mentioned among firms in France in *Guide Sam* 1930: 283.

84 E.g., the Greek Demetr. Joannides and the Jewish D. Angel in 1932. YIVO, RJCS, Greece, RG 207, FO. 156ff. For detailed cases from the YIVO Archives, see Chapter 7, below.

85 Free translation: "Exempted from stamp duty according to article 8, law of 31 December 1924". YIVO, RJCS, Greece, RG 207, FO. 156, Les Tanneries Lyonnaises, SA (Lyon), Depôt Paris, to Banque Union, SA, Salonica, 4 August 1932.

86 Joseph M Molho (Appendix 4.1, no. 619; Appendix 5, no. 557). Old Maison (est. 1907), which engaged in foreign trade had *références de tout premier ordre* (*Guide Sam* 1930: 910), was proud of its superior commercial relations with the largest export–import houses in Greece and Serbia. *Annuaire Commercial* 1922: 27.

87 For instance, Jacques Nahum from Salonica married Sophie Cohen of Belgrade, a Sephardic Jewess who owned an estate in Serbia. See Morin 1989: 53. See also Meron 2005b.

88 On the affluent Jewish bankers belonging to the Scialom family of Yugoslavia, see Freidenreich 1979: 19. On Russo, see ibid.: 33.

89 YIVO, Greece, RG 207, FO. 156, Technisches Unternehmen "Technokommerz" Ing. Albert Gattegno, Skoplje, to Banque Union, SA, Salonica, 12 July 1932.

90 Meron 2006; Meron 2008b.

91 Meron 2006.

92 Mazower 1991.

93 As the British Consul Rawlins remarked, "The Greeks are naturally a sea-faring race." HMSO 1920: 30; see also Eddy 1931: 114–115.

94 Harlaftis 1996: 207–225; 277.

95 Ben-Zvi 1967 [1914]: 340.

96 Baxevanis 1963: 27.

97 Frenzl 1927: 119.

98 The firm officially managing the firm was transformed into a government agency only in 1953. See Baxevanis 1963: 23–25; see also <http://www.thpa.gr/index.php?option=com _content&task=view&id=23&Itemid=46&lang=en>.

99 See also Ben-Zvi's 1914 report: "The shipping industry in Salonica is a Jewish stronghold, passed down from father to son for hundreds of years. Only a few Greeks are employed in this occupation. Exact numbers are difficult to come by; apparently, the number of sailors owning small boats approaches 200, with a higher number owning large boats, of which only about fifteen or twenty were Greeks. . . . Shipping is divided into two vocations: seamen who own small boats to transport passengers from the wharf to the boat . . . ; the others haul freight from the boat to the shore, or vice versa. Owners of large boats . . . are wealthier and can hire workers, or family members who earn a salary" [Hebrew, trans. OM] (Ben-Zvi 1967:340).

100 Refael 1997: 79–81.

101 For detailed data, see Meron 2008b.

102 For a comprehensive description of Salonica's Jewish alcoholic beverages industry as provided by two veteran wine merchants, Yoseph Ha-Elion and Eliahu Angel, see *Salonique, Ville-Mère en Israël* 1967: 237–238. The famous firm mentioned in that survey, Nahmias Maor (Mair) Cie., was the only Jewish firm engaged in spirits production in 1926. See the CD attached to Dagkas 2003: Table 112.

103 On the four newly established Greek-owned flour mills after 1924, see Dagkas 2003: 265.

104 CAHJP Gr/Sa Fils de David Hasson BA/4376, 7/10/1936.

105 Imports were channelled via Hamburg due to the relatively convenient credit terms provided by the city's banks. DOT 1927: 21.

106 See Freris 1986: 48.

107 CAHJP Gr/Sa FO 346 Makedoniki Kaltsopiia (ex-Modiano Frères) BA/161, 21 February 1936; this firm, bearing the name Modiano J S, was already operating in the last decades of the Ottoman regime (*Austrian Report* 1915: 182).

108 Roupa and Hekimoglou 2004: 31–32; on the developing metal industries including manufacture of electric lamps, electric wires, and locks in Greece during the 1920s, see DOT 1927:
26.
109 Angel and Levi, *Almanach Israélite* 5683 [1923]: 128–135.
110 Richard Turner, the British Commercial Secretary, counted the manufacture of gramo-
phone discs within the small new factories erected in Greece during 1926. DOT 1927: 26.
111 *Guide Sam* 1930: 902.
112 On the legal framework of the tobacco industry, see Dagkas 2003: 301–305.
113 The privilege of selling tobacco and cigarettes at retail was reserved for families of disabled
war veterans (Dagkas 2003: 302). Due to their lack of participation in the army during
World War I (section 3.2), indirectly supported by this category's absence from *Guide Sam*
1930, Jewish retailers in Salonica appear to have been excluded from this market at this
point.
114 Mazower 1991: 85–86; Pelt 1998: 27–28.
115 *Guide Sam* (1930: 933) excluded the Commercial Company of Salonica, Ltd. (section 2.2.3)
from its list of tobacco firms operating in Salonica. Yet, this firm was included within the
Kavalla list of tobacco companies, together with Hermann Spierer & Cie. (*Guide Sam* 1930:
964). The latter, also included among the tobacco companies listed in Salonica (but
excluded from the Jewish-owned firms of Appendix 5), processed the tobacco leaves from
Greek central and western Macedonia before exporting the manipulated leafs to Germany.
(Dagkas 2003: 383–384). According to a "legend" introduced by Yehuda Hacohen Perah-
ia, one of the former Allatini employees, Hermann and Carlo Spierer were the sons of
Allatini's nanny. These talented brothers were nurtured and educated by Carlo Allatini,
served as managers of the Commercial Company of Salonica, Ltd., and replaced the
Allatinis in the tobacco business after the Allatinis left Salonica. *Salonique, Ville-Mère en
Israël* 1967: 239. Even if we do not accept this story verbatim, Hermann Spierer & Cie. was
related to the Jewish entrepreneurial family from Germany that operated in Smyrna as well.
See also Molho and Nehama 1965: 31; for the company operating in Smyrna, see *Guide
Sam* 1930: 851. On the Spierer family in Smyrna, see Avner Levi 1992.
116 Fleischer 1995.
117 This Jewish-Islamic sect (the *Selânikli*) maintained relations with Salonica's large Jewish
community, some of whose members sympathised with them. See Landau 2007.
118 H. Recanati 1984: 16–17. Harry Recanati was born in Salonica in 1919 to Leon Recanti
and Matilde Saporta. The Recanati (of Italian origin) and Saporta (of Spanish origin) families were both well-known, prominent families. In 1937, following extensive studies abroad,
Harry Recanati joined the then-modest Palestine Discount Bank, Ltd., Tel-Aviv, founded
by his father in 1935. See <http://harryrecanati.org/>, accessed March 2008.
119 Hassiotis 2002.
120 *Guide Sam* 1930: 933.
121 *Guide Sam* 1930: 964.
122 *Guide Sam* 1930: 964.
123 *Guide Sam* 1930: 898.
124 *Guide Sam* 1930: 964. N. Mayer had tobacco factories in Kavalla, managed by Vartan Bey,
a Turk, even before 1919. See Mayer 1913: 7.
125 The advertisement in *Guide Sam* gives only the Hamburg office address, telegraph, and telephone numbers. *Guide Sam* 1930: 948.
126 The firm had also agencies in Constantinople and Smyrna (*Guide Sam* 1930: 800).
127 German-owned cigarette companies in 1926 included Reemtsma AG (est. 1921), which
employed 828 managers and labourers in 1924, and Jasmatzi, Batschari, Manoli, Greiling,
Mal-Kah, and Muratti. See Dagkas 2003: 374–379, and in the CD attached to Dagkas 2003:
Tables 157–158.
128 Meron 2006.
129 Avdela 1998: 423.
130 On the tobacco sector within the Jewish-controlled economy during the 1910s, see Meron
2006.
131 All of the members of the Association des Ouvriers de la Manufacture de Papier à Cigarettes
et des Boîtes in Salonica were Jews: Solomon Sarphati, Solomon Coenca, Mousson Sarphati,

David Botton, Nissim Tabah, Mosson Barzilai, Avraam Molho, Alegra Mordehai Beza, Solomon Molho, Roza Hané, Rachel Amar, Samouel Kapon, Zaco Avraam Sabetai, Sara E. Hané, and Anna Petilon. See the CD attached to Dagkas 2003: Table 216a.

132 Attempts to Hellenise the Socialist Federation in Salonica by deposing Benaroya in July 1919, prior to the 1920 elections, failed. Starr 1945: 331–332.

133 Grèce, Departement Hellénique de l'Information [n.d.], *Le drame des juifs hellènes*.

134 TARK was established by law on 11 July 1925, and began functioning by 11 August 1926. On its operations, see Dagkas 2003: 602–623.

135 On Jewish representatives in the association of tobacco workers in Salonica in 1926 (e.g., Avram Soustiel and Solomon Levi) as well as in 1928 (e.g., Yacco Cabilli), see the CD attached to Dagkas 2003: Table 216a.

136 For comprehensive demographic research on tobacco workers in Northern Greece, see Dagkas 2003: 484–492. For the number of Jewish workers see Table 222 in the CD attached to Dagkas 2003. For estimates based on the 1928 census see Meron 2005d.

137 Mavrogordatos 1983: 254.

138 DOT 1927: 16.

139 Due to the small size of the new plots, tobacco cultivation became even more profitable and preferable to opium and other cash crops. Mazower 1991: 120–121; Dagkas 1996: 25–106; Kontogiorgi 2006: 312.

140 DOT 1925: 21, Mavrogordatos 1983: 146–147.

141 Mazower 2004: 389–390.

142 Following the decrease in exports due to rising prices, driven by heavy taxes and high wages, the government consented to merchants' demands for the repeal of the prohibition against export of un-manipulated tobacco, a step related to the industry's rationalisation through introduction of new bale-packing methods. DOT 1927:17.

143 Two methods of manipulation and packing were used: (1) treatment of leaves in pieces of paper (*feuilles: basma, bachi bagli*), or (2) a simplified system, *Tonga*, related to new trends in the industry, which did not distinguish between qualities of leaf, and produced what were known as *sira pastal* [*série pastal*], or peasant bales. On tobacco production methods, see Dagkas 2003: 292–297.

144 Specialisations had previously been gendered, with the processing of top-quality tobacco a male preserve and the handling of poorer leaf a female preserve, consistent with the generally inferior position of women workers. Moreover, the transfer of women workers to the privileged occupations was restricted by statute, a mechanism that not only maintained their inferior working conditions but also prohibited women's admission into the sector's union. A gendered-segregated labour market was thus created in the industry. Avdela 1998: 424.

145 Avdela 1998: 433.

146 Avdela 1998: 433.

147 Cigarette production was an almost exclusively female realm. See Avdela 1998: 424.

148 Dagkas 2003: 298–301; on the cigarette factories in Macedonia, including those in Salonica, see Dagkas 2003: 305–311; on the Nahmias factory, see ibid: 309. This firm was classified in Appendix 5 in "tobacco trade" category according to *Guide Sam* original classification. The Greek Census 1928 classified tobacco processing and cigarette manufacturing under the same category "tobacco", see: Greek Census 1928, III, part 1, Table Ie: 351.

149 Hirschon 1989: 82; Mazower 1991: 263; Mazower 2004: 374–375.

150 In 1927, this company was one of the four main tobacco manufactureres in Salonica. Dagkas 2003: 310–311.

151 This firm is not present in the listed firms of the Salonica Chamber of Commerce and Industry of 1922. Yet, the firm advertised itself in the *Annuaire Commercial* (1922: 238). D. Arditti was considered "La première fabrique des tabacs & Cigarettes, Xanthie". Its was known throughout Greece for its aromatic cigarettes until 1934. Molho and Nehama 1965: 31.

152 In reality it functioned as an anti-labour act. Dritsas 2003: 304 note 16.

153 Kritikos 2000: 205; Mavrogordatos 1983: 147–152; Mazower 1991: 128.

154 Mazower 1991: 227. For the increasing misery in the tobacco towns during the late 1920s and the beginning of the 1930s, see ibid.: 126–127.

155 Between 1923 and 1930, the textile industry was transformed into the largest industrial sector in Greece, with annual production exceeding 20 percent of total industrial production. DOT 1925: 27–29; Pentzopoulos 1962: 160–167.

156 Small-scale carpet ventures using wool – a locally available raw material – were established by individual male refugee entrepreneurs who tried to exploit the pre-migratory skills practiced exclusively by their female compatriots, beginning with the placing of scattered looms in the workers' homes. Government encouragement thus stimulated the growth of carpet weaving into a large-scale industry, controlled exclusively by refugees but supported by repatriation agency resources. DOT 1925: 28–29; Kritikos 2000: 196–201.

157 Kritikos 2000: 196–201; Dagkas 2003. For the regional economic policy, see Simmons and Kalantaridis 1994: 655; Kamaras 2004.

158 Hastaoglou-Martinidis 1997b: 501.

159 Mazower 1991: 97, 109; Pentzopoulos 1962: 161–162.

160 Lampe and Jackson 1982: 371–375.

161 On the biased socio-demographic structure of the Greek metropolitan labour market following the Transfer, see Kritikos 2000; Meron 2005d.

162 Kritikos 2000: 198–199.

163 The *Statistical Yearbook* for 1930 still placed textiles and clothing into separate categories. Missing from the tables providing industrial production data was garment manufacture, while the category "clothing articles" (*articles d'habillement*) was divided into "hats" and "felt hats". Greece 1931, *Annuaire Statistique de la Grèce* (1930): 125–128. It appears that the ready-made garment industry in Greece was still very small in scope and incapable of influencing the national economy. Separation of textiles into the sub-branches of textiles and clothing therefore helps us assess the nation's industrial growth during the interwar period. If we look at the index weighted by value-added shares for 1938, the index for textiles moves from 0.286 to 0.217, whereas the index for clothing moves only from 0.003 to 0.002. Christodoulaki 2001.

164 See figures 1 and 2 in Roupa and Hekimoglou 2004: 26, 31.

165 According to the *Austrian Report* (1915), the fourteen knitting plants in Salonica were ethnically distributed as follows: Turkish (5): Baldji Frères, Caracache Fils de Mehm., Halet Hassan et Djemal, Mohmad Caracache Zadé Ruchdi, and Moustapha Chamli & Fils; Jewish (4): Fils de Abram Bivasch & Cie., Errera Fils de G.A. & Cie., Marcos J. & Cie., and Nahmias Joseph; Greek (2): Dalenga A. & Cie., Panajotides P. F.; the three other firms were of undetermined or mixed ethnicity: Orosdi-Back (Jewish partnership), The Anglo-Hellenic Society of Salonica, Société Commercial du Levant. *Austrian Report* 1915: 175. On the initial transition towards mass production of fashion during the last decades of the Ottoman Empire, see Jirousek 2000.

166 *Austrian Report* 1915: 52.

167 See section 8.4.2.

168 Roupa and Hekimoglou 2004: 28. These researchers emphasised that the new knitting enterprises "were all Greek".

169 Compare with Kupferschmidt 2007: 38.

170 Green 1997: 76 163–165.

171 For such advertisements, see *Guide Sam* 1930: 908, 920, and 922.

172 During the 1920s, local manufacturers of hosiery could compete with French, German, and British imports in former Ottoman markets. See Kupferschmidt 2007: 38 note 186.

173 DOT 1928: 24.

174 The Jewish-owned firms were: R. Assael (Palais Hermion); Torres & Anastassiadis (Palais Hermion); and Sam Sarfati (Baicou 2); the Greek-owned firms were: Kosmides & Co.; E. Charalampides & Fils; Joseph Lascaridis; and N. Demetriades & Chr. Economou (Paicou 4). YIVO, RJCS, Greece, RG 207, FO. 156, Vereinigte Strick- und Wirkmaschinennadel-Fabriken, GMBH, Chemnitz, to Banque Union, SA, Salonica, 14/7/1932; 21/7/1932; 28/7/1932; 8/8/1932.

175 Sewing machines were imported into Salonica at the beginning of the twentieth century by the following firms: J. Roubin, Orosdi-Back, Abdurahman Iskender Pasche et Yahia Ali, Ali Bin Abdi Fils, Bayaltzalieff Th., and Singer. See *Austrian Report* 1915: 167.

176 Roupa and Hekimoglou 2004: 23.

177 The growth in Jewish firms trading in clothing and listed in *Guide Sam* 1930 was compared with the *Annuaire Commercial* 1922. The final list was also derived after considering the absence of the category "manufacturers' agents" in *Guide Sam*; participants in this category frequently acted as textile and clothing traders. To illustrate, Matalon Sabetay (Appendix 4.1, no. 454) (est. 1907), acted as wholesalers, manufacturers file cards (*fiches*), headscarves of cotton, wool, and silk as well as silk notions. *Annuaire Commercial* 1922: 190.

178 The term *Nouveautés* (novelty goods) emerged around 1900 in Paris and came to cover a wide range of items typically available in department stores. It implied being up-to-date with the latest Parisian fashions but also expressed a strong desire to emulate the world's cultural standards. See Kupferschmidt 2007: 31. Since the category "*Modes*" in *Guide Sam* 1930 included firms simultaneously listed under "*Nouveautés*" in addition to fashionable clothing and accessories producers (e.g., Moskovitz Haim, Appendix 5, no. 397, listed under "*Modes*" [*sic*] but not hat producers), we eliminated the repetitions in Appendix 5. Yet, in Table 5.6b, when the categories again included repetitious, we preferred to differentiate between the two categories to show the similarity between *Nouveautés* and *Haberdashery*, or the supply of inputs for the clothing industry versus ready-made imported products targeted at stores (including department stores) engaged in mixed commodities commerce.

179 Translation: Haberdashery and hosiery.

180 *Annuaire Commercial* 1922: 173.

181 *Annuaire Commercial* 1922: 240. This fashion house/clothing store had been mentioned in the daily *Journal de Salonique* already in (1909). See Cooperman 1991: 209.

182 See above notes 180 and 181.

183 *Annuaire Commercial* 1922: 109. Similarly, Nahmias & Massoth (no. 259), sold cotton threads, finished products, perfumery items (*Annuaire Commercial* 1922: 6); Raphael & Benveniste (no. 265), participated in the wholesale/retail sale of draperies and clothing (*Annuaire Commercial* 1922: 291).

184 *Annuaire Commercial* 1922: 127.

185 *Guide Sam* 1930: 908.

186 *Annuaire Commercial* 1922: 108.

187 Kupferschmidt 2007: 37–38.

188 Matarasso, Saragoussi & Rousso, whose department store sold hosiery and many other textile goods (Appendix 4.1, no. 219).

189 *Guide Sam* 1930: 892.

190 Vidal Nahoum, a Jewish emigrant from Salonica, gave a simple, practical explanation for his preference for hosiery over the tissue trade in the new Parisian "hostess society": "*Et pourquoi tous dans la bonneterie? . . . [workers in the tissue trade required apprenticeship to distinguish between laine, cotton, and mixed fabrics, whereas] dans la bonneterie c'était plus facile. On achetait des chaussettes, bon. Les chaussettes coûtaient 3 francs la douzaine . . . on les vendait 3.50 francs. On achetait des bas, la même chose, On achetait des culottes de coton. . . . L'affaire est beaucoup plus riche dans les tissus que dans la bonneterie, mais enfin, dans la bonneterie, on se défendait, la preuve . . .*" Morin 1989: 122.

191 CAHJP Gr/Sa FO 346 Makedoniki Kaltsopiia (the former Modiano Frères) BA/161, 21 February 1936. This firm, bearing the name Modiano J S, had operated a brick factory before the demise of the Ottoman regime (*Austrian Report* 1915: 182). According to Modiano (2000: 57), before establishing this factory, Pepo [Joseph] also served as an official interpreter for the Italian Consulate in Salonica. For his numerous services he was made a *Cavaliere* of the Italian Crown.

192 CAHJP Gr/Sa FO 346 Daniel S. Modiano BA/4628, 29/03/1937.

193 The firm does not appear in *Guide Sam*. CAHJP Gr/Sa 346 Fils de Samuel Florentin BA/473 19/10/1937; BA/428, 16/6/1937.

194 CAHJP Gr/Sa Haim Isac Nissim Succ. BA/4605, 17/03/1937.

195 Kritikos 2000: 197.

196 *Guide Sam* 1930: 907.

197 In Athens, 315 female refugees enjoyed absolute domination of this sector. For total employees in Athens, see Greek Census 1928, Vol. III, Part 1; for refugees in Athens, see ibid., Table Iie: 705. See also Meron 2005d.

198 A small gap emerged between indigenous females (including Jewesses) (ERI=0.848) and refugee females (ERI=1.117), favouring the latter in the representation indices for the 1928 census category "lace-making and embroidery industry". Greek Census 1928, Vol. III, Part 1; for total employment in Salonica see Table Ie: 314; for Refugees in Salonica, see Table Iie: 741.

199 The Jewish benevolent society Tifereth Yisrael, (i.e., Splendour of the Jewish People), founded by middle- and upper-class Jewish women, promoted and supported female vocational training in the needle trades. Molho 2005b.

200 Dagkas 2003: 544–546.

201 CZA S6/2533 [January 1932]; according to her birth certificate (*Acte de Naissance*) issued on 29 January 1932, Daisy-Doudoun Broudo, the daughter of Isac Emmanuel Broudo and the late Esther Broudo, née Tazartes, was born in Salonica in 1912. Her father, who is mentioned in the document, had been a teacher.

202 Born & Cie., Avenue Constantin, see *Annuaire Commercial* 1922: 324.

203 On the innovative methods that Singer used to penetrate the market, see Godley 2006.

204 Dagkas 2003: 544–546.

205 On the labour shortage during the 1910s, see Quataert 1995.

206 According to the testimony of the late Shlomo Calderon (3 February 2009), the Jewish owner of a factory producing riding breeches and suits for export to Europe employed Jewish seamstresses, who worked at home and supplemented the factory work force during periods of high demand.

207 Handeli 1992: 16; Hirschon 1989.

208 According to this concept, women were not the main breadwinners. This argument, which women themselves tended to believe in, gave both employers and trade unions a justification to pay women wages below those of men for the same work, among other discriminatory practices. See De Groot and Schrover 1995: 3.

209 Kritikos 2000.

210 Strumza 1995: 10.

211 See Ironi 1967: 208.

212 The following example was derived from the *Bulletin of Information c.*1934, published in reference to the two new Jewish neighbourhoods, Quarter Number 6 and Karagach. Fakima, is a clerk at Abravanel and Benveniste (Appendix 5, no. 444) and earns GRD 1,200 per month; Esther works regularly "in house" (*en kaza*) as a tailoress and earns from GRD 80 to 100 daily (i.e., GRD 1,600–2,000 per month). Naar 2006: 20.

213 Sewing, like knitting and embroidery, were eminently suitable occupations for women during this period because they allowed them to be employed while maintaining the social norms of modesty. Mazower considers this analysis relevant for refugee seamstresses into the 1930s. Mazower 2004: 389.

214 Similarly, the only women entrepreneurs mentioned for 1912 were the Jewish Rahel Pinhas (*Austrian Report* 1915: 146) and two Greek female furriers (*Austrian Report* 1915: 160). See also Meron 2005b.

215 Mazower 2004: 417–418.

216 Refael 1988: 378; Strumza 1995: 10.

217 For the refugee space distribution in the city, see Hastaoglou-Martinidis 1997b.

218 YIVO, Greece, RG 207, FO. 156, Unione Manifatture, Milano; Headquarters: Parabiago, to Banque Union, SA, Salonica, 4 August 1932.

219 YIVO, RJCS, Greece, RG 207, FO. 156, Henry Mason (Shipley) Ltd., Shipley, England, to Bank Union, SA, Salonica, 7 July 1932; YIVO, RJCS, Greece, RG 207, FO. 156 G. A. Badenoch, woollen goods merchant, London, to Bank Union, SA, Salonica, 8 July 1932.

220 In contrast, the share of food, tobacco, and tanning (all low-technology industries) dropped from 53 percent to 26 percent of total manufactured production. For data on industrial growth, see Louri and Pepelasis Minoglou 2002: 329–330.

221 Morin 1989: 120–127.

222 The Jewish population in the department of Kavalla was 2,165; in Drama 597; and in Serres 583. Greek Census 1928, Vol. IV, Table 5*.

Chapter 6

1 *Financial default* is to be distinguished from *bankruptcy* and *insolvency*. Default occurs when a debtor (a private person or institution) cannot meet his financial obligations, such as a loan repayment, according to the agreed-upon debt contract schedule. In such cases, the creditor can require the debtor to repay the loan immediately. However, in the majority of the cases, the creditors will attempt to restructure the debt in order to allow the debtor to remedy this situation before taking other steps. *Insolvency* is a legally defined situation in which it is clear the debtor's assets or cash flow will be insufficient to meet the contractual payment schedule. *Bankruptcy*, in contrast, involves a legal declaration that a debtor is unable to pay his debts and thus needs to have debts forgiven or reorganised. It is a legal proceeding in which a person or corporation (firm) has become insolvent. In bankruptcy proceedings, one's assets and debts are evaluated and debts are repaid according to the debtor's ability to pay, what the creditors will accept, and what the court and the law decide.

2 Kontogiorgi 2006: 320.

3 Constantopoulou and Veremis 1998, No. 24: 107.

4 According to a contemporary's comments on the conditions of the initial loan, obtained in 1924: "[A] refugee loan [the first from 1924] was placed on the market, amounting in all to ten million sterling, three-fourths of which was obtained from England." Cunliffe-Owen 1927: 13. On the costs of the war and immigrant absorption in general, see Mazower 1991: 60–65.

5 According to Kostis [Costis], the damage caused by the entry of a wave of Greek refugees was greater than their contribution to the economic development attributed to them by public opinion. See Kontogiorgi 2003: 74, 77. On similar processes in the Balkan nation-states, see also Mazower 2002: 128–130.

6 Pelt 1998: 50.

7 Remittances rose again between 1934 and 1938. Pelt 1998: 47–48.

8 See Dertilis and Costis 1995: 467–469.

9 The first loan (1924) was for £12.3 million at a real interest rate of 8.71 percent; the second loan (1927) was for £7.5 million at a real interest rate of 7.05 percent; see Kontogiorgi 2003: 74, 77; Mazower 1991: 191.

10 Mazower 1991: 143–176.

11 Between 1909 and 1920, only partial convertibility was maintained. See Dritsas 1999.

12 The negotiators from the League of Nations' financial committee imposed severe institutional conditions: reform of the Greek banking system and stabilisation of the drachma. Although the new Greek central bank received (from the government) the right to handle the public debt, yet, it lacked the real power to effectively intervene in the market through open-market operations and the discount-rate policy. In October 1928, just six months after the Bank of Greece began operating, the leading commercial banks established the Union of Greek Banks. The Union's purpose was to regulate competition between its members but also to present a common front against the central bank. Thus, the local public market for government bonds was shallow due to the highly oligopolistic credit market as well as the high cost of money, which was still controlled by the commercial banks led by the National Bank of Greece. Mazower 1991: 145–160; Dertilis and Costis 1995: 463–465.

13 Mazower and Veremis 1993: 112–113.

14 When the drachma was stabilised *de jure* in 1928, it had lost almost 95 percent of its pre-war value. Christodoulaki (2001) mentions this monetary instability as a hindrance to industrial expansion during the 1920s.

15 Venizelos was compelled to meet the terms set by his foreign creditors, which required keeping reserves in gold and foreign currency at 40 percent of the loans' value. Kontogiorgi 2003.

16 Dertilis and Costis 1995: 466–467.

17 Freris 1986: 78. For the exact chronology, see http://www.bankofgreece.gr/en/bank/history.asp, accessed 4 February 2008.

18 These steps did nothing to halt the decline in the drachma's value. That value dropped from GRD 305 = £1 on 31 March 1932 to GRD 539 = £1 on 5 May 1932, immediately after

passage of the new measures, only to level out in January 1933 at GRD 628 = £1. Freris 1986: 78–80. Dertilis and Costis (1995: 467) indicated 27 April 1932 as the law's date; see also section 7.1 here.

19 Freris 1986: 78–80; Mazower 1991: 143–176; Dertilis and Costis 1995: 466–467.

20 Dertilis and Costis 1995: 468; for an overview on the emergence of European autarkies between the wars, see Feinstein et al. 1995.

21 Greek migrant remittances shrank from $88 million (1920) to $41 million (1930) to $6 million (1935); see Bostas 1987: 218.

22 Mazower 1991: 89–91, 120.

23 Mavrogordatos 1983: 163–168; Mazower 1991: 79–91. Greek rural protectionism, considered stronger than that in other European countries, became a structural element of the country's economy and politics. Dertilis and Costis 1995: 464.

24 Annual average production of grain grew from 282,000 tons (1919–1927) to 532,500 tons (1928–1937), while annual consumption increased from 30 percent (1920–1924) to 60 percent (1935–1939) of total production. See Freris 1986: 94–96.

25 Mavrogordatos 1983: 163–168; Mazower 1991: 79–91; Kontogiorgi 2003: 73.

26 DOT 1937.

27 Nationally, these two branches of manufacturing consisted of 335 and 17,803 units of production, respectively; Dritsas 1992: 203–217.

28 The pre-war industrial growth in Greece has recently been disputed on the basis of new indices. By adopting the New Index of Industrial Output, Christodoulaki (2001) was able to confirm that Greece enjoyed high rates of growth in the 1920s and 1930s. However, in contrast to the dominant view held in the literature, the New Index shows that industrial output fell from 1929 to 1932, with the early and strong devaluation being the main factor stimulating the industrial sector's robust recovery from the Great Depression. See Christodoulaki 2001.

29 Pelt 1998: 78–82.

30 Pelt 1998: 126–130.

31 Freris 1986: 92–93; Mazower and Veremis 1993: 126.

32 Mazower 1991: 86–88; 116–128; Mazower and Veremis 1993: 116.

33 DOT 1934: 28.

34 Bostas 1987: 215–218.

35 Freris 1986: 82.

36 The clearing system was conducted as follows: The importer deposited the goods' purchase price in his own currency at the national clearing agency of his country, which deposited the same amount to the credit at the clearing agency of the exporting country. The latter institution then paid the exporter in his own currency. Thus, if trade between two countries was not balanced, the clearing agency of one acquired a claim against the agency of the other. That claim, however, was satisfied only when a shift in the balance of trade gave rise to an offsetting claim. Mazower 1991: 203–235.

37 Mazower 1991: 218–224.

38 Germany, faced with dwindling revenues from taxation and apparently unable to raise money through either external or internal loans, was economically exhausted by early 1933. See Freris 1986: 82; Feinstein et al. 1995: 57–61; Hardach 1995.

39 Pelt 1998: 40–41.

40 Hjalmar Horace Greeley Schacht was appointed acting Minister of Economics by Hitler in August 1934, and resigned from this post in November 1937. On 19 March 1938, Schacht was reappointed (firstly on 16 March 1937) for a four-year term as President of the Reichsbank. Hilter dismissed him from this post on 20 January 1939 but he remained as Minister without Portfolio until January 1943. His main achievements were: (1) credit-based funding of armaments production; (2) the "New Plan" for economic recovery; (3) control of production; and (4) plans and preparations for the imposition of economic controls during World War II. See Weitz 1997; Hardach 1995.

41 Mazower and Veremis 1993: 124.

42 Pelt 1998: 102.

43 On the unique methods enforced by the Nazis within the bilateral exchange clearing system, see Feinstein et al. 1995: 57–61.

44 Freris 1986: 88.
45 Freris 1986: 89; for the similar cases of Germany's trading partners in Southeast Europe, see Feinstein et al. 1995: 59.
46 On the Greek–German arms negotiations, see Pelt 1998: 142–156.
47 Pelt 1998: 130–132.
48 Capt. Vivian Dering Vandeleur Robinson (during his adult life he went by Vandeleur Robinson) (1902–1990), the son of an army colonel, was briefly a military cadet before leaving to study history at Emmanuel College, Cambridge. He was active during the interwar period within the League of Nations Union and may have resided for a period in Czechoslovakia. He was the author of several books on the Balkans as well as a number of plays. He became a captain in the army during World War II and was probably involved in political intelligence work. See <http://www.ssees.ac.uk/archives/rob.htm>.
49 Robinson 1939: 351.
50 Pelt 1998: 50–54.
51 Mavrogordatos 1983.
52 Ioannis Metaxas died on 28 January 1941, less than three months before German troops invaded Salonica on 9 April 1941. See Pierron 1996: 217–218.
53 For a detailed account of these political events, see Mavrogordatos 1983: 203–214; Pierron 1996: 207–208.
54 Lagos 2005: 406.
55 Mazower 2004: 409–410.
56 The temporal proximity between the Bolshevik Revolution (1917) and the Greek Transfer (1923) – for more on accusations of Jewish instigation of the Transfer, see Chapter 3 – was perceived as evidence of the power of the Jews to threaten national stability. The Jewish minority was therefore accused of communism and the "Jewish threat" was held responsible for the rise of the totalitarian regime. See Chirot 1997: 19.
57 Mazower 1991: 116–128.
58 Constantopoulou and Veremis 1998: No. 50:165.
59 Constantopoulou and Veremis 1998: Nos. 48–51.
60 Lagos 2005: 404–406.
61 Constantopoulou and Veremis 1998: 175–192; Mazower 2004: 414–415.
62 Kallis 2006: 39.
63 On the Salonica police and its battles against communism and workers, see Mazower 2004: 378–380.
64 Moisis 1972; Reuven 1967; Toledano 1972.
65 Kallis 2006: 43, 48.
66 Fleischer 1995: 5.
67 On the small number of Zionist publications in Greek, see Moisis 1972: 387–388.
68 Kallis 2006: 39.
69 The Turkish property abandoned in "New Greece" was transferred to the Greek government by the Refugee Settlement Commission and from there to the Greek National Bank, which held the property in trust against the refugees' debentures. See Eddy 1931: 165; Hirschon 1989: 47.
70 On the riots in the Jewish suburbs and the Campbell pogrom, see Rozen 2005a: 277–288, whose research is based on the testimony of Jewish witnesses; Rena Molho 2005: 237–238; Fleming 2008: 94–100.
71 Vassilikou 1993; Vassilikou 2003: 113–114.
72 Abatzopoulou 1997: 222.
73 Constantopoulou and Veremis 1998: No. 67, pp. 216–217.
74 Fleischer 1995: 7.
75 Mazower 2004: 409, 416.
76 Pierron 1996: 213.
77 Translation of: "*En Grèce rien de semblable ne se produisit, et les Israélites hellènes continuèrent a bénéficier jusqu'à l'occupation allemande des droits qui leur avaient été accordés par une constitution libérale.*" Pierron 1996: 210.
78 On the expropriation of the ancient Jewish cemetery according to Law 890 from 29 September 1937, see Pierron 1996: 199–203.

79 In this way the authorities also solved the burning problem of the Alliance schools, which they categorised as foreign schools. They later compelled them to integrate into the community's main education system. Pierron 1996: 213–218.

80 Fleischer 1995: 3.

81 Fleischer 1995: 4–5; Pelt 1998.

82 Fleischer 1995: 5–6.

83 Fleischer 1995: 4–5; Pelt 1998.

84 Pelt 1998: 118–124.

85 See: Meron 2008b.

86 Bonnet 1976.

87 Rozen 2005a: 298–300.

88 Transmission from the Director of Salonica's Press Bureau to the Minister of Foreign Affairs, Salonica, 20 December 1932. Constantopoulou and Veremis 1998: no. 68, p. 218.

89 Following the denial of entry to three young men, unemployed workers of the Jewish enterprise Alfred Sarfatty & Marco Matalon (Rue Ermou 11), into the Mikveh Yisra'el agricultural school in Mandatory Palestine, these young men asked for assistance "to take us out of this poverty, and to settle us up in our Holy Land". CZA KKL5/5265 Azaria Sarfatty, Avraham Moshe, and Avraham Perahia to the Keren Kayemet representative in Salonica, 29/11/31.

90 Mazower 2004: 406–407.

91 The Director of the Salonica Press Bureau submitted a French translation of its lead article, "To the Ministry of Foreign Affairs", originally published in Salonica's Ladino newspaper *Pueblo*, 5 January 1933, Constantopoulou and Veremis 1998: No. 70, pp. 222–223.

92 M. Molho 1986: 29. Molho and Nehama (1955: 30) mention slightly different figures for that year: 52,350 total and 5,061 foreigners.

93 Gil 1950: Table 4, p. 28.

94 Similar estimates had already been circulated by P. Dragoumis, Governor General of Macedonia, in a 1934 report addressed to the Ministry of Foreign Affairs: "The Jews of Greece do not number more than 65,000, of whom approximately 40,000 reside in Salonica (whose total population is 250,000)." The report's aim was to minimise the importance of the Jewish component to the city's character and thus rationalise the enforcement of Sunday as the day of rest on Jewish residents. Constantopoulou and Veremis 1998: No. 80, p. 236.

95 M. Molho claimed that the 49,000 Jews indicated in the 1940 municipal census did not accord with reality. Based on Danuta Czech's estimates (1973: 183), more than 54,533 Jews arrived at Auschwitz from Greece, while 48,533 were deported from Salonica to the Nazi concentration camps as of 1943. This estimate may include Jews from the provincial towns of Macedonia. According to Ben (1977), 46,091 Salonican Jews were deported; see also Mazower 1993: 256–257; Benbassa and Rodrigue 1995: 169–170.

96 Dublon-Knebel, 2007: 77: 30/11/38, Consul Schönberg, Salonica to FO, Berlin, on the anti-Jewish atmosphere in Salonica and the activity of the Ethniki Etaireia.

97 Dublon-Knebel, 2007: 76–78: 30/11/38, Consul Schönberg, Salonica to FO, Berlin, on the anti-Jewish atmosphere in Salonica and the activity of the Ethniki Etaireia. Jews originally from Salonica were numbered among the 3,500 Athenian Jews on the eve of the German occupation. According to Yacoel's diary (Bowman 2002: 80), rich Salonican Jews settled in Athens.

98 In 1933, about 70 percent of the Jewish community's members (35,000 out of 50,000) needed relief assistance. See *American Jewish Year Book* 1934: 195.

99 This special tax was also imposed on wine and cheese, see Naar 1997.

100 In 1932, the death rate increased, as the birth rate decreased among city dwellers. Hekimoglou and Roupa 2004: 45–46.

101 For 1934–1935 data, see Meron 2010; for 1936 data, see Emmanuel 1972: 233.

102 Compare with Skourtis 1992: 238, cited by Vassilikou 2003: 114

103 Constantopoulou and Veremis 1998: No. 74, p. 229.

104 Constantopoulou and Veremis 1998: No. 74, pp. 229–231.

105 The ethnic public sector should include administrative and professional jobs. Lewin-Epstein and Semyonov 1994: 625–627.

106 D. Levi [1941] 1986.

107 For the analysis of the Jewish community's budgets (1933–1934), see Meron 2010.
108 Pierron 1996: 165–166.
109 See Meron 2010.
110 Reuven 1967: 231.
111 Rozen 2005a: 288–299.
112 Rozen 2005a: 298.
113 Constantopoulou and Veremis 1998: No. 53, pp. 169–172.
114 To the Assimilationists with the exclusion of the communists and parties representing limited interest groups (local, professional, etc.).
115 Constantopoulou and Veremis 1998: No. 81, 237–239.
116 Constantopoulou and Veremis 1998: Attachment to No. 52, pp. 168–169; Rozen 2005a: 266–267.
117 Author's loose translation: "Eliminate the Jewish monopolisation of the French intellectual influence." Fleischer 1995: 16, n.8.
118 Constantopoulou and Veremis 1998: No. 80, pp. 236–237.
119 Constantopoulou and Veremis 1998: Nos. 48, 51, 54, 59, and 72.
120 Constantopoulou and Veremis 1998: No. 72.
121 On Rabbi Zvi Koretz, see Rozen 2005b.
122 Constantopoulou and Veremis 1998: Nos. 48 and 51. On the consternation aroused among the leaders of the Jewish Community, see ibid: No. 54.
123 Toledano 1986: 174. Author's translation.
124 See Refael 1988: 116. On the society, established in 1901, see also Matanoth Laévionim 1909.
125 René Molho 1994: 2.

Chapter 7

1 According to the British Consul's report: "The principal Banks are: Bank of Greece, National Bank of Greece, Ionian Bank Limited, Popular Bank, and the American Express Company." DOT 1934: 9.
2 On the commercial banks during the period 1929–1932, see also Kostis 1986; Hekimoglou 1987.
3 The bank was paid its charges and commissions in Greece and abroad, respectively. Receipt of these fees directly into a special account kept abroad may have bypassed Greek regulation. For instance, Midland Bank, Ltd., Bradford, paid Banque Union for the credit it extended to the London & Eastern Trade Bank, Ltd. See YIVO, RJCS, Greece, RG 207, FO. 156 Midland Bank, Ltd., Bradford, Foreign Branch, to Banque Union, SA, Salonica, 25 July 1932.
4 Hekimoglou 1987; 2004.
5 The German text reads: "*Unwichtig. Ein schreiben an die Kommission des Devisenschutzer der Bank von Griechenland von seiten der Bank Union. Die Wegen Devisenschmuggel angeklagt Bank Union will ihre unschuldigkeit beweisen. Sprache: Griechisch, dasselbe Fransösisch. Jahr: 1935.*" CAHJP Gr/Sa FO 102.
6 Translation of the author from YIVO, Greece, RG 207, FO. 156 J. Gattegno, Marseille, to Banque Union, SA, Salonica, 6 July 1932.
7 The Greek government hoped to negotiate a satisfactory solution with its Greek creditors at the Lausanne Conference, held in June 1932. Mazower 1991: 170–171.
8 The French text reads: "*Non seulement le Ministre de Commerce, Le Ministre des affaires Etrangères, mais aussi Chambre de Commerce de Paris nous ont fait savoir que des pourparlers très actifs sont poursuivis entre la France et la Grèce et que tout fait supposer qu'on arrivera très bientôt a un arrangement donnant tout satisfaction aux créanciers de France.*" YIVO, Greece, RG 207, FO. 156 J. Gattegno, Marseille, to Banque Union, SA, Salonica, 6 July 1932.
9 Ibid.
10 The French text read: "*les nouvelles, dispositions de la dernière loi ne permettent par*

*actuellement le règlement des dettes envers l'étranger contractées avant le 27 Avril par conséquent le règlement aura lieu aux termes de la loi du 27 avril no. 5422 (qui fixe le règlement de dettes à raison de 10% chaque semestre)."*YIVO, Greece, RG 207, FO. 156 Nollesche Werke, Weissenfels, Berlin, to Banque Union, SA, Salonica, 25 July 1932.

11 For the distribution of Greek importers according to clearing agreements, see Mazower 1991: 220–221.

12 Mazower 1991: 213.

13 Samuel Ghedalia Yeni represented Italian cement suppliers in Salonica and was involved in the payment of debts by Greek firms (Jean G. Roussis; Yannoulis & Souris). YIVO, RJCS, Greece, RG 207, FO. 156, Banco di Roma, Milano, to Banque Union, SA, Salonica, 15 July 1932;19 July 1932; 1, 2 August 1932;YIVO, Greece, RG 207, FO. 156 G. Bassani, Venezia, to Banque Union, SA, Salonica, 25 July 1931; 19 July 1932.

14 The French text reads: *"nous pouvons avoir notre monnaie par l'entremise d'une autre maison allemande qui a un débit à payer dans votre pays pour tabac, par exemple, et nous avons cuit [sic] que la maison Reemtsma Zigarrettenfabriken, GmbH a Altona Bahrenfeld, fait des affaires avec votre pays et peut-être on peut avoir sa monnaie par l'entremise de cette maison."* YIVO, Greece, RG 207, FO. 156 Nollesche Werke, Weissenfels, Berlin, to Banque Union, SA, Salonica, 13 August 1932.

15 YIVO, RJCS, Greece, RG 207, FO. 156, Vincenz Werner, Merzdorf, to Banque Union, SA, Salonica, 22 July 1932.

16 YIVO, RJCS, Greece, RG 207, FO. 156, Storchwerke Brückmann, Boysen & Weber, Köln, to Banque Union, SA, Salonica, 12 August 1932.

17 The three members of Kyder family were still free in Salonica during mid-May 1943. Dublon-Knebel 2007: S80, 31.5.1943 World Service, International Institute for the Elucidation of the Jewish Question, Frankfurt/Main, to von Thadden, FO, Berlin on the Jewish Question in Greece, p. 151.

18 YIVO, Greece, RG 207, FO. 156, H. Schemel BMBH, Guben [Germany], to Banque Union, SA, Salonica, 4–7 July 1932.

19 In this case, a draft was to be remitted to Lewis Is. Nahmias, who would provide instructions. Freight would be paid by Nahmias. YIVO, RJCS, Greece, RG 207, FO. 156, Kurt Schubert, Fabrik und Export Chirurgischer Glasinstrumente, Frankenhain, to Banque Union, SA, Salonica, 22 July 1932.

20 Dublon-Knebel 2007: 19–20.

21 The French text reads: *"mais si je vous ai bien compris, je ne puis pas toucher à mon argent qui me sera remboursé avec toute probabilité aux calendes grecques. Dans ces conditions je crois inutile de vous dire que je refuse catégoriquement de me prononcer d'accord et je vous prie de délivrer les dits documents à Mr. Mano contre remise de sa part d'une traite pour le dit montant de Frcs Fr. [sic] 1910.-payable après 2 mois."* YIVO, Greece, RG 207, FO. 156, Clement Cohen, Strumpfwaren-Fabrikation, Chemnitz, to Banque Union, SA, Salonica, 19 July 1932; 15 August 1932.

22 YIVO, Greece, RG 207, FO. 156 IAFA, Genova, to Banque Union, SA, Salonica, 25 July 1932.

23 Mazower 1991: 183.

24 Subsequent to this step, taken to prevent devaluation of the drachma and following the dollar's devaluation, the flow of emigrants' remittances from the US, which had dried up in 1932, began once more. See Mazower 1991: 186.

25 Mazower 1991: 180–186.

26 Translation: "About 30 francs." YIVO, Greece, RG 207, FO. 156 Graemiger Frères SA, Bazenheid, to Banque Union, SA, Salonica, 3 August 1932.

27 YIVO, RJCS, Greece, RG 207, FO. 156, Spalato, Société Anonyme des Ciments Portland, Solin, Yugoslavia, to Banque Union, SA, Salonica, 27 July 1932; 1 and 12 August 1932.

28 Apparently identified with Zakai [sic] Frères (Appendix 5, no. 155: metals).

29 YIVO, RJCS, Greece, RG 207, FO. 156, Banco di Roma, Milan, to Banque Union, SA, Salonica, 9 August 1932.

30 YIVO, Greece, RG 207, FO. 156, IAFA, Società a.g.l. di Produzione e di Esportazione, Genova, to Banque Union, SA, Salonica, 19 July 1932.

31 YIVO, RJCS, Greece, RG 207, FO. 156. Helios Società Cartaria a G. L., Trieste, to Banque Union, SA, Salonica, 8 and 25 July 1932.

32 The same document also referred to the drafts of Zacai [*sic*] & Co. YIVO, RJCS, Greece, RG 207, FO. 156, Verheyden & Biemans SA, Belgium, to Banque Union, SA, Salonica, 27 October 1932.

33 YIVO, RJCS, Greece, RG 207, FO. 156, Usines Spindler, Mont par Plancher-Bas, Maison de vent, Paris, to Banque Union, SA, Salonica, 25 July 1932.

34 YIVO, RJCS, Greece, RG 207, FO. 156, Spécialité de Poulies, P. Poitou, Saint-Florent, to Banque Union, SA, Salonica, 25 , 26 July 1932 ; 4 August 1931; 1 July 1932.

35 YIVO, RJCS, Greece, RG 207, FO. 156, Gattefosse, Lyon, to Banque Union, SA, Salonica, 1 August 1932; 10 August 1932.

36 YIVO, RJCS, Greece, RG 207, FO. 156, Les Tanneries Lyonnaises, SA, Depôt Paris, to Banque Union, SA, Salonica, 28 April 1932; 19, 20, 25 July 1932; 4 August 1932.

37 YIVO, RJCS, Greece, RG 207, FO. 156, Les Tanneries Lyonnaises, SA, Depôt Paris, to Banque Union, SA, Salonica, 8 July, 1932.

38 Mazower 1991: 218–220.

39 YIVO, RJCS, Greece, RG 207, FO. 156, Bern, Fried & Sohne, export–import, Budapest, to Banque Union, SA, Salonica, 8 July 1932.

40 Nevertheless, the greater part of all imports from the Balkan states, especially of wheat and coal, continued to be paid for in foreign currency. Mazower 1991: 219.

41 YIVO, RJCS, Greece, RG 207, FO. 156, Dioni arsko društvo za Eksploatacÿu drua - Société Anonyme d'Exploitation Forestière, Zagreb, to Banque Union, SA, Salonica; 16, 20, 22, 23 July 1932; 6, 16 August 1932.

42 DOT 1937: 10.

43 Mazower 1991: 220–221.

44 YIVO, RJCS, Greece, RG 207, FO. 156 J. & S. Rhodes Ltd., Morley, York, to Banque Union, SA, Salonica, 25, 26 July 1932 and 12 August 1932.

45 The same Hector Capuano also had to collect the debts due to another British manufacturer from Pessah Frères & Danon. YIVO, RJCS, Greece, RG 207, FO. 156 J & S Rhodes Ltd., Morley, York, to Banque Union, SA, Salonica, 25 and 26 July 1932; 8 August 1932.

46 CAHJP Gr/Sa FO 346 Mentech S. Arama BA/none 05/07/1935.

47 YIVO, RJCS, Greece, RG 207, FO. 156 A. & S. Henry Co., Ltd., Textile Manufacturers, Bradford, to Banque Union, SA, Salonica, 25 and 26 July 1932; 5 August 1932.

48 Author's translation from YIVO, RJCS, Greece, RG 207, FO. 156 S. Selka, Lumb Lane Mills, Bradford, to Banque Union, SA, Salonica, 25, 26 and 28 July 1932; 14 August 1932.

49 YIVO, RJCS, Greece, RG 207, FO. 156 Lloyds Bank, Ltd., Colonial & Foreign Department, Bradford, to Banque Union, SA, Salonica, 25 and 26 July 1932; 14 August 1932.

50 E.g., a postcard protesting bill no. 796: YIVO, RJCS, Greece, RG 207, FO. 156 Midland Bank, Ltd., Bradford, to Banque Union, SA, Salonica, 18 July 1932.

51 Examples: YIVO, RJCS, Greece, RG 207, FO. 156 Westminster Bank, Ltd., London, to Banque Union, SA, Salonica, 25 and 26 July 1932; 8 August 1932; YIVO, RJCS, Greece, RG 207, FO. 156 Midland Bank, Ltd., Bradford, to Banque Union, SA, Salonica, 25, 26 July 1932; 15, 18, 26 July 1932; 10 August 1932; YIVO, RJCS, Greece, RG 207, FO. 156 Kessler & Co., Ltd., Manchester & Bradford, to Banque Union, SA, Salonica, 25 and 26 July 1932; 14 August 1932. For Carasso Frères, see Appendix 5, no. 326.

52 YIVO, RJCS, Greece, RG 207, FO. 156 National Bank of India, Ltd., Aden, to Banque Union, SA, Salonica, 9 August 1932.

53 Apparently related to Aroesti Haim Frères (Appendix 5, no. 211), a firm dealing in leather goods.

54 YIVO, RJCS, Greece, RG 207, FO. 156, N.V. Chroomlederfabriek "De Hinde", Tilburg, Holland, to Banque Union, SA, Salonica, 20 July 1932; 12, 13 August 1932.

55 DOT 1937: 10.

56 YIVO, RJCS, Greece, RG 207, FO. 156, Henry Mason (Shipley), Ltd., Shipley, England, to Banque Union, SA, Salonica, 7 July 1932. For Matarasso & Rousso, see Appendix 5, no. 392: Matarasso, Saragossi et Rousso.

57 Author's translation from YIVO, RJCS, Greece, RG 207, FO. 156, National Provincial Bank, Ltd., Bradford, to Banque Union, SA, Salonica, 8 July 1932.
58 YIVO, RJCS, Greece, RG 207, FO. 156, National Provincial Bank, Ltd., Bradford, to Banque Union, SA, Salonica, 18 July 1932.
59 YIVO, RJCS, Greece, RG 207, FO. 156, National Provincial Bank, Ltd., Bradford, to Banque Union, SA, Salonica, 3 August 1932.
60 YIVO, RJCS, Greece, RG 207, FO. 156, Gaetano Lanza, SA, Milano, to Banque Union, SA, Salonica, 8 August 1932.
61 Mazower 1991: 219.
62 A letter of credit is a letter issued by the bank in the destination country, in which the bank promises the exporter payment for the merchandise even if the foreign recipient finds it difficult to pay.
63 Author's translation from YIVO, Greece, RG 207, FO. 156, Technisches Unternehmen "Technokommerz", Ing. Albert Gattegno, Skopje, to Banque Union, SA, Salonica, 12 July 1932.
64 YIVO, RJCS, Greece, RG 207, FO. 156, Dresdner Bank, Dresden, to Banque Union, SA, Salonica, 6 July 1932.
65 YIVO, RJCS, Greece, RG 207, FO. 156, Hermann Seeber, Langenviesen, Thuringia, to Banque Union, SA, Salonica, 13 August 1932.
66 YIVO, RJCS, Greece, RG 207, FO. 156, Chemische Fabrik Lehrte, GmbH, Lehrte/Hannover, to Banque Union, SA, Salonica, 26 July 1932.
67 A similar example, also related to the pharmaceutical trade: the German firm requested the transfer of payment (the client's name was not mentioned) in cash, by means of Greek banks authorised to conduct foreign exchange transactions, despite the availability of full clearing agreements. The transaction was to be conducted by transfer of the respective payment to Bank Populaire, SA, Salonica, or alternatively to Banque de Grèce, Athens, and then on to Berlin. YIVO, RJCS, Greece, RG 207, FO. 156, Georg König, Fabrik Pharmazeutischer Präparate, Bückeburg, to Banque Union, SA, Salonica, 22 July 1932.
68 His address was Rue Syngrou-Paikou, Stoa de Mayo. YIVO, RJCS, Greece, RG 207, FO. 156, Chininfabrik Braunschweig Buchler & Co, Braunschweig, to Banque Union, SA, Salonica, 26 July 1932. For a similar payment made through Bernard Landau, see YIVO, RJCS, Greece, RG 207, FO. 156, Union de Banques Suisses, Zurich, to Banque Union, SA, Salonica, 9 July 1932.
69 The address was Tsimiski 52, Salonica. YIVO, RJCS, Greece, RG 207, FO. 156, Corneliussen & Stahgold, SA, Automotive Manufactures Representatives Brussels, Belgium (from their Antwerp warehouse), to Banque Union, SA, Salonica, 22, 28 July 1932.
70 YIVO, RJCS, Greece, RG 207, FO. 156, Romeiser F. és Fiai R.T. (F. Romeiser & Fils SA), Budapest, to Banque Union, SA, Salonica, 15 and 23 July 1932, 10 August 1932.
71 YIVO, RJCS, Greece, RG 207, FO. 156 The Barr Rubber Products Co., Sandusky, Ohio, US, to Banque Union, SA, Salonica, 25, 26 July 1932; 10 August 1932. Yakar & Ovadia were not mentioned under this name in the *Guide Sam* 1930. The writer is probably referring to the firm of Yacar E. Ovadia.
72 CAHJP Gr/Sa FO 346 Sam E. Varsano BA/79 26/4/1935.
73 CAHJP Gr/Sa FO 346 Nahmias & Gattegno BA/4653 9/4/1937.
74 Dritsas 2003.
75 CAHJP Gr/Sa FO 346 Vital Cohen BA/205 13/6/1936; CAHJP Gr/Sa FO 346 Vital Albert Cohen BA/4734 8/5/1937.
76 Vita Amar was also appointed procurator for the late Samuel Modiano in 1910, eight years after he had begun handling Modiano's real estate investments; CAHJP Gr/Sa FO 346 Vita B Amar BA/ none 19/8/1935.
77 This may explain why Vidal Nahum delayed his own naturalisation in the mid-1920s (section 3.4), and chose Greek nationality instead, despite the fact that Greece was culturally foreign to him. The family business was still active in Salonica (Appendix 4.1, nos. 630, 631). Only in 1931, when France raised barriers to immigration (section 6.3) did he finally accept naturalisation. See Morin 1989: 87–88, 120, 137–142, and 148–149.
78 If the émigrés provided their new foreign addresses, they would be considered "foreigners" by the Greek government, which would then freeze their accounts.

79 See Appendix 4.1, Jewish-Gentile Joint Ventures, no. 687.
80 Author's translation from YIVO, Greece, RG 207, FO. 156 J. Gattegno, Marseille, to Banque Union, SA, Salonica, 6 July 1932.
81 Similarly see Morin 1989.
82 YIVO, Greece, RG 207, FO. 156, I.H. Covo to Banque Union, SA, Salonica, 13 July 1932. Covo is registered under this Paris address in *Guide Sam* 1930: 189 (for Paris).
83 Haim Mechoulam apparently also relied on the financial assistance given by his father-in-law, Elie S. Angel. Moise Mechoulam, Haim Mechoulam's father, likewise worked in the firm but was constantly away on business in other parts of Greece. CAHJP Gr/Sa 346 179 Moïse Mechoulam & Fils BA/ 30/03/1936; BA/4800 12/06/1937.
84 CAHJP Gr/Sa 346 Mano & Co. BA/4629 29/03/1937.
85 CAHJP Gr/Sa FO 346 Fratelli Mahel BA/none 05/07/1935; Mahel Rousso & Cie. BA/none 14/12/1935.
86 On the family relationship between the Fernandez and Allatini of Salonica and the Bloch family in Paris, see Assouline 1999: 15. The Jewish Bloch family originated in Alsace and was active in the Alliance Israélite Universelle, Paris. On David Bloch, see Rodrigue 1993: 34.
87 Gino Fernandez, who resided in Paris, established an *anonymous society*, Fernandez & Derin (15 May 1936) that operated a factory for producing automobile parts (*carrosseries*). CAHJP Gr/Sa FO 346 Gino Mario Fernandez BA/4784 31/05/1937.
88 CAHJP Gr/Sa FO 346 Gino Mario Fernandez BA/4784 31/05/1937.
89 CAHJP Gr/Sa FO 346 Fils de David Hasson BA/4376 7/10/1936.
90 CAHJP Gr/Sa FO 346 Albert D. Saporta BA/4368 02/10/1936.
91 YIVO, RJCS, Greece, RG 207, FO. 156, Spalato, Société Anonyme des Ciments Portland in Solin, Yugoslavia, to Banque Union, SA, Salonica, 12 August 1932.
92 The debtor was Elie Abastado. YIVO, RJCS, Greece, RG 207, FO. 156, Alb Muylle de Muelenaere, Brussels, Belgium, to Banque Union, SA, Salonica, 25, 26 July 1932; 19 July 1932.
93 Author's translation from H. Recanati 1984: 23.
94 Author's translation from H. Recanati 1984: 22.
95 CAHJP Gr/Sa FO 346 Isac Saporta BA/128 08/01/1936.
96 The firm was founded by Iomtov Is. Saporta's sons, Isac and Meir, following his death in May 1936. CAHJP Gr/Sa FO 346 Société pour la Commerce du Bois, Iomtov Is Saporta BA/4387 15/10/1936; 22/11/1938.
97 Meron 2008.
98 The firm itself was founded by Elie Allalouf in 1919. Following the expansion of its affairs, it was transformed into a partnership (*société en nom collectif*) in 1922 under the above-mentioned name. Among the firm's clients were the Poland–Palestine Line and KLM. CAHJP Gr/Sa FO 346 Allalouf & Co. BA/245 5/9/1936; BA/4525 25/1/1937. On the history of Allalouf & Co. Shipping, Ltd. in Israel, see also http://www.allalouf.com/Articles/Article.asp?ArticleID=5&CategoryID=17, retrieved 30 May 2008.
99 CAHJP Gr/Sa FO 346 Allalouf & Co. BA/4525 25/1/1937.
100 Jewish shipping and maritime service firms (e.g., Sarfati, Maritime Transport; Morris Rafael and Isaac Elbo) had, as early as 1930, begun offering stevedore services in order to employ Salonican longshoremen. They were joined in 1935 by other Jewish port service firms. To illustrate, Avraham Kimchi, based in Salonica, had acquired special permission from the Greek Minister of the Interior to relocate their advertising staff to the Port of Haifa (see Meron 2008b: 220–221).
101 CAHJP Gr/Sa FO 346 Revah, Mattia & Co. BA/4715 28/04/1937.
102 It should be noted that there were only a few cases where emigration to Mandatory Palestine caused financial problems for the Jewish firms left in Salonica. For instance, the emigration of Elie Angel, who settled in Tel Aviv, was considered the reason for the impaired financial situation of Sevy & Aelion. The firm had already suffered losses when the firm's vast property holdings, whose initial capital in 1918 was abundant, was entirely liquidated in 28 May 1936. CAHJP Gr/Sa FO 346 Sevy & Aelion BA/482126/06/1937.
103 YIVO, RJCS, Greece, RG 207, FO. 156 The Anglo-Palestine Bank, Ltd. in Jaffa, to Banque Union SA, Salonica, 12 August 1932. For similar requests for information on Jewish firms,

see YIVO, RJCS, Greece, RG 207, FO. 156 Barclays Bank (Dominion, Colonial and Overseas), which was amalgamated with The Anglo-Egyptian Bank, Ltd. in Tel Aviv, to Banque Union, SA, Salonica, 18 July 1932.

104 YIVO, RJCS, Greece, RG 207, FO. 156 Dresdner Bank, Elberfeld, to Banque Union, SA, Salonica, 22 July 1932.

105 YIVO, RJCS, Greece, RG 207, FO. 156 Société Laitière des Alpes Bernoises (Stalden, Emmenthal, Swisse) in Bern, to Banque Union, SA, Salonica, 6 July 1932.

106 Roupa and Hekimoglou 2004: 37.

107 Small tradesmen were hardest hit. The number of tailors and shoemakers fell from 1,534 in 1929 to only 435 in 1935, although tradesmen dealing in food products (grocers, bakers, butchers, greengrocers, etc.) managed to survive the crisis and even grow in number, from 2,355 in 1926 to 2,645 in 1935. Hekimoglou 1997: 146.

108 CAHJP Gr/Sa FO 346 Leon A. Juda BA/4678 13/04/1937.

109 CAHJP Gr/Sa FO 346 Vidal Is. Tiano BA/144 12/02/1936; BA/ 4396 19/10/36.

110 CAHJP Gr/Sa FO 346 Hananel E. Naar & Co. BA/4478 04/12/1936.

111 CAHJP Gr/Sa FO 346 Francés & Menache BA/141 8/2/1936.

112 CAHJP Gr/Sa FO 346 Fratelli Mahel BA/none 05/07/1935.

113 The original firm was established in 1912 under the name Francès & Saltiel. Following its dissolution in late 1918, Abram Elie Francès left and established an independent firm while Abram E. Saltiel became a partner in Saltiel Frères & Cohen. CAHJP Gr/Sa FO 346 Abram Elie Francès BA/112 18/10/1935; Saltiel S. Cohen BA/468 8/10/1937; BA/222 A. Arianoutsos & Co. 7/8/1936.

114 Each of the two brothers possessed considerable real estate, registered in their wives' names. CAHJP Gr/Sa FO 346 Fils de Moise Saltiel BA/4447 16/11/1936.

115 CAHJP Gr/Sa FO 346 Altcheh & Co. BA/4686 15/04/1937.

116 Isac settled in Tel Aviv, where he participated in construction and mortgage loan (*prêts sur hypothèques*) activities. CAHJP Gr/Sa FO 346 Aron J. Florentin BA/107 12 October 1935; BA/4635 30/03/1937. It is highly likely that Isac J. Florentine was the cousin of another Isac, son of David Florentin, who also settled (1933) in Mandatory Palestine; *CZA* KKL5/5265 Letter from David Isac Florentin, Zionist Federation of Greece, Salonica, to Menachem Ossishkin, President, The Jewish National Fund (Keren Hakayemet LeYisrael), 10 February 1933.

117 CAHJP Gr/Sa FO 346 Sefiha Frères BA/182 31/03/1936; Sefiha Frères BA/438 26/06/1937.

118 In an earlier incarnation the company had been Fils d'Abram de Mayo & Roussos, established in 1924 and dissolved in 1926. CAHJP Gr/Sa FO 346 Fils d'Abram de Mayo BA/337 28/3/1937.

119 In 1911, Humbert Scialom undertook the management of his father's affairs, while in 1912, Hassid became a partner in Acher Hassid & Co. In 1930, both founded this commercial representation agency, investing in fabrics, metals and ironworks. Scialom, who possessed a fortune valued at GRD 10 million, including fixed property, generally resided abroad while Hassid ran the company. The partners enjoyed a good reputation in commerce and were recommended *pour l'entrée en relations*. CAHJP Gr/Sa FO 346 Humbert Scialom & Hassid BA/none 02/01/1936.

120 CAHJP Gr/Sa FO 346 Salomon S. Mordoh Successors BA/4817 22/06/1937.

121 The original trading house was established in 1904; CAHJP Gr/Sa FO 346 S.A. Nehama BA/400 28/5/1937.

122 Previously Haim & Salomom Saltiel & Co. dissolved following Haim's emigration. CAHJP Gr/Sa FO 346 Salomom Saltiel & Co. BA/4380 14/10/36.

123 CAHJP Gr/Sa FO 346 Pepo Juda Menahem BA/4464 23/11/1936.

124 "Elle s'occupe d'opérations de banque sur une très petite échelle vu qu'elle a cesse de faire partie de l'Union des Banques et qu'elle ne possède pas le privilège de faire des transactions en change." CAHJP Gr/Sa FO 346 Haim et Joseph Salomon Salem BA/4758 13/05/1937.

125 CAHJP Gr/Sa FO 346 Ipalliliki Micropistossis, Albert Jacob Houlli BA/4779 28/05/1937.

126 They had two mortgages for fixed property, one of which (GRD 300,000), due to the widow Aslanian, were reimbursed. The rest (£2,000) was owed to Moise Abram Botton. CAHJP Gr/Sa FO 346 Oikos Mikropistosseos, Ouziel & Hazan BA/4786 1/6/1937; BA/4819 25/6/1937.

127 "Keren Le'halvaot Ktanot", *Zikhron Saloniki*, II: 215.
128 See Ossoskin 1967: 214.
129 The JDC was founded in 1914 to assist Jews in Eretz Yisra'el caught in the throes of World War I. The JDC has since aided millions of Jews in more than eighty-five countries. The JCA was founded by Baron Maurice Hirsch in 1891 for the purpose of assisting East European Jews to settle in America. See Kadosh 2006.
130 This firm, founded in 1921 with initial capital of GRD 1,000,000, was meant to create commercial contacts between Greece and Mandatory Palestine (import–export, land purchasing, and housing construction in Palestine). See Ossoskin 1967: 214.
131 For similar small loan funds that supported Jewish immigrant entrepreneurs in the US, see Godley 1996; Tennenbaum 1986.

Chapter 8

1 To illustrate, the state's wheat marketing agency (KEPES) protected Greek farmers from the deflationary effects of falling world prices. Yet in Macedonia, where labour was plentiful, mono-cultivation of wheat suffered due to a scarcity of land. On the complexity of self-sufficiency in cereals during 1932–1936, see Mazower 1991: 238–250.
2 See Roupa and Hekimoglou 2004: 47.
3 In the original French, "*La firme est enregistrée à la Chambre de Commerce et d'Industrie de notre ville*".
4 For example see CAHJP Gr/Sa FO 346 Mentech S. Arama BA/none 05/07/1935; Isac Nahmias and Albert Gattegno set up a new partnership (no. 136) in the same sector where the firm owned by Joseph Francès was dissolved following Francès' emigration to London (1931). CAHJP Gr/Sa FO 346 Nahmias & Gattegno BA/4653 9/4/1937. See Appendix 8 for a list of all the firms dealt with in this chapter. Unless otherwise indicated, the numbers in parentheses indicate the firm's position in the Appendix.
5 Legislative measures against Jewish businesses were not instituted in Germany before 1938. Yet, preparation for future radical expropriation (the November 1938 Kristallnacht pogrom) was already under way in 1936, when a "Jewish business" came to be defined as a business having at least one Jewish proprietor, or alternatively a Jewish minority interest of at least 25 percent. In view of the high degree of state regulation of all types of market transactions, such labels virtually marked these enterprises; the second step was a decree forcing Jews to register their private resources, which were examined by the tax offices and later confiscated. See Ziegler et al. 2003: 188–196.
6 On the distribution of the total firms registered in the Salonica Chamber of Commerce and Industry by ethnic ownership in 1938, see Dublon-Knebel 2007: 78.
7 See Dublon-Knebel 2007: 78.
8 The "natural" sample includes the available registered firms (see Appendix 8).
9 See Dublon-Knebel 2007: 78.
10 In order to conduct a goodness-of-fit chi-square analysis for a single variable (ethnic origin) for the purpose of determining whether the differences between the branch distributions of the Jewish and the Greek firms were significant, the number of branches was reduced from thirteen to seven (food; chemicals; construction material, metals and wood; hides and leather; textiles and clothing; paper; large-scale commerce = luxuries, agricultural products, foreign trade, and tobacco). The results indicated that the differences between these distributions were not statistically significant, $\chi^2(6) = 11.32$, $p > .05$. In both distributions, the percentage for paper, leather, chemicals, and food was relatively small (below 10 percent) while the percentage for textiles and clothing was largest (about 30 percent).
11 For example, in January 1932, the Jewish-owned tobacco warehouse belonging to Hermann Spierer & Cie. located in Drama (Macedonia) was sold to a Greek-owned tobacco company. See: <http://www.tachydomi.gr/en/projects_for_development>, accessed February 2010.
12 I would like to thank my colleague, Alexandros Dagkas, for his assistance in the translation of the tobacco industry's French terminology.

13 CAHJP Gr/Sa FO 346 Salomon Is. Amariglio BA/4818 23/6/1937.
14 CAHJP Gr/Sa FO 346 Raphaël Jakob Varsano & Co. BA/ 4660 07/04/1937.
15 Reetsma Cigarettenfabriken, GmbH, a Hamburg-based cigarette manufacturer.
16 According to the testimony of Baruh Elimelech, a former tobacco worker in this firm, the factory was sold by Avram Nahmias (Nahmias & Cie: see Appendix 5, no. 451) to Raphaël Varsano, who belonged to one of Salonica's richest families. The factory was very well-known. Only a few Jewish-owned tobacco factories remained by then, e.g., Leon Recanati. See Refael 1988, Testimony of Baruh Elimelech: 88.
17 Pelt 1998: 41; Fleischer 1995: 4.
18 H. Recanati 1984: 22.
19 Pelt 1998: 110–113.
20 Pelt 1998: 112–113.
21 Pelt 1998: 142–145.
22 While Venizelists and anti-Venizelists struggled for power, Greek middlemen were annoyed by plans to organise the arms trade directly between governments, an arrangement that would reduce their profits. Beginning in June 1937, the Schacht–Tsouderos agreement, signed 8 December 1936, provided a framework for concluding contracts between German arms producers and the Greek government. Pelt 1998: 142–151.
23 Pelt 1998: 147.
24 Fleischer 1995: 6.
25 H. Recanati 1984: 23.
26 CAHJP Gr/Sa FO 346 Raphaël Jakob Varsano & Co. BA/ 4660 07/04/1937.
27 The thirteen Greek owners of tobacco firms included Theodoros Arzoglou, Georges Ch. Christoforides, Antigonos Hadjigeorgiou, Georges Hadjigeorgiou, Gregoire Karayannides, Ermokratis Khristoforidis, Constantin Moscoff, Panagopoulos Frères, Pantelis Pantazis, Papadopoulos Bros, Jean Protopapas, and Thomas Vlahopoulos, Stelios Voivodas. In addition, G. Tsikos was a cigarette retailer (and thus included in the category "tobacco", Table 8.1).
28 Pelt 1998: 39. On the famous Ottoman Greek entrepreneur Prodromos Bodosakis-Athanasiadis, see idem: 177–181; on his activities in the Greek arms trade, see idem: 161–177.
29 For another example of a Greek tobacco trader who was a "*victime de la crise*" in the early 1930s, see CAHJP Gr/Sa FO 346 Thomas Vlahopoulos BA/105 11/9/1935.
30 CAHJP Gr/Sa FO 346 Ermokratis Khristoforidis BA/83 23/5/1935; see also BA/117 Eftimios Dimitriou 3/11/1935.
31 Author's translation of: "*La situation de cette firme, comme du reste de tous les négociants de tabacs, avant quelques années et notamment de 1930 à 1933 était mauvaise et n'inspirait aucune confiance. Toutefois, grâce à des affaires lucratives qu'elle a traité en 1933 et 1934 sa situation s'est sensiblement améliorée. Néanmoins elle ne peut-être encore considérée comme tout à fait prospère, car ceci dépendrait de la demande de tabacs acheteurs de l'Etranger.*" This merchant, originally from eastern Macedonia, had previously competed with the long-established and well-known firm of Maison de Tabacs Hassan Akif. CAHJP Gr/Sa FO 346 Antigonos Hadjigeorgiou BA/68 26/3/1935; BA/349 1/4/1937.
32 CAHJP Gr/Sa FO 346 Panagopoulos Frères BA/121 23/11/1935.
33 He dispersed his goods from vast warehouses in both Old and New Greece, specifically, in Salonica, Volo, and Agrinion. CAHJP Gr/Sa FO 346 Stelios Voivodas BA/432 17/6/1937.
34 CAHJP Gr/Sa FO 346 Georges Hadjigeorgiou BA/302 5/2/1937.
35 CAHJP Gr/Sa FO 346 Theodoros Arzoglou BA/263 3/11/1936.
36 The owners of Papadopoulos Frères worked closely with a former general in the Greek army, a Mr. Vernardos, then living in Hamburg. Through the latter, they signed a contract with a German shipyard to purchase two oil-powered passenger vessels. According to the contract, the Greek purchaser would transfer a down payment of 40 percent of the vessels' cost by transporting tobacco goods worth that amount to the shipyard. CAHJP Gr/Sa FO 346 Papadopoulos Bros. BA/194 7/5/1936.
37 Fleischer 1995: 5.
38 Fleischer 1995: 17 n. 24.
39 Greece imposed heavy taxes on tobacco exports; Egypt imposed heavy taxes in imports of

tobacco from Macedonia, which increased the costs of local cigarette manufacture; heavy taxes were also imposed by countries importing Egyptian-made cigarettes as soon as a local cigarette industry began to emerge. Kitroeff 1989: 100–101.

40   Only on the eve of World War II did the UK expend any additional efforts to buy Greek goods; see Freris 1986: 89.

41   Yet, in 1927, the export of Greek cigarettes to Alexandria amounted to 10,510 kg, with Italy in second place with 7,423 kg of Greek cigarettes. See Table 182 in the attached CD to Dagkas 2003.

42   Greek merchants, especially holders of Greek citizenship (the majority were originally from Constantinople) who had chosen to reside in British Mandatory Egypt, established the Egyptian cigarette industry. Their success depended in good part on their easy access to imported Macedonian tobacco leaf and cheap Egyptian labour, essential for this labour-intensive industry. On the Greek cigarette industry in Egypt, see Kitroeff 1989: 96–112.

43   "*Traite de bonnes affaires ayant réussi à avoir des commandes importantes et fermes principalement d'une forte Compagnie anglaise d'Egypte*" (The making of good deals have succeeded in producing important and firm orders in most cases, primarily with the one of the most robust English companies in Egypt.) CAHJP Gr/Sa FO 346 Constantin Moscoff BA/274 12/11/1936.

44   The Eastern Tobacco Company (a subsidiary of British–American Tobacco, which took over Egypt's Greek-owned tobacco firms in the 1920s) compelled Greek distributors to provide the cheaper Virginia leaf, suited to British tastes. Kitroeff 1989: 109.

45   Author's summary of: "*Ces tabacs gagés auprès de la Banque Nationale de Grèce de notre ville sous la garantie de son frère Dimos Christoforides (tannerie) ont déjà été exportés et régulièrement liquidés.*" CAHJP Gr/Sa FO 346 George Ch. Christoforides BA/153 17/2/1936.

46   On the preferred status of the Greek elites, who were represented mainly by the National Bank of Greece or some other authorised Greek banks, see Dritsas 2003; Pelt 1998: 112–118.

47   One such Greek firm was Caradimos & Stamoulis, which operated a vast shop for hosiery, leather goods, perfumery, capeskin (soft sheepskin leather for gloves), and related items in addition to a factory for trousseau items (e.g., lingerie and linens). CAHJP Gr/Sa FO 346 Caradimos & Stamoulis BA/66 22/3/1935.

48   Author's translation of: "*L'affaire marche bien ce qui est la conséquence de la plus value du stock en marchandises au moment de la dissolution de l'ancienne Société en nom collectif.*" CAHJP Gr/Sa FO 346 Hananel E. Naar & Co. BA/4478 04/12/1936.

49   The firm Haim J[acob] Benrubi was established in 1919 by the two cousins just named. Haim Jacob Benrubi had acquired twenty years of experience in his father's firm, Modiano & Benrubi. The firm operated a vast store for the wholesale and retail sale of household utensils, glassware, porcelain, light fixtures, etc. CAHJP Gr/Sa FO 346 Haim J[acob] Benrubi BA/198 14/5/36; BA/4360 24/9/36.

50   Abravanel & Benveniste was mentioned in other records as La Maison de Verrerie. Elie Benveniste operated the cinemas Pathe and Apollon in the name of his son-in-law Elie Pinhas. See CAHJP Gr/Sa FO 346 Albert Levy BA/215 26/6/1936.

51   Like other commercial mergers, e.g., Albion, this firm is not registered separately in Appendix 8 due to missing details.

52   Mazower 1991: 214.

53   Author's free translation of the two phrases as one: "One of the biggest commercial enterprises for glassware in Salonica and in Greece."

54   Although the firm's total capital equalled only GRD 4,000,000, Benrubi (GRD 1,600,000), Abravanel and Benveniste were listed as equal partners. We can therefore conclude that the firm of Abravanel & Benveniste also contributed GRD 1,600,000. Furthermore, it was well known that Asséo Frères & Fils, the third partner, was registered as contributing GRD 1,000,000, even though by 12 November 1936 the firm had actually transferred only GRD 400,000. These figures, if correct, exceeded the firm's total capital of GRD 4,000,000. We have no way of explaining this difference; we can only quote from the documents, which may contain errors. The capital invested in stock reached GRD 10,000,000. The firm also owned the building that contained its warehouses, valued at GRD 4,000,000, against a

mortgage held by the Banque de Salonique. CAHJP Gr/Sa FO 346 Haim J[acob] Benrubi BA/198 14/5/36; BA/4360 24/9/36; CAHJP Gr/Sa FO 346 Asséo Frères & Fils BA/4434 12/11/36.

55 CAHJP Gr/Sa FO 346 Eliezer & Chimchi BA/none 14/8/35; BA/4450 17/11/1936.

56 The firm's total capital, GRD 1,200,000, was approximately equal to that of Eliezer & Chimchi & Cie. CAHJP Gr/Sa FO 346 N. Constantinides BA/154 18/2/1936.

57 The President, Conrad Weynandt (a former delegate of the Banque Belge pour l'Etranger in Salonica and then Director of Compagnie Générale Financière des Tabacs) as well as the Nehama brothers, were considered experienced financiers. CAHJP Gr/Sa FO 346 Eletan SA, Salonica–Athens BA/218, 6 November 1935; BA/208 16 June 1936 and a letter dated 26 November 1936.

58 H. A. Altshey was previously known as H. Altshey & Co. (est. 1920); the firm was renamed in 1932 after the death of one of its associates (1927). The deceased, H. Altshey, the former Secretary and Chief Accountant of La Cunard Line (later the Saporta Agency, Ltd.) and Standard Oil Co. of New York (later Socony-Vacuum Oil Corp.) had established several agencies in Salonica. The source of this information is a confidential letter found in the firm's files. CAHJP Gr/Sa FO 346 A. Altshey 30/05/1936.

59 Permission to be listed in the Import Entitlements Registry was granted by the Ministry of National Economy as a means to regulate import activity following the Greek default (1932).

60 Mazower 1991: 213.

61 Established in 1908 by Mentech J. Hassid, who died in 1934 in Lausanne, and his brother-in-law, Moise J. Aélion; CAHJP Gr/Sa FO 346 Aélion & Hassid BA/4520 21/1/1937.

62 Author's translation of: "*Cette réalisation, jointe au produit de la vente d'une partie du livret d'importation, permit non seulement de régler à terme les dettes sur base du compromis, mais de laisser encore disponible un certain lot de merchandise.*" CAHJP Gr/Sa FO 346 Aélion & Hassid BA/4520 21/1/1937.

63 Ibid., "*Depuis lors, la situation de la Firme s'est sensiblement améliorée grâce a l'activité de son personnel et de ses dirigeants.*" (Since then, the firm's situation has improved significantly thanks to its staff and management.)

64 British exporters of refined cotton thread and wool yarn to Greece competed successfully with suppliers in clearing countries and represented the lion's share of the products traded. Britain's share in coal and printed cotton textiles imported to Greece eventually dropped, with German goods taking their place, but only beginning in 1934. The change was based mainly on competitive prices rather than any clearing arrangement. Mazower 1991: 220–224.

65 The firm also imported some items for direct sale: leather belts, rubber products (*caoutchouc*) as well as automobile accessories. CAHJP Gr/Sa FO 346 H. Pardo & M. Carasso BA/none 15/11/1937.

66 Fleischer 1995: 4–5.

67 Uskub (Skopje) is now part of modern Macedonia.

68 Author's translation of: "*C'est pour des raisons fiscales que la Firme travaille sous des raisons différentes à Thessaloniki et à Uskub. . . . A Thessaloniki, elle s'occupe de l'exportation de files de coton à la succursale d'Uskub et en contre partie celle-ci lui expédiee [sic] des légumes secs, etc.*"

69 The firm was sufficiently profitable to make cash purchases – it never used bank credit. CAHJP Gr/Sa FO 346 David S. Asséo BA/4434 12/11/1936.

70 CAHJP Gr/Sa FO 346 Salomon Pinhas Pardo BA/4417 09/11/1936.

71 Nefussy & Cie. (est. 1917) had previously been engaged in trade in metals and construction materials. CAHJP Gr/Sa FO 346 Albert Elie Nefussy BA/4616 27/05/1939.

72 CAHJP Gr/Sa FO 346 Isac A. Aroesti BA/484 2/11/1937.

73 See also Chapter 6. CAHJP Gr/Sa FO 346 Menahem Rousso & Fils. BA/none 29/8/35; BA/4436 12/11/36.

74 CAHJP Gr/Sa FO 346 Salomon S. Mordoh Successors BA/4817 22/06/1937.

75 CAHJP Gr/Sa FO 346 Humbert Scialom & Hassid BA/none 02/01/1936.

76 CAHJP Gr/Sa FO 346 Isaac Scialoum BA/369 19/04/1937. Similarly, S. Moché & Co.

(1930) exported raw skins, mainly to Skopje. See CAHJP Gr/Sa FO 346 S. Moché & Co. BA/4437 12/11/1936.

77 Author's free translation of: "*Depuis lors, elle s'est rattrapée et n'a cessé [sic] d'être correcte en affaires [sic] et régulier en ses payements.*" CAHJP Gr/Sa FO 346 Nissim Frères BA/4624 24/03/1937.

78 CAHJP Gr/Sa FO 346 Fils de Levy Simha BA/4820 25/06/1937.

79 For a list of the nations concluding clearing agreements with Greece, see Mazower 1991: 220.

80 Bostas (1987: 218) argues that trade statistics underestimate the value of the commerce conducted between Egypt and Greece while indicating demand for Greek nautical transport services. The latter was provided in part by the Greek merchant diaspora in the Levant during the Great Depression. On the reshaping of the Egyptian economy by foreigners, including Jews and Greeks, after World War I, see Tignor 1980.

81 The firm Moise D. Massarano (1902) was transformed into a partnership in 1920, when Moise added his son Dario as a partner. CAHJP Gr/Sa FO 346 Moise Massarano & Fils BA/4706 [n.d.].

82 CAHJP Gr/Sa FO 346 Fils d'Isac S. Saltiel BA/4565 16/02/1937.

83 The Jewish knitwear manufacturer Sam Sarfati (no. 152), for instance, suggested to Elie Modiano, proprietor of Cité Saul [the estate of late Saul Modiano] that they construct a one-storey shop at Rue Ermou 12 and thereby transform the premises occupied by Maison Mano & Co. and Salomon Saltiel. CAHJP Gr/Sa FO 346 Sam A. Sarfati BA/4569 17-18/2/1937.

84 The Jewish community's expenditures in 1929 listed a debt to Si[gnor] Elie Modiano in payment of the construction of Kazes School. LA 0059 Komunita Israelita Saloniko 1929.

85 On the drainage and reclamation projects completed in Macedonia as well as the resettlement of the refugees, see Kontogiorgi 2003: 72; Kontogiorgi 2006: 277–284.

86 CAHJP Gr/Sa FO 346 BA/220 E. Guikas 6/7/1936.

87 On the interrelationship between economic and political patronage in Greece during the inter-war period, see Dritsas 2003: 295–300.

88 For a broad discussion of Jewish engineers in Greece in the 1930s, see Meron 2008d.

89 CAHJP Gr/Sa FO 346 Elie J.[acob] Modiano BA/58 3/3/1935. See also Colonas 2002.

90 Author's translation of: "*La Société en question travaille exclusivement avec l'Etat, étant donné que tous les fleuves sont propriété de l'Etat.*" CAHJP Gr/Sa FO 346 SA Technique Hellenique de Defense Fluviale BA/61 5/03/1935.

91 For similar difficulties as experienced by foreign corporations, see Pepelasis Minoglou 2002.

92 CAHJP Gr/Sa FO 346 SA Technique Hellenique de Defense Fluviale BA/61 5/03/1935.

93 The head office of Errera Frerès was located in Salonica, on the same block as Modiano's engineering firm. Moise Errera managed the firm's Salonica office while his brother Joseph managed the Athens branch. Moise Errera and Elie Modiano were thus forced to travel frequently between Athens and Salonica. CAHJP Gr/Sa FO 346 Elie Modiano & Errera Frerès BA/59 3/3/1935; Elie J.[acob] Modiano BA/58 3/3/1935; Elie Modiano & Errera Frerès BA/42012/06/1937.

94 Compare Pepelasis Minoglou 2002.

95 Author's free translation of: " . . . *sa situation financière était un peu difficile ces derniers temps du fait qu'il a à recevoir de sommes importantes du Gouvernement pour des travaux effectues dézà [sic]. On me rapporte toutefois que le susnommé contracte des emprunts avec la garantie de son père, grand propriétaire d'immeubles et dont la fortune est évalue a Lstg. 50,000 environ.*" No information is given as to the value of the debt. CAHJP Gr/Sa FO 346 Elie J.[acob] Modiano BA/58 3/3/1935.

96 See also Pepelasis Minoglou 1998.

97 Compare Dritsas 2003.

98 DOT 1937: 18. The index of industrial production in Greece rose from 100 (the standardised base value) in 1928 to 127.8 in 1934 and 143.17 in 1935, with a slight drop to 141 in 1936.

99 These majority elites created the Federation of Greek Industries and through it demanded

legislation of an industrial policy (1922, 1935, and 1937; import restrictions were enforced in 1932) affecting the imports of machinery and raw material. Dritsas 2003.

100 Author's translation of: "*Marche de l'affaire satisfaisante grâce à la protection . . . a tout industrie viable.*" CAHJP Gr/Sa FO 346 Isac Carasso & Co. BA/4566 16/02/1937.

101 Author's translation of: "*Tout fait croire que sa demande sera prise en considération, la programme de gouvernement Métaxas prévoyant la protection et l'encouragement des industries qui apparaissent viables.*" (Very many believed that his request would be taken into consideration; farsighted programs of the Métaxas government envisaged protection and encouragement of the industries which appeared viable.) CAHJP Gr/Sa FO 346 Moise Perahia & Fils BA/none 01/01/1935; Pepo Moise Perahia (E.B.G.Y) BA/4783 01/05/1937.

102 DOT 1937: 16.

103 Freris 1986.

104 CAHJP Gr/Sa FO 346 BA/228 Pantis 21/7/1936.

105 CAHJP Gr/Sa FO 346 BA/296 Tsicas Frères 27/1/1937.

106 Since the 1920s, alcohol manufactured exclusively from currants was supported by the large surplus of fruit that was usually produced. The Greek treasury enjoyed high revenues from the alcohol consumption tax. Tariffs protected local distilleries. DOT 1925: 30; Mazower 1991: 56.

107 CAHJP Gr/Sa FO 346 BA/358 Georgiades Frères 15/4/1937; BA/ 272 Georgiades & Coniordou 12/11/1936.

108 It cannot be confirmed whether the firm Coniordou Frères relocated to Salonica in 1914 before the Transfer, when the brothers settled in Salonica, or in 1925, as there are contradictory reports on the subject: BA/282 Coniordou Frères 25/11/1936; BA/ 272 Georgiades & Coniordou 12/11/1936.

109 Mazower 1991: 81–86.

110 CAHJP Gr/Sa FO 346 BA/358 Georgiades Frères 15/4/1937. Based on the *Austrian Report* 1915: 53, Georgiades Frères established their brewery in 1911 (section 4.5.2), which started operating in 1912.

111 The commercial affairs of Mahel Rousso & Cie. were continued after its dissolution in 1930 by Rousso & Gavios, which later (1934) changed its name to Aron Gavios CAHJP Gr/Sa FO 346 Mahel Rousso & Cie BA/none 14/12/1935.

112 CAHJP Gr/Sa FO 346 Marco Matarasso Romani & Co. BA/none 14/12/1937.

113 Beraha & Cie was owned by S[abbetai] J[uda] Beraha and his partner Joseph Haim. In 1924 it was located in Ladadika area (between Rue Tsimiski and the Port), motorised ten horsepower; six workers; produced 6,000 oke (oke = approx. 1.3 kg, or 7,800 kg) of macaroni per a day. Roupa and Hekimoglou 2004: 346.

114 The Greek partners were Couscouras & Mocas, Hadjiyannis & Verrou and G. Micas Fréres. CAHJP Gr/Sa FO 346 "AVEZ" BA/267 11/9/1936. Compare with Roupa and Hekimoglou 2004: 29–30.

115 Author's translation of "*A englobé toutes les affaires des fabriques des pâtes alimentaires . . . et donner fin à la concurrence qu'elles se faisaient.*"

116 By 1936 this corporation included the Greek pasta-producing factory and its large attached shop, which employed about sixty workers. CAHJP Gr/Sa FO 346 "AVEZ" BA/267 11/9/1936.

117 According to testimonies, the AVEZ pasta factory could compete also with Italian and French pasta producers factory. Roupa and Hekimoglou 2004: 354.

118 CAHJP Gr/Sa FO 346 Fils de David Hasson BA/4376 7/10/1936.

119 CAHJP Gr/Sa FO 346 BA/37 Nektar 9 February 1935.

120 CAHJP Gr/Sa FO 346 Pliancas, Castritsis & Co. BA/287 14/12/1936.

121 CAHJP Gr/Sa FO 346 Chocolaterie Floca, SA BA/414 08/06/1937.

122 See notes 120 and 121.

123 Given the diversity of the goods produced, this discussion also includes a review of the trade in iron under the category of "trade in construction materials" (see Table 8.1).

124 DOT 1927: 26, 30.

125 Pelt 1998: 126–130.

126 CAHJP Gr/Sa FO 346 Gheorgiki Eteria Thrakis & Makedonias SA BA/443 9/7/1937.

127 CAHJP Gr/Sa FO 346 Leon A. Juda BA/4678 13/04/1937.

128 CAHJP Gr/Sa FO 346 Anastassios Kazgandjoglou BA/185 21/4/1936.

129 CAHJP Gr/Sa FO 346 BA/86 D. Hovaghimian & Co. 27/5/1935; BA/165 29/2/1936.

130 CAHJP Gr/Sa FO 346 BA/81 Agop Keklikian 8/5/1936.

131 Benrubi was previously employed by Alvo & Bendavid; CAHJP Gr/Sa FO 346 Moise Benrubi.

132 CAHJP Gr/Sa FO 346 Ouziel & Menaché BA/4746 11/05/1937.

133 CAHJP Gr/Sa FO 346 Joseph Sabetay Saadi BA/ 4743 11/05/1937; BA/none7/12/1935.

134 Roupa and Hekimoglou 2004: 480–485.

135 Victor Zadok also owned a chain of boutiques; CAHJP Gr/Sa FO 346 Galeries Modernes – S. Zadok & Cie. BA/132 21/01/1936; BA/4435 10/11/1936.

136 CAHJP Gr/Sa FO 346 Revah, Levy & Co. BA/4652 09/04/1937.

137 Previously Frances & Menaché (1928), reconstituted in 1935 under the cited name. CAHJP Gr/Sa FO 346 A. Ménaché & Co. BA/4544 9/2/1937.

138 Pepo Yacoël (aka Jacoël) & Cie. (Appendix 5 no. 445), founded in 1918 by Pepo Yacoël, was transformed into a partnership in 1923 when Nehama Mallah, a tissue merchant and Pepo's brother-in-law, became an associate. CAHJP Gr/Sa BA/none 04/03/1935; BA/none January 1937; CAHJP Gr/Sa FO 346 Pepo Yacoël & Co BA/4545. 9/2/1937.

139 On the arms trade see Pelt 1998: 133–181.

140 The firm was founded in 1912 by their father, Haim Alvo. CAHJP Gr/Sa FO 346 Alvo Frères BA/130 21/01/1936.

141 CAHJP Gr/Sa FO 346 Clouterie et Tréfilerie Macédonienne SA BA/483 01/11/1937.

142 Leon Isac Navarro had settled in Paris in 1924. The Navarro brothers, who traded in construction materials, were also involved in the hotel business, thanks to their small interest in the Hotel Majesty; CAHJP Gr/Sa FO 346 M. & A. Navarro BA/ 4669 10/04/1937.

143 Author's translation of: *"Leurs affaires marchent bien et ils ont réalise d'excellents bénéfices par suite du stock qu'ils détenaient et la hausse des métaux."* Similarly, the Jewish firm Nefussy, which traded in construction materials, realised considerable profits following the unexpected rise in metal prices. See CAHJP Gr/Sa FO 346 Albert Elie Nefussy BA/4616 27/05/1939

144 CAHJP Gr/Sa FO 346 Benico and Isac Angel & Cie. BA/4393 15/10/1936.

145 The firm succeeded (1926) the old firm of Maison Jacob D. Frances. CAHJP Gr/Sa FO 346 Joseph Isac Hassid & Frères BA/503 30/11/1937.

146 Compare with the Armenian-owned firm Keklikian, also a nail producer, which employed only ten workers, a reflection of its relatively small market share. BA/81 Agop Keklikian 8/5/1936.

147 This procedure required receipt of an invoice against payment of a bill of lading. Banque Union was later to collect Dario Assael's matured debt: YIVO, RJCS, Greece, RG 207, FO; 156 Bremer Bank (a branch of Dresdner Bank), Bremen, on behalf of Wagner & Co., Altena (Westf.) Stahldrahtwerke, to Banque Union, SA, Salonica, 29 July 1932 (in English). A confirmation obtained from the tax authorities (1932) indicates that Dario Assael imported these goods in 1932 by means of a ship bearing the German flag. YIVO, RJCS, Greece, RG 207, FO. 156 Salonica Customs House 16/9/1932.

148 CAHJP Gr/Sa FO 346 Dario Joseph Assael BA/4633 30/03/1937.

149 Pelt 1998: 127.

150 Dritsas 2003.

151 Pelt 1998: 34–35.

152 This entrepreneurial branch was also included under large-scale trade.

153 Pelt 1998: 127.

154 DOT 1937: 18–19. On fluctuations in the Greek bauxite and chrome trade to Germany (1937–1940), see Pelt 1998: p. 132, Table 19. Expanded mining and exports to free currency markets made possible growth in the export of bauxite to Germany. Pelt 1998: 289 n. 549.

155 DOT 1937: 16.

156 Based on data from the National Bank of Greece. Papastefanaki 2007: Table 6. The absence of state supervision, the paucity of research and geological knowledge, and the inadequacy of local technical education impeded the efficient operation of mines but did not their profitability.

157 Author's free translation of: *"Les affaires minières, qui tendent à se developer de jour en jour*

d'avantage, ont tout mon attention. Je m'en occupe trèactivement [*sic*]." CAHJP Gr/Sa FO 346 Vita B. Amar BA/ none 19/8/1935.

158 CAHJP Gr/Sa FO 346 Pepo Yacoël & Co. BA/none 04/03/1935;

159 Mentioned in CAHJP Gr/Sa FO 346 Pepo Yacoël & Co. BA/4545 9/2/1937.

160 CAHJP Gr/Sa FO 346 Pepo Yacoël & Co. BA/4545 9/2/1937.

161 CAHJP Gr/Sa FO 346 BA/124 Eteria Asvestopiias "Enossis" 7/12/1935.

162 Roupa and Hekimoglou 2004: 37.

163 CAHJP Gr/Sa FO 346 Pepo Is. Joseph & Co. BA/4662 06/04/1937.

164 Pelt 1998: 114.

165 Landau had previously served (1912–1915) with the Deutsche Levante Linie in Salonica. In 1915, he left for a stint in Hamburg. He returned to Salonica in 1919 and established the firm of Landau & Benveniste (Commercial Representation) (Appendix 4.1, no. 595). This partnership was dissolved in 1921. CAHJP Gr/Sa FO 346 Bernard Landau BA/250 8 October 1936. Bernard Landau was not an outsider to the Sephardic business community in Salonica despite his German origins. Although married to a woman named Olga – a non-Sephardic name – his relatives were important members of the Sephardic community. A rich correspondence between Landau and the Alvo brothers of the Salonica diaspora in Paris shows that he was deeply involved in Jewish social life. The Alvo brothers in fact helped him arrange the funeral of his younger sister, Carolina (the wife of Leon Hazan), who died in Paris on 15 November 1937 of rheumatic fever. She was buried in a Jewish cemetery and had a tombstone engraved in Hebrew. CAHJP Gr/Sa FO 80 9 February 1938.

166 In an informant's words: " . . . *en association d'après certaines sources avec la fabrique de parfumerie allemande Drall de Hamburg*" (. . . in association, according to certain sources, with the firm of the German perfumery Drall of Hamburg). CAHJP Gr/Sa FO 346 Bernard Landau BA/250 8 October 1936.

167 In an informant's words: "*S'occupe aussi de renseignements commerciaux, ce qui provoque, paraît-il, l'indignation des maisons de représentations de notre ville étant donne qu'il n'est pas jugé impartial dans ses informations*" (His stratagems arouse anger among the city's [commercial] representatives, given the fact that he is never neutral in his assessment of any information about them.).

168 Dagkas 2003: 270–271.

169 CAHJP Gr/Sa FO 346 Joseph Menahem Hassid BA/4697 19/04/1937.

170 It appears that this date was chosen because September, the month in which the Jewish New Year generally fell, was the time when Jews traditionally renewed contracts (e.g., rental agreements). CAHJP Gr/Sa FO 346 Gheorgacopoulos, Asséo & Capon BA/none 31/03/1936.

171 CAHJP Gr/Sa FO 346 Nahama B. Capon & Cie BA/none 30/03/1936.

172 CAHJP Gr/Sa FO 346 Abram Pelossof & Amariglio BA/4386 12/10/1936.

173 Société Anonyme, fondée en 1929, autorisée par Décret du Ministère de l'Economie Nationale de 22 Mars 1929. Its board included Vassilio G. Yacou (president), Georges J. Yacou & Juda Isac Leon (administrative representative), Vassilio I. Yacou, Abram Sam Leon, and Jacob Isac Leon (administrators). CAHJP Gr/Sa FO 346 SA Macedonienne pour l'Industrie de Savon BA/347 01/04/1937.Compare with Roupa and Hekimoglou 2004: 500–511.

174 CAHJP Gr/Sa FO 346 Hassid & Cuenca BA/none 15 February 1935; BA/335 28/03/1937.

175 Author's translation of: "*Sa production assez intéressante est vendue dans le Pays même.*" CAHJP Gr/Sa FO 346 Moise J. Hassid BA/4647 1/4/1937; BA/none 13/6/1936.

176 By 1927, the British consul was reporting on new industries being established in Greece. These included rubber factories (excluding automobile tires and tubes). In 1928, he sent details of "a new factory of 25 HP for rubber articles, one of 175HP for cellulose [sic] goods, and three nail factories of 207 H[orse] P[ower]". DOT 1927: 26; DOT 1928: 24.

177 CAHJP Gr/Sa FO 346 Isac David Tiano BA/4796 11/06/1937.

178 CAHJP Gr/Sa FO 346 "Hermes" S. Benveniste, H. Pardo 7 co. 2/10/1936.

179 For example, the national rubber factory, which provided rubber for Greek gas mask production, was a vertical extension of the huge Greek Powder and Cartridge Company (established in the mid-1930s), owned by the former Ottoman Greek Prodromos-Bodosakis-Athanasiadis. Similarly, the Chemical Products and Fertiliser Company

supplied the concern with the basic chemicals needed for powder and explosives production. See Pelt 1998: 78–82.

180 CAHJP Gr/Sa FO 346 Albert J. Ammir BA/4521 [n.d].

181 Author's free translation of: *[L]a branche bois de construction a pu réaliser ces dernières années des affaires assez lucratives à la suite des restrictions imposées par l'Etat pour l'importation de cet article.* CAHJP Gr/Sa FO 346 Kokou & Co. 14/1/1937.

182 CAHJP Gr/Sa FO 346 Alexandre B[asile] Zahariades 15/6/1937. For correspondence between Serbian timber suppliers and Banque Union regarding Zahariades's debts, see YIVO, RJCS, Greece, RG 207, FO. 156 Fr. Premrov & Sin, Martinjak P. Cerknica, Jugoslavia to Banque Union, SA, Salonica, 12 August 1932; YIVO, RJCS, Greece, RG 207, FO. 156 Dioni arsko društvo za Eksploatacÿu drua – Société Anonyme d'Exploitation Forestière, Zagreb, to Banque Union, SA, Salonica; 16, 20, 22, 23 July 1932; 6, 16 August 1932; YIVO, RJCS, Greece, RG 207, FO. 156 A. Sciaky, Bois de Construction, Sarajevo, Bosnia, Yugoslavia, to Banque Union, SA, Salonica, 12 August 1932.

183 This firm was originally founded (1893) under the name of Moise Semtov Saltiel. It was later transformed (1924) into a partnership owned by Semtov Moise Saltiel, Isac Moise Saltiel, and Benico Semtov Saltiel. Following a notary act dated 6 February 1936, the partnership expanded to include Albert Semtov Saltiel, Moise Isac Saltiel, and Moise Semtov Saltiel, who were the founder Moise Saltiel's grandsons; CAHJP Gr/Sa FO 346 Moise Saltiel Fils & Cie. BA/4753 12/5/1937.

184 Author's translation of: "*La marche de leur affaire est normale avec tendance à la progression dûe à la protection par l'Etat à toute entreprise reconnue viable.*" CAHJP Gr/Sa FO 346 Beja Frères BA/240 20/08/1936.

185 Originally from Monastir, Yugoslavia, Barouh later settled in Athens, where he was employed by the Bank of Piraeus. CAHJP Gr/Sa FO 346 M.I. Barouh BA/201 18/5/1936.

186 Yahiel was a Yugoslav national whose city of origin was Bitolj, the former Ottoman Monastir. CAHJP Gr/Sa FO 346 Yahiel Jacob Alevy BA/4844 15/7/1937.

187 According to Banque Amar's records, the only three Greek firms registered with the bank were Castrinakis & Georgantas (typographies), Papeterie Hermes (paper milling, printers, and registry manufacture), and Elliniki Kytiopita Makedonias (cardboard boxes). CAHJP Gr/Sa FO 346 ff.

188 Benveniste Haim & Albert (est. 1909) (Appendix 5, no. 421) had previously been dissolved (1933) for fiscal reasons. Given the commercial milieu, the two brothers continued to be effective partners in the 'new' firm, Haim Benveniste. CAHJP Gr/Sa FO 346 Haim Benveniste BA/4631 29/3/1937.

189 CAHJP Gr/Sa FO 346 Errico Jakob Arones BA/4856 29/07/1937.

190 CAHJP Gr/Sa FO 346 Pepo Moise Perahia (E.B.G.Y.) BA/4783 01/05/1937; Moise Perahia & Fils BA/none 01/01/1935.

191 CAHJP Gr/Sa FO 346 Abram J. Juda BA/330 24/03/1937.

192 Dagkas 2003: 302. The cigarette paper demanded for hand-made cigarettes was generally of a higher quality (i.e., lighter) than was paper for industrially produced cigarettes. Ibid., note 873.

193 YIVO, RJCS, Greece, RG 207, FO. 156. The Italian paper factory Helios Società Cartaria, G.L., Trieste to Banque Union, SA, Salonica, 8 July, 1932; 25 July 1932.

194 According to the informant's report: "*En 1931 a la suite d'un différent avec la Fisc qui découvrit chez Mr. Hassid du papier a cigarette contenant 1.52% au lieu du minimum de 2% requis par la loi.*" (Following the firm's deviation (1931) from government standards regarding the composition of cigarette paper, Abram Hassid was forced to change the firm's name and transfer it to his son, Isac Abram Hassid (24)). CAHJP Gr/Sa FO 346 Isac Abram Hassid BA/none 22/1/1935

195 Author's translation of: "*Al suite de la forte concurrence existant dans la branche, et de la crise générale. . . .*"

196 CAHJP Gr/Sa FO 346 Isac Abram Hassid BA/none 22/1/1935; Abram H. Hassid BA/339 29/3/1937.

197 CAHJP Gr/Sa FO 346 Georges Darveris BA/225 14/07/1936.

198 CAHJP Gr/Sa FO 346 Theodoros Hadjinacou BA/217 26/06/1936.

199 CAHJP Gr/Sa FO 346 Benico Segura BA/216 26/06/1936.

200 The Jewish economist and Nobel Prize winner (1976) Milton Friedman explained the substantial presence of Jews in the US movie industry in the first half of the twentieth century by its competitive character as well as its ease of entry. This "was a new industry and for that reason open to all", being free of government regulation in its early days. Friedman 1988: 388.

201 Saby Nissim Mallah became an attaché at the Consulat Honoraire of Portugal in Salonica beginning in 1919. CAHJP Gr/Sa FO 346 Saby Nissim Mallah BA/4828 1/7/37.

202 Prior to 1933, he and his brother Victor were partners. CAHJP Gr/Sa FO 346 Yacoel Jacques BA/ none 28/03/1935.

203 Author's translated summary of: "*Les affaires sont satisfaisantes, comme l'ailleurs celles de tous les commerçants de la branche. Les résultants obtenus ces années doivent donc être intéressantes.*" CAHJP Gr/Sa FO 346 Nahmias & Mordoh BA/none 7/12/1935.

204 DOT 1937: 17.

205 The narrow profit margin of the steam-powered spinning mills derived from a restricted internal market, the lack of industrial credit, and the availability of cheap refugee labour; these were probably the main reasons for the delayed mechanisation of the factories. Despite the protective tariff regime and the currency devaluation, production cost reduction became crucial. Greek industrialists consequently intensified exploitation of the workforce by extending the work day, reorganising labour, vertically integrating production, and reducing wages. See Papastefanaki 2007; 2009.

206 Mazower 1991: 253–256.

207 CAHJP Gr/Sa FO 346 Mario Lezer Salmona BA/4815 19/6/1937.

208 CAHJP Gr/Sa FO 346 Salomon A. Mordoh BA/none 10/1935; 02/01/1936.

209 CAHJP Gr/Sa FO 346 Salomon Menahem Rousso BA/246 10/09/1936.

210 Daniel Sidés and his brother Jacques held 1,152 firm shares, valued at GRD 1,152,000, about one-third of the firm's capital, valued at GRD 3,200,000. CAHJP Gr/Sa FO 346 Sidés Frères BA/4667 10/4/1937; see also Stavroulakis et al. (n.d.).

211 Female refugees, who had the advantage of low-cost yet pre-migratory skills, entered the industry. This led to the industry's vertical expansion from the agricultural breeding of silk cocoons to the weaving of silk floss, manufacture of fabric, international exports, and, for some, knitting of stockings. DOT 1925: 27.

212 Greece, *Annuaire Statistique de la Grèce 1931*, Table 5, p. 95.

213 CAHJP Gr/Sa FO 346 Saltiel Bros. 6/2/1935.

214 CAHJP Gr/Sa FO 346 BA/4605 [Fils d'Isac M. Nissim] Haim Isac Nissim Succ. 17/03/1937; "HERMES" H. Pardo & M. Carasso BA/none 15/11/1937.

215 The partners took over all liquid as well as immovable capital and assumed all the obligations (*assumèrent l'actif et le passif de*) of the firm of Fils de Jacob Saltiel & Cie. CAHJP Gr/Sa FO 346 Fils de Jacob Saltiel & Broudo BA/none 6/2/1937.

216 The sewing and knitting machine merchants Benmayor, Molho & Cohen, Maison "Veritas" (est. 1919) underwent two transitions. In 1931, after Bension Cohen settled in Paris, the firm continued as a partnership under its new official name, Benmayor & Molho; in 1932, this partnership was dissolved. CAHJP Gr/Sa FO 346 BA/93 Ino Benmayor, Maison "Veritas" 7/8/1935.

217 The brothers Haim and Samuel Af[f]ias were equal partners in a shop selling cotton material and scarves to peasants; see A. Recanati 2000: 41: 2/304; 2/306.

218 CAHJP Gr/Sa FO 346. Asséo & Capuano BA/4716 28/4/1937.

219 Author's translation of: "*de tissus manufacturés de qualité inférieure à l'usage des classes laborieuses.*" CAHJP Gr/Sa FO 346 Juda Noah & Fils BA/4656 7/4/1937.

220 In index numbers: from 61.6 for 1924–1930 to 201.1 for 1931–1937. For a detailed analysis of the textile sector's recovery in Greece, see Mazower 1991: 251–256.

221 A mixed liability partnership (*société en commandite*). Whereas Elie's son Salomon Elie Pinhas was the Director of Procurement for the enterprise, Guedalia Pinhas represented the old (74) silent partner Haim Elie Pinhas. In spite of the firm's reconstitution on new foundations in 1933, the banks still restricted its credit (1936) in order to discount their commercial bills from their incomes. CAHJP Gr/Sa FO 346 Elie Pinhas & Cie. BA/4016 28/2/1936.

222 Because its nominal invested capital was only GRD 60,000, it officially continued to be

listed under small-scale firms, i.e., firms with less than GRD 100,000 in assets, such as Haim Mano (see section 9.4 below). CAHJP Gr/Sa FO 346 Elie Pinhas & Cie. BA/4016 28/2/1936.

223 Compare Hekimoglou 2004: 22.

224 Based on their fishing tradition, new refugee communities developed the fishing industry in rural Macedonia, e.g., the village of Ammouliani. See Salamone 1987.

225 CAHJP Gr/Sa FO 346 Saltiel & Elie Angel & Fils, BA/4683 14/04/1937.

226 Author's translation of: "*Elle* [i.e., this firm] *vient d'être agrandie et actuellement la production répond aux besoins de la demande.*"

227 DOT 1937: 17.

228 For example, the solely Greek-owned firm Lazar Vogas Fils (est. 1885), which operated a factory and shop for the manufacture and sale of braiding (*passementerie*) and other sewing notions, did very well thanks to the restrictions imposed on similar imports. CAHJP Gr/Sa FO 346 Lazar Vogas Fils BA/249 2/10/1936.

229 Author's translation of: "*Ses affaires marchent depuis plus de deux ans très bien à la suit de restrictions prises par l'Etat pour l'importation d'articles similaires de l'Etranger.*" CAHJP Gr/Sa FO 346 Moise I. Mordoh BA/204 8/6/1936.

230 CAHJP Gr/Sa FO 346 R[osa]. Kellermann (Sam Sarfati & Co.) BA/88 26 June 1935; A. Guelermann BA/511 16/12/1937.

231 This firm continued to manage the fire insurance portfolio of Company Patriotic following the death of Daniel's father. CAHJP Gr/Sa FO 346 Daniel S. Modiano BA/4628 29/03/1937.

232 Author's translated summary of: "*La fabrique est considérée comme une de plus importantes de la branche dans toute la Macédoine.*" CAHJP Gr/Sa FO 346 Makedoniki Kaltsopiia SA BA/161, 21 February 1936.

233 Author's translation of: "*Cettes* [sic] *sociétés ont fusionné pour mettre fin a la concurrence qu'elles se faisaient entre elles.*" The Anonymous Society (12 November 1936) represented the merger of four factories manufacturing socks and stockings: A. Korexenides (est. 1930), Sam Sarfati & Co. (est. 1925), Anastassiades & Dimopoulos (est. 1933), and Lazarides Frères (est. 1935). Its board of directors included Sam Sarfati (administrative delegate), Anesti Korexenides, Ioannis Korexenides, Nicolaos Dimopoulos, Emmanuel Lazarides, and Lélémaque Lazarides. The records note that the merger between Sam Sarfati, Anesti Korexenides, Nicolaos Dimopoulos, and Emmanuel Lazarides was useful to the company. Sarfati's total interests amounted to GRD 1,128,000 (1,128 shares valued at GRD 1,000 each). CAHJP Gr/Sa FO 346 Sam A. Sarfati BA/4569 17-18/2/1937; Fabriques Réunies de Bas et Chaussettes de Sal/Que SA, BA/426 15/06/1937.

234 CAHJP Gr/Sa FO 346 Sam A. Sarfati BA/4569 17-18/2/1937.

235 CAHJP Gr/Sa FO 346 Papadimitriou & Assael BA/506 12/12/1937; BA/none 24/9/1935; BA/none 12/4/1937.

236 The firm had been active in Salonica's market since 1915, even though the partnership was officially registered only in 1922. CAHJP Gr/Sa FO 346 Tchico & Bitran BA/none 5/2/1936; BA/4733 08/05/1937.

237 CAHJP Gr/Sa FO 346 Saltiel & Guilidi BA/ none 24/01/1935.

238 CAHJP Gr/Sa FO 346 Barouh S. Venezia BA/4634 30/30/37.

239 As of the late 1920s, the sale of woollen fabrics declined by about 10 percent and the sale of cotton fabrics by about 25 percent in relation to the early 1920s. Roupa and Hekimoglou 2004: 35.

240 Author's free translation of: "*Marche de l'affaire: intéressante depuis l'application des mesures de restriction sur l'importation d'articles fabriqués dans le Pays. A noter qu'avant l'application de ces mesures, les tourniquets étaient importes de l'étranger.*" CAHJP Gr/Sa FO 346 Moise Paladino Fils & Cie BA/4440 14/11/1936.

241 CAHJP Gr/Sa FO 346 Simon S. Molho BA/4640 31/03/1937.

242 CAHJP Gr/Sa FO 346 Makedoniki Pilopiia Moscovitch, Frances & Cie BA/4453 18/11/1936; BA/64 17/3/1935.

243 This firm is identified with the hat producer Arianoutsos, rue Tsimiski. *Guide Sam* 1930: 907.

244 N.K. Arianoutsos was originally founded in 1924 as a branch of Arianoutsos SA of Athens, a hat manufacturer. Following the corporation's dissolution in about 1933, N.K.

Arianoutsos independently continued the Salonica branch's activity. CAHJP Gr/Sa FO 346
A. Arianoutsos & Co. BA/70 29/3/1935; BA/222 08/07/1936.

245 CAHJP Gr/Sa FO 346 Saltiel S. Cohen BA/468 8/10/1937.

246 CAHJP Gr/Sa FO 346 Constantin Zografakis BA/401 31/5/1937.

247 CAHJP Gr/Sa FO 346 Seraphimides Frères BA/69 29/3/1935.

248 For ostrich feather hat decoration as a Jewish speciality in the Mediterranean, see also
Abrevaya Stein 2007; idem 2008.

249 E.g., CAHJP Gr/Sa FO 346 Samuel Avayou & Frères BA/4722 01/05/1937.

250 But despite its high profits following the inflation, its debts were still unpaid in 1936. Its
group of stores still had mortgages held by Banque Union and Banque Populaire. " . . . *se
procure sur place des peaux brutes et une partie de sa production est exportée." "Durant l'ex-
ercice 1936 elle a réalisé d'intéressants bénéfices à la suite de la hausse survenue sur les peaux.
Cependant des dettes restent toujours en suspense."* (. . . procures rawhide on site and part
of its production is exported. In the fiscal year 1936 the company has made extremely good
profits as a result of increased demand for skins. However, [the company] still debts hanging
over it.) CAHJP Gr/Sa FO 346 Ammir & Mevorah BA/4553 11/02/1937.

251 Nehama was previously a partner in Nehama & Florentin, dissolved in 1931; CAHJP Gr/Sa
FO 346 Sabetay I. Nehama BA/4777 28/5/1937. A careful comparison of the documents
leads to the conclusion that this firm was not identical to that of Sabetay J. Nehama (no.
119), even though their addresses were the same. We cannot, however, exclude some family
relationship between the two. CAHJP Gr/Sa FO 346 Sabetay J. Nehama BA/none 7/1/1935.

252 CAHJP Gr/Sa FO 346 Liaou Camhi BA/406 1/6/1937; BA/77 26/4/1935.

253 *Guide Sam* 1930: 940.

254 The firm even didn't change its address even though Rue Roi Constantin was renamed as
Rue Venizelos. CAHJP Gr/Sa FO 346 Cohen Frères. BA/4644 1/4/1937.

255 Previously David Angel & Cie., a partnership. After its dissolution (1928) following the
death of its founder, Angel's nephews Benico and Isac and his brother Lezer formed a new
partnership which took over his affairs. CAHJP Gr/Sa FO 346 Benico & Isac Angel & Cie,
BA/4393 15/10/1936.

256 Grèce, Departement Hellénique de l'Information [n.d.], *Le Drame des Juifs Hellènes*, p. 2.

257 On the politics characterising this branch, see Mazower 1991.

258 These majority elites created the Federation of Greek Industries and through it demanded
legislation of industrial policy (1922, 1935, and 1937) and institution of import restrictions
(1932) on machinery and raw material. Dritsas 2003.

259 Grèce, Département Hellénique de l'Information [n.d.], *Le Drame des Juifs Hellènes*.

260 Dritsas 2003: 296–297.

261 Dritsas 2003: 299–300.

262 Veteran Greek elite networks were connected to land ownership whereas the new networks,
formed by refugees, were based on the internal cohesion growing from shared education,
professions, and social qualifications. Dritsas 2003: 295–300.

263 Dritsas 1992: 210.

264 It is symbolic that the Nazi invaders chose to begin closing Jewish shops with the famous
Molho bookstore in Salonica and the Kaufman bookstore in Athens. See Fleischer 1995:
10.

265 Dublon-Knebel 2007: 77. T3: Consul Schönberg, Salonika, to FO, Berlin, on the anti-
Jewish atmosphere in Salonika and the activity of Ethniki Etaireia. 30 November 1938

266 Molho and Nehama 1965: 31.

267 For the citation from Israel Kirzner, see Ioannides and Pepelasis – Minoglou 2005: 175–176.

268 Kitroeff 1989.

269 CAHJP Gr/Sa FO 346 Moise Sal Abastado BA/4756 13/05/1937.

270 CAHJP Gr/Sa FO 346 David & Joseph Abastado BA/76 22/04/1935.

271 On Torrès SA and the Torrès family tree, see Roupa and Hekimoglou 2004: 548–553.

272 CAHJP Gr/Sa FO 346 Raphaël Jakob Varsano & Co. BA/ 4660 07/04/1937.

273 CAHJP Gr/Sa FO 346 Salomon Is. Amariglio BA/4818 23/6/1937.

Chapter 9

1   The remaining firms consisted of 68 foreign firms and 40 Armenian firms. See Dublon-Knebel, 2007: 78.
2   Foreman-Peck 1985; Foreman-Peck 2005: 81.
3   As in the book's other chapters, the numbers in parentheses indicate the firm's position in Appendix 8 unless otherwise indicated.
4   CAHJP Gr/Sa FO 346 Joseph S. Djahon BA/ [none] 21/9/1936.
5   CAHJP Gr/Sa FO 346 Joseph R. Hazan BA/29 08/01/1935.
6   CAHJP Gr/Sa FO 346 Fils d'Azriel Frances BA/98 13/08/1935.
7   Author's free translation of: "*Ses neveux lui ont accordé ce privilège pour sa collaboration appréciée, étant donné ses connaissances de la branche.*" CAHJP Gr/Sa FO 346 Benico & Isac Angel & Cie. BA/4393 15/10/1936.
8   CAHJP Gr/Sa FO 346 Abram M. Mattia BA/4750 12/05/1937.
9   CAHJP Gr/Sa FO 346 Joseph Mordohai Nahmias BA/4721 01/05/1937.
10 CAHJP Gr/Sa FO 346 Dario Pinhas BA/355 12/4/1937.
11 CAHJP Gr/Sa FO 346 Pinto & Barzilai BA/445 13/07/1937.
12 CAHJP Gr/Sa FO 346 Samuel Sion BA/470 19/10/1937.
13 Between 1931 and 1934, Marcel was a member of the firm of De Mayo & Zadok, commercial representatives. CAHJP Gr/Sa FO 346 Marcel Abram de Mayo BA/none 9/1/1935.
14 Author's translation of: " . . . *pendant une vingtaine d'années, Mr Asséo a été attaché à la maison Affias Frères ou il acquis une grande expérience de la branche.*" CAHJP Gr/Sa FO 346 Asséo & Capuano BA/4716 28/4/1937; BA/none 17/1/1935.
15 CAHJP Gr/Sa FO 346 Salvator J. Varsano BA/ 331 24/03/1937.
16 CAHJP Gr/Sa FO 346 Haim J. Moché & Fils BA/503 9/12/1937.
17 CAHJP Gr/Sa FO 346 Moïse S. Francès BA/ none 07/08/1936; 18/11/1937. The Franco-Serb Bank was a consortium of four Paris banks, which had been recruited by several Serbian political parties. The bank, established in Paris during the late 1900s to arrange a new loan to the Municipality of Belgrade on the Paris capital market, opened its doors in Belgrade only in the mid-1910s. The bank facilitated state loans supporting infrastructure development, such as Belgrade's water system. See Lampe and Jackson 1982: 230–231, 260. CAHJP Gr/Sa FO 346 Moïse S. Francès BA/ none 07/08/1936; 18/11/1937.
18 E.g., Sam A. Saporta (no. 229) employed two people, including his partner's son, Salomon Broudo. CAHJP Gr/Sa FO 346 Sam A. Saporta BA/4654 [date erased]/04/1937.
19 His father, Hanania Mardoché, had "*très larges moyens financiers*" (very large financial resources). CAHJP Gr/Sa FO 346 Henri Mardoché BA/none/ 1/3/1933.
20 Paraphrased in the text from the following: "*MM. Mardoché financent avec les fonds de leur père certaines entreprises industrielles s'occupant de la fabrication de bas et chaussettes contre certains privilèges, indépendamment des intérêts perçus a un taux modéré.*" CAHJP Gr/Sa FO 346 Mardoché Frères BA/4636 31/03/1937.
21 Previously Fils de Sam Florentin (1870–1937) when Salomon had only a 68 percent ownership. CAHJP Gr/Sa FO 346 Fils de Sam Florentin BA/428 16/6/1937; CAHJP Gr/Sa FO 346 Salomon S. Florentin BA/428 16/6/1937; BA/473 19/10/1937.
22 See *Austrian Report* 1915: 50.
23 Stoianovich 1994: 196, 292–293; Mazower 2004: 268–271.
24 Gounaris 1998: 2.
25 CZA S6/2535, 6 January 1939, a survey on Zionist activities in Greece, sent by Dr. Zvi Zohar from the Head Office of the Jewish National Fund in Prague to the organisation's headquarters in Jerusalem.
26 Among the Jewish-Gentile joint ventures (excluding corporations) active in 1912, we can include Carvonides, G.I. & Morpugo; Jenny (also spelled Yenny) & Vock; Mano Haim & Nouri Abdurahman; Pandeli & Matalon; Peneuchlieff & Gattegno; Rowel et Molho. The majority of these ethnically mixed ownerships did not involve Greeks. See Meron 2005b, Appendix A.
27 On sesame cultivation in Macedonia, see Dagkas 2003: 206.
28 Bourla 1986: 212 (in Hebrew).
29 Similarly, two of the Jewish partnerships created with non-Jewish partners involved ethnic

groups already residing in the new Balkan states. Like the Greek case, Jewish-Serbian (Dobrovolski & Livada, insurance) or Jewish-Romanian partnerships (e.g., Salamonesco & Segura, import–export) helped Jews penetrate the Serbian and Romanian trading arenas by activating middlemen belonging to the respective countries' resident ethnic majorities.

30 See for example: Alexandre Spiliotis, Pandelis Nicolaou (also a consignor), K. Antipas et Filides (also consignors), Apostolides et Georgiades, Rossis Tsounis et Cie. *Annual Report* 1922, pp. 337–338.

31 Zvi Zohar also noted that Jewish non-acculturationist behaviour prevented formation of a "forthright and honourable relationship with the Greek authorities". CZA S6/2535, 6 January 1939, survey on Zionist activities in Greece sent by Dr. Zvi Zohar from the Jewish National Fund's Head Office in Prague to the organisation's headquarters in Jerusalem.

32 In the context of the uncertain world of early industrialisation, family firms were also found to be attractive in Spain, Italy, and Britain. See Colli et al. 2003: 35–38.

33 Formerly a *société en nom collectif* owned by Hananel Naar and his brothers Moise and Abram (1910). By the Notary Act of 1 December 1932, a *société en commandite* was constituted between Hananel E. Naar and Maïr S. Amariglio. CAHJP Gr/Sa FO 346 Hananel E. Naar & Co. BA/4478 04/12/1936.

34 Author's free translation of: "*Depuis la création de la nouvelle Société en commandite l'affaire marche bien ce qui est la conséquence de la plus value du stock en marchandises au moment de la dissolution de l'ancienne Société en nom collectif et aussi parce que la Firme Hananel Naar & Cie. Trouve auprès de son commanditaire l'argent nécessaire à assurer le bon fonctionnement de l'entreprise . . . les bénéfices nets réalises en 1935 ont été de l'ordre de 20%.*" CAHJP Gr/Sa FO 346 Hananel E. Naar & Co. BA/4478 04/12/1936. In addition the company also realised its assets, increasing its capital worth (stock) from an estimated GRD 500,000 (1936) to at least 1,200,000 by November 1937, following the sale of the building at Saint Minas 4, the firm's location, to Maison Alvo Frères.

35 Previously a partner in the firm of Fils d'Abram de Mayo & Roussos (1924), dissolved in 1926. CAHJP Gr/Sa FO 346 Fils d'Abram de Mayo BA/337 28/03/1937.

36 Paraphrased in the text from the following: "*Au ralenti en raison de ce qu'elle ne peut pas tenir tête a la concurrence qui dispose de capitaux bien plus importants*". CAHJP Gr/Sa FO 346 Jacob Joseph & Cohen, Maison "Camelia" BA/4625 24/3/1937.

37 CAHJP Gr/Sa FO 346 M. S. Matalon BA/169 05/03/1936.

38 The Commercial Law and the Greek legal system greatly retarded the development of business risk-taking. See Pepelasis 1959: 194–196.

39 For example, until 1923, the Roman law that demanded partnerships to automatically dissolve with the death of a partner made agreements to continue the arrangement illegal, a situation boding disaster for family-based partnerships. Pepelasis 1959.

40 Compare Colli et al. 2003.

41 The family's predominance as the centre of social, political, and economic identity impacted on the business organisation models that the entrepreneurial elite adopted: The great majority of businesses were small if not tiny family enterprises. When "formalised", they generally took the shape of either private proprietorships or partnerships. No strict division of labour between business and politics was observed. The most prominent entrepreneurs and members of their families were expected to seek political power. Pepelasis-Minoglou 2007b.

42 Based on advertisements, the following firms belonged to the category *société anonyme*: Banque Amar, Banque de Salonique, and Fils de G.A. Errera & Co., Ltd. (see Appendix 4.1). The latter was sold to G. Matalon & Cie. during the 1920s. See *Guide Sam* 1930: 908.

43 Pepelasis 1959: 194–196.

44 Lampe and Jackson 1982: 415–417.

45 Mazower 2004: 373.

46 Pepelasis Minoglou 2007a: 536.

47 The nine SAs out of 328 firms (or 0.0274 percent) in 1935–1938 were, according to Appendix 8: "Hermes" SA Pâtes Alimentaires (no. 13), Macédonienne pour l'Industrie de Savon SA (no. 33), Clouterie et Tréfilerie Macédonienne SA (no. 59), Eletan SA. – Elliniki Eteria Antibrossopion An. Et. (no. 89), Fabriques Réunies de Bas et Chaussettes de Sal/Que SA (no. 144), Makedoniki Kaltsopiia SA (formerly Modiano Frères, no. 148), Abram

Benveniste SA (no. 201), AGETRA, General Agency of Transport, Alain Hassid & Co., SA (no. 284), and S.A. Technique Hellénique de Défense Fluviale (no. 328). In addition, the following two companies were mentioned without details of their charters, and thus were not included in the sample: Trabout SA (shareholders: the Jewish brothers Trabout, Benjamin Benforado, Nahama Mallah, Pepo Yacoel, and Haim Mathia, all of them small metalware merchants; its capital, GRD 1,500,000), see CAHJP Gr/Sa FO 346 Benjamin Jacob Benforado BA/4555 12/2/1937; and Société Anonyme Hellénique de Papeterie Aighion had Jewish shareholders (see section 8.3).

48   "AVEZ" SA Industrielle de Pâtes Alimentaires (est. 12/1926), Floca Chocolaterie SA (est. 1/1934), Gheorgiki Eteria Thrakis & Makedonias SA, Société Anonyme d'Entreprises Techniques et Agricoles, Psorulla & Co. (est. 1929), Makedoniki Ifantourghia SA (est. 1937), and Khatzitolios & Rakas SA (est. 09/1932). For a description of their activities, see section 8.3.

49   Pepelasis Minoglou 2007a: 535.

50   Dritsas 1994: 229–230.

51   CAHJP Gr/Sa FO 346 AGETRA, General Agency of Transport, Alain Hassid & Co., SA BA/none 13/4/1935. Although the decree fixed its time horizon or duration to twenty years, this firm, which was managed by Nahman Saadi, was dissolved by December 1936. CAHJP Gr/Sa FO 346 "Hermes" Société de Transports Internationaux BA/ 304 9/2/1937.

52   Pepelasis-Minoglou (2007b) indicates five features that made the modern corporation a superior form of business organisation: (1) limited liability of shareholders and transfer-ability of ownership, (2) external financing, (3) separation of ownership from control (management), (4) accountability to owners/shareholders, and (5) a long-term horizon. According to Pepelasis-Minoglou (2007a: 528–529), with the notable exception of banks and railways, nearly all Greek SAs were private joint-stock companies (or private corporations) whose original shareholders were drawn from among family members and a tightly knit group of business associates or social acquaintances.

53   Thirty years: CAHJP Gr/Sa FO 346 Chocolaterie Floca SA BA/414 8/6/1937; fifty years: CAHJP Gr/Sa FO 346 Société Anonyme d'Entreprises Techniques et Agricoles, Psorulla & Co. BA/392 18/5/1937.

54   Chocolaterie Floca SA: GRD 1,000 x 25,000 shares; SA Psorulla & Cie: GRD 100 x 40,000 shares; SA "Avez": GRD 100 x 75,000 shares; Georgiki Eteria Thrakis & Makedonias SA: GRD 100 x 800 shares; Khatzitolios & Rakas SA: GRD 1000 x 6,000 shares.

55   In 1937 Rodolphe Mazlliah became a partner and manager of the new partnership formed by Nahman Saadi in Athens, with a branch in Piraeus. The firm's invested capital had already almost tripled (GRD 300,000), with the Salonican firm's capital at GRD 120,000. CAHJP Gr/Sa FO 346 "Hermes" Société de Transports Internationaux BA/304 9/2/1937.

56   Tignor 1980: 431.

57   Conrad Weynandt, President (a former delegate of the Banque Belge pour l'Étranger in Salonica and currently Director, Compagnie Générale Financière des Tabacs); Weynandt's wife Marie C. Weynandt and the Jewish brothers Jacques Nahama, Director of the Athens office, and Albert Nahama (see section 7.1), Director of the Salonica branch. CAHJP Gr/Sa FO 346 Eletan SA, Salonica–Athens BA/218, 6 November 1935; BA/208 16 June 1936, and a letter dated 26 November 1936. For the history of the American tyre giant Goodrich (est. 1870) and its participation in international trade, see: http://www.goodrich.com/CDA/GeneralContent/0,1277,67,00.html.

58   The board of directors for the second five-year period included: Petros Lenis (president), and the widow Zissis J. Verrou, managing director (*administrateur délégué*). CAHJP Gr/Sa FO 346 "AVEZ" BA/267 11/9/1936.

59   Pepelasis 1959: 194–196; Nicholas G. Karambelas (2007) "Greek Legal Entities", http://ngklaw.com/index.php?page=greek-commercial-and-company-law, downloaded 24 February 2008.

60   This corporation was founded in November 1935, following issuance of Official Decree 299 and Notary Act 6725 for the wholesale and retail trade in draperies for twenty years. CAHJP Gr/Sa FO 346 Abram Benveniste SA BA/4452 17/11/1936.

61   Author's free translation of: "*Que lors de la constitution de la société, les marchandises qui se*

trouvaient en magasin ont été inventories à des prix inférieurs a ceux de revient et ce pour des raisons fiscales." CAHJP Gr/Sa FO 346 Abram Benveniste SA BA/4452 17/11/1936.

62   David Hasson, the firm's founder and a Spanish subject, retired in 1924. However, according to the documents, "*Mr. David Hasson conserve toujours la haute direction de l'affaire*", i.e., he became the senior manager of the new partnership or, alternatively, he (rather than a grandson with the same name) was appointed president. Compare Hekimoglou 2004 IV: 253–254.

63   Banque Amar documents indicate that Jewish entrepreneurs were wont to take large mortgages from Greek banks. See below.

64   H. Recanati 1984: 23.

65   CAHJP Gr/Sa FO 346 Sam A. Saporta BA/4654 [date erased]/04/1937.

66   On transplanted networks, see Tilly 1990.

67   The firm enjoyed a good reputation in Greece as well as abroad. See CAHJP Gr/Sa FO 346 Maison Jacques Nahmias & Fils BA/4661 07/04/1937.

68   This type of organisation is similar to expatriate multinational free standing companies, wherein the headquarters takes full control of overseas operations. See Casson 1994.

69   Casson and Godley 2005: 38–39.

70   Author's translation of: "*La firme [Fils de Sam. Florentin] jouit d'une très bonne réputation sur place. Les susnommés sont réputes très honnêtes, actifs et ponctuels à leurs engagements.*" CAHJP Gr/Sa FO 346 Fils de Sam. Florentin BA/428 16/6/1937.

71   Author's translation of: "*La Firme jouit en Grèce et à l'Etranger d'une très bonne réputation. Elle est considérée comme de premier ordre, solvable et d'après les avis recueillis elle mérite pleine confiance.*" CAHJP Gr/Sa FO 346 Maison Jacques Nahmias & Fils BA/4661 07/04/1937.

72   Author's translation of: "*tous les milieux de considération . . . Il ne fait pas usage du crédit des Banques.*" CAHJP Gr/Sa FO 346 David S. Molho BA/4745 12/5/1937.

73   Other Jewish entrepreneurs who served as consuls were Edw. Saltiel, Honorary Consul of Japan; S. Arditi, Honorary Consul of Portugal; S. Ezratty (also spelled Ezratti), Consul of Honour for Brazil; [first name not indicated] Benveniste, General Consul for Belgium. *Guide Sam* 1930: 909.

74   Mourghianni-Estela 1996: 598.

75   Dritsas 1992: 211–213; idem 1994: 231–232.

76   In the wake of the increasing commitment to industrial entrepreneurship, the National Bank of Greece established a new department in 1927 to gather information. Its activities included investigating clients and firms. Following visits to plants, bank officials prepared detailed reports evaluating company performance in addition to estimating value and credit required. Although considered confidential, these reports became a source of industrial intelligence. Dritsas 1992: 211–213; Dritsas 1994.

77   Dritsas 1992: 210.

78   Casson and Godley 2005: 37.

79   CAHJP Gr/Sa FO 346 Isac S. Saltiel BA/4699 19/4/1937.

80   Author's translation of: "*Chiffre d'affaires relativement restreint en raison de ce que la Firme ne dispose pas de capital de roulement. . . . la firme ne se serait pas encore complètement libérée de ses dettes à l'étranger.*" CAHJP Gr/Sa FO 346 Moise Sciaky & Frères BA/4799 12/06/1937.

81   On similar situations among Jewish-owned banks that avoided granting loans to potential Greek clients in the late Ottoman era, see Hekimoglou 1999.

82   Author's partial translation of: "*D'après les renseignements recueillis auprès des sources autorisées, leur capital présumé est celui indiqué. Tel n'est pas l'avis de Me. Samuelidés [the notary] qui m'a assuré que le capital de chacune des deux Firmes dépasse les £3000 – ce qui prouve que leurs affaires marchent bien. Cet avis doit être pris en considération puisque la constitution et la dissolution de la Société en nom collectif I Raphaël & Benveniste et Moise I. Benveniste ont été enregistrées auprès de lui.*" CAHJP Gr/Sa FO 346 M. J. Bourla BA/none 16/6/1937.

83   Author's translation of: "*Inclus le rapport demandé sur la Maison Erricou J. Arones d'Athènes. Mon correspondant en cette ville a enquêté auprès de deux sources différentes, dont les renseignements diffèrent [sic] entre eux. Il vous appartient de fixer votre décision en tenant*

compte de tous les détails fournis."CAHJP Gr/Sa FO 346 M.J. Bourla no. 2/1622 29/7/1937; Errico Jacob Arones BA/4856 29/7/1937.

84 Author's paraphrase of a rather difficult text: "*On le dépeint comme caractère plutôt difficile et enclin à la chicane. De ce fait bien poser les conditions en traitant.*" The information on this firm is inconsistent. I adopted the official version from 1937. The original firm was established in 1901 but transformed into a partnership (*société en nom collectif*) in 1922. The dissolution of Marcos Frères, owned by Daniel, Isac, and Joseph Marcos in 1928/9 was motivated mainly by internal disagreements. Daniel's firm also suffered from huge operating losses, especially in its Beirut operation (his brother Isac emigrated to Beirut prior to settling in Volos in Old Greece). Joseph, another brother, emigrated to Mandatory Palestine (1935). Daniel consequently remained the sole owner of a registered firm bearing his name. He continued to sell fruit in the market but later sold dried legumes in his shop, located in Rue d'Egypte. CAHJP Gr/Sa FO 346 Daniel Marcos BA/none 6/2/1935; BA/ 4680 12/04/1937; BA/464 25/9/1937.

85 Author's translation of: "*Ce qui n'est pas à son honneur, vu que d'autres firmes moins importantes qu'elle se sont déjà libérées de leurs engagements . . . et voilà pourquoi nos sources d'information conseillent la prudence.*" CAHJP Gr/Sa FO 346 Fils de Moise Saltiel BA/4447 16/11/1936.

86 CAHJP Gr/Sa FO 346 Salomon S. Mordoh Successors BA/4817 22/06/1937.

87 CAHJP Gr/Sa FO 346 Saltiel & Elie Angel & Fils BA/4683 14/04/1937.

88 CAHJP Gr/Sa FO 346 Isac Saporta BA/128 08/01/1936.

89 The original text read: "*Elle [the firm] travaille avec la Banca Commerciale Italiana & Greca en compte courant présentant actuellement un solde créditeur en faveur de MM. Hasson.*" CAHJP Gr/Sa FO 346 Fils de David Hasson BA/4376 7/10/1936. David Hasson, the founder of the original firm and a Spanish subject, retired in 1924 to become the senior manager of this new partnership. Compare Hekimoglou 2004 IV: 253–254.

90 CAHJP Gr/Sa FO 346 Haim Salem & Frères BA/4672 12/04/1937.

91 CAHJP Gr/Sa FO 346 Nissim Gheledi & fils BA/4377 7/10/1936.

92 Ya'akov (Jacky) Allalouf, interview conducted 28 January 2009 in the office of Allalouf & Co. (est. 1919, Salonica), Tel Aviv. Allalouf, the only son of Natan Allalouf, was born in Salonica on 28 January 1934. He was a boy when his family was compelled to leave Salonica. See also Allalouf 2006: 45.

93 For example, British gold sovereigns were usually of 22 karat (91.7%) gold; their value could be a little over the gold value depending on their condition and demand.

94 Nahmia 2006: 50.

95 In contrast to token money, which was made of inferior metals or of alloys containing expensive metals, or coins of regular issue whose face value was greater than their intrinsic value. On the development of this dichotomous monetary system in Ottoman Palestine during the nineteenth century, see Gross 1999: 55.

96 DOT 1925: 9.

97 This expression was used by a British consular officer in 1922, after passage of the capital levy. On the increase in firm taxation, see DOT 1925:9. On the tax measures introduced in 1922, see DOT 1925: 8–10.

98 Nehama 1989: 244–245.

99 Author's free translation of: "*La capital investi dans l'affaire selon contrat notarié s'élève à Drs. 370,000.- Cette somme a été fixé par mesure fiscale, vu que les membres qui composent la Société, notamment Mme. Bourla et Mr. Mathius Carasso, disposent personnellement d'une fortune mobilière assez intéressante.*" CAHJP Gr/Sa FO 346 Mano & Co. BA/4629 29/03/1937.

100 CAHJP Gr/Sa FO 346 Viktor Almosnino BA/34 26/1/1936.

101 CAHJP Gr/Sa FO 346 S. Damkou & M. Beraha BA/197 12/5/1936 [1/4/1936].

102 CAHJP Gr/Sa FO 346 Elie Sarfati & Ovadia Ezratti BA/207 16/6/1936.

103 A chi-square analysis for goodness of fit (one variable) was used to examine whether the differences between the distribution of the Jewish firms by size (the firm's estimated nominal assets) and the distribution of the Greek firms by size were significant. The results yielded significant chi-square values: $\chi^2(4) = 19.18$, $p < .001$.

104 Recall the number of branches was reduced from thirteen to seven (food, chemicals,

construction material, metals and wood, hides and leather, textiles and clothing, paper, large scale commerce = luxuries, agricultural products, foreign trade, and tobacco). Two chi-square tests for contingency (two variables) were conducted for Jewish and for Greek firms separately to examine whether a statistical link could be established between economic activity (branch) and firm size (estimated nominal assets). Although non-significant results were obtained ($\chi^2(24) = 27.81$, $p > .05$) for the Jewish firms – i.e., for firms of all sizes, the leading branches were textiles and clothing, wood, metal and construction materials, and large-scale commerce – the association between firm branch and size was statistically significant ($\chi^2(24) = 45.49$, $p < .005$) for the Greek firms as follows. The leading firms in the medium size range were in textiles and clothing; wood, metal and construction materials and large-scale commerce; small-sized firms were abundant in chemicals, hides and leather, and large-scale commerce; as to very large size, these were commonly found in food, textiles and clothing, and large-scale commerce.

105   These brothers were partners in Lanaras, Kyrtsis & Co., which operated a modern spinning mill in Naoussa, together with a factory for fine fabrics, Lanaras Fréres SA (a combed wool factory), Gregoire Tsitsis & Co. (three spinning mills), and Gregoire Tsitsis & Fils (producers of hydrophile, *cabot* [a cheap sort of grey-coloured cotton cloth], and other cotton cloth). In addition, the two brothers were partners in a company that ran two hotels in Athens and also represented Chevrolet automobiles in Athens. CAHJP Gr/Sa FO 346 Panayotis G. Kyrtsis BA/209 19/6/1936.

106   CAHJP Gr/Sa FO 346 Théodore Hadjiparaskévas BA/4632 30/3/1937.

107   The firm, which had ten employees, was not included within the twenty-five Greek firms in the sample having nominal capital above GRD 5,000,000. CAHJP Gr/Sa FO 346 N. Krallis & Fils BA/269 11/11/1936.

108   CAHJP Gr/Sa FO 346 Eteria Asvestopiias "Enosis" BA/124 7/12/1935.

109   CAHJP Gr/Sa FO 346 Chocolaterie Floca SA BA/414 8/6/1937.

110   CAHJP Gr/Sa FO 346 Alexandre P. Karapanayotis.

111   This firm was previously D. Serefas, founded in 1881. In 1926, A. D. Serefas continued his late father's business but only in 1930 was the firm's name changed to A. D. Serefas. In 1935, A. D. Serefas' wealth was estimated at GRD 12,000,000, including GRD 5,000,000 million in fixed assets. CAHJP Gr/Sa FO 346 D. Serefas; BA/63 14/3/1935; A.D. Serefas BA/351 2/4/1937.

112   CAHJP Gr/Sa FO 346 Constantin Moscoff BA/274 12/11/1936.

113   CAHJP Gr/Sa FO 346 Stelios Voivodas BA/432 17/6/1937.

114   One of the leading German armament producing firms involved in Greek–German cooperation as well as exports to the Middle East. See Pelt 1998: 71, 89, 157, 170, 175, 205–206.

115   CAHJP Gr/Sa FO 346 G. Gregoriadés Frères BA/4385 12/10/1936.

116   For additional information on Greek middlemen in the arms trade, see Pelt 1998: 114, 142–145, 150, 161, 175–181.

117   The jute firm developed by E. Torres – Iutificio (also possibly Jutificio) E. Torres SA, exclusively owned by the Dino Fernandez, Enrico Misrachi, and Elia Torres families – is missing from Banque Amar records. Its industrial value was estimated by the Italian consul of Salonica as GRD 32,000,000 in pre-war values. Carpi 1999: 94.

118   Bowman, 2002: 84.

119   CAHJP Gr/Sa FO 346 Botton, Saias & Co. BA/4432 12/11/1936. The De Botton family held Spanish citizenship. Nahmia [1996] 2006: 30.

120   At the outbreak of World War II, Greece was home to some 670 Sephardic Jews holding Spanish citizenship; 550 of these Jews lived in Macedonia. See Rother 2002: 47; Avni 1982: 82.84, 161.

121   On Britain's protection of the national minorities, see Finney 1995.

122   Yet, sixty Italian Jewish families were without any means. Carpi 1999: 89–94.

123   Dublon-Knebel 2007: 80.

124   For the value of Calzificio IEKA Soc. Ano. di proprieta esclusiva dei Sig. Giacomo, Umberto e Armando Modiano, see Carpi 1999: 94. For the estimated capital of Eliia di Giacobbe, see ibid.: 93.

125   Following the Campbell district riots, the leather merchant Arouestis (*sic*) appealed to Yugoslav consul general for protection, which was extended to all Jews holding Serbian citi-

zenship. Similarly, Jews holding Italian citizenship, led by the pharmacist Isaac Tivoli, sought the protection of the Italian consul. Constantopoulou and Veremis 1998: 192–193.

126 D. de Sola Pool (1912–1913), in referring to the compulsory military service during the Young Turks era (1909), wrote: "It [military service] introduced an innovation for our co-religionists in the East that increased the difficulties of supporting a family and interfered with religious observance" (*American Jewish Year Book* 1912–1913: 210). Similar considerations motivated non-Muslims not to enter the Ottoman army once it was opened to this group; they preferred to pay a tax (*bedel-i askeri*) in lieu of military service. See Issawi 1982.

127 According to Yomtov Yacoel (1943), the prohibition on purchasing real estate, which was imposed on foreign nationals, was targeted mainly at Jewish entrepreneurs. See Bowman, 2002: 84. Yacoel was apparently referring to the legislated restrictions on foreigners' property rights in the areas bordering New Greece, a step aimed at protecting its territorial consolidation. Yet, based on registered documents, it appears that these entrepreneurs ignored this law and purchased property through their Greek national co-religionists. As an alternative, they purchased real estate in Old Greece (e.g., Volos), where this prohibition was not in effect. I thank Stella Salem, Adv., for providing this information, which is based on her legal experience in Salonica.

128 Nevertheless, in contrast to the late Ottoman era when all foreign Jews belonged to the richest level of society, by the eve of the German occupation only about 46 percent (52 out of 112) of Italian Jewish heads of households were classified as "with means". Italian Diplomatic Documents, Salonika [*sic*] 23 July 1942. Consul General Zamboni to the Italian Diplomatic Mission to Athens. Carpi 1999: 89–94.

129 Compare Skourtis 1992: 238, cited by Vassilikou 2003: 114.

130 Mazower 2004: 406–407.

131 CZA S6/2535, 6 January 1939, a survey on Zionist activities in Greece, sent by Dr. Zvi Zohar from the Head office of the Jewish National Fund in Prague to the organisation's headquarters in Jerusalem.

132 Older Jewish workers spoke Ladino almost exclusively, a practice that functioned as an entry barrier into the mainstream Greek labour market. According to Jacky Allalouf, his family employed office workers who all spoke Ladino. Interview, Tel Aviv, 2009. See also p. 356 n. 92 above..

133 Kahan 1975: 87–88.

134 As the contemporary Jewish journalist Eliyahu Veissi wrote in November 1936, "Nowadays, everyone in Salonica works on the Sabbath. Even in the markets, vendors and fruit and vegetable sellers . . . go to pray in the synagogues in the morning, and afterward open their shops. Everyone claims that it is impossible to survive on [the earnings of] a five-day work-week. In the port, the porters, carters, tobacco factory workers, commercial establishments, the sons of judges and rabbis – all open their businesses on the Sabbath." Toledano 1986: 173.

135 In 1929, Saltiel & Elie Angel (1895) entered a partnership that included their sons. CAHJP Gr/Sa FO 346 Saltiel & Elie Angel & Fils BA/468314/04/1937.

136 Excluding the store on Rue Comninon for which they paid rent, the facilities located on this street were mortgage-free; see ibid.

137 Victor Zadok also owned a chain of boutiques; CAHJP Gr/Sa FO 346 Galeries Modernes – S. Zadok & Cie. BA/132 21/01/1936; BA/4435 10/11/1936.

138 CAHJP Gr/Sa FO 346 Clouterie et Tréfilerie Macédonienne SA BA/483 01/11/1937.

139 Bessantchi [1936]: 210.

140 Among the 153 female concentration camp prisoners whose occupations were indicated, the majority were housewives, with only a few connected to the clothing industry: Afias, Mathilde (umbrellas & socks); Almosnino, Esterina (day labourer); Almosnino, Estrea (day labourer); Angel, Djamila (day labourer); Cohen, Gilda (shirt maker); Cohen, Riketta (dressmaker, day labourer); Cuenca, Lea (day labourer); Eliezer, Rachel (small repairs); Frangi, Sarah (shirt maker); Lappas, Lucie (Loutchia) (dressmaker); Molh'o, Marie (haberdashery shop owner); Nah'mias, Esterina (haberdashery shop co-owner; tailoring supplies); Nah'mias, Riketta (home-based shirt maker); Rosa, Tamara (milliner); Rotsas, Bea (factory worker); Sarfati, Reina (worker); Sasson, Esther (invisible mender); Sasson, Riketta (house-

keeper and dressmaker); Tzerasi, Eda (textile shop co-owner); Yacoel, Rachel (dry cleaning and laundry worker). See Recanati 2000.

141 On the geographic clustering of refugees in Salonica's periphery, see Hastaoglou-Martinidis 1997b: 501.

142 The aim of the Jewish Association established in 1924 by Isac Joseph Molho in the Harilaos quarter was to further the interests of its residents in order to improve living conditions, maintain their health, and ensure internal solidarity. See Aharon Rousso's manuscript, *The Jewish Societies in Salonica.*

143 CAHJP Gr/Sa FO 346 Makedoniki Kaltsopiia SA BA/161, 21 February 1936.

144 On the geographic clustering of refugees in Salonica's periphery, see Hastaoglou-Martinidis 1997b: 501.

145 CAHJP Gr/Sa FO 346 Sam A. Sarfati BA/4569 17–18/2/1937.

146 CAHJP Gr/Sa FO 346 Ladas & Djadjas, Société "Melissa", BA/266 6/11/1936.

147 In the late 1930s, the Greek government, like that in Germany and the US, initiated infrastructure projects in Macedonia as a solution for the vast unemployment. DOT 1937: 12–13; Mazower and Veremis 1993: 126.

148 He was in partnership with his brother Mario until June 1936. CAHJP Gr/Sa FO 346 Jacques Juda Moché BA/4401 24/10/1936.

149 For more on this strategy, adopted by Jewish bankers in northern Italy since the late Middle Ages, see Meron 1998.

150 CAHJP Gr/Sa FO 346 David S. Sarrano BA/482 01/11/1937.

151 CAHJP Gr/Sa FO 346 Moise Sciaky & Frères BA/4799 12/06/1937.

152 CAHJP Gr/Sa FO 346 Léon Josué Amaraggi BA/4671 10/4/1937.

153 Ruben Beja & Nehama (est. 1913) had been transformed into Ruben, Nehama & Cie. (1918), and again transformed into Ruben, Tchénio & Nehama in 1919 before being dissolved in 1932. CAHJP Gr/Sa FO 346 Ruben Fils & Tchénio BA/none 21/01/1935; BA/4668 10/4/1937.

154 CAHJP Gr/Sa FO 346 Joseph Mordohai Nahmias BA/4721 01/05/1937.

155 CAHJP Gr/Sa FO 346 Maurice Dav. Sasson BA/none 01/02/1935; BA/none 4/2/1937.

156 The partners took over all the firm's liquid and solid assets (long-term capital) as well as all the obligations due (*assumèrent l'actif et le passif de*) Fils de Jacob Saltiel & Cie. CAHJP Gr/Sa FO 346 Fils de Jacob Saltiel & Broudo BA/none 6/2/1937.

157 CAHJP Gr/Sa FO 346 Yomtov, Franco & Cie BA/4455 10/11/1936.

158 Previously Joseph Paladino & Fils (1905–1933). Following his son's emigration to Paris in 1933 – from which he eventually returned – "*l'affaire n'ayant pas bien marché ces derniers temps*" (the business had not gone well of late). See CAHJP Gr/Sa FO 346 Joseph Samuel Paladino BA/4775 25/5/37.

159 His share of the property was estimated at GRD 600,000. CAHJP Gr/Sa FO 346 Joseph Samuel Paladino BA/4775 25/5/37.

160 CAHJP Gr/Sa FO 346 David Isac & Fils BA/4623 29/3/1937.

161 CAHJP Gr/Sa FO 346 Gabriel E. Nissim BA/328 23/03/1937; BA/none 30/10/1935.

162 Previously the partnership of David Angel & Cie. After its dissolution (1928) following the death of its founder, Angel's nephews Benico and Isac and his brother Lezer formed a new partnership, which took over his affairs. CAHJP Gr/Sa FO 346 Benico & Isac Angel & Cie, BA/4393 15/10/1936.

163 Abram Benveniste also operated a drapery shop in St. Minas Street, CAHJP Gr/Sa FO 346 BA/158; 18/2/1936; BA/4803 16/06/1937.

164 His activity raised questions in some circles since his ethics " . . . *est critiquée dans certains milieux*" (. . . was criticised in certain quarters). He also possessed a plot in the Istira quarter (the old cereal market), which was mortgaged. CAHJP Gr/Sa FO 346 Ino Jakob Matalon BA/none 11/12/1935; BA/4648 1/4/1937.

165 CAHJP Gr/Sa FO 346 Haim M. Mano BA/371 21/04/1937.

166 CAHJP Gr/Sa FO 346 Nahama B. Capon & Cie BA/none 30/03/1936.

Chapter 10

1 Pierron 1996: 217.
2 Jews declared that they were employed as porters by the municipal authorities. Among those providing this information were H'alegoua Seh'aya (b. 1900), a resident of Regie Verdar (A. Recanati 2000: 210) and David Aaron (b. 1915), whose father and grandfather were stevedores (Matsas 1997: 306–308).
3 On the massive numbers of Jewish paupers in 1940, see Hekimoglou 2002.
4 Entrepreneurial and occupational activity in the formal sector is characterised by entry barriers, large-scale entrepreneurial activity, imported technology, capital-intensive investment, corporate ownership, and markets protected by government-controlled quotas and trade concessions. See Meier 1984: 183–190.
5 Such as the Cercle de Salonique established in 1873. In 1936 the Jewish minority was still over-represented in the Cercle de Salonique, representing about 44 percent (57 out of 129) of Salonica's business elite in comparison with the Greek majority, which was represented by only about 47 percent (60 out of 129) of its members. These figures should nevertheless be compared with those for 1887, when Jews formed the dominant component (44 percent, or 63 out of 142) within a multi-ethnic social structure (the *Cercle* was comprised of fifteen Germans, fourteen Italians, eleven Muslims, six Frenchmen, six Slavs, four Englishmen, three Armenians, and one Scandinavian). By 1936 Jewish entrepreneurs had lost their advantage to the Greeks, who almost tripled their absolute strength in the Cercle, from 19 (out of 142) to 60 (out of 142), with the negligible representation (12 out of 142) of other ethnic groups. Data adapted from Rena Molho 2005: 155, Table 1.
6 See the advertisement placed by the Jewish-owned merchant house Fils de N[ehama] A. Mal[l]ah. *Annuaire Commercial* 1922: 126.
7 By the 1920s Jewish entrepreneurs had voluntarily chosen to place bi-lingual (French and Greek) or solely Greek advertisements in the almanac of the Chamber of Commerce and Industry of Salonica. Pinhas Salomon & Cie. engaged in the grocery products trade, especially chocolate, sweets, and jams, placed a bi-lingual (French–Greek) advertisement. *Annuaire Commercial* 1922: 346; Pelossof Abram & Rousso, trade in colonial commodities, advertised in Greek only. *Annuaire Commercial* 1922: 33. The huge soap manufacturer, Leon Samuel & Yomtov (also by the name, Into) advertised only in Greek due to the Greek characteristics of the industry (Greek partners, workers, clients, etc.). *Annuaire Commercial* 1922: 295. (Appendix 4.1, nos. 11, 52 and 90). For advertising in Greek from the 1930s, see Stavroulakis et al. 2006: passim.
8 Based on the YIVO sources, banking institutions conducted their correspondence with local tax authorities in the official language, Greek.
9 Gans 2007: 157. See also Chin 2005.
10 Gans (2007: 158) referred to ethnic commuters when considering transnationalism as a form of assimilation resistance in the contemporary US.
11 French continued to be used as a common language for Jewish and Greek businessmen at least until the beginning of the 1930s: " . . . *l'éclat aristocratique du cercle . . . conservait, même en 1932, la langue française comme moyen d'expression.*" (. . . the remnant of aristocratic circle . . . retained, even in 1932, the French language as a means of expression.) R. Molho 2005: 157.
12 On the development of the Judéo-Fragnol, see Quintana-Rodriguez 1999: 596–598; for Edgar Morin's comment that his father "*Vidal écrit en 'fragnol'* " (Vidal writes in "Fragnol"), see Morin 1989: 109; Kerem 1996: 586.
13 For the linguistic dimension of diasporas, see Ben-Rafael 2001: 337.
14 See Trivellato 2009; excluding two partnerships with British firms, business partnerships between Jewish Baghdadis and non-Jews were rare during the colonisation phase (Chiara Betta 2005: 274–279).
15 Don 1992: 271.
16 Hamilton and Waters 1997: 260.
17 Kuznets 1960; on Hungary see Don 1992: 270–271; on Iraq see Darvish 1985.
18 For example, the government-owned Thai rice corporation was established during the

1930s to deprive the Chinese of their status as rice wholesalers and exporters; see Yambert 1981: 192. Similarly, nationalisation of cereals at all production levels (agriculture, milling, and distribution) within the emerging nation-state in the Philippines (1946) also hurt the Chinese minority. See Eitzen 1968: 224–225.

19 Discrimination against non-Muslim Turkish businesses included the obligation to keep accounts (ledgers) in Turkish, forced dismissals of non-Muslim employees, and the hiring of Muslim Turks in their place. On the Turkification of the economy, see Aktar 2003.

20 *American Jewish Year Book* 1925: 468.

21 See for example Light et al. 1993: 590–591; Zenner 1982: 463–465.

22 On the Jewish-Muslim coalition in the municipal council in 1906, the seven-year business partnership that rented the great gardens of the White Tower, and other examples of Jewish-Turkish partnerships, see Cooperman 1991: 214–220.

23 Hamilton and Waters 1997.

24 For the ethnic cohesion resulting from intra-marriage among Jewish minorities until World War II, see Kuznets 1960; Don 1990. On Greek cohesion based, *inter alia*, on ethnic endogamy, see Dritsas 1994: 229; Harlaftis 1996; on the Jews in Salonica, see above, sections 2.4 and 8.5; also Chapter 9.

25 Participating non-Jews in the organisation and operation of Jewish-owned firms was also witnessed among Jews in Hungary following the Anti-Jewish Acts legislated from April 1938 up to the Nazi occupation (1944). Jewish firms in Hungary before the Nazi occupation (1944) countervailed attempts to oust their original directors and key workers by bringing in fictitious or genuine – though usually redundant – directors with clear Christian pasts, preferably with aristocratic pedigrees. On this "straw man system", see Don 1986.

26 Keyder 1994: 134.

27 Keyder 1994: 137.

28 On the history and legacy of the Greek diaspora, emphasising its cohesiveness, see Harlaftis 2005; Pepelasis-Minoglou 2005.

29 These majority elites created the Federation of Greek Industries and through it demanded legislation on industrial policy (1922, 1935, 1937; import restrictions were enforced in 1932) affecting the imports of machinery and raw material. Dritsas 2003.

30 Kahan 1986b: 101; the Jewish historian Salo Baron (1973: 167) reached a similar conclusion during the Eichmann trial: "In contrast to the Middle Ages, when the authorities protected the Jews even when their blood was shed by the masses, the events of Kristallnacht were perhaps the first, outside precedents that had occurred in Tsarist Russia, when the government had actually encouraged pogroms against the Jews. This was no return to the Middle Ages but something new" (author's translation).

31 Pelt 1998: 211–214.

32 From 1936 on, Hitler explicitly adopted a crude neo-mercantilist view of the economy in which the requirements for food, raw materials, and living space could be fulfilled not by raising the domestic economy's productivity but by creating a German-ruled economic area in the East. This economy would function as a kind of siege economy, self-dependent, or "autarkic". See Overy 2003: 182–183.

33 As of 1936, foreign currency and gold had to be handed over to the state on pain of severe punishment. Businesses refusing to collaborate with rearmament priorities found themselves nationalised. Economic racism manifested itself, above all, in the dispossession of the Jews. See Overy 2003. On Aryanisation, see also Stallbaumer 1999; James 2001; Bajohr 2002.

34 Pelt 1998: 211–212. This may explain why the German consul reported in 1943 that family relations existed between the Jewish merchant Broudo and the tobacco merchant representing *Reemstma.mann* [*sic*], Zalidis (given names unknown). The latter was the brother-in-law of Broudo. Dublon-Knebel 2007: 151. 31.5.1943 World Service, International Institute for the Elucidation of the Jewish Question, Frankfurt/Main, to von Thadden, FO, Berlin on the Jewish Question in Greece.

35 The Austro-Hellenic tobacco factory also employed Jewish workers.

36 Pelt 1998: 213–214.

37 Based on lists processed by Aure Recanati (2000: passim). At least 45 Jewish males and seven Jewish females declared their occupation as "tobacco workers" including

unemployed or retired tobacco workers; two Jewish females and a dozen Jewish males declared their occupation as " tobacco shopkeepers/shop employees"; in addition the list contains a tobacco mill technician for and a tobacco preparation worker.

38 The original firm's management, which was transformed into an SA in 1931, included a Greek notary as long as it was directed by Hanz Heitmann (the former principal partner). CAHJP Gr/Sa FO 346 John Campbell Succ. S.A. BA/248, 16/09/1936.

39 A. Recanati 2000: 79, 81–82.

40 CZA S6/2535, 6 January 1939, a survey on Zionist activities in Greece, sent by Dr. Zvi Zohar from the Head office of the Jewish National Fund in Prague to the organisation's headquarters in Jerusalem.

41 A. Naar 1997: 204.

42 CZA S6/2535, 6 January 1939, a survey on Zionist activities in Greece, sent by Dr. Zvi Zohar from the Head office of the Jewish National Fund in Prague to the organisation's headquarters in Jerusalem.

43 CZA S6/2535, 6 January 1939, a survey on Zionist activities in Greece, sent by Dr. Zvi Zohar from the Head office of the Jewish National Fund in Prague to the organisation's headquarters in Jerusalem.

44 Allalouf 2006.

45 Dublon-Knebel, 2007: 76–78: 30/11/38 Consul Schönberg, Salonica to FO, Berlin on anti-Jewish atmosphere in Salonica and the activity of the Ethniki Etaireia.

46 Ibid.

47 Dublon-Knebel 2007: 74–75: 24 November 1937, Envoy Viktor, Prinz von Erbach-Schönberg, Athens, to the Foreign Office, Berlin, on Greek Jewry.

48 Dublon-Knebel, 2007: 78–79: 16/12/1938 Consul Schönberg, Salonica, to Foreign Office, Berlin, on the anti-Jewish hostilities in Salonica.

49 Dublon-Knebel, 2007: 75: 11 November 1938, Consul Schönberg, Salonica, to FO, Berlin, on the anti-Jewish atmosphere in Salonica.

50 Dublon-Knebel, 2007: 77: 30 November 1938, Consul Schönberg, Salonica, to FO, Berlin, on the anti-Jewish atmosphere in Salonica. The Greek business elites were graduates of French education, and had absorbed liberal values.

51 Dublon-Knebel, 2007: 77: 30 November 1938, Consul Schönberg, Salonica, to FO, Berlin, on the anti-Jewish atmosphere in Salonica.

52 CZA KKL5/11089, a report on the Jews in Greece in April 1940 written by Yaacov Tshernovitz, in Sofia to the Keren Kayemet LeYisrael headquarters in Jerusalem (n.d.).

53 CZA KKL5/11089, a report on the Jews in Greece (April 1940) written by Yaacov Tshernovitz in Sofia to the Keren Kayemet LeYisrael headquarter in Jerusalem (n.d.).

54 CZA S6/2535, 6 January 1939, a survey on Zionist activities in Greece, sent by Dr. Zvi Zohar from the Head office of the Jewish National Fund in Prague to the organisation's headquarters in Jerusalem. According to the "then unknown census" of October 1940 (p. cxvii), only 67,591 inhabitants (including foreigners) of the "Israelite" faith were in Greece (excluding 2,000 Jews from the Dodecanese and refugees). Of 53,125 who declared "Spanish or Judeo-Spanish" as their mother tongue, 52,731 were Jewish. From the difference, the 327 Greek Orthodox were obviously converted Sephardim. Fleischer 1995: 11; 20 n. 60.

55 Don 1986.

56 Hekimoglou 2002.

57 CZA S6/2535, 6 January 1939, a survey on Zionist activities in Greece, sent by Dr. Zvi Zohar from the Head office of the Jewish National Fund in Prague to the organisation's headquarters in Jerusalem.

58 See chapter 2 above.

59 Author's translation from CZA S6/2535, 6 January 1939, a survey on Zionist activities in Greece, sent by Dr. Zvi Zohar from the Head office of the Jewish National Fund in Prague to the organisation's headquarters in Jerusalem.

60 Bowman 2002: 83–88.

61 On Salonican Jewry during the Nazi occupation and on the fate of Jewish business in Greece

during World War II, see Molho and Nehama 1965, Emmanuel 1972, Ben 1985, Carpi 1999, Mazower 1993, Dublon-Knebel 2007, Bowman 2009, and Tomai 2009; for some of the testimonies of survivors, see S. Refael 1988, Handeli 1992, Ha-Elion 19972, Matsas 1997, H. Refael 1997, and Lewkowicz 2006.

Bibliography

Unpublished Archival Sources

Austria

Austrian Report 1915 (K. K. Österreichisches Handelsmuseum, Dezember, 1915), Salonik, Topographisch-Statistische Übersichten, Wien (II.41.821) (200 pp.).

Britain

Public Record Office [PRO], Kew
Foreign Office
FO, *Diplomatic and Consular Reports on Trade and Finance, Turkey* (Trade of the District of Salonica) Annual Series (1888) no. 394; (1889) no. 623; (1891) no. 822; (1892) no. 962; (1893) no. 1310; (1896) no. 1837. London.
FO 371/1135.
FO 371/9894.
FO 371/9888.
FO 371/16764.

France

Archives de l'Alliance Israélite Universelle [AAIU], Paris

Greece, II/C.53-54, 1 April 1919, Response au questionnaire de la Mission Hoover (unsigned).

Israel

Central Archives for the History of the Jewish People (CAHJP), Jerusalem
Gr/Sa [Thessaloniki] 346 (Original material Xerox, 775 pp.).
Gr/Sa [Thessaloniki] 370.
Gr/Sa [Thessaloniki] 102.
Gr/Sa [Thessaloniki] 80.

Central Zionist Archives (CZA), Jerusalem
KKL5; S6; Z3; Z4.
Ben-Zvi Institute, Jerusalem: Ladino Collection
Angel, Joseph Vidal and A. Levi (eds.) *Almanach Israélite* 5683 [1923].
Thessaloniki: Edition "Renasinsia".
Perez, Alexandro (1929). *Almanac commercial de las provincias.* Thessaloniki: Edition "El
     Tiempo".
Private Archives, Tel Aviv
Rousso, Aharon (manuscript). *The Jewish Societies in Salonica* [s.n.].

USA

Archive of the YIVO Institute for Jewish Research, New York
Records of the Jewish Community of Salonica, Greece, RG 207, FO. 156.
Records of the Jewish Community of Salonica, Greece, RG 207, FO. 157.

Judaica Collection, Harvard University, Cambridge, Massachusetts
LA 0638
Komunita Israelita Saloniko (1928). *Prozeto de Budgeto dela Komunita . . . por el anio 1928*
     [Saloniko: s.n.].
LA 0059
Komunita Israelita Saloniko (1929). *Budgeto ordinario dela Komunita Israelita por el egser-
     sisio 1929.* Saloniko: Emprimeria "Estrumsa".
LA 0625
Federasion delas uniyones mutualas Guida de Grega (1925). *Statutos.* Saloniko [s.n.].
LA 0566
Matanoth Laévionim (Thessaloniki) (1909). *Matanoth Laevionim: sosiedad fundada el 14
     Adar shenat 5661.* [Saloniko: Tip. "Moderna"].
LA 0154–0155
De Botton, Yitshak Avraham (1919). *El insendio del 18–19 augusto 1917 suvenires involvid-
     ables . . . / por C. Nott, T. Yaliz.* Saloniko: [s.n.].
LA 0340-0341
Molkho, Michael (1932). *Kontribusion a la istoria de Saloniko.* Saloniko: [s.n.].

Library of Congress - Manuscript Division, Washington, DC
Morgenthau, Henry (1916?). The Jews in the Balkan States and Salonica. In the Henry
     Morgenthau Papers, Container no. 34, reel no. 28. (36 pp.).

Statistics and Official Sources

Britain

Gillard, David; Bourne, Kenneth; Watt, Donald Cameron (1984). *British Documents on
     Foreign Affairs: Reports and Papers from the Foreign Office Confidential Print.* Part I:
     From the Mid-Nineteenth Century to the First World War. Series B: The Near and
     Middle East, 1856–1914, vols. 5 and 20.
HMSO [His Majesty's Stationery Office] (1920). *Report on the Commercial and Industrial
     Situation of Greece for the Year 1919.* London.

Department of Overseas Trade [DOT]

DOT (1921). *General Report on the Industrial and Economic Situation in Greece, Dated February 1921*. London: His Majesty's Stationery Office.

DOT (1922). *Report on the Industrial and Economic Situation in Greece to April 1922*. London: His Majesty's Stationery Office.

DOT (1923). *Report on the Industrial and Economic Situation in Greece, Dated July 1923*. London: His Majesty's Stationery Office.

DOT (1925). *Report on the Industrial & Economic Situation in Greece, For the Years 1923 and 1924*. London: His Majesty's Stationery Office.

DOT (1927). *Report on the Industrial & Economic Situation in Greece, Dated May 31st, 1927*. London: His Majesty's Stationery Office.

DOT (1928). *Report on Economic Conditions in Greece, Dated May 1928*. London: His Majesty's Stationery Office.

DOT (1934). *Report on Economic Conditions in Greece, 1932–33*.
London: His Majesty's Stationery Office.

DOT (1937). *Report on the Economic and Commercial Conditions in Greece, April 1937*. London: His Majesty's Stationery Office.

Greece

Vecris, Jean (1922). *Annuaire Commercial*. Thessaloniki: Chambre de Commerce et d'Industrie de Salonique.

Christodoulou, Georgios K. (1936). *I Thessaloniki kata tin teleftea ekatontaetia: Emborio-Viomihania-Viotehnia* (Thessaloniki during the Last Century: Commerce-Industry-Crafts). Thessaloniki [s.n.]. (334 pp.) (Greek).

Royaume de Grèce, Ministère de l'Économie Nationale – Direction de la Statistique (1923). *Renseignements généraux sur la population de la Grèce d'après le recensement de 1920*. Athens, Imprimerie Nationale.

Republique Hellénique, Ministère de l'Economie Nationale, Statistique Générale de la Grèce (1928). *Recensement de la Population de la Grèce au 19 Décembre 1920–1 Janvier 1921. Résultats Statistiques Généraux:* A. Population B. Familles. Athens, Imprimerie Nationale.

Vol. I. *Résultats Statistiques pour la Grèce Centrale et Eubée* (1927).

Vol. II. *Résultats Statistiques pour Thessalie et Arta* (1929).

Vol. III. *Résultats Statistiques pour les Iles Ioniennes* (1924).

Ministère de L'Economie Nationale - Statistique Générale de la Grèce (1927).

Recensement des Entreprises Industrielles au 18 Décembre 1920. Vol. D. *Nombre, personnel et force motrice des entreprises recensées en général*. Athens, Imprimerie Nationale.

République Hellénique, Ministère de l'Economie Nationale, Statistique Générale de la Grèce,(1933–1937). *Résultats statistiques du recensement de la population de la Grèce du 15–16 mai 1928*. Athens: Imprimerie Nationale.

Vol. 1: *Population de fait et de droit - Refugiés* (1933).

Vol. 2: *Age - Etat matrimonial - Instruction* (1935).

Vol. 3: *Professions* (in two parts, 1932 and 1937).

Vol. 4: *Lieu de naissance – Religion et langue – Sujetion* (1935).

Greece (1931–1937). *Annuaire Statistique de la Grèce (1930–1936)*. Athens:
Imprimerie Nationale.

Grèce, Departement Hellénique de l'Information [n.d.], *Le Drame des Juifs Hellènes*. Le Caire [s.n.].

Document Collections, Journals, Testimonies and Other Published Primary Sources

—— (1967). *Salonique, Ville-Mère en Israël*. Jerusalem and Tel Aviv: Centre de recherches sur le Judaïsme de Salonique. (Hebrew).

—— (1967). *Hayey HaKalkala BeSaloniki* (Economic Life in Salonica). In *Salonique, Ville-Mère en Israël*. Jerusalem and Tel Aviv: Centre de Recherches sur le Judaïsme de Salonique, 233–240. (Hebrew).

—— (1986). *Keren LeHalva'ot Ktanot* (Small Loans Fund). In D. Recanati (ed.), *Zikhron Saloniki* (A Memoir of Salonica). Tel Aviv: The Committee for Publishing the Book of the Jewish Community of Salonica, vol. II, 215. (Hebrew).

Abbot, George Frederick (1903). *The Tale of a Tour in Macedonia*. London: Edward Arnold.

Adler, Elkan Nathan (1905). *Jews in Many Lands*. Philadelphia: The Jewish Publication Society of America.

Aelion, Jacques (1997). Quelques souvenirs sur des banquiers saloniciens à Paris. In Elie Carasso (ed.), *Les voix de la mémoire*. Trarascon: Elie Carasso, pp. 65–113.

Allalouf, Ya'akov (Jacky) (2006). *Memories*. Tel Aviv: published by the author.

Allatini, Moise (1875). *A Sketch of the of Primary Education among the Jews of the East and Especially among the Jews of Salonica: Addressed to the Anglo-Jewish Association*. Trans. from Italian by James Picciotto. London: Wertheimer.

Alvo, Yitshak (1967). *Aharei HaDleka* (After the Fire). In *Salonique, Ville-Mère en Israël*. Jerusalem and Tel Aviv: Centre de Recherches sur le Judaïsme de Salonique, 226–227. (Hebrew).

American Jewish Year Book 1912–1939. Philadelphia: The Jewish Publication Society of America.

Assouline, Pierre [1997] (1999²). *Le dernier des Camondo*. Paris: Gallimard.

Baron, Salo W. (1973). An Outline of European Jewish History between the Two World Wars: A Testimony at the Eichman Trial. In Yisrael Gutman and Livia Rothkirchen (eds.), *The Holocaust: Background, History, Implications*. Jerusalem: Yad Vashem, 143–174.

Ben-Shanji, Mentesh (1986) [September-October 1936]. *Ba'alei Mikzo'ot be-Kehilat Saloniki* (Craftsmen in the Jewish Community of Salonica). In David A. Recanati (ed.), *Zikhron Saloniki* (A Memoir of Salonica). Tel Aviv: The Committee for Publishing the Book of the Jewish Community of Salonica, vol. II, 208–210. (Hebrew).

Ben-Zvi, Yitzhak (1967). *Lekorot Aliyyat Ha Yama'im HaSalonika'im le'Erets Yisra'el* (The Immigration of the Salonican Seamen to Erets Yisra'el). In *Salonique, Ville-Mère en Israël*. Jerusalem and Tel Aviv: Centre de Recherches sur le Judaïsme de Salonique, 339–341. (Hebrew).

Ben-Yaakov, Yair (February 2003). Uzo, Brothers. *Massa Olami* 14: 32–36. (Hebrew).

Blanchard, Raoul (1925). The Exchange of Populations between Greece and Turkey. *Geographical Review* 15(3), 449–456.

Bourla, Yosef (1986). *Yehudey Saloniki BeIskey HaSapanut VehaTovala HaYamit* (The Jews of Salonica in Shipping and Maritime Transport Business). In David A. Recanati (ed.), *Zikhron Saloniki* (A Memoir of Salonica). Tel Aviv: The Committee for Publishing the Book of the Jewish Community of Salonica, vol. II, 211–212. (Hebrew).

Bowman, Steven (ed.) (2002). The Holocaust in Salonika: Eyewitness Accounts. Trans. from Greek and Judeo-Spanish with introductions and notes by Isaac Benmayor. New York: Sephardic House and Bloch Publishing Company.

Broudo, Yitzhak (1967). *HaSabalim BeSaloniki LeMinehem UleIrgunehem* (Salonica's Porters: Their Specializations and Organizations). In *Salonique, Ville-Mère en Israël*. Jerusalem and Tel Aviv: Centre de Recherches sur le Judaïsme de Salonique, 242–243. (Hebrew).

Carpi, Daniel (ed.) (1999). *Italian Diplomatic Documents on the Holocaust in Greece*

(1941–1943). Tel Aviv: The Chair for the History and Culture of the Jews of Salonika and Greece, The Diaspora Research Institute, Tel Aviv University.

Constantopoulou, Phontini and Thanos Veremis (1998). *Documents on the History of the Greek Jews: Records from the Historical Archives of the Ministry of Foreign Affairs.* Athens: Kastaniotis.

Convention Relative to Transit through Salonica Concluded between Greece and Serbia. Supplement: Official Documents (1919). *The American Journal of International Law* 13(4), 441–456.

Cunliffe-Owen, Betty (1927). *Silhouettes of Republican Greece: Romances and Refugees* (Forward by H. Morgenthau). London: Hutchinson.

Dublon-Knebel, Irith (2007). *German Foreign Office Documents on the Holocaust in Greece (1937–1944)*. Tel Aviv: Chair for the History and Culture of the Jews of Salonika and Greece, Goldstein-Goren Diaspora Research Centre, Tel Aviv University.

Eddy, Charles B. (1931). *Greece and the Greek Refugees.* London: George Allen & Unwin.

Emmanuel, Isac Samuel (1936). *Les grands juifs de Salonique.* Tel Aviv: Strud & Sons Press. (Hebrew).

Emmanuel, Isac Samuel (1972). *Toldot Yehudey Saloniki* (The History of the Jews of Salonica). In David A. Recanati (ed.), *Zikhron Saloniki* (A Memoir of Salonica). Tel Aviv: The Committee for Publishing the Book of the Jewish Community of Salonica, vol. I, 1–272. (Hebrew).

Frenzl, M. (ed.) (1927). Salonika. In *The Marine Underwriter: An International Marine Insurance Review.* Berlin: The International Union of Marine Insurance, vol. 6, 119–120.

Ha-Elion, Moshe (1997²). *Metsarey She'ol* (The Straits of Hell). Bat-Yam: Self-published by author. (Hebrew).

Handeli, Ya'acov (Jack) (1992). *A Greek Jew From Salonica Remembers.* Trans. from Hebrew by Martin Kett. New York: Herzl Press.

Ironi, A. (1967). *Mivne HaKehila UMosdoteha* (The Jewish Community and its Institutions). In *Salonique, Ville-Mère en Israël.* Jerusalem/Tel Aviv: Centre de Recherches sur le Judaïsme de Salonique, 207–208. (Hebrew).

Kounio-Amariglio, Erika Myriam (2000). *From Thessaloniki to Auschwitz and Back: Memories of a Survivor from Thessaloniki.* London and Portland, Oregon: Vallentine Mitchell.

League of Nations (1926). Greek Refugee Settlement. Geneva.

Lefeuvre-Méuelle, M. (1916). *La Grèce économique et financière.* Paris: Librairie Felix Alcan.

Levi, David (Daut) [1941] (1986). *Skira Al Mosdot HaKehila Hayehudit BeSaloniki, 1870–1940* (A Survey on the Institutions of the Jewish Community in Salonica, 1870–1940). In D. Recanati (ed.), *Zikhron Saloniki* (A Memoir of Salonica). Tel Aviv: The Committee for Publishing the Book of the Jewish Community of Salonica, vol. II, 127–142. (Hebrew).

Lévy, Sam (ed.) (1930). *Le Guide Sam: Le Livre d'Or de l'Orient.* France: Garches (S. & O.).

Lévy, Sam (1937). Les grandes familles Séphardites: Les Allatini. *Le Judaisme Sephardi* 51, 24–25 and 58–59.

Matsas, Michael (1997). *The Illusion of Safety: The Story of the Greek Jews during the Second World War.* New York: Pella.

Mayer, N. (1913). *The Jews of Turkey: A Lecture Delivered by N. Mayer before the Jewish Literary Society at the Beth Hamidrash.* London: [s.n.].

Mears, E. G. (1929). *Greece To-day.* Stanford, California: Stanford University Press.

Megas, Yannis (1993). *Souvenir: Images of the Jewish Community of Salonika 1897–1917.* Athens: Kapon.

Menasche, Albert (1947). *Birkenau: Auschwitz II (Memories of an Eyewitness): How 72,000 Greek Jews Perished*. New York: Isaac Saltiel.

Miller, William (1928). *Greece*. London: Ernst Brown.

Modiano, Mario (2008). *Hamehune Modillano: The Genealogical Story of the Modiano Family from 1570 to Our Days*. 7th edition. Athens: M. Modiano. Available at <http://www.themodianos.gr/The_Story.pdf>.

Moisis, Asher R. (1972a). *Yehudim BiTsva Yavan* (Jews in the Greek Army). In D. Recanati (ed.), *Zikhron Saloniki* (A Memoir of Salonica). Tel Aviv: The Committee for Publishing the Book of the Jewish Community of Salonica, vol. I, 331–333. (Hebrew).

Moisis, Asher R. (1972b). *Makabi UFra'ot Campbell* (Maccabi and the Campbell Riots). In D. Recanati (ed.), *Zikhron Saloniki* (A Memoir of Salonica). Tel Aviv: The Committee for Publishing the Book of the Jewish Community of Salonica, vol. I, 361–365. (Hebrew).

Moisis, Asher R. (1972c). *HaTnu'a HaTsionit BeSaloniki Uve Yeter Kehilot Yavan* (The Zionist Movement in Salonica and Other Communities in Greece). In D. Recanati (ed.), *Zikhron Saloniki* (A Memoir of Salonica). Tel Aviv: The Committee for Publishing the Book of the Jewish Community of Salonica, vol. I, 366–394. (Hebrew).

Molho, Yitzhak R. (1951). *Yama'im Salonika'im Be Yisra'el: Hazon VeHagshama*. (Salonican Seamen in Israel: Vision and Realization). Jerusalem: Hahevel Hayami LeYisra'el. (Hebrew).

Molho, Michael (1967a). *Toldot Yehudey Saloniki* (The History of the Jews in Salonica). In *Salonique, Ville-Mère en Israël*. Jerusalem/Tel Aviv: Centre de Recherches sur le Judaïsme de Salonique, 1–26. (Hebrew).

Molho, Michael (1967b). *Ha'Eda HaAshkenazit BeSaloniki* (The Ashkenazi Congregation in Salonica). In *Salonique, Ville-Mère en Israël*. Jerusalem/Tel Aviv: Centre de Recherches sur le Judaïsme de Salonique, 27–31. (Hebrew).

Molho, Michael (1967c). *HaKehilot (Batey HaKneset) BeSaloniki* (The Synagogues in Salonica). In *Salonique, Ville-Mère en Israël*. Jerusalem/Tel Aviv: Centre de Recherches sur le Judaïsme de Salonique, 174–184. (Hebrew).

Molho, Michael (1974). *Matsevot Bet Ha'Almin Shel Yehudey Saloniki* (The Epitaphs of the Old Jewish Cemetery of Salonica). Tel Aviv: The Institute for Research of Salonica Jewry. (Hebrew).

Molho, Michael (1986). *HaShkhunot Ha Yehudiyot BeSaloniki* (The Jewish Neighbourhoods in Salonica). In *Zikhron Saloniki* (A Memoir of Salonica). Tel Aviv: The Committee for Publishing the Book of the Jewish Community of Salonica, vol. II, 5–31. (Hebrew).

Molho, Michael and Joseph Nehama (1965). *The Destruction of Greek Jewry, 1941–1944*. Jerusalem: Yad Vashem. (Hebrew).

Molho, René [with Rebecca Camhi Fromer] (1994). *They Say Diamonds Don't Burn: The Holocaust Experiences of René Molho of Salonika, Greece*. Berkeley, CA: Judah L. Magnes Museum.

Morin, Edgar (1989). *Vidal et les siens*. Paris: Editions du Seuil.

Morin, Edgar (2009). *Vidal and His Family: From Salonica to Paris*. Trans. Deborah Cowell. Foreword by Alfonso Montuori. Brighton/Portland: Sussex Academic Press.

Naar, Devin E. (ed.) (2006). *With Their Own Words: Glimpses of Jewish Life in Thessaloniki before the Holocaust*. Thessaloniki: The Jewish Community of Thessaloniki.

Nahmia, Nina [1996] (2006). *Kelipot Shel Ke-ev* (Peels of Pain). Trans. from Greek by Amir Zukerman. Jerusalem: Yad Vashem. (Hebrew).

Ossoskin, Moshe (1967). *Pe'ulot HaKehila BeShetah HaDiyur, HaHinukh VeHa'Ezra HaSotsialit Al Saf Milhemet Ha'Olam HaShniyya* (The Jewish Community's Activity in Housing, Education and Social Welfare on the Brink of the Second World War). In

Salonique, Ville-Mère en Israël, Jerusalem/Tel Aviv: Centre de recherches sur le Judaïsme de Salonique, 211–214. (Hebrew).

Pallis, Alexandros A. (1925). Racial Migrations in the Balkans during the Years 1912–1924. *The Geographical Journal* 66(4), 315–331.

Pallis, Alexandros A. (1929). The Greek Census of 1928. *The Geographical Journal* 73(6), 543–548.

Pallis, Alexandros A. (1948). *Social and Labor Legislation in Greece*. London: Greek Information Office.

Recanati, David A. (ed.) (1971–1986). *Zikhron Saloniki* (A Memoir of Salonica). 2 vols. Tel Aviv: The Committee for Publishing the Book of the Jewish Community of Salonica.

Recanati, David A. (1972). *Ha-Milhama Le-Ma'an Ha-Shabat* (The Struggle for the Sake of the Sabbath). In D. Recanati (ed.), *Zikhron Saloniki* (A Memoir of Salonica). Tel Aviv: The Committee for Publishing the Book of the Jewish Community of Salonica, vol. I. 334– 356. (Hebrew).

Recanati, Aure (2000). *Jewish Community of Salonika 1943 . . . Based on Microfilms from U.S. Holocaust Memorial Museum* (1997–A0220). Jerusalem: Erez.

Recanati, Harry (1984). *Recanati, Father and Son*. Jerusalem: Kana. (Hebrew).

Refael, Haim (1997). *Shirat Haim*. Israel: Self-published by the author. (Hebrew).

Refael, Shmuel (interviewer and ed.) (1988). *Routes of Hell: Greek Jewry in the Holocaust (Testimonies)*. Tel Aviv: The Institute for Research of Salonica Jewry and the Organization of Jewish Survivors of Greece in Israel.

Reuven, S[olomon] (1967). *Mishpat Campbell* (The Campbell Trial). In *Salonique, Ville-Mère en Israël*. Jerusalem/Tel Aviv: Centre de Recherches sur le Judaïsme de Salonique, 229–231. (Hebrew).

Risal, Pierre (pseudonym of Joseph Nehama) (1917) [1914]. *La ville convoitée: Salonique*. Paris: Perrin.

Robinson, Vandeleur (1939). Greece Faces the Axis. *The Political Quarterly* 10(3), 351–364.

Rodrigue, Aron (1993). *Images of Sephardi and Eastern Jewries in Transition: The Teachers of the Alliance Israélite Universelle, 1860–1939*. Seattle/London: University of Washington Press.

Schibi, Baruch (1967). *Ha-Status Ha-Huki Shel Yahadut Saloniki* (The Legal Status of Salonican Jewry). In *Salonique, Ville-Mère en Israël*. Jerusalem/Tel Aviv: Centre de Recherches sur le Judaïsme de Salonique, 209–210. (Hebrew).

Sciaky, Leon (1946). *Farewell to Salonica: Portrait of an Era*. New York: Current Books.

Stavroulakis, Nicholas Hannan, Eleni M. Tsouka and Dimitris Vlahos (s.n). *The Entrepreneurial Activity of the Jews of Thessaloniki, 1920–1940*. Catalog of the exhibition presented in the Jewish Museum of Thessaloniki.

Strumza, Jack (1995). *And You Choose Life: From Salonica to Jerusalem via Auschwitz and Paris*. Tel Aviv: The Institute for the Research of Saloniki Jewry. (Hebrew).

Toledano, Haim (1972). *Ha-28 VeHa-29 Be Yuni 1931* (The 28th and 29th of June 1931). In D. Recanati (ed.), *Zikhron Saloniki* (A Memoir of Salonica). Tel Aviv: The Committee for Publishing the Book of the Jewish Community of Salonica, vol. I, 357–360. (Hebrew).

Toledano, Haim (1986a). *Igrot Meha'Itonay Eliyahu Veissi Al HaMatsav Shel HaKehila HaYehudit 1935–1939* (Letters of the Journalist Eliyahu Veissi on the Situation of the Jewish Community 1935–1939). In D. Recanati (ed.), *Zikhron Saloniki* (A Memoir of Salonica). Tel Aviv: The Committee for Publishing the Book of the Jewish Community of Salonica, vol. II, 168–176. (Hebrew).

Toledano, Haim A. (1986b). *HaYehudim BeHayey HaMishar VehaTa'asiyya Shel Saloniki* (The Jews in the Commercial and Industrial Life of Salonica). In D. Recanati (ed.),

Zikhron Saloniki (A Memoir of Salonica), Tel Aviv: The Committee for Publishing the Book of the Jewish Community of Salonica, vol. II, 202–207. (Hebrew).

Tomai, Photini (2009). *Auschwitz-Birkenau: About the Destruction of Jewish Sephardic Communities in Greece*. The Greek Ministry of Foreign Affairs: Papazisis. (Greek).

Uziel, Baruch (1967). *Ha-Dayagim Ha-Yehudim BeSaloniki* (The Jewish Fisheries in Salonica). In *Salonique, Ville-Mère en Israël*. Jerusalem/Tel Aviv: Centre de Recherches sur le Judaïsme de Salonique, 244–248. (Hebrew).

Uziel, Yossef (1967a). *Ha-Yehasim ben Yehudey Saloniki La'Amim ShebiSvivatam* (The Relationship between the Salonica's Jews and Other National Groups in Their Environment). In *Salonique, Ville-Mère en Israël*. Jerusalem/Tel Aviv: Centre de Recherches sur le Judaïsme de Salonique, 53–56. (Hebrew).

Uziel, Yossef (1967b). *Mo'adonim Va'Agudot LeSugehem* (Clubs and Associations). In *Salonique, Ville-Mère en Israël*. Jerusalem/Tel Aviv: Centre de Recherches sur le Judaïsme de Salonique, 127–129. (Hebrew).

Uziel, Yossef (1967c). *Saloniki Ola BeLehava* (Salonica on Fire). In *Salonique, Ville-Mère en Israël*. Jerusalem/Tel Aviv: Centre de Recherches sur le Judaïsme de Salonique, 223–225. (Hebrew).

Uziel, Yossef [1929] (1978). *HaMigdal HaLavan* (The White Tower) (2nd Edition). Tel Aviv: The Institute for Research of Salonica Jewry. (Hebrew).

Varsano, Samuele (1997). Des juifs de Salonique à Naples (1917–1940): un témoignage. In E. Carasso (ed.), *Les voix de la mémoire*. Tarascon: Elie Carasso, 95–102.

Secondary Sources

Abatzopolou, Fragiski (1997). The Image of the Jew in the Literature of Salonica. In P. Mackridge and E. Yannakakis (eds.), *Ourselves and Others: The Development of a Greek Macedonian Cultural Identity since 1912*. Oxford/New York: Berg, 217–224.

Abravanel, Nicole (1996). Paris et le sépharadisme ou l'affirmation sépharadiste à Paris dans les années trente. *Sephardica* 1, 497–523.

Abrevaya Stein, Sarah (2002). Introduction: Ladino in Print. *Jewish History* 16(3), 225–233.

Abrevaya Stein, Sarah (2004). *Making Jews Modern: The Yiddish and Ladino Press in the Russian and Ottoman Empires*. Bloomington: Indiana University Press.

Abrevaya Stein, Sarah (2007). Mediterranean Jewries and Global Commerce in the Modern Period: On the Trail of the Jewish Feather Trade. *Jewish Social Studies: History, Culture, Society* 13(2), 1–39.

Abrevaya Stein, Sarah, (2008). *Plumes: Ostrich Feathers, Jews, and a Lost World of Global Commerce*. New Haven: Yale University Press.

Ahmad, Feroz (1982). Unionist Relations with the Greek, Armenian and Jewish Communities of the Ottoman Empire, 1908–1914. In B. Braude and B. Lewis (eds.), *Christians and Jews in the Ottoman Empire*. New York: Holmes & Meier Publishers, vol. I, 401–434.

Aktar, Ayhan (2003). Homogenising the Nation, Turkifying the Economy. In Renée Hirschon (ed.), *Crossing the Aegean: An Appraisal of the 1923 Compulsory Population Exchange between Greece and Turkey*. Oxford/New York: Berghahn Books, 79–95.

Aldrich, Howard and Roger Waldinger (1990). Ethnicity and Entrepreneurship. *Annual Review of Sociology* 16: 111–135.

Alexandris, Alexis (2003). Religion or Ethnicity: The Identity Issue of the Minorities in Greece and Turkey. In R. Hirschon (ed.), *Crossing the Aegean: An Appraisal of the 1923*

Compulsory Population Exchange between Greece and Turkey. Oxford/New York: Berghahn, 117–132.

Anastassiadou, Meropi (1992–1994). Artisans juifs à Salonique au début des Tanzimat. *Revue du Monde Musulman et de la Méditerranée* 66, 65–72.

Anastassiadou, Meropi (1993). Les Occidentaux de la place. In G. Veinstein (ed.), *Salonique, 1850–1918: La 'ville des juifs' et le réveil des Balkans*. Paris: Éditions Autrement, 143–156.

Anastassiadou, Meropi (1997). *Salonique, 1830–1912*. Leiden/New York/Koln: Brill.

Anker, Richard. (1998). *Gender and Jobs: Sex Segregation of Occupations in the World*. Geneva: International Labour Office.

Anthias, Floya (1992). *Ethnicity, Class, Gender and Migration*. Aldershot: Avebury.

Armstrong, John A. (1976). Mobilized and Proletarian Diasporas. *The American Political Science Review* 70(2), 393–408.

Avdela, Efi (1998). Class, Ethnicity and Gender in Post-Ottoman Thessaloniki: The Great Tobacco Strike of 1914. In B. Melman (ed.), *Borderlines, Gender and Identities in War and Peace, 1870–1930*. New York: Routledge, 421–438.

Avni, Haim (1970). Spanish Nationals in Greece and their Faith during the Holocaust. *Yad Vashem Studies on the European Jewish Catastrophe and Resistance* 8, 31–68.

Baer, Marc (2007). Globalization, Cosmopolitanism, and the Dönme in Ottoman Salonica and Turkish Istanbul. *Journal of World History* 18(2), 141–170.

Bailey, Tomas and Roger Waldinger (1991). Primary, Secondary, and Enclave Labor Markets: A Training System Approach. *American Sociological Review* 56(4), 432–445.

Bajohr, Frank (2002). *'Aryanisation' in Hamburg: The Economic Exclusion of Jews and the Confiscation of Their Property in Nazi Germany, 1933–1945*. Trans. George Wilkes. New York: Berghahn.

Banton, Michael (1983). *Racial and Ethnic Competition*. Cambridge: Cambridge University Press.

Baron, Salo W. (1973). An Outline of European Jewish History between Two World Wars: A Testimony at the Eichman Trial. In Yisrael Gutman (ed.), *The Holocaust: Background, History, Implications*. Jerusalem: Yad Vashem, 143–174. (Hebrew).

Barth, Frederick (1969). Introduction. In F.Barth (ed.), *Ethnic Groups and Boundaries: The Social Organization of Culture Difference*. Boston: Little, Brown, 9–38.

Barutciski, Michael (2003). Lausanne Revisited: Population Exchange in International Law and Policy. In R. Hirschon (ed.), *Crossing the Aegean: An Appraisal of the 1923 Compulsory Population Exchange between Greece and Turkey*. Oxford/New York: Berghahn, 23–37.

Bashan, Eliezer (1989). The Rise and Decline of the Sephardi Communities in the Levant: The Economic Aspects. In R.D. Barnett and W.M. Schwab (eds.), *The Sephardi Heritage: Essays on the Historical and Cultural Contribution of the Jews of Spain and Portugal*. Grendon (Northants): Gibraltar Books, vol. II, 128–178.

Baxevanis, John (1963). *The Port of Thessaloniki*. Thessalonili: Institute for Balkans Studies.

Becker, Gary S. (1971²). *The Economics of Discrimination*. Chicago: Chicago University Press.

Ben, Joseph (1985). *The Greek Jewry in the Holocaust and Resistance, 1941–1944*. Tel Aviv: s.n. (Hebrew).

Benayahu, Meir (1971–1978). Hatnu'a HaShabta'it BeYavan (The Sabbatean Movement in Greece), *Sefunot* 14(4), entire issue. (Hebrew).

Ben-Rafael, Eliezer (2001). The Transformation of Diasporas: The Linguistic Dimension. In Eliezer Ben-Rafael and Yitzhak Sternberg (eds.), *Identity, Culture and Globalization*. Leiden: Brill, 337–352.

Ben-Rafael, Eliezer, E. Olshtain and I. Geijst (1998). Identity and Language: The Social

Insertion of Soviet Jews in Israel. In Elazar Leshem and Judith T. Shuval (eds.), *Immigration to Israel: Sociological Perspectives, Studies of Israeli Society*. New Brunswick (USA): Transaction, vol. VIII, 333–356.

Benbassa, Esther (1994). Associational Strategies in Ottoman Jewish Society in the Nineteenth and Twentieth Centuries. In Avigdor Levi (ed.), *The Jews of the Ottoman Empire*. Princeton, N.J.: The Darwin Press, 457–484.

Benbassa, Esther and Aron Rodrigue (1995). *The Jews of the Balkans: The Judeo-Spanish Community, 15ᵗʰ to 20ᵗʰ Centuries*. Oxford, UK/Cambridge, USA: Blackwell.

Bergesen, Albert and Ronald Shoenberg (1980). Long Waves of Colonial Expansion and Contraction. In Albert Bergesen (ed.), *Studies of the Modern World-System*. New York: Academic Press, 231–277.

Betta, Chiara (2005). The Trade Diaspora of Baghdadi Jews: From India to China's Treaty Ports, 1842–1937. In Baghdiantz McCabe, Gelina Harlaftis and Ioanna Pepelasis Minoglou (eds.), *Diaspora Entrepreneurial Networks: Four Centuries of History*. Oxford/New York: Berg, 269–285.

Blalock, Hubert M. (1967). *Toward a Theory of Minority-Group Relations*. New York: Capricorn Books.

Bloemraad, Irene (2006). Citizenship Lessons from the Past: The Contours of Immigrant Naturalization in the Early 20th Century. *Social Science Quarterly* 87(5), 927–953.

Bonacich, Edna (1973). A Theory of Middleman Minorities. *American Sociological Review* 38(5), 583–594.

Bonacich, Edna (1993). The Other Side of Ethnic Entrepreneurship: A Dialogue with Waldinger, Aldrich, Ward and Associates. *International Migration Review* 27(3), 685–692.

Bonacich, Edna and John Modell (1981). *The Economic Basis of Ethnic Solidarity*. Berkeley: University of California Press.

Bonnet, Jean-Charles (1976). *Les pouvoirs publics français et l'immigration dans l'entre-deux-guerres*. Lyon: Centre d'histoire économique et sociale de la région lyonnaise.

Bostas, Eleftherios N. (1987). Greece and the East: The Trade Connection, 1851–1984. *Journal of Modern Greek Studies* 5(2), 207–235.

Boswell, Terry E. (1986). A Split Labor Market Analysis Theory of Discrimination against Chinese Immigrants, 1850–1882. *American Sociological Review* 51(3), 352–371.

Bowman, Steven (1990). The Great Powers and the Jews: British and French Consuls on Interwar Greek Jewry. In *Proceedings of the Tenth World Congress of Jewish Studies*, Division B, Jerusalem: The World Union of Jewish Studies, vol. II, 379–386.

Bowman, Steven (2009). *The Agony of Greek Jews, 1940–1945*. Stanford: Stanford University Press.

Braude, Benjamin (1983). The Cloth Industry of Salonica in the Mediterranean Economy. *Pe'amim: Studies in Oriental Jewry* 15, 82–95. (Hebrew)

Braude, Benjamin and Bernard Lewis (1982). Introduction. In B. Braude and B. Lewis (eds.), *Christians and Jews in the Ottoman Empire*. New York: Holmes & Meier, vol. I, 1–34.

Brezis, Elise S. and Peter Temin (1999). Elites, Minorities and Economic Growth in an Interdisciplinary Perspective. In E. S. Brezis and P. Temin (eds.), *Elites, Minorities and Economic Growth*. Amsterdam: Elsevier, 3–16.

Cable, Vincent (1972) [1969]. The Asians of Kenya. In A.M. Rose and C.B. Rose (eds.), *Minority Problems*. 2nd edn., New York: Harper and Row, 103–111.

Çağaptay, Soner (2003). Citizenship Policies in Interwar Turkey. *Nations and Nationalism* 9(4), 601–619.

Campbell, John and Philip Sherrard (1968). *Modern Greece*. London: Ernest Benn.

Carabott, Philip (1997). The Politics of Integration and Assimilation vis-à-vis the Slavo-Macedonian Minority of Inter-War Greece: From Parliamentary Inertia to Metaxist

Repression. In P. Mackridge and E. Yannakakis (eds.), *Ourselves and Others: The Development of a Greek Macedonian Cultural Identity since 1912*. Oxford/New York: Berg, 59–77.

Cassis, Youssef and Ioanna Pepelasis Minoglou (2005). Entrepreneurship in Theory and History: State of the Art and New Perspectives. In Y. Cassis and I. Pepelasis Minoglou (eds.), *Entrepreneurship in Theory and History*. London/New York: Palgrave Macmillan, 3–21.

Casson, Mark (1982). *The Entrepreneur: An Economic Theory*. Oxford: Martin Robertson.

Casson, Mark (1994). Institutional Diversity in Overseas Enterprise: Explaining the Free-Standing Company. *Business History* 36(4), 95–108.

Casson, Mark and Andrew Godley (2005). Entrepreneurship in Historical Explanation. In Y. Cassis and I. Pepelasis Minoglou (eds.), *Entrepreneurship in Theory and History*. London and New York: Palgrave Macmillan, 25–60.

Colli, Andrea, Paloma Fernández Pérez, and Mary Rose (2003). National Determinants of Family Firm Development? Family Firms in Britain, Spain and Italy in the Nineteenth and Twentieth Centuries. *Enterprise and Society* 4(1), 28–64.

Chase-Dunn, Christopher and Thomas D. Hall (1997). Rise and Demise - Comparing World-Systems. USA and UK: Westview Press, a division of HarperCollins Publishers.

Chatziioannou, Maria Christina (2008). Relations between the State and the Private Sphere: Speculation and Corruption in Nineteenth-Century Greece. *Mediterranean Historical Review* 23(1), 1–14.

Chin, Margaret M. (2005). *Sewing Women: Immigrants and the New York City Garment Industry*. New York: Columbia University Press.

Chin, Ku-Sup, In-Jin Yoon and David Smith (1996). Immigrant Small Business and International Economic Linkage: A Case of the Korean Wig Business in Los Angeles, 1968–1977. *International Migration Review* 30(2), 485–510.

Chirot, Daniel (1997). Conflicting Identities and the Dangers of Communalism. In Daniel Chirot and Anthony Reid (eds.), *Essential Outsiders: Chinese and Jews in the Modern Transformation of Southeast Asia and Central Europe*. Seattle/London: University of Washington Press, 3–32.

Chiswick, Barry R. and Michael Wenz (2006). The Linguistic and Economic Adjustment of Soviet Jewish Immigrants in the United States. *Research in Labor Economics* 24, 179–216.

Christodoulaki, Olga (1999). Industrial Growth Revisited: Manufacturing Output in Greece during the Interwar Period. Economic History Working Papers 50/99, London School of Economics, Department of Economic History. (Downloaded 11 December 2006 from <http://www.lse.ac.uk/collections/economicHistory/pdf/wp5099.pdf>.

Christodoulaki, Olga (2001). Industrial Growth in Greece between the Wars: A New Perspective. *European Review of Economic History* 5(1), 61–89.

Christov, Christo (1964). *The Land Problem in Macedonia in the XIX. and at the Beginning of the XX. Century*. Sofia: Bulgarian Academy of Sciences Press. (Bulgarian).

Clogg, Richard [1979] (1986²). *A Short History of Modern Greece*. Cambridge: Cambridge University Press.

Clogg, Richard (1992). *A Concise History of Greece*. Cambridge: University Press.

Coleman, James S. (1988). Social Capital in the Creation of Human Capital. *American Journal of Sociology*, vol. 94, Supplement, *Organizations and Institutions: Sociological and Economic Approaches to the Analysis of Social Structure*, S95–S120.

Colonas, Vassilis (2002). The Contribution of the Jewish Community to the Modernisation of Salonika at the end of the Nineteenth Century. In M. Rozen (ed.), *The Last Ottoman Century and Beyond: The Jews in Turkey and the Balkans, 1808–1945*. Tel Aviv: Tel Aviv University, pp. 165–172.

Cooperman, Eugene Abraham (1991). Turco-Jewish Relations in the Ottoman City of

Salonica, 1889–1912: Two Communities in Support of the Ottoman Empire. Ph.D. diss., New York University.

Crouzet, François (1999). Business Dynasties in Britain and France. In E. S. Brezis and P. Temin (eds.), *Elites, Minorities and Economic Growth*. Amsterdam: Elsevier, 41–54.

Czech, Danuta (1973). *Hashmadat Yehudey Yavan BeAuschwitz* (The Extermination of the Jews of Greece in Auschwitz). In *Dapim LeHeker HaSho'ah VeHaMered*, Beit Lohamei HaGeta'ot, Israel: Hakibuts HaMe'uhad, vol. II, 181–194. (Hebrew).

Dagkas, Alexandros (2003). *Recherches sur l'histoire sociale de la Grèce du Nord: le mouvement des ouvriers du tabac, 1918–1928*. Paris: Association Pierre Belon.

Dakin, Douglas (1966). *The Greek Struggle in Macedonia, 1897–1913*. Thessaloniki: Institute for Balkan Studies.

Darvish, Tikva (1985). The Economic Structure of the Jewish Minority in Iraq vis-à-vis the Kuznets Model. *Jewish Social Studies* 47 (3–4), 255–266.

Darvish, Tikva (1987). The Jewish Minority in Iraq: A Comparative Study of Economic Structure. *Jewish Social Studies* 49(2), 175–180.

Darvish, Tikva (1987). *The Jews in the Economy of Iraq*. Ramat Gan: Bar-Ilan University Press. (Hebrew).

Davison, Roderic H. (1982). The *Millets* as Agents of Change in the Nineteenth-Century Ottoman Empire. In B. Braude and B. Lewis (eds.), *Christians and Jews in the Ottoman Empire*. New York: Holmes & Meier, vol. I, 319–337.

De Groot, Gertjan and Marlou Schrover (1995). General Introduction. In G. De Groot and M. Schrover (eds.), *Women Workers and Technological Change in Europe in the Nineteenth and Twentieth Centuries*. London: Taylor & Francis, 1–16.

Della Pergola, Sergio (1983). *La transformazione demografica della diaspora ebraica*. Turin: Loescher.

Delivanis, D. J. (1980). Thessaloniki on the Eve of World War I and Its Aftermath. *Balkan Studies* 21(2), 191–201.

Deringil, Selim (2002). Jewish Emigration to the Ottoman Empire at the Time of the First Zionist Congresses: A Comment. In M. Rozen (ed.), *The Last Ottoman Century and Beyond: The Jews in Turkey and The Balkans 1808–1945*, Tel Aviv: Tel Aviv University, vol. II, 141–150.

Dertilis, George B. and Constantine Costis (1995). Banking, Public Finance and the Economy: Greece, 1919–1933. In Charles H. Feinstein (ed.), *Banking, Currency and Finance in Europe between the Wars*, Oxford: Clarendon Press, 458–471.

Deutsch, Karl W. (1966²). *Nationalism and Social Communication*. Cambridge, Mass./ London: The MIT Press.

Diehl, C. and R. Schnell (2006). 'Reactive Ethnicity' or Assimilation? Statements, Arguments, and First Empirical Evidence for Labor Migrants in Germany. *International Migration Review* 40(4), 786–816.

Dimitriadis, Vassilis (1983a). *Topografia tis Thessalonikis kata tin periodo tis Turkokratias, 1430–1912* (A Topography of Thessaloniki under the Turks, 1430–1912). Thessaloniki: Hetaireia Makedonikon Spoudon. (Greek).

Dimitriadis, Vassilis (1983b). O plythismos tis thessalonikis kai i elliniki koinotita tis kata to 1913 (The Population of Salonica and Its Greek Community in 1913). *Makedonika* 23, 88–116. (Greek).

Dishon Judith (2006). A Travel Account of Salonika at the Beginning of the Twentieth Century. *Pe'amim: Studies in Oriental Jewry* 107, 39–66. (Hebrew)

Don, Yehuda (1986). Economic Effects of Anti-Semitic Discrimination. *Jewish Social Studies* 48(1), 63–82.

Don, Yehuda (1990). Economic Behaviour of Jews in Central Europe Before World War II. In E. Aerts and F.M.L. Thompson (eds.), *Ethnic Minority Groups in Town and*

Countryside and Their Effects on Economic Development (1850–1940). Leuven: Leuven University Press, 114–124.

Don, Yehuda (1992). Patterns of Jewish Economic Behavior in Central Europe in the Twentieth Century. In M.K. Silber (ed.), *Jews in the Hungarian Economy, 1930–1945*. Jerusalem: The Magnes Press, The Hebrew University, 247–273.

Dritsas, Margarita (1992). Bank-Industry Relations in Inter-War Greece: The Case of the National Bank of Greece. In Philip L. Cottrell, Hakan Lindgren and Alice Teichova (eds.), *European Industry and Banking between the Wars*. Leicester/London/New York: Leicester University Press, 203–217.

Dritsas, Margarita (1994). Networks of Bankers and Industrialists in Greece in Interwar Period. In Alice Teichova, Terry Gourvish and Agnes Pogány (eds.), *Universal Banking in the Twentieth Century: Finance, Industry and the State in North and Central Europe*. Aldershot: Edward Elgar, 229–245.

Dritsas, Margarita (1999). Monetary Modernisation in Greece: Bimetallism or the Gold Standard 1833–1920. *Journal of European Economic History* 28(1), 9–48.

Dritsas, Margarita (2003). Business and Politics: The State and the Networks in Greece. In Terry Gourvish (ed.), *Business and Politics in Europe, 1900–1970*. Cambridge, UK: Cambridge University Press, 289–306.

Dumont, Paul (1979). The Social Structure of the Jewish Community of Salonica at the End of the Nineteenth Century. *Southeastern Europe* 5(2), 33–72.

Dumont, Paul (1984). La franc-maçonnerie d'obédience française à Salonique au début du xxe siècle. *Turcica* 16, 65–94.

Dumont, Paul (1994). A Jewish Socialist and Ottoman Organisation: The Workers' Federation of Thessaloniki. In M. Tuncay & E.J. Zürcher (eds.), *Socialism and Nationalism in the Ottoman Empire, 1876–1923*. London: British Academic Press, 49–75; 178–183.

Eisenstadt, Shmuel N. (1954). *The Absorption of Immigrants: A Comparative Study Based Mainly on the Jewish Community in Palestine and the State of Israel*. London: Routledge.

Eisenstadt, Shmuel N. (1998). The Construction of Collective Identity – Some Analytical and Comparative Indications. *Israeli Sociology: A Journal for the Study of Israeli Society* 1(1), 13–38.

Eitzen, Stanley D. (1968). Two Minorities: The Jews of Poland and the Chinese of the Philippines. *Jewish Journal of Sociology* 10(2), 221–240.

Elazar, Daniel J. (1984). The Sunset of Balkan Jewry. In D. Elazar, H.P. Friendenreich, B. Hazzan and A. Weiss (eds.), *The Balkan Jewish Communities: Yugoslavia, Bulgaria, Greece, and Turkey*. Lanham, Md.: University Press of America, and Jerusalem: The Center for Jewish Community Studies of the Jerusalem Center for Public Affairs, 1–11.

Eldem, Edhem (1999). *A History of the Ottoman Bank*. Istanbul: Ottoman Bank Historical Research Centre.

Eldem, Edhem, Daniel Goffman, and Bruce Master (2004). *The Ottoman City between East and West: Aleppo, Izmir, and Istanbul*. Cambridge and New York: Cambridge University Press.

Elmlund, Peter and Charles C. Bohl (2006). Places of Ethnic Commerce across the Transect. *Places* 18(1), 26–29. Available at: <http://www.escholarship.org/uc/item/0xg9g3p6>.

Farhi, David (1971–1981). Yehudey Saloniki BeMahapekhat Ha-Turkim Ha-Tse'irim (The Jews of Salonica during the Young Turks' Revolution). *Sefunot* 15, 135–152. (Hebrew).

Feinstein, Charles H., Peter Temin and Gianni Toniolo (1995). International Economic Organization: Banking, Finance and Trade in Europe between the Wars. In Charles H.

Feinstein, (ed.), *Banking, Currency and Finance in Europe between the Wars*. Oxford: Clarendon Press, 9–76.

Filippini, Jean Pierre (1989). Le rôle des négociants et des banquiers juifs de Livourne dans le grand commerce international en Méditerranée au XVIII siècle. In A. Toaff and S. Schwarzfuchs (eds.), *The Mediterranean and the Jews*. Ramat Gan: Bar-Ilan University Press, 123–150.

Findley, Carter V. (1982). The Acid Test of Ottomanism: The Acceptance of Non-Muslims in the Late Ottoman Bureaucracy. In B. Braude and B. Lewis (eds.), *Christian and Jews in the Ottoman Empire: The Functioning of a Plural Society*. New York/London: Holmes & Meier, vol. 1, 339–368.

Fink, Carole (2004). *Defending the Rights of Others: The Great Powers, the Jews, and International Minority Protection*. New York: Cambridge University Press.

Finney, Patrick B. (1995). 'An Evil for All Concerned': Great Britain and Minority Protection after 1919. *Journal of Contemporary History* 30(3), 533–551.

Fleming, Katherine Elizabeth (2008). *Greece: A Jewish History*. Princeton, N.J.: Princeton University Press.

Fleischer, Hagen (1995). Greek Jewry and Nazi Germany: The Holocaust and Its Antecedents. *Etairea Meletes Ellenikou Evraismou, Oi Evraioi ston elleniko choro: Zetemata istoriaas ste makra dirkeia, Praktika tou Alpha Symposiou Istorias, Thessalonike, 23–24 Noemvriou 1991* (Society for the Study of Greek Jewry, The Jews in Greek Territory: Historical Issues of Long Duration: Proceedings of the First Historical Symposium, Salonica, 23–24 November 1991). Athens: Gavrielides Publishing, 185–206.

Foreman-Peck, James (1985). Seedcorn or Chaff? New Firm Formation and the Performance of the Interwar Economy. *Economic History Review* 38(3), 402–422.

Foreman-Peck, James (2005). Measuring Historical Entrepreneurship. In Y. Cassis and I. Pepelasis Minoglou (eds.), *Entrepreneurship in Theory and History*. London/New York: Palgrave Macmillan, 77–108.

Frank, Andre G. (1993). Transitional Ideological Modes: Feudalism, Capitalism, Socialism. In A.G. Frank and B.K. Gills (eds.), *The World System: Five Hundred Years or Five Thousand?* London/New York: T.J. Press, 200–221.

Fredman Cernea, Ruth (2007). *Almost Englishmen: Baghdadi Jews in British Burma*. Lanham, Md.: Roman and Littlefield.

Freris, A. F. (1986). *The Greek Economy in the Twentieth Century*. New York: St. Martin's Press; London/Sydney: Croom Helm.

Freidenreich, Harriet Pass (1979). *The Jews of Yugoslavia*. Philadelphia: The Jewish Publication Society of America.

Friedman, Milton (1988). Capitalism and the Jews. *The Freeman* 38(1), 385–394.

Friedman, Thomas L. (2000). *The Lexus and the Olive Tree*. New York: Anchor Books.

Furnival, J.S. (1948). *Colonial Policy and Practice: A Comparative Study of Burma and Netherlands India*. Cambridge: Cambridge University Press.

Gans, Herbert J. (2007). Acculturation, Assimilation and Mobility. *Ethnic and Racial Studies*, 30(1), 152–164.

Garncarska-Kadary, Bina (1985). *The Role of Jews in the Development of Industry in Warsaw 1816/20–1914*. Tel Aviv: The Diaspora Research Institute and the Centre for Research on the History of Polish Jewry. (Hebrew).

Gelber Nachum Michael (1955). An Attempt to Internationalize Salonika, 1912–1913. *Jewish Social Studies* 17(2), 105–120.

Georgeon, François (1993). Selanik musulmane et deunmè. In G. Veinstein (ed.), *Salonique, 1850–1918: La 'ville des juifs' et le réveil des Balkans*. Paris: Éditions Autrement, 105–118.

Gil, Benjamin (1950). *Dapey Aliyya: Shloshim Shnot Aliyya LeIsra'el, 1919–1949* (Pages of

Immigration: Thirty Years of Immigration to Israel, 1919–1949). Jerusalem: Jewish Agency. (Hebrew).

Gilbar, Gad G. (2003). The Muslim Big Merchant-Entrepreneurs of the Middle East, 1860–1914. *Die Welt des Islams* 43, 3–28.

Ginio, Eyal (2002). 'Learning the Beautiful Language of Homer:' Judeo-Spanish Speaking Jews and the Greek Language and Culture between the Wars. *Jewish History* 16(3), 235–262.

Glaser, Richard (1976). The Greek Jews in Baltimore. *Jewish Social Studies* 38(3–4), 321–336.

Godley, Andrew (1996). Jewish Soft Loan Societies in New York and London and Immigrant Entrepreneurship, 1880–1914. *Business History* 38(3), 101–116.

Godley, Andrew (2001). *Jewish Immigrant Entrepreneurship in New York and London 1880–1914: Enterprise and Culture.* Basingstoke and New York: Palgrave Macmillan.

Godley, Andrew (2006). Selling the Sewing Machine around the World: Singer's International Marketing Strategies, 1850–1920. *Enterprise & Society* 7(2), 266–314.

Goffman, Daniel (1990). *Izmir and the Levantine World, 1550–1650.* Seattle/London: University of Washington Press.

Goffman, Daniel (2002). *The Ottoman Empire and the Early Modern Europe.* Cambridge, UK: Cambridge University Press.

Gold Steven J. (1994). Patterns of Economic Cooperation among Israeli Immigrants in Los Angeles. *International Migration Review* 28(1), 114–135.

Gold, Steven J. (2001). Gender, Class, and Network: Social Structure and Migration Patterns among Transnational Israelis. *Global Networks* 1(1), 19–40.

Gold, Steven J. (2004). Using Photography in Studies of Immigrant Communities. *American Behavioral Scientist* 46(10), 1–21.

Gold, Steven J. (2005). Migrant Networks: A Summary and Critique of Relational Approaches to International Migration. In Mary Romero and Eric Margolis (eds.), *The Blackwell Companion to Social Inequalities.* Malden, Mass.: Blackwell, 257–285.

Goldscheider, Calvin and Alan S. Zuckerman (1984). *The Transformation of the Jews.* Chicago/London: The University of Chicago Press.

Goody, Jack (1996). Rationality and Ragioneria: The Keeping of Books and the Economic Miracle. In J. Goody, *The East in the West.* Cambridge: Cambridge University Press, 49–81.

Gordon, Milton M. (1964). *Assimilation in American Life: The Role of Race, Religion, and National Origins.* New York: Oxford University Press.

Gounaris, Basil C. (1989). Emigration from Macedonia in the Early Twentieth Century. *Journal of Modern Greek Studies* 7, 133–153.

Gounaris, Basil C. (1993). *Steam Over Macedonia, 1870–1912: Socio-Economic Change and the Railway Factor.* Boulder, Colo.: East European Monographs.

Gounaris, Basil C. (1997). Thessaloniki, 1830–1912: History, Economy and Society. In I. K. Hassiotis, (ed.), *Queen of the Worthy, Thessaloniki, History and Culture.* Vol. I: *History and Society.* Thessaloniki: Paratiritis, 111–126.

Gounaris, Basil C. (1998). Doing Business in Macedonia: Greek Problems in British Perspective (1912–1921). *European Review of History* 5(2), 169–180.

Gounaris, Basil C. (2001). From Peasants into Urbanites, from Village into Nation: Ottoman Monastir in the Early Twentieth Century. *European History Quarterly* 31(1), 43–63.

Green, Nancy L. (1977). *Ready-to-Wear and Ready-to-Work: A Century of Industry and Immigrants in Paris and New York.* Durham: Duke University Press.

Greenberg, Stanley B. (1980). *Race and State in Capitalist Development.* New Haven and London: Yale University Press.

Gross, Nachum (ed.) (1975). *Economic History of the Jews.* Jerusalem: Keter.

Gross, Nahum T. (1999). *Not by Spirit Alone: Studies in the Economic History of Modern Palestine and Israel.* Jerusalem: Hebrew University Magnes Press and Yad Yizhak Ben-Zvi Press.

Gross, Nahum T. (2000). Introduction: On Jewish Entrepreneurship. In Ran Aharonsohn and Shaul Stampfer (eds.), *Jewish Entrepreneurship in Modern Times: East Europe and Eretz Israel.* Jerusalem: Hebrew University Magnes Press, 17–24. (Hebrew).

Gutman, Israel (ed.) (1990). *Encyclopedia of the Holocaust.* New York: Macmillan.

Guarnizo, Luis Eduardo, Alejandro Portes and William Haller (2003). Assimilation and Transnationalism: Determinants of Transnational Political Action among Contemporary Migrants. *American Journal of Sociology* 108(6), 1121–1148.

Hacker, Joseph R. (1993). *Yots'ey Sefarad BaImperia HaOtmanit BaMe'ot 15–18* (Jews from Spain in the Ottoman Empire, 15th –18th Centuries). In M. Avitbol, J. Hacker, R. Bonfil, Y. Kaplan and E. Benbassa (eds.), *Hapezura Hayehudit Hasepharadit Le'ahar HaGerush* (The Sephardic Jewish Diaspora following the Expulsion from Spain). Jerusalem: The Zalman Shazar Centre, 27–72. (Hebrew).

Halamish, Aviva (2003). Immigration According to the Economic Absorptive Capacity: The Guiding Principals, the Implementation and the Demographic Ramifications of the British and the Zionist Immigration Policy in Palestine between the World Wars. *Iyunim Bitkumat Israel, Thematic Series: Economy and Society in Mandatory Palestine, 1918–1948,* 179–216. (Hebrew).

Hamilton, Gary G. and Tony Waters (1997). Ethnicity and Capitalist Development: The Changing Role of the Chinese in Thailand. In Daniel Chirot and Anthony Reid (eds.), *Essential Outsiders: Chinese and Jews in the Modern Transformation of Southeast Asia and Central Europe.* Seattle/London: Washington University Press, 258–284.

Hardach, Gerd (1995). Banking in Germany, 1918–1939. In Charles H. Feinstein, (ed.), *Banking, Currency and Finance in Europe between the Wars.* Oxford: Clarendon Press, 269–295.

Harlaftis, Gelina (1996). *A History of Greek-Owned Shipping: The Making of an International Tramp Fleet, 1830 to the Present Day.* London/New York: Routledge.

Harlaftis, Gelina (2005). Mapping the Greek Diaspora from the Early Eighteenth to the Late Twentieth Centuries. In Baghdiantz McCabe, Gelina Harlaftis and Ioanna Pepelasis Minoglou (eds.). *Diaspora Entrepreneurial Networks: Four Centuries of History.* Oxford/New York: Berg, 147–171.

Hassiotis, Ioannis. K. (1997). The Armenian Community in Thessaloniki: Origin, Organisation and Ideological Evolution. In I. K. Hassiotis (ed.), *Queen of the Worthy: Thessaloniki, History and Culture.* Vol. I: *History and Society.* Thessaloniki: Paratiritis, 296–305.

Hassiotis, Ioannis K. (2002). The Extermination of the Jewish Community of Drama (1941–1943). *Chronika* 25(178), 6–12. Downloaded 14 November 2006 from <http://www.macedonian-heritage.gr/Contributions/20020726_Hassiotis_Jews.html>.

Hastaoglou-Martinidis, Vilma (1997a). On the Jewish community of Salonica after the Fire of 1917: An Unpublished Memoir and Other Documents from the Papers of Henry Morgenthau, Sr. In I. K. Hassiotis (ed.), *The Jewish Communities of Southeastern Europe from the Fifteenth Century to the End of World War II.* Thessaloniki: Institute for Balkan Studies, 147–174.

Hastaoglou-Martinidis, Vilma (1997b). A Mediterranean City in Transition: Thessaloniki between the Two World Wars. *Facta Universitatis: Architecture and Civil Engineering* 1(4), 493–507. Downloaded 14 November 2006 from <http://facta.junis.ni.ac.yu/facta/aace/aace97/aace97-04.pdf>.

Heim, Carol E. (1994). Comments on Godley, Lai, and Taylor. *Journal of Economic History* 54(2), 441–445.

Hekimoglou, Evangelos A. (1987). *Trapezes kai Thessaloniki, 1900–1936* (Banks and Thessaloniki, 1900–1936). Thessaloniki: [s.n.]. (Greek).

Hekimoglou, Evangelos A. (1997a). The Jewish Bourgeoisie in Thessaloniki, 1906–1911. In I. K. Hassiotis (ed.), *The Jewish Communities of Southeastern Europe from the Fifteenth Century to the End of World War II*. Thessaloniki: Institute for Balkan Studies, 175–184.

Hekimoglou, Evangelos A. (1997b). Thessaloniki 1912–1940: Economic Developments. In I. Hassiotis (ed.), *Queen of the Worthy: Thessaloniki, History and Culture*. Thessaloniki: Paratiritis, 142–154.

Hekimoglou, Evangelos A. (1999). Hazakah: Land Market Practices in Ottoman Thessaloniki. *Remember Salonika. Justice* (special issue, spring), 35–37.

Hekimoglou, Evangelos A. (2002). Jewish Pauperism in Salonika, 1940–1941. In M. Rozen (ed.), *The Last Ottoman Century and Beyond: The Jews in Turkey and the Balkans (1808–1945)*. vol. 2, Tel Aviv: Tel Aviv University Press, 195–206.

Hekimoglou, Evangelos A. (2004). *Istoria tis Epicheirimatikotitas sti Thessaloniki apo tin idrysi tis polis mechri to 1940* (The History of Entrepreneurship in Thessaloniki from the Establishment of the City to the Year 1940). vol. D: *Lexiko Epicheirimation tis Thessalonikis, 1900–1940* (Dictionary of the Entrepreneurs of Thessaloniki, 1900–1940). Thessaloniki: Politistiki Etaireia Epichireimation Voreiou Ellados. (Greek).

Hirschman, Charles (1975). *Ethnic and Social Stratification in Penisular Malaysia*. Washington: American Sociological Association.

Hirschon, Renée (1989). *Heirs of the Greek Catastrophe: The Social Life of Asia Minor Refugees in Piraeus*. Oxford: Clarendon Press.

Hirschon, Renée (2003). Introduction: Background and Overview. In R. Hirschon (ed.), *Crossing the Aegean: An Appraisal of the 1923 Compulsory Population Exchange between Greece and Turkey*, Oxford/New York: Berghahn Books, 3–20.

Inalcık, Halil and Donald Quataert (eds.) (1994). *An Economic and Social History of the Ottoman Empire, 1300–1914*. Cambridge/New York: Cambridge University Press.

Ioannides, Stavros and Ioanna Pepelasis Minoglou (2005). Diaspora Entrepreneurship between History and Theory. In Y. Cassis and I. Pepelasis Minoglou (eds.), *Entrepreneurship in Theory and History*. London/New York: Palgrave Macmillan, 163–189.

Issawi, Charles (ed.) (1980). *The Economic History of Turkey, 1800–1914*. Chicago: University of Chicago Press.

Issawi, Charles (1982). The Transformation of the Economic Position of the Millets in the Nineteenth Century. In B. Braude and B. Lewis (eds.), *Christian and Jews in the Ottoman Empire: The Functioning of a Plural Society*. New York/London: Holmes and Meier, vol. 1, 262–285.

Iyer, Gopalkrishnan R. and Jon M. Shapiro (1999). Ethnic Entrepreneurial and Marketing Systems: Implications for the Global Economy. *Journal of International Marketing* 7(4), 83–110.

Jackson, Marvin R. (1985). Comparing the Balkan Demographic Experience: 1860–1970. *Journal of European Economic History* 14(2), 223–272.

Jain, Parakash C. (1988). Towards Class Analysis of Race Relations: Overseas Indians in Colonial/Post-Colonial Societies. *Economic and Political Weekly* 23(3), 95–103.

James, Harold (2001). *The Deutsche Bank and the Nazi Economic War against the Jews: The Expropriation of Jewish-Owned Property*. Cambridge: Cambridge University Press.

Jelavich, Charles and Barbara Jelavich (1977). *The Establishment of the Balkan National States, 1804–1920*. Seattle and London: University of Washington Press.

Jirousek, Charlotte (2000). The Transition to Mass Fashion System Dress in the Later

Ottoman Empire. In Donald Quataert (ed.), *Consumption Studies and the History of the Ottoman Empire, 1550–1922: An Introduction*. Albany: State University of New York Press.

Kadosh, Sara (2006). American Jewish Joint Distribution Committee (JDC or The Joint). In *Encyclopedia Judaica*, 2nd edition. Philadelphia: Coronet Books, vol. 2, 59–64.

Kahan, Arcadius (1975). The Modern Period. In N. Gross (ed.), *Economic History of the Jews*. Jerusalem: Keter, 83–104.

Kahan, Arcadius (1986a). The Impact of Industrialization in Tsarist Russia on the Socioeconomic Conditions of the Jewish Population. In R.W. Weiss (ed.), *Essays in Jewish Social and Economic History*. Chicago/London: The University of Chicago Press, 1–69.

Kahan, Arcadius (1986b). Economic Opportunities and Some Pilgrims' Progress: Jewish Immigrants from Eastern Europe in the United States, 1890–1914. In *Essays in Jewish Social and Economic History*. Chicago/London: The University of Chicago Press, 101–117.

Kallis, Aristotle A., (2006). The Jewish Community of Salonica under Siege: The Antisemitic Violence of the Summer of 1931. *Holocaust and Genocide Studies* 20(1), 34–56.

Kamaras, Antonis (2001). A Capitalist Diaspora: The Greeks in the Balkans. Hellenic Observatory Discussion Paper No. 4, Hellenic Observatory, London School of Economics and Political Science.

Kamaras, Antonis (2004). Market Reforms and Urban Disparity: the cases of Athens and Thessaloniki. E-Paper No. 3, Hellenic Observatory, London School of Economics and Political Science. Downloaded on 23 August 2007 from <http://www.lse.ac.uk/collections/hellenicObservatory/pubs/DP_oldseries.htm>.

Kansu, Aykut (1997). *The Revolution of 1908 in Turkey*. Leiden/New York/Köln: Brill.

Kaplan, David H. (1997). The Creation of an Ethnic Economy: Indochinese Business Expansion in Saint Paul. *Economic Geography* 73(2), 214–233.

Karpat, Kemal H. (1978). Ottoman Population Records and the Census of 1881/2–1893. *International Journal of Middle East Studies* 9(2), 237–274.

Karpat, Kemal H. (1982). Millets and Nationality: The Roots of the Incongruity of Nation and State in the Post-Ottoman Era. In B. Braude and B. Lewis (eds.), *Christian and Jews in the Ottoman Empire: The Functioning of a Plural Society*. New York/London: Holmes & Meier, vol. 1, 141–169.

Karpat, Kemal H. (1985). *Ottoman Population, 1830–1914: Demographic and Social Characteristics*. Madison, Wisc.: The University of Wisconsin Press.

Karpat, Kemal H. (1994). Jewish Population Movements in the Ottoman Empire, 1862–1914. In Avigdor Levi (ed.), *The Jews of the Ottoman Empire*. Princeton, N.J.: The Darwin Press, Inc., 399–422.

Kashima, Tetsuden (1982). Review of Bonacich and Modell, *The Economic Basis of Ethnic Solidarity*. *American Historical Review* 87: 1476.

Kerem, Yitzchak (1993). The Influence of Anti-Semitism on Jewish Immigration Patterns from Greece to the Ottoman Empire in the Nineteenth Century. In C. E. Farah (ed.), *Decision Making and Change in the Ottoman Empire*, Kirksville, Mo.: Thomas Jefferson University Press at Northeast Missouri State University, 305–314.

Kerem, Yitzchak (1996). The Influence of European Modernizing Forces on the Development of the Judeo-Spanish Press in the 19th Century in Salonika. *Sephardica* 1: 581–591.

Keyder, Çağlar (1994). Manufacturing in the Ottoman Empire and in Republican Turkey, ca. 1900–1950. In D. Quataert (ed.), *Manufacturing in the Ottoman Empire and Turkey, 1500–1950*. Albany: State University of New York Press.

Kieval, Hillel J. (1997). Middleman Minorities and Blood: Is There a Natural Economy of the Ritual Murder Accusation in Europe? In Daniel Chirot and Anthony Reid (eds.), *Essential Outsiders: Chinese and Jews in the Modern Transformation of Southeast Asia and Central Europe*. Seattle/London: University of Washington Press, 208–233.

Kitroeff, Alexander (1989). *The Greeks in Egypt, 1919–1937: Ethnicity and Class.* London: Published for the Middle East Centre, St. Antony's College, Oxford, by Ithaca Press.

Kloosterman, Robert and Jan Rath (2001). Immigrant Entrepreneurs in Advanced Economies: Mixed Embeddedness Further Explored. *Journal of Ethnic and Migration Studies* 27(2), 189–202.

Koliopoulos, John S. and Thanos M. Veremis [2002] (2004²). *Greece: The Modern Sequel.* London: Hurst.

Kontogiorgi, Elisabeth (2003). Economic Consequences Following Refugee Settlement in Greek Macedonia 1923–1932. In R. Hirschon (ed.), *Crossing the Aegean: An Appraisal of the 1923 Compulsory Population Exchange between Greece and Turkey.* Oxford/New York: Berghahn Books, 63–77.

Kontogiorgi, Elisabeth (2006). *Population Exchange in Greek Macedonia: The Rural Settlement of Refugees 1922–1930.* Oxford/New York: Clarendon Press.

Kostis, Kostas (1986). *The Banks and the Crisis, 1929–1932.* Athens: Historical Archives of the Commercial Bank of Greece. (Greek).

Kostis, Kostas (1990). *Economie rurale et la Banque Agraire. Aspects de l'économie de la Grèce pendant l'entre-deux-geurres (1919–1928): Les documents.* Athens: Cultural Foundation of the National Bank of Greece.

Kostis, Kostas (1992). The Ideology of Economic Development: The Refugees in the Interwar Period. *Bulletin of the Centre for Asia Minor Studies [DKMS]* 9, 31–46. (Greek).

Krausz, Ernest (1971). *Ethnic Minorities in Britain.* London: MacGibbon and Kee.

Kritikos, George (2000). State Policy and Urban Employment of Refugees: The Greek Case (1923–30). *European Review of History* 7(2), 189–206.

Kritikos, George (2001). Motives for the Compulsory Population Exchange in the Aftermath of the Greek-Turkish War (1922–1923). *Bulletin of the Centre for Asia Minor Studies [DKMS]* 13, 209–224.

Kupferschmidt, Uri M. (2007). *European Department Stores and Middle Eastern Consumers: The Orosdi-Back Saga.* Istanbul: Ottoman Bank Archives and Research Centre.

Kural Shaw, Ezel (1993). Integrity and Integration: Assumptions and Expectations Behind Nineteenth-Century Decision Making. In C.E. Farah (ed.), *Decision Making and Change in the Ottoman Empire,* Kirksville, Mo.: Thomas Jefferson University Press at Northeast Missouri State University, 39–52.

Kuznets, Simon (1960³). Economic Structure and Life of the Jews. In L. Finkelstein (ed.), *The Jews, Their History Culture and Religion.* New York: Harper & Brothers Publishers, vol. 2, 1597–1666.

Lagos, Katerina (2005). The Hellenization of Sephardic Jews in Thessaloniki in the Interwar Period, 1917–1941. In M. Aradas and N.C.J. Pappas (eds.), *Themes in European History: Essays from the 2nd International Conference on European History.* Athens: The Athens Institution for Education and Research, 401–406.

Lampe, John R. and Marvin R. Jackson (1982). *Balkan Economic History 1550–1950: From Imperial Borderlands to Developing Nations.* Bloomington: Indiana University Press.

Lapavitsas, Costas (2006). Social and Economic Underpinnings of Industrial Development: Evidence from Ottoman Macedonia. *Journal of European Economic History* 35(3), 661–710.

Landau, Jacob M. (1994). Relations between Jews and Non-Jews in the Late Ottoman Empire: Some Characteristics. In Avigdor Levi (ed.), *The Jews of the Ottoman Empire,* Princeton, N.J.: The Darwin Press, Inc., 539–545.

Landau, Jacob M. (2004). *Exploring Ottoman and Turkish History*. London: Christopher Hurst.

Landau, Jacob M. (2007). The Dönmes: Crypto-Jews under Turkish Rule. *Jewish Political Studies Review* 19(1–2), 109–118.

Lawrence, Paul (2001). Naturalization, Ethnicity and National Identity in France between the Wars. *Immigrants and Minorities* 20(3), 1–24.

Leighton, Neil O. (1979). The Political Economy of a Stranger Population. In William A. Shack and Elliot P. Skinner (eds.), *Strangers in African Societies*. Berkeley: University of Caifornia Press, 85–103.

Levene, Mark (1993). Nationalism and its Alternatives in the International Arena: The Jewish Question at Paris, 1919. *Journal of Contemporary History* 28: 511–531.

Levene, Mark (2001). Port Jewry of Salonika: Between Neo-Colonialism and Nation-State. *Jewish Culture and History* 4(2), 125–154.

Levene, Mark (2003). 'Ni grec, ni bulgare, ni turc': Salonika Jewry and the Balkan Wars, 1912–1913. *Jahrbuch des Simon-Dubnow-Instituts* 2, 65–97.

Levi, Avner (1992). *Toledot HaYehudim BaRepublica HaTurkit: Ma'amadam HaPoliti VeHamishpati* (History of the Jews in Turkish Republic: Their Political and Legal Status). Jerusalem: Self-published by the author.

Levitt, Peggy and Nadya B. Jaworsky (2007). Transnational Migration Studies: Past Developments and Future Trends. *Annual Review of Sociology* 33, 129–156.

Lewin-Epstein, Noah and Moshe Semyonov (1994). Sheltered Labor Markets, Public Sector Employment and Socio-Economic Returned to Education of Arabs in Israel. *American Journal of Sociology* 100(3), 622–651.

Lewis, Bernard (1961). *The Emergence of Modern Turkey*. London/New York/Toronto: Oxford University Press.

Lewis, Bernard (1964). *The Middle East and the West*. London: Weidenfeld and Nicolson.

Lewis, Bernard (1984). *The Jews of Islam*. Princeton, N.J.: Princeton University Press.

Lewkowicz, Bea (2006). *The Jewish Community of Salonika: History, Memory, Identity*. London/Portland, Ore.: Vallentine Mitchell.

Light, Ivan (1984). Immigrant and Ethnic Enterprise in North America. *Ethnic and Racial Studies* 7(2), 195–216.

Light, Ivan. (2005). The Ethnic Economy. In Neil Smelser and Richard Swedberg (eds.), *The Handbook of Economic Sociology*, 2nd edition. New York: Russell Sage Foundation, chap. 28, 650–677.

Light, Ivan, Georges Sabagh, Mehdi Bozorgmehr and Claudia Der-Martirosian (1993). Internal Ethnicity in the Ethnic Economy. *Ethnic and Racial Studies* 16(4), 581–597.

Light, Ivan, Richard B. Bernard and Rebecca Kim (1999). Immigrant Incorporation in the Garment Industry of Los Angeles. *International Migration Review* 33(1), 5–25.

Light, Ivan and Stavros Karageorgis (1994). The Ethnic Economy. In Neil Smelser and Richard Swedberg (eds.), *The Handbook of Economic Sociology*. New York: Russell Sage Foundation, chap. 16, 647–671.

Light, Ivan and Steven Gold (2000). *Ethnic Economies*. San Diego/San Francisco/New York/Boston/London/Sydney/Tokyo: Academic Press.

Loukatos, Spyros D. (1985). Statistical Elements of the City and Prefecture of Salonica, during the Decade of 1910. In *Actes du Colloque, 'Salonique après 1912'*. Thessalonika: Centre d'histoire de Salonique, 101–128. (Greek).

Louri, Helen and Ioanna Pepelasis Minoglou (2002). A Hesitant Evolution: Industrialisation and De-industrialisation in Greece Over the Long Run. *Journal of European Economic History* 31(2), 321–348.

Lowry, Heath W. (1986). From Lesser Wars to the Mightiest War: The Ottoman Conquest and Transformation of Byzantine Urban Centers in the Fifteenth Century. In Anthony

Bryer and Heath Lowry (eds.), *Continuity and Change in Late Byzantine and Early Ottoman Society*. Birmingham, UK: University of Birmingham, 323–338.

Lowry, Heath W. (1994). When Did the Sephardim Arrive in Salonica? The Testimony of the Ottoman Tax-Registers. In Avigdor Levi (ed.), *The Jews of the Ottoman Empire*. Princeton, N.J.: The Darwin Press, 203–214.

Macartney, C.A. (1934). *National States and National Minorities*. London: Oxford University Press.

Mackridge, Peter and Eleni Yannakakis (1997). Introduction. In P. Mackridge and E. Yannakakis (eds.), *Ourselves and Others: The Development of a Greek Macedonian Cultural Identity since 1912*. Oxford/New York: Berg, 1–22.

Malino, Frances and David Sorkin (eds.) (1990). *From East and West: Jews in a Changing Europe, 1750–1870*. Oxford, UK/Cambridge, Mass.: Basil Blackwell.

Marantzidis, Nicos and Mavroudi Georgia (2004). The neglected sons of nationalism: 'Repatriated refugees' in Greece and Germany. *Central and East European Studies Review* 6(2–3), 1–19.

Mathias, Peter (1997). How do Minorities Become Elites? In E. S. Brezis and P. Temin (eds.), *Elites, Minorities and Economic Growth*. Amsterdam: Elsevier, 115–127.

Mavrogordatos, George Th. (1983). *Stillborn Republic: Social Coalitions and Party Strategies in Greece, 1922–1936*. Berkeley/Los Angeles: University of California Press.

Mazower, Mark (1991). *Greece and the Inter-War Economic Crisis*. Oxford: Clarendon Press.

Mazower, Mark (1992). The Refugees, the Economic Crisis and the Colapse of Venizelist Hegemony, 1929–1932. *Bulletin of the Centre for Asia Minor Studies [DKMS]* 9, 119–134. (Greek).

Mazower, Mark (1993). *Inside Hitler's Greece: The Experience of Occupation, 1941–1944*. New Haven/London: Yale University Press.

Mazower, Mark (2002). *The Balkans: A Short History*. New York: Random House.

Mazower, Mark (2004). *Salonica City of Ghosts: Christians, Muslims and Jews 1430–1950*. London: Harper Collins.

Mazower, Mark and Veremis Thanos (1993). The Greek Economy 1922–1941. In Robin Higham, and Thanos Veremis (eds.), *The Metaxas Dictatorship: Aspects of Greece, 1936–1940*. Athens: Hellenic Foundation for Defense and Foreign Policy, 111–130.

McCabe, Baghdiantz, Gelina Harlaftis and Ioanna Pepelase Minoglou (eds.) (2005). *Diaspora Entrepreneurial Networks: Four Centuries of History*. Oxford/New York: Berg.

McCarthy, Justin (1990). The Population of Ottoman Europe Before and After the Fall of the Empire. In R. S. Hattox and H. W. Lowry, *Proceedings of the Third International Conference on the Social and Economic History of Turkey*. Princeton University, 24–26 August 1983, Istanbul: Isis Press, 275–311.

McCarthy, Justin (1994). Jewish Population in the Late Ottoman Period. In Avigdor Levi (ed.), *The Jews of the Ottoman Empire*, Princeton, N.J.: The Darwin Press, 375–397.

Megas, Yannis (1993). *Souvenir: Images of the Jewish Community of Salonika 1897–1917*. Athens: Kapon Editions.

Meier, Gerald (1984). *Leading Issues in Economic Development*. New York/Oxford: Oxford University Press

Meron, Orly C. (1990). The Decline of Jewish Banking in Milan and the Establishment of the S. Ambrogio Bank (1593). Were the Two Interrelated? *Nuova Rivista Storica* 74, 369–384.

Meron, Orly C. (1992). Il prestito ebraico nel Ducato di Milano nel periodo spagnolo (1535–1597). *Annuario di Studi Ebraici* 12, 69–87.

Meron, Orly C. (1998). The Dowries of Jewish Women in the Duchy of Milan (1535–1597): Economic and Social Aspects. *Zakhor. Rivista di Storia degli Ebrei d'Italia* 2, 127–137.

Meron, Orly C. (1999). The Jewish Community of Salonica (1881–1936): Middleman Minority in a Process of Peripheral Incorporation into the Capitalist World-Economy. Ph.D. diss., Ramat Gan, Bar-Ilan University. (Hebrew).

Meron, Orly C. (2005a). Jewish Entrepreneurship in Salonica during the Last Decades of the Ottoman Regime in Macedonia (1881–1912). In Colin Imber (ed.), *Frontiers of Ottoman Studies: State, Province, and the West*. London: I.B. Tauris, vol. 1, 265–286.

Meron, Orly C. (2005b). Sub-Ethnicity and Elites: Jewish Italian Professionals and Entrepreneurs in Salonica (1881–1912). *Zakhor. Rivista di Storia degli Ebrei d'Italia* 8, 177–220.

Meron, Orly C. (2005c). The Jewish Economy of Salonica (1881–1912). *Jewish Journal of Sociology* 47(1–2), 22–47.

Meron, Orly C. (2005d). Minority within Minority: Jewish Women in the Greek Labor Force (1928). In T. Cohen and S. Regev (eds.), *Woman in the East, Woman from the East: The Story of the Oriental Jewish Woman*. Ramat Gan: Bar-Ilan University Press, 163–189. (Hebrew).

Meron, Orly C. (2006). An Ethnic-Controlled Economy in Transition: Jewish Employment from European Semi-Colonialism in Ottoman Macedonia to Greek Nation-State. *Sociological Papers* 11, 1–58.

Meron, Orly C. (2008a). The Demographic Development of the Jewish Population in Northern Greece (1893–1928). *Pe'amim* 116, 7–78. (Hebrew).

Meron, Orly C. (2008b). Economic Nationalism from a Comparative Perspective: Jewish Port Workers between Salonika and Haifa, 1923–1936. *Iyunim Bitkumat Israel* 18, 193–235. (Hebrew).

Meron, Orly C. (2008c). Jewish Commerce in Salonica: 1881–1912. In Avrum Ehrlich (ed.), *Encyclopedia of the Jewish Diaspora*, Vol. 3, *Countries, Regions and Communities*. Santa Barbara: ABC-CLIO, 860–864.

Meron, Orly C. (2008d). Jewish Engineers in Salonica, 1912–1940. Paper presented at the Second Memorial Day for Eng. Aharon H. Rousso sponsored by The Chair for the History and Culture of the Jews of Salonika and Greece, Tel Aviv University, 4 December 2008.

Meron, Orly C. (2010). Crisis and Budgeting: Salonica's Jewish Community, 1928–1934. 16th British Conference on Judeo-Spanish Studies, Queen Mary, University of London, 15–17 July 2010. Unpublished paper.

Metzer, Jacob (1978). Economic Structure and National Goals: Jewish National Home in Interwar Palestine. *The Journal of Economic History* 38(1), 101–119.

Milano, Attilio (1949). *Storia degli Ebrei Italiani nel Levante*. Florence: Casa Editrice Israel.

Minns, Chris and Marian Rizov (2005). The Spirit of Capitalism? Ethnicity, Religion, and Self-Employment in Early 20th Century Canada. *Explorations in Economic History* 42, 259–281.

Model, Suzanne (1993). Ethnic Niches and the Structure of Opportunity: Immigrants and Minorities in New York City. In M. B. Katz (ed.), *The Underclass Debate*. Princeton: Princeton University Press, 161–193.

Moissis, Konstantinis (2006). *Holocaust of the Greek Jews: Monuments and Memories*. Athens: KIS.

Molho, Rena (1988). The Jewish Community of Salonika and its Incorporation into the Greek state (1912–1919). *Middle Eastern Studies* 24(4), 391–403.

Molho, Rena (1988/1993). Popular Antisemitism and State Policy in Salonika during the City's Annexation to Greece. *Jewish Social Studies* 50(3–4), 253–264.

Molho, Rena (1992). Salonique après 1912: propagandes étrangères et la communauté juive. *Revue Historique* 287(1), 126–140.

Molho, Rena (1997). La réforme éducative et le renouveau des Juifs de Salonique (1850–1918). In Elie Carasso (ed.), *Les voix de la mémoire*. Tarascon: Elie Carasso.

Molho, Rena (2002). Jewish Working-Class Neighborhoods Established in Salonika Following the 1890 and 1917 Fires. In M. Rozen (ed.), *The Last Ottoman Century and Beyond: The Jews in Turkey and The Balkans 1808–1945*. Tel Aviv: Tel Aviv University, vol. 2, 173–194.

Molho, Rena (2005a) [1993]. Education in the Jewish Community of Salonica in the Beginning of the Twentieth Century. In R. Molho, *Salonika and Istanbul: Social, Political and Cultural Aspects of Jewish Life*. Istanbul: Isis, 127–137.

Molho, Rena (2005b). Female Jewish Education in Salonica at the End of the 19th Century. In R. Molho, *Salonika and Istanbul: Social, Political and Cultural Aspects of Jewish Life*. Istanbul: Isis, 139–150.

Molho, Rena (2005c). Le Cercle de Salonique 1873–1958: Club des Saloniciens. In R. Molho, *Salonika and Istanbul: Social, Political and Cultural Aspects of Jewish Life*. Istanbul: Isis, 151–164.

Morin, Edgar (1989). *Vidal et les siens*. Paris: Editions du Seuil.

Morin, Edgar [1989] (2009). *Vidal and His Family from Salonica to Paris: The Story of a Sephardic Family in the Twentieth Century*. Trans. Debora Cowell. Brighton/Portland: Sussex Academic Press.

Mosse, Werner Eugen (1987). *Jews in the German Economy: The German-Jewish Economic Elite 1820–1935*. Oxford: Clarendon Press.

Mourghianni-Estela, Anna (1996). Salonique années '20: Le déclin. *Sephardica* 1, 595–602.

Moutsopoulos, N. K. (1981). *Thessaloniki, 1900–1917*. Thessaloniki: M. Molho Publications.

Mouzelis, Nicos P. (1978). *Modern Greece: Facets of Underdevelopment*. London: Macmillan.

Naar, Albertos (1997). Social Organisation and Activity of the Jewish Community in Thessaloniki. In I. K. Hassiotis (ed.), *Queen of the Worthy: Thessaloniki, History and Culture*. Vol. 1, *History and Society*. Thessaloniki: Paratiritis, 191–209.

Naar, Devin E. (2007). From the 'Jerusalem of the Balkans' to the Goldene Medina: Jewish Immigration from Salonika to the United States. *American Jewish History* 93(4), 435–473.

Nahon, Yaacov (1984). *Trends in Occupational Status: The Ethnic Dimension 1958–1981*. Jerusalem: The Jerusalem Institute for Israel Studies. (In Hebrew with an introduction in English).

Nehama, Joseph (1935–1978). *Histoire des Israélites de Salonique*. Thessaloniki: The Jewish Community of Thessaloniki, vols. VI–VII.

Nehama, Joseph (1989). The Jews of Salonika and the Rest of Greece under Hellenic Rule: The Death of a Great Community. In R. D. Barnett and W. M. Schwab (eds.), *The Sephardi Heritage: Essays on the Historical and Cultural Contribution of the Jews of Spain and Portugal*. Vol. II, *The Western Sephardim*. Grendon, UK: Gibraltar Books, 243–282.

Overy, Richard J. (2003). German Business and the Nazi Order. In Terry Gourvish (ed.), *Business and Politics in Europe, 1900–1970*, Cambridge: Cambridge University Press, 171–186.

Pamuk, Şevket (1984). The Ottoman Empire in the 'Great Depression' of 1873–1896. *The Journal of Economic History* 44(1), 107–118.

Pamuk, Şevket (1987). *The Ottoman Empire and European Capitalism, 1820–1913: Trade, Investment, and Production*. Cambridge: Cambridge University Press.

Papagiannopoulos, Apostolos (1982). *History of Thessaloniki*. Trans. Pantazidou Anastasia. Thessaloniki: Rekos.

Papastefanaki, Leda (2007). Division of Labour, Technology and Gender in Greece. The Cases of Cotton and Mining Industry, 1870–1940. Paper presented at the Seventh

European Historical Economics Society Conference, Lund University, Sweden, 29 June–1 July, 2007.

Papastefanaki, Leda (2009). *Ergasia, technologia kai fylo stin helleniki viomichania. I klostoyfantourgia tou Pirea 1870–1940* (Labour, Technology and Gender in Greek Industry: The Textile Industry of Piraeus, 1870–1940). Herakleion: Crete University Press. (Greek).

Pelt, Mogens (1998). *Tobacco, Arms and Politics: Greece and Germany from World Crisis to World War, 1929–1941*. Copenhagen: Museum Tusculanum Press, University of Copenhagen.

Pentzopoulos, Dimitri (1962). *The Balkan Exchange of Minorities and its Impact upon Greece*. Paris: Mouton.

Pepelasis, Admantios A. (1959). The Legal System and Economic Development of Greece. *The Journal of Economic History* 19(2), 167–198.

Pepelasis, Admantios, Leon Mears and Irma Adelman (1961). *Economic Development: Analysis and Case Studies*. New York/London/Tokyo: Harper and Row.

Pepelasis Minoglou, Ioanna (2002). Between Informal Networks and Formal Contracts: International Investment in Greece during the 1920s. *Business History* 44(2), 41–66.

Pepelasis Minoglou, Ioanna (2005). Toward a Typology of Greek-diaspora Entrepreneurship. In Baghdiantz McCabe, Gelina Harlaftis and Ioanna Pepelasis Minoglou (eds.), *Diaspora Entrepreneurial Networks: Four Centuries of History*, Oxford/New York: Berg, 173–189.

Pepelasis Minoglou, Ioanna (2007a). Women and Greek Family Capitalism, 1780–1940. *Business History Review* 81, 517–538.

Pepelasis Minoglou, Ioanna (2007b). (In)corporation in Greek Business: Between Tradition and Modernity, c. 1780–1910. Paper delivered at the EAEPE 2007 Conference, Porto, Portugal, 1–3 November 2007. Accessed 17 May 2009 at <http://www.fep.up.pt/conferencias/EAEPE2007/Papers%20and%20abstracts_CD/MINOGLOU.pdf>.

Perez, Avner and Gladys Pimienta (2007). *Diksionario Amplio Djudeo-espanyol-Ebreo, Lashon me-Aspamia*. Maale Adumim, Israel: Sefarad, El Instituto Maale Adumim: La Autoridad Nasionala del Ladino i su Kultur. (Ladino).

Petridis, Pavlos B. (1997). Thessaloniki, 1912–1940: A Period of Political and Social Transition. In I. K. Hassiotis (ed.), *Queen of the Worthy: Thessaloniki, History and Culture*. Vol. I, *History and Society*. Thessaloniki: Paratiritis, 129–141.

Phizacklea, Annie and Monder Ram (1995). Ethnic Entrepreneurship in Comparative Perspective. *International Journal of Entrepreneurial Behaviour & Research* 1(1), 48–58.

Pierron, Bernard (1996). *Juifs et Chrétiens de la Grèce Moderne: Histoire des relations inter-communautaires de 1821 à 1945*. Paris: L'Harmattan.

Plaut, Joshua Eli (1996). *Greek Jewry in the Twentieth Century, 1913–1983*. Madison: Fairleigh Dickinson University Press, and London: Associated University Presses.

Quataert, Donald (1993a). Premières fumées d'usines. In G. Veinstein (ed.), *Salonique, 1850–1918: La 'ville des juifs' et le réveil des Balkans*. Paris: Éditions Autrement, 177–194.

Quataert, Donald (1993b). *Ottoman Manufacturing in the Age of the Industrial Revolution*. Cambridge: Cambridge University Press.

Quataert, Donald (1995). The Workers of Salonica, 1850–1912. In D. Quataert and E. Zürcher (eds.), *Workers and the Working Class in the Ottoman Empire and the Turkish Republic, 1839–1950*. London/New York: Tauris Academic Studies, 59–74, 171–173.

Quataert, Donald (ed.) (2000). *Consumption Studies and the History of the Ottoman Empire, 1550–1922: An Introduction*. Albany: State University of New York Press.

Quataert, Donald (2002). The Industrial Working Class of Salonica, 1850–1912. In A. Levi (ed.), *Jews, Turks, Ottomans: A Shared History, the Fifteenth through the Twentieth Century*. New York: Syracuse University Press, 194–211.

Quataert, Donald (2005). *The Ottoman Empire, 1700–1922*. New York: Cambridge University Press.

Quintana Rodrigues, Aldina (1999). Proceso de Recastellanización del Judezmo. In Judith Targarona Borras and Angel Saenz-Badillos (eds.), *Jewish Studies at the Turn of the Twentieth Century*. Proceedings of the 6th EAJS Congress Toledo, July 1998, Leiden/Boston/Köln: Brill, vol. II, 593–602.

Rath, Jan (2002). A Quintessential Immigrant Niche? The Non-Case of Immigrants in the Dutch Construction Industry. *Entrepreneurship and Regional Development* 14(4), 355–372.

Razin, Eran and Dan Scheinberg (2001). Immigrant Entrepreneurs from the Former USSR in Israel: Not the Traditional Enclave Economy. *Journal of Ethnic and Migration Studies* 27(2), 259–276.

Reich, Nathan (1955²). The Economic Structure of Modern Jewry. In L. Finkelstein (ed.), *The Jews: Their History, Culture and Religion*. New York: Harper & Brothers Publishers, vol. 2, 1239–1266.

Reid, Anthony (1997). Enterpreneurial Minorities, Nationalism, and the State. In Daniel Chirot and Anthony Reid (eds.), *Essential Outsiders: Chinese and Jews in the Modern Transformation of Southeast Asia and Central Europe*. Seattle/London: University of Washington Press, 33–71.

Rex, John (1970). *Race Relations in Sociological Theory*. London: Weidenfeld and Nicolson.

Rodrigue, Aron (1990a). *French Jews, Turkish Jews: The Alliance Israélite Universelle and the Politics of Jewish Schooling in Turkey, 1860–1925*. Bloomington: Indiana University Press.

Rodrigue, Aron (1990b). Abraham de Camondo of Istanbul: Transformation of Jewish Philanthropy. In Frances Malino and David Sorkin (eds.), *From East and West: Jews in a Changing Europe, 1750–1870*. Oxford, UK/Cambridge, Mass.: Basil Blackwell, 46–56.

Rodrigue, Aron (1994). The Beginning of Westernization and Community Reform among Istanbul's Jewry, 1854–1865. In Avigdor Levi (ed.), *The Jews of the Ottoman Empire*. Princeton, N.J.: The Darwin Press, Inc., 439–456.

Rodrigue, Aron (1995). From Millet to Minority: Turkish Jewry. In Pierre Birnbaum and Ira Katznelson (eds.), *Paths of Emancipation*. Princeton: Princeton University Press, 238–261.

Rodrigue, Aron (2002). Preface. *Jewish History* 16, 221–223.

Rother, Bernd (2002). Spanish Attempts to Rescue Jews from the Holocaust: Lost Opportunities. *Mediterranean Historical Review* 17(2), 47–68.

Roupa, Efrosini and Evangelos A. Hekimoglou (2004). *Istoria tis Epicheirimatikotitas sti Thessaloniki apo tin idrysi tis polis mechri to 1940* (The History of Entrepreneurship in Thessaloniki from the Establishment of the City to the Year 1940), vol. C: *Megales epicheiriseis kai epicheirimatikes oikogeneies* (Big Enterprises and Families of Entrepreneurs). Thessaloniki: Politistiki Etaireia Epichireimation Voreiou Ellados. (Greek).

Rozen, Minna (1993a). Strangers in a Strange Land: The Extraterritorial Status of Jews in Italy and the Ottoman Empire in the Sixteenth to Eighteenth Centuries. In M. Rozen, *In the Mediterranean Routes: The Jewish-Spanish Diaspora from the Sixteenth to Eighteenth Centuries*, Tel Aviv: Tel Aviv University, 24–64.

Rozen, Minna (1993b). Contest and Rivalry in Mediterranean Maritime Commerce in the First Half of the Eighteen Century: The Jews of Salonica and the European Presence.

In M. Rozen, *In the Mediterranean Routes: The Jewish-Spanish Diaspora from the Sixteenth to Eighteenth Centuries*, Tel Aviv: Tel Aviv University, 65–113. (Hebrew).

Rozen, Minna (1993c). Individual and Community in Jewish Society in the Ottoman Empire: Salonika in the Sixteenth Century. In M. Rozen, *In the Mediterranean Routes: The Jewish-Spanish Diaspora from the Sixteenth to Eighteenth Centuries*, Tel Aviv: Tel Aviv University, 114–167.

Rozen, Minna (2005a). *The Last Ottoman Century and Beyond: The Jews in Turkey and the Balkans, 1808–1945*. Tel Aviv: Tel Aviv University Press.

Rozen, Minna (2005b). Jews and Greeks Remember Their Past: The Political Career of Tzevi Koretz (1933–1943). *Jewish Social Studies: History, Culture, Society* 12(1), 111–166.

Rozen, Minna (ed.) (2008). *Homelands and Diasporas: Greeks, Jews and Their Migrations*. London: I.B. Tauris.

Sebag, Paul (2002). *Les noms des juifs de Tunisie: Origins et significations*. Paris: L'Harmattan.

Salamone, Stephen D. (1987). *In the Shadow of the Holy Mountain: The Genesis of a Rural Greek Community and its Refugee Heritage*. Boulder: East European Monographs.

Sandis, Eva E. (1973). *Refugees and Economic Migrants in Greater Athens: A Social Survey*. Athens: National Centre of Social Research.

Schermerhorn, R. A. (1970). *Comparative Ethnic Relations: A Framework for Theory and Research*. New York: Random House.

Schrover, Marlou (2001). Immigrant Business and Niche Formation in the Nineteenth Century. *Journal of Ethnic and Migration Studies* 27(2), 295–311.

Schwarzfuchs, Simon (1995). The Sicilian Jewish Communities in the Ottoman Empire. In *Italia Judaica: Gli ebrei in Sicilia sino all'espulsione del 1492, Atti del V convegno internazionale, Palermo, 15–19 giugno 1992*. Rome: Ministero per i beni culturali Ambientali, Ufficio Centrale per i beni archivistici, 397–411.

Scott, A. J. (1998). *Regions and the World Economy: The Coming Shape of Local Production, Competition and Political Order*. Oxford: Oxford University Press.

Şeni, Nora (2007). Camondo. In *Encyclopedia Judaïca*, 2nd edition. Philadelphia: Coronet Books, vol. 4, 382.

Sfika, Angeliki-Theodosiou (1990). The Founding of the Branch of the National Bank of Greece in Thessaloniki and Greek-Bulgarian Relations (1912–1913). *Makedonika* 27: 63–77. (Greek).

Shaw, Stanford J. (1975). The Nineteenth-Century Ottoman Tax Reforms and Revenue System. *International Journal of Middle East Studies* 6(4), 421–459.

Shaw, Stanford J. (1978). The Ottoman Census System and Population, 1831–1914. *International Journal of Middle East Studies* 9(3), 325–338.

Shaw, Stanford J. (1991). *The Jews of the Ottoman Empire and the Turkish Republic*. New York: New York University Press.

Shaw, Stanford J. and Ezel Kural Shaw (1976–1979). *History of the Ottoman Empire and Modern Turkey*. London/New York/Melbourne: Cambridge University Press.

Shibutani, Tamostu and Kian M. Kwan (1965–1972). *Ethnic Stratification: A Comparative Approach*. New York: Macmillan.

Simmons Colin P. and Christos Kalantaridis (1994). Garment Manufacturing in Peonia County, Greece. *Comparative Studies in Society and History* 36 (4 October), 649–675.

Smith, Anthony D. (ed.) (1976). *Nationalist Movements*. London/Basingstoke: The Macmillan Press.

Smith, Anthony D. (1986). *The Ethnic Origins of Nations*. Oxford: Blackwell.

Smith, Anthony D. (ed.) (1992). *Ethnicity and Nationalism*. Leiden: E.J. Brill.

Smith, Anthony D. (1994). The Problem of National Identity: Ancient, Medieval and Modern? *Ethnic and Racial Studies* 17(3), 375–399.

Smith, M. G. (1986). Pluralism, Race and Ethnicity in Selected African Countries. In J. Rex and D. Mason (eds.), *Theories of Race and Ethnic Relations.* Cambridge: Cambridge University Press, 187–225.

Stallbaumer, L. M. (1999). Big Business and the Persecution of the Jews: The Flick Concern and the 'Aryanization' of Jewish Property before the War. *Holocaust and Genocide Studies* 13(1), 1–27.

Starr, Joshua (1945). The Socialist Federation of Saloniki. *Jewish Social Studies* 7(4), 323–336.

Stavrianos, L. S. (1963). *The Balkans, 1815–1914.* New York: Holt, Rinehart and Winston.

Stavroulakis, Nicholas P. (1993). *Salonika: Jews and Dervishes.* Athens: Talos Press,

Stoianovich, Traian (1960). The Conquering Balkan Orthodox Merchant. *Journal of Economic History* 20(2), 234–313.

Stoianovich, Traian (1994). *Balkan Worlds: The First and Last Europe.* New York: M.E. Sharpe.

Sugar, Peter F. (1977). *Southeastern Europe under Ottoman Rule, 1354–1804.* Seattle/London: University of Washington Press.

Sussnitzki, Alphons J. [1917] (1966). Ethnic Division of Labor. In C. Issawi (ed.), *The Economic History of the Middle East, 1800–1914.* Chicago and London: Chicago University Press, 114–125.

Svennilson, Ingvar (1954). *Growth and Stagnation in the European Economy.* Geneva: United Nations Economic Commission for Europe.

Svoronos, Nicholas (1991). Administrative, Social and Economic Developments, 1430–1821. In M. B. Sakellariou (ed.), *Macedonia: 4000 Years of Greek History and Civilization* (English edition supervised by H. L. Turner). Athens: Ekdotike Athenon S.A., 354–386.

Syrquin, Moshe (1985). The Economic Structure of the Jews in Argentina and Other Latin America Countries. *Jewish Social Studies* 47(2), 115–134.

Teichova, Alice (1992). Rivals and Partners: Reflections on Banking and Industry in Europe, 1880–1938. In Philip L. Cottrell, Hakan Lindgren and Alice Teichova (eds.), *European Industry and Banking between the Wars.* Leicester/London/New York: Leicester University Press, 17–29.

Temin, Peter (1999). The American Business Elite in Historical Perspective. In E. S. Brezis and P. Temin (eds.), *Elites, Minorities and Economic Growth.* Amsterdam: Elsevier, 19–39.

Tennenbaum, Shelly (1986). Immigrants and Capital: Jewish Loan Societies in the United States, 1880–1945. *American Jewish History* 76(1), 67–77.

Theophanides, Stavros (1991). The Economic Development of Greek Macedonia after 1912. In M.B. Sakellariou (ed.), *Macedonia: 4000 Years of Greek History and Civilization.* Athens: Ekdotike Athenon, 509–527.

Tignor, Robert (1980). The Economic Activities of Foreigners in Egypt, 1920–1950: From Millet to Haute Bourgeoisie. *Comparative Studies in Society and History* 22(3), 416–449.

Tilly, Charles (1990). Transplanted Networks. In Virginia Yans-McLaughlin (ed.), *Immigration Reconsidered: History, Sociology and Politics.* New York: Oxford University Press, 79–95.

Todorov, Nikolai (1983). *The Balkan City, 1400–1900.* Seattle/London: University of Washington Press.

Todorov, Nikolai (1985). Social Structures in the Balkans during the Eighteenth and Nineteenth Centuries. *Études balkaniques* 21(4), 48–71.

Trivellato, Francesca (2009). *The Familiarity of Strangers: The Sephardic Diaspora, Livorno, and Cross-Cultural Trade in the Early Modern Period.* New Haven: Yale University Press.

Tsukashima, R. T. (1991). Cultural Endowment, Disadvantaged Status and Economic Niche: The Development of an Ethnic Trade. *International Migration Review* 25(2), 333–354.

Tulea, Gitta and Ernest Krausz (1993). Changing Approaches in Postmodern Sociological Thought. *International Journal of Comparative Sociology* 34(3–4), 210–221.

Turner, Jonathan H. and Edna Bonacich (1980). Toward a Composite Theory of Middleman Minorities. *Ethnicity* 7(2), 144–158.

Vacalopoulos, Apostolos P. (1963). *A History of Thessaloniki*. Trans. from Greek by T. F. Carney. Thessaloniki: Institute for Balkan Studies.

Vafopoulos, G. Th. (1993). Dans la Guerre mondiale. In G. Veinstein (ed.), *Salonique, 1850–1918: La 'ville des juifs' et le réveil des Balkans*, Paris: Éditions Autrement, 255–260.

Van Amersfoort, Hans (1982). *Immigration and the Formation of Minority Groups: the Dutch Experience, 1945–1975*. Trans. from Dutch by Robert Lyng. Cambridge: Cambridge University Press.

Van den Berghe, Pierre L. (1981). *The Ethnic Phenomenon*. New York: Elsevier.

Van den Berghe, Pierre L. (1986). Ethnicity and Sociobiology Debate. In J. Rex and D. Mason (eds.), *Theories of Race and Ethnic Relations*. Cambridge: Cambridge University Press, 246–263.

Vassilikou, Maria (1993). The Anti-Semitic Riots in Thessaloniki (June 1931) and the Greek Press: A Case-Study of 'Scapegoating' Theory. M.A. diss. (P. Carabott, Supervisor). London, King's College, Department of Byzantine and Modern Greek Studies.

Vassilikou, Maria (2003). Post-Cosmopolitan Salonika: Jewish Politics in the Interwar Period. *Simon Dubnow Institute Yearbook* 2: 99–118.

Venistein, Gilles (1997). La draperie juive de Salonique. Une relecture critique de Joseph Nehama. In I. K. Hassiotis (ed.), *The Jewish Communities of Southeastern Europe from the Fifteenth Century to the End of World War II*. Thessaloniki: Institute for Balkan Studies, 579–589.

Voutira, Eftihia (2003). When Greeks Meet Other Greeks: Settlement Policy Issues in the Contemporary Greek Context. In R. Hirschon (ed.), *Crossing the Aegean: An Appraisal of the 1923 Compulsory Population Exchange between Greece and Turkey*. Oxford/New York: Berghahn Books, 145–159.

Ward, Robin (1996⁴). Middleman Minority. In Ellis Cashmore (ed.), *Dictionary of Race and Ethnic Relations*. New York: Routledge & Kegan Paul, 237–238.

Waldinger, Roger (1993). The Two Sides of Ethnic Entrepreneurship. *International Migration Review* 27(3), 692–701.

Waldinger, Roger (1996). *Still the Promised City? African-Americans and New Immigrants in Postindustrial New York*. Cambridge, Mass.: Harvard University Press.

Waldinger, Roger (2000). The Economic Theory of Ethnic Conflict: A Critique and Reformation. In J. Rath (ed.), *Immigrant Businesses: The Economic, Political and Social Environment*. London: Macmillan, 124–141.

Walker, C. E. (1931). The History of the Joint Stock Company. *The Accounting Review* 6(2), 97–105.

Wallerstein, Immanuel (1974). *The Modern World-System*. New York: Academic Press.

Wallerstein, Immanuel (1980). Imperialism and Development. In A. Bergesen (ed.), *Studies of the Modern World-System*. New York, London: Academic Press, 13–23.

Wallerstein, Immanuel (1993). World System versus World-Systems: A Critique. In A. G. Frank and B. K. Gills (eds.), *The World System: Five Hundred Years or Five Thousand?* London/New York: T. J. Press, 292–296.

Wallerstein, Immanuel, Hale Decdeli and Reşat Kasaba (1987). The Incorporation of the

Ottoman Empire into the World-Economy. In H. Islamoglu-Inan (ed.), *The Ottoman Empire and the World-Economy*. Cambridge: Cambridge University Press, 88–97.

Weiker, Walter F. (1992). *Ottomans, Turks and the Jewish Polity: A History of the Jews of Turkey*. Lanham: University Press of America.

Weill, Georges (1987). L'Alliance Israélite Universelle et la condition sociale des communautés juives méditerranéennes à la fin du XIX siècle (1860–1914). In S. Schwarzfuchs (ed.), *L'Alliance dans les communautés du bassin méditerranéen à la fin du 19ème siècle et son influence sur la situation sociale et culturelle*. Jerusalem: Misgav Yerushalayim, pp. vii–lii.

Weill, Georges (1982). The Alliance Israélite Universelle and the Emancipation of the Jewish Communities in the Mediterranean. *The Jewish Journal of Sociology* 24: 117–134.

Weitz, John (1997). *Hitler's Banker: Hjalmar Horace Greeley Schacht*. New York: Little, Brown and Company.

Wilson, F. D. (2003). Ethnic Niching and Metropolitan Labor Markets. *Social Science Research* 32(3), 429–466.

Yambert, Karl A. (1981). Alien Traders and Ruling Elites: The Overseas Chinese in Southeast Asia and the Indians in East Africa. *Ethnic Groups* 3(3), 173–198.

Yerolympos, Alexandra and Vassilis Colonas (1993). Un urbanisme cosmopolite. In G. Veinstein (ed.), *Salonique, 1850–1918: La 'ville des juifs' et le réveil des Balkans*. Paris: Éditions Autrement, 158–176.

Yerolympos, Alexandra (1993). La part du feu. In G. Veinstein (ed.), *Salonique, 1850–1918: La 'ville des juifs' et le réveil des Balkans*. Paris: Éditions Autrement, 261–270.

Yerolympos, Alexandra (1997). New Data Relating to the Spatial Organisation of the Jewish Communities in the European Provinces of the Ottoman Empire (19th c.). In I.K. Hassiotis (ed), *The Jewish Communities of Southeastern Europe from the Fifteenth Century to the End of World War II*. Thessaloniki: Institute for Balkan Studies, 623–630.

Yerolympos, Alexandra (2003). Inter-War Town Planning and the Refugee Problem in Greece: Temporary Solution and Long-Term Dysfunctions. In R. Hirschon (ed.), *Crossing the Aegean: An Appraisal of the 1923 Compulsory Population Exchange between Greece and Turkey*. Oxford/New York: Berghahn Books, 133–143.

Yinger, Milton J. (1981). Toward a Theory of Assimilation and Dissimilation. *Ethnic and Racial Studies* 4(3), 249–264.

Yinger, Milton J. (1986). Intersecting Strands in the Theorisation of Race and Ethnic Relations. In J. Rex and D. Mason (eds.), *Theories of Race and Ethnic Relations*. Cambridge: Cambridge University Press, 20–41.

Yoon, In-Jin (1991). The Changing Significance of Ethnic and Class Resources in Immigrant Business: The Case of Korean Immigrant Business in Chicago. *International Migration Review* 25(2), 303–332.

Zenner, Walter P. (1982). Arabic-Speaking Immigrants in North America as Middleman Minorities. *Ethnic and Racial Studies* 5(4), 457–477.

Zhou, Min (2004). Revisiting Ethnic Entrepreneurship: Convergencies, Controversies, and Conceptual Advancements. *International Migration Review* 38(3), 1040–1074.

Ziegler, Dieter, Harald Wixforth and Jörg Osterlon (2003). 'Aryanisation' in Central Europe, 1933–1939: A Preliminary Account for Germany (the 'Altreich'), Austria and the 'Sudeten' Area. In Terry Gourvish (ed.), *Business and Politics in Europe, 1900–1970*. Cambridge: Cambridge University Press, 187–214.

Index

Note: Page numbers in italics refer to entries which appear in the appendices, tables or figures.